THE OF[ICIAL]
AUTOGRAPH
COLLECTOR
PRICE GUIDE

Fourth Edition

by Mark Allen Baker

"Trusted by Collectors and Dealers"

ODYSSEY PUBLICATIONS

A Collectors Universe Company

NASDAQ: CLCT

www.AutographCollector.com

Publisher: Odyssey Publications
Publisher: A Collectors Universe Company
Publisher: NASDAQ: CLCT

Cover Design: Jackie Floyd, Type "F"
Author: Mark Baker
Edited By: Ev Phillips

Printed in the United States of America
First Edition, First Printing
10 9 8 7 6 5 4 3 2 1

ISBN#0-9669710-9-4

Library of Congress Catalog Card Number: 2004101364

Odyssey Publications
A Collectors Universe Company
510-A So. Corona Mall
Corona, CA 92879-1420

1-800-996-3977 or (909)734-9636

www.AutographCollector.com

Printed in the United States

Contents

SECTION THREE - References

Dedication

To Matthew Robert Baker
Take time to think,
Take time to love and be loved,
Take time to give,
Take time to play,
Take time to pray
Take time to laugh,
and always take time to spend with me.

In Memory of Gloria S. Long (1926-2002)

ACKNOWLEDGMENTS

Taking on the task of writing this book was not an easy decision for me to make. If it weren't for the encouragement of others, belief in a purpose and the commitment of the publisher, I would not have undertaken the challenge.

First, I would like to thank Al Wittnebert. Many of you know Al through the UACC – The Universal Autograph Collectors Club, where he serves as treasurer – but he is far more than that. Al represents everything good about the hobby of autograph collecting. He believes in education through the courses he has taught, and through the books he has written, such as *The Study of Star Trek Autographs.* I had the fortunate opportunity to attend one of his classes on authentication and was impressed by his knowledge, thoroughness and duty.

I would be remiss if I didn't thank all of my readers who have bought so many of my books over the years. I have always believed that I am writing for you and not for myself.

As my books exemplify, and my readers can attest to, I am committed to the hobby through the education of the collector. When I began collecting some four decades ago, I had few resources to turn to for education. Through my mistakes and the limited information I could glean through dealers and other collectors, I persevered and remained steadfast to my goals in collecting. Today, novice collectors have a wealth of information to turn to, and I am proud to have played a small part in their education.

Odyssey Publications – a Collectors Universe Company – through its many publications is committed to the hobby. Trust me when I say, "If they were not, I wouldn't be writing this book." Without question *Autograph Collector* magazine has been the finest publication of its kind and a fantastic resource for the hobby.

A special thanks to Bill Miller, Darrell Talbert, Trish Hessey, Ev Phillips, David Laurell, Joanne Lindsey, John Treworgy and all the contributing editors of *Autograph Collector.* Also to the many dealers who have contributed through their advertisements, catalogs and auctions, your prices have been included. To Shannon Watson and all the people at MastroNet Inc., thank you for your support.

A very special thanks to Harold L. Esch, Gil Griggs, Larry Rosenbaum, David M. Beach and Al Hallonquist.

To Aaron A. Baker, Elizabeth M. Baker and Rebecca J. Baker, I miss you!

Also to Alison Long for allowing me to finish this book before I lose my Florida sunshine.

INTRODUCTION

There is simply no hobby like collecting autographs and manuscripts. To think that a memory can be invoked, often instantaneously, through a simple signature still entices me. To realize that, as participants, many of us hold information that is a part of history. A great collector once told me that if you could manage to put the top twenty five private document collections together it would alter hundreds, if not thousands, of history books. As a novice collector, I didn't believe him. As an experienced collector, I now realize he was right.

As an author, I have had the great fortune of having many wonderful people give an introduction to one of my books. They have ranged from sparring partners of Ernest Hemingway to New York Yankee great and Baseball Hall of Famer Joe Sewell. Many have had the unique ability to transport me through time to a place I never knew, a time I never saw, and experiences I could only dream about. This book, if you read it carefully, is more than just a price guide; it's a book of memories, a treasury of thoughts from an earlier time.

My choice for this book is Harold L. Esch, an author, sportswriter and autograph collector. Harold may not be familiar to most of you, but he is a reflection of us all. A testament to all that is good about the hobby, especially in its purest form. Using baseball as a familiar vehicle, if not a common denominator for many of us, he reflects from his own experiences on the glory days of our "National Pastime."

Memories Are A Wonderful Thing

by Harold L. Esch

Getting Started

My first introduction to baseball came at an early age. My dad, being an avid fan, took me to a spring training game at Tinker Field in Orlando, Florida. The Cincinnati Reds were based there at the time, and although I don't recall the opponent, the thrill of just being there is when I became a true fan.

It was through my dad's suggestion that I became an autograph collector. By the time that occurred the Brooklyn Dodgers had replaced the Reds in Orlando. In those days, access to the playing field during practice was no problem and players were generous in signing my cards. From Al Lopez, Tony Cuccinello and Van Mungo to Sam Leslie and Joe Stripp, boy, what a thrill for a collector! Dazzy Vance signed a card and when returning it to me said, "Hey kid, I've got tobacco juice on your card, give me another." I did, but I still have that treasured card.

The Washington Nationals

It wasn't long before the Washington Nationals moved to Orlando. Making new friends on the club was easy. My dad would take me out to Tinker Field early in the morning and I would stay all day. I watched batting practice, and after the batting cage was removed, I would head for the dugout. At that time (1941) the

Tigers were in for a game and Steve O'Neill was manager. While in the dugout, O'Neill turned to me and said, "I thought I'd gone to heaven when our bus drove us up through the orange groves." On another occasion when a game was about to begin, Birdie Tebbetts, the high-voiced, talkative backstop, stood in front of me, hands on his hips. "Who are you?" he asked. When my reply seemed satisfactory, he said, "OK, you can stay – but no interviews with my players."

During this time the game had its share of antics. I remember Washington coach Nick Altrock, who was often joined by Al Schacht, do a comedy routine as fans waited for the game to start. I'll never forget Walter "Cuckoo" Christensen, who had a short major league career (1926-27, Cincinnati, National League), thrill American Association fans by standing up and catching fly balls in the outfield while riding in the side-car of a motorcycle.

The Players

Joseph Valentine Stripp, who played eleven years in the National League with the Reds, Dodgers, Cardinals and Braves, retired and became a full time Florida resident. He opened up Jersey Joe Stripp's Baseball School in Orlando, a development school for Depression-era boys who wanted to make a living playing baseball. He brought in several players as instructors such as Zack Taylor, John Ganzel, Jeff Heath and others. Joe Tinker even agreed to be an advisor. The successful venture not only yielded many major leaguers, but also was a treasure trove for autograph collectors.

Zack Taylor and I grew into good friends. Florida-born (Yulee, Fla.), Zack devoted his entire life to baseball. He spent half a century in organized baseball, sixteen of them as a major league catcher (1920-35). He coached, managed and scouted until 1970 and was often a source of clinics for high school-age prospects. Having spent many hours with Zack in his home, it was a real education. While I remember him as a friend, many recall him as the man who sent pinch hitter Eddie Gaedel to the plate on August 18, 1951, the day the midget had his one famous at-bat. Zack's statistics might not help for Hall of Fame consideration, but his personal devotion to the game adds many points.

Hall of Fame Encounters

Obtaining an autograph from Lou Gehrig was probably one of the highlights of my early collecting years. It was in St. Petersburg at the Seminole Hotel – spring base for the Yankees. After dinner one evening several players were enjoying the city's famous "green benches" ... Gehrig was included ... what a thrill!

The mention of Gehrig brings Babe Ruth to mind. Just a few months prior to Ruth's demise, he made a personal appearance at Tinker Field. One of the local radio announcers had the good fortune to be able to interview him there. The babe's voice was so very weak and strained. It was so very sad to witness.

Chance encounters were common during this time. Finding Connie Mack – or Mr. Mack as he was universally addressed – and Clark Griffith together in the hotel lobby was always a plus as they would reminisce over early times as keen opponents. Naturally this combination drew a group of fans and even players. To Mack baseball was always a business and Griffith admired him for that.

My lone person-to-person encounter with Ted Williams (other than getting him to sign autographs for me) was one day in Orlando at the "old" Tinker Field. Having been on the field taking pictures, it was just about time for the game to begin. Heading out behind the visitors dugout I heard his very distinct voice – similar to John Wayne: "Anyone have a pocket knife?" I turned around and it was Ted carrying a bat. I quickly handed him mine and he proceeded to scrape the handle. He thanked me and went back to the dugout. Needless to say I carefully wrapped my knife in my handkerchief to "keep the fingerprints." I still have it!

The Pittsburgh Pirates had an exhibition game at Tinker Field in 1972. Among those on the field was an older gentleman in full uniform. Unable to identify him, I introduced myself. It turned out to be Harold Joseph "Pie" Traynor. We had a very memorable conversation, Traynor speaking with his New England accent (which he never lost), and afterward he graciously signed a couple items for me. He then inquired where the bullpen was, as he wanted to watch some of the Pirates' rookie pitchers. Not only was Traynor popular, but John McGraw himself called him the greatest team player in the game. After the Pirates bus returned to Bradenton, Traynor suffered a heart attack that evening and had to be rushed back to Pittsburgh, where he passed away on March 16th.

The Sports Reporters

Over a period of several years, I had the pleasure of being on the sports staff of the *Orlando Sentinel* and *Reporter Star.* It was during this time that I had assignments for baseball coverage during spring training and the Class D Florida State League Orlando Senators.

What an opportunity and pleasure to work alongside the many media personnel. The top of the list had to be sitting next to Mel Allen whenever the Yankees were in town. People forget that there was no private box for radio in those days.

One of the writers I remember most was Wirt Gammon of the *Chattanooga Times.* With the Chattanooga Lookouts being a farm club of the Senators and the big club in training at nearby Winter Garden, Gammon was doing double duty. Since Wirt was also an avid collector of baseball memorabilia, we struck up a strong friendship. Gammon had a special "in" with Ty Cobb, and the two frequently exchanged correspondence. It was my good fortune to share that privilege.

Just a few months prior to the passing of author and sportswriter Fred Lieb, I had the pleasure of visiting him at his home in St. Petersburg. His many books and other works were recognized through his election to the Baseball Hall of Fame (1972). We had a wonderful visit together and I discovered that he, too, was a collector. He said, "Look under my bed." Believe it or not, there must have been at least a hundred autographed baseballs. Later he mentioned that he had just recently sent his vast collection of baseball press pins to the Hall of Fame.

"Stengelese"

Looking back, I now realize the 1934-35 era played an important role in my interest in the game. Brooklyn had as its manager one Charles Dillon "Casey" Stengel – "The Old Professor." Casey struggled with the Dodgers for three years, with a sixth-place finish in 1934, a fifth-place finish in 1935 and a seventh-place finish in 1936. Discovering that Casey was born on the same date as myself, I took particular pride in every opportunity to visit with him. He was a very special person indeed.

Being sorry to see the Dodgers move their spring base to Clearwater in 1936 didn't turn out so bad after all, because when Casey later managed the Boston Braves – then called the Bees – I had ample opportunity to resume our friendship. Casey managed the team for six years from 1938 through 1943, never finishing higher than fifth place. After being let go in the spring of 1944, he went back to managing in the minor leagues. That same year he took over the helm of the

Harold L. Esch

Milwaukee Brewers (American Association) and led them to a first-place finish. Stengel loved to coach at third base, and I can see him to this day swinging his arms like a windmill bringing in the runs.

I have many memorable Stengel moments, but the one that sticks in my mind is sitting in on a long exchange of conversation between Casey and Yogi Berra. Can you imagine? I should have taped it! One of my favorite quotes from Stengel was when he was asked, "How can you handle so many men and keep them satisfied? Stengel's reply was, "It's like this ... I try to keep the seven or eight men who hate me away from those who haven't made up their minds."

Making a Difference

Luis Clemente Tiant Vega began his career with Cleveland. Tiant's father, Luis Tiant Sr., was one of Cuba's greatest pitchers, so needless to say, expectations for his son's baseball career were high. He was a hot property early in his career and the Indians knew it, but after missing his usual stint in winter ball, he led the American league with 20 losses and 129 walks in 1969. After the season, Cleveland traded him to Minnesota. Tiant started the 1970 season with six straight wins, but suffered a hairline fracture in his shoulder and finished with a 7-3 record. At the beginning of the 1971 season near the close of spring training, Minnesota released him.

The very next morning, I ran into Luis in the post office and had a long chat with him. He was obviously very upset and indicated that his career might be over. I tried very hard to encourage Luis and felt certain that some club would sign him and things would be different. He faltered in the minor league system the following year, but never gave up. Whether our talk made any difference or not, I'm not sure. He was the Comeback Player of the Year in 1972 for a very competitive Red Sox team. He picked up a second ERA title with a 1.91 mark and was 15-6. The rest is simply history.

PREFACE

An Autograph Collector Price Guide

When a buyer enters a bookstore looking for some reading material, he is confronted with a variety of choices and a number of terms. They include "Fiction" – meaning invented stories, "Best-Sellers" – meaning books whose sales are among the highest of their class, and "Collectibles" – books that deal with objects collected by fanciers or enthusiasts. Chances are that you found this book in a "Collectibles" section.

Collectible books come in all shapes and sizes, but what they all have in common is a market for a specific subject matter. A "market" as defined by this author is the course of commercial activity by which the exchange of commodities is effected – the extent of demand. There is an "autograph market." It is not finite, such as The New York Stock Exchange, but it is equally dynamic.

Before we elaborate, let's talk about this book.

Definition

An "Autograph" is a single word, used as both a noun and verb, and defined by this author as a noun and something written in one's own hand, such as a person's handwritten signature or an original manuscript or work of art.

Add to "Autograph" the term "Collector" and you have "Autograph Collector," the latter being defined as one that makes a collection.

A "Price Guide" is defined by two words, not one. The term "price," as defined by this author, is the amount of money given or set as a consideration for the sale of a specific thing. The term "guide," as defined by the author, is something that provides a person with guiding information.

So what you have in your hand is a book that provides you with information about the amount of money given or set as a consideration for the sale of a person's handwritten signature. Let me add to this, "at a given period of time."

Pricing

Since the autograph market does not operate like the New York Stock Exchange, it cannot be defined in the same terms. A definitive list of subjects – the number of autographs in existence, the number of signatures traded on a particular day, or price to earnings ratio – doesn't exist. Therefore pricing, as listed in this guide, is based on a "data base" developed and maintained by the author. This "data base," or collection of data organized for rapid search and retrieval, is based on the participants in the autograph market. These participants range from auction houses and major dealers to auctioneers, serious collectors and casual participants. Thousands of catalogs, advertisements and auction results over the last twenty-five years were used as a basis for this information. Market data was collected, organized, analyzed and interpreted. It was an objective process based on fact, not fiction.

To determine an accurate price, certain processes had to be employed, such as not including the highest and lowest prices, etc. Many other concerns are taken into consideration, such as location, wholesale versus retail, known signing habits, etc. What you end up with is a completely original work based on available market data and all of the market concerns that impact value.

About Price Guides

If you just want to get an idea of how much the only autograph you own might be worth, then numerous resources can be found. From books and magazines to even the Internet, a "ballpark price range" can be easily determined. Such is the case for common signatures in their simplest form, such as signed photograph. For uncommon signatures in unusual forms, however, the task isn't as simple. You may have to do additional research, such as contacting dealers, institutions, organizations, or even specialists in certain areas. And yes, you may have to purchase an autograph price guide.

Typically, both collectors and dealers will purchase or reference the book they feel most comfortable with. This could be based on a number of reasons – format, accuracy, ease of use, available references or reputation, just to name a few. Whatever the case, it's nice to know you have some options.

The Official Autograph Collector Price Guide is structured as a buyer's guide – a resource to assist you when purchasing an object in the open market from a dealer or collector. It is *not* a seller's guide to prices. Don't deceive yourself by thinking anything else.

Naturally, if someone is selling an autograph, they will choose to refer to the price guide with the highest price in that form. However, with so many price guides available in the market, a buyer will counter with a reference source at the lowest possible value. If you have an item listed in this book, you can expect to receive approximately 35 to 40 percent of the value following a proper evaluation. The evaluation process will take into consideration all the elements that determine value.

The most confrontational element during the purchasing process is determining value. In fact, it is so much a conflict that I have included a separate chapter on the topic. This information will assist both buyer and seller in determining a fair market price.

Structure

This price guide has been formatted for the collector. The valuable information given to me by collectors has allowed me to structure a guide based on their needs. Time and time again, I listened to criticism about the existing guides in the market – including my own – and what collectors wanted to see changed.

Hopefully this book has taken into consideration all of their concerns. For example, the book is segmented by subject matter, not alphabetical. This is because collectors wanted easy access to evaluate related material. Each chapter head begins with bulleted points that can inform a reader in just a few minutes, "What You Need To Know," "Market Facts" and "Trends." This is done because research has proven that the average user of a price guide spends less than five minutes utilizing it for their needs.

Special features also have been added on collectors' behalf. Past price guides just haven't met their needs – needs that have changed with time and circumstance. For example, the chapter on the Presidents of the United States provides you first with key information, followed by a segmented valuation based on available formats, and lastly with recent offerings. A common criticism of price guides has been that they don't accurately reflect the market. What better way than to publish recent market offerings and the prices asked? Naturally these prices are already included in the listing, but this provides you with some of my references. It gives you a chance to cross-check any information you have with what has currently been offered.

Regarding the large number of references, every collector that I spoke to said, "I want to take only one book to an autograph show, not a half a dozen." I thought about it for awhile, looked down at my stack of references, and determined they were right. The references included are based on collector needs for each individual area of collecting. Naturally they differ. If you collect material signed by Supreme Court Justices, your needs are different than someone purchasing an autographed Babe Ruth baseball. If you read the chapter on market perspectives, you will realize that we all view collecting differently. These references will improve with subsequent editions, but for now they are the first step in meeting your needs.

In every price guide, this one included, there are names listed without prices; this is because they could not be determined. This is done because collectors would rather see that no price has been determined than assume a person has been overlooked. Also, as one collector pointed out to me, "Give me space in the guide to write down a price that I encountered or a checklist I can use for, say, Academy Award Winners." Well, you got it!

A Final Sentence

All price guides, especially those that contain elements of subjectivity to determine value, are controversial. Collecting autographs is a wonderful hobby in many ways, but it is not as definitive as stamp or coin collecting. Comparing "apples to oranges" is often a routine occurrence for those attempting to determine an accurate price for an autographed item.

Remember, what you have in your hand is a book that provides you with information about the amount of money given or set as a consideration for the sale of a person's handwritten signature at a given time.

If you have any comments, feel free to contact me through the publisher of this book.

A Final Word

As an elder statesman of this hobby, I speak with credentials that I am very proud of. Heading toward my fifth decade as a collector and having sold a few books along the way, I have had the opportunity to meet some of the finest and most dedicated individuals you would ever want to meet. Extraordinary people who spend relentless hours researching, dedicating themselves to the hobby and preserving history.

As a group, this is the one hobby where I could stick twelve people in a room and have them come out with artifacts and evidence that could change history. Imagine – unpublished stories from Ernest Hemingway, eyewitness accounts to the assassination of President Kennedy, a letter from one Hall of Famer to another saying they don't know what they are talking about when it comes to baseball.

The list is endless.

We live in a society that regularly broadcasts meaningless award shows on television, yet as a group we are seldom acknowledged. When we are, it is often at a "flea market level" rather than a level that we, as a group, deserve. We have lost many pioneers in this industry in recent years, wonderful people who lived and believed in this hobby. We need to continue to work together and to maintain the spirit of our predecessors. Let's believe in us, believe in our work, and believe in this wonderful hobby.

Section One

CHAPTER ONE
UNDERSTANDING THE VALUE
OF AN AUTOGRAPH

Finding out how much your autographed Dwight Eisenhower or Arnold Schwarzenegger photograph is worth usually means turning to a certain page in a price guide, but understanding just how that value was determined requires a greater understanding of the hobby.

The most common misconception in the hobby is that age determines value. In fact, only documents dated before the year 1400 are done so due to age. The key factors that influence the value of autographed celebrity memorabilia are condition, supply/scarcity, demand, form/content, source and subject. The source of an item, although paramount for authenticity purposes, is considered a secondary factor. In recent years, many dealers have put a premium on "in-person" signatures. To what extent this will play in the market remains to be seen. For those individuals who are in the business of buying and selling autographed celebrity memorabilia, understanding these factors is essential to their success. To a novice or casual collector they are important, but far less significant than the pure enjoyment of the hobby.

There is a demand for celebrity autographs and individuals willing to sell them, therefore a market exists. Where there is market, there is a need to understand value, by both the buyer and seller. Most of us started collecting because of an interest in a particular area, occupation or individual. The value of an autograph wasn't even a consideration. Collecting autographs gave us an opportunity to share in the achievements of the celebrities we cherished. To preserve those moments, we often wrote a celebrity and asked for their autograph, or tried to acquire a signature in-person. It was our assurance that the memory wouldn't fade and, of course, our proof that we really did have contact with the person or persons we admired.

As a market, the pricing of autographs can be traced back hundreds of years, probably a surprise to many of you participating in the hobby today. Unfortunately – or fortunately depending upon your perspective – it took the explosion in the sports autograph market to really bring the hobby of autograph collecting into the forefront. With this growth in the hobby came a greater need for communication, even dedicated magazines and, of course, more sophisticated price guides. Those of us who had participated for decades prior to this phenomenon were complacent to pull out old auction catalog results or our copy of Charles Hamilton's *The Book of Autographs* to update ourselves on autograph prices.

The Introduction of Television

During the 1950s most casual autograph collectors weren't interested in values, because many of their autographs were obtained in-person, and the value was in the moment and not on the paper. There was radio and cinema, but it took television to really bring many of our heroes to life and for collectors to finally see for themselves the faces of Joe DiMaggio, Bob Hope, Judy Garland, and Groucho Marx from a different perspective. As television evolved, we were treated to an increased number of shows on a variety of subjects. Television became a maternity ward for Hollywood's next biggest and brightest stars.

The mark of a great television show is its profound impact on our culture and its uncanny ability to mimic an era. Characters such as Archie Bunker and "Hawkeye" Pierce take on bigger-than-life roles, catapulting the actors who play them into almost instant celebrities, and therefore valuable autographs.

The Boom in Sports Autographs

Although the attendance of some sports waned during the 1960s, it began to flourish again in the 1970s. The word "athlete" was slowly being replaced by the term "sports personality" or "sports celebrity." The growing interest in professional sports prompted an increase, and often renewed interest, in collectibles, especially sports trading cards and autographs. Companies not only began to wonder about what new products they could sell into this market, but also became more interested in the appeal of the sports celebrity to sell those products. We knew "Broadway Joe" Namath could throw a football, but could he convince men watching television to buy a brand of shaving cream?

The competitive cable market, new and affordable satellite equipment, and what seemed to be a never-ending appetite for this visual medium, was the enticement needed for the birth of many new networks, including FOX, ESPN and numerous others. Increased competition meant higher fees for the rights to broadcast certain events, especially professional sports. Then, of course, there was the celebrity, who felt that he, too, was entitled to his share of the revenues. Lucrative multi-million dollar contracts soon became necessary to assure that a team's "sports celebrities" would remain in town for another season, or that a particular character wouldn't disappear from an actor's repertoire.

Professional athletes-turned-celebrities were even turning up in magazine advertisements, syndicated television shows, commercials, shopping networks and even movies. The growth in sports trading cards, specifically baseball, led to the increased number of sports trading card shows. These shows soon found themselves expanding to include autograph guests to boost revenues and increase attendance. The additional cost of getting sports celebrities to attend a show meant that a promoter often was forced to charge a fee for an autograph. With greater exposure came an increase in the number of autograph requests and the need for to find out where and how to contact the person. The growth in sports autographs soon found many collectors branching out into other fields such as entertainment, politics and music.

Major League Baseball was the first of the four major sports to combine all the necessary ingredients to entice autograph collectors. For a market to be viable, collectors need access to their subjects – at the ballpark or at home *(Baseball Address List No.1);* a cost-effective method of acquisition (through dealers, in-person or by mail); a price guide to validate an autograph's value (numerous sources); a way to confirm a signature's authenticity (numerous resources); and a vehicle to monitor the market, such as *Sports Market Report* or *Autograph*

Collector.

As the market matured, in-person access to many major players has been reduced, while indirect sources such as satellite shopping networks and product catalogs have expanded. You may not be able to obtain a free Cal Ripken signature at the ballpark, but at least you still have the opportunity to obtain an autograph, despite the purchase price. Recently there have been signs that the market for autographed sports memorabilia is beginning to lose some steam. However, over the past twenty-five years, autographed photos in this niche have shown the greatest increase in value.

The Dichotomy in the Autograph Market

The boom in signed sports memorabilia created a second tier to the already established autograph market. This traditional market, made up of hundreds of dealers, has catered to the needs of those participants in the Manuscript Society, Universal Autograph Collectors Club and Antiquarian Booksellers Association of America. While there are parallels to both market segments, there are also significant differences. The traditional market offers material in a wide variety of fields from signed opera photos to land grants signed by Presidents of the United States. Naturally, as an established market segment, their business practices, ethics and organizations are held to a higher standard than those of newer segments. Their views on autograph values are also much different, with many of the major dealers choosing to sell only a handful of sports autographs, if any at all. A traditional autograph dealer walking around a sports collectibles show would find only a few signed items of interest and would certainly disagree with the majority of prices. This dichotomy is being addressed here because, as an autograph collector, there are going to be some instances where the values of certain pieces conflict between these two segments.

The Definition of Value

The definition of value itself has two different meanings to collectors. Many collectors perceive the word value to mean "that quality of a thing that makes it more or less desirable, having an intrinsic or inherent worth." These celebrity autograph collectors can't put a value on their collections, because there is no monetary equivalent to the satisfaction they have derived from building them. It is this definition that I hear the most from satisfied collectors and hobbyists who still have fun.

The other definition some collectors use is "estimated worth." Dealers participating in this market often find themselves trying to accurately price a wide variety of autographed items. Since pricing autographed items is far from an exact science, dealers will often refer to a number of sources for pricing assistance. These sources can be other dealers, experienced collectors, auction houses, advertisements and a variety of price guides. The buyer – who wishes to pay a fair and not an inflated price – also will find many of these resources useful. Whether you like it or not, your definition of value is going to affect how you collect celebrity autographs.

The Factors That Influence Value

Not all collectors are fortunate enough to have a professional-level team, major concert hall or museum located in the city where they live. These collectors are forced to acquire most celebrity autographs indirectly, some of which will be purchased from dealers. To efficiently purchase celebrity autographs from dealers, it is necessary to have an understanding of value. Understanding the key factors that influence value will help prevent you from being overcharged for an item.

As mentioned previously, there are five key factors that determine the value of a celebrity autograph: condition, supply/scarcity, demand, form/content, and the source, or whom you purchase from.

Condition

The condition of an autographed celebrity collectible is considered by most dealers to be the paramount factor effecting an item's value. When assessing the value of an autographed celebrity collectible, the condition of the signature as well as the condition of the material that was signed are both thoroughly examined. The signature should be bold, clear and unobstructed by any portion of the material that was signed or any other signatures that appear with it. The material that was signed should reflect, as much as possible, the original state of that object. The only exception would be some costumes and game/event-worn equipment that naturally would show some indication of wear. For those collectors of autographed game-worn equipment or costumes, it is important to understand that severe damage to the item, such as uniform tears or large pieces missing from certain items, can negatively affect the value of the autographed item.

It is not unusual for some autographed items to reflect certain aging characteristics. The aging characteristics of paper-based collectibles are probably the most familiar to collectors. These include light stains, discoloration due to fading and inconsistent wear due to folding. Sports equipment, such as hockey sticks and baseball bats, typically will exhibit discoloration due to the aging of the finish applied to them during the final stages of production. Jerseys will exhibit loose threads and some fading. Certain aging characteristics are anticipated by collectors and thus have little or no effect on value. Any flaw that is not part of the normal aging process will have a negative impact on the value of the piece. For example, autographed baseballs, costumes or playbills that show excessive wear due to mishandling will detract from the value of the piece.

The type of ink and the writing device used for an autograph can effect an item's condition, thus impacting its value. All material has a level of porosity, or a degree to which fluids, air or light can pass through or into them. The higher the level of porosity, the greater the chance of deterioration that takes place in the item. Unfinished wood and certain fabrics are very porous, thus when certain inks are applied to them the fluid spreads into the surface. This is why so many collectors of autographed baseballs prefer ballpoint pen ink signatures over those produced by other porous tip markers. Many inks react negatively to the surfaces they come in contact with, causing dramatic discoloration over a short period of time.

Supply/Scarcity

The supply or scarcity of a form of autographed celebrity memorabilia typically will have a reciprocal effect on the demand for the piece. This is particularly true with the signatures of deceased individuals and many of the pioneers in certain fields. In the sport of baseball, the autograph of Babe Ruth has always been in great demand. Even though he signed frequently, the supply continues to be insufficient to meet the demand of the collector. Although "Shoeless" Joe Jackson is not a member of the Baseball Hall of Fame, his signature is highly sought after. This is due not only to the mystique created by the movie *Eight Men Out,* but also because for many years he was considered an illiterate and didn't learn to sign his name until late in life.

The Jacksons owned a liquor store in Greenville, South Carolina. When accompanied by his wife, Joe never would never sign anything or, if forced, would sign with an "X". On the occasions when he was left alone, his wife would leave a piece of paper with his name written on it, just in case he needed to sign for merchandise or possibly an autograph. Mr. Jackson would essentially draw his autograph, sometimes taking close to a minute to complete it. Today the autograph of "Shoeless" Joe Jackson is considered the most valuable sports autograph in history. The first Jackson clipped signature that entered the market sold for $23,000. A few years ago, an 8x10-inch photograph of "Shoeless" Joe sold for $28,000 at an Odyssey Auctions sale in Corona, California.

Scarcity is often difficult to determine. Many times the market will move based on a rumor, and a celebrity's signature will immediately skyrocket in value, even though there has been no confirmation that the information is indeed true. A few years ago a collector I knew began buying Stan Musial autographed baseballs at twice the current market price because he heard a rumor that he wasn't going to sign baseballs any more. The rumor was incorrect and the collector ended up spending an awful lot of money foolishly.

Fluctuations in supply are often temporary, as is the case with most celebrities who are actively involved in their field. The demand for the signatures of the field's biggest stars or contributors builds during certain seasons, and is typically met during the "off" season when many celebrities are more accessible. Many entertainers do sign during tours, but at a lesser frequency. There are also occasions when a dealer has purchased a large number of signed checks or documents from an estate and offered them for resale to the market. This flooding of material will fill current demand and drive values down for that type of autographed item. In this case it may take many years for the market to replenish the demand and drive values upward.

Demand

The current demand for many celebrity autographs has been so strong that some athletes, entertainers and musicians have had to resort to facsimile (stamped), secretarial, or machine signed (autopen) autographs. The massive correspondence received by celebrities like Michael Jordan, Tiger Woods, Britney Spears and Julia Roberts, if attended to personally, would leave little time for their own everyday needs. To reduce the response time to signature requests received by mail, some celebrities will only sign one item per person. Many celebrities use this technique, including Alan Alda, Shirley Temple Black and Norman Mailer. This helps meet current market demand without frustrating collectors, or resorting to unauthentic responses, which only serve to confuse the public. Some television shows, such as *Beverly Hills 90210,* will try to hamper demand by responding to collectors' requests for cast autographs with 4x 6-inch color postcards bearing facsimile signatures on the back. Although collectors are grateful that their requests are at least acknowledged, this method only serves to increase demand.

Significant achievements, such as reaching a career milestone, winning an Emmy, Oscar or Golden Globe, can immediately affect demand. An example of this is certainly Tom Hanks, who was accessible to collectors for many years both through the mail and in-person during his television days. It wasn't until he won the Best Actor Oscar for *Philadelphia* (1993) that anyone saw a noticeable increase in the demand for his signature. This increase will remain until all public demand has been met.

Changes in a celebrity's popularity, for whatever reason, also affect demand. While a poor performance, poor judgment or a career-threatening injury usually triggers these changes, they also can be caused by an event that the public may consider distasteful. For example, O.J. Simpson, Michael Jackson, Tonya Harding, Paul Reubens, Mike Tyson and Hugh Grant have all seen the demand for their signature reduced because they have not met the public's performance expectations. These demand changes are often cyclical and, as you can see by some of the names on this list, any of these celebrities has the potential to put together a tremendous year. For the contrarian in the autographed celebrity memorabilia market, this represents the best time to buy these stars' signatures, because they are probably at the lowest possible prices.

The signatures of recently deceased celebrities, especially former or current stars, are always in demand, often commanding two or three times what an average autograph from these individuals would have commanded prior to their deaths. In the case of an unpredictable circumstance claiming a celebrity's life, demand can be enormous, as exemplified by the reaction of collectors following the deaths of Natalie Wood, River Phoenix, Princess Diana, John F. Kennedy Jr. and Brandon Lee.

Form/Content

The type of material the collector has the celebrity sign and its relevance to the subject has an impact on the item's value. This is why a Sylvester Stallone autographed boxing glove is worth more than his signature on a photograph. This is not to say that you can't be creative – like having a baseball signed by Kevin Costner, Charlie Sheen and Michael Jordan (you can) – but try to avoid having foolish or unrelated items autographed. How many times have we all seen unprepared fans flock to request the signature of a celebrity on a napkin? In all my years of collecting, I have never met a collector of napkins, either the dinner or cocktail varieties. If you are going to collect autographed celebrity memorabilia, try to choose a form that at least is appealing and accepted by the majority of others already participating in the hobby. While popular forms of collecting may be less creative, they offer a greater range of acquisition possibilities. Adding to an autographed sports trading card, baseball, movie script or personal check collection is easier than more bizarre forms of collectibles, such as clocks, furniture and glassware.

Baseball collectors believe in having only "Official League" baseballs autographed, mainly because they are datable and subject to less authentication scrutiny. Additionally, "Official League" baseballs are identical to those used by the professionals. Because this has become an accepted form of collecting, "Official League" autographed baseballs have greater value than non-"Official League" baseballs. Whenever an autographed sports collectible can be dated, it reduces a collector's concern for authenticity, and thus increases the value of that item. Collectors of autographed baseballs also prefer single-signature baseballs, or balls with only one autograph on the "sweet spot," or side opposite the name of the league's president, over multiple signature balls. This is why a single-signature baseball of Lou Gehrig is worth more than an equivalent Gehrig signature on a baseball accompanied by the names of Johnny Allen, Frank Crosetti, Bill Dickey and Doc Farrell. In this case "less is more" in terms of value.

Autographed letters containing "great," extremely relevant, or even controversial content are highly sought after forms by collectors. A letter from Bob Hope discussing his style of golf is far more intriguing than a simple note thanking someone for an autograph request. Admittedly, most celebrities are not known for their letter writing prowess, but if you pick this form to collect, remember that value is a function of content.

Source

When mentioning celebrity and sports autograph values in my other books, I have been reluctant to acknowledge the source where the item was acquired because it could have an impact on the value of a piece. Increasing market concerns for authenticity have forced me to reconsider its absence. Although the source of a signature can impact an autograph's value, I believe it has a lesser effect than any of the factors listed previously. Recently, advertisements in many of the autograph collecting periodicals have put an increased value on in-person signatures. Whether or not this trend continues remains to be seen, but it is certainly worth taking note of.

Additionally, it is getting extremely difficult for the average collector to authenticate many of the sports autographs he is buying. Therefore, he is not afraid to spend the extra money to purchase an autographed Roger Staubach football directly from the Dallas Cowboys' recognized source for $129.99. Yes, he could have saved himself as much as $40 by choosing an alternative source, but his level of purchasing confidence would have been reduced. In this case, his lack of expertise in authentication determined his purchasing source.

What scares me about including source as an impact on value is that I have already seen many larger companies intimidate smaller collectors into purchasing their products by using a "forgery fear" in their marketing tactics. Let me state it clearly to all collectors that the signature you receive in-person, be it at a show, or in the arena, is of equal, if not greater, value than a purchase you make from a major autograph memorabilia supplier. "Letter of Authenticity" or not, if a major company or dealer files for bankruptcy, what do you honestly think it's going to take in terms of time and finances to redeem your autographed Reggie Jackson baseball that you paid $79.95 for just because you have authenticity concerns?

Subject

The demand for autograph-related items is not equal throughout all fields – Sports, Presidential, Entertainment, etc. – or forms such as signed photographs, handwritten letters, etc. Not only is it not equal, it is also variable. Who and what was "hot" twenty years ago probably has little demand now. While this is of little concern to the casual autograph collector, it is paramount to dealers and investors. Collecting for value is another field of it's own and, like speculating in stocks and mutual funds, can be very volatile.

A Final Word on Value

Remember, it is not the dealer, celebrity, or promoter who determines value, it is the collector. Your willingness, justifiable or not, to pay a certain price for an autographed celebrity item has an impact on value. While there is little doubt in my mind that an autographed photograph of Paul Newman will eventually increase in value, there is a point at which the collector refuses to purchase an item. You – the collector – make that decision. These major dealers and companies are in business to make money, or they won't be around for long. If they cannot get the price they are asking for an autographed sports item, there is only one alternative – lower it. Stagnant inventory doesn't pay bills or impress investors, but sales do. My father once told me, "An item is only worth what someone is willing to pay for it."

CHAPTER TWO
MARKET PERSPECTIVES

A friend of mine once said, "If you don't like people criticizing your work, write a phone book!" It's no secret that price guides are dissected like frogs in biology class. Add to the criticism the dynamics and subjectivity of autograph collecting and any author has a significant challenge. While I have chosen to tackle the job in the past with my own view as a collector, it's time for some different perspectives.

Every participant in this hobby has a different view. A perspective is a person's capacity to see things in a certain light or relative importance – a viewpoint. To understand the autograph market is to acknowledge these participants. Whether you agree or disagree, all of these individuals determine value and impact pricing.

There are six primary market participants: the casual collector, shop owner, auctioneer, auction house/dealer, obsessed collector and the person whose autograph is being sought – typically a celebrity.

Since price guides and their formats don't appeal to every participant, I have also decided to include a differing perspective. I believe that everyone in this hobby has a voice, and in future editions perhaps this can be a forum for their opinions.

The views expressed here are copyright the individuals chosen for inclusion. They do not necessarily reflect the views of the author or publisher, but are provided for a comparison and contrasting viewpoints that we feel are beneficial to our readers.

The Casual Collector – Introduction

Having formerly owned a memorabilia shop, encountering the casual autograph collector was a daily occurrence, yet an event that I always looked forward to. After all, the casual collector represents the innocence and purity of the hobby. Unaltered by greed, they collect for the sheer pleasure – a virtue I pray that we never lose. The person I chose for this section wishes to remain anonymous. I not only respect this choice, but also feel it's appropriate. Here is what he wrote:

The Casual Collector

"Collecting for us has always been fun and, in many cases, an afterthought. My sons first got me into collecting by attending baseball games. They would bring their cards to the game and hand them to the players for an autograph. We never thought about the value a signature would add to the card, only the value of the card itself. At that time there were many people who didn't have cards signed for fear it would decrease the value. For my sons and me, it wasn't even a concern.

When we shopped for signatures at the local shops, pricing wasn't a big concern. It's not to say we wanted to be "ripped off" if we bought something, only to say it wasn't our primary focus. If we had the money, trusted who we bought the item from, then we added it to our collection. For me (the father) it was a way to bond with my kids, like baseball.

When all the cable stations started to offer memorabilia, we got hooked again. Instead of having to travel all over town to find an item for our collection, we spent hours in front of the television. If we wanted an item and it fit into our budget – which we needed at the time – we bought it. We never consulted price guides, but assumed the amount we were paying was about right. Looking back, I'm not sure if that was the right decision at the time, but it was easy to get caught up in the excitement. We had to establish a budget because it became too easy to spend money. Not to mention it taught the kids about finances and setting parameters.

We have an area in the house dedicated to our autograph treasures. From Cal Ripken signed baseballs and Ken Griffey Jr. bats to signed programs and even hats, all are there for our viewing pleasure. As the kids have gotten older, their interests have changed and we find ourselves adding fewer items. To me the items have little value other than a memory. We do realize that they are worth money, but we'll never sell them. We've never collected to make money, so why start now?"

The Shop Owner – Introduction

Having collected autographs for nearly four decades, I have been in my fair share of memorabilia shops. Although they vary considerably in size and shape, they never vary in intrigue. Whether you're a casual collector or dealer, the experience is often memorable. For a shop owner's perspective I chose Uncle Al's Time Capsule in Mount Dora, Florida. It's a wonderful shop, owned and operated by Al Wittnebert. Having published autograph books and been a key participant in the hobby for many years, Al is far from your average shop owner. But as a resource, he is invaluable.

RUNNING A SMALL AUTOGRAPH GALLERY
by Al Wittnebert

You travel through rolling hills and orange groves in what seems to be a remote portion of Florida. After all there are no amusement parks or water slides, only country roads with the occasional gas station along the way. You pass postings that read "Beware of Bears Crossing" and "Eagle Sanctuary" until you see a sign that states very plainly "Welcome to Mount Dora."

Founded in the 1870s, the city of Mount Dora lies about 40 miles due north of Orlando, and is as off the beaten path as one can get. The city itself has a population of about 9,000 and overlooks rolling hills and large lakes in the center of Florida. This may seem like a place to open a bait store or a Bed and Breakfast. But my wife and I – ever the optimists – opened an autograph gallery. Having worked in the hustle and bustle of big cities, traffic, high taxes and pollution for the last twenty-five years, we both felt it was time for change. Both of us took early retirement from our jobs and moved to Mount Dora. To keep ourselves busy, we acquired what was once an old doctor's office built in 1921 in the quaint downtown district (three blocks by three blocks) and converted it into a gallery.

Al Wittnebert with Cammie King

Having been involved in autographs for over forty years, I wanted to work in an environment that afforded me the opportunity to talk and interact with other collectors. I wanted to open a place that catered to the needs of collectors. Having sold autographs at shows and on the Internet gave me some idea what the market was and where I could find a place. I asked myself, "What do collectors need?" Having experience in appraisals and being a member of the International Society of Appraisers, I set up offices in the back of the gallery to provide appraisal services for collectibles. That was our first associated business with the gallery. My wife of over thirty years and the love of my life, Irene has a good eye for merchandising and display. The gallery itself was put in her charge. She decorates, buys stock and determines the direction of the gallery itself. We saw early on that framing the material ourselves would cut our overhead and add a new dimension to our business. So we attached a frame shop to the gallery that specializes in archival framing of autograph material.

Name and reputation brought in our initial business. After that, we used television and strategic advertising to promote our business as a destination. This way we were not dependent on walk-in traffic. We occasionally bring in guest celebrities to sign autographs and meet our customers. Over the years these promotions have been very successful and have attracted new customers from all over.

Since my wife and I have a love for old movies, the gallery focuses on autographs from Hollywood's Golden Era. Our material is tastefully framed and presented in a number of rooms where the customers can freely roam and view

the merchandise. We also have an ample stock of movie-related items like posters, photographs and such to complement the autographs we have in stock. All of our material is on view and for sale on our Web site www.sign-here.com, which also serves as our record of inventory.

Autograph sales make up only 25

percent of our total revenue for the business. The rest of the balance sheet is filled with non-autographed items as well as services we provide. The autographs serve in other capacities and are attractions that serve as decoration, curiosity and atmosphere. This is achieved by creative presentation. How you present the collectible is directly proportional to its salability.

We keep a number of signed photos and such in binders for our customers to peruse, but it is the framed items that sell best. We also carry a number of autograph reference books for the serious collector as well as magnifiers and microscopes. All are essential tools for the hobby.

Since we offer discounts to all UACC members on any purchase in the gallery, I have found that I meet more collector members here than at any show or on my travels. They come in and we talk autographs. I always have UACC literature and copies of *The Pen and Quill* to give out. This is the best part of owning a gallery. Talking with collectors and hearing about how they started and what they collect is just indescribable. I always make time to talk autographs.

I am sure I could make more money and have a bigger, better business if I had my gallery in a large metropolitan area, but the pace of a small town suits my family and me. We are part of the community and the community is part of us. I can't imagine doing anything else.

The Auctioneer – Introduction

In it's simplest terms, an auctioneer is defined as an agent who sells goods at an auction. But this definition is a far cry from describing the person I have chosen to write this section. Gil Griggs, a member of IADA, UACC and The Manuscript Society, operates Signature House in Bridgeport, West Virginia. Gil and Karen Griggs, along with their talented staff of Jerry Reames, Mike McBee and James R. Bucheimer, manage to put together one of the finest auction catalogs in the business. Gil is a fascinating individual who will easily charm you with his wealth of knowledge and appreciation of history. As a gifted auctioneer, he provides you with a unique perspective:

The Auctioneer

"Why have auctions become the main source of autograph collecting? Good question. I think we have to look back at the history of autographs and collecting and see how a hobby enjoyed by a few select collectors and dealers evolved into what it is today – an industry.

Autograph collecting goes way back. One of the first recorded collectors was Cicero. All through history there are stories about the scripts and scribbling of famous people being hoarded by collectors. One such notable is Napoleon. Because he had five or six secretaries writing letters at the same time, he is very rare as an ALS. However, his entire career can be traced by the manner in which he signed his name. At the beginning, he signed "Bouneparte" (his family name), later on as the French general "Bonaparte" (dropping the Italian spelling), then "Napoleon" as Emperor and, as his career began to wane, "Nap," and finally the very brief "Np."

During his time as General of the Continental Army, George Washington signed every soldier's discharge himself. If a man invested his time and willingly endured the hardships with the real possibility of losing his life in the Continental cause, the revered general felt he could do no less than sign his name to the discharge. One of the reasons you do not find many such documents in good condition is that the proud Revolutionary soldiers carried them on their person for years.

Stories abound from Thomas Jefferson and his autograph copy machine to Franklin D. Roosevelt who himself was an autograph collector as well as an avid stamp collector. Dealers from whom FDR purchased his stamps would not cash his payment checks – which would play havoc with the President's banking records. To his amusement, Roosevelt's inquires regarding receipt of a check were met with, 'Oh yes, Mr. President, we did.' 'Then why did you not cash the check?' FDR persisted. He knew, of course, that his signature on the checks would in time be more valuable than the amount of the checks themselves.

A similar tale is told about Pablo Picasso. While living in Madrid, the great artist brought an Italian cabinetmaker to his villa. In the course of explaining where he wanted the cabinet and what he desired, he quite naturally took a piece of paper and drew the image he envisioned. 'Now do you comprehend?' Picasso then questioned the cost of such a cabinet in oak wood. 'No charge,' the cabinetmaker said. 'Just sign the drawing.'

For many years six or seven New England dealers controlled the collecting of autographs in America. There were no price guides. If one wanted an autograph, whether it was a letter or signature, you paid the dealer's price or you went without. The only accepted authority regarding the authenticity of autographs was the late Charles Hamilton. I believe he should have the title 'Father of American Autographs.' He was one of the most interesting men I ever met. He wrote most of the books on autographs. He loved collecting. There is a story that during the 1970s he was invited to a house warming. It seems the host had bought a lovely old house on Cape Cod and invited Hamilton and others to his new home. Hamilton had someone drive him there. After partaking of the white wine and cheeses, Hamilton finally met the host, who, upon hearing Hamilton's name, said, 'So you are the Charles Hamilton who writes all those books on autographs?' 'I am,' Hamilton replied. 'When I bought this house we found a trunk which had a bunch of old letters from George Washington, John Adams, Thomas Jefferson ...' Hamilton's eyes lit up. 'And where are they now?' Seeking to impress his guest, the new homeowner said, 'We burned them, I think, to start a fire in the fireplace.' Whereupon Hamilton's face reddened and, turning over his wine glass, he told his driver that he wished to leave. He then turned to his host and commented, 'You, Sir, are a fool. You would have been better off to burn this beautiful old house and keep the autographs.'

The Eighties came and so did a boom in the economy. Two things caused an explosion in the autograph market, allowing it to leap from hobby to industry. The first was world traveler George Sanders of Asheville, North Carolina and his wife Helen. Always avid autograph collectors, they realized the need for a basic resource to share with the growing number of hobby enthusiasts. Their *Sanders Price Guide* became a benchmark. About the same time, a few established auction houses were going out of business due to the owner's death, bankruptcy, etc. A new auction house then appeared in Acton, Maine called Remember

When. Not only was it successful, but owner Jim Smith brought other new people into the auction business. He personally sponsored five new auction houses, and Signature House was one of the recipients of his generosity. Someone asked him if he was not afraid of diluting his business ... 'after all, there are only so many slices to the pie.' Jim saw it differently. 'I'm just making it a bigger pie,' he replied. All of these factors contributed to the boom in the autograph market. But what really drove market share was the advent of eBay and Internet auctions. With the seismic advent of the Internet, the wide world of commerce, as well as information, had indeed become a global 'village.' Auctions have become the preferred method of marketing. Everyone likes a bargain, and it's fun! Bidding at auction evokes a universal spirit of competition. And the expanding niche of autograph auctions has been hugely affected. Whether it's for good or ill is the subject of ongoing debate.

Specialty auctions have gained market share. The Civil War category saw increased interest generated by the Ken Burns film *Gettysburg.* Increased interest in other categories made special interest auctions worthwhile – Literature, Composers, Artists, Americana, etc. The most expensive category – and the most difficult to find – is Colonial, including Revolutionary War American and British Generals. Interest in Signers of the Declaration of Independence remains high. That is why the most expensive autograph is Button Gwinnett of Georgia, who was killed at age 45 in a duel only a year after he signed. Any collection of Signers must include this elusive autograph. Last year a document signed by him sold at auction for $240,000.

The best-selling categories, in my opinion, are Presidents, War Between the States, Sports and Entertainment (tie), Military, Aviators and Astronauts, The Arts, Colonial, Heads of State and Royalty, and Science and Technology.

The most sought after Presidents are Washington, Lincoln, Jefferson and Kennedy. However, the most expensive as President is William Henry Harrison, who was in office only 31 days. Then comes Garfield, who was in office for a matter of months, and Zachary Taylor, who was in office a little over a year.

In the War Between the States, generally the Confederate autographs are the most expensive – three times their Yankee counterparts. The most popular are Robert E. Lee and, of course, 'Stonewall' Jackson and J.E.B. Stuart, both of whom were killed in action. Of the Federals, the most sought after are George Armstrong Custer of Little Big Horn fame and Ulysses S. Grant, along with other Presidents who participated in the war – Hayes, Garfield and Arthur.

Entertainment and Sports, I feel, are equally desirable. Each genre has its superstars – Babe Ruth and Lou Gehrig and other vintage Hall of Fame members – Honus Wagner, Cy Young and John McGraw. Latter-day members make a nice living signing their names. Mickey Mantle quipped, 'Shucks, I get more money signing autographs than I got playing baseball.' Joe DiMaggio was interested in how much money was going to be made on his signature. However, collectors must be very wary of authenticity in sports autographs. Fraudulent autographs have become a cottage industry. The most expensive baseball autograph is 'Shoeless' Joe Jackson. He couldn't write his name and relied on his wife to sign his signature while he would draw the letters. Hollywood has its superstars as well – Marilyn Monroe, Humphrey Bogart, John Wayne. The really rare ones such as Jean Harlow, Buster Keaton and Fatty Arbuckle are often not that desirable to new collectors. They just don't know who they are. Academy Award winners are usually safe to buy or sell, especially anyone who appeared in *Gone with the Wind* and *The Wizard of Oz.* In entertainment, one must be aware of secretarial and studio signatures.

In buying or selling at auction, the most important factor is proving authenticity. With the emergence of eBay and a host of Internet and small auction houses, it is paramount to know whom you are doing business with and to 'get it in writing.' Buy what you like and read this book. Use it. Research the numbers – what an autograph you are contemplating buying is worth and what you are willing to pay for it. There are those who buy from one auction, pay the premium, consign it to another auction and pay the consignor's commission – and still make money. As a matter of fact, they make a living at it. But before you place your bid, find out about the auctioneer's guarantee. Is it for life or for 30 days? Either an autograph is good forever or it's bad forever. With some auction houses, the bidder buys "as is." Either the authenticity is not known or the auctioneer doesn't care. Don't bid with them. One big auction house states, 'All sales are final. Because of the due diligence we perform, it is our firm policy that any autograph lot sold with a letter of authenticity will be considered final. We will not engage in dueling experts, nor will we simply accept a contrary opinion as grounds for canceling a sale regardless of the perceived qualifications of another expert. In other words, even if you have an army of experts agreeing that an autograph is not authentic, the sale is still final.' In this same catalog was offered a land grant signed by Franklin Pierce – it was obviously secretarial. There was no recourse to the buyer. The moral of the story: Read the guarantee. Do business only with dealers who offer a lifetime guarantee, not a limited one. If a signature is good, it will be good for life. Before I bid with a new auction house, I talk with the owner – or at least the manager – someone in authority. I don't want to talk with a clerk, someone who only takes my bid.

Buy what you like, whether it is George Washington, Babe Ruth or David Ben Gurion. That should be evident. If you like the person, or are interested in a particular era, you will feel good about your purchase.

As you do your research, realize that there are three different market prices available. The most expensive market is retail. You are buying a Cadillac at the sticker price. When you are ready to sell, will you make a profit or even get your money back? I believe auction price is the true value of an autograph. It reflects the overall marketplace value. The time you invest in studying this book will help you make a wise investment. Ask for Prices Realized from the catalogs available to you. This is an additional tool to help you become aware of market prices. The third price point is the dealer's price – the amount the dealer will pay for your autograph. The benefit to you is quick payment. The downside is that it is usually less than auction price. He is going to make a profit on it. He is entitled to that. After all, he is in the business to earn a living.

It is your choice in buying or selling an autograph. This book can be a valuable tool. The more you do your homework, the more profitable it will be. It is your hobby – enjoy it!"

The Auction House – Introduction

EAC Gallery, a division of Emrose Art Corporation, is located in Roslyn Heights, New York. It is a charter member of the International Autograph Dealers Alliance, a member of The Manuscript Society and a UACC Registered Dealer. Under the watchful eye of Vice President Larry Rosenbaum – a member of the Appraisers Association of America – the gallery conducts numerous sales in a variety of formats.

Rosenbaum's expertise made him a perfect choice for an auction house perspective. For the reader's benefit, I asked him to focus on value and his interpretation of its factors. Here is what he had to say:

The Auction House

"One of the questions we at EAC Gallery are frequently asked regarding our auction catalogs and fixed priced catalogs – often right after, 'Where do you find all these wonderful items?' is 'How do you determine pricing?' In reality, that question is two questions: First, what factors determine value and second – and equally important – is how does one determine changes in value?

In determining value, both objective and subjective factors come into play. Some of the most significant objective factors are rarity, physical condition and state of the item. Ironically, in many cases, two subjective factors – content (subject matter) and connection (who written to) – have far greater influence on value than the objective ones.

Rarity, which in essence is the basic law of supply and demand, can be easily understood by the example of an item we sold earlier this year (2003) for $95,000 – the only known free franked full envelope signed by William Henry Harrison as President. Harrison caught a cold at his Presidential inauguration on March, 4, 1841, which developed into pneumonia, leading to his death exactly one month later, on April 4, 1841. Although Harrison's stature is far from that of a Washington, Jefferson or Lincoln, the rarity (shortness of supply) and, in this case, the uniqueness of the free frank due to the brief nature of Harrison's term in office, determined its phenomenal value – far in excess of free franks by Washington, Jefferson or Lincoln.

Condition is undoubtedly the most easily understood of the objective factors, as quite obviously a pristine baseball with a perfect Babe Ruth signature will be far more valuable than one that is scuffed and stained with a smudged signature, all other factors being equal. Because of this, as an important tool to help my clients determine value, I include an overall condition rating as well as a specific detailed condition report on each item I catalog.

The state of an item, with some exceptions, generally is divided into four major categories: (a) signatures, (b) letters signed or documents signed, (c) photographs signed and (d) autographed letters signed or autograph documents signed. A 'clipped' or 'cut' signature is placed at the bottom of the value hierarchy, as obviously it is simply the individual's signature and nothing more. A letter signed or document signed not only contains the individual's signature, but also additional content, either in someone else's hand, typed or printed, and therefore holds more value. How much more will be addressed later, as that relates to a subjective factor. At the top of the value hierarchy are autograph letters signed and autograph documents signed, which contain not only the signature, but also all writing in the individual's hand.

The factor that strongly differentiates autograph collecting from other collecting arenas is the great importance placed on subjective rather than objective criteria. The true importance, and associated value, of content and connection can best be demonstrated by a simple example – comparing two hypothetical typed letters signed by John F. Kennedy as President on official White House stationery. The first, sending birthday wishes, might sell in the $2,000-$2,500 range. The second, of equal length, but discussing the Bay of Pigs incident (significant content), would easily sell in excess of $100,000. If the second example is written to Nikita Khrushchev, the value increases further as this would add significant connection.

No marketplace is static, and therefore values are not permanent, but are subject to change by conditions both within and without our industry. Thus changing conditions also must be taken into account.

One factor affecting changes in pricing that I consider to be perhaps the most significant, is the huge growth in the collecting population. Once an almost secretive few collectors, autograph collecting has now become a mainstream pursuit, attracting daily press right alongside fine art, coins, stamps and other collectible arenas. This can best be summed up by a recent quote in *L.A. Business:* 'Investors hunting for the next sure thing have unearthed the historical document.' With demand increasing yearly and supply diminishing at an even greater rate, prices have been escalating for several decades now. There is an old maxim, often quoted by Charles Hamilton and other renowned dealers, which sums up this phenomena well: 'The high prices of today are the bargains of tomorrow.' It is therefore necessary to chart sales both in our auctions and other auctions to account for such changes. For example, we have been working with the Topps Trading Card Company recently in the acquisition of presidential autographs to be placed as promotions in packs of their cards. This provides exposure of presidential collectibles to an entire new base of sports collectors, and we have seen an immediate increase in prices realized as increasing numbers of collectors vie for the same property.

In addition to factors directly related to autograph collecting, there are also factors such as general economic conditions that affect pricing. As a general rule, in times of inflation prices of all collectibles tend to increase, and conversely decline in times of recession. Following the double whammy of the tech bubble bursting and the tragedy of September 11th, we witnessed a decline in pricing through the end of 2001 and into the start of 2002. However, 2002 ended on a very strong, positive, upward direction in pricing, and 2003 has seen the continuation of that trend, with EAC Gallery posting sales in excess of $5 million for that period.

Simply stated, but not simply accomplished, today's collector must be cognizant of both objective and subjective characteristics of an autograph collectible, both directly related to the collectibles industry as well as external to collecting. All factors must be taken into account and constantly reviewed and updated to successfully develop an equation that leads to the price value of an autographed item."

The Obsessed Collector – Introduction

The obsessed collector plays a pivotal role in the field of autograph collecting. It is through them that valuable information regarding their field of expertise enters the hobby. This knowledge is typically far more extensive than that of the casual collector. These participants have dedicated themselves not only to collecting autographs, but also to the field itself. Value to them is relative, and no price guide can accurately define the importance they place on a particular item.

The participant of choice for this section is Al Hallonquist. Al holds memberships in the following organizations: National Aviation Hall of Fame, Flight Test Historical Foundation, American Fighter Aces Association, Roadrunners Internationale, Air Force Association, Space Walk of Fame, Experimental Aircraft Association, Aircraft Owners and Pilots Association, National Aeronautical Association, National Air-racing Group and Silver Wings Fraternity. He also serves as an aerospace historian, author and contributing editor for a number of publications.

Like many dedicated collectors, Al's passion for his field began as a youth. He grew up in South Florida watching launches, attending AF JROTC Military School, learning to fly and Aerospace Education. The seeds were sewn early, and it wasn't long before they would bear fruit.

2003 UACC Executive Board with astronaut Wally Schirra (sixth from left)

SPACE AND AVIATION AUTOGRAPH COLLECTING
by Al Hallonquist

My first astronaut signature was not obtained through the mail, attending shows, or wherever. In 1986 during my career as a police officer, I answered an alarm at the residence of Al Worden, command module pilot on Apollo 15. Being the space and aviation geek that I am, and through Worden's kindness, we became friends and enjoy this friendship to this day. He signed some things for me, which to this day are still treasured pieces in my collection. He also put me in touch with my first test pilot, Chuck Yeager.

Attending Events

Each year I attend the Flight Test Historical Foundation's "Gathering of Eagles" in Lancaster, California. The event is attended by the likes of Yeager, Joe Engle, Fitz Fulton, Pete Knight, Joe Cotton, Bob Cardenas, and the list goes on. I have become friendly with these gents over the years, and it is so much fun not only to have them sign items for me in person, but to sit in the lobby as Joe Cotton and Fitz Fulton "hold court" and listen to the stories.

The U.S. Astronaut Hall of Fame at Kennedy Space Center has induction ceremonies and other celebrations as well. Living a two-hour drive south makes it easy for me to attend these events, and I do every opportunity I can get. This has afforded me a few opportunities to meet these heroes. One of the highlights of my collection is a stack of photos taken with the pre-shuttle astronauts and test pilots.

The best event I have attended yet for diverse opportunities is the National Aviation Hall of Fame's celebration last year in Dayton, Ohio. They held two events over the weekend, and I finally got to meet Neil Armstrong! I now have pictures with him, Buzz Aldrin, Tom Stafford, John Young, Al Worden (of course), John Glenn, Charlie Duke, Ed Mitchell, Dick Gordon, Joe Engle, Gene Cernan, Bill Anders, Ken Mattingly and many, many more.

A Change in Attitudes

It used to be easy to acquire signatures in this area, and in some cases, such as current astronauts, it still is. But by the late Eighties and early Nineties, attitudes had changed. The early astronauts were just not as forthcoming.

The first astronaut to charge for signing a photo was Jim Irwin. The charge at the time was a whopping $3 per signature. However, this was for the litho *he* provided and printed, not one of NASA's lithos, so he truly did not charge for his signature and would still sign your item for free and a SASE.

In the early Nineties Neil Armstrong started to slow down his signing and then quit altogether. Many people complained, but they didn't take into consideration that he was one of the best signers up to that point. Arguably the most sought after autograph from our modern era, Armstrong simply found the task overwhelming. Other astronauts soon followed suit. Bill Anders, while never a freely signing type through the mail, was not impossible prior to this time, but soon became a significant challenge.

Private signings and astronauts charging for their signatures through the mail soon became common. Early on, Pete Conrad charged a ridiculously low $10 fee and kept it there until his death. Dick Gordon, Alan Bean, Charlie Duke, Gene Cernan, Frank Borman, Tom Stafford and Ed Mitchell, along with others, also began to charge manageable fees. Others like Jim Lovell began signing only his book.

Enterprising individuals emerged during this time. Folks such as Kim Poor of Novaspace Galleries began the idea of having astronauts sign at his store either in a private signing, or in a reception/private signing. Kim is a class act and probably has done this the best so far. For a short time, The Space Source was the exclusive agent for some astronauts, but with the exception of Tom Stafford, they did not stay with them for long. Then Sims/Hankow put together a UACC show in America and Autographica in England. Both were very well done and proved to be excellent sources for collectors.

Today it is nearly impossible to obtain the autographs of most of the surviving pre-shuttle astronauts except through private signings, shows or the odd chance to catch them in-person. For example, Cernan and Aldrin sign exclusively through Kim Poor and Novaspace at announced private signings and for a good-sized fee. This is in contrast to their appearance at the Aviation Hall of Fame event in Dayton last summer, where they both signed freely and with a smile.

The advent of the online auction eBay was a key contributor to the change in attitude of many of the astronauts. There were some unscrupulous folks, using multiple post office boxes and pseudo names, who would write the astronauts for autographs only to turn around and offer them at auction. This process, which was easily unmasked, changed the attitudes of many astronauts, causing some to stop signing altogether.

Test Pilots

Collecting the signatures of test pilots is still a viable alternative for aviation enthusiasts. They never received the publicity given to astronauts and many aren't household or common names, but are no less essential. Without test pilots like Bob White, Scott Crossfield, "Slick" Goodlin and Joe Kittinger, believe me, the astronauts would never have made it into space. Their research and accomplishments were invaluable, and many of their aviation records are still standing today.

Collecting challenges in this area also exist. One of my goals is to collect a flight cover (cover commemorating a particular flight) from each X-15 pilot. There are 12 of them, and while this may be impossible, why not try? So far I have the autographs of Scott Crossfield, Robert Rushworth, Forrest Petersen, Bob White, Joe Walker, Milt Thompson, Jack McKay, Joe Engle, Pete Knight and Bill Dana. That leaves only Neil Armstrong and Mike Adams, with Adams – who died very early in the program – being far tougher to obtain. The thought of completing this task is just one of the thrills of collecting items from the X-15 program.

Every Picture Tells a Story

To date I have portrait pictures from the following pre-shuttle astronauts (either in their space suits, flight suits, EVA, on the moon or business suits): Shepard, Glenn, Carpenter, Schirra, Cooper and Slayton from Mercury, and Cunningham, Anders, Borman, Lovell, McDivitt, Schweikart, Scott Cernan, Stafford, Young, Armstrong, Collins, Aldrin, Conrad, Gordon, Bean, Haise, Mitchell, Worden, Irwin and Mattingly from Gemini and Apollo, plus many more.

A goal of some folks is to collect all the white space suit (WSS) portraits. This is a terribly difficult goal to reach, and not just because of the elusiveness of Armstrong. John Young signed very few of these, and has quit signing anything sent to him or in-person. In today's market, a signed John Young Gemini or

Apollo white space suit photo, or a picture of him on the moon is valued in the $3,000-$5,000 range depending on your source. The same is true for Jim Irwin in his white space suit, as he didn't care for the picture and would substitute a picture of him on the moon instead. The price for Irwin's white space suit portrait can be around $5,000. I am just happy to have a portrait or other picture of whomever I can get and am realistic that I will never see a collection such as all WSS portraits or on the moon pictures.

Complicating matters is that there is only one picture of Neil Armstrong on the moon and he signed very, very few of these. Also, some astronauts – Frank Borman and Bill Anders, for example – never had a WSS portrait. I am still looking for portraits of some style for Swigert (expensive), Roosa (expensive), Grissom (very expensive) and Evans.

Signed pre-shuttle crew pictures are not easy to find, either, and with the death of some of the astronauts and some simply not signing any more, your best bet is to purchase them should you desire to complete all Gemini, Apollo, Skylab and Apollo-Soyuz crews. I have managed to accumulate many, but it hasn't been an easy process. Some I have purchased, some I completed by mail or in-person, and others I traded for. While the process is fun, I have been realistic in my goals. I understand that completing the GT8 (Gemini/Titan) with Armstrong's signature will be nearly impossible, the GT10 of John Young and Mike Collins equally impossible, and that I'll never have an Apollo 1. Also, I will have to buy or trade for an Apollo 14 some day.

Another option for collectors is obtaining the WSS portrait of those that did not fly or didn't fly until the shuttle era. In this area, I have been successful with John Bull, Don Lind, Bob Crippen, Joe Engle and Don Holmquest. Also, collecting those peripheral folks to the space program can prove fascinating. Individuals such as Chris Kraft, Dee O'Hara, Geunter Wendt, Max Faget, George Ludwig, James Van Allen, Jesco von Putthamer, Lee Scherer, Jack King, Rocco Petrone, John Houbolt and Farouk el Baz are all great signers.

Collecting space and aviation over the years has been a lot of fun. Of course there is the monetary value of collecting, and frankly I've been very fortunate to collect some of these during a time when the values were very low. I realize that many items in my collection have risen in price, but I don't collect for the monetary value, but, rather, for the small piece of history I grew up with. Through meeting so many of my heroes I have developed friendships that are worth more than the monetary value of an autograph collection.

The Celebrity – Introduction

A celebrity is simply "a celebrated person," someone who is widely known and often referred to. Celebrities come in all shapes and sizes, from all parts of the world, from all age brackets, and from all fields of endeavor. They can be famous, infamous, or even both. As celebrated people, sometimes the only common denominator they have with other celebrities is that they are often unaware of how long their public adoration will last. While some celebrities are forever immortalized, many slip into obscurity and may never be heard from again.

Since celebrities are the primary targets in the field of autograph collecting, it is always interesting to hear their views on the hobby.

The Celebrity

"When fans send photos or memorabilia I sign them. I get approximately 250 pieces a month." – Robert Englund, a.k.a. Freddy Krueger

" I try to set aside one day a month to sign autographs through the mail – I receive several hundred a week – (from all of the world)." – Gary Owens, *Rowan & Martin's Laugh-In*

"Many requests: They cost $20 each, including USA postage. Outside of USA, add cost of postage and/or send postpaid envelope." - Karen Lynn Gorney, *Saturday Night Fever*

"Yes I sign autographs (through the mail). Mostly if they are handwritten by people, not collectors. If they are form letters with my name added, sometimes I pass." – Frank Stallone, *Rocky*

"Yes (signing in-person) – Sometimes I do when one person has 10 or 20 items (limiting items)." – Florence Henderson, *The Brady Bunch*

"Yes, I do. Every three to four weeks I receive a package containing requests from both the Miss America Organization & my parents ... the amount is always a surprise." – Katie Harmon, Miss America 2002

"You gotta get more specific – snail mail, email, fan mail, charity – I sign tons of autographs for myriads of reasons – many for free, many for profit, many for charity." – Sean Astin, *Rudy, The Lord of the Rings*

"Yes, I sign requests (in-person). I sometimes limit the number of items." – Robert Englund, a.k.a. Freddy Krueger

"Yes, I try to limit them to two per person." – Gary Owens, *Rowan & Martin's Laugh-In*

" I always do (in-person requests). If I'm in a hurry, I have to keep it to a limit." – Frank Stallone, *Rocky*

"I was not aware of how popular autograph collecting was until I received my first stack of requests after being named Miss America." – Katie Harmon, Miss America 2002

"Even though I worked with him I was too shy to ask Walt Disney for his (autograph) – I wish I had done so. On Hollywood's Walk of Fame – my star is next to his at 6743 Hollywood Boulevard." – Gary Owens, *Rowan & Martin's Laugh-In*

"As long as they pay they don't have to pose as fans. I use the money to support

my acting, painting and music and dance projects. The fans are my "backers"! They are my creative partners." – Karen Lynn Gorney, *Saturday Night Fever*

"Yes I do, but I charge $10 per autograph (with discounts on multiple items)." – Victoria Zdrok, *Playboy* Playmate

"Yes – almost always (signing in-person), unless I'm late or the people are engaging in a pure profit exchange." – Sean Astin, *Rudy, The Lord of the Rings*

A DIFFERENT PERSPECTIVE – Introduction

While writing a price guide for a different publisher a few years ago, I was contacted by David M. Beach. Beach believes that price guides, in their current form, do not fairly address value when it comes to the area of finance. Since he specializes in this area, I felt giving him an opportunity to express his views in this book would prove useful for collectors.

Collecting the Robber Barons, "The Builders and The Rascals of History"
by David M. Beach

Before there was television and movies, the public loved to follow the almost unbelievable exploits of that group of mostly men called "the Robber Barons." They were the movie stars and celebrities of their era. This was a time when America was entering the great Industrial Age. Millions migrated from the farms and rural communities to the great cities to work in the factories and new industries. This was a time when there were few laws governing business and Wall Street. Laws against "insider trading" and other activities that are illegal today did not exist.

"Smart Men" knew how to work the system and became the wealthiest men in America. Most were basically honest men who just operated in a time when the rules were being developed and were frequently changing. A good example is the most famous of the Robber Barons, Jay Gould. Known as the "Great Mephistopheles of Wall Street" and, of course, "The Devil," Gould has been proven to be a decent man and some of his letters have revealed him to be very ethical. However, while he was alive and until very recently, his reputation was terrible. He was the most hated man in America. He was vilified in satirical cartoons weekly in *Puck* and *The Judge* and most other newspapers and magazines, but Gould knew the angles and he thought of them before anyone else did. He was simply smarter than those around him, and on Wall Street, for every winner there is at least one loser. Since Gould did not often lose, there was always someone to bad-mouth him and frequently distort the truth. He was crucified in the press as a wrecker of companies, but in reality he was a great builder.

The Scarlet Woman of Wall Street and *The Gold Ring* are two books that are easy to read and almost unbelievable in content – as the exploits of Gould and James Fisk are so spectacular that one may think they must be fiction. *The*

Scarlet Woman of Wall Street was not a woman at all, but the Erie Railroad. The battle for the Erie was front-page news around the world, and the exploits of the participants are almost beyond your wildest imagination. *The Gold Ring* tells the story of how Gould and Fisk, with the assistance of President Grant's brother-in-law, cornered the gold supply of the United States and caused "Black Friday" in 1869 and the depression that followed.

Collecting Gould's autograph material can be most exciting, as can Fisk's. Others worth exploring are Cornelius Vanderbilt (known as "The Commodore"), Daniel Drew ("The Great Bear of Wall Street"), John D. Rockefeller, Andrew Carnegie and "The Big Four of Railroads" – Leland Stanford, Collis P. Huntington, Charles Crocker and the most elusive Mark Hopkins (not to be confused with the educator). While these are only a few, others can be gleaned from the good books listed at the end of this article.

In addition to collecting the Robber Barons' letters, contracts and other financial documents, you may also want to collect some of their antique stock

certificates. Of course, I am talking about stocks that are 75 to 175 years old. These stocks can be extremely beautiful, as they come with engraved or lithographed vignettes or pictures on them to prevent counterfeiting. Some of the financial people can be found on stocks either signing as an officer of the company or by endorsing the backside of a stock that was issued to them. It will take a little experience or the help of a knowledgeable collector or dealer to recognize those that are really rare from ones that are frequently available. As an example, Gould signed a large number of Missouri, Kansas and Texas railroad stocks and there are some on the market. You can get one in the $350-$500 range depending on how nice it is. However, Gould's signature on many other stocks can be very rare, with several railroad stocks having only 1-5 certificates signed by him, making them much more valuable. Beyond this form, Gould letters are almost impossible to find.

Collis P. Huntington is similar to Gould with many less expensive stocks somewhat available, but letters are extremely rare. A reverse example is Andrew Carnegie, whose routine content letters only bring $500-$1,000. However less than ten or so of his stock certificates have ever been discovered. One such certificate sold for more than $100,000 several years ago at the height of the last stock boom. Cyrus Field, founder of the Atlantic Telegraph, was world famous when he was still very young, so his letters are fairly easy to obtain. However, he became a partner of Jay Gould later in life, and only two stock certificates signed by Field are known to exist.

Collecting financial autographs does not have to be expensive, as many important railroad and industry presidents have signed stock certificates and bonds that are beautiful, yet very inexpensive ($20-$50 range). For example, an 1885 certificate can be purchased for about $25 and includes not only the signature of a president of the particular company, but the stock may have been issued to a prominent individual whose signature may also appear. In such cases, the certificate may be worth ten times what you have paid for it. So collecting antique stocks is like being on a treasure hunt with many important discoveries still being made. With many people paying hundreds or even thousands of dollars for so-called limited edition prints, why not collect antique stocks and bonds? They are certainly original limited editions, as each certificate has its own individual number. Collecting antique stocks is known as "Scripophily" and more information can be obtained from myself or other knowledgeable collectors and dealers or by contacting the International Bond and Share Society.

Useful resources: *The Scarlet Woman of Wall Street* by Gordon, *The Gold Ring* by Ackerman, *The Age of Moguls* by Holbrook, *The Robber Barons* by Josephson and *Jay Gould* by Klein. Another source is The Museum of American Financial History, 28 Broadway, New York, NY 10004 or (212) 908-4110. David Beach can be reached at (407) 688-7403.

CHAPTER THREE
A MARKET ANALYSIS

Now that we have gleaned some understanding of value and have been given various perspectives from some participants in the hobby, let's take it a step further. Let's paint a picture of the hobby using twenty-five years worth of data. We're going to analyze each field of collecting in the market to see which realized the greatest gains in value. Through this analysis we should be able to determine which, if any, areas have been overlooked. We can answer the following questions: Does the autograph market favor a particular form, such as handwritten letters over signed photographs? Is there a market bias toward race, religion or gender?

I have provided my readers with similar information in the past and they have found it extremely useful. To simplify matters, numbers and formulas have been removed.

A Twenty-Five Year Market Analysis

To understand the answers to these questions, we only need to look back two and a half decades to see where we have been and where we stand today. Without going too far into detail, here is how we accomplished our task. Each segment of the autograph market has "market drivers" – those key individuals whose signed material affects their particular niche. For example, Babe Ruth for baseball, George Washington, Abraham Lincoln and John F. Kennedy for Presidents of the United States, and so on. Using a variety of sources, we were able to determine prices for these individuals in 1978 and compare them to their prices today. Using a variety of mathematical formulas, we were able to then apply a rating to these segments based on several parameters. The rating also assists us in determining characteristics of the market. For example, do certain niches favor a particular form, such as signed photographs?

This is by no means an investment guide, but simply a look back at where we have been.

TOP TEN BEST MARKET SEGMENTS IN VALUE, 1978-2003

Market Segment

1. Athletes and Sports Figures (all forms including SP)
2. Famous Women (all forms – AF)
3. Entertainment Personalities (all forms with SP)
4. Athletes and Sports Figures (all forms minus SP)
5. Financiers, Philanthropists, Jurists and Lawyers (all forms with SP)
6. Financiers, Philanthropists, Jurists and Lawyers (all forms minus SP)
7. Inventors, Aviators, Explorers and Architects (AF)
8. Military Leaders (all forms with SP)
9. Black Leaders (AF)
10. Composers (all forms with SP)

COMMENTS:

* Not a surprise to those of us who participated in the autograph sports memorabilia boom of the 1980s and early 1990s, however this market has slowed down significantly. Whether this is a matter of supply catching up with demand, or fear of forgery, it appears to be both.

* Famous Women was probably a surprise to many, but not when you really look at the area and see the significant increases in people like as Eva Peron and Susan B. Anthony, not to mention the increased respect we now have for the many pioneers of human rights. Speaking of which, the increased interest in African-American culture and the many prominent black leaders of the 1960s is certainly evident here. The respect this area has achieved has enabled it to out-value American Authors and even U.S. Presidents.

* It is particularly interesting to note how certain autographed forms impact value. Were it not for signed photographs, the first and second positions would be reversed.

TOP TEN WORST MARKET SEGMENTS IN VALUE, 1978-2003

Market Segment

1. Colonial and Revolutionary Leaders (All forms - AF)
2. Signers of the Declaration of Independence (AF)
3. Royalty (AF)
4. Nazi and Fascist Leaders (AF)
5. Continental Authors (AF)
6. Religious Leaders (AF)
7. British Authors (AF)
8. Artists and Photographers (AF)
9. Scoundrels (AF)
10. Scientists and Doctors (AF)

COMMENTS:

* No surprise here when you realize that these are the oldest and most established segments in the hobby. In many of these areas, autograph collecting has had hundreds of years to experience the trials and tribulations associated with the particular segment.

* Twenty-five years ago, thanks to many of the outstanding dealers and collectors, our knowledge base was strong in these areas and, as such, many of the items were fairly and consistently priced.

* These areas have had the most consistent value increases in all forms. This was determined through a stability factor.

TOP TEN MARKET SEGMENTS IN VALUE, BY FORM, 1978-2003

Market Segment

1. Athletes and Sports Figures (SP)
2. Famous Women (SIG)
3. World Leaders and Politicians (SP)
4. Financiers, Philanthropists, Jurists and Lawyers (DS/LS)
5. Entertainment Personalities (SIG)
6. Athletes and Sports Figures (ALS)
7. Inventors, Aviators, Explorers and Architects (DS/LS)
7. Athletes and Sports Figures (AF)
8. Famous Women (AF)
9. Financiers, Philanthropists, Jurists and Lawyers (SP)

Comments:

* It is worth noting that half of these include photographs as a form. We have become a very visual-oriented society, even in our autograph collecting. The advances in photography have given collectors access to better and cheaper photographs for signing purposes, especially in the areas of Sports and Entertainment.

* Signed photographs, followed by simple signatures, are the desired forms.

TOP TEN WORST MARKET SEGMENTS IN VALUE, BY FORM, 1978-2003

Market Segment

1. Colonial and Revolutionary Leaders (ALS)
2. Colonial and Revolutionary Leaders (All forms)
3. Colonial and Revolutionary Leaders (Sig.)
4. Royalty (ALS)
5. Signers of the Declaration of Independence (ALS)
6. Royalty (SIG)
7. Scoundrels (ALS)
8. Signers of the Declaration of Independence (All forms)
9. Nazi and Fascist Leaders (ALS)
10. Signers of the Declaration of Independence (SIG)

Comments:

* Older, consistent and established segments occupy this list. A contrarian thinker might view all of these segments as bargains, or laggards in a market that has exploded in popularity.

* Some dealers view a segment's appearance on this list as an area with limited

price ranges. For example, a signature of Roger Sherman is harder to push to a higher value than a signed photograph of Winston Churchill.

* Popularity, price and location could be factors in a segment's appearance in this chart. Certainly the signatures of Royalty are far better appreciated in Europe and Asia than in the United States.

* Another factor for lack of performance is familiarity. While many Americans can list twenty popular athletes or actors, few can even name five Signers of the Declaration of Independence.

A common concern of most participants in the hobby is stability. Since not everyone is a casual collector, many are concerned with protecting and preserving the value of their collections. Unlike stocks, bonds and mutual funds, autograph collecting is not considered a viable investment option or a form of financial security. However, like other hobbies where a great deal of money is transacted, value is a factor and a characteristic of that is stability.

THE TEN MOST STABLE AUTOGRAPH MARKET SEGMENTS 1978-2003

Market Segment
1. Signers of the Declaration of Independence
2. Royalty
3. Nazi and Fascist Leaders
4. Religious Leaders
5. Colonial and Revolutionary Leaders
6. British Authors
7. Continental Authors
8. American Authors
9. Scientists and Doctors
10. Artists and Photographers

THE FIVE LEAST STABLE AUTOGRAPH MARKET SEGMENTS 1978-2003

Market Segment
1. Sports Figures
2. World Statesman and Political Leaders
3. Entertainment Personalities
4. Military Leaders
5. Financiers, Philanthropists, Jurists and Lawyers

Over the last twenty-five years the hobby of autograph collecting has experienced phenomenal growth, with the value of autographed items increasing nearly tenfold. The influx of new hobbyists, fueled in many cases by the boom in autographed sports memorabilia, has contributed significantly to the demand for many items. As the sports market has slowed, many of its participants have migrated to other areas of autograph collecting. To what extent this will assist or detract from the hobby remains uncertain. Most of the current participants in the traditional autograph market, while somewhat apprehensive with the changes, are also enticed by the new opportunities those changes bring.

Perhaps I'm bullish, but I believe the autograph market will continue to thrive over the next decade. While the "forgery factor" has been detrimental to both the sports market and the hobby in general, the traditional market participants are older, wiser and less prone to the mistakes experienced in the sports market. Many of these dealers are far better versed on the autograph market, authentication methods and acceptable business practices. Also, traditional market participants will play an integral role in stabilizing many segments in the hobby, including sports. As has always been the case, "quality autographs" – the cream of the hobby – will always rise to the top!

Section Two

ARTISANS

WHAT YOU NEED TO KNOW

* Collectors in this niche must familiarize themselves with the various terminology associated with form, such as types of print proofs and photographic images.

* For many years, The Getty Museum aggressively sought and purchased everything written by artists causing a temporary market drought in material.

* There is a parallel between the popularity and quality of an artists's work and the value of their autographed material.

* There are many collectors who specialize in artists associated with various art movements.

* Institutions are extremely active in this niche and often specialize in certain areas such as the Hudson River School.

* Although material signed by some artists is uncommon, it may not be in great demand and availability and prices will reflect this.

MARKET FACTS

* Similar to artwork, the market for autographed art items is driven by "The Masters" and those artists popular during certain periods.

* The interest in illustration has grown dramatically in recent years. Artists such as Maxfield Parrish, Norman Rockwell, Howard Pyle and N.C. Wyeth continue to command significant interest with collectors.

* The market for autographed architectural material is driven primarily by Frank Lloyd Wright, followed by that of James Hoban, Benjamin Latrobe and a handful of others.

* According to many industry analysts, with the exception of Frank Lloyd Wright material, the architectural market is undervalued. This could be due to the lack of material and interest in this area.

MARKET TRENDS

* Due to cost and availability, much of the interest in this area is focusing toward illustration and other more affordable areas of artwork.

* Institutions continue to play an important role in this market by accumulating significant collections and driving the value of certain material upward.

* The market for autographed material in the architectural niche remains undefined with many subjects and therefore values continue to fluctuate unpredictably.

Abbreviations: ESPV = exhibits significant pricing variations, FA = forgery/facsimile alert, PU = pricing undetermined, RS = responsive signer, SD = strong demand

ARCHITECTS

Name	db/dd	Sig.	DS	ALS	SP	Comments
Abramovitz, Max	1908-	20	40		30	Avery Fisher Hall
Bacon, Henry	1866-1924	80	175	350		Lincoln Memorial
Belluschi, Pietro	1899-1994	35	75		60	Julliard School, Lincoln Ctr.
Breuer, Marcel	1902-1981	70	165		150	Whitney Museum
Bulfinch, Charles	1763-1844					Capitol (part), rare, PU
Bunshaft, Gordon	1909-1990	30	60		50	Hirshhorn Museum
Burnham, Daniel H.	1846-1912	115	240	375		Union Station, Wash., D.C.
Chanin, Irwin	1892-1988	30	60		45	NYC, theaters, skyscrapers
Costa, Lucio	1902-1998	25	50		50	Brasilia
Cram, Ralph Adams	1863-1942	40	80			U.S. Military Academy (part)
Fuller, R. Buckminster	1895-1983	30	75	150	60	Author, U.S. Pavilion - 1967, RS
Gehry, Frank O.	1929-	25	50		50	Experience Music Project, RS
Gilbert, Cass	1859-1934	50	100		75	Supreme Court Bldg.
Goodhus, Bertram G.	1869-1924	30	60	110		Capitol, NE
Graves, Michael	1934-	15	40		20	Humana Bldg., KY
Gropius, Walter	1883-1969	100	150		125	Pan Am Bldg., NYC
Halprin, Lawrence	1916-	20	50		30	FDR Memorial
Harrison, Peter	1716-1775					Redwood Library, PU
Harrison, Walter K.	1895-1981	45	100		60	Lincoln Center, NYC
Hastings, Thomas	1860-1929	60	125	260		NY Public Library
Hoban, James	1762-1831	250	500	850		White House
Hood, Raymond	1881-1934	40	75	150	70	Rockefeller Center (part)
Hunt, Richard M.	1827-1895					Metropolitan Museum (part), PU
Jahn, Helmut	1940-	20	45		30	O'Hare Airport, RS
Jenny, William L.	1832-1907	50	100			Home Insurance
Johnson, Phillip C.	1906-	20	40		25	AT&T Hdqtrs.
Kahn, Albert	1869-1942	35	70	150		GM Bldg., MI
Kahn, Louis	1901-1974	40	115		65	Yale Art Gallery
LaFarge, Christopher G.	1862-1938	50	125	235		R. Catholic Chapel, West Point
Latrobe, Benjamin	1764-1820	300	600			Capitol (part), rare in some forms
Le Corbusier	1887-1965	100	200		150	(C-E Jeanneret)

Name	db/dd	Sig.	DS	ALS	SP	Comments
Lescaze, William	1896-1969	80	175		125	Borg-Warner Bldg., Chicago
Lin, Maya	1959-	40	100			Vietnam Vet. Memorial
Mackintosh, Charles R.	1868-1928	35	70	130		Hill House
Maybeck, Bernard R.	1862-1957	25	50		35	Hearst Hall, US at Berkeley
McKim, Charles F.	1847-1909	45	90	165		Public Library, Boston
McKim, Charles M.	1920-	15	30		25	L. Church of Redeemer, TX
Meier, Richard	1934-	20	50		35	Getty Ctr. Museum
Mies van der Rohe, Lud.	1886-1969	60	115		75	Seagram Bldg.
Mills, Robert	1781-1855					Washington Monument, PU
Moore, Charles	1925-1993	25	50		30	Sea Ranch, CA
Neutra, Richard J.	1892-1970	30	60		45	Mathematics Park, NJ
Niemeyer, Oscar	1907-	20	45		35	Brasilia Palace Hotel
Obata, Gyo	1923-	25	50		35	Dallas-Ft. Worth Airport
Olmstead, Frederick L.	1822-1903	100	200	300		Central Park, rare
Pei, I.M.	1917-	50	100		75	Rock 'n' Roll Hall of Fame
Pelli, Cesar	1926-	25	65		50	Carnegie Hall Tower
Pereira, William	1909-1985	30	100		75	Transamerica Bldg.
Pope, John R.	1874-1937	60	120		75	National Gallery
Portman, John	1924-	20	45		25	Peachtree Center, GA
Post, George B.	1837-1913	100	200	275		NYSE
Renwick, James, Jr.	1818-1895					St. Patrick's Cath., PU
Richardson, Henry H.	1838-1886	160	205	340		Trinity Church, MA
Roche, Kevin	1922-	20	45		25	Oakland Museum, CA
Rogers, James G.	1867-1947	30	60		45	Northwestern Univ.
Root, John W.	1887-1997	25	50		30	Palmolive Bldg.
Rudolph, Paul	1918-1997	20	40		25	Jewitt Art Ctr., MA
Saarinen, Eero	1910-1961	50	100		65	Gateway Arch, MO
Skidmore, Louis	1897-1962	25	50		35	Terrace Pl. Hotel, OH
Stein, Clarence S.	1882-1975	25	50		35	Temple Emanu-El, NYC
Stone, Edward D.	1908-1978	50	125		70	Gallery Modern Art, NYC
Sullivan, Louis H.	1856-1924	50	115			Auditorium Bldg., IL
Upjohn, Richard	1802-1878	70	145	275		Trinity Church, NYC
Urbahn, Max O.	1912-1995	20	45		25	Vehicle Assembly Bldg., FL
Venturi, Robert	1925-	15	30		20	Gordon Wu Hall, NJ
Walker, Ralph T.	1889-1973	25	50		35	IBM Research Lab, NY
Wank, Roland A.	1898-1970	20	45		30	Cin. Union Terminal, OH
White, Stanford	1853-1906					First MSG, NYC, ESPV, PU
Wright, Frank Lloyd	1867-1959	1000	1750			Strong demand, ESPV
Wurster, William	1895-1973	30	75		40	Ghirardelli Sq.
Yamasaki, Minoru	1912-1986	75	200		150	World Trade Center, NYC

ARTISTS, PHOTOGRAPHERS AND SCULPTORS - Selected Entries

1700 - present

Name	db/dd	Sig.	DS	ALS	SP	Comments
Abbott, Berenice	1898-1991	25	50	100		Photographer
Adams, Ansel E.	1902-1984	125	200	350	200	Photographer, RS
Allston, Washington	1779-1843					Landscapist, PU
Arbus, Diane	1923-1971					Photographer, scarce, PU
Archipenko, Alexsandr	1887-1964	75	150	300		Sculptor
Atget, Eugene	1856-1927					Photographer, PU
Audubon, James J.	1785-1851	750	1500	3000		"Birds of America"
Avedon, Richard	1923-	25	50	125	100	Photographer, RS
Barlach, Ernst	1870-1938	100	200	300		Sculptor
Bartholdi, Frederic-Aug.	1834-1904	400	600	750	900	
Beardon, Romare	1911-1988	50	100	200	150	Mixed media
Beardsley, Aubrey	1872-1898					Illustrator, scarce, PU
Beckmann, Max	1884-1950	125	250	450		Expressionist
Bellows, George W.	1882-1925	100	225	350		Sports artist
Benton, Thomas Hart	1889-1975	100	200		210	American regionalist
Bierstadt, Albert	1830-1902	125	250	500		Landscapist
Bingham, George C.	1811-1879	150	275	400		
Blake, William	1752-1827					Engraver, PU
Bonheur, Rosa	1822-1899	100	175	300		
Bonnard, Pierre	1867-1947	100	250		200	Intimist
Borglum, Gutzon	1871-1941	225	400	500	750	Sculptor, RS
Bourke-White, Margaret	1906-1971	100	125	200		Photographer
Brady, Matthew	1823-1896	400	1000	2000		Photographer
Brancusi, Constantin	1876-1957	100	200	300		Sculptor
Braque, Georges	1882-1963	350	650	1200		Cubist
Burne-Jones, Edward	1833-1898	125	250	500		Artis, craftsman
Calder, Alexander	1898-1976	125	225		150	Sculptor
Cameron, Julia	1815-1879	150	300			Photographer
Capa, Robert	1913-1954	75	150		125	Photographer
Carr, Emily	1871-1945	80	165	250		Landscapist
Carra, Carlo	1881-1966	50	120	200		Metaphysicalist
Cassatt, Mary	1844-1926	250	500	750		Impressionist, scarce
Catlin, George	1796-1972	55	125	250	100	American Indian Life
Cezanne, Paul	1839-1906	1125	2500			Rare, ALS - $2,500
Chagall, Marc	1887-1985	200	350		350	Jewish life and folklore
Church, Frederick	1826-1900	150	400	750		Hudson River School
Cole, Thomas	1801-1848					Hudson River School, PU
Constable, John	1776-1837	300	600			Landscapist, rare, SD
Copley, John Singleton	1738-1815	350	700			Portraitist
Corinth, Lovis	1858-1925	75	150			Expressionist
Corot, Jean-Baptiste-C.	1796-1875	250	500	1000		Landscapist, available
Courbet, Gustave	1819-1877	250	500	1000		Realist, difficult to find

Name	db/dd	Sig.	DS	ALS	SP	Comments
Cunningham, Imogen	1883-1976	35	70	150	50	Photographer
Currier, Nathaniel	1813-1888	250	750	1125		Lithographer, w/Ives
Curry, John S.	1897-1946	100	200	300	165	Americana
Dali, Salvador	1904-1989	200	425	700	800	Surrealist, ESPV, FA
Daumier, Honore	1808-1879	250	500	1000		Caricaturist, very rare
David, Jacques-Louis	1748-1825	175	350	500		Neoclassicist, not common
Davies, Arthur	1862-1928	70	150	250		Landscapist
de Kooning, Willem	1904-1997	100	225	450	125	Abstract
Degas, Edgar	1834-1917	700	1250	2300		Rare
Delacroix, Eugene	1798-1863	200	400	600		Romantic, available
Delaroche, Paul	1797-1856	175	325	500		Historical themes
Dubuffet, Jean	1902-1985	40	75		70	Painter, sculptor
Duchamp, Marcel	1887-1968	150	350	600		Dada artist
Dufy, Raoul	1877-1953	275	450	750	425	Fauvist
Durand, Asher Brown	1796-1886	100	200	275		Hudson River School
Eakins, Thomas	1844-1916	225				Realist, ESPV
Eisenstaedt, Alfred	1898-1995	25	60		150	Photographer
Emerson, Peter H.	1856-1936	75	150	250		Photographer
Epstein, Jacob	1880-1959	125	250	400		Sculptor
Ernst, Max	1891-1976	200	300	500		Surrealist
Fenton, Roger	1819-1868					Photographer, PU
Feuerbach, Anselm	1829-1880	100	200	275		Romantic Classicist
Flannagan, John B.	1895-1942	75	150	250		Animal sculptor
Fragonard, Jean-Honre	1732-1806					Rococo, PU
French, Daniel Chester	1850-1931	100	200	375		Lincoln Memorial, available
Friedrich, Caspar David	1774-1840					Landscapes, PU
Gainsborough, Thomas	1727-1788					Portraitist, rare, PU
Gardner, Alexander	1821-1882	125	250	500		Photographer
Gaugin, Paul	1848-1903	625	1300	4000		Post-imp., very rare, recluse
Giacometti, Alberto	1901-1966					Sculptor, rare, PU
Gogh, Vincent van	1853-1890					Dutch, extremely rare, PU
Gorky, Arshile	1905-1948	100	200	300		Surrealist
Goya y Lucientes, Fran.	1746-1828	2500	4500			Etcher
Greenough, Horatio	1805-1852	100	225	325		Sculptor
Hansen, Austin	1910-1996	20	50		55	Photographer
Hassam, Childe	1859-1935	175	350	600		Impressionist, ALS - rare
Hicks, Edward	1780-1849	200	400	500		Folk painter
Hine, Lewis W.	1874-1940	60	110		100	Photographer
Hofmann, Hans	1880-1966	60	125		120	Abstract expressionist
Hokusal, Katsushika	1760-1849					Printmaker, PU
Homer, Winslow	1836-1910	350	600	900		Naturalist, rare
Hopper, Edward	1882-1967	225	500			Realistic urban sce., ALS - rare
Horst, Horst P.	1906-1999	25	60		60	Photographer
Ingres, Jean -A-D	1780-1867	200	425	1000		Classicist, available
Inness, George	1825-1894	100	200	400		Landscapist

Name	db/dd	Sig.	DS	ALS	SP	Comments
Jackson, William Henry	1843-1942	50	100		100	Photographer
Judd, Donald	1928-1994	30	75			Sculptor
Kahlo, Frida	1907-1954	80	165	300		Painter
Kandinsky, Vasily	1866-1944	175	650	1300		Abstractionist
Karsh, Yousof	1908-	40	80	150	100	Photographer
Kent, Rockwell	1882-1971	50	100		75	
Klee, Paul	1879-1940	225	600	1500		Abstractionist
Klimt, Gustav	1862-1918	200	500	1000		Austrian
Kokoschka, Oscar	1886-1980	100	200	350	250	Expressionist
Kollwitz, Kathe	1867-1945	100	200	300		Printmaker
Lachaise, Gaston	1882-1935	65	120	250		Sculptor
La farge, John	1835-1910	50	100	200		Muralist
Landseer, Edwin	1802-1873	35	70	225		Painter
Lange, Dorothea	1895-1955	135	250		225	Photographer
Leger, Fernand	1881-1955	100	250	300		Machine art
Leutze, Emanuel	1816-1868	100	200	300		Historical themes
Lichtenstein, Roy	1923-1997	35	75	150	60	Pop artist
Lipchitz, Jacques	1891-1973	125	225	300		Cubist sculptor
Louis, Morris	1912-1962	125	250	435		Abstract expressionist
Magritte, Rene	1898-1967	200	400	800		Surrealist
Maillol, Aristide	1861-1944	225	450	800		Sculptor
Manet, Edouard	1832-1883		2000			Impressionism, rare, SD
Marc, Franz	1880-1916					Expressionist, scarce, PU
Marin, John	1870-1953	100	225	450		Expressionist
Marsh, Reginald	1898-1954	130	250		200	Satirical artist
Matisse, Henri	1869-1954	500	750	1250		Fauvist
Millet, Jean-Francois	1814-1875	250	500			French, difficult to find
Miro, Joan	1893-1983	200	550	700	300	Spanish, FA
Modiglianl, Amedeo	1884-1920	300	800	1500		Italian
Mondrian, Piet	1872-1944	250	600	1500		Abstractionist
Monet, Claude	1840-1926	550	1200	2250		Impress., prolific, ALS - $4,500
Moore, Henry	1898-1986	50	200	500	125	Sculptor, RS
Moreau, Gustave	1826-1898	175	350	600		Symbolist
Morrice, James W.	1865-1924	100	200	400		Landscapist
Morris, William	1834-1896	125	300	500		Decorative artist, SD
Moses, Grandma	1860-1961	225	500	900		Folk painter, CC available
Munch, Edvard	1863-1944	100	250	475		Expressionist, rare, SD
Muybridge, Eadweard	1830-1904	300	600	900		Photographer
Nadar	1820-1910	100	200	300		Photographer
Newman, Barnett	1905-1970	60	150		75	Abstract expressionist
Noguchi, Isamu	1904-1988	35	70		50	Abstract sculptor
O'Keeffe, Georgia	1887-1986	325	650			Southwest motifs, ALS - rare
Orozco, Jose Clemente	1883-1949					Mexico frescoes, PU
O'Sullivan, Timothy H.	1840-1882					Photographer, PU
Parirsh, Maxfield	1870-1966	250	500	800		Illustrator, ALS/TLS - 2X
Peale, Charles Willson	1741-1827	275	500	800		Portraitist, rare

Name	db/dd	Sig.	DS	ALS	SP	Comments
Peale, Rembrandt	1778-1860	250	500	1200		Portraitist, rare
Picasso, Pablo	1881-1973	750	1500		1500	Painter, sculptor, available
Pissarro, Camille	1830-1903	250	500	1200		Impressionist, available
Pollock, Jackson	1912-1956					Abstract expressionist, PU
Prendergast, Maurice	1860-1924	250	475	625		Post-impressionist
Prud'hon, Pierre-Paul	1758-1823					Romanticist, PU
Pyle, Howard	1853-1911	175	350	700	600	Illustrator
Ray, Man	1890-1976	250	500		400	Dada artist
Redon, Odilon	1840-1916	100	200	300		Symbolist
Remington, Frederic	1861-1909	575	800	1750		Painter, sculptor, rare
Renoir, Pierre-Auguste	1841-1919	325	700	2225		Impressionist, rare
Reynolds, Joshua	1723-1792	200	350	600		Portraitist, scarce
Ritts, Herb	1952-2002	25	75		60	Photographer
Rivera, Diego	1886-1957	300	600	800	1200	Frescoes
Rivers, Larry	1923-2002	50	100		100	Painter
Robinson, Henry P.	1830-1901					Photographer, PU
Rockwell, Norman	1894-1978	150	300	500	400	Illustrator
Rodin, Auguste	1840-1917	250	450	1575		Sculptor, ALS - $3,500
Rothko, Mark	1903-1970	150	300		350	Abstract expressionist
Rouault, Georges	1871-1958	225	500	750		Expressionist
Rousseau, Henri	1844-1910	150	300	600		Primitive
Rousseau, Theodore	1812-1867	100	200	450		Landscapist
Russell, Charles M.	1866-1926	300	700	1500		Western life, rare
Ryder, Albert P.	1847-1917	100	250	500		Seascapes
Saint-Gaudens, Augus.	1848-1907	225	500	900		Memorial statues, SD
Sargent, John Singer	1856-1925	125	250	425		Portrait., ALS - $1,250; $1,750
Segal, George	1924-2000	30	60		50	Sculptor
Seurat, Georges	1859-1891					Pointillist, unavailable, PU
Severini, Gino	1883-1966	75	150		120	Futurist, cubist
Shahn, Ben	1898-1969	60	125	225	125	Social and political themes
Sheeler, Charles	1883-1965	100	175		150	Abstractionist
Siqueiros, David A.	1896-1974	55	100	220		Muralist
Smith, David	1906-1965	50	100	175		Metal sculpture
Steichen, Edward	1879-1973	100	200	300	400	Photographer
Stieglitz, Alfred	1864-1946	225	450	650		Photographer
Strand, Paul	1890-1976	40	100	200		Photographer
Stuart, Gilbert	1755-1828	230	500	750		Portraitist
Sully, Thomas	1783-1872	175	350	500		Portraitist
Talbot, William H.F.	1800-1877	75	150	250		Photographer
Tames, George	1919-1994	30	75	150		Photographer
Tanguy, Yves	1900-1955	110	200	275		Surrealist
Toledo, Jose Rey	1916-1994	40	80	150		Native American artist
Toulouse-Lautrec, Hen.	1864-1901	1225	2500			French, rare, SD
Trumbull, John	1756-1843	150	300	750		Histor. themes, SD, uncommon
Turner, J.M.	1775-1851	225	475	900		Landscapist, SD, rare
Utrillo, Maurice	1883-1955	350	600			Impressionist, ESPV
Vanderlyn, John	1775-1852	225	400	500		Neo-classicist

Name	db/dd	Sig.	DS	ALS	SP	Comments
Vlaminck, Maurice de	1876-1958	75	150	300		Fauvist
Warhol, Andy	1928-1987	125	250	500	250	Pop art
Watts, George F.	1817-1904	75	150	300		Painter, sculptor
West, Benjamin	1738-1820	225	600	1200		Historical themes, scarce
Weston, Edward	1886-1958	40	100	200		Photographer
Whistler, James A. M.	1834-1903	250	500	675		US, uses butterfly signature
Willard, Archibald M.	1836-1918	125	275			US
Wood, Grant	1891-1942	200	400	625		Regionalist
Wyeth, Andrew	1917-		250	500	700	900	Realist, ALS - scarce
Wyeth, Jamie	1946-	100	225	375	225	s. Andrew
Wyeth, Newell Convers	1882-1944	175	450	900		Illustrator, family collects letters
Zadkine, Ossip	1890-1967					Russian sculptor, PU

AUTHORS

WHAT YOU NEED TO KNOW

* Collecting literary autographs has been popular for over a century. Beginning first with book collectors who savored signed limited and first editions, literary autograph collecting then migrated toward the now traditional forms.

* Increasingly book dealers realized the value of letters associated with a certain body of work, therefore it wasn't unusual to drop by a distinguished book store and find a letter written by an author tipped into one of his bestselling works.

* As no other occupation lends itself more toward the written form of communication, most authors are quite prolific during their lifetime.

* During the last century many very distinguished literary collections were sold and resold for very handsome profits. While these collections typically begin in private hands, they eventually find a home at a major institution or library.

* During the latter half of the last century, it became increasingly evident - and thus prestigious, that autograph letters and manuscripts had tremendous research value. Many major institutions began contacting both authors and collectors to persuade them to present or donate their manuscripts.

* While institutions have soaked up a considerable amount of material, changes in the tax laws have have had a negative effect on many donations, therefore increasing the amount of material available in the autograph market.

MARKET FACTS

* Constantly in demand have been the works of contemporary writers. As the generations pass, Eliot, Faulkner, Frost and Hemingway are replaced by Updike, Mailer, Kerouac and Bellow. It's not to say that the former are in any lesser demand, only that both the supply and price have somewhat restricted the market for their material.

* Many private collections of authors such as Hemingway, Faulkner, Ginsburg and Fitzgerald can rival many of the major institutional holdings in this country.

* Some literary collectors prefer to collect only unpublished letters or manuscripts.

TRENDS

* Advances in internet, printing and publishing technology now makes alternative forms of collectibles more cost-effective. This includes typescripts, portions of

books and online articles which could then be signed.

* High-end publishers now offer both authors and collectors affordable quality limited editions, some of which are signed. A good example is The Easton Press (Norwalk, CT) who offers a fine series of signed collector's editions.

* Bookplates remain popular with collectors for their ease of use when mailed to have signed and for the ability to be tipped-into a fine edition.

Abbreviations: ES = elusive signer, ESPV = exhibits significant pricing variations, PU = pricing undetermined, RS = responsive signer

Name	db/dd	Sig.	DS	ALS	SP	Comments
Achebe, Chinua	1930-	15	25	45	20	Nigerian, "Things Fall Apart"
Adams, Alice	1926-	10	20	30	15	U.S., RS
Agee, James	1909-1955					U.S., "A Death in the Family"
Aiken, Conrad	1889-1973	35	100	165	50	U.S. poet, critic, "Ushant"
Albee, Edward	1928-	10	30	55	20	U.S. writer, RS
Alcott, Louisa May	1832-1888	225	300	450		U.S. novelist, "Little Women"
Aleichem, Sholom	1859-1916	800	2000	4000		Russian, "The Old Country"
Alexandre, Vicente	1898-1984					Spanish poet, PU
Alger, Horatio	1832-1899	150	200	350	250	U.S. author, clergyman
Amado, Jorge	1912-	20	30	50	25	Brazilian, "The Violent Land"
Amis, Kingsley	1922-1995	20	30	75	50	British, critic, "Lucky Jim"
Amis, Martin	1949-	15	20	40	20	British writer, "Success"
Anderson, Hans Christ.	1805-1875					Danish, "The Ugly Duckling," PU
Anderson, Maxwell	1888-1959	35	50	150	60	U.S. playwright, "Key Largo"
Anderson, Sherwood	1876-1941	50	125	200	75	U.S. , writer, "Winesburg, Ohio"
Angelou, Maya	1928-	30	40	50	45	U.S. writer, poet
Arias Sanchez, Oscar	1941-	40	60	100	50	Costa Rican writer
Arnold, Matthew	1822-1888	45	70	130		British poet, critic, "Thrysis"
Ashbery, John	1927-	10	20	30	20	U.S. writer, "Flow Chart"
Asimov, Issac	1920-1992	50	100	225	100	U.S. sci-fi, "I Robot," RS
Atwood, Margaret	1939-	10	25	50	25	Canadian, "Surfacing," RS
Auchincloss, Louis	1917-	10	25	60	25	U.S., "A World of Profit," RS
Auden, Wyston Hugh	1907-1973	110	300	550	450	British poet, playwright, ESPV
Austen, Jane	1775-1817	1000	2500	4000		British, SALS-2X, ESPV
Babel, Issac	1894-1941					Russian, "Odessa Tales," PU
Baldwin, James	1924-1987	100	350	400	200	"Just Above My ..."SALS-2X
Balzac, Honore de	1799-1850	800	1650	3000		French, "Le Pere Goriot," ESPV
Barrie, James M.	1860-1937	100	250	350	300	British, "Peter Pan," SB-$250
Barth, John	1930-	20	40	100	35	U.S., "The End of the Road"
Baudelaire, Charles	1821-1867	400	1000	1500		French, "Les Fleurs du Mal"
Baum, Lyman Frank	1856-1919	600	2000	2250		"The Wizard of Oz," SALS-2X
Beattie, Ann	1947-	10	20	35	15	U.S. , Love Always," RS
Beauvior, Simone de	1908-1986	35	70	150		French , "The Second Sex"
Beckett, Samuel	1906-1989	175	500	425	400	"Waiting for Godot," TS - $450
Behan, Brendan	1923-1964	175	365	700	400	Irish playwright, "The Hostage"
Bellow, Saul	1915-	30	100	100	50	U.S., "Humboldt's Gift" - $175

Name	db/dd	Sig.	DS	ALS	SP	Comments
Benchley, Robert	1889-1945	40	65	150	60	U.S. humorist
Benchly, Peter	1940-	20	30	65	30	U.S., "Jaws,"shark sk. - $30
Benet, Stephen Vin.	1898-1943	100	175	240	150	U.S. poet, "John Brown's Body"
Berger, Thomas	1924-	10	25	40	15	U.S. writer, "Killing Time"
Berryman, John	1914-1972	30	75	150		U.S. poet, "Homage to Mist..."
Bierce, Ambrose	1842-1914	300	600	600		U.S. , "The Devil's Dictionary"
Bishop, Elizabeth	1911-1979	40	130	200	50	U.S. poet
Blake, William	1757-1827					British, "Songs of Inn...," PU
Blume, Judy	1938-	15	25	50	20	U.S., "Are You There God?..."
Boccacclo, Giovanni	1313-1375					Poet, "Decameron," PU
Boll, Heinrich	1917-1985	50	100	175	70	German, "Group Portrait ..."
Borges, Jorge Luis	1900-1986	100	375	525		Short-story , "Labyrinths"
Boswell, James	1740-1795	1000	2000	4500		Biographer
Boulle, Pierre	1913-1994	20	35	50	30	French, "Planet of the Apes"
Bradbury, Ray	1920-	30	130	225	45	U.S. writer, "Fahrenheit 451"
Bradford, Barbara Taylor	1933-	10	20	30	15	British writer, "Angel," RS
Bradstreet, Anne	1612-1672					U.S. poet, scarce, PU
Brecht, Bertolt	1898-1956	500	1625	2650		German, "The Threepenny..."
Brodsky, Joseph	1940-1996	20	30	55	25	Russian-U.S, "To Urania," RS
Bronte, Charlotte	1816-1855					British, "Jane Eyre," PU
Bronte, Emily	1818-1848					British, "Wuthering Heights," PU
Brooks, Gwendolyn	1917-	30	50	75	40	U.S., "Primer For Blacks" - $75
Browning, Elizabeth B.	1806-1861	525	1250	2750		British poet, "Aurora Leigh"
Browning, Robert	1812-1889	325	550	1150	1255	British, AMsS- $3250
Buck, Pearl S.	1892-1973	50	175	225	65	U.S., "The Good Earth," RS
Bulgakov, Mikhail	1891-1940					Russian, "The Heart...Dog," PU
Bunyan, John	1628-1688					British, "Pilgrim's Progress," PU
Burgess, Anthony	1917-1993	50	125	245	100	British, "A Clockwork Orange"
Burnet, Frances H.	1849-1924	100	200	300		British/US, "The Secret Garden"
Burns, Robert	1759-1796	750	1500	3000		"Auld Lang Syne," ESPV-ALS
Burroughs, Edgar Rice	1875-1950	275	500	800	750	U.S., "Tarzan ...," STLS-4X
Burroughs, William S.	1914-1997	35	55	100	50	U.S., "Naked Lunch,"elusive
Burton, Virginia Lee	1909-1968	35	75	125		U.S., "Mike Mulligan and ..."
Byron, Lord (G.Gordon)	1788-1824	1750	2575	3000		British, "Don Juan," ESPV-ALS
Calisher, Hortense	1911-	10	20	40	15	U.S. writer, "Collected Stories"
Calvino, Italo	1923-1985					Italian, "If On a Winter's ...," PU
Camus, Albert	1913-1960	100	275	600		French writer, "The Stranger"
Capek, Karel	1890-1938					Czech. playwright, novelist, PU
Capote, Truman	1924-1984	150	350	1000	300	U.S., "In Cold Blood"
Carroll, Lewis (Dodgson)	1832-1898	360	1000	1550		British, "Alice's Adventures ..."
Cather, Willa	1873-1947	245	500	835	325	U.S., "O Pioneers!," SALS-3X
Cervantes (Saavedra), M	1547-1616					Spanish, "Don Quixote," PU
Chandler, Raymond	1888-1959	365	900			U.S., "Philip Marlowe" series
Chaucer, Geoffrey	c.1340-1400					Br., "The Canterbury Tales," PU
Cheever, John	1912-1982	55	125	265	125	U.S. poet, "The Wapshot..."
Chekhov, Anton	1860-1904	1000	2500	5500		Russian, SALS-2X, ESPV
Chesterton, Gilbert K.	1874-1936	100	200	300	200	British, "F. Brown," STLS-2X
Chopin, Kate	1851-1904					U.S., "The Awakening," PU
Christie, Agatha	1890-1976	215	500			British, "Murder on ..." ESPV
Clancy, Tom	1947-	10	20	30	15	U.S., "The Hunt for ..." , RS
Clark, Mary Higgins	1931-	10	20	35	20	U.S. , "Remember Me," RS

Name	db/dd	Sig.	DS	ALS	SP	Comments
Clavell, James	1925-1994	20	50	65	35	British-U.S., "Shogun," RS
Cleary, Beverly	1916-	10	20	30	20	U.S., "Ramona" series, RS
Cocteau, Jean	1889-1963	150	300	750		French, "The Beauty ... Beast"
Coleridge, Samuel T.	1772-1834	300	600	1200		British, "Kubla Khan," ESPV
Colette, (Sidonie)	1873-1954	100	275	400		French, "Gigi"
Connell, Evan S.	1924-	10	25	35	15	U.S., "Mr. Bridge"
Conrad, Joseph	1857-1924	200	875	1200		British, "Lord Jim"
Conroy, Pat	1945-	12	30	45	20	U.S., "The Prince of Tides," RS
Cook, Robin	1940-	10	15	25	15	U.S. writer, RS
Cooper, J. Fenimore	1789-1851	80	175	750		U.S., "The Last ...," SALS-2-3X
Cornelle, Pierre	1606-1684					French dramatist, PU
Crane, Hart	1899-1932	200	500	1250		U.S. poet, "The Bridge"
Crane, Stephen	1871-1900	1000		4500		U.S., "The Red ...Courage"
Crews, Harry	1935-	12	20	40	20	U.S., "Where Does ..." - $75
Crichton, Michael	1942-	15	40	100	25	U.S., "Jurrasic Park," RS, FA
Cummings, E.E.	1894-1962	225	400	500	600	U.S., "Tulips and Chimneys"
D'Annunzio, Gabriele	1863-1938	85	125	165		Poet, novelist, "The Victim"
Dahl, Roald	1916-1990	30	75		75	British-U.S.,
Dailey, Janet	1944-	10	20	35	15	U.S., "Aspen Gold"
Davies, Robertson	1913-1995	20	35	60	25	Canadian, playwright
De Vries, Peter	1910-1993	25	40	60	30	U.S., "The Tunnel of Love," RS
Defoe, Daniel	1660-1731					British, "Robinson Crusoe," PU
Dickens, Charles	1812-1870	650	1500	1225	1600	British, "O. Twist," SALS - 2.5X
Dickey, James	1923-1997	20	40	75	50	U.S., "Deliverance," RS
Dickinson, Emily	1830-1886	700	2250	6500		U.S. lyric poet, ESPV
Didion, Joan	1934-	10	25	45	25	U.S. writer, "Run River"
Dinesen, Isak (K.Blixen)	1885-1962	125				Danish, "Winter's Tales"
Doctorow, E.L.	1931-	10	30	35	25	U.S., "Billy Bathgate" - $75
Doi, Takako	1928-					Japanese writer, PU
Donne, John	1573-1631					British, "Songs...Sonnets," PU
Donoso, Jose	1924-1996					Novelist,"The Obscene...," PU
Dos Passos, John	1896-1970	30	60	100	50	U.S. novelist, "U.S.A."
Dostoyevsky, Fyodor	1821-1881	2000				Russian, "Crime and Pun..."
Dove, Rita	1952-	25	35	70	30	U.S., "Mandolin," SB - $60
Doyle, Arthur Conan	1859-1930	500	700	1500	1850	British nov., Sherlock Holmes"
Dreiser, Theodore	1871-1945	75	175	280	225	U.S. novelist, "Sister Carrie"
Dryden, John	1631-1700					British poet, "All for Love," PU
Dumas, Alexandre	1802-1870	150	300	650	700	French, "The Three Musk..."
Dumas, Alexandre	1824-1895	40	150	200		French, "Le Demi-Monde"
Dunne, John Gregory	1932-	15	25	50	25	U.S. writer, "True Confessions"
Ehrenburg, Ilya G.	1891-1967					Russian writer, "The Thaw," PU
Eliot, George	1819-1880	175	550	1100		British novelist
Eliot, Thomas Stearns	1888-1965	200	550	2250	750	British poet, "Dante" - $1250
Elkin, Stanley	1930-1995	15	30	50	30	U.S. novelist, short-story writer
Ellison, Ralph	1914-1994	55	200	415		U.S. writer, "Invisible Man"
Emerson, Ralph Waldo	1803-1882	225	375	550		U.S. poet, essayist, SALS-4-5X
Erdich, Louise	1954-	10	20	30	15	U.S. writer
Esquivel, Laura	1950-	15	25	45	20	Mexican writer
Farrell, James T.	1904-1979	25	35	50	30	U.S. novelist, "Studs Lonigan"

Name	db/dd	Sig.	DS	ALS	SP	Comments
Fast, Howard	1914-	25	65		40	U.S. writer, "Spartacus," RS
Faulkner, William	1897-1962	400	1250	2550		U.S., "The Sound and the Fury"
Ferber, Edna	1887-1968	125	275	450		U.S., "Show Boat," SDS-2X
Fielding, Henry	1707-1754					British, "Tom Jones," PU
Fitzgerald, F. Scott	1896-1940	400	1500	3000	2600	U.S., SALS 2X-3X, ANS-$1500
Flaubert, Gustave	1821-1880	200	575	1350		French, "Madame Bovary"
Fleming, Ian	1908-1964	350	800			British, creator of James Bond
Foote, Horton	1916-	15	30	50	20	U.S. writer, "Night Seasons"
Ford, Ford Madox	1873-1939					British, "The Good Soldier," PU
Forester, Cecil Scott	1899-1966	100	200		125	British, Horatio Hornblower
Forster, Edward Morgan	1879-1970	75	200	300	150	British novelist, "Howards End"
Forsyth, Frederick	1938-	15	40	75	25	British, "The Day of the Jackal"
Fox, Paula	1923-	10	35	55	15	U.S. writer, "A Place Apart," RS
France, Anatole	1844-1924	60	125	200		French, "Penguin Island"
French, Marilyn	1929-	12	25	50	25	U.S., "The Women's Room"
Frost, Robert	1874-1963	175	650	2000	550	STLS-2X, ANS-$250
Fuentes, Carlos	1928-	25	50		30	Mexican writer, "Aura"
Fuller, Charles	1939-	10	25	40	25	U.S., "A Soldier's Play," RS
Gaddis, William	1922-	10	20	35	20	U.S. writer, "The Recognitions"
Galsworthy, John	1867-1933	50	100	200	200	British, "The Forsyte Saga"
Garcia Marquez, Gabriel	1928-	30	60		40	Columbian, "One Hundred..."
Gardner, Erle Stanley	1889-1970	100	200	300	200	Mystery writer, Perry Mason
Genet, Jean	1911-1986					French, "The Maids," PU
Gibran, Kahlil	1883-1931	175	400	800		Mystical novelist, "The Prophet"
Gide, Andre	1869-1951	200	400	600		French, "The Immoralist"
Gilroy, Frank	1925-	15	35	60	25	U.S. writer, "Little Ego"
Ginsberg, Allen	1926-1997	65	200	250	130	U.S. Beat poet, elusive signer
Giraudoux, Jean	1882-1944					French, "Tiger at the Gate," PU
Godwin, Gail	1937-	5	30	50	20	U.S. writer, "Violet Clay," RS
Goethe, Johann W.v	1749-1832	1500	3000	6000		German poet, novelist, "Faust"
Gogol, Nikolai	1809-1852	1000	3000	5650		Novelist, "Dead Souls," PU
Golding, William	1911-1993	75	250	500	100	British, "Lord of the Flies"
Goldman, William	1931-	20	35	80	50	U.S. writer, "Marathon Man"
Goldsmith, Oliver	c.1730-1774					"The Vicar of Wakefield," PU
Gordimer, Nadine	1923-	30	50	75	35	S. African, "A Guest of Honour"
Gordon, Mary	1949-	10	20	30	15	U.S. writer, "Men and Angels"
Gorky, Maxim	1868-1936	500	1100	1575	1000	Russian, "The Lower ..."
Grafton, Sue	1940-	15	25	40	20	U.S. writer, RS
Grass, Gunter	1927-	45	100	185	100	German writer, "Dog Years"
Grau, Shirley Ann	1929-	10	25	40	20	U.S. writer, "The Condor...," RS
Graves, Robert	1895-1985	70	150	275	100	British, "The White Goddess"
Gray, Thomas	1716-1771	1000	2000			British, "The Progress of Poesy"
Gray, Zane	1872-1939	125	300	600		U.S. western writer
Greene, Graham	1904-1991	100	300	500	300	British, "The Heart of the Matter"
Grimm, Jakob	1785-1863	650	1600	3500		German, "Grimm's Fairy Tales"
Grimm, Wilhelm	1786-1859	675	1725	3650		German, "Grimm's Fairy Tales"
Grisham, John	1955-	30	75		50	U.S., "The Firm"
Guare, John	1938-	15	30	60	25	U.S., "Two Gentleman of..."
Hailey, Arthur	1920-	20	40	60	30	U.S. writer, "Airport," RS
Haley, Alex	1921-1992	50	150	165	100	U.S., "Roots," SALS - 10-12X

Name	db/dd	Sig.	DS	ALS	SP	Comments
Hammett, Dashiell	1894-1961	425	1200	2500	600	U.S., "The Maltese ..."
Hamsun, Knute	1859-1952	45	125	175	100	Novelist, "Hunger"
Hardy, Thomas	1840-1928	275	750	1500		British,"Jude the Obscure"
Harris, Joel Chandler	1848-1908	200	350	700		U.S., Uncle Remus series
Hart, Moss	1904-1961	30	55	120	40	U.S., "The Man ... Dinner"
Harte, Bret	1836-1902	100	175	200		U.S. short-story writer, poet
Hasek, Jaroslav	1883-1923					Czech., "The Good ...". PU
Hass, Robert	1941-					U.S. writer, PU
Havel, Vaclav	1936-	25	100	150	50	Czech. writer
Hawkes, John	1925-	20	40	60	25	U.S. writer, "Lunar Landscape"
Hawthorne, Nathaniel	1804-1864	500	1275	2250		U.S., "The Scarlet Letter"
Heine, Heinrich	1797-1856					German, "Book of Songs," PU
Heller, Joseph	1923-	25	50		35	U.S., "God Knows" - $150
Hellman, Lillian	1905-1984	50	150	275	115	U.S., "The Little Foxes"
Helprin, Mark	1947-	15	30	60	25	U.S. writer, "Swan Lake"
Hemingway, Ernest	1899-1961	1000	3500	4500	2750	U.S. , SB - $2500

Ernest Hemingway

* U.S. novelist and short-story writer, Ernest Hemingway was one of the most commanding personalities of the age.

* Hemingway's voluminous and diversified correspondence typically included gossip, anecdotes, boasts, self-recriminations, character sketches, fishing stories, advice and an almost daily weight record.

* By some estimates he probably wrote six or seven thousand letters during the half century before his death in 1961.

* Hemingway was a poor speller his entire life and his gramatic errors became a trademark of his personal style.

* "Hemingstein" had a gift as a spinner of yarns, therefore not all the stories communicated in his letters can be trusted as true.

* "Papa" wrote to many figures, including family, literary greats, publishers, correspondents, painters, literary critics, military heroes, close friends and current and future wives.

* A must reference for all Hemingway collectors is "Ernest Hemingway, Selected Letters, 1917-1961" edited by Carlos Baker and published by Charles Scribner's Sons, New York, 1981.

* Hemingway's distinctive handwriting has many anomalies that should be studied before purchasing an ALS. Unique characters include "f, g, and t".

* Hemingway signed his name in many ways including, "Papa," "Ernie," "Hem," "Hemmy," "Stein," "Ernest M. Hemingway," "Hemingway," "Ernesto," "Pappy," "Mister Papa," "E.H." and many others.

* Until his Cuban years, where he used La Finca Vigia letterhead, Hemingway did not view paper as a commodity and often wrote on a variety of papers. His letters would often flow into margins rather than opting for another sheet of paper.

* He often wrote standing up with the paper tilted to one side.

Name	db/dd	Sig.	DS	ALS	SP	Comments
Henry, O. (W.S. Porter)	1862-1910	325	750	1500		U.S., "The Gift of the Magi"
Herriot, James (Wright)	1916-1995	25	50	90	35	British, "All Creatures Great ..."
Hersey, John	1914-1993	25	60	125	30	U.S. novelist, "Hiroshima," RS
Hesse, Hermann	1877-1962	175	375	500	350	German novelist, SDS/LS-2X
Hilton, James	1900-1954	50	150	250	65	British novelist, "Lost Horizon"
Hinton, S.E.	1948-	10	20	35	15	U.S. writer, "Rumble Fish"
Holmes, Oliver Wendell	1809-1894	100	225	450		U.S. poet, novelist, ESPV-ALS
Housman, Alfred	1859-1936	75	180	350		British poet, SALS-2X
Howells, William Dean	1837-1920	55	150			U.S. novelist, "The Rise of ..."
Hughes, Langston	1902-1967	265	425	900		U.S. poet, SB - $865
Hughes, Ted	1930-1998	25	50	80	35	Poet, author, "A Dancer to God"
Hugo, Victor	1802-1885	250	400	800		French poet, "Les Miserables"
Hurston, Zora Neale	1903-1960					U.S., PU, "Mules and Men"
Huxley, Aldous	1894-1963	75	250	375	400	Brit. writer, STLS-2-6X, ESPV
Ibsen, Henrik	1828-1906	225	500	1350		Dramatist, "A Doll's House"
Inge, William	1913-1973	60	140	215		U.S. playwright, "Bus Stop"
Ionesco, Eugene	1910-1994	40	100	225		French dramatist, "The Chairs"
Irving, John	1942-	15	30	70	50	U.S. writer, "The World ..."
Irving, Washington	1783-1859	200	450			U.S. writer, "Rip Van Winkle"
Isherwood, Christopher	1904-1986	50	150	250	200	British, "The Berlin ..."
Jackson, Shirley	1919-1965					U.S. writer, "The Lottery," PU
Jakes, John	1932-	10	20	30	15	U.S. writer, RS
James, Henry	1843-1916	125	375	750		U.S. novelist, "Daisy Miller"
James, P.D.	1920-	25	50	100		British, "The Black Tower"
Jeffers, Robinson	1887-1962	75	280	400	100	U.S. poet, "Tamar and Other ..."
Johnson, Samuel	1709-1784	1800	4500			British, "Vanity of Human ..."
Jong, Erica	1942-	10	25		15	U.S. writer, "Fear of Flying"
Jonson, Ben	1572-1637	3000				British dramatist, "Volpone"
Joyce, James	1882-1941	450	600	2750		Irish writer, "Ulysses"
Kafka, Franz	1883-1924	1000				German novelist, "Tha Castle"
Kaufman, George S.	1889-1961	35	70	150	40	U.S, "The Man Who Came to ..."
Kazantzakis, Nikos	c.1883-1957					Greek novelist, "Zorba ...," PU
Keats, John	1795-1821					British poet, "Ode on ...," PU
Keillor, Garrison	1942-	10	25	30	15	U.S. writer, RS
Kennedy, William	1928-	10	25	35	20	U.S. writer, "Ironweed"
Kerouac, Jack	1922-1969	550	3000	5000	6000	U.S., poet, "On The Road"
Khayyam, Omar	c.1028-1122					Poet, PU
Kilmer, Joyce	1886-1918	225	500	750		U.S. poet, "Trees"
King, Stephen	1947-	50	125	400	100	U.S. writer, "Carrie"
Kingsolver, Barbara	1955-	10	20	30	15	U.S. writer, "Animal Dreams"
Kingston, Maxine Hong	1940-	10	25	35	15	U.S. writer, "The Woman ..."
Kinnell, Galway	1927-	15	30	50	25	U.S., $150 (FE, SB)
Kipling, Rudyard	1865-1936	240	400	600		British, "The Jungle Book"
Knowles, John	1926-	20	35	60	30	U.S., "A Separate Peace"
Koch, Kenneth	1925-	15	25	45	20	U.S., "The Red Robins," RS
Koontz, Dean	1945-	10	20	40	20	U.S. , "Winter Moon," RS
Krantz, Judith	1928-	10	25	40	20	U.S. , "Scruples," RS
Kumin, Maxine	1925-	15	25	45	25	U.S., "Up Country: ..."

Name	db/dd	Sig.	DS	ALS	SP	Comments
L'Amour, Louis	1908-1988	80	250	500	140	U.S., screenwriter, "Hondo"
L'Engle, Madeleine	1918-	15	25	50	25	U.S. writer, "Wintersong"
la Fontaine, Jean de	1621-1695					French, "Fables choisies," PU
Lagerkvist, Par	1891-1974	40	80	160	75	Swedish poet, "The Sybil"
Lagerlof, Selma	1858-1940	100	275	500	150	Swedish novelist, "Jerusalem"
Lamartine, Alphonse de	1790-1869	120	225	300		French poet, "Meditations ..."
Lamb, Charles	1775-1834	125	275	600		British, "Essays of Elia"
Lampedusa, Giuseppe	1896-1957					Italian, "The Leopard," PU
Langland, William	c.1332-1400					English, "Piers Plowman," PU
Lardner, Ring	1885-1933	75	200	300	100	U.S. short-story writer, humorist
Lasage, Alain-Rene	1668-1747					French novelist, PU
Lawrence, David Herbert	1885-1930	300	675	2500		British, "Sons and Lovers"
Le Carre, John	1931-	20	40	80	25	British, "The Honourable ...," RS
LeGuin, Ursula	1929-	15	25	45	25	U.S. writer, The Dispossessed"
Leonard, Elmore	1925-	10	25	40	25	U.S. writer, "Get Shorty"
Lermontov, Mikhail	1814-1841	750	2000	4500		Russian, "Hero of Our Time"
Lessing, Doris	1919-	25	50	75	40	English, "The Grass is Singing"
Lessing, Gotthold	1729-1781					German, "Miss Sara ...," PU
Levin, Ira	1929-	25	45		30	U.S., "Rosemary's Baby," RS
Lewis, Clive Staples	1898-1963	250	500	1250		British, "Out of the Silent ..."
Lewis, Sinclair	1885-1951	120	275	600	275	U.S. novelist, "Babbitt"
Lindsay, Vachel	1879-1931	65	150	475	100	U.S. poet, "The Congo"
Lofting, Hugh	1896-1947	115	265	500		British, Dr. Doolittle series.
London, Jack	1876-1916	340	750	2400		U.S., "Call of the Wild"
Longfellow, Henry W.	1807-1882	175	350	400		U.S., "The Song of Hiawatha"
Lowell, Amy	1874-1925	40	110	225		U.S. , poet, "Lilacs"
Lowell, James Russell	1819-1891	55	150	250	325	U.S., "The Biglow Papers"
Lowell, Robert	1917-1977	50	125	200		U.S., "Lord Weary's Castle"
Ludlom, Robert	1927-	10	25	40	20	U.S., "The Scarlatti Inheritance"
Lurie, Alsion	1926-	10	25	40	15	U.S., "Love and Friendship," RS
MacLeish, Archibald	1892-1982	40	125	150	50	U.S. poet "Conquistador"
Mahfuz, Nagib	1911-	20	35	55	25	Egyptian writer
Mailer, Norman	1923-	15	100	200	60	U.S. , "An Amer ...," RS
Mairaux, Andre	1901-1976					French novelist, "Man's Fate"
Malamud, Bernard	1914-1986	30	55	125	30	U.S., novelist, "The Magic..."
Mallarme, Stephane	1842-1898	165	400	950		French poet, "Poesies"
Malory, Thomas	?-1471					British, "Morte d'Arthur," PU
Mamet, David	1947-	10	25	45	20	U.S. writer, RS
Mandelstam, Osip	1891-1938					Russian poet, "Stone," PU
Mann, Thomas	1875-1955	150	400	1100	800	German, "The Magic Mountain"
Mansfield, Katherine	1888-1923	115	250	460		British, "Bliss"
Marlowe, Christopher	1594-1593					British, "Dr. Faustus," PU
Mason, Bobbie Ann	1940-	10	25	30	15	U.S., "Feather Crowns,"RS
Massefield, John	1878-1967					British poet, "Sea Fever," PU
Masters, Edgar Lee	1869-1950	60	175	225	60	U.S., AMsS - $600
Maugham, William S.	1874-1955	75	200	350		British, "The Moon and Six..."
Maupassant, Guy de	1850-1893	300	700	1000		French, "The Necklace"
Mauriac, Francois	1885-1970					French, "Viper's Tangle," PU
Mayakovsky, Vladimir	1893-1930					Russian, "The Cloud...," PU
McCarthy, Cormac	1933-	10	20	35	20	U.S., "All the Pretty Horses"
McCarthy, Mary	1912-1989	50	100	165	65	U.S., "Memories of a Catholic..."

Name	db/dd	Sig.	DS	ALS	SP	Comments
McCourt, Frank	1930-	15	30	60	25	U.S. writer
McCullers, Carson	1917-1967	50	175	440	75	U.S., "Clock ..." - $125 (SB)
McCullough, Colleen	1937-	25	75	135	40	U.S. writer, "The Grass Crown"
McGuane, Thomas	1939-	10	25	30	15	U.S., "Missouri Breaks," RS
McMurtry, Larry	1936-	10	25	40	20	U.S., "Terms of Endearment"
Melville, Herman	1819-1891	700	2500	10000		U.S., "Billy Budd," SALS- 2-4X
Mencken, Henry Lewis	1880-1956	100	200	400	375	U.S., "Prejudices"
Meredith, George	1828-1909					British, "The Egoist," PU
Merimee, Prosper	1803-1870					French, "Carmen," PU
Merrill, James	1926-1995	25	50	65	35	U.S., "Divine Comedies," RS
Michener, James	1907-1998	40	250	300	100	U.S. writer, "Tales ... RS
Millay, Edna St. Vincent	1892-1950	150	300	725	1000	U.S. poet, "A Few ...Thisties"
Miller, Arthur	1915-	25	100	200	70	U.S., "Death...," SB - $75
Miller, Henry	1891-1980	100	200	350	130	U.S., "Tropic of Cancer"
Milne, Alan Alexander	1882-1956	225	500	900	450	British, "Winnie-the-Pooh"
Milton, John	1608-1674					British, "Areopagitica," PU
Mishima Y. (H. Kimitake)	1925-1970					Japan, "Confess....Mask," PU
Mistral, Gabriela	1889-1957	30	50	75	35	Poet, "Sonnets of Death"
Mitchell, Margaret	1900-1949	600	3000	3250		U.S., GWTW - $7500 (FE,SB)
Moliere, Jean Baptiste	1622-1673					French, "Le Misanthrope," PU
Molnar, Ferenc	1878-1952	85	150	300		Novelist, "The Swan"
Montaigne, Michel de	1533-1592					French, "Essais," PU
Montale, Eugenio	1896-1981	20	50	75	35	Italian poet
Moore, Clement C.	1779-1863	200	450	1250		U.S., "A Visit...Saint Nicholas"
Moore, Marianne	1887-1972	75	175	300	100	U.S., $250 (FE, SB)
More, Sir Thomas	1478-1535					British writer, PU
Morris, Wright	1910-	20	35	50	25	U.S. writer, "My Uncle Dudley"
Morrison, Toni	1931-	25	50	100	30	U.S. writer, "Beloved"
Munro, Alice	1931-	15	30	50	20	Canadian writer, "Lives of..."
Murdoch, Iris	1919-	20	35	50	25	Irish writer, "The Bell"
Musset, Alfred de	1810-1857					French poet, dramatist, PU
Nabokov, Vladimir	1899-1977	300	850		900	Russian-U.S. novelist
Naipaul, V.S.	1932-	25	50	75	30	Trinidad, "The Mystic Masseur"
Nash, Ogden	1902-1971	50	100	150	50	U.S. poet
Neruda, Pablo	1904-1973					Poet, "Toward the ...," PU
O'Casey, Sean	1884-1964	125	225	400	275	Irish dramatist, "The Plough..."
O'Connor, Flannery	1925-1964	350	1000			U.S., 'Wise Blood"
O'Connor, Frank	1903-1966					"Guests ...," (M. Donovan). PU
O'Hara, John	1905-1970	150	400	700		U.S. novelist, "Pal Joey"
O'Neill, Eugene	1888-1953	265	400	500		U.S., "Long Day's Journey ..."
Oates, Joyce Carol	1938-	10	30	40	25	U.S., "The Poisoned Kiss"
Odets, Clifford	1906-1963	40	75	150	80	U.S. playwright, "Golden Boy"
Orwell, George	1903-1950					British, "Animal Farm," PU
Osborne, John	1929-1995	15	30	50	25	British, "The Entertainer"
Ozick, Cynthia	1928-	15	25	45	25	U.S., "Fame and Folly," RS
Paley, Grace	1922-	10	25	40	20	U.S., "Later the Same Day," RS
Parker, Dorothy	1893-1967	30	45	100	35	U.S., "Enough Rope"
Pasternak, Boris	1890-1960	400	800	1650		Russian,, SB- $1500
Paz, Octavio	1914-1998	40	75	120	50	Mexican writer

Name	db/dd	Sig.	DS	ALS	SP	Comments
Pepys, Samuel	1633-1703					British diarist, PU
Perelman, Sidney J.	1904-1979	30	60	85	50	U.S. humorist
Perrault, Charles	1628-1703			3000		"Sleeping Beauty,"scarce
"Cinderella"Petrarch	1304-1374					Poet, (Francesco Petraca), PU
Piercy, Marge	1936-	10	30	50	20	U.S. writer, "Available Light"
Pinsky, Robert	1940-	10	25	40	20	U.S. writer, "The Want Bone"
Pirandello, Luigi	1867-1936	75	200	450	300	Italian, "Six Characters in ..."
Plath, Sylvia	1932-1963					U.S., poet, "The Bell Jar," PU
Poe, Edgar Allan	1809-1849					U.S. poet, "The Raven," PU
Pope, Alexander	1688-1744	650	1600	2250		British poet, "An Essay on Man"
Porter, Katherine Anne	1890-1980	75	150	400	125	U.S. novelist, "Ship of Fools"
Potok, Chaim	1929-2002	25	50	75	40	U.S. writer, "The Promise"
Pound, Ezra	1885-1972	225	890	1175		U.S. poet, "Cantos"
Price, Reynolds	1933-	10	20	40	20	U.S., "A Long and Happy Life"
Proulx, E. Annie	1935-	10	20	35	20	U.S., "The Shipping News," RS
Proust, Marcel	1871-1922	550	750	2150		French, "Rememberance..."
Pushkin, Aleksandr	1799-1837	850	2750	000		Russian, "Eugene Onegin"
Puzo, Mario	1920-1999	25	80	175		U.S. writer, "The Godfather"
Pynchon, Thomas	1937-	10	25	40	20	U.S. writer, "V"
Rabe, David	1940-	10	25	30	15	U.S. writer, "Streamers"
Rabelais, Francois	1495-1553					French, "Gargantua," PU
Racine, Jean	1639-1699	5000				French dramatist, "Britannicus"
Rand, Ayn	1905-1982	525	1100		700	Russian-U.S. novelist "Atlas..."
Reed, Ishmael	1938-	10	20	35	15	U.S., "Yellow Back Radio ..."
Remarque, Erich Maria	1898-1970	60	135	400	75	German-U.S., "All Quiet on ..."
Rice, Anne	1941-	10	30		25	U.S., "Interview... Vampire," RS
Rich, Adrienne	1929-	15	20	40	20	U.S., "Diving into the Wreck"
Richardson, Samuel	1689-1761					British, "Pamela," PU
Rilke, Rainer Maria	1875-1926	150	300	1000		German, "Life and Songs"
Rimbaud, Arthur	1854-1891					French, "A Season in Hell," PU
Robinson, Edwin A.	1869-1935	50	150	200		U.S. poet, "Merlin"
Roethke, Theodore	1908-1963	45	150	250	50	U.S. poet, "The Far Field"
Rolland, Romain	1866-1944	35	100	150	40	French novelist, biographer
Ronsard, Pierre de	1524-1585					French poet, PU
Rostand, Edmond	1868-1918	75	200	500	750	French, "Cyrano de Bergerac"
Roth, Philip	1933-	10	30	75	25	U.S., "Portnoy's..." - $315 (TS)
Runyon, Damon	1880-1946	175	375	400	200	U.S., "Guys and Dolls"
Rushdie, Salaman	1947-	30	75	150	50	Indian, "The Satanic Verses"
Ruskin, John	1819-1900	65	125	275		British, "Modern Painters"
Saint-Exupery, Ant. de	1900-1944	75	150	250	150	French, "The Little Prince"
Saki (H. Munro)	1870-1916					British, "The Chron....," PU
Salinger, J.D.	1919-	750	3250	4000		U.S., "The Catcher in the Rye"
Sand, George	1804-1876	125	250	500		French novelist, "Indiana"
Sandburg, Carl	1878-1967	100	250	325	400	U.S. poet, "The People"
Sanders, Lawrence	1920-	15	30	50	25	U.S., "The Anderson Tapes"
Saroyan, William	1908-1981	75	200	275	100	U.S., "The Human Com."
Sarton, May	1914-1995	15	25	50	25	Belg/U.S. poet, "Anger"
Sayers, Dorothy L.	1893-1957	225	400	500	130	British mystery writer
Scarry, Richard	1920-1994	30	50	100	50	U.S. author of children's books
Schiller, Friedrich von	1759-1805					German, poet, historian, PU

Name	db/dd	Sig.	DS	ALS	SP	Comments
Scott, Sir Walter	1771-1832	125	550	800		Novelist, poet "Ivanhoe"
Seifert, Jaroslav	1902-1986					Poet, PU
Seuss, Dr. (T.Geisel)	1904-1991	145	450	550	425	U.S. , $745 (SBP)
Shakespeare, William	1564-1616					British, "Hamlet," only 6 known
Shaw, George Bernard	1856-1950	325	740	1650		Playwright, critic, "Pygmalion"
Sheldon, Sidney	1917-	15	25	50	20	U.S., "Bloodline," RS
Shelley, Mary W.	1797-1851	700	1000	1400		Novelist, "Frankenstein"
Shelley, Percy Bysshe	1792-1822	1250	2500	5250		British, "Ode to the West Wind"
Shepard, Sam	1943-	30	55	100	45	U.S., "Chicago," elusive signer
Sheridan, Richard B.	1751-1816	75	125	300		British, "The Rivals"
Sherwood, Robert	1896-1955	35	100	175	50	U.S., "Abe Lincoln in Illinois"
Shields, Carol	1935-	15	20	40	20	U.S., "The Box Garden," RS
Shikibu, Murasaki	c.978-1031?					Japanese novelist, PU
Sholokhov, Mikhail	1906-1984					Russian, "The Silent Don," PU
Silverstein, Shel	1932-	25	50	100	50	U.S., "Drain My Brain," elusive!
Simon, Neil	1927-	20	50	100	25	U.S. writer, RS
Sinclair, Upton	1878-1968	50	100	150	120	U.S. novelist, "The Jungle"
Singer, Issac Bashevis	1904-1991	45	165	275	150	Pol./U.S. novelist
Smiley, Jane	1949-	10	20	30	15	U.S. writer, "At Paradise Gate"
Snow, Charles Percy	1905-1980	30	65	130	45	British novelist
Solzhenitsyn, Alek.	1918-	100	350	440	150	Russian writer, "Cancer Ward"
Soyinka, Wole	1934-	30	65	100	40	Nigerian, "The Interpreter"
Spender, Stephen	1909-1995	75	150	200	100	British poet, critic, novelist
Spenser, Edmund	1552-1599					British poet, PU
Spillane, Mickey	1918-	15	30	60		U.S. writer, "The Deep"
Standhal	1783-1842					Frenc, (Marie H. Beyle), PU
Stead, Christine	1903-1983					Australian, PU
Steel, Danielle	1947-	10	25	50	25	U.S. writer, "Wings," RS
Steele, Richard	1672-1729	240	575	1150		British essayist, playwright
Steffens, Lincoln	1866-1936	35	100	150	50	U.S. editor, writer
Stein, Gertrude	1874-1946					U.S. writer, "Three Lives," PU
Steinbeck, John	1902-1968	425	2000	3000	1000	U.S., "East of Eden" - $2875, SB
Stern, Richard	1928-	10	25	30	15	U.S. , "Golk," RS
Sterne, Laurence	1713-1768					British, "Tristram Shandy," PU
Stevens, Wallace	1879-1955	225	800	1275		U.S. poet, "Harmonium"
Stevenson, Robert L.	1850-1894	350	1250	1725		British, "Treasure Island"
Stewart, Mary	1916-	25	50	75	40	British writer, "The Ivy Tree"
Stoker, Bram	1845-1910	300	600	750		British writer, "Dracula"
Stone, Robert	1937-	10	25	30	15	U.S. writer, "Dog Soldiers,"RS
Stoppard, Tom	1937-	25	45	60	30	U.K. Writer, "Billy Bathgate"
Stout, Rex	1886-1975	30	75	160	45	U.S. mystery writer
Stowe, Harriet Beecher	1811-1896	275	475	1000		U.S., "Uncle Tom's Cabin"
Strachey, Lytton	1880-1932	80	150	450		British biographer, critic
Strindberg, August	1849-1912					Swedish, "The Father," PU
Styron, William	1925-	20	40	100	45	U.S., "Sophie's Choice" - $150
Swift, Jonathan	1667-1745	2650	6500	12500		British, "Gulliver's Travels"
Swinburne, Alge.C.	1837-1909	200	300	535		British, "Atalanta in Calydon"
Synge, John M.	1871-1909					Poet, "Riders to the Sea," PU
Tagore, Rabindranath	1861-1941	130	275	425	280	Author, poet, "Sadhana"
Tan, Amy	1952-	20	30	50	30	U.S. writer, "The Moon Lady"
Tarkington, Booth	1869-1946	45	140	240	100	U.S. novelist, "Seventeen"

Name	db/dd	Sig.	DS	ALS	SP	Comments
Taylor, Peter	1917-1994	25	40	60	30	U.S., "A Summons to Memphis"
Teasdale, Sara	1884-1933					"Rivers to the Sea," PU
Tennyson, Alfred Lord	1809-1892	225	650	800	1000	British poet, "Idylls of the King"
Thackery, William M.	1811-1863	125	350	640		British novelist, "Vanity Fair"
Theroux, Paul	1941-	20	35	50	25	U.S. writer, "The Family Arsenal"
Thomas, Dylan	1914-1953	525	1250	1650		Welsh poet, "Under Milk Wood"
Thoreau, Henry David	1817-1862	2380	4850	8000		U.S. writer, "Walden"
Thurber, James	1894-1961	125	265	475	140	U.S., "The Secret... Mitty"
Tolkien, J.R.R.	1892-1973	500	1200	2500		British writer, "The Hobbit"
Tolstoy, Leo	1828-1910	1000	2350	3150	2250	Russsian, short-story writer
Trollope, Anthony	1815-1882	100	250	750		British novelist, "The Warden"
Turgenev, Ivan	1818-1883	225	500	1250		Russian novelist, "First Love"
Turow, Scott	1949-	25	50	75	30	U.S., "The Burden of Proof"
Tutuola, Amos	1920-1997	30	50	60	40	Nigerian novelist
Twain, Mark	1835-1910	935	1560	2500	2000	U.S. novelist, "Tom Sawyer"
Tyler, Ann	1941-	10	25	50	25	U.S. writer, "Breathing ...," RS
Udset, Sigrid	1881-1949					Novelist, poet, PU
Updike, John	1932-	25	100	175	50	U.S. writer,RS, "The Coup"
Uris, Leon	1924-2003	25	45	65	30	U.S. writer, "Exodus," RS
Valery, Paul	1871-1945	50	125	200	75	French poet, critic
Verne, Jules	1828-1905	200	700	1275		French, "Twenty Thousand..."
Vidal, Gore	1925-	25	40	75	30	U.S. writer, "Washington D.C."
Villon, Francois	1431-c.1463					French poet, "The Lays," PU
Voltaire (F.M. Arouet)	1694-1778	500	2000	3750		French writer, philosopher
Vonnegut, Jr., Kurt	1922-	25	75		60	U.S., "Slapstick" - $215 (TS)
Walker, Alice	1944-	25	60	80	50	U.S. writer, "The Color Purple"
Waller, Robert James	1939-	15	30	50	25	U.S., "The Bridges ...County"
Wambaugh, Joseph	1937-	15	25	45	20	U.S., "The Onion Field," RS
Warren, Robert Penn	1905-1989	35	125	150	75	U.S., "All the King's Men," RS
Wasserstein, Wendy	1950-	15	25	35	20	U.S., "The Heeidi Chronicles"
Waugh, Evelyn	1903-1966	50	185	300	65	British, "The Loved One"
Wells, H.G.	1866-1946	160	350	550		British, "The Invisible Man"
Welty, Eudora	1909-2001	50	150	250	75	U.S., "The Ponder Heart"
West, Rebecca	1893-1983	20	50	100	35	British, "Black Lamb... Falcon"
Wharton, Edith	1862-1937	215	500	1150		U.S., "Ethan Frome"
White, E.B.	1899-1985	35	125	265	75	U.S. , "Charlotte's Web"
White, Patrick	1912-1990					Australian, "The Tree ...," PU
White, T.H.	1906-1964					British, "The ...Future King," PU
Whitman, Walt	1819-1892	825	2750	3750	3250	U.S. poet, "Leaves of Grass"
Whittier, John Greenleaf	1807-1892	100	300	450		U.S. poet, "Snow-Bound"
Wideman, John Edgar	1941-	10	20	30	20	U.S., "Sent ... Yesterday," RS
Wilde, Oscar	1854-1900	850	1700	2750		Irish novelist, playwright
Wilder, Laura Ingalls	1867-1957					U.S., "Little House...," PU
Wilder, Thornton	1897-1975	75	200	425	225	U.S. playwright, "Our Town," RS
Williams, Tennessee	1911-1983	175	400	600	300	U.S., "Cat on ...," TMS - $550
Williams, William Carlos	1883-1963	250	350	425	300	U.S. poet
Wilson, August	1945-	20	40	60	30	U.S. writer, "Fences"
Wilson, Edmund	1895-1972	30	100	200	65	U.S. critic, novelist
Wilson, Lanford	1937-	15	25	40	20	U.S. writer, "Angels Fall"

Name	db/dd	Sig.	DS	ALS	SP	Comments
Wodehouse, P.G.	1881-1975	150	225	325		British/U.S. humorist
Wolfe, Thomas	1900-1938	450	2250	3000		U.S. novelist, rare
Wolfe, Tom	1931-	20	45	100	40	U.S. writer, "The Right Stuff"
Wolff, Tobias	1945-	10	20	30	15	U.S. writer, "The Barracks Thief"
Woolf, Virginia	1882-1941	400	1500	2500		British, "The Waves"
Wordsworth, William	1770-1850	230	1225	2150		British poet
Wouk, Herman	1915-	35	100	150	100	U.S., "The Caine Mutiny"
Wright, Richard	1908-1960	75	200	300	215	Novelist,
Yeats, William Butler	1865-1939	225	725	800		Irish poet, playwright
Zola, Emile	1840-1902	175	365	575		French novelist, "Nana"

AVIATION

WHAT YOU NEED TO KNOW

* As of September, 2003, there have been 113 shuttle flights, 88 since the 1986 Challenger disaster. Both totals include the final Columbia flight; the Columbia completed 28 flights, counting its final mission.

* There are three remaining shuttles: the Discovery (30 flights), the Atlantis (26) and the Endeavour (19). The Challenger completed nine missions in all.

*Four Soviets are known to have died in space flights: Komarov was killed on Soyuz 1 (1967); the three-person Soyuz 11 crew (1971) was asphyxiated. Six Americans and an Israeli astronaut died aboard the Columbia (2003); Seven Americans died in the Challenger explosion and three astronauts (Apollo 1)- Grissom, White and Chaffee died in 1967

* Since the field of aviation is relatively new, when compared to other niches, amassing a significant collection remains feasible and often cost-effective.

* Facsimile signed material, often machine generated, is common with autographed space material. This includes cards along with individual and crew photographs.

* Many outstanding research materials, in the form of books, periodicals and articles, have documented this area of collecting and are highly recommended.

* Participants in this niche of collecting are typically responsive to autograph requests.

MARKET FACTS

* The Centennial of the first man-flight (12/17/1903) has drawn more collectors to this area of collecting.

* The signatures of space pioneers and those who have walked on the surface of the moon, continue to be the most sought.

* The collecting form of choice is the signed photograph.

* The signatures of some early cosmonauts remain scarce and are difficult to value.

* This market niche has been a viable area of collecting for years.

MARKET TRENDS

* Many astronauts continue to remain active on the autograph show circuit.

* Many books have been published in recent years from the staff and crews of NASA active in the early years of the space program. Therefore signed editions can often be encountered.

* Market value continues to escalate for the signatures of deceased participants of the space program.

* Collecting options in this area, such as the signatures of test pilots or aces, remain popular with collectors.

* Specialization, both in form - SP's of astronauts in specific flight suits or on certain missions, and during certain programs - Mercury, Apollo, etc., continue to be popular with collectors.

Abbreviations: ASTP = Apollo-Soyuz Test Project, ESPV = exhibits significant price variation, EVA = extravehicular activity, FA = facsimile/forgery alert, MW = moonwalker, NAHOF = National Aeronautic Hall of Fame, NASA = National Aeronautics and Space Administration, PU = pricing undetermined, RS = responsive signer, SB = signed book, STS = Space Transportation System, SDS = significant document signed

Note: Bold = those individuals who have walked on the moon.

Name	db/dd	Sig.	LS/DS	ALS	SP	Comments
Bleriot, Louis		250	500	600	500	First to fly English Channel
Crossfield, A. Scott		10	30	60	40	National Aviation Hall of Fame
Earhart, Amelia	1898-1937	750	1500	2000	1725	NAHOF, SB-$850, SDS-2X, ESPV
Lindbergh, Charles	1902-1974	800	2000	3435	1625	ALS-2X, SB-$900, 675, VSP-$2350, ESPV
Lindbergh, Anne M.		25	60	150	50	NAHOF
Piccard, Auguste	1884-1962	50	120	175	100	Swiss physicist
Post, Wiley	1900-1935	275	800	600	750	Sig. w/H. Gatty-$595(FDC),
Richthofen, Manfred	1882-1918	2250			6500	German airman, rare
Rickenbacker, Edward	1890-1973	150	250	575	280	NAHOF, TLS-$125-$695-ESPV
Sikorsky, Igor	1889-1972	100	200	300	275	Aeronautical engineer
Tibbets Jr., Paul W.		20	100		75	NAHOF, RS
Von Braun, Wernher	1912-1977	150	400	500	375	German rocket expert
Whittle, Sir Frank	1907-	15	40		45	English aeronautical engineer
Wright, Orville	1871-1948	500	1250	2000	2000	American pioneer aviator
Wright, Wilbur	1867-1912	1000	2000	5000	4500	American pioneer aviator
Yeager, Charles E.	1923-	25	60	100	50	NAHOF, RS
Zeppelin, Ferdinand	1838-1917	300	500			German soldier, aeronaut

OUTER SPACE

Name	Sig.	LS/DS	ALS	SP	Comments
(Abdul) Ahad (Mohmand)					Soyuz TM-6, first Afghan in space, PU
Acton, Loren W.	5	15	25	10	Challenger, 7/29/85
Adamson, James C.	8	20	30	15	Columbia, 8/9/89, Atlantis, 8/3/91, FA
Afansev, Viktor	15	40	40	20	Soyuz TM-11, 12/2/90
Akers, Thomas D.	5	10	20	10	Discovery, 10/6/90, Endeavour, 5/7/92
Akiyama, Toyohiro	20	30	45	25	Soyuz TM-11, 12/2/90, Japanese
Aksenov, Vladimir					Soyuz 22, PU
Aldrin, Edwin E., Jr.	**65**	**225**	**300**	**140**	**Gemini 12, 2nd MW, TSS**
Aleksandrov, Aleksandr					Soyuz T-9, 6/27/83, PU
Alexandrov, Aleksandr					(different person), Soyuz TM-5, PU
Allen, Andrew M.	5	10	20	10	Atlantis, 7/31/92, Columbia, 3/4/94, RS
Allen, Joseph P.	10	15	30	20	Columbia, 11/11/82, Discovery, 11/8/84
Anders, William A.	45	100		100	Apollo 8

Focus On the Apollo Program

Date-Mission	Crew (# of flights)	SP	Comments
10/11/68- Apollo 7	Schirra (3), Donn F. Eisele, R. Walter Cunnigham	200	1st piloted flight
12/21/68-Apollo 8	Borman (2), Lovell (3), William A. Anders	500	1st lunar orbit
3/3/69-Apollo 9	McDivitt (2), D. Scott (2), Russell L. Schweickart	200	1st piloted LM
5/18/69 - Apollo 10	Stafford (3), Young (3), Cernan (2)	300	LM moon orbit
7/16/69-Apollo 11	Armstrong (2), Collins (2), Aldrin(2)	1500	1st lunar land.
11/14/69 - Apollo 12	Conrad (3), Richard F. Gordon Jr. (2), Alan L. Bean	300	2nd lunar land.
4/11/70 - Apollo 13	Lovell (4), Fred W. Haise Jr., John L. Swigert, Jr.	1400	Aborted
1/31/71-Apollo 14	A. Shepard (2), Stuart A. Roosa, Edgar D. Mitchell	1350	3rd lunar land.
7/26/71 - Apollo 15	D. Scott (3), James B. Irwin, Alfred M. Worden	500	4th lunar land.
4/16/72 - Apollo 16	Young (4), Charles M. Duke, Jr., Thomas K. Mattingly II	200	5th lunar land.
12/7/72 - Apollo 17	Cernan (3), Ronald E. Evans, Harrison H. Schmitt	200	Last lunar land.

Name	Sig.	LS/DS	ALS	SP	Comments
Apt, Jay	5	10	25	10	Endeavour, 9/12/92, 4/9/94,RS
Apt, Jerome	10	15	30	15	Atlantis, 4/5/91
Armstrong, Neil A.	**275**	**1000**		**535**	**Gem. 8, TLS-$1,000, MW - 1st.**
Artebarsky, Anatoly					Soyuz TM-12, 5/18/91, PU
Artukhin, Yuri P.	35	75		70	Soyuz 14
Atkov, Oleg					Soyuz T-10B, 2/8/84, PU
Aubakirov, Toktar O.					Soyuz TM-13, 10/2/91, PU
Avdeyev, Sergei					Soyuz TM-15, 7/27/92, PU
Bagian, James P.	5	20	25	10	Discovery, 3/13/89, Columbia, 6/5/91
Baker, Ellen S.	5	20	25	10	Atlantis, 10/18/89, Columbia, 6/25/92
Baker, Michael A.	5	20	25	10	Atlantis, 8/3/91, Columbia, 10/22/92,
Balandin, Aleksandr					Soyuz TM-9, 2/11/90, PU
Bartoe, John-David F.	5	15	30	20	Challenger, 7/29/85
Baudry, Patrick	10	20	40	25	Discovery, 6/17/85
Bean, Alan	**50**	**150**		**100**	**Apollo 12, SL 3, MW, TLS - $500**

Name	Sig.	LS/DS	ALS	SP	Comments
Belyayev, Pavel I.					Voskhod 2, PU
Beregovoi, Georgi T.					Soyuz 3, PU
Berezovoy, Anatoly					Soyuz T-5, PU
Blaha, John E.	8	20	25	15	Discovery, 3/13/89, 11/22/89, Atlantis
Bluford, Guion S., Jr.	15	30	35	25	Challenger, 8/30/83, first black Amer.
Bobko, Karol J.	10	20	25	20	Challenger, 4/4/83, FA
Bolden, Charles F., Jr.	5	25	30	15	Discovery, 4/24/90, 2/3/94, Atlantis
Bondar, Roberta L.	5	15	25	10	Discovery, 1/22/92, RS, send sm. SP
Borman, Frank	35	150	250	125	Gemini 7, Apollo 8
Bowersox, Kenneth D.	8	20	25	15	Columbia, 6/25/92, Endeavour, 12/2/93
Brand, Vance D.	15	45		200	ASTP, Columbia, 12/2/90
Brandenstein, Daniel C.	10		30	20	Challenger, 8/30/83, Discovery, FA
Bridges, Roy D., Jr.	5	10	15	10	Challenger, 7/29/85, RS
Brown, Curtis L., Jr.	7	20	25	15	Endeavour, 9/12/92, Atlantis, 11/3/94
Brown, Mark N.	5	15	25	10	Columbia, 8/9/89, Discovery, 9/12/91
Buchi, James F.	10	20	15	20	Discovery, 1/24/84, 3/13/89, FA
Budarin, Nikolai M.	7	20	30	15	Atlantis, 6/27/95
Bursch, Daniel W.	7	15	20	15	Discovery, 9/1/93, Endeavour, 9/30/94
Bykovsky, Valery F.					Vostok 5, Soyuz 22, Soyuz 31, PU
Cabana, Robert D.	8	15	25	12	Discovery, 10/6/90, 12/2/92, RS
Cameron, Kenneth D.	5	15	20	12	Atlantis, 4/5/91, Discovery, 4/8/93
Carpenter, M. Scott	50	100	200	100	Mercury-Atlas 7,
Carr, Gerald P.	10	25	30	20	Skylab 4, RS
Carter, Jr., Manley Lanier	7	15	20	15	Discovery, 11/22/89
Caspar, John H.	10	35	55	25	Atlantis, 2/28/90, Endeavour, 1/13/93
Cenker, Robert J.	5	10	20	15	Columbia, 1/12/86
Cernan, Eugene A.	**35**	**100**	**200**	**100**	**Gem. 9A, Apollo 10 & 17, MW**
Chaffee, Roger	225	500		450	Apollo 1, perished in launch fire
Chang-Diaz, Franklin R.	10	30	40	15	Columbia, 1/12/86, Atlantis, 10/18/89
Chiao, Leroy	5	10	20	15	Columbia, 7/8/94
Chilton, Kevin B.	8	20	25	12	Endeavour, 5/7/92, 4/9/94, varied res.
Chretien, Jean-Loup					Soyuz T-6, TM-7, first Fr. cosmo., PU
Cleave, Mary L.	10	15	20	25	Atlantis, 11/26/85, 5/4/89
Clervoy, Jean-Francois	5	15	25	15	Atlantis, 11/3/94
Clifford, Michael R.	7	15	25	15	Discovery, 12/2/92, Endeavour, 4/9/94
Coats, Michael L.	10	20	25	20	Discovery, 8/30/84, 3/13/89, FA
Cockrell, Kenneth D.	5	15	20	10	Discovery, 4/8/93, RS
Collins, Eileen M.	5	10	20	15	Discovery, 2/3/95
Collins, Michael	125	300	460	275	Gemini 10, Apollo 11, book - $300
Conrad, Charles, Jr.	**35**	**200**	**300**	**100**	**Gem. 5, Apollo 12, RS, MW, TSS**
Cooper, L. Gordon	30	75	150	75	Mercury-Atlas 9, Gemini 5, TSS
Covey, Richard C.	5	15	20	10	Discovery, 8/27/85, Atlantis, RS
Creighton, John O.	10	20	20	25	Atlantis, 2/28/90, Discovery, FA
Crippen, Robert L.	25	75	200	80	Columbia, 4/12/81, first flight of shut.
Culbertson, Frank L., Jr.	5	10	20	15	Atlantis, 11/15/90, Discovery, 9/1/93
Cunningham, R. Walter	20	40	60	40	Apollo 7, TSS
Currie, Nancy J.	5	10	15	10	STS-57, 70, 88, RS
Davis, N. Jan	5	10	20	15	Endeavour, 9/12/92, D 2/3/94
DeLucas, Lawrence J.	10		30	15	Columbia, 6/25/92, FA
Demin, Lev					Soyuz 15, PU

Name	Sig.	LS/DS	ALS	SP	Comments
Dezhurov, Vladimir					Soyuz TM-21, 3/14/95, PU
Dobrovolsky, Georgi T.					Soyuz 11, all 3 cosmonauts killed , PU
Duffy, Brian	5		25	10	Atlantis, 3/24/92, E 6/21/93, RS
Duke, Charles M., Jr.	**35**	**150**	**200**	**75**	**Apollo 16, MW, TSS**
Dunbar, Bonnie J.	5		25	10	Challenger, 10/30/85,Columbia, 1/9/90
Durrance, Samuel T.					Columbia, 12/2/90, Endeavour, PU
Dzhanibekov, Valdimir					Soyuz 27, PU
Eisele, Donn F.	50	100		100	Apollo 7
England, Anthony W.	5	10	20	15	Challenger, 7/29/85, RS
Engle, Joe H.	10	30		40	Columbia, 11/12/81, Discovery, RS
Evans, Ronald E.	45	100		85	Apollo 17, RS
Fabian, John M.	5	15	25	10	Challenger, 6/18/83
Faris, Muhammad					Soyuz TM-3, first Syrian in space, PU
Farkas, Bertalan					Soyuz 36, PU
Feoktistov, Konstantin P.	30			75	Voskhod 1
Fettman, Martin J.	5	10	20	10	Columbia, 10/18/93
Filipchenko, Anatoly V.					Soyuz 7, PU
Fisher, Anna L.	10	20	30	20	Discovery, 11/8/84
Fisher, William F.	5	15	20	10	Discovery, 8/27/85
Flade, Klaus-Dietrich					Soyuz TM-14, a German, PU
Foale, Michael	10	20	35	20	Atlantis, 3/24/92, Discovery, 4/8/93
Frimout, Dirk D.	5	15	25	10	Atlantis, 3/24/92
Fullerton, C. Gordon	5	15	25	15	Columbia, 3/22/82, Challenger, 7/29/85
Furrer, Reinhard	20	35		70	Challenger, 10/30/85
Gaffney, Francis A.	5	15	25	10	Columbia, 6/5/91
Gagarin, Yuri A.	700			1500	Vostock 1, first human orbital flight
Gameau, Marc	8		30	12	Challenger, first Canadian astronaut
Gardner, Dale A.	10	20	20	25	Challenger, 8/30/83, Discovery, FA
Gardner, Guy S.	5		20	10	Atlantis, 12/2/88, Columbia, RS
Garn, Jake	12	35	50	15	Discovery, 4/12/85, USS, FA (USS)
Garriott, Owen K.	12		30	22	Skylab 3, Columbia, 11/28/83, RS
Gemar, Charles D. (Sam)	8		30	12	Atlantis, 11/15/90, Discovery, RS
Gibson, Edward G.	10	30	40	20	Skylab 4
Gibson, Robert L.	10		30	15	Challenger, 2/3/84, Columbia, RS
Glazkov, Yuri N.					Soyuz 24, PU
Glenn, John H., Jr.	50	200	500	100	Mercury-Atlas 6, 1st American in orbit
Godwin, Linda M.	5		20	10	Atlantis, 4/5/91, Endeavour, 4/9/94, RS
Gorbatko, Viktor V.	30			65	Soyuz 7
Gordon, Richard F., Jr.	25	40	70	50	Gemini 11, TSS
Grabe, Ronald J.	10		25	15	Atlantis, 10/4/85, 5/4/89, Discovery
Grechko, Georgi M.					Soyuz T-14, 9/17/85, Soyuz 17, PU
Gregory, Frederick D.	8		25	12	Discovery, 11/22/89, Atlantis, 11/24/91
Gregory, William G.	5	15	20	10	Endeavour, 3/2/95
Griggs, S. David	50	100		125	Discovery, 4/12/85
Grissom, Virgil I.	450	1000		1200	Mercury-Redstone 4
Grunsfeld, John M.	5	10	20	10	Endeavour, 3/2/95
Gubarev, Alexi A.					Soyuz 17, PU
Gurragcha, Jugderdemuduyn					Soyuz 39, first Mongolian, PU
Gutierrez, Sidney M.	5		20	10	Columbia, 6/5/91, Endeavour, RS

Name	Sig.	LS/DS	ALS	SP	Comments
Haignere, Jean-Pierre					Soyuz TM-17, 7/1/93, French, PU
Haise, Fred W.	40	120		100	Apollo 13
Halsell, James D., Jr.	5	10	20	10	Columbia, 7/8/94
Hammond, L. Baine, Jr.	5		20	10	Discovery, 4/28/91, 9/9/94, RS
Harbaugh, Gregory J.	8		25	12	Discovery, 4/28/91, Endeavour, RS
Harris, Bernard A., Jr.	5	15	25	10	Columbia, 4/26/93, Discovery, 2/3/95
Hart, Terry	5	10	15	15	Challenger, 4/6/84, FA
Hartsfield, Henry W.	5		20	10	Columbia, 6/27/82, RS
Hauck, Frederick H.	10	20	25	20	Challenger, 6/18/83
Hawley, Steven A.	5		20	10	Discovery, 8/30/84, Columbia, RS
Heinze, Karl G.	10	20		20	Challenger, 7/29/85
Helms, Susan J.	10	25		20	Endeavour, 1/13/93
Hennen, Thomas J.	5		20	10	Atlantis, 11/24/91, RS
Henricks, Terence T.	5	15	25	10	Atlantis, 11/24/91, Columbia, 4/26/93
Hermaszewski, Miroslav					Soyuz 30, PU
Hieb, Richard J.	5		20	10	Discovery, 4/28/91, Endeavour, RS
Hilmers, David C.	5		20	10	Atlantis, 10/4/85, 2/28/90,FA
Hoffman, Jeffrey A.	10	25	30	20	Discovery, 4/12/85, Columbia, 12/2/90
Hughes-Fulford, Millie	5		25	10	Columbia, 6/5/91, RS
Irwin, James	**55**	**175**		**150**	**Apollo 15, RS, MW**
Ivanchenkov, Alexander S.	50	140	250	75	Soyuz 29
Ivanov, Georgi					Soyuz 33, PU
Ivins, Marsha S.	5		20	10	Columbia, 1/9/90, Atlantis, 7/31/92, RS
Jahn, Sigmund					Soyuz 31, PU
Jarvis, Gregory B.	150			300	Challenger, killed during launch
Jemison, Mae Carol					Endeavour, 9/12/92, 1st black fem., PU
Jernigan, Tamara E.	5		20	12	Columbia, 6/5/91, Columbia, 10/22/92,
Jones, Thomas D.	5		20	10	Endeavour, 4/9/94, 9/30/94, RS
Kaleri, Aleksandr					Soyuz TM-14, PU
Kerwin, Joseph P.	10	30	40	20	Skylab 2
Khrunov, Yevgeni V.	50	130		75	Soyuz 5
Kirkalev, Sergi M.					Discovery, 1st Russian aboard STS, PU
Kizim, Leonid					Soyuz T-15, one of first aboard Mir, PU
Klimuk, Pyotr I.	50	150		75	Soyuz 13, Soyuz 18B
Komarov, Vladimir M.					Soyuz 1, first fatality space program, PU
Kondakova, Yelena					Soyuz TM-20, 10/3/94, PU
Kovalyonok, Vladimir					Soyuz 25, Soyuz 29, PU
Krikalev, Sergei M.					Soyuz TM-12, 5/18/91, Soyuz TM-7, PU
Kubasov, Valery N.	50	115	225	60	Soyuz 6, Soyuz 19, TSS
Laveykin, Aleksandr					Soyuz TM-2, PU
Lawrence, Wendy B.	10		30	20	Endeavour, 3/2/95
Lazarev, Vasily G.					Soyuz 12, PU
Lebedev, Valentin					Soyuz 13, Soyuz T-5, PU
Lee, Mark C.	6		25	10	Endeavour, first married couple
Leestma, David C.	8		30	12	Challenger, 10/5/84, Columbia, 8/9/89
Lenoir, William B.	10	20	25	20	Columbia, 11/11/82, RS
Leonov, Aleksei A.	125	200		250	Voskhod 2, made first "space walk", TSS

Name	Sig.	LS/DS	ALS	SP	Comments
Levchenko, Anatoly					Soyuz TM-4 - set longevity record, PU
Lichtenberg, Byron K.	5	15	25	15	Columbia, 11/28/83, Atlantis, 3/24/92
Lind, Don L.	10	20	15	20	Challenger, 4/29/85, FA
Lineger, J.M.	5	15	25	10	Discovery, 9/9/94
Lounge, John M.	5		20	10	Discovery, 8/27/85, Columbia, 12/2/90
Lousma, Jack R.	10	30	40	25	Skylab 3, Columbia, 3/22/82
Lovell, James A., Jr.	25	100		85	Gemini 7, Apollo 13, charges fee
Low, G. David	5		20	10	Columbia, 1/9/90, Atlantis, 8/3/91, RS
Lucid, Shannon W.	10		45	40	Discovery, 6/17/85, Atlantis, 10/18/89
Lyakhov, Vladimir					Soyuz T-9, 1983, TM-6, Soyuz 32, PU
MacLean, Glenwood	5	15	25	10	Columbia, 10/22/92
Makarov, Oleg G.					Soyuz 12, PU
Malenchenko, Yuri					Soyuz TM-19, 7/3/94, PU
Mallerba, Franco					Atlantis, 7/31/92, first Ital. astronaut, PU
Malyshev, Yuri					Soyuz T-11, 4/2/84, Soyuz T-2, PU
Manakov, Gennadi					Soyuz TM-10, Soyuz TM-16, 1993, PU
Manarov, Musa					Soyuz TM-4 - set longevity record, PU
Mattingly, Thomas K. II	50	100	165	125	Apollo 16
McArthur, William S., Jr.	5	15	25	10	Columbia, 10/18/93
McAuliffe, Christa	500	1000	1500	750	Challenger, 1986, killed during launch
McBride, Jon A.	10	20	25	20	Challenger, 10/5/84, FA
McCandless, Bruce	5		20	10	Challenger, 2/3/84, Discovery, RS
McCulley, Michael J.	10	20	25	20	Atlantis, 10/18/89, FA
McDivitt, James A.	35	75		50	Gemini-Titan 4
McMonagle, Donald R.	5		25	10	Discovery, 4/28/91, Endeavour, RS
McNair, Robert E.	200	325		300	Challenger, 1986, killed during launch
Meade, Carl J.	10	25	35	20	Atlantis, 11/15/90, Columbia, 6/25/92
Melnick, Bruce E.	5	15	25	10	Discovery, 10/6/90, Endeavour, 5/7/92
Merbold, Ulf D.	10	25	35	20	Columbia, 11/28/83, Discovery, 92, S94
Messerschmid, Ernst	10		40	20	Challenger, 10/30/85, RS
Mitchell, Edgar D.	**30**	**125**	**200**	**60**	**Apollo 14, MW, TSS**
Mohri, Mamoru	15	30		30	Endeavour, first prof. Japanese Ast.
Mullane, Richard M.	8		25	10	Discovery, 8/30/84, Atlantis, 2/28/90
Musabayev, Talgat					Soyuz TM-19, 7/3/94. PU
Musgrave, F. Story	8		30	15	Challenger, 4/4/83, Atlantis, RS
Nagel, Steven R.	5		20	10	Discovery, 6/17/85, Challenger, A91
Naito-Mukai, Chiaki	10	20	20	10	Columbia, first Japanese woman, RS
Nelson, George	5	15	25	15	Challenger, 4/6/84, Columbia, 1/12/86
Newman, James H.	5	15	25	10	Discovery, 9/1/93
Nicollier, Claude	15	30		30	Atlantis, first Swiss astronaut, E1993
Nikolayev, Andrian G.	125	250		175	Vostok 3, Soyuz 9
O'Conner, Bryan D.	5	15	25	10	Atlantis, 11/26/85, Columbia, 6/5/91
Ochoa, Ellen	5		20	10	Discovery, 4/8/93, RS
Ockels, Wubbo J.	8		25	12	Challenger, 10/30/85, RS
Onizuka, Ellison S.	200			275	Challenger, 1986, killed during launch
Oswald, Stephen S.	5		20	10	Discovery, 1/22/92, Discovery, RS
Overmyer, Robert F.	25	50		100	Columbia, 11/11/82
Pailes, William A.	5	15	25	10	Atlantis, 10/4/85

Name	Sig.	LS/DS	ALS	SP	Comments
Parazynski, Scott E.	5	15	25	10	Atlantis, 11/3/94
Parise, Ronald A.	5	15	25	15	Columbia, 12/2/90, Endeavour, 3/2/95
Patsayev, Viktor I.	3400				Soyuz 11, all 3 cosmonauts killed
Payton, Gary E.	5	15	25	10	Discovery, 1/24/84
Peterson, Donald H.	10	20	30	15	Challenger, 4/4/83
Pogue, William R.	10	30	40	20	Skylab 4
Polishchuk, Alexander					Soyuz TM-16, 1/24/93, PU
Polyakov, Valery					Soyuz TM-6, Soyuz TM-18, 1/8/94, PU
Popov, Leonid					Soyuz 35, PU
Popovich, Pavel R.	85	200	400	175	Vostok 4, Soyuz 14
Precourt, Charles J.	5	10	15	10	Columbia, 4/26/93, Atlantis, RS
Prunariu, Dumitru					Soyuz 40, PU
Readdy, William F.	5		20	10	Discovery, 1/22/92, 9/1/93, RS
Reightler, Kenneth S., Jr.	5		20	10	Discovery, 9/12/91, FA, Discovery
Remek, Vladimir					Soyuz 28, PU
Resnik, Judith A.	150			300	Discovery, killed on Challenger 1/86
Richards, Richard N.	10		25	15	Discovery, 10/6/90, Columbia, 8/9/89
Ride, Sally K.	20		100	50	Challenger, first U.S. woman in space
Romanenko, Yuri V.					Soyuz 26, TM-2
Roosa, Stuart A.	25			75	Apollo 14, ESPV
Ross, Jerry L.	8		25	12	Atlantis, 4/5/91, 11/26/85, Colum., RS
Rozhdestvensky, Valery					Soyuz 23, PU
Rukavishnikov, Nikolai N.					Soyuz 16, Soyuz 10, PU
Runco, Mario, Jr.	5		20	10	Atlantis, 11/24/91, Endeavour, RS
Ryumin, Valery					Soyuz 26, Soyuz 32, PU
Salman al-Saud					Discovery,1985, 1st Arab. in space, PU
Sarafanov, Gennady					Soyuz 15, PU
Savinykh, Viktor					Soyuz T-13, 6/6/85, Soyuz T-4, PU
Savitskaya, Svetlana					Soyuz T-12, first woman spac. walk, PU
Schirra, Walter M.	25	75	175	65	Mercury 8, Gemini 6A, TSS
Schlegel, Hans					Columbia, 4/26/93, Ger. scientist, PU
Schmitt, Harrison H.	**25**		**200**	**70**	**Apollo 17, RS, MW**
Schriver, Loren J.	10	20	30	20	Discovery, 1/24/84, Atlantis, 7/31/92
Schweickart, Russell L.	20	50		40	Apollo 9
Scobee, F. Richard	125			250	Challenger, killed during launch
Scott, David R.	**50**	**160**		**150**	**Gem. 8, Apoll 9 &15, MW, TSS**
Scully-Power, Paul D.	5	15	25	10	Challenger, 10/5/84
Searfoss, Richard A.	5	15	25	10	Columbia, 10/18/93
Seddon, Margaret Rhea	10		25	20	Discovery, 4/12/85, Columbia, RS
Sega, Ronald	5	15	25	10	Discovery, 2/3/94
Serebov, Alexander A.					Soyuz TM-8, T-7, Soyuz TM-17, PU
Sevastyanov, Vitaly I.					Soyuz 18B, PU
Sharma, Rakesh					Soyuz T-11, first Indian cosmonaut, PU
Sharman, Helen					Soyuz TM-12, first Briton in space, PU
Shatalov, Vladimir A.					Soyuz 4, Soyuz 8, PU
Shaw, Brewster H., Jr.	10	30	40	20	Columbia, 11/28/83, 8/9/89, Atlantis
Shepard, Alan B. , Jr.	**75**	**150**	**200**	**200**	**Mer-Red. 3, 1st US in space, MW**
Shepherd, William M.	10	20	30	20	Atlantis, 12/2/88, Discovery, 10/6/90
Sherlock, Nancy Jane	10	20	30	20	Endeavour, 6/21/93
Shonin, Georgi S.	40	100	200	65	Soyuz 6

Name	Sig.	LS/DS	ALS	SP	Comments
Shriver, Loren J.	8		25	12	Discovery, 4/24/90, RS
Slayton, Donald K.	40	125		150	ASTP, RS
Smith, Michael J.	250			375	Challenger, 1986, killed during launch
Smith, Steven L.	5	10	15	10	Endeavour, 9/30/94, RS
Solovyev, Anatoly					Soyuz TM-9, 2/11/90, Soyuz TM-15, PU
Solovyev, Vladimir					Soyuz T-15, one of first aboard Mir, PU
Spring, Sherwood C.	10	20	30	15	Atlantis, 11/26/85
Springer, Robert C.	5	15	25	10	Discovery, 3/13/89, Atlantis, 11/15/90
Stafford, Thomas P.	25	75	140	50	Gemini 6A, Gemini 9A, RS, TSS
Stewart, Robert	10	20	30	20	Challenger, 2/3/84, Atlantis, 10/4/85
Strekalov, Gennadi M.					Soyuz T-3, Soyuz T-11, 4/2/84, T-8, PU
Sullivan, Kathryn D.	10	30	40	25	Challenger, 10/5/84, Discovery
Swigert, John L., Jr.	40	80		125	Apollo 13
Tamayo-Mendez, Arnaldo					Soyuz 37, first Cuban in space, PU
Tanner, Joseph R.	5		15	10	Atlantis, 11/3/94, res. signer!
Tereshkova, Valentina V.	175	375	525	300	Vostok 6, 1st woman in space
Thagard, Norman E.	8		30	10	C 6/18/83, Atlantis, 5/4/89, Discovery
Thomas, Donald A.	5	15	25	10	Columbia, 7/8/94
Thornton, Kathryn C.	5		25	10	Discovery, 11/22/89, Endeavour, RS
Thornton, William	5		25	10	Challenger, 8/30/83, Challenger, RS
Thout, Pierre J.	5		20	10	Atlantis, 2/28/90, Endeavour, RS
Titov, Gherman S.					Vostok 2, first spaceflight - 24 hrs. +, PU
Titov, Vladimir G.					Soyuz T-8, 4/20/83, Discovery, PU
Tognini, Michael					Soyuz TM-15, 7/27/92, French, PU
Trinh, Eugene H.	5	15	25	15	Columbia, 6/25/92
Truly, Richard H.	25	80		50	Columbia, 11/12/81
Tsiblyev, Vasily					Soyuz TM-17, 7/1/93, PU
Tuan, Pham					Soyuz 37, first Vietnamese in space, PU
Usachyov, Yuri					Soyuz TM-18, 1/8/94, PU
Van Den Berg, Lodewijk	10	20	30	15	Challenger, 4/29/85
Van Hoften, James D.	10	25	35	20	Challenger, 4/6/84
Vasyutin, Vladimir					Soyuz T-14, 9/17/85, PU
Veach, Charles Lacy	5		25	10	Discovery, 4/28/91, Columbia, FA
Vela, Rudolfo Neri					Atlantis, 1985, 1st Mex. in space, PU
Viehboeck, Franz					Soyuz TM-13, first Austrian in space, PU
Viktorenko, Aleksandr S.					Soyuz TM-3, Soyuz TM-8, PU
Volk, Igor					Soyuz T-12, 7/18/84, PU
Volkov, Aleksandr N.					Soyuz T-14, 9/17/85, Soyuz TM-13, PU
Volkov, Vladislav N.	100			200	Soyuz 11, killed in reentry, S7, ESPV
Volynov, Boris V.					Soyuz 5, Soyuz 21, PU
Voss, James S.	5		25	10	Atlantis, 11/24/91, Discovery, RS
Voss, Janice E.	5		25	10	Endeavour, 6/21/93, Discovery, 2/3/95
Walker, Charles D.	5	15	25	10	Discovery, 8/30/84, RS
Walker, David M.	10	25	40	20	Discovery, 11/8/84, Discovery, 12/2/92
Walter, Ulrich	10		30	20	Columbia, 4/26/93, Ger. scientist, RS
Walz, Carl E.	5	15	25	10	Discovery, 9/1/93, Columbia, 7/8/94
Wang, Taylor G.	10	25	30	20	Challenger, 4/29/85
Weitz, Paul J.	8		25	10	Skylab 2, Challenger, 4/4/83, RS

Name	Sig.	LS/DS	ALS	SP	Comments
Wetherbee, James D.	5		25	12	Columbia, 1/9/90, Columbia, RS
White, Edward H. II	250	325		600	Gemini-Tit. 4, 1st Amer. to "space walk"
Williams, Donald E.	5	15	25	10	Discovery, 4/12/85, Atlantis, 10/18/89
Wisoff, Peter J.K.	5	15	25	10	Endeavour, 6/21/93, Endeavour
Wolf, David	5	15	25	10	Columbia, 10/18/93
Worden, Alfred M.	15	40		30	Apollo 15, RS
Wulcutt, Terrence W.	5		15	10	Endeavour, 9/30/94, RS
Yegorov, Boris B.					Voskhod 1, PU
Yeliseyev, Alexei S.					Soyuz 5, Soyuz 8, PU
Young, John W.	**75**	**150**		**200**	**Gem. 10, Apollo 10, 1st shuttle**
Zholobov, Vitaly					Soyuz 21, PU
Zudov, Vyacheslav					Soyuz 23, PU

BASEBALL

WHAT YOU NEED TO KNOW

* Entire books have been written and published about baseball autographs, including many by this author.

* The market for single-signed autographed official league baseballs has dominated this area of collecting and has even played a pivotal role in the overall valuation of the hobby.

* A majority of interest in this area centers around those elite members of the Baseball Hall of Fame.

* Signatures of living members of the Baseball Hall of Fame are extremely plentiful, while those deceased over the last few decades remain abundant.

* Just because a player is in the Baseball Hall of Fame, doesn't mean his signature is worth more than any player who has ever played the game.

* The signatures of newly inducted Hall of Fame members are inflated until demand is met.

MARKET FACTS

* The market for baseball autographs has been extremely volatile over the last twenty-five years.

* The market has exhibited significant price variations in all forms.

* Single-signed official league baseballs are the form in greatest demand.

* There are simply not enough signature transactions for some of the individuals included here to accurately list a value. Some signatures,particularly those of baseball pioneers, are so scarce that offering at auction is perhaps the only way to command the maximum value.

* The market is driven by the signatures of the greatest players - Babe Ruth, Lou Gehrig, Ty Cobb, Honus Wagner, Rogers Hornsby, Tris Speaker, Cy Young, Walter Johnson, Christy Mathewson, etc...

* Forgeries, although curtailed significantly over the past few years, are still prevalent.

* Obtaining a full set of signatures from every member of the Baseball Hall of Fame is extremely difficult.

TRENDS

* Collectors have been far more apprehensive to enter this niche in the market due to "forgery fear."

* Players who charged for their signatures at shows twenty-five years ago, have seen a dramatic decrease in demand.

* The value of baseball autographs is extremely inflated, with few exceptions.

* Due to volatility, supply, demand, subjectivity, and lack of precise information, NO price guide, nor individual can accurately value this market sector.

Notes:
    * Recent Offerings include buyer's premium.
    * Single-signed Baseballs:

    * A signature on the "sweet spot," will often double the value of a baseball (same condition); (Grades: 5-7)
    * A signature on the "sweet spot" (9), could nearly double in value from the next lowest grade (8).
    * A signature on the "sweet spot" (10), could double in value from the next lowest grade (9).
    * A signature on the "sweet spot" (10) from a major player is a key indicator of market value.
    * A single-signed baseball, graded less than (7), is typically of little demand unless it is autographed by a prominent player or by a player seldom encountered.

Abbreviations: Sig. = signature, SP = signed photograph, HP = Baseball Hall of Fame Plaque (Various types), BB = single-signed official league baseball, bat = autographed bat (not game-used), Comments include recent prices realized that include buyer premiums, ESPV = exhibits significant pricing variations, (s) = side, (ss) = sweet spot, grades may be listed in parenthesis, RS = player is/was a responsive signer, Hall of Fame induction year is listed only when space permits, ALS = autographed letter signed (handwritten), TLS = typed letter signed, Players whose autographed material in many forms always finds its way into the market is detailed.

Name	Sig.	SP	HP	BB	BAT	Comments
Aaron, Hank	25	50	40	65	165	HOF 1982, sig. var., FA
Adcock, Joe	10	20	N/A	50	100	
Alexander, Grover Cleveland	575	840	3275	4250		BB (ss) - $16,642; ALS - $4,710
Allen, Dick	17	30	N/A	35	55	
Alomar, Roberto	18	25	N/A	30	55	
Alou, Felipe	10	20	N/A	30	50	
Alston, Walter	50	85	150	600	UNK	HOF 1983, scarce in HP
Amoros, Sandy	25	40	N/A	100	200	
Anderson, Garret	10	20	N/A	25	65	
Anderson, Sparky	10	20	20	30	65	HOF 2000, RS
Anson, Cap	1750					BB (s) $70, 366; ALS - $1,761
Aparicio, Luis	15	25	25	35	75	HOF 1984
Appling, Luke	10	25	25	85	175	HOF 1964, RS
Ashburn, Richie	15	30	50	75	150	HOF 1995
Averill, Earl	15	60	30			HOF 1975, RS
Bagwell, Jeff	15	25	N/A	40	100	
Baines, Harold	10	20	N/A	35	50	
Baker, Dusty	10	20	N/A	25	50	
Baker, Frank	250	625	2000	3500		HOF 1955
Bancroft, Dave	130	225	1000	1800		HOF 1971
Banks, Ernie	15	35	25	40	100	HOF 1977
Barlick, Al	10	25	25	35	75	HOF 1989, RS
Barrow, Ed	200	375		3500		HOF 1953, BB (ss) - $12,368
Bauer, Hank	10	15	N/A	25	45	
Baylor, Don	10	20	N/A	25	45	
Beckley, Jake	3275					HOF 1971, scarce, FA
Bell, Buddy	10	20	N/A	20	45	
Bell, Gus	30	50	N/A	100	200	
Bell, Cool Papa	25	55	40	225		HOF 1974, sig. var., RS
Bench, Johnny	20	30	25	40	100	HOF 1989
Bender, Chief	250	500			2850	HOF 1953
Berg, Moe	175					ESPV - all forms, spy
Berkman, Lance	10	20	N/A	30	60	
Berra, Yogi	15	40	25	45	110	HOF 1972
Biggio, Craig	12	25	N/A	30	60	
Blue, Vida	10	20	N/A	25	50	
Blyleven, Bert	15	20	N/A	25	50	
Boggs, Wade	20	30	N/A	35	110	
Bonds, Barry	50	75	N/A	175	500	ESPV - all forms, FA, sig. var.
Bonds, Bobby	20	30	N/A	35	75	
Bottomley, Jim	350	600			3000	HOF 1974
Bouton, Jim	10	20	N/A	25	45	
Boudreau, Lou	12	25	25	35	75	HOF 1970, RS
Bowa, Larry	10	15	N/A	20	40	
Boyer, Clete	10	20	N/A	25	45	
Boyer, Ken	60	180	N/A	400	750	
Branca, Ralph	10	15	N/A	25	45	
Bresnahan, Roger	575	1000		5000		HOF 1945, DS - $1550
Brett, George	20	40	40	50	125	HOF 1999
Brock, Lou	15	30	20	40	80	HOF 1985
Brouthers, Dan	1650					HOF 1945, scarce - all forms

Name	Sig.	SP	HP	BB	BAT	Comments
Brown, Bobby	10	20	N/A	25	50	
Brown, Kevin	10	25	N/A	30	70	
Brown, Mordecai	400	1400	N/A	4250		HOF 1949
Buckner, Bill	10	20	N/A	25	55	
Bulkeley, Morgan	1250					DS - $2500, SB - $1,298
Bunning, Jim	10	25	25	35	70	HOF 1996, USS
Burdette, Lew	10	20	N/A	20	45	
Burgess, Smoky	25	70	N/A	100	150	
Burkett, Jesse	675	1250	2800			HOF 1946, BB (side) - $25,775
Burrell, Pat	10	20	N/A	30	80	
Campanella, Roy	450	900	1000	4500		HOF 1969, sig. var., ESPV

Roy Campanella
Recent Sales: BB (ss), (5/6) - $1,814, program - $452

Name	Sig.	SP	HP	BB	BAT	Comments
Campaneris, Bert	12	25	N/A	25	50	
Canseco, Jose	10	25	N/A	30	100	
Carew, Rod	15	30	30	35	100	HOF 1991, RS
Carey, Max	25	60	125	1150		HOF 1961
Carlton, Steve	15	30	30	40	100	HOF 1994
Carter, Gary	20	30	30	45	75	HOF 2003
Carter, Joe	10	25	N/A	30	60	RS
Cartwright, Alexander	1200					HOF 1938, DS - $2500; $3,892
Carty, Rico	12	20	N/A	25	50	
Cash, Norm	40	60	N/A	265		BB (ss), (10) - $1072
Cavarretta, Phil	10	20	N/A	30	50	
Cepeda, Orlando	15	30	35	40	80	HOF 2000
Chadwick, Henry	3250					DS - $3500, SB - $1360
Chance, Frank	1650	3200				HOF 1946, SALS - $15,154
Chandler, Happy	20	45	25	130	200	HOF 1982, RS
Charleston, Oscar						HOF 1976, ESPV - all forms
Chesbro, Jack	2250					HOF 1946, scarce all forms
Chylak, Nestor	200	500		600		HOF 1999, BB - $506
Cicotte, Eddie	600	700	N/A			Sig. - $805; contract - $35,187
Clark, Will	12	25	N/A	25	75	
Clarke, Fred	250	500	750	2000		SP - $5,032; BB (ss) - $1201
Clarkson, John	4000					HOF 1963, scarce all forms
Clemens, Roger	25	50	N/A	60	125	
Clemente, Roberto	465	770		3500		HOF 1973, see below

Roberto Clemente
Recent Sales: SP - $2,536, postcard - $1,761, BB (ss) (6/7) - $5,182

Name	Sig.	SP	HP	BB	BAT	Comments
Cobb, Ty	575	1450				HOF 1936, see below

Ty Cobb
Recent Sales:
ALS: 7 pp., - good content - $5,829
Baseballs:
Single-signed: BB , (side) - $23,431; BB , (ss) (10) - $5,701, BB, (side), (10) - $4, 485,
BB, (side), (10) - $13,225

Name	Sig.	SP	HP	BB	BAT	Comments

Combination: SB, TC (side) & w/H. Wagner (ss) - $5,372
Cards: Exhibit - $1,995
Checks: SC - $1,497, SC - $700, SC - $845
First Day Covers: FDC, 1939, Cooperstown - $928; $1,648; $1428
Index card: $805
Photographs: SP - $1,497, SP - $6,090
Press Ticket: $886
TLS : TLS - strong content - $4, 281; TLS - $675; TLS - $1,298

Name	Sig.	SP	HP	BB	BAT	Comments
Cochrane, Mickey	225	500	800	2620		HOF 1947, BB (ss) (7) - $1,995
Colavito, Rocky	10	25	N/A	30	100	
Collins, Eddie	350	825		3500		HOF 1939, ESPV
Collins, Jimmie						HOF 1945, scarce all forms
Combs, Earle	55	200	150	1650		HOF 1970
Comiskey, Charles	600	1675		2000		TLS - $991; SB - $1,995
Concepcion, Dave	15	22	N/A	30	50	
Cone, Dave	20	40		45		
Conigliaro, Tony	89	200	N/A	625		
Conlan, Jocko	20	40	30	150		HOF 1974
Connelly, Tom	425	975	1500	3100		HOF 1953
Connor, Roger	2500	5000				HOF 1976
Connors, Chuck	30	60	N/A	100		
Coveleski, Stan	20	55	30	465		HOF 1969
Cox, Bobby	5	15	N/A	25	50	
Crawford, Sam	150	350	400	2225		HOF 1957
Cronin, Joe	25	55	50	500		HOF 1956, BB (ss) - $1,454
Crosetti, Frank	12	25	N/A	55	120	RS
Cummings, Candy						HOF 1939, ESPV all forms
Cuyler, Kiki	325	675	N/A	4250		HOF 1968
Dandridge, Ray	20	45	35	100	225	HOF 1987, sig. variations.
Davis, George						HOF 1998, PU
Davis, Tommy	10	20	N/A	30	60	
Davis, Willie	10	20	N/A	30	50	
Dawson, Andre	10	25	N/A	30	80	
Day, Leon	25	50	N/A	100	200	HOF 1995
Dean, Dizzy	125	340	240	1000		BB (side) - $914; $557
Delahanty, Ed						HOF 1945, scarce in all forms
Delgado, Carlos	15	30	N/A	35	75	RS
Dent, Bucky	5	15	N/A	25	45	
Dickey, Bill	30	60	70	250		HOF 1954, elusive signer
Dihigo, Martin	900					HOF 1977, scarce
DiMaggio, Dom	10	25	N/A	40	75	
DiMaggio, Joe	150	185	200	315	2150	HOF 1955, $
DiMaggio, Vince	50	100	N/A	335		
Doby, Larry	20	30	35	35	75	HOF 1998, $
Doerr, Bobby	5	15	15	25	55	HOF 1986, RS
Drysdale, Don	25	50	45	125	200	HOF 1984
Duffy, Hugh	350	850	2000	2600		HOF 1945, sig, variations
Durocher, Leo	25	50	N/A	150	250	HOF 1994
Dykstra, Lenny	5	15	N/A	20	50	

Name	Sig.	SP	HP	BB	BAT	Comments
Eckersley, Dennis	10	20	N/A	30	55	HOF 2004
Edmonds, Jim	15	25	N/A	35	75	
Ennis, Del	15	30	N/A	50		
Erskine, Carl	10	20	N/A	25	50	
Evans, Billy	300	750	N/A			HOF 1973
Evans, Darrell	5	10	N/A	20	40	
Evans, Dwight	10	20	N/A	25	50	
Evers, Johnny	550	1325	N/A			HOF 1946, ESPV - BB
Ewing, Buck						HOF 1939, scarce all forms
Faber, Red	40	140	150	1500		Used red ink, BB (side) - $1,091
Fain, Ferris	10	20	N/A	40		
Feller, Bob	10	20	20	35	50	HOF 1962, RS
Ferrell, Rick	10	25	20	50	110	HOF 1984, RS
Fidrych, Mark	10	20	N/A	25	55	RS
Fielder, Cecil	10	25	N/A	40	75	Often illegible sig.
Fingers, Rollie	10	20	20	25	60	HOF 1992, $
Fisk, Carlton	25	40	30	40	100	HOF 2000, elusive
Flick, Elmer	70	200	440	1650		BB (ss) (10) - $1,600
Flood, Curt	50	75	N/A	225		Can be tough to find!
Ford, Whitey	15	30	N/A	40	100	HOF 1974, $
Foster, George	10	20	N/A	25	60	Elusive signer
Foster, Rube	2850					HOF 1981, scarce in all forms
Foster, Willie	1125					ALS - $2,346, note - $2,839
Fox, Nellie	185	400	N/A			HOF 1997, see below

Nellie Fox
> Recent Sales: BB (side) - $1,600; Check - $981

Name	Sig.	SP	HP	BB	BAT	Comments
Foxx, Jimmie	400	1150	1500			See below

Jimmie Foxx
> Recent Sales: SP - $991, BB (ss) - $20,363, SP - $1,201, SP - $2,839, SP - $2,346

Name	Sig.	SP	HP	BB	BAT	Comments
Frick, Ford	50	150	150	1500		HOF 1970, plentiful DS
Frisch, Frankie	65	150	150	1750		SV, BB (ss) - $1,091
Furillo, Carl	25	65	N/A	215		
Galarraga, Andres	12	25	N/A	30	70	
Galvin, Pud						HOF 1965, scarce in all forms
Garagiola, Joe	10	20	N/A	25	60	$
Garciaparra, Nomar	20	45	N/A	65	125	
Garvey, Steve	10	20	N/A	25	50	RS
Gehrig, Lou	2275	7250	N/A			HOF 1939, see below

Lou Gehrig
> Recent Sales:
> Album page: album page - $1,938
> ALS: ALS - $6,600; ALS, 2pp., - $18,055,   ALS - $11,244,   ALS, 1 p. - $5,829
> Baseballs:
>   Single-signed: BB (side) - $7, 464, BB (ss) - $61,047,
>   Combination: (see babe Ruth)

Name	Sig.	SP	HP	BB	BAT	Comments
						Book: SB - $14,967,
						Index card: $2,839
						Photographs: SP - $4,817, SP - $4,210, SP (small) - $1761
Gehringer, Charley	20	40	40	125		HOF 1949, RS
Giambi, Jason	25	60	N/A	80		
Gibson, Bob	20	35	30	40	110	HOF 1981
Gibson, Josh						HOF 1972, scarce
Gibson, Kirk	10	20	N/A	25	60	Refuses mail!
Giles, Warren	45	150	N/A			HOF 1979, RS
Gilliam, Jim	55	125	N/A			
Glavine, Tom	20	35	N/A	40	80	
Gomez, Lefty	25	65	40	175		HOF 1972
Gonzalez, Juan	15	30	N/A	35	75	
Gooden, Dwight	10	20	N/A	25	60	ESPV - all forms
Gordon, Joe	45	75	N/A			
Goslin, Goose	140	375		2250		HOF 1968, ESPV - HP
Gossage, Rich	10	20	N/A	25	50	RS
Grace, Mark	15	30	N/A	40	75	
Green, Shawn	10	30	N/A	50	100	
Greenberg, Hank	70	285	75	1500		BB (s) - $991, BB (ss) - $1,761
Griffey, Ken, Jr.	30	60	N/A	75	225	
Griffith, Clark	175	440	1000	2225		HOF 1946, prolific
Grimes, Burleigh	25	70	45	250		HOF 1964, RS
Groat, Dick	10	25	N/A	25	50	
Grove, Lefty	50	160	150	1625		HOF 1947, BB (ss) - $1,600
Guerrero, Vladimir	15	30	N/A	45	90	Sig. variations
Guidry, Ron	10	25	N/A	25	50	
Gwynn, Tony	20	45	N/A	50	125	FA
Haddix, Harvey	15	30	N/A	60	100	
Hafey, Chick	50	200	400	2225		HOF 1971
Haines, Jesse	30	150	90	1325		HOF 1970, RS
Hamilton, Billy						HOF 1961
Hanlon, Ned	2500					HOF 1996, DS most likely form.
Hargrove, Mike	5	10	N/A	20	45	
Harrelson, Bud	5	12	N/A	25	50	
Harrelson, Ken	10	25	N/A	30	65	"The Hawk"
Harridge, Will	125	325	N/A			BB (side) - $417, SP - $460
Harris, Bucky	55	165	160	2000		HOF 1975, RS
Hartnett, Gabby	65	150	320	2000		BB (side) - $2,581; $974
Heilmann, Harry	400	1250	N/A	2775		HOF 1952, SP - $2,619
Helton, Todd	15	30	N/A	50	100	
Henderson, Ricky	20	40	N/A	45	110	
Henrich, Tommy	7	20	N/A	30	60	RS
Herman, Billy	15	30	15	80	145	HOF 1975, RS, sig. variations
Hernandez, Orlando	15	25	N/A	30	65	
Hershiser, Orel	10	25	N/A	30	50	Reluctant signer
Hodges, Gil	175	330	N/A	1575		BB (ss) - $3,123
Hoffman, Trevor	15	30	N/A	30	60	
Hooper, Harry	30	125	125			HOF 1971, RS
Hornsby, Rogers	265	600	1400	3175		BB (s) - $4,158,BB (ss) - $2,984

Name	Sig.	SP	HP	BB	BAT	Comments
Houk, Ralph	10	20	N/A	30	70	
Howard, Elston	100	225	N/A	1650		BB (ss) - $1,454; con. - $2,305
Howard, Frank	10	20	N/A	30	75	
Hoyt, Waite	25	75	40	450		HOF 1969, RS
Hubbard, Cal	60	250	850	1300		HOF 1976
Hubbell, Carl	25	75	50	200		HOF 1947, RS, sig. variations
Hubbs, Ken	185	325	N/A	850		Scarce in all forms
Huggins, Miller	1265	2785	N/A	4265		HOF 1964, contract - $2,717
Hulbert, William						HOF 1995
Hunter, Catfish	20	40	35	70	150	HOF 1987
Irvin, Monte	10	20	20	30	65	HOF 1973, RS
Jackson, Bo	15	30	N/A	40	75	Elusive signer
Jackson, Joe						"Black Sox scandal", rare, SV
Jackson, Reggie	25	50	50	60	150	HOF 1993, $
Jackson, Travis	30	55	50	300		HOF 1982, RS
Jenkins, Ferguson	10	20	15	25	55	HOF 1991
Jennings, Hughie	1140	2200	N/A	6000		HOF 1945, BB (ss) - $5,299
Jensen, Jackie	25	100	N/A	265		
Jeter, Derek	50	100	N/A	150		$, signed often in minors
John, Tommy	10	20	N/A	25	50	
Johnson, Ban	430	1250	N/A			HOF 1937, DS common form
Johnson, Davey	10	20	N/A	25	50	
Johnson, Judy	30	50	50	135	250	HOF 1975, sig. variations
Johnson, Randy	25	45	N/A	50	125	Typically small signature
Johnson, Walter	700	1400	N/A			HOF 1936, ESPV - BB

Walter Johnson
Recent Sales: BB (side) - $2,470; BB (ss) - $3,980, BB (ss) (7) - $4,810

Name	Sig.	SP	HP	BB	BAT	Comments
Jones, Andruw	15	25	N/A	30	65	
Jones, Chipper	20	40	N/A	35	100	
Joss, Addie						HOF 1978, rare in all forms
Justice, Dave	15	25	N/A	35	75	Sig. variations
Kaat, Jim	10	25	N/A	30	60	
Kaline, Al	15	30	20	35	110	HOF 1980, RS
Karros, Eric	10	20	N/A	25	50	
Keefe, Tim						HOF 1964, rare in all forms
Keeler, Willie	1375					HOF 1939
Kell, George	10	20	15	25	55	HOF 1983, RS
Kelley, Joe	2250	4780	N/A			ESPV, BB (ss) - $20, 138
Kelly, George	12	30	30	220		HOF 1973, RS
Kelly, Mike "King"	2775					HOF 1945
Kent, Jeff	20	35	N/A	40	80	
Killebrew, Harmon	10	25	25	35	75	HOF 1984
Kiner, Ralph	10	20	20	30	75	HOF 1975
Kingman, Dave	12	25	N/A	30	60	
Klein, Chuck	325	650	N/A			HOF 1980, BB (side) - $411
Klem, Bill	430	820	N/A	3175		HOF 1953, BB (side) - $818
Kluszewski, Ted	40	105	N/A	300		BB (ss) - $549

Name	Sig.	SP	HP	BB	BAT	Comments
Koosman, Jerry	10	20	N/A	30	50	
Koufax, Sandy	30	65	65	85	175	HOF 1972
Kubek, Tony	25	50	N/A	80	150	
Kuenn, Harvey	25	40	N/A	300		BB (ss) (10) - $891
Lajoie, Nap	375	800	1500	5675		HOF 1937, SP - $6,090
Landis, Kenesaw	365	700	N/A	3800		SP - $1,454, check - $2922
Larkin, Barry	15	25	N/A	30	65	
LaRussa, Tony	10	15	N/A	30	50	
Larsen, Don	10	20	N/A	30	50	"Perfect Game" material higher
Lasorda, Tommy	15	30	35	40	75	HOF 1997, RS
Lazzeri, Tony	650	1200	N/A	3500		HOF 1991
Lemon, Bob	10	15	15	30	75	HOF 1976, RS, HP common
Leonard, Buck	20	40	40	60	125	HOF 1972, sig. variations
Lindstrom, Fred	30	65	65			HOF 1976, ESPV-BB, RS
Lloyd, John Henry						HOF 1977, scarce in all forms
Lombardi, Ernie	55	135	N/A	1250		HOF 1986
Lopez, Al	15	30	30	60	120	HOF 1977, ESPV-BB
Lopez, Javy	10	20	N/A	25	60	
Lyle, Sparky	10	20	N/A	25	50	
Lyons, Ted	20	40	40	230		HOF 1955, RS
Mack, Connie	250	600	1200	1325		HOF 1937, RS, prolific

Connie Mack

Recent Sales: BB (ss),$675; BB (ss), (6/7) - $460; SB - $414; signed program - $278; SP - $891

Name	Sig.	SP	HP	BB	BAT	Comments
MacPhail, Larry	125					HOF 1978, ESPV - most forms
MacPahil, Lee	15	25	25	50		HOF 1998, RS
Maddux, Greg	25	50	N/A	65	130	
Maglie, Sal	25	50	N/A	300		
Mantle, Mickey						HOF 1974, ESPV-all forms

Mickey Mantle

Recent Sales:

Baseballs:

Single-signed:

OAL (ss) (10) $3,181 - early style

Combination:

OAL (ss)w/Maris (side) $2,195

OAL (side)w/Maris (10) $2,839

Cards: 1953 Bowman - $1730, bundle 100 not cards - $17,022

First Day Covers: $498

Photographs: vintage - $1072;,wire photo - $805, SP - vintage - $2,790

Replica Jersey: $2094

Yearbook: 1951 Commerce, OK - $731, $2,536

OAL - Official American League Baseball, (ss) - "sweet spot", (?) - condition

Name	Sig.	SP	HP	BB	BAT	Comments
Manush, Heinie	60	200	300	1725		HOF 1964; BB (ss) - $743
Maranville, Rabbit	310	625	N/A	1895		HOF 1954, SP - $2,381
Marichal, Juan	15	25	25	35	75	HOF 1983

Name	Sig.	SP	HP	BB	BAT	Comments
Maris, Roger	225	450	N/A	2250		See below

Roger Maris

Recent Sales: BB (ss), (8/9) - $2,132; BB (side) , (9) - $3,436, BB (side) (10) - $3,069, BB (side) (9) - $2,305, BB (ss) (10) - $3,069, BB (side) (9/10) - $2,346

Name	Sig.	SP	HP	BB	BAT	Comments
Marquard, Rube	40	75	60	750		HOF 1971, RS, HP - common
Martin, Billy	70	140	N/A	425		BB (ss) - $981
Martin, Pepper	150	300	N/A			
Martinez, Dennis	10	20	N/A	25		
Martinez, Edgar	15	30	N/A	35	70	
Martinez, Pedro	25	65	N/A	85	165	
Martinez, Tino	20	35	N/A	45	95	
Mathews, Eddie	20	35	35	55	145	HOF 1978, prolific signer
Mathewson, Christy	1500					ESPV - all forms, see below

Christy Mathewson

Recent Sales: SP - $19, 861, SB - $6,167, Contract - $4,934, check - $9,607, ALS - $8,536

Name	Sig.	SP	HP	BB	BAT	Comments
Matsui, Hideki	50	100	N/A	200		ESPV-all forms
Mattingly, Don	15	30	N/A	50	125	RS
Mays, Willie	30	50	60	75	150	HOF 1979, $, reluctant signer
Mazeroski, Bill	10	20	20	30	75	HOF 2001, RS
McCarthy, Joe	50	100	100	1000		HOF 1957, RS, BB (ss) - $1,021
McCarthy, Tom	1650					HOF 1946, ESPV - all forms
McCarver, Tim	10	20	N/A	25	50	
McCovey, Willie	15	30	30	50	100	HOF 1986
McDougald, Gil	10	20	N/A	30	50	
McDowell, Sam	10	20	N/A	25	50	
McGinnity, Joe						HOF 1946
McGowan, Bill	400	800	N/A			HOF 1992
McGraw, John	700	1675	N/A	6000		SP - $2,245; check - $5,536
McGraw, Tug	10	15	N/A	25	50	
McGriff, Fred	15	25	N/A	30	80	
McGwire, Mark	75	150	N/A			ESPV - all forms
McKechnie, Bill	170	300	800			HOF 1962
McLain, Denny	15	30	N/A	40	80	Controversial
McNally, Dave	15	30	N/A	45	90	
Medwick, Joe	50	120	150	1450		HOF 1968, RS
Minoso, Minnie	10	25	N/A	30	65	
Mize, Johnny	15	25	25	75	215	HOF 1981, RS
Molitor, Paul	15	25	N/A	50	150	RS, HOF 2004
Mondesi, Raul	10	20	N/A	25	55	
Morgan, Joe	15	30	30	40	80	HOF 1990
Munson, Thurman	330	700	N/A			ESPV , BB (ss) - $4,158
Murcer, Bobby	10	25	N/A	30	60	
Murphy, Dale	10	20	N/A	30	65	
Murray, Eddie	20	40	45	60	120	HOF 2003, elusive signer
Musial, Stan	20	40	35	60	125	HOF 1969, RS
Mussina, Mike	15	30	N/A	35	75	
Nettles, Graig	10	20	N/A	30	55	

Name	Sig.	SP	HP	BB	BAT	Comments
Newcombe, Don	10	20	N/A	30	50	
Newhouser, Hal	12	25	20	35	75	HOF 1992, RS
Nichols, Kid	340	800	1750			HOF 1949
Niekro, Phil	10	25	25	35	75	HOF 1997
Nomo, Hideo	25	50	N/A	65	110	
O'Doul, Lefty	100	200	N/A	1100		
O'Neill, Paul	20	40	N/A	45	75	Reluctant signer
O'Rourke, Jim	3275					HOF 1945, scarce in all forms
Oates, Johnny	7	15	N/A	20	45	
Olerud, John	15	30	N/A	35	70	
Oliva, Tony	10	25	N/A	35	65	
Oliver, Al	10	20	N/A	30	60	
Ott, Mel						See below

Mel Ott
Recent Sales: ALS - $1,236,BB (ss) - $26, 435, SP - $4,158, BB (side) (9) - $24,032, HOF plaque - $2,415

Name	Sig.	SP	HP	BB	BAT	Comments
Paige, Satchel	125					BB (side) - $5,536, SP - $1,180
Palmeiro, Rafael	25	40	N/A	50	100	
Palmer, Jim	15	30	25	35	75	HOF 1990, RS
Parker, Dave	12	25	N/A	30	60	
Parrish, Lance	7	15	N/A	30	60	RS
Pennock, Herb	450	1000	N/A	5250		HOF 1948, ESPV - BB
Pepitone, Joe	10	20	N/A	25	50	
Percival, Troy	12	25	N/A	30	60	
Perez, Tony	20	35	35	40	85	HOF 2000
Perry, Gaylord	10	25	25	35	75	HOF 1991, $
Perry, Jim	7	15	N/A	25	50	
Pesky, Johnny	10	20	N/A	25	50	
Pettitte, Andy	20	40	N/A	50	100	
Piazza, Mike	20	50	N/A	65	175	
Pierce, Billy	7	15	N/A	25	50	
Piersall, Jimmy	10	20	N/A	25	50	
Pinella, Lou	12	25	N/A	30	60	
Pinson, Vida	30	70	N/A			ESPV - BB
Plank, Eddie						HOF 1946, PU
Podres, Johnny	7	15	N/A	25	50	
Powell, Boog	10	20	N/A	25	50	
Prior, Mark	12	25	N/A	30	65	
Puckett, Kirby	20	30	30	50	110	HOF 2001
Pujols, Albert	15	30	N/A	50	100	RS
Radbourn, Hoss						HOF 1939, rare in all forms
Raines, Tim	12	25	N/A	25	50	$
Ramirez, Manny	15	40	N/A	50	110	
Randolph, Willie	10	20	N/A	25	50	
Raschi, Vic	25	50	N/A			
Reese, Pee Wee	25	40	40	60	150	HOF 1984, check - $160
Reynolds, Allie	20	35	N/A	60	125	
Rice, Jim	15	25	N/A	35	70	
Rice, Sam	75	150	150	1500		HOF 1963

Name	Sig.	SP	HP	BB	BAT	Comments
Richard, J.R.	12	25	N/A	30	60	$
Richardson, Bobby	10	15	N/A	25	50	RS
Rickey, Branch	225	450	N/A	2250		HOF 1967, DS - common form
Ripken, Cal, Jr.	30	60	N/A	100	225	ESPV
Rivera, Mariano	20	45	N/A	40	75	Distinct signature
Rixey, Eppa	275	525	N/A	2500		HOF 1963
Rizzuto, Phil	15	25	25	35	70	HOF 1994
Roberts, Robin	10	25	20	30	55	HOF 1976, RS
Robinson, Brooks	10	25	15	35	75	HOF 1983, RS
Robinson, Frank	20	40	30	40	125	HOF 1982
Robinson, Jackie	375	725	1100	3500		HOF 1962, see below

Jackie Robinson
Recent Sales:
    Baseballs:
        Single-signed:
            OAL(side)   (7/8) $2,581
            OAL(side)   (8) $2,195
        Combination:
      Book: SB - "Wait Til Next Year" - $1,454
      Postcard: Postcard - $1,475,
      Program : $1,938
      TLS: $3,892, $1,072

Name	Sig.	SP	HP	BB	BAT	Comments
Robinson, Wilbert	1000	1500	N/A	6250		HOF 1945, scarce
Rodriguez, Alex	30	60	N/A	75	150	Sig. variations
Rodriguez, Ivan	15	35	N/A	40	75	
Roe, Preacher	10	20	N/A	30	60	
Rogan, Bullet						HOF 1998
Rolen, Scott	15	35	N/A	40	80	
Rose, Pete	20	30	N/A	50	125	$
Rosen, Al	10	25	N/A	30	60	
Roush, Edd	20	45	40	300		HOF 1962, RS
Rudi, Joe	12	25	N/A	30	60	
Ruffing, Red	35	75	75	540		HOF 1967, RS
Rusie, Amos						SP - $6,981, BB (s) - $45,667
Ruth, Babe				18500		HOF 1936, see below

Babe Ruth
Recent Sales:
    Baseballs:
        Single-signed:
            OAL (ss)   (7) $7,216
            OAL(side) (7/8) $4,817
            OAL(side) (7/8) $4,379
            OAL(side) (8) $3,058
            OAL (ss)   (8) $6,406
            OAL (ss)   (8) $8,745
            ONL (ss)   (8) $5,768
            OAL (ss)   (8/9) $8,733
            OAL(side) (9) $4,817
            OAL (ss)   (9) $16,812

Name	Sig.	SP	HP	BB	BAT	Comments
	OAL (ss)	(9)	$9,031			
	OAL (ss)	(9)	$32,816 - early			
	OAL (ss)	(9/10)	$14,920			
	ONL (ss)	(10)	$13,563 - as coach			
	OAL (ss)	(10)	$16,837			
	OAL (ss)	(10)	$21,847			
	OAL (ss)	(10)	$42, 576			

Combination: OAL (7)w/Gehrig $5,420
OAL (9)w/Gehrig $19,861
OAL (10)w/Gehrig $32,816

Books: SB - "The Babe Ruth Story" - $5,829; $6,346; $1,572
Checks: Personal - $10,221; Personal w/Claire - $3,436; Payroll - $6, 785; To Claire - $4,158;
Personal - $2,922; $3,215
Cut: w/Gehrig - $3,069
First Day Covers: Cooperstown, 1939 - $3,537
Photographs: $10, 221; $4,333 (side portrait); SP - $2,839; SP -small - $1,938; SP - $2,415
Postcard: 1942 - $1,600

OAL - Official American League Baseball, (ss) - "sweet spot", (?) - condition

Name	Sig.	SP	HP	BB	BAT	Comments
Ryan, Nolan	30	65	50	75	150	HOF 1999, FA
Sain, Johnny	10	15	N/A	25	50	
Salmon, Tim	15	30	N/A	35	70	
Sandberg, Ryne	20	30	N/A	50	100	
Santo, Ron	10	20	N/A	35	70	
Sax, Steve	10	20	N/A	30	60	
Schalk, Ray	75	150	325	1300		HOF 1955, BB (ss) - $1,600
Schilling, Curt	15	30	N/A	60	120	
Schmidt, Mike	25	50	45	60	125	HOF 1995
Schoendienst, Red	15	25	20	35	70	HOF 1989
Score, Herb	10	20	N/A	30	60	
Seaver, Tom	20	40	40	50	100	HOF 1992
Selee, Frank						HOF 1999
Sewell, Joe	20	40	20	125	250	HOF 1977
Shantz, Bobby	10	15	N/A	25	40	
Simmons, Al	325	600	1200	2250		HOF 1953
Simmons, Ted	10	15	N/A	30	45	
Sisler, George	55	150	150	1650		HOF 1939, BB(s) - $817
Skowron, Bill	10	15	N/A	25	40	
Slaughter, Enos	10	20	15	30	60	HOF 1985
Smith, Hilton						HOF 2001, TLS - $900
Smith, Lee	12	25	N/A	35	75	
Smith, Ozzie	20	35	35	45	125	HOF 2002
Smoltz, John	15	25	N/A	40	75	
Snider, Duke	15	30	25	50	115	HOF 1980
Soriano, Alfonso	15	30	N/A	55	110	
Sosa, Sammy	35	70	N/A	150	350	
Spahn, Warren	10	25	20	40	100	HOF 1973
Spalding, Al	1350					SB - $2,132, receipt - $1,995
Speaker, Tris	300	725	1000	4225		BB (s) - $2,839, BB (ss) - $7,938

Name	Sig.	SP	HP	BB	BAT	Comments
Stanky, Eddie	15	30	N/A	40	80	
Staub, Rusty	10	20	N/A	25	50	
Stargel, Willie	15	25	25	40	125	HOF 1988
Stengel, Casey	100	225	175	1000		HOF 1966
Strawberry, Daryl	10	20	N/A	25	50	Controversial
Stuart, Dick	20	30	N/A	50	100	
Sutter, Bruce	15	25	N/A	30	60	
Sutton, Don	20	30	30	35	75	HOF 1998
Suzuki, Ichiro	50	100	N/A	130	200	ESPV - all forms
Tejada, Miguel	10	30	N/A	40	80	
Terry, Bill	20	50	40	175		HOF 1954, RS
Terry, Ralph	10	20	N/A	25	55	
Thomas, Frank	20	40	N/A	50	125	
Thome, Jim	10	25	N/A	40	85	
Thompson, Sam						HOF 1974, PU
Thomson, Bobby	10	20	N/A	30	75	
Tiant, Luis	10	20	N/A	30	60	
Tinker, Joe	750	1400	N/A	3650		HOF 1946
Torre, Joe	15	30	N/A	35	100	
Trammell, Alan	15	25	N/A	35	70	
Traynor, Pie	150	300		1865		HOF 1948, BB (ss) - $1,500
Tresh, Tom	10	20	N/A	25	50	
Uecker, Bob	15	25	N/A	35	70	
Valenzuela, Fernando	15	25	N/A	30	60	
Van Slyke, Andy	10	20	N/A	25	55	Often unpredictable
Vance, Dazzy	265	540	1230	2400		BB (ss) - $1,995, BB (s)- $1,454
VanderMeer, Johnny	20	40	N/A	70	140	
Vaughan, Arky	450	850	N/A			HOF 1985, BB (side) - $8,918
Vaughn, Mo	20	35	N/A	40	100	
Veeck, Bill	125	300	N/A	750		HOF 1991, DS - common form
Vizquel, Omar	15	30	N/A	30	75	
Waddell, Rube						BB (s)-$29,786, SP - $6484
Wagner, Honus	400	920	1800	4000		Check - $731, contract - $3,070
Walker, Larry	20	40	N/A	35	75	
Wallace, Bobby	450	1200	1500	3200		HOF 1953
Walsh, Ed	275	675	800	4000		HOF 1946, BB (side) - $3,255
Waner, Lloyd	25	60	40	575		HOF 1967, RS
Waner, Paul	300	600	750	3350		HOF 1952, SP - $3,255
Ward, John						Check - $7,054, SB - $27,104
Weaver, Earl	15	30	30	40	75	HOF 1996
Weiss, George	150	300	4000	2000		HOF 1971, HP - rare
Welch, Mickey	3000					HOF 1973, scarce in all forms
Wells, David	20	40	N/A	50	100	
Wells, Willie	300	600	N/A			ALS - $1201, SP - $900
Wheat, Zach	75	225	300	2150		HOF 1959, BB (side) - $1,454
Whitaker, Lou	15	25	N/A	30	50	
Wilhelm, Hoyt	15	30	20	40	75	HOF 1985, $
Williams, Bernie	25	45	N/A	50	75	

Name	Sig.	SP	HP	BB	BAT	Comments
Williams, Billy	15	25	20	30	70	HOF 1987
Williams, Ted	125	225	150			HOF 1966, $
Willis, Vic						HOF 1995
Wills, Maury	15	25	N/A	30	60	Elusive signer!
Wilson, Hack	575	1000	N/A	4000		HOF 1979, BB (ss) - $3,289
Winfield, Dave	20	40	35	45	125	HOF 2001
Wood, Joe	35	80	N/A	400		RS
Wood, Kerry	20	40	N/A	50	100	
Woodling, Gene	15	30	N/A	45	100	RS
Wright, George						HOF 1937, SP (c)- $10,996
Wright, Harry						HOF 1953, SP (c)- $10, 582
Wynn, Early	25	40	35	50	135	HOF 1972
Wynn, Jimmy	10	20	N/A	25	50	
Yastrzemski, Carl	25	40	40	50	125	HOF 1989
Yawkey, Thomas	225	400	N/A			HOF 1980
Young, Cy	475	900	1750	6000		HOF 1937, BB (side) - $6,412
Youngs, Ross						HOF 1972, scarce all forms
Yount, Robin	20	40	40	50	150	HOF 1999
Zimmer, Don	10	20	25	40		
Zito, Barry	15	30	N/A	50	75	

TEAM BASEBALLS

WHAT YOU NEED TO KNOW

* There are six factors that affect the value of authentic autographed team baseballs: ball type, medium or writing material, completeness, condition, scarcity and demand, and signature form, style and placement.

* Of the six factors listed above that affect value, condition is paramount in most cases.

*The ball type of choice is an "Official League" baseball dated to the particular era.

* Grading is subjective and based on a particular source.

* Grading has a substantial impact upon value and should be thoroughly reviewed before any purchase.

* Multiple-signed baseballs can be difficult to identify especially those signed during Spring Training where many non-roster players are in attendance.

* Multiple-signed baseballs can be difficult to accurately value if an unassociated signature also appears on the item.

* Combination signed baseballs, such as "Mantle & Maris", "Ruth & Gehrig", etc., are popular with many collectors.

* The inclusion of a deceased player or manager on a ball will naturally increase the value of the item, particularly if the individual had a significant impact on the game.

MARKET FACTS

* The market for team baseballs lagged for many years behind that of single-signed baseballs. This was primarily attributed to the absence of information necessary to properly identify, grade and value the item.

* As the market for single-signed baseballs escalated, more interest turned toward team baseballs.

* Value continues to be impacted by popularity. Certain teams have a boundless appeal and lasting impact on baseball fans - New York Yankees, Brooklyn Dodgers, Los Angeles Dodgers, etc.

* World Champion autographed team baseballs are always in demand.

* The absence of key signatures, such as Mickey Mantle and Roger Maris, on a team baseball, such as a 1961 New York Yankee item, can reduce value by as much as seventy-five percent.

TRENDS

* Condition, condition, condition remains key with collectors of team baseballs.

* Condition is not the primary factor on value only when a key signature appears on the item, such as Joe Jackson on a 1919 Chicago White Sox baseball. It is at this point that scarcity and demand become paramount issues with regard to value.

* The frequency of autographed team baseballs appearing in the market from the last twenty-five years is far less than their predecessors.

Year	#S	Grade	Team	Price Realized
1910-1925				
1916	12	7	Chicago White Sox	1938
1919	11	7-9	Cincinnati Reds	11625
1920	18	4-6	Chicago White Sox	17603
1923	27	6-7	New York Giants	10102
1923	21	4-5	New York Yankees	4710
1924	24	7-10	Boston Red Sox	900
1924	23	5-7	Detroit Tigers	1497
1924	26	4-8	St. Louis Browns	613
1925	27	2-8	Philadelphia A's	818
1925	25	5-7	Cincinnati Reds	743
1926-1929				
1926	25	5-7	Detroit Tigers	1834
1926	21	3-6	Brooklyn Dodgers	675
1927	21	3-7	New York Yankees	3058
1927	16	6-9	New York Yankees	9607
1927	14	7-9	New York Yankees	5244
1927	27	6-8	St. Louis Browns	743
1927	24	8-10	Cleveland Indians	675
1927	19	6-8	Philadelphia Athletics	1360
1928	10	7-8	Philadelphia Athletics	2132
1928	19	7	Boston Braves	818
1928	26	6-8	Chicago Cubs	1252
1928	25	5-8	New York Giants	1497
1929	25	8-10	New York Yankees	9292
1929	20	6-9	New York Yankees	4333
1929	26	2-8	Philadelphia Athletics	3537
1929	29	5-8	Washington Senators	991
1930-1939				
1930	20	6-9	Philadelphia Athletics	743

Year	#S	Grade	Team	Price Realized
1930	23	4-8	New York Yankees	3215
1930	28	6-10	St. Louis Cardinals	900
1931	23	9-10	New York Giants	1903
1932	25	7-10	Pittsburgh Pirates	1091
1932	20	6-8	New York Yankees	8733
1932	12	8-10	Philadelphia Athletics	3123
1932	21	5-8	Chicago Cubs	1072
1932	22	5	New York Yankees	3974
1933	28	7-8	Brooklyn Dodgers	900
1933	24	8-9	New York Yankees	12368
1933	24	7-8	New York Giants	8108
1933	23	5-9	Washington Senators	1124
1933	24	7-8	New York Giants	8108
1933	19	3-7	New York Yankees	3255
1934	26	6-8	New York Yankees	4767
1935	24	6-9	Detroit Tigers	1648
1935	21	5-7	Pittsburgh Pirates	675
1935	22	5-8	New York Yankees	3255
1936	24	5-7	New York Yankees	3123
1936	16	8-10	St. Louis Cardinals	1761
1936	23	5-8	New York Giants	1600
1936	22	6-8	St. Louis Browns	557
1936	16	8-10	St. Louis Cardinals	1761
1937	25	7-9	Detroit Tigers	675
1937	23	7	New York Giants	2305
1937	21	2-3	New York Yankees	743
1937	22	4-7	New York Yankees	1761
1938	18	6-8	New York Yankees	5244
1938	24	10	Cleveland Indians	830
1939	21	6-9	Boston Red Sox	2346
1939	21	6-8	Pittsburgh Pirates	900
1939	20	6-9	Pittsburgh Pirates	991
1939	20	6-9	Pittsburgh Pirates	991
1939	23	7-9	Detroit Tigers	557
1940-1949				
1941	28	5-7	New York Yankees	3436
1942	23	8	New York Yankees	1600
1942	21	7-9	Pittsburgh Pirates	622
1944	29	6-8	St. Louis Browns	622
1944	24	5-8	Chicago Cubs	1091
1945	24	8-10	Pittsburgh Pirates	1787
1946	26	5	St. Louis Cardinals	665
1947	29	8-9	New York Yankees	3436
1947	20	8-10	New York Yankees	1201
1947	27	6-7	Boston Red Sox	900
1947	16	8-10	New York Yankees	1321
1947	22	8-10	New York Yankees	1454
1948	25	7-9	New York Yankees	557
1949	28	8-10	Brooklyn Dodgers	2839
1949	29	8	New York Yankees	1108
1949	23	6-8	Brooklyn Dodgers	974

Year	#S	Grade	Team	Price Realized
1949	28	7-8	Brooklyn Dodgers	4575
1949	24	5-8	Brooklyn Dodgers	830

1950-1959

Year	#S	Grade	Team	Price Realized
1950	23	7-10	Philadelphia Phillies	1219
1950	22	8-10	Philadelphia Athletics	805
1950	22	6-9	Brooklyn Dodgers	1600
1950	26	6-7	Brooklyn Dodgers	805
1950	21	7-10	New York Yankees	3436
1950	18	8-9	New York Yankees	2132
1951	25	6-9	Brooklyn Dodgers	1600
1951	25	7-8	New York Giants	1201
1952	26	8	Brooklyn Dodgers	1938
1952	29	6-10	Brooklyn Dodgers	1600
1952	26	6-10	New York Yankees	2581
1952	26	8	Brooklyn Dodgers	1938
1953	24	6-7	Brooklyn Dodgers	613
1953	28	7-8	New York Yankees	1648
1953	31	8-10	Detroit Tigers	498
1953	29	8	New York Yankees	2132
1953	33	7-8	New York Yankees	1321
1953	25	8	Brooklyn Dodgers	818
1953	26	8	New York Yankees	6899
1954	26	8-10	New York Yankees	818
1954	29	7-8	Cleveland Indians	1219
1954	26	8-9	Boston Red Sox	1072
1955	26	8-10	New York Yankees	1180
1955	26	9-10	Milwaukee Braves	886
1955	28	7-9	New York Yankees	1072
1955	24	8-10	Brooklyn Dodgers	3436
1955	27	7-9	New York Yankees	991
1955	27	8-10	Brooklyn Dodgers	7054
1955	25	9-10	Brooklyn Dodgers	21300
1955	26	7-8	New York Yankees	1428
1955	30	7-9	New York Yankees	1938
1955	25	8-10	Brooklyn Dodgers	6412
1956	23	9-10	New York Yankees	8348
1956	27	9-10	New York Yankees	4281
1956	23	8-9	Brooklyn Dodgers	1321
1956	29	7-10	Brooklyn Dodgers	2581
1956	25	8-9	Brooklyn Dodgers	1600
1956	24	8-9	Brooklyn Dodgers	4575
1956	27	9-10	New York Yankees	5032
1956	28	8-9	Milwaukee Braves	342
1957	25	8-10	Pittsburgh Pirates	1600
1957	31	7-8	Cleveland Indians	665
1959	29	8-9	New York Yankees	4086
1959	27	10	New York Yankees	3780

1960-69

Year	#S	Grade	Team	Price Realized
1960	28	9-10	Pittsburgh Pirates	2381
1960	30	9-10	New York Yankees	9811

Year	#S	Grade	Team	Price Realized
1960	30	6-10	Pittsburgh Pirates	1321
1960	25	7-9	Los Angeles Dodgers	1572
1961	32	7-10	New York Yankees	20138
1962	31	9-10	New York Yankees	11873
1962	32	10	Los Angeles Dodgers	1428
1962	27	9	Pittsburgh Pirates	1298
1962	32	10	Los Angeles Dodgers	1298
1963	27	6-9	Los Angeles Dodgers	818
1963	31	9	New York Yankees	4710
1963	28	9-10	Los Angeles Dodgers	2839
1963	29	8-10	Los Angeles Dodgers	1938
1963	29	9-10	Pittsburgh Pirates	1201
1963	29	8-10	Los Angeles Dodgers	2839
1963	28	8-10	Cincinnati Reds	1180
1964	25	9-10	Pittsburgh Pirates	1201
1966	25	8-10	Los Angeles Dodgers	805
1967	27	9-10	Boston Red Sox	1572
1967	20	9-10	Boston Red Sox	743
1967	28	8-10	St. Louis Cardinals	2839
1968	24	7-10	Detroit Tigers	974
1968	27	7-9	Detroit Tigers	1572
1968	25	8-10	St. Louis Cardinals	1454
1969	26	10	Baltimore Orioles	1298
1969	31	8-10	Washington Senators	1428
1969	27	9	New York Mets	3715

1970-1979

Year	#S	Grade	Team	Price Realized
1971	17	9-10	New York Yankees	886
1971	34	10	Baltimore Orioles	731
1972	28	10	Cincinnati Reds	1072
1972	25	10	Oakland Athletics	1072
1975	23	10	New York Yankees	2094
1975	26	10	Cincinnati Reds	2536
1976	29	9	New York Yankees	1072
1976	22	9-10	New York Yankees	2132

1980-89

Year	#S	Grade	Team	Price Realized
1980	28	10	Philadelphia Phillies	1180
1982	27	9-10	Milwaukee Brewers	407
1984	30	9-10	Detroit Tigers	1180
1984	30	10	Detroit Tigers	1730
1986	32	10	New York Mets	549

1990- present

Year	#S	Grade	Team	Price Realized
1991	25	9/10	Minnesota Twins	736
2001	26	10	Arizona Diamondbacks	1428
2001	24	6-8	Arizona Diamondbacks	1730
2001	31	10	New York Yankees	886
2002	28	10	New York Yankees	1428

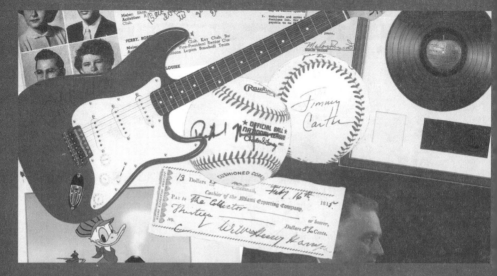

Auctioning Your Autographs?

No auction house can market your high value collectibles like MastroNet.

Our only concerns are to offer your material in the most ideal manner possible and to make sure that the value of your material is maximized. Furthermore, MastroNet is a consignment auction house. Many other auctions are run by dealers offering material they own, exposing consignors to numerous unreconcilable conflicts of interest. We succeed when we do the best possible job for you. If you have material you think might be of interest, call **630-472-1200** or visit *www.mastronet.com* and click on *Consignments*.

 MASTRONETinc. *Premier Auctions*

10S660 Kingery Highway   Willowbrook, IL 60527
630.472.1200   www.mastronet.com

BASKETBALL

WHAT YOU NEED TO KNOW

* Basketball was invented in 1891 by James A. Naismith (1861-1939). When compared to sports such as boxing, it is relatively new. Naismith was inducted as the first member of the Basketball Hall of Fame in 1959.

* The Basketball Hall of Fame did not have a physical home until February 17, 1968. In 1985 the Hall of Fame was moved to Springfield, Mass.

* The Naismith Memorial Basketball Hall of Fame includes players from all basketball levels, including college, women's, and foreign leagues.

* Much of this area of collecting focuses upon those who have competed in the National Basketball Association (NBA).

MARKET FACTS

* The market has shown significant price variations in the form of official league basketballs signed by the greatest players of the game.

* The market is driven by the signatures of the greatest players such as Larry Bird, Wilt Chamberlain, Magic Johnson, Michael Jordan, and Bill Russell.

* Forgeries are common for the names listed above.

* Obtaining a full set of signatures from every member of the Basketball Hall of Fame is challenging but feasible.

TRENDS

* The increased frequency of drafting high school players for the NBA causes authentication concerns for collectors. Collectors typically remain unfamiliar with a player's autograph until supply has meant demand.

* Although dissipating, the negative publicity surrounding the arrest and prosecution of many individuals responsible for the forgery of basketball memorabilia continues to impact collecting interest.

Abbreviations: BB = signed official league basketball, ESPV = can exhibit signifigant price variations, FA = facsimile alert, RS = responsive signer, Sig. = signature, SP = signed photograph, USS = United States Senate

Name	Sig.	SP	BB	Comments
AbdulJabbar, Kareem	45	65	165	HOF 1995, FA
Allen, Ray	10	20	100	
Anthony, Carmelo	15	25	125	
Archibald, Nate	10	20	100	HOF 1991
Arizin, Paul	8	20	100	HOF 1977, RS
Artest, Ron	10	20	100	
Auerbach, Red	12	25	145	HOF 1968
Barkley, Charles	22	40	155	Very temporamental
Barry, Rick	8	17	115	HOF 1987, RS
Baylor, Elgin	10	20	125	HOF 1976
Bellamy, Walt	10	20	115	HOF 1993
Belov, Sergei	8	15		HOF 1992
Biasone, Danny	20	30		HOF 2000
Bing, Dave	10	25	130	HOF 1990
Bird, Larry	30	50	185	HOF 1998, ESPV BB
Blazejowski, Carol	10	20		HOF 1994, RS
Bradley, Bill	25	50	165	HOF 1982, USS, FA
Brown, Larry	10	20		HOF 2002
Bryant, Kobe	30	60	185	ESPV BB, controversial
Camby, Marcus	10	20	95	
Carter, Vince	22	38	165	
Chamberlain, Wilt	125	185	350	HOF 1978
Chaney, John	10	20	100	HOF 2001
Cousy, Bob	10	35	155	HOF 1970, RS
Cowens, Dave	10	20	100	HOF 1991, RS
Crum, Denny	10	20		HOF 1994
Cunningham, Billy	10	20	120	HOF 1986
Daley, Chuck	10	20	95	HOF 1994
Davies, Bob	38	65	250	HOF 1969
DeBusschere, Dave	15	25	150	HOF 1982, RS
Donovan, Anne	7	15	75	HOF 1995
Drexler, Clyde	15	30	125	
Dumars, Joe	10	20	85	
Duncan, Tim	25	45	125	
Embry, Wayne	10	20	75	HOF 1999
English, Alex	10	20	100	HOF 1997
Erving, Julius	25	60	210	HOF 1993
Ewing, Patrick	20	40	145	FA
Frasier, Walt	15	25	125	HOF 1987
Fulks, Joe	30	100		HOF 1977
Gallatin, Harry	10	20	100	HOF 1991, RS
Garnett, Kevin	20	40	125	
Gervin, George	12	25	125	HOF 1996, RS
Gola, Tom	10	20	110	HOF 1975, RS
Goodrich, Gail	10	20	100	HOF 1996
Greer, Hal	10	20	100	HOF 1981
Hagan, Cliff	10	20	100	HOF 1977, RS
Hardaway, Anfernee	10	25	100	
Hardaway, Tim	10	20	100	
Havlicek, John	20	32	165	HOF 1983
Hawkins, Connie	10	20	100	HOF 1992
Hayes, Elvin	10	20	100	HOF 1990

Name	Sig.	SP	BB	Comments
Heinsohn, Tom	10	20	130	HOF 1986
Hill, Grant	20	40	125	
Holman, Nat	20	40	150	HOF 1964
Holzman, Red	25	45	170	HOF 1985
Howard, Juwan	10	20	100	
Iba, Henry	20	50		HOF 1968
Issel, Dan	10	20	110	HOF 1993
Iverson, Allen	25	40	150	
Jackson, Mark	10	22	100	
Jackson, Phil	20	40	110	
James, LeBron	25	50	150	
Jamison, Antwan	10	20	95	
Jeannette, Buddy	10	20	100	HOF 1994
Johnson, Magic	20	65	250	HOF 2002, RS, ESPV BB
Jones, K.C.	10	20	100	HOF 1989, RS
Jones, Sam	10	20	100	HOF 1983
Jordan, Michael	125	300		ESPV BB, FA
Kidd, Jason	15	25	120	
Knight, Bobby	10	25	100	HOF 1990, controversial
Krzyzewski, Mike	10	25	110	HOF 2001
Lanier, Bob	10	20	100	HOF 1992, RS
Lovellette, Clyde	10	20	85	HOF 1987
Lucas, Jerry	10	20	90	HOF 1979
MacCauley, Ed	10	20	110	HOF 1960, Rs
Malone, Karl	20	45	160	
Malone, Moses	15	25	150	HOF 2001
Maravich, Pete	200	425		HOF 1987, ESPV
Marbury, Stephon	10	20	100	
Martin, Kenyon	10	20	100	
Martin, Slater	10	20	110	HOF 1981, RS
McAdoo, Bob	12	24	110	HOF 2000
McGrady, Tracy	20	40	150	
McGuire, Dick	10	20	100	HOF 1993, RS
Meyer, Ray	12	25	110	HOF 1978
Mikan, George	15	40	175	HOF 1959
Miles, Darius	10	20	80	
Mikkelsen, Vern	10	20	100	HOF 1995
Miller, Cheryl	10	25	100	HOF 1995
Miller, Reggie	15	30	125	
Ming, Yao	25	50	150	
Monroe, Earl	15	25	115	HOF 1990
Mourning, Alonzo	10	20	75	
Mullin, Chris	12	25	100	
Murphy, Calvin	10	25	110	HOF 1993
Nash, Steve	10	20	75	
O'Neal, Jermaine	10	25	100	
O'Neal, Shaquille	50	100	225	
Olajuwon, Hakeem	20	40	130	
Parrish, Robert	15	30	125	HOF
Payton, Gary	10	20	100	
Pettit, Bob	10	25	100	HOF 1970, RS
Phillip, Andy	10	20	100	HOF 1961

Name	Sig.	SP	BB	Comments
Pippen, Scottie	25	50	165	
Pollard, Jim	25	45	200	HOF 1977
Price, Mark	10	20	100	
Ramsey, Frank	10	20	100	HOF 1981, RS
Reed, Willis	12	25	120	HOF 1981
Rice, Glen	10	20	100	
Riley, Pat	15	30	110	
Robertson, Oscar	30	60	175	HOF 1979
Robinson, David	25	50	150	
Robinson, Glenn	10	22	100	
Rodman, Dennis	20	30	100	Controversial
Russell, Bill	100	200	500	HOF 1974, elusive, ESPV
Schayes, Dolph	10	20	125	HOF 1972, RS
Sharman, Bill	10	20	100	HOF 1975
Smith, Dean	15	25	120	HOF 1982, RS
Sprewell, Latrell	10	22	100	
Stackhouse, Jerry	10	20	100	
Stockton, John	25	50	155	Elusive signer
Stoudamire, Damon	10	25	100	
Strickland, Rod	10	20	100	
Thomas, Isiah	10	25	125	HOF 2000
Thompson, John R.	20	40	125	HOF 1999
Thurmond, Nate	7	15	100	HOF 1984
Twyman, Jack	5	15	80	HOF 1982
Unseld, Wes	10	25	110	HOF 1988
Van Exel, Nick	10	25	100	
Van Horn, Keith	10	25	100	
Walker, Antoine	10	25	100	
Wallace, Rasheed	10	25	100	
Walton, Bill	10	25	125	HOF 1993
Wanzer, Robert	10	20	100	HOF 1987, RS
Webber, Chris	10	30	125	
West, Jerry	15	25	130	HOF 1979
Wilkens, Lenny	10	15	100	HOF 1989
Wilkins, Dominique	10	25	125	
Williams, Jason	10	25	100	
Wooden, John	15	30	150	HOF 1960
Worthy, James	10	25	110	
Yardley, George	10	20	100	HOF 1996

BOXING

WHAT YOU NEED TO KNOW

* Despite its often controversial status, the sport of boxing has always had –
albeit limited compared to baseballl or football, an appeal to autograph
collectors.

* The advent of the International Boxing Hall of Fame in Canastota, New York has
done much to legitimize this area of collecting.

* By some estimates, there are only a few dozen serious boxing autograph
collectors.

* Until recent years, participants in this area of the hobby have shared little
information regarding the availability of autographed material.

* Most autograph collectors focus on the fighters included in the "modern"
category of the International Boxing Hall of Fame.

* Many of the signatures of fighters in the "pioneer" category of the International
Hall Boxing Hall of Fame are extremely scarce, especially in the United States.

* Often overlooked are those members in the "non-participant" category of the
International Hall Boxing Hall of Fame.

MARKET FACTS

* The market is driven by the signatures of the greatest fighters, name such as
Sullivan, Fitzsimmons, Corbett, Dempsey, Tunney, Johnson, Armstrong, Louis,
Robinson, Marciano and Ali.

* The market has shown signifigant price variations in obscure forms, such as
contracts, licenses, early programs, etc.

* Autographed boxing gloves are the form in greatest demand.

* Forgeries are scarce, especially when compared to sports such as baseball.

* Interest in boxing memorabilia continues to lag that of other sports. With limited
transactions, compared to the four major sports, pricing can very signifigantly
especially with deceased fighters.

* Obtaining a full set of signatures from every member of theInternational Boxing
Hall of Fame is nearly impossible.

TRENDS

* The signatures of living members of the International Boxing Hall of Fame are plentiful.

* While there is lttle demand for the signatures of living Hall of Fame members, there is a steady demand for many of the deceased inductees.

* The seemingly perpetual controversy surrounding the sport has hurt interest in collecting boxing autographs.

* Participants in the sport are generally very obliguing to autograph requests.

Abbreviations: ESPV = exhibits significant pricing variation, FA = forgery/ facsimile alert, F = featherweight, H = heavyweight, L = lightweight, LH = light heavyweight, M= middleweight, RS = responsive signer, SV = signature variations, W = welterweight, SSP = significant/vintage signed photograph

Name	db/dd	Sig.	SP	SG	Comments
Ali, Muhammad	1942 -	35	150	275	USA, H, "Cassius Clay", SV, SSP-2X
Ambers, Lou	1913-1995	25	45	150	USA, L, RS
Angott, Sammy	1915-1980	45	75		USA, L
Apostoli, Freddie	1913-1973	100	175		USA, M
Arcel, Ray	1899-1994	25	50	155	USA, trainer
Arguello, Alexis	1952-	10	25	60	Nicaragua, L, F, SV, RS
Armstrong, Henry	1912-1988	100	200	800	USA, W, L, F
Arum, Bob	1931-	5	10	40	USA, Promoter
Attell, Abe	1884-1970	125	250	700	USA, F, RS, sought by baseball fans
Baer, Max	1909-1959	150	300	1250	USA, H, RS
Basilio, Carmen	1927-	10	25	65	USA, W, M, RS
Benitez, Wilfred	1958-	15	30	90	USA, JW, W, RS
Benn, Nigel	1964-	10	20	40	England, M, SM
Benvenuti, Nino	1938-	15	60	200	Italy, JM, M, often elusive
Berg, Jackie "Kid"	1909-1991	35	75	275	England, JW
Bivins, Jimmy	1919-	15	25	60	USA
Blackburn, Jack	1883-1942	125	300		USA, trainer, "Chappie"
Bowe, Riddick	1967-	10	25	50	USA, H. controversial
Brady, William A.	1863-1950				USA, manager, PU
Brenner, Teddy	1917-2000	20	40	85	USA, matchmaker, RS
Britton, Jack	1885-1962	100	175	600	USA, W
Brown, Joe	1926-1997	25	50	100	USA, L
Brown, Panama Al	1902-1951	140	315		Panama, B
Bruno, Frank	1961-	15	25	55	England, H
Burley, Charley	1917-1992	25	45	120	USA, M, rRS
Burns, Tommy	1881-1955	320	750		Canada, H,ESPV, SSP-2X
Buchanan, Ken	1945-	10	20	40	Scotland, L
Canto, Miguel	1949-	10	25	60	Mexico, FL, RS
Canzoneri, Tony	1908-1959	125	235	800	USA, F, L, JW, RS

Name	db/dd	Sig.	SP	SG	Comments
Carpentier, Georges	1894-1975	125	250	1000	France, LH, RS
Carter, Jimmy	1923-1994	25	50	100	USA, L
Carter, Ruben	1937-	10	25	75	USA, M
Cerdan, Marcel	1916-1949	400	775	3225	Algeria, M, scarce signature
Cervantes, Antonio	1945-	15	30	75	Columbia, JW
Chamber, John Graham	1843-?				England, Queensberry rules author, PU
Chandler, Jeff	1956-	5	15	50	USA
Charles, Ezzard	1921-1975	125	350	1000	USA, H
Chavez, Julio Cesar	1962-	15	35	75	Mexico, JL, L, JW
Chocolate, Kid	1910-1988	130	235	650	Cuba, JL, F
Choynski, Joe	1868-1943				USA, H, PU
Clancy, Gil	1922-	5	10	45	USA, trainer, manager, RS
Coffroth, James W.	1872-1943	85	150		USA, promoter
Cokes, Curtis	1937-	5	10	40	USA, W, RS
Conn, Billy	1917-1993	35	120	300	USA, LH, RS
Cooper, Henry	1934 -	10	25	55	England, H
Cuevas, Pipino	1957-	10	25	50	Mexico, W
Corbett, James J.	1866-1933	450	900		USA, H
D'Amato, Cus	1908-1985	55	100		USA, manager
De la Hoya, Oscar	1973-	15	25	75	
Delaney, Jack	1900-1948	150	300		Canada, LH
Dempsey, Jack	1895-1983	100	200	750	USA, H, RS
Dillon, Jack	1891-1942	150	320		USA, LH
Dixon, George	1870-1909				Canada, B, F, PU
Donovan, Arthur	1891-?				USA, referee, RS, PU
Donovan, Mike	1847-1918				USA, M, PU
Downes, Terry	1936-				England, M, PU
Driscoll, Jim	1880-1925				Wales, F, PU
Duffy, Paddy	1864-1890				USA, W, PU
Dundee, Angelo	1923-	10	20	45	USA, trainer
Dundee, Chris	1908-1998	30	50	125	USA, manager, promoter
Dundee, Johnny	1893-1965	60	125	450	Italy, F, JL
Dunphy, Don	1911-1998	20	40	75	USA, broadcaster, RS
Duran, Roberto	1951-	15	30	75	Panama, L, W, JM, M, SM
Duva, Lou	1922-	5	15	50	USA, trainer, manager, RS
Ellis, Jimmy	1940-	5	15	45	USA, H, singer, RS
Elorde, Gabriel "Flash"	1935-1985	55	110	250	Philippines, JL
Fenech, Jeff	1964-	15	25	50	Australia, B, SB, F
Fitzsimmons, Bob	1863-1917	1965	4000		England, M, H, LH
Fleischer, Nat S.	?-1972	25	45	150	USA, writer, publisher
Flowers, Tiger	1895-1927	300	1100		USA, M
Foreman, George	1948 -	20	55	165	USA, H, RS
Foster, Bob	1938-	5	15	60	USA, LH, RS
Fox, Richard K.	1846-1922	85	125		Ireland, writer, publisher
Frazier, Joe	1944-	10	50	125	USA, H, RS
Fullmer, Gene	1931-	5	15	45	USA, M, RS
Futch, Eddie	1911-2001	15	25	50	USA, trainer, manager
Galindez, Victor	? - 1980				Argentina, LH, PU

Name	db/dd	Sig.	SP	SG	Comments
Galaxy, Khaosai	1959-	10	15	50	Thailand, B
Gans, Joe	1874-1910	600	1500		USA, L
Gavilan, Kid	1926-2003	20	40	125	Cuba, W, RS, sig. variations
Genaro, Frankie	1901-1966	125	150	575	USA, F
Giardello, Joey	1930-	10	20	50	USA, M, RS
Gibbons, Mike	1887-1956	100	200		USA, M
Gibbons, Tommy	1891-1960	80	175	1400	USA, H
Goldman, Charley	1888-1968	125	235	600	Poland, trainer
Goldstein, Ruby	1907-1984	50	110		USA, referee
Gomez, Wilfredo	1956-	15	30	70	Puerto Rico, SB, F, JL, elusive signer
Graham, Billy	1922-1992	30	55	200	USA, W
Graziano, Rocky	1922-1990	45	125	260	USA, M, prolific
Greb, Harry	1894-1926	750	2425		USA, M
Griffith, Emile	1938-	5	15	50	Virgin Islands, W, M, RS
Hagler, Marvelous M.	1954-	20	50	100	USA, M, can be elusive, lives in Italy
Harada, Masahiko	1943-	10	25	65	Japan, FL, B, RS
Herman, Pete	1896-1973	85	165		USA, B
Holmes, Larry	1949 -	10	30	60	USA, H
Humphreys, Joe	1872-1936	60	120		USA, announcer
Jack, Beau	1921-2000	15	40	75	USA, L, RS, sig. variations
Jackson, Peter	1861-1901				West Indies, H, PU
Jacobs, Jimmy	1930-1988	50	100		USA, manager, film historian
Jacobs, Mike	1880-1953	75	160		USA, promoter
Jeannette, Joe	1879-1958	365			USA, H, ESPV
Jeffries, James J.	1875-1953	380	850		USA, H
Jenkins, Lew	1916-1981	25	50	100	
Jofre, Eder	1936-	15	30	70	Brazil, B, F,RS
Johansson, Ingemar	1932 -	15	30	65	Sweden, H
Johnson, Harold	1928-	10	20	60	USA, LH, RS
Johnson, Jack	1878-1946	600	1450	6250	USA, H
Jones, Roy, Jr.	1969-	15	30	75	USA, M, SM
Kearns, Jack		50	100	275	USA, manager
Ketchel, Stanley	1886-1910				USA, M, scarce in all forms, PU
Kilbane, Johnny	1889-1957	100	265		USA, F
King, Don	1931-	5	15	45	USA, promoter
Labarba, Fidel	1905-1981	25	45	110	USA, FL
Laguna, Ismael	1943-	15	30	65	Panama, L
LaMotta, Jake	1921-	15	25	75	USA, M, charges for signatures
Langford, Sam	1883-1956				Canada, H, PU
Lavigne, Kid	1869-1928				USA, L, PU
Leonard, Benny	1896-1947	150	300		USA, L, RS
Leonard, Sugar Ray	1956-	15	30	75	USA, W-LH, RS
Lewis, John Henry	1914-1974	70	170	700	USA, LH
Lewis, Lennox	1965-	15	50	120	England, H
Lewis, Ted "Kid"	1894-1970	60	125		England, W
Liebling, A.J.	? - 1963	45	75		USA, writer
Liston, Charles "Sonny"	1932-1970	420	1575		USA, H, very scarce in all forms, FA
Locche, Nicolino	1939-	15	30	70	Argentina, L

Name	db/dd	Sig.	SP	SG	Comments
Loughran, Tommy	1902-1982	60	125	375	USA, LH
Louis, Joe	1914-1981	200	425		USA, H, prolific, ESPV - SG
Lynch, Benny	1913-1946	250	500		Ireland, FL, ESPV
Mace, Jem	1831-1910				England, PU
Mandell, Sammy	1904-1967	40	80	235	USA, L
Marciano, Rocky	1923-1969	250	700	3450	USA, H, RS
Markson, Harry	1907-1998	20	40	75	USA, publicist, promoter
Maxim, Joey	1922-2001	20	40	80	USA, LH, RS
McAuliffe, Jack	1866-1937	150	400		Ireland, L
McCallum, Mike	1956-	10	20	50	
McCoy, Charles "Kid"	1872-1940	125	250		USA, M
McFarland, Packey	1888-1936	150	300		USA, L
McGovern, Terry	1880-1918	400	1000		USA, F, B
McGuigan, Barry	1961-	10	25	45	Ireland, F
McLarnin, Jimmy	1906-	30	65	150	Ireland, W
Mercante, Arthur	1920-	5	15	45	USA, referee, RS
Miller, Freddie	1911-1962	60	125		USA, F
Montgomery, Bob	1919-1998	25	55	80	USA, L, RS
Monzon, Carlos	1942-1995	50	150	275	Argentina, M, elusive signer, "tough"
Moore, Archie	1913-1998	25	45	100	USA, LH, RS
Morrissey, John	1831-1878	600			Ireland
Muhammad, Matthew S.	1954-	5	15	50	USA, LH, "Matthew Franklin", RS
Muldoon, William	1845-1933	50	115		USA, trainer, official
Napoles, Jose	1940-	15	30	75	Cuba, W, elusive signer
Nelson, Battling	1882-1954	85	185		Denmark, L
Norton, Ken	1943-	15	30	75	USA, H, reluctant, yet RS
O'Brien, Philadelphia J.	1878-1942	100	200		USA, LH
Odd, Gilbert	1902- ?	30	70		England, writer, prolific
Olivares, Ruben	1947-	5	15	45	Mexico, B, F, RS
Olson, Carl "Bobo"	1928-2002	15	30	60	
Ortiz, Carlos	1936-	5	10	45	Puerto Rico, JW, L, RS
Ortiz, Manuel	1916-1970	70	150		USA, B
Papp, Lazlo	1926-2003	20	35	75	Olympic legend
Parker, Dan	1893-1967	35	60		USA, sports editor, columnist
Parnassus, George	1897-1975	35	70		Greece, promoter
Pastrano, Willie	1935-1997	25	55	120	USA, LH
Patterson, Floyd	1935-	15	30	75	USA, H, reluctant, yet RS
Pedroza, Eusebio	1953-	15	30	75	Panama, F
Pep, Willie	1922-	15	30	65	USA, F, RS
Perez, Pascual	1926-1977	60	135		Argentina, FL
Pryor, Aaron	1955-	5	15	45	USA, JW, RS
Ramos, "Sugar"	1941-	15	30	65	Cuba, F, L, RS
Rickard, George "Tex"	1871-1929	175	375		USA, promoter
Robinson, Sugar Ray	1920-1989	45	160	750	USA, W, M, RS
Rodriguez, Luis	1937-1996	15	40	175	Cuba, W
Rosenbloom, Maxie	1904-1976	45	150		USA, LH, RS
Ross, Barney	1909-1967	45	150	375	USA, W, JW, L

Name	db/dd	Sig.	SP	SG	Comments
Ryan, Tommy	1870-1948	165	370		USA, W, M
Saddler, Sandy	1926-2001	20	45	100	USA, F, JL, RS, SV
Salidivar, Vicente	1943-	15	35	75	Mexico, L
Sanchez, Salvador	1959-1982				Mexico, F, extremely scarce, PU
Schmeling, Max	1905-	30	75	200	Germany, H, RS
Sharkey, Jack	1902-1994	65	165	400	USA, H
Siler, George	1846-1908				USA, referee, PU
Solomons, Jack	?-1979	50	100		England, promoter
Spinks, Leon	1953-	5	15	40	USA, H
Spinks, Michael	1956-	10	25	60	USA, LH, H, can be elusive, FA
Steward, Emanuel	1944-	5	10	45	USA, trainer, manager
Stribling, Young	1904-1933	500	1250		USA, LH, H
Sullivan, John L .	1858-1918	1100	1800		USA, H
Taub, Sam	?-1979	50	110		USA, broadcaster
Taylor, Herman	1887-1980	35	85		USA, promoter
Terrell, Ernie	1939-	5	15	40	USA, H
Tiger, Dick	1929-1971	125	250	700	Nigeria, M, LH
Torres, Jose	1936-	5	15	50	Puerto Rico, LH, RS
Tunney, Gene	1897-1978	100	225	800	USA, H, RS
Turpin, Randy	1928-1966				England, M, scarce in all forms
Tyson, Mike	1966-	30	75	150	USA, H, controversial
Villa, Pancho	1901-1925	600			Philipines, FL, extremely scarce
Walcott, Jersey Joe	1914-1994	50	100	350	USA, H, RS
Walcott, Joe (Barbados)	1873-1935				Brit. West Indies, W, PU
Walker, James J.	1881-1946	35	50		USA, politician
Walker, Mickey	1901-1981	60	175	700	USA, W, M, RS
Welsh, Freddie	1886-1927				Wales, L, PU
Wilde, Jimmy	1892-1969	100	225		Wales, FL
Williams, Ike	1923-1994	25	50	175	USA, L, RS
Williams, Kid	1893-1963	80	165		Denmark, B
Wills, Harry	1889-1958	125	275		USA, H
Wright, Chalky	1912-1957	100	200		Mexico, F
Zale, Tony	1913-1997	25	50	200	USA, M, RS
Zarate, Carlos	1951-	25	55	135	Mexico, B, can be an elusive signer
Zivic, Fritzie	1913-1984	35	100		USA, W, RS

BUSINESS LEADERS, ECONOMISTS, FINANCIERS & PUBLISHERS

WHAT YOU NEED TO KNOW

* Names such as William C. Durant (General Motors), Ray Kroc (McDonalds), and Henry Ford (Ford Motor Co.), are just some of the examples of businessman whose lives have left a lasting impression on our society.

* Economists such as John Maynard Keynes, played a central role in British war finances during World War II and his economic theories, such as advocacy of a government-sponsored policy of full employment as a key to the recovery from a recession, are often quoted.

* Financiers such as August Belmont, a leading private banker in his time,were critical to the success of many influential businessman and to the international banking market.

* Publishers, such as Dewitt and Lila Acheson Wallace, founders of "The Reader's Digest," who focused on the literary needs of Middle America, through truncated articles published in a unique format.

* A now-accepted terminology for a popular form in this niche is "scripophily," which comes from the Greek: ophily (love of) and scrip (stock).

MARKET FACTS

* Popular with collectors in this niche of the hobby is the autographs of those business leaders who founded some of the most popular and recognizable corporations of our time.

* Popular forms in this market segment include photographs, stock certificates, bank checks, business cards and letters on corporate letterhead.

* Financiers's signatures appear in many forms including personal correspondence, business letters, legal documents, stocks, bonds, business cards, photographs, etc. The rarity of form and legibility of the signature - limited cancellation (punch holes, lines, etc...) are paramount considerations of value. The value of a security also derives from its historical importance.

* Forgeries, printed and secretarial signatures are commonly encountered.

MARKET TRENDS

* A word of caution, however, this segment of the market is prone to significant pricing variations particularly in the DS form. For example, stock certificates and mortgage bonds signed by "Wells & Fargo" and Jay Gould have shown major pricing variations.

* While it's probably no surprise that autographed material from John D. Rockefeller, Cornelius Vanderbilt, and Meyer Guggenheim have exhibited consistent and strong gains over the past twenty-five years, it may startle you when you see some of the prices commanded by individuals such as Howard Hughes, J. Paul Getty and Aristotle Onassis.

Abbreviations: ESPV = exhibits significant pricing variations, LU = letters uncommon, PU = pricing undetermined, RS = responsive signer

Name	db/dd	Sig.	DS	ALS	SP	Comments
Adams, Charles F., Jr.	1835-1915					Railroad executive, historian, PU
Adams, Henry C.	1851-1921					Economist, PU
Agnelli, Giovanni	1921-2003					Industrialist, Fiat, PU
Andreas, Dwayne O.	1918-	6	15		10	Honeymead Products CEO
Annenberg, Walter	1908-2002					Founder TV Guide, PU
Applebaum, Irwyn	1955-	5	10		8	Bantam Books President
Arden, Elizabeth	1884-1966	35	55	120	50	Founder of cosmetics empire
Arledge, David A.	1945-	5	10		5	Coastal Corporation President
Armour, Phillip D.	1832-1901	50			80	Industrialist, ev. meatpacking
Arrow, Kenneth	1921-	5	10		10	Economist
Artzt, Edwin L.	1930-	5	15		10	Procter & Gamble Director
Ash, Mary Kay	1915-	10	30	65	30	Mary Kay Cosmetics founder
Ashley, William H.	c.1788-1838					Businessman, political ldr., PU
Astor, John Jacob	1763-1848	350	1750	5000		Real estate magnate, banker
Astor, William B.	1792-1875	150				Heir of J.J. Astor, ANS - $145
Augustine, Norman R.	1935-	5	10		10	Lockheed Martin Chairman
Ayer, Francis W.	1848-1923	15	30	65	30	Ad industry pioneer
Bache, Jules		350	950	1450		Wall Street Founder
Baer, George F.	1842-1914	20	30	50	35	Financier
Barnum, Phineas T.	1810-1891	180	450	500	1100	Impresario, museum pass - $800
Barton, Bruce	1886-1967	20	45	50	30	Advertising executive, writer
Baruch, Bernard	1870-1965	80	275	400	250	Financier
Belasco, David	1853-1931	30	40	60	75	Theatrical producer
Belmont, August	1816-1890	200	675	830	400	Financier
Bennett, James G.	1795-1872	50	150	225		Editor
Bennett, James G., Jr.	1841-1918	35	60	100	40	Publisher
Bergson, Abram	1912-	5	10	20	15	Economist
Biddle, Nicholas	1786-1844	115	400	535	250	Banker
Bloch, Henry W.	1922-	15	30	100	40	H & R Block founder
Bose, Amar	1929-	10	20	55	15	Bose Corporation founder
Boskin, Michael	1942-	5	10	25	10	Economist, author

Name	db/dd	Sig.	DS	ALS	SP	Comments
Brady, James B.	1856-1917	500	1125	1280	875	U.S. financier, philanthropist
Bram, Leon	1931-	5	10	20	10	Funk & Wagnalls Vice president
Bryan, John Henry Jr.	1936-	5	10	20	10	Sara Lee chairman
Busch, Adolphus	1839-1913	375	2265	3000		German-born businessman
Campbell, Robert H.	1937-	5	10	25	10	Sun Company Inc. executive
Candler, Asa	1851-1929	600	1700	2250		Founded Coca-Cola Co.
Carey, Henry C.	1793-1879	30	50	70		Economist
Carey, Matthew	1760-1839	25	50	65		Publisher
Carnegie, Andrew	1835-1919	240	675	1150	1000	Industrialist, SALS - 2-4X, ESPV
Carney, Frank L.		10	20	40	25	Pizza Hut Restaurant founder
Carvel, Tom	1908-1989	35	65	100	60	Ice cream chain founder
Chapman, Morris H.	1940-	5	10	15	10	Southern Baptist Conven. CEO
Chrysler, Walter	1875-1940	365	1000	1000	700	Automotive executive
Colgate, William	1783-1857	30	110	145		Industrialist, philanthropist,
Cook, Lodwrick M.	1928-	5	15	20	10	Atlantic Richfield CEO
Cooke, Jay	1821-1905	275	1150	1875		Financier
Cooper, Peter	1791-1883	135	475	645		Industrialist, inventor, Cooper U
Cooper, Roger	1953-	5	10	15	10	Doubleday Book vice president
Cornell, Ezra	1807-1874	40	150	225	100	Bus.philan, ALS - con. $1100
Corning, Erastus	1794-1872	75	160	300		U.S. financier, N.Y. Central
Creighton, John W. Jr.	1932-	5	10	15	10	Weyerhaeuser Co. executive
Crocker, Charles	1822-1888					U.S. railroad, ESPV, PU
Cunard, Samuel	1787-1865	100	155	240		Pioneered trans-Atlantic steam
Curley, Tom	1948-	5	10	25	10	Pub. and Pres. of USA Today
Daly, Marcus	1841-1900	20	50	100		Irish-born copper magnate
Daniell, Robert F.	1934-	5	15	25	10	United Technologies executive
Darehshori, Nader	1936-	5	10	20	10	Houghton Mifflin Co. executive
Decrane, Alfred C.	1941-	5	15	30	10	Texaco CEO
Deere, John	1804-1886	425	1340	1500		Inventor, manufacturer
Delacorte, George T.	1893-1991	25	45	100	50	U.S. publisher
Dell, Michael S.	1965-	5	20	35	12	Dell Computer executive
Deming, W. Edwards	1900-1993	20	35	50	25	U.S. quality-control guru
Derr, K.T.	1936-	5	10	20	10	Chevron Corporation executive
Desimone, L.D.	1936-	5	12	25	10	3M executive
Dodge, Grenville M.	(see Civil War - Union Generals)					
Dow, Herbert H.	1866-1930	45	100	165	75	U.S. chemical company founder
Drew, Daniel	1797-1879	1250				American financier, DS - $8500
Drew, Ernest H.	1937-	5	10	15	10	Hoechst Celanese Corp. exec.
du Pont, Eleuthere	1771-1834					French/U.S. gunpowder, PU
Du Pont, Pierre S.	1870-1954	150	300		250	Business leader
Duke, James	1856-1925	215				Amer. Tobacco fdr., SDS-$2000
Durant, Thomas	1820-1885	45	250	400		U.S. railroad official, financier
Durant, William C.	1861-1947	275	750	1100		U.S. industrialist, formed GM
Eastman, George	1854-1932	300	1000	2650	1500	U.S. inventor, photo. equip.
Eaton, Robert J.	1940-	5	10	15	10	Chrysler Corporation exec., RS
Eccles, Marriner S.	1890-1977	30	55	80	45	Businessman, banker
Eiger, Richard	1933-	5	10	15	10	Publisher
Fargo, William G.	1818-1881	435	800	1450		American Express founder

Name	db/dd	Sig.	DS	ALS	SP	Comments
Field, Cyrus W.	1819-1892	150	375	865		Merchant, financier
Field, Marshall	1834-1906	325	850	1125	600	U.S. merchant, dept. store Fdr.
Fink, Albert	1827-1897	60	140	300		Railroad engineer
Firestone, Harvey	1868-1938	325	1000	1275	500	U.S. tire company fdr., SDS-3X
Fisher, Avery	1906-1994	25	60	115	40	U.S. industrialist, philanthropist
Fisher, George M. C.	1940-	5	10	20	10	Eastman Kodak CEO, RS
Fisk, James Jr.	1834-1872					Financier, ESPV - all forms, PU
Flagler, Henry M.	1830-1913	1000	2100	5650		U.S. fin., S.Oil, dev. , SDS - 6X
Fletcher, Philip B.	1933-	5	10	15	10	ConAgra Inc. executive
Fogel, Robert W.	1926-	10	15	20	15	Economist
Forbes, John M.	1813-1898	35	75	125		Financier, merchant
Forbes, Malcolm	1919-1990	40	75	150	80	U.S. magazine publisher, RS
Ford, Edsel	1893-1943	250	500		500	Ford Motor Co.
Ford, Henry	1863-1947	995	3000	4000	2650	U.S. auto maker, ESPV
Ford, Henry II	1917-1987	15	30	75	50	U.S. auto maker head, RS
Frick, Henry C.	1849-1919	200	425	875		U.S. magnate, recluse
Friedman, Milton	1912-	5	15	30	10	Economist, Nobel Prize winner
Fuller, Alfred C.	1885-1973	100	150	200	160	Canadia-born businessman
Gaines, William	1922-1992	25	55	125	50	Mad mag. creator, ANS - $95
Galbraith, John Kenneth	1908-	20	40	75	25	Economist
Gallup, George	1901-1984	25	275	300	50	Pollster
Gannett, Frank E.	1876-1957	35	175	200	50	Newspaperman
Gardner, John	1912-	5	10	15	10	Carnegie Corporation president
Gary, Elbert H.	1846-1927	115	375	525	220	U.S Steel chairman 1903-1927
Gates, Bill	1955-	25	75		50	Microsoft founder
Gault, Stanley	1926-	5	15	20	10	Goodyear Tire & Rubber Co.
Gerstner, Louis V.	1941-	10	30	75	25	I.B.M. CEO
Getty, Jean Paul	1892-1976	225	650	1750	430	U.S. oil empire head
Giannini, Amadeo P.	1870-1949	125	250	500	275	Founded Bank of America
Girard, Stephen	1750-1831	140	300	350		French-born financier, philan.
Goizueta, Robert C.	1931-	20	50		50	Fmr. Coca-Cola Company CEO
Goldenson, Leonard H.	1905-1999					PU
Gould, Jay	1836-1892	200	625		1500	U.S. RR, fin.., RR pass - $425
Grann, Phyllis E.	1937-	5	10	15	10	Publisher
Green, Hetty	1834-1916	1450	3000			U.S. financier, "Witch of ..."
Greenspan, Alan	1926-	5	15	30	10	Federal Reserve chairman
Gregg, William	1800-1867	25	50	70		Launched south. textile industry
Grove, Andrew S.	1936-	10	20	25	15	Intel executive
Guggenheim, Daniel	1856-1930	45	100	130	60	Industrialist
Guggenheim, Meyer	1828-1905	100	325	465	225	Swiss-born merchant, philan.
Hagelstein, Robert	1942-	5	10		10	Greenwood Publishing Group
Hammer, Armand	1898-1990	60	200	300	150	Occidental Petroleum, BC - $45
Hansen, Alvin H.	1887-1975	20	45	70	25	Economist
Hardymon, James F.	1934-	5	10	20	10	Textron CEO
Harper, James	1795-1869	50	230	415		Publisher
Harriman, Edward H.	1848-1909	170	475			U.S. rail. pioneer, Union Pacific
Havemeyer, Henry O.	1847-1907	40	75	140		Manufacturer
Hayward, Charles	1950-	5	10	15	10	Publishing executive
Hearst, George	1820-1891	300	600	900		
Hearst, William R.	1863-1951	240	590	600	600	Built U.S. publishing empire

Name	db/dd	Sig.	DS	ALS	SP	Comments
Hefner, Hugh M.	1926-	25	75	100	50	Pub. Playboy, STLS- 9X
Heimbold, Charles	1933-	5	10	20	10	Bristol Myers Squibb CEO
Heinz, Henry J.	1844-1919	125	250	725	300	Founded U.S. food empire
Hewlett, William R.	1913-	20	50	125	25	Hewlett Packard co-founder
Hill, James J.	1838-1916	365	1000	2000		Canadian-born railroad magnate
Hilton, Conrad N.	1888-1979	75	130	205	150	U.S. hotel chain founder
Hopkins, Johns	1795-1873	200	650	2100		American financier
Hopkins, Mark	1813-1878	1250				CA RR, letters common form
Hughes, Howard	1905-1976	1750	4500	7000	2500	U.S. industrialist, aviator
Hunt, H.L.	1889-1974	100	320	410	200	Oil magnate
Huntington, Collis P.	1821-1900	150	450		750	Letters-rare, AQS - $175
Huntington, Henry E.	1850-1927	75	150	265		U.S. railroad builder
Hyde, H.B.	1834-1899	10	20	35		Insurance executive
Iacocca, Lido (Lee) A.	1924-	10	35	65	25	Automotive executive
Insull, Samuel	1859-1938	135	625	800		Businessman
Irani, Ray R.	1935-	5	10	15	10	Occidental Petroluem Corp
Jacobs, Walter L.	1898-1985	30	70	100	50	Fdr. first car rental agency - Hertz
Jobs, Steven	1955-	20	30	60	25	Co-founder Apple Computer
Johnson, Howard	1896-1972	75	150	220	100	U.S. restaurant founder
Johnson, John H.	1918-	20	45	100	40	Publisher
Jordan, Jerry L.	1941-	5	15	20	10	Economist
Jordan, Michael	1936 -	10	20	25	15	Westinghouse Elec. Corp.
Judah, Theodore D.						Trans. RR fdr., rare in all forms
Junkins, Jerry R.	1937-	5	12	20	10	Texas Instruments CEO
Kahn, Otto H.	1867-1934	30	75	100	65	Wall Street banker, broker
Kaiser, Henry J.	1882-1967	170	575		250	U.S. industrialist, steel alum.czar
Kalikow, Peter	1848-1929	55	180		100	U.S. railroad mag., United Fruit
Kellogg, Will K.	1860-1951	125	200	350	200	U.S. businessman, philan.
Keynes, John Maynard	1883-1946	100	395	700	250	Economist, STLS - 4X
King, Richard	1825-1885	25	50	75		U.S. cattleman, rancher
Kndleberger, II, Chas. P.		5	10	20	10	Economist
Knight, Charles F.	1936-	5	10	20	10	Emerson Elec. Co. executive
Knight, Philip H.	1938-	20	30	75	25	Nike Inc. founder
Knott, Walter		25	75	100	135	Founder Knotts Berry Farm
Knudsen, William S.	1879-1948	25	50	100	50	Danish-born auto executive
Kress, Samuel H.	1863-1955	35	75	115	75	U.S. buisnessman, "dime store"
Kroc, Ray A.	1902-1984	75	200	275	225	Founded McDonald's , RS
Krupp, Alfred	1812-1887	150	400	500		German armaments magante
Kuznets, Simon Smith	1901-1985	20	45	60	25	Economist
Larsen, Ralph S.	1938-	5	10	15	10	Johnson & Johnson executive
Lawrence, Amos	1786-1852	40	100	150		Merchant
Lazarus, Charles		15	25	75	25	Toys 'R' Us founder
Lee, Ivy L.	1877-1934	25	50	100		Businessman, publicist
Leland, Henry M.	1843-1932	825	1680			Lincoln Motor Co.
Lever, William	1851-1925	40	100	230	125	British philanthropist
Levitt, William	1907-1994	20	50	80	30	Industrialist, "suburb maker"
Lippencott, Jr., Walter	1919-	5	10	20	10	Publisher
Lipton, Thomas	1850-1931	100	375	600	350	Built tea empire, merchant

Name	db/dd	Sig.	DS	ALS	SP	Comments
Long, Elizabeth	1950-	10	25	45	20	Publisher, "People"
Lowell, Francis C.	1775-1817	45	80	125		Industrialist, inventor
Luce, Henry R.	1898-1967	60	125	250	100	Publisher
Mackay, John W.	1831-1902	95	200	300	150	Mining Czar
Madigan, John	1937-	5	15	20	10	Tribune Newspaper Co. exec.
Mahoney, Richard J.	1934-	5	10	20	10	Monsanto Co. CEO
Mark, Reuben	1934-	5	10	25	10	Colgate-Palmolive Co. CEO
Markowitz, Harry	1927-	10	20	25	20	Economist, responsive signer
McDonald, Richard J.		95	250	400	190	Hamburger chain founder
McGill, James	1744-1813	80	175	250		University founder
McGowan, William C.		10	25	25	20	MCI Communications Corp.
McKay, Donald	1810-1880	50	100	200		Shipbuilder
Mellon, Andrew W.	1855-1937	200	625	865	300	Industrialist, fin., National Gallery
Merrill, Charles E.	1885-1956	35	100	150	75	U.S. financier, Merrill Lynch
Miles, Michael A.	1939-	10	20	25	15	Philip Morris CEO
Milken, Michael	1946-	10	35	60	25	Financier
Miller, Robert L.	1949-	10	20	25	15	Time Inc. president
Mitchell, Wesley C.	1874-1948	20	35	50	60	Economist
Monaghan, Thomas S.	1937-	10	25	65	25	Domino's Pizza founder
Morgan, John Pierpoint	1837-1913	255	1000	1750		M. Bond - $600, SP - rare
Morgan, John Pier., Jr.	1867-1943	155	245		200	Financier
Morita, Akio	1921-1999	30	100		75	Co-founded SONY
Muir, Malcolm	1885-1979	40	80	150	65	Created Bus. Week, Newsweek
Munsey, Frank A.	1854-1925	25	50	70	65	Publisher, financier
Murdoch, Rupert	1931-	10	25	50	30	News Corporation Ltd. CEO
Murray, Allen E.	1929-	5	10	20	10	Retired Mobil Corp. executive
Musgrave, Richard A.	1910-	10	25	50	20	"The Theory of Public Finance"
Newhouse, Samuel	1895-1979	25	60	125	60	U.S. publishing, broadcast mag.
North, Douglass C.	1920-	10	25	40	15	Economist, educator
Nyren, Neil S.		5	10	15	15	G.P. Putnam's Sons executive
O'Reilly, Anthony F.J.	1936-	5	10	20	10	H.J. Heinz Co. executive
Ochs, Adolph S.	1858-1935	50	100	200	75	Publisher
Olsen, Kenneth H.	1929-	10	20	45	20	Digital Equipment Corp. founder
Onassis, Aristotle	1906-1975	200	400	1000	250	Shipping Magnate
Osborne, Burl	1937-	5	10	15	10	Publisher
Pace, Arrow K.	1921-	10	20	30	15	Economist, educator
Paley, William S.	1901-1990	25	45	75	40	Built CBS com. empire
Parker, Louis	1906-	10	20		15	Parker Instrument Co. executive
Parkinson, Roger	1942-	5	10	15	10	Globe and Mail CEO
Peabody, George	1795-1869	50	115	415		U.S. financier, philanthropist
Penney, James C.	1875-1971	75	275	325	255	U.S. businessman, dept. store
Penniman, Nicholas G.	1938-	5	10	20	10	Publisher
Perkins, George W.	1862-1920	20	40	50	30	Businessman, political leader
Perot, Henry Ross	1930-	15	35	130	50	EDS Corp. founder
Pfeiffer, Eckhard	1941-	10	20	30	10	Compaq Computer Corp CEO
Phelps, Ashton Jr.	1945-	5	10	15	10	Publisher
Philipson, Morris	1926-	5	10	20	10	Publisher
Picard, Dennis J.	1932-	10	15	25	10	Raytheon Co. CEO

Name	db/dd	Sig.	DS	ALS	SP	Comments
Pinkerton, Allan	1819-1884	250	575	1400	1000	Detective
Pinkham, Lydia Estes	1819-1883	40	100	125		Businesswoman
Platt, Lewis E.	1942 -	5	10	20	10	Hewlett-Packard Co. CEO
Poole, William	1937-	10	25	45	15	Economist, educator
Poor, Henry W.	1812-1905	25	50	60		Business leader
Popoff, Frank P.	1935-	5	10	25	10	Dow Chemical Co. CEO
Post, Marjorie M.		30	95	145	50	Philanthropist
Procter, William C.	1862-1934	40	100	200	75	Headed U.S. soap company
Pulliam, Eugene	1914-	5	10	15	10	News America Publishing CEO
Pullman, George M.	1831-1897	250	500	600		Industrialist, inventor
Quinson, Bruno A.	1938-	5	10	15	10	Henry Holt & Co. CEO
Raymond, Lee	1938-	10	20	25	15	Exxon CEO
Ricciardi, Lawrence R.	1941-	5	10	20	10	RJR Nabisco Inc. executive
Ringling, John	1866-1936	130	555		600	Showman
Ringling, Otto	1858-1911	250	500		650	Showman
Rockefeller, John D.	1839-1937	425	1500	1850	1500	Standard Oil, SB-$1500
Rockefeller, John D., Jr.	1874-1960	65	100	250	75	Industr., UN, T. Deed - $2200
Rockefeller, John Dav.	1906-1978	50	100		75	
Rosenwald, Julius	1862-1932	300	850	1275	640	Business leader, philanthropist
Rostow, Walt	1916-	10	25	30	15	Economist, advisor to JFK
Rothschild, Amschel M.	1773-1855	150	325			Frankfurt Est., LU
Rothschild, James	1792-1868	150	325	580		Paris Est., LU
Rothschild, Karl M.	1788-1855	150	300			Naples Est., LU
Rothschild, Mayer A.	1743-1812	200	365	525		Founded inter. banking house
Rothschild, Nathan	1777-1836	355	715	1425		Banker, ICSF bond available
Rothschild, Salomon M.	1774-1855	160	300			Vienna bank, LU
Rubin, Robert	1938-	10	25	40	25	Economist, Clinton advisor
Rubin, Stephen E.	1941-	10	25		20	Doubleday CEO
Rubinstein, Helena	1870-1965	70	200	275	295	Cosmetics
Ruml, Beardsley	1894-1960	10	20	25	20	Economist, banker
Ryan, Thomas Fortune	1851-1928	30	75	165	80	U.S. , Fndr. American Tobacco
Safrs, Edmond J.	1932-1999					Republic National Bank of NY
Sage, Russell	1816-1906	185	6400	1260		U.S. financier
Samuelson, Paul A.	1915-	10	30	50	25	Economist, educator
Sanders, Colonel Har.	1890-1980	50	125	175	125	KFC founder, RS
Sanders, Wayne R.	1947-	5	10	20	10	Kimberly-Clark CEO
Sarnoff, David	1891-1971	75	360		100	U.S. broadcasting pioneer, NBC
Schiff, Jacob H.	1847-1920	120	440	500		Financier
Schmalensee, Richard	1944-	5	15	20	10	Economist
Schultz, Theodore W.	1902-	10	20	25	15	Economist, educator
Schumpeter, Joseph A.	1883-1950	15	30	55	25	Economist
Schwab, Charles M.	1862-1939	40	80	125	100	Industrialist
Schwab, Charles R.	1937-	15	25	35	25	Charles Schwab & Co. founder
Scott, Thomas A.	1823-1881	24	40	55	40	Businessman
Sears, Richard	1863-1914					Fnd. U.S. mail-order co., PU
Shrontz, Frank A.	1931-	5	15	20	10	Boeing CEO
Siemens, Werner von	1816-1892	150	425			German industrialist, inventor
Silas, C.J.	1932-	10	15	15	15	Phillips Petroleum Company
Sisler, William P.	1947-	5	10	15	10	Publisher

Name	db/dd	Sig.	DS	ALS	SP	Comments
Slater, Samuel	1768-1835	160	450	600		Manufacturer
Sloan, Alfred P.	1875-1966	50	75	125	65	Industrialist, philanthropist, GM
Smith, Frederick	1944-	10	25	35	20	Federal Express Corp. founder
Solow, Robert M.	1924-	10	25	50	20	Economist, educator, RS
Sperry, Elmer A.	1860-1930	175	350	500	200	Inventor, engineer
Sprinkel, Beryl	1923-	10	20	40	15	Economist, Reagan advisor, RS
Stafford, John R.	1937-	5	15	20	10	American Home Products Corp.
Stanford, A. Leland	1824-1893	250	1600		450	U.S. RR official, philan.ESPV
Stapleton, Joan		10	20	40	15	New Republic president,
Steere, William C., Jr.	1936-	5	10	25	10	Pfizer Inc. CEO
Stein, Herbert	1916-	5	10	20	10	Economist, s. of Ben Stein, RS
Steinway, Henry	1797-1871	135	300	600		Industrialist
Steinway, Christian	1825-1889	80	145	300		Industrialist
Steinway, William	1835-1896	65	125	240		Industrialist
Stigler, George	1911-1991	10	20	40	20	Economist, educator
Stiritz, William P.	1934-	5	10	15	10	Ralston-Purina Co. executive
Straus, Nathan	1848-1931	115	165		75	German-born merchant, Macy's
Straus, Roger W.	1917-	15	30	55	25	Farrar, Starus, & Giroux, pub.
Strauss, Levi	c.1829-1902					U.S. pants manufacturer, PU
Strong, Benjamin	1872-1928	25	70	100		Banker
Strothman, Wendy J.	1950-	5	10	20	15	Publisher
Strutton, Larry D.	1940-	5	10	15	10	Publisher, Rocky Mt. News CEO
Studebaker, Clement	1831-1901	175	445	550		U.S. wagon and carriage man.
Sulzberger, Arthur O.	1926-	15	40	60	20	New York Times CEO
Swift, Gustavus	1839-1903	100	265	400		U.S. pioneer meatpacker
Swift, Louis F.	1861-1937	65	125	300		U.S. meatpacker
Swops, Gerard	1872-1957	50	120	135	100	U.S. industrialist, head G.E.
Taylor, Frederick W.	1856-1915	20	40	50	35	Manufacturer, social scientist
Taylor, William		5	10	15	10	Publisher
Tellep, Daniel M.	1931-	5	10	20	10	Aviation executive
Thierot, Richard		5	10	20	10	Publisher
Thomas, Dave	1932-2002	20	50		45	Wendy's founder, RS
Thompson, James W.	1847-1928	30	75	150	50	U.S. ad executive
Thomson, John E.	1808-1874	30	65	110		Financier, railroad leader
Tobin, James	1919-	10	20	30	15	Economist, educator, RS
Tooker, Gary L.	1939-	10	25		15	Motorola Inc. CEO
Trotman, Alexander J.	1933-	10	30		20	Ford Motor Co. president
Trump, Donald	1946-	20	75	100	35	Businessman
Tugwell, Rexford G.	1891-1979	15	25	40	20	Economist
Tully, Alice	1902-1993	25	45	75	45	Philanthropist, art patron
Turner, Ted	1938-	10	60	125	30	Cable News Network founder
Tyson, Laura D.	1947-	5	15	30	15	Economist, Clinton advisor
Urbanowski, Frank	1936-	5	10	15	10	Publisher, MIT Press
Vagelos, Pindaros R.	1929-	5	10	25	10	Merck & Comapny, Inc. CEO
Vail, Theodore N.	1845-1920	50	160	225		Organized Bell Telephone
Valenti, Carl		10	15	30	15	Publisher, The W. St.Journal
Vanderbilt, Cornelius	1794-1877	500	2250		3000	U.S. financier, est. railroad emp.
Vanderbilt, Cornelius, J.	1843-1899	200	750		450	Financier, railroad president
Vanderbilt, Frederick W.	1856-1938	155	400		375	Railroad leader

Name	db/dd	Sig.	DS	ALS	SP	Comments
Vanderbilt, George W.	1862-1914	225	465	800	300	Biltmore House
Vanderbilt, Harold S.	1884-1970	75	200		125	NY Central lines, Americas Cup
Vanderbilt, William H.	1821-1885	225	700		450	Railroad leader
Vanderbilt, William K.	1849-1920	200	500	1000	400	Railroad leader, yachtsman
Villard, Henry	1835-1900	30	65	125		U.S./German born railroad exec.
Walgreen, Charles R.	1873-1939	50	75	150	80	Founded drugstore chain
Wallace, DeWitt	1889-1981	55	175	225	150	Reader's Digest
Wallace, Lila	1889-1984	55	175	225	150	Cofounder of Reader's Digest
Walton, Sam	1918-1992	75	150	275	120	U.S. founder of Wall-Mart stores
Wanamaker, John	1838-1922	60	100	200	100	U.S. depat.-store pioneer
Warburg, Paul M.	1868-1932	25	40	55	45	Banker
Ward, Aaron Mont.	1843-1913	65	150	240	125	Established first mail-order firm.
Watson, Thomas J.	1874-1956	100	350		175	Head of IBM 1914-1956
Weidenbaum, Murray L.	1927-	10	20	40	15	Economist, educator, author
Weil, Louis A. III	1941-	5	10	20	10	Publisher, The Arizona Rep.
Welch, John F., Jr.	1935-	15	50	100	25	General Electric Co. CEO
Westinghouse, George	1846-1914	300	650	775	400	Inventor, Westingjhouse Elec.
Whitney, John Hay	1905-1982	25	75	150	75	U.S. publisher, sportsman
Whitwan, David R.	1942-	5	10	20	10	Whirpool Corp. executive
Will, George	1884-1946	140	325	475	250	American Tobacco
Wilson, Charles E.	1890-1961	25	45		40	U.S. auto industry executive
Wilson, Kemmons		35	100	135	95	Holiday Inn chain founder, RS
Winter, Alan	1937-	5	10	15	10	fm.Publisher, Cam.Univ. Press
Woolard, Edgar S., Jr.	1934-	10	30		20	Du Pont chairman
Woolworth, Frank W.	1852-1919	415	1600			Created five and dime store
Wrigley, Philip K.	1894-1977	75	150	225	150	Cubs owner, RS
Wrigley, William, Jr.	1861-1932	150	350	430	200	U.S. chewing gum founder
Young, Jane		5	10	15	15	Publisher, The Atlantic Monthly

CARTOONISTS

WHAT YOU NEED TO KNOW

* A cartoon is typically a drawing intended as satire, caricature, or humor and even political.

* There are many forms in this area popular with collectors including caricatures, comic strips, comic book panels, character studies, and production cels. The form of choice in this area is typically that most associated with the subject.

* A popular response from cartoonists to autograph requests is often a quick signed drawing or sketch.

* Collectors in this area should familiarize themself with the common forms associated with their subject and its availability.

* Many animation studios and magazines have strict rules regarding the creation, use and disposal of material.

MARKET FACTS

* The value for a signed drawing (SD) depends on the character(s) drawn, detail, medium (pen, ink, etc.), and the period. Drawings done at the pinnacle of a cartoonists career are the most sought.

* While uncommon, forgeries in this area may be encountered.

* With so many diverse forms available in this market, pricing is often inconsistent.

* Material encountered in this area is far more sporadic than that in other niches.

TRENDS

* While popular current material is favored with collectors, the market continues to be driven by major contributors such as Disney Studios.

* Political cartooning, typically fueled by controversy, continues to be a very popular area of collecting.

* Most cartoonists are aware of the market value for their work in many forms, so many have opted for generic answers to autograph requests.

Notes/Abbreviations: PU = pricing undetermined, SD = signed drawing refers to those done for collectors and not for published work, RS = responsive signer

Name	Dates	Sig.	DS	ALS	SD	Comments
Adams, Scott	1957-	20	40		55	"Dilbert"
Addams, Chas.	1912-1988	60	125		450	Macabre cartoons, "The Addams Family"
Anderson, Brad	1924-	10	15	20	25	"Marmaduke", RS
Aragines, Serg.	1937-					MAD magazine, PU
Armstrong, Tom		10			35	"Marvin", RS
Arno, Peter	1904-1968	25	40	60	50	New Yorker contributor
Arriola, Gus		10			25	Gordo
Avery, Tex	1908-1980	30	50		450	Animator of Bugs Bunny, Porky Pig
Babbitt, Arthur	1907-1992	15	30			Disney cartoonist
Baker, George	1915-1975	35	70		300	"The Sad Sack"
Banks, Carl	1901-2000					Donald Duck comic books, PU
Beck, C.C.	1910-1989	25	50		150	"Captain Marvel"
Berg, Dave	1920-2002	15	35			MAD magazine, PU
Berry, Jim	1932-	10	20		25	"Berry's World"
Blake, Bud		10			25	"Tiger", RS
Block, Herb	1909-	15	35		125	Political cartoonist
Booth, George	1926-	10	25		45	New Yorker cartoonist
Brady, Pat		10	20		25	"Rose is Rose"
Breathed, Berk.	1957-	15	30		155	"Bloom County"
Briggs, Clare	1875-1930	25	50		65	"Mr. & Mrs."
Browne, Dik	1917-1989	15			45	"Hi & Lois", "Hagar the Horrible", RS
Buell, Marjorie	1904-1993	15	30			"Little Lulu"
Bushmiller, Ern.	1905-1982	25	50	100	150	"Nancy"
Caniff, Milton	1907-1988	30	100		175	"Terry and the Pirates", "Steve Canyon"
Capp, Al	1909-1979	100	200		275	"Li'l Abner"
Chast, Roz	1954-	10	25		35	New Yorker, "bonfire of the banalities"
Clokey, Art		15	30		30	"Gumby", RS
Conrad, Paul	1924-	10	25		50	Political cartoonist
Crane, Roy	1901-1977	40	75		200	"Captain Easy", "Buz Sawyer"
Crumb, Robert	1943-	30	50		100	"Underground" cartoonist
Culhane, Sham.	1908-1996	15	30			Animator
Darling, Jay N.	1876-1962	30	75		175	Political cartoonist
Davis, Jack	1926-	10	30			"MAD" magazine
Davis, Jim	1945-	30	60		150	"Garfield"
DeBeck, Billy	1890-1942	35			200	"Barney Google"
Dirks, Rudolph	187-1968	80			425	"The Katzenjammer Kids"
Disney, Walt	1901-1966	1650	3500			Producer cartoons, Mickey Mouse
Ditko, Steve	1927-	15	60			"Spider-man"
Drucker, Mort	1929-	20	55			"MAD" magazine
Eisner, Will	1917-	10	30			"The Spirit"
Feiffer, Jules	1929-	10			70	Village Voice cartoonist
Fisher, Bud	1884-1954	125	150		275	"Mutt & Jeff"
Fisher, Ham	1900-1955	125			300	"Joe Palooka"
Flagg, James M.	1877-1960	100	200		500	Illustrator, "Uncle Sam" recruiting poster

Name	Dates	Sig.	DS	ALS	SD	Comments
Fleischer, Max	1883-1972	55	325		450	"Betty Boop"
Foster, Hal	1892-1982	60			420	"Tarzan", "Prince Valiant"
Fox, Fontaine	1884-1964	40			225	"Toonerville Folks"
Freleng, Isadore	1905-1995	40	75		225	Animator, Porky Pig, Yosemite Sam
Frueh, Al	1880-1968	55	130			New Yorker cartoonist
Gallo, Bill		15			50	
Goldberg, Rube	1883-1970	65			160	"Boob McNutt"
Gould, Chester	1900-1985	55			400	"Dick Tracy"
Gray, Harold	1894-1968	125			525	"Little Orphan Annie"
Groening, Matt	1954-	30	75		175	"The Simpsons", unresponsive signer
Guisewite, Ca.	1950-	15	40		70	"Cathy", responsive signer
Hanna, Bill	1910-	35	75		150	Animators, "Tom & Jerry", "Flintstones"
Barbera, Joe	1911-	35	75		150	Animators, "Tom & Jerry", "Flintstones"
Hart, Johnny	1931-	10	35		155	"BC", "Wizard of Id", RS
Harrington, Oliv.	1912-1995					"Bootsie", PU
Harvey, Alfred	1913-1994					"Casper the Friendly Ghost", PU
Hatio, Jimmy	1898-1963	15	60		100	"Little Iodine"
Held, John Jr.	1889-1958	175			600	"Jazz Age" cartoonist
Herriman, Geo.	1881-1944	75			700	"Krazy Kat"
Hershfield, Har.	1885-1974	25			145	"Abie the Agent"
Hirschfeld, Al	1903-2003	40	125		400	NY Times Entertainment caricaturist
Hobart, Nick		10			30	
Hoest, Bunny		10			25	
Hogarth, Burne	1911-1996	30			270	"Tarzan"
Hokinson, Hel.	1900-1949	30			125	Satirized clubwomen
Hollander, Nic.	1939-	10	40		65	"Sylvia"
Johnston, Lynn	1947-	25			100	"For Better or For Worse"
Jones, Chuck	1912-2002	30			200	Animator, Bugs Bunny, Porky Pig
Judge, Mike	1962-	25				"Beavis & Butt-head", "King of the Hill"
Kane, Bob	1916-1998	65			525	"Batman"
Keane, Bill	1922-	10	30		45	"The Family Circus", RS
Kelly, Walt	1913-1973	65	175		450	"Pogo"
Kelley, Steve		10	20		25	Editotrial cartoonist, RS
Ketcham, Hank	1920-2001	30	75		125	"Dennis the Menace", RS
Key, Ted	1912-	10	25		35	"Hazel", RS
King, Frank	1883-1969	40	100		200	"Gasoline Alley"
Kirby, Jack	1917-1994	50	150		225	'Fantastic Four", "The Incredible Hulk"
Kirby, Rollin	1875-1952	25	50		110	Political cartoonist
Kliban, Bernard	1935-1991	25	115		225	Cat books
Koren, Edward	1935-	10	30		80	New Yorker cartoonist
Kurtzman, Harv.	1921-1993	25	60			"MAD" magazine, PU
Lantz, Walter	1900-1994	75	100		165	"Woody Woodpecker"
Larson, Gary	1950-	25	75		150	"The Far Side", elusive signer
Lazarus, Mell	1929-	15	30		35	"Momma", "Miss Peach"
Lee, Stan	1922-			25	100	200 Marvel Comics
Levine, David	1926-	10	35		125	"N.Y. Review of Books" caricatures

Name	Dates	Sig.	DS	ALS	SD	Comments
MacNelly, Jeff	1947-2000	25	60		165	Political cartoonist, "Shoe"
Margulies, Jimmy		10	20		25	Editorial cartoonists
Mariette, Doug	1949-	10	20		50	Editorial cartoonist, "Kudzu"
Martin, Don	1931-	15	35			"MAD" magazine
Mauldin, Bill	1921-	50	135		300	"GI" cartoonist of WWII
McCay, Winsor	1872-1934	75	175		700	"Little Nemo"
McCutcheon, JT.	1870-1949	20			60	Midwestern rural life cartoonist
McGruder, Aaron	1974-	15	30		50	"The Boondocks"
McManus, Geo.	1884-1954	50	100		225	"Bringing Up Father"
Messick, Dale	1906-	25	60		150	"Brenda Starr"
Mingo, Norman	1896-1980	40	100			"Alfred E. Neuman"
Montana, Bob	1920-1975	50	100		200	"Archie"
Moores, Dick	1909-1986	25	50		100	"Gasoline Alley", RS
Mullin, Willard	1902-1978	20	40		60	Sports cartoonist
Murphy, John C.		10	20		25	
Myers, Russell	1938-	10	25		75	"Broom Hilda", RS
Nast, Thomas	1840-1902	145	315		950	Political, created pol. party symbols
Oliphant, Pat	1935-	15	25		35	Political cartoonist
Opper, Fredrick	1857-1937	40	100		300	"Happy Hooligan"
Outcault, Rich.	1863-1928	100	200		465	"Yellow Kid", "Buster Brown"
Parker, Brant	1920-					"Wizard of Id", PU
Parker, Trey	1969-	30	60		100	"South Park"
Peters, Mike	1943-	15	30		50	Editorial, "Mother Goose" & "Grimm"
Price, George	1901-1995	20	30		45	New Yorker cartoonist
Prohias, Anton.	1921-1998					"Spy vs. Spy", PU
Raymond, Alex	1909-1956	50	200		500	"Flash Gordon", "Jungle Jim"
Sagendorf, F.(Bud)	1915-1994	50	120		275	"Popeye"
Sansom, Art	1920-1991	20	30		40	"The Born Loser"
Scaduto, Al		10	20		25	RS
Schultz, Charles	1922-2000	125	250		1250	"Peanuts", ESPV
Sears, Bart		10	20		25	Comic book artist
Segar, Elzie C.	1894-1938	140	275		625	"Popeye" creator
Shuster, Joe	1914-1992	175	350		1200	
Siegel, Jerry	1914-1996	175	335		1200	"Superman"
Smith, Sydney	1887-1935	60	100		215	"The Gumps"
Soglow, Otto	1900-1975	30	75		125	"Little Kings", "Canyon Kiddies"
Spiegelman, Art	1948-	10	20		35	Raw, Maus
Steig, William	1907-	25	40		115	New Yorker cartoonist
Stone, Matt	1971-	30	50		100	"South Park", PU
Swinnerton, Jas	1875-1974	40	75		200	"Little Jimmy"
Szep, Paul	1941-	20	30		50	Political cartoonist
Terry, Paul	1887-1971	70	125		300	Mighty Mouse animator
Thaves, Bob	1924-	10	15		30	"Frank and Ernest"
Thurber, James	1894-1961	125	230		610	New Yorker cartoonist
Trudeau, Garry	1948-	25	60		200	"Doonesbury"
Turner, Morrie		10	15		20	RS

Name	Dates	Sig.	DS	ALS	SD	Comments
Wagner, John		15	20		35	"Maxine", RS
Walker, Mort	1923-	10	30		60	"Beetle Bailey"
Watterson, Bill	1958-	25				"Calvin and Hobbes", SD - scarce
Westover, Russ	1887-1966	30	60		120	"Tillie the Toiler"
Wilder, John		10	15		20	"Crock"
Wilkinson, Sign.	1950-	20	30		50	Political cartoonist
Willard, Frank	1893-1958	45	100		255	"Moon Mullins"
Williams, J.R.	1888-1957	30	75		140	"Out Our Way"
Wilson, Gahan	1930-	15	40		70	Macabre cartoonist
Wilson, Tom	1931-	15	30		55	"Ziggy"
Young, Art	1866-1943	30	65		165	Political cartoonist, satirist
Young, Chic	1901-1973	45	100		225	"Blondie"

The Generals of The Civil War

While controversies have raged even decades after the Civil War as to who was, or wasn't, entitled to be called "General," such has been the case with nearly every war. As the line of demarcation in many individual cases still fluctuates, you as a collector may be forced to make an addition or deletion, but consider this your "Executive Privilege." The record, for what it's sometimes worth, states 425 individuals received appointments by the President to one of the four grades of general. When the war ended 126 had fallen prey to attrition, while 299 remained.

Acquiring the signatures of the Generals of the Confederacy has been a task undertaken for decades by many outstanding and dedicated collectors. While many collectors prefer "war-dated" signatures, many C.S.A. generals signatures in any form have become so scarce that date simply doesn't matter. Similar to collecting the "Signers" of the Declaration of Independence, acquiring this finite set of 425 reflects one of the most difficult tasks in the hobby. Fortunately for collectors, many examples from this era have been preserved by both institutions and individuals, aspiring to chronicle this rich portion of our history.

Collectors are also fortunate that autograph dealers for years have recognized this portion of the hobby and routinely catered to it by offering fine examples for sale. While it is natural to expect that some of the obscure signatures may have slipped out of the collecting arena, it is doubtful that many authentic examples of the primary players have been overlooked.

As the first war with many literate, or at least semi-literate, participants, it is typical to find numerous forms of written or printed communication. Documentation was critical, with the primary source of interchange often handwritten. Collectors who wish to attack this area of collecting should familiarize themselves with the many routine forms used and the anticipated signatures that would adorn these examples.

Additionally, collectors should acquaint themselves with the handwriting habits and idiosyncrasies of all the key individuals/generals, as in addition to often paying a hefty sum for their autograph, you may also find a fair amount forged or "ghost-signed" examples. For example, it was common for Varina Davis, wife of the confederate president, to routinely affix his signature to late-dated war documents.

Confederate-generated military documents are scarcer than those of the Union, primarily due to the destruction of the South, the need to destroy military information and the lack of resources. The advent of photography makes this form an option - albeit expensive, in some cases. While a collector may often find carte de vistes reflective of this era, other forms should parallel the life of the subject.

The signatures of Patrick Romayne Cleburne, James Dearing, John Herbert Kelly, William Dorsey Pender, and John Calhoun C. Sanders should provide the most significant challenges of your conquest. As facsimiles of their signatures have been published in the market, anticipate encountering your fair share of forgeries. The two most commonly encountered forgeries in this niche of the market are Robert E. Lee and Thomas J. "Stonewall" Jackson.

Abbreviations: ANV = Army of Northern Virginia, DPW = distinguished post-war career, ESPV = exhibits signifigant pricing variations, G = Governor/state, KIA = Killed in action, MW = Mexican War, NE = numerous engagements, PM - Postmaster, PU = pricing undetermined, SALS = Signifigant autograph letter signed, SL = state legislature, WP = West Point, USHR = United States House of Represenatives, USS = United States Senate

C.S.A. Generals of The Civil War

Name	DB/DD	SIG	LS/DS	ALS	Comments
Adams, Daniel W.	1821- 1872	175	300	450	Shiloh, Chickamauga, SALS-2X
Adams, John	1825-1864	525	1125	2500	Vicksburg, Atlanta, WP, MW,KIA.
Adams, William Wirt	1819-1888	300	600	900	Vicksburg, SL, PM/Jackson.
Alexander, Edward P.	1835-1910	600	1125	2000	ALS - $525, Gettysburg, WP
Allen, Henry Watkins	1820-1866	225	450	900	Shiloh,SL, TW, G/LA
Allen, William Wirt	1835-1894	215	450	600	Shiloh, Atlanta,U.S. Marshall,SALS-2X
Anderson, George B.	1831-1862				Williamsburg, Sharpsburg, PU
Anderson, George T.	1824-1901	125	200	450	Second Manassas, Gettysburg,
Anderson, James P.	1822-1872	150	300	450	Shiloh, Murfreesboro, MW, SL
Anderson, Joseph R.	1813-1892	125	300	600	Seven Days, WP, check - $150
Anderson, Richard H.	1821-1879	80	200	300	Sayler's Creek, WP, MW
Anderson, Robert H.	1835-1888	150	400	500	Numerous engagements ,WP
Anderson, Samuel R.	1804-1883	150	300	400	West. Virginia, MW, PM-Nashville
Archer, James Jay	1817-1864	375	475	800	NE, Princeton,DS - $370, MW.
Armistead, Lewis A.	1817-1863				Gettysburg, WP, MW, PU
Armstrong, Frank C.	1835-1909	200	400	750	First Manassas, Holy Cross, Indian Insp.
Ashby, Turner	1828-1862	500	1000	2000	Shenandoah Valley,KIA, SALS-2X
Baker, Alpheus	1828-1891	150	300	500	Vicksburg, Baker's Creek
Baker, Laurence S.	1830-1907	100	200	400	Peninsular, Gettysburg, Bentonville, WP
Baldwin, William E.	1827-1864	500	1000	3000	Vicksburg, Had fatal fall from a horse
Barksdale, William	1821-1863	500	1000	1750	First Manassas, Gettysburg, ,USHR, KIA
Barringer, Rufus	1821-1895	150	300	500	NE, Brother-in-law S.Jackson & D.H. Hill
Barry, John D.	1839-1867				Seven Days, Pricing undetermined
Barton, Seth M.	1829-1900	125	250	500	Vicksburg, SALS & SDS/LS - 2X
Bate, William B.	1826-1905	100	200	300	USS, MW, G/TN, check - $150, ALS-3X
Battle, Cullen A.	1829-1905	200	400	600	Sharpsburg, Gettysburg , USHR
Beale, Richard L.T.	1819-1893	125	250	450	NE, Univ of VA, USHR. lawyer
Beall, William N.R.	1825-1883	200	400	800	West.frontier, Gen.commiss. merchant
Beauregard, Pierre G.T.	1818-1893	475	1000	1600	First Manassas, ALS - $695, WP, MW.
Bee, Barnard E.	1824-1861				Manassas, WP, MW, PU, rare

Name	DB/DD	SIG	LS/DS	ALS	Comments
Bee, Hamilton P.	1822-1897	100	200	400	Red River, SL, MW.
Bell, Tyree H.	1815-1902	70	150	250	Belmont, Shiloh, Richmond.
Benning, Henry L.	1814-1875	150	300	400	Second Manassas ,GASupreme Court.
Benton, Samuel	1820-1864	350	600	875	SL, Nephew of Thomas Hart Benton
Blanchard, Albert G.	1810-1891	70	175	275	WP, MW, ESPV
Boggs, William R.	1829-1911	125	250	450	Trans-Mississippi., WP, taught at VPI.
Bonham, Milledge L.	1813-1890	150	225	450	MW, SL, G/SC
Bowen, John S.	1830-1863				Shiloh, Vicksburg, WP, PU
Bragg, Braxton	1817-1876	400	700	1125	Shiloh, Chickamauga, WP, MW.
Branch, Lawrence O.	1820-1862	400	600	1200	Seven Days, USHR,KIA, stock - $445
Brandon, William L.	1801-1890	70	150	250	Malvern Hill, Chickamauga, SL
Brantley, William Felix	1830-1870	500	1000		Chickamauga, Chattanooga, ESPV
Bratton, John	1831-1898	150	300	450	Fort Sumter, Seven Pines, USS, USHR.
Breckinridge, John C.	1821-1875	300	500	1000	VP - Buchanan, USHR, USS, CSA/SOW
Brevard, Theodore W.	1835-1882	150	300	420	Sayler's Creek, Univ. of VA
Brown, John C.	1827-1889	100	200	400	NE, G/TN, railroad executive, DS - $245
Browne, William M.	1823-1883	150	300	500	Savannah, Personal staff of J. Davis,
Bryan, Goode	1811-1885	150	300	500	Seven Days, Gettysburg , WP, MW.
Buckner, Simon B.	1823-1914	150	300		Kentucky, WP, MW, G/KY, ESPV
Buford, Abraham	1820-1884	150	300	600	WP, MW, SL, SDS & SALS - 2-3X
Bullock, Robert	1828-1905	70	165	250	Chickamauga, Atlanta, Tennessee, SL
Butler, Matthew C.	1836-1909	100	200	300	SL, USS, executive, SALS-2X
Cabell, William L.	1827-1911	200	400	500	WP, Mayor ,CSA flag, SALS-2-3X
Campbell, Alexander W.	1828-1893	70	150	250	Shiloh
Cantey, James	1818-1874	125	250	315	Richmond, Atlanta , SL (SC), MW
Capers, Ellison	1837-1908	100	200	300	Fort Sumter, minister,SALS-2X
Carroll, William H.	1810-1868	70	160	245	Fishing Creek, PM Memphis
Carter, John C.	1837-1864				Shiloh, Perryville,KIA, PU, scarce
Chalmers, James R.	1831-1898	175	350	500	Shiloh, Murfressboro,USHR, Sig. - $150
Chambliss, Jr., John R.	1833-1864				Maryland, WP, KIA, PU
Cheatham, Benjamin F.	1820-1886	200	400	500	Shiloh, Atlanta. MW,PM/Nashville,TN
Chesnut, Jr., James	1815-1885	175	325	450	SL, USS, Staff of Pres. Davis.
Chilton, Robert Hall	1815-1879	200	500	750	WP, MW, SDS/LS & SALS-5-6X
Churchill, Thomas J.	1824-1905	100	150	300	Wilson's Creek, MW, G/Ark., SALS-2X
Clanton, James H.	1827-1871	150	275	450	Shiloh, Farmington, Booneville, MW, SL
Clark, Charles	1811-1877	125	250	350	Shiloh. SL, MW, G/Miss.
Clark, Jr., John B.	1831-1903				Pea Ridge, Trans-Mississippi, USHR, PU
Clayton, Henry D.	1827-1889	100	200	450	Murfreesboro, Chickamauga, Atlanta,SL
Cleburne, Patrick R.	1828-1864	1200	2150	4500	NE, Savage fighter, highly regarded
Clingman, Thomas L.	1812-1897	100	250	400	SL, USHR, USS, ALS - $195
Cobb, Howell	1815-1868	160	300	600	USHR, G/GA, Sec. Tres.,SDS/ALS-2-3X
Cobb, Thomas Reade	1823-1862				Seven Days, KIA, Bros.H.Cobb, PU
Cocke, Phillip St. Geo.	1809-1861				First Manassas, WP, Va. Agric. Soc., PU
Cockrell, Francis M.	1834-1915	75	150	250	Carthage, Wilson's Creek , USS
Colquitt, Alfred H.	1824-1894	100	200	300	NE, USS, MW, USHR, SL, G/ GA
Colston, Raleigh E.	1825-1896	135	200	300	Chancellorsville, ESPV - all forms
Conner, James	1829-1883	100	175	300	First Manassas, Seven Pines, DSDA
Cook, Phillip	1817-1865	125	250	350	Seven Days, Sharpsburg, USHR, SL
Cooke, John R.	1833-1891	200	450	575	NE,Outstanding record, highly regarded
Cooper, Douglas H.	1815-1879	200	450	600	Elkhorn, MW, U.S. agent, SALS-2-3X
Cooper, Samuel	1798-1876	125	200	400	No field command,WP, Adj & Insp. Gen.

Name	DB/DD	SIG	LS/DS	ALS	Comments
Corse, Montgomery D.	1816-1895	160	325	500	NE,Blind in final years, great soldier
Cosby, George B.	1830-1909	75	150	240	Jackson , WP
Cox, William R.	1832-1919	75	125	200	Stock - $225 ,USHR, Sec. of the Senate
Crittenden, George B.	1812-1880	100	225	300	WP, MW, librarian of KY, Bros.Un. Gen.
Cummings, Alfred	1829-1910	100	300	400	NE, WP, uncle of the same name G/UT
Daniel, Junius	1828-1864				Seven Days, Gettysburg, WP, KIA, PU
Davidson, Henry B.	1831-1899	125	240	435	Island No. 10, MW, WP, Dept. Sec. NC
Davis, Joseph Robert	1825-1896	350	750	1350	NE, ESPV, SDS/LS/ALS-2-3X, N/JDavis
Davis, William G. M.	1812-1898	70	165	300	Lawyer.
de Lagnel, Julius A.	1827-1912	75	150	230	Rich Mountain,Pacific steamship service
Dearing, James	1840-1865				NE, WP, KIA, V.SCARCE, PU
Deas, Zachariah C.	1819-1882	100	200	400	Shiloh, NE, MW, cotton & stockbroker
Deshler, James	1833-1863				NE,WP, KIA (Chickamauga), PU
Dibrell, George G.	1822-1888	150	350	430	Merchant, financier, USHR, rail pres.
Dockery, Thomas P.	1833-1898	150	300	425	Wilson's Creek, Corinth Civil engineer
Doles, George P.	1830-1864	675	850	1475	NE, Gettysburg, outstanding brig., KIA
Donelson, Daniel S.	1801-1863	355	450	750	Murfressboro,SL, Neph.of A. Jackson
Drayton, Thomas F.	1808-1891	145	250	340	NE,WP, SL, inefficient as a field cmdr.
DuBose, Dudley M.	1834-1883	140	300	475	Gettysburg, Richmond, USHR
Duke, Basil Wilson	1838-1916	130	250	650	NE, author,SDS/LS & SALS - 5-6X
Duncan, Johnson K.	1827-1862				Forts Jackson and St. Phillip,WP, PU
Dunovant, John	1825-1864				Virginia,MW , PU
Early, Jubal A.	1816-1894	400	750	1300	NE,WP, SL, MW,ESPV, SALS-2X
Echols, John	1823-1896	125	200	400	NE, Harvard, SL,SDS & SALS - 2-3X
Ector, Matthew D.	1822-1879	225	400	500	NE,SL, judge,SDS & SALS - 2-3X
Elliott, Jr., S.	1830-1866				Primarily SC,SL, yachtsman,PU
Elzey (Jones), A.	1816-1871	275	500	800	NE,WP, MW, SALS- 2X, ESPV
Evans, Clement A.	1833-1911	150	400	750	NE, judge, author & editor,SDS-2X
Evans, N. G."Shanks"	1824-1868	200	400	600	Manassas, WP, principal, controversial
Ewell, Richard S.	1817-1872	500	700	1750	NE,WP, MW, controversial, SALS-2X
Fagan, James F.	1828-1893	350	800		NE, MW, SL, ESPV, LS/DS - 2X
Featherston, Winfield S.	1820-1891	100	200	325	NE,USHR, SL, judge ,ESPV
Ferguson, Samuel W.	1857-1917	200	400	800	Shiloh, Vicksburg, Miss. River Com.
Field, Charles W.	1828-1892	125	250	430	NE, WP, varied post-bellum career
Finegan, Joseph	1814-1885	125	200	400	Cold Harbor, Florida,SL, cotton broker
Finley, Jesse J.	1812-1904	100	200	300	NE,SL, Mayor of Memphis, TN, USHR
Floyd, John B.	1806-1863	100	200	300	SL, Gov. of VA, Sec. of War,SALS-2-3X
Forney, John H.	1829-1902	150	300	500	NE,WP, bros. W.H.Forney, SALS-2X
Forney, William H.	1823-1894	150	200	300	MW, SL, USHR, SALS -2-3X, Sig. - $245
Forrest, Nathan B.	1821-1877	1000	2000	5000	NE, legendary commander, SALS-2-3X
Frazer, John W.	1827-1906	125	265	315	Kentucky, E. Tennessee,WP
French, Samuel G.	1818-1910	150	275	375	NE - w/Army of TN, WP, MW
Frost, Daniel M.	1823-1900	120	200	400	Prairie Grive, WP, MW, SL
Fry, Birkett Davenport	1822-1891	175	400	500	NE,Grad. VMI, attended WP, MW
Gano, Richard M.	1830-1913	75	150	225	Tullahoma, Camden, doctor, SL
Gardner, Franklin	1823-1873	250	500		Shiloh, Kentucky, farmer
Gardner, William M.	1824-1901	85	200	300	First Manassas, Olustee,WP, MW
Garland, Jr., Samuel	1830-1862				Manassas, KIA, disting.commander, PU

Name	DB/DD	SIG	LS/DS	ALS	Comments
Garnett, Richard B.	1817- 1863?	700			NE,WP, KIA (Gettysburg), cousin of R.S.
Garnett, Robert S.	1819-1861	1000			WP, MW, First general to fall in battle.
Garrott, Isham W.	1816-1863	425	600	850	Port Gibson, Baker's Creek, SL, KIA
Gartrell, Lucius J.	1821-1891	100	300	400	First Manassas, SL, USHR
Gary, Martin W.	1831-1881	220	400	800	First Manassas, Richmond,Harvard,SL
Gatlin, Richard C.	1809-1896	125	300	400	North Carolina coast, WP, MW, farmer
Gholson, Samuel J.	1808-1883	150	300	600	Alabama, Mississippi,SL, USHR, judge
Gibson, Randall L.	1832-1892	115	275		USHR, USS, SALS-3-4X, check - $170
Gilmer, Jeremy F.	1818-1883	200	500	650	Shiloh, engineer, WP, ESPV
Girardey, Victor J. B.	1837-1864				Seven Days, KIA, skilled fighter, PU
Gist, States Rights	1831-1864				First Manassas, KIA, well respected, PU
Gladden, Adley H.	1810-1862	450	1575	3150	Shiloh, MW, KIA, SALS-2X, ESPV
Godwin, Archibald C.	1831-1864				NE, in charge Libby Prison, KIA, PU
Goggin, James M.	1820-1889	150	300	450	VA Peninsula, Cedar Creek, NE,WP
Gordon, George W.	1836-1911	260	400	500	Murfressboro, Chickamauga, NE,USHR
Gordon, James Byron	1822-1864				Bethesda Church, Dumfries, NE,SL, PU
Gordon, John Brown	1832-1904	250	400	750	NE, USS, author, SDS & SALS-2-5X
Gorgas, Josiah	1818-1883	250	600	700	WP, key player in CSA, SDS-2-3X
Govan, Daniel C.	1829-1911	125	300	640	NE- western army ,Indian agent / WA
Gracie, Jr., Archibald	1832-1864				Chickamauga, NE,WP, KIA, PU
Granbury, Hiram B.	1831-1864				Vicksburg, NE,county chief justice, PU
Gray, Henry	1816-1892	100	200	300	Red River, lawyer, SL
Grayson, John B.	1806-1861				WP, MW,brig. general Prov. Army, PU
Green, Martin E.	1815-1863	365	455	800	NE, KIA, Bros. U.S.S. J.S. Green
Green, Thomas	1814-1864				Valverde, Galveston, MW, KIA, PU
Greer, Elkanah B.	1825-1877	135	270	375	Wilson's Creek, Elkhorn Tavern, MW
Gregg, John	1828-1864				First Manassas, NE, judge, KIA, PU
Gregg, Maxcy	1814-1862	500	1000	2000	NE, Manassas, MW, KIA, SDS/LS-2-4X
Griffith, Richard	1814-1862				Seven Days, MW, U.S. marshal, KIA, PU
Grimes, Bryan	1828-1880				ANV, fierce fighter, assassinated, PU
Hampton, Wade	1818-1902	350	500	1000	NE, USS, SALS-4-5X, SLS/DS-3-4X
Hanson, Roger W.	1827-1863				Murfreesboro, MW, SL, KIA, PU
Hardee, William J.	1815-1873	475	1000	2000	NE,WP, author, outstanding general
Hardeman, W.P "Gotch"	1816-1898	100	200	350	Red River, MW, railroad inspector
Harris, Nathaniel H.	1834-1900	165	325	450	Chancellorsville, Gettysburg
Harrison, James E.	1815-1875	100	200	300	Louisiana, SL
Harrison, Thomas	1823-1891	100	225	300	Chickamauga, NE, MW, SL
Hasgood, Johnson	1829-1898	100	200	400	First Manassas, Drewry's Bluff, G/SC
Hatton, Robert H.	1826-1862	150	300	400	Cheat Mt.,SL, USHR
Hawes, James M.	1824-1889	100	250	355	Shiloh, Vicksburg, WP, MW
Hawthorn, Alexander T.	1825-1899	150	300	400	Shiloh, Helena, Baptist minister
Hays, Harry T.	1820-1876	225	500	1000	First Manassas, Valley,NE, MW, SDS-2X
Hebert, Louis	1820-1901	150	375	465	Wilson's Creek, Elkhorn, WP, SL
Hebert, Paul O.	1818-1880	100	200	300	Vicksburg, Milliken's Bend, WP, G/LA
Helm, Benjamin H.	1831-1863	200	300	400	Chickamauga, WP, SL, KIA, scarce
Heth, Henry	1825-1899	100	200	400	Western Virginia, Gettysburg, WP,
Higgins, Edward	1821-1875	100	200	300	Forts Jackson and St. Phillip, Vicksburg
Hill, Ambrose P.	1825-1865	2500	6000	12000	NE, WP, MW, "APHill", ALS - $9000
Hill, Benjamin J.	1825-1880	100	200	300	Shiloh, Chickamauga, SL
Hill, Daniel H.	1821-1889	300	500	600	NE, MW, won the first battle, SALS-3X
Hindman, Thomas C.	1828-1868	375	500	1000	NE, SL, USHR, assassinated

Name	DB/DD	SIG	LS/DS	ALS	Comments
Hodge, George B.	1828-1892	100	215	275	SW Mississsippi, E. Louisiana, SL
Hogg, Joseph L.	1806-1862	350	450	775	Shiloh, MW, SL, son was Texas Gov.
Hoke, Robert F.	1837-1912	100	225	325	NE, "R. F. Hoke"
Holmes, Theophilus H.	1804-1880	225	500	600	Seven Days, WP, MW, SALS-2X
Holtzclaw, James T.	1833-1893	145	275	400	Shiloh, Chickamauga, Chattanooga
Hood, John Bell	1831-1879	1000	2000	4000	NE, WP, sig. w/rank - $1600, SALS-4-5X
Huger, Benjamin	1805-1877	140	325	400	Norfolk, Seven Days, WP, MW, SDS-2X
Humes, William Y.C.	1830-1882	150	300	400	N. Georgia, Tennessee, "WYCHumes"
Humphreys, Ben. G.	1808-1882	240	440	575	NE, ANV,WP, SL, first elect. G/MI
Hunton, Eppa	1822-1908	125	250	375	NE, ANV, USHR, USS
Imboden, John Daniel	1823-1895	175	400	500	NE,SL,SDS-2X, SALS - 7-9X, ESPV
Iverson, Alfred, Jr.	1829-1911	175	400	500	Seven Days, S. Mountain, Sharpsburg
Jackson, Alfred E.	1807-1889	75	200	425	Greenville, paymaster, SALS-2X
Jackson, Henry R.	1820-1898	100	200	400	Western Virginia, Atlanta,Min. to Mexico,
Jackson, T. J."Stonewall"	1824-1863	4200	9000	15000	NE, WP, MW, SALS - 2-3X, SDS-2X
Jackson, W.H. "Red"	1835-1903	100	200	300	Belmont, Vicksburg, Atlanta, WP,
Jackson, W. L."Mudwall"	1825-1890	165	350	500	NE, SL, lt. gov., 2nd. cousin "Stonewall"
Jenkins, Albert G.	1830-1864				Western Virginia, Ohio,Gettysburg, PU
Jenkins, Micah	1835-1864				First & Second Manassas, NE, PU
Jerome Bonaparte R.	1815-1891				Second Manassas, Gettysburg, SL, PU
Johnson, A.R.	1834-1922				Totally blind after the war, PU
Johnson, Bradley T.	1829-1903	130	400	500	NE, SL,SDS-3-4X, SALS-7-10X, ESPV
Johnson, Bushrod R.	1817-1880	125	300	540	NE, WP, MW, teacher
Johnson, Edward	1816-1873	140	300	525	NE, Gettysburg, WP, MW,
Johnston, Albert S.	1803-1862	500	2000	2500	WP, MW, controversial, SDS-4-5X
Johnston, George D.	1832-1910	100	250	350	NE, Mayor Marion, AL, SL
Johnston, Joseph E.	1807-1891	300	600	1150	NE, USHR,SDS -2X, SALS-3X, ESPV
Johnston, Robert D.	1837-1919	60	125	260	NE, Gettysburg, one of last generals
Jones, D. R. "Neighbor"	1825-1863				First Manassas, Peninsular, NE, MW, PU
Jones, John Marshall	1820-1864	375	740	1200	Gettysburg, ANV, WP, ESPV - ALS
Jones, John Robert	1827-1901	150	320	500	First Manassas, Valley, Chancellorsville
Jones, Samuel	1819-1887	150	460	800	First Manassas, Corinth MW, farmer
Jones, W. E. "Grumble"	1824-1864				Manassas, WP, KIA, PU, check - $295
Jordan, Thomas	1819-1895	110	225	465	NE, WP, MW, writer, SDS/SALS-2X
Kelly, John Herbert	1840-1864				NE, WP, KIA, youngest gen. in CSA, PU
Kemper, James L.	1823-1895	200	300	400	First Manassas, NE, MW, G/VA
Kennedy, John D.	1840-1896	130	300	430	First Manassas, NE, SL, diplomat
Kershaw, Joseph B.	1822-1894	230	750	800	NE, , MW, SL,SALS-2X, ESPV - LS/DS
Kirkland, William W.	1833-1915				NE, WP,invalided later in life, PU
Lane, James H.	1833-1907	120	240	360	NE, ANV
Lane, Walter P.	1817-1892	70	160	300	Red River, Mansfield, MW, merchant
Law, Evander M.	1836-1920	100	225	300	NE, Manassas, writer
Lawton, Alexander R.	1818-1896	125	370	550	NE, WP,SL, minister of Austria
Leadbetter, Danville	1811-1866	240	500	600	WP, engineer officer
Lee, Edwin Gray	1836-1870	200	300	400	NE, Seven Days, Second Manassas
Lee, Fitzhugh	1835-1905	160	300	400	NE, WP, G/VA, diplomat, neph. R.E.Lee
Lee, George W. C.	1832-1913	225	600	1250	Davis staff, son R.E. Lee, ESPV - ALS
Lee, Robert Edward	1807-1870	4000	6750	20000	SP - 8500, ANV, WP, MW, ESPV

Name	DB/DD	SIG	LS/DS	ALS	Comments
Lee, Stephen D.	1833-1908	200	400	500	Mississippi, Alabama, WP, ESPV
Lee, W.H.F. "Rooney"	1837-1891	200	450	725	300 - SP, ANV, USHR, son of R. E. Lee
Leventhorpe, Collett	1815-1889	80	150	400	ANV, NE, SALS-2-3X
Lewis, Joseph H.	1824-1904	75	175	300	NE, SL, USHR
Lewis, William G.	1835-1901	80	160	260	Gettysburg, Petersburg, Valley
Liddell, St. John R.	1815-1870	115	270		NE, WP, murdered by C.S.A. colonel
Lilley, Robert D.	1836-1886	100	200	300	Western Virginia, NE
Little, Lewis Henry	1817-1862	425	600		Elkhorn, MW, KIA, ESPV
Logan, Thomas M.	1840-1914	100	225	340	First Manassas, Seven Days,Sharpsburg
Lomax, Lunsford L.	1835-1913	100	225	300	Gettysburg,NE, WP, ins. general, writer
Long, Armistead L.	1825-1891	120	240	350	Lee's mil.sec., WP, totally blind by 1870
Longstreet, James	1821-1904	925	2150	4300	2000 - SP, NE, WP, MW, diplomat,
Loring, William W.	1818-1886	135	250	320	NE, SL, MW, served in Egyptian army
Lovell, Mansfield	1822-1884	125	250	300	Corinth, WP, MW, engineer
Lowrey, Mark P.	1828-1885	100	210	245	Kentucky, Chickamauga, Atlanta
Lowry, Robert	1830-1910	70	125	200	Shiloh, Vicksburg, Atlanta, G/Miss.
Lyon, Hylan Benton	1836-1907	75	150	225	Holly Springs, Vicksburg, WP
Mackall, William W.	1817-1891	100	265	440	Chickamauga, Atlanta, WP, SALS-2-3X
MacRae, William	1834-1882				Seven Days, Second Manassas, PU
Magruder, John B.	1807-1871	230	475	500	Peninsular, Seven Days WP, MW, ESPV
Mahone, William	1826-1895	150	275	430	ANV, railroad superintendent, USS
Major, James P.	1836-1877				Vicksburg, Red River, WP, PU
Maney, George E.	1826-1901	150	270	365	Cheat Mt., MW, SALS-2X
Manigault, Arthur M.	1824-1886	115	250	300	Shiloh, Corinth MW, inspector general
Marmaduke, John S.	1833-1887	130	300	400	NE, WP, G/Miss.,ESPV - SALS - 5-6X
Marshall, Humphrey	1812-1872	110	225	300	WP, MW, USHR, SALS - 5 - 6X, ESPV
Martin, James G.	1819-1878	150	270	400	Churubusco, N. Carolina, MW, popular
Martin, William T.	1823-1910	125	300	450	Seven Days, Sharpsburg, SL
Maury, Dabney H.	1822-1900	100	230	320	NE, WP, MW, writer, SALS-4-5X
Maxey, Samuel B.	1825-1895	150	250	325	NE, WP, MW, USS,SALS-6-7X, ESPV
McCausland, John	1836-1927	75	130	175	Shenandoah Valley, Petersburg
McComb, William	1828-1918	100	225	350	Cedar Mt., Second Manassas, ANV
McCown, John P.	1815-1879	125	275	325	WP, MW, teacher, SDS-4X
McCulloch, Ben	1811-1862	375	500	800	Wilson's Creek, MW, U.S. marshal, KIA
McCulloch, Henry E.	1816-1895	80	175	285	Sheriff, MW, SL, U.S. marshal,
McGowan, Samuel	1819-1897	100	200	330	ANV, SL, MW
McIntosh, James M.	1828-1862				Arkansas Mounted Rifles, WP, KIA, PU
McLaws, Lafayette	1821-1897	135	340	365	ANV, WP, MW, neph. Z.Taylor
McNair, Evander	1820-1902	100	200	250	NE, Murfreesboro, MW
McRae, Dandridge	1829-1899	100	225	275	Wilson's Creek, Elkhorn, Red River
Mercer, Hugh W.	1808-1877	100	200	260	Savannah, Atlanta, Jonesboro, WP
Miller, William	1820-1909	70	135	200	Kentucky, Murfreesboro, MW, SL
Moody, Young M.	1822-1866				Kentucky, Chickamauga, PU
Moore, John C.	1824-1910	100	200	250	Shiloh, Corinth, Vicksburg
Moore, Patrick T.	1821-1883	110	200	250	First Manassas merchant, insur. agent
Morgan, John H.	1825-1864	1200	3000		NE, legend of the CSA, SDS - 3-4X
Morgan, John T.	1824-1907	150	245	400	First Manassas, USS, ESPV, SALS-3-4X
Mouton, J.J.A.A.	1829-1864				Shiloh, Red River, WP, KIA, PU
Nelson, Allison	1822-1862	415	500		Devall's Bluff, SL, MW, mayor of Atlanta
Nicholls, Francis R.	1834-1912	75	150	200	First Manassas, NE, WP, G/LA

Name	DB/DD	SIG	LS/DS	ALS	Comments
Northrup, Lucius B.	1811-1894	100	200	300	Commissary general C.S.A., WP,
O'Neal, Edward Asbury	1818-1890	70	160	275	Peninsular, NE, G/AL
Page, Richard L.	1807-1901	150	250	550	Port Royal, cousin R.E. Lee
Palmer, Joseph B.	1825-1890	100	200	255	NE, SL, mayor of Murfreesboro
Parson, Mosby M.	1822-c.1865	265	400	800	Carthage, MW, SL, SALS - 2X
Paxton, Elisha F."Bull"	1828-1863	750	2250		NE, Staff of S. Jackson, ESPV - LS/DS
Payne, William H.F.	1830-1904	150	300	400	ANV, ESPV - LS/DS
Peck, William R.	1818-1871	165	350		ANV, ESPV
Pegram, John	1832-1865	700	1400		Rich Mountain, WP, KIA, ESPV
Pemberton, John C.	1814-1881	200	425	550	WP, MW, originator of Coca-Cola
Pender, William D.	1834-1863				NE, Gettysburg,WP, PU, scarce
Pendleton, William N.	1809-1883	240	375	450	ANV, WP, teacher, rector, ESPV - Sig.
Perrin, Abner M.	1827-1864				NE, MW, KIA, PU
Perry, Edward A.	1831-1889	100	225	300	Seven Days, Chancellorsville, G/FL
Perry, William F.	1823-1901	80	175	280	NE, Gettysburg, Sharpsburg
Pettigrew, James J.	1828-1863	400			NE, SL, illegible handwriting, ESPV
Pettus, Edmund W.	1821-1907	75	150	400	NE, USS, SDS- 8X
Pickett, George E.	1825-1875	1000	1500	3000	NE, Gettysburg , WP, ESPV
Pike, Albert	1809-1891	75	175	250	Elkhorn Tavern, editor, MW
Pillow, Gideon J.	1806-1878	130	375	500	Belmont, MW, law partner J.K. Polk
Polignac, C.A.J.M.	1832-1913				NE, PU
Polk, Leonidas	1806-1864	400	550		NE, WP, friend of J. Davis, KIA, ESPV
Polk, Lucius E.	1833-1892	110	240	275	Murfreesboro, Chickamauga, SL
Posey, Carnot	818-1863	420			ANV, MW, ESPV
Preston, John S.	1809-1881	75	150	225	First Manassas, SL
Preston, William	1816-1887	125	250	400	Murfreesboro, NE, MW, SL, SDS-2X
Price, Sterling	1809-1867	275	375	600	NE, SL, USHR, MW, ALS-7-10X, ESPV
Pryor, Roger A.	1828-1919	140	275	385	NE, SALS - 1.5 - 2X
Quarles, William A.	1825-1893	75	165	270	Vicksburg, , SL
Rains, Gabriel J.	1803-1881	100	300		Seven Pines, WP, ESPV - LS/DS
Rains, James E.	1833-1862				Murfreesboro, KIA, PU
Ramseur, Stephen D.	1837-1864				Seven Days, Malvern Hill, WP, KIA, PU
Randolph, George W.	1818-1867	275	550	650	Big Bethel, CSA Sec. of War for CSA
Ransom, Jr., Robert	1828-1892	150	285	325	Seven Days, Maryland, WP, ESPV
Ransom, Matt Whitaker	1826-1904	100	240	300	Seven Pines, NE, SL, diplomat
Reynolds, Alexander W.	1816-1876	100	200	240	NE, WP, fought in Egypt after war
Reynolds, Daniel H.	1832-1902	100	225	340	Wilson's Creek, Chickamauga, Atlanta
Richardson, Robert V.	1820-1870	400	800		Shiloh, Corinth, assassinated, ESPV
Ripley, Roswell S.	1823-1887	200	250	500	Seven Days, NE, MW, SDS & SALS - 2X
Roane, John S.	1817-1867	275	500		Prairie Grove, SL, MW, G/AK, ESPV
Roberts, William P.	1841-1910	100	300	500	ANV, SL, SDS & SALS - 2-3X
Robertson, Beverly H.	1827-1910	70	140	200	Jackson's Valley, ANV, WP
Robertson, Felix H.	1839-1928	70	140	200	Murfreesboro, NE,, WP
Roddey, Philip D.	1826-1897	135	300	450	North Alabama, SDS - 3X, SALS - 4 - 5X
Rodes, Robert E.	1829-1864	475	1200	1500	NE, KIA, SDS - 4X, SALS - 5 - 6X
Ross, Lawrence S.	1838-1898	200	550	800	NE, G/Texas, popular, SALS-2X
Rosser, Thomas L.	1836-1910	150	300	500	First Manassas, NE, WP
Ruggles, Daniel	1810-1897	125	300	600	Corinth, WP, MW, SDS & SALS - 2X

Name	DB/DD	SIG	LS/DS	ALS	Comments
Rust, Albert	1818-1870	100	200	245	Cheat Mt., Corinth, SL, USHR
Sanders, John C.C.	1840-1864				Seven Pines, Seven Days, NE, KIA, PU
Scales, Alfred M.	1827-1892	145	265	350	Peninsular, SL, USHR, G/NC
Scott, Thomas M.	1829-1876	145			Vicksburg, Atlanta, ESPV
Scurry, William R.	1821-1864	575			Galveston, Red River, Mansfield, scarce
Sears, Claudius W.	1817-1891	70	165	250	Chicksaw Bayou,NE, WP
Semmes, Paul J.	1815-1863	1275	1875		Yorktown, NE, KIA, ESPV
Sharp, Jacob H.	1833-1907	160	275		Shiloh, Murfreesboro, Chickamauga
Shelby, Joseph O.	1830-1897	350	1750	2000	NE, U.S. marshal, well respected, ESPV
Shelley, Charles M.	1833-1907	70	150	215	First Manassas, architect, builder, sheriff
Shoup, Francis A.	1834-1896	100	200	325	Shiloh, NE, WP
Sibley, Henry H.	1816-1886	125	350	425	Army of New Mexico, WP, MW, inventor
Simms, James P.	1837-1887	125	225		Seven Days, NE, SL, ESPV
Slack, William Y.	1816-1862	400	500		Elkhorn, Carthage, MW, ESPV
Slaughter, James E.	1827-1901	120	200		Shiloh, Kentucky, related to J. Madison
Smith, Edmund K.	1824-1893	350	500	600	Shenandoah, NE, WP, MW, SALS- 2X
Smith, Gustavus W.	1821-1896	125	300	500	ANV, WP, MW, engineer, SALS-2X
Smith, James A.	1831-1901	125	165	265	Shiloh, Perryville, Murfreesboro , WP
Smith, Martin L.	1819-1866	100	150	300	New Orleans, Vicksburg, ANV, WP
Smith, Preston	1823-1863	540			Shiloh, Kentucky, Chickamauga, KIA
Smith, Thomas B.	1838-1923	100	150		Mill Springs, Shiloh, NE
Smith, William	1797-1887	125	250	320	NE, Gettysburg, G/VA
Smith, William D.	1825-1862	500			Secessionville WP, MW
Sorrel, Gilbert M.	1838-1901	200	400	500	First Manassas,writer, SDS-4-5X
St. John, Isaac M.	1827-1880	100	160	250	Captain of engineers, com. gen.
Stafford,Leroy A.	1822-1864	415			Seven Days, NE, ESPV
Starke, Peter B.	1815-1888	160	250		Atlanta,SL, sheriff
Starke, William E.	1814-1862				Seven Days, KIA, PU
Steele, William	1819-1885	100	200	300	Red River, WP, adj. gen. TX
Steuart, G. H. "Maryland"	1828-1903	160	350		Valley,Gettysburg , WP, farmer
Stevens, Clement H.	1821-1864	400	2000	2750	NE, KIA, SDS-2X, ESPV
Stevens, Walter H.	1827-1867	300	600		Engineer ANV, WP
Stevenson, Carter L.	1817-1888	100	200	450	Kentucky, WP, MW,
Stewart, Alexander P.	1821-1908	175	300	400	Tennessee Army, WP
Stovall, Marcellus A.	1818-1895	125	250	345	Murfreesboro, ESPV-ALS
Strahl, Otho French	1831-1864				Shiloh, Murfreesboro, KIA, PU
Stuart, James E,B,"Jeb"	1833-1864	4275	7500	15000	ANV, WP, legendary, ESPV
Taliaferro, William B.	1822-1898	125	250	400	Valley, SL, SDS-2X
Tappan, James C.	1825-1906	60	110	150	Shiloh, Kentucky, NE, SL
Taylor, Richard	1826-1879	300	750	1175	NE, MW, s. Z. Taylor, SDS-2-3X
Taylor, Thomas H.	1825-1901	75	140	275	Peninsular, MW, marshal
Terrill, James B.	1838-1864				Manassas, Valley, KIA, PU
Terry, William H.	1824-1888	100	200	250	Manassas, Seven Days, USHR
Terry, William R.	1827-1897	125	250	300	First Manassas, Gettysburg, SL
Thomas, Allen	1830-1907	70	150	265	Vicksburg, diplomat
Thomas, Bryan M.	1836-1905	125	280	350	Shiloh, NE, WP, U.S. marshal
Thomas, Edward L.	1825-1898	115	250	330	Seven Days, ANV, NE, MW
Tilghman, Lloyd	1816-1863	175	350	600	NE,WP, MW, KIA , SALS-2X
Toombs, R. A."Bob"	1810-1885	150	300	400	NE, popular,ESPV-ALS

Name	DB/DD	SIG	LS/DS	ALS	Comments
Toon, Thomas F.	1840-1902	115	265	300	Seven Pines, NE
Tracy, Edward D.	1833-1863	500	1000		Shiloh, Manassas, KIA, scarce
Trapier, James H.	1815-1865	150	300	400	Corinth WP, engineer
Trimble, Isaac R.	1802-1888	325	800		NE, Gettysburg , WP,ESPV
Tucker, William F.	1827-1881	80	175		Perryville,NE, SL, assassinated
Twiggs, David E.	1790-1862	165	330	750	MW, ESPV
Tytler, Robert C.	1833-1865				Shiloh, Missionary Ridge,, PU
Van Dorn, Earl	1820-1863	325			NE, MW, assassinated, ESPV
Vance, Robert B.	1828-1899	75	150	280	Cumberland Gap, clerk, USHR
Vaughan, Jr., Alfred J.	1830-1899	115	200	400	Fought in all west battles
Vaughn, John C.	1824-1875	150	375		First Manassas, MW, SL, ESPV
Villepigue, John B.	1830-1862	350	500	700	Pensacola, Mobile, WP, ESPV
Walker, James A.	1832-1901	140	250		Valley, Spotsylvania, USHR
Walker, John G.	1822-1893	100	200	275	ANV, MW, diplomat
Walker, Leroy P.	1817-1884	200	400	585	No battles, SL, Sec. of War
Walker, Lucius M.	1829-1863	400	500		Corinth WP,nep.Pres. J. K. Polk
Walker, Reuben L.	1827-1890	115	200	300	First Manassas, Seven Days
Walker, William H.T.	1816-1864	200	450	600	NE, MW, KIA, SDS & ALS - 3X
Walker, William S.	1822-1899	125	235	335	Petersburg, North Carolina, MW
Wallace, William Henry	1827-1901	125	250	365	Second Manassas, NE, SL
Walthall, Edward C.	1831-1898	100	200	300	NE, USS, SDS & ALS - 2, ESPV
Waterhouse, Richard	1832-1876	175	350	600	Red River, Arkansas, MW
Watie, Stand	1806-1871				Wilson's Creek, PU
Waul, Thomas N.	1813-1903	115	250		Vicksburg, Red River
Wayne, Henry C.	1815-1883	150	250	350	Insp.Gen. GA, WP, MW
Weisiger, David A.	1818-1899	115	250	500	NE, MW,SDS & ALS - 2X
Wharton, Gabriel C.	1824-1906	100	225	265	New Market, SL, SDS-2X
Wharton, John A.	1828-1865	285	600	1450	Shiloh, Murfreesboro, ESPV
Wheeler, Joseph	1836-1900	175	375	600	NE, WP, USHR, SDS- 5X
Whitfield, John W.	1818-1879	125	200		NE, MW, Indian agent, SL
Whiting, William H.C.	1824-1865	400	975	1400	NE, WP, KIA
Wickham, Williams C.	1820-1888	100	280	400	First Manassas, Maryland,SL
Wigfall, Louis T.	1816-1874	115	225	325	SL, USS, controversial
Wilcox, Cadmus M.	1824-1890	160	325	375	ANV, WP, MW, well-respected
Williams, J.S.	1818-1898	75	150	275	Kentucky, MW, SL, USS
Wilson, Claudius C.	1831-1863				Vicksburg, solicitor-general, PU
Winder, Charles S.	1829-1862				NE, WP, well-respected, PU
Winder, John H.	1800-1865	100	225	365	WP, MW,SDS-2-3X, ESPV
Wise, Henry A.	1806-1876	75	150	250	NE, USHR, diplomat, G/VA
Withers, Jones M.	1814-1890	70	165	270	Shilo, WP, MW, mayor of Mobile
Wofford, William T.	1824-1884				Manassas, MW., PU
Wood, Sterling A.	1823-1891	100	225	280	Shiloh, Murfreesboro, NE, SL
Wright, Ambrose R.	1826-				ANV, newspaper man, PU
Wright, Marcus Joseph	1831-1922	75	130	175	Shiloh, Murfreesboro, NE
York, Zebulon	1819-1900				Peninsula, Seven Days, NE, PU
Young, Pierce M.B.	1836-1896	75	155	285	Maryland, Carolinas, WP, USHR
Young, Wiliam H.	1838-1901				Shiloh, Perryville, NE, PU
Zollicoffer, Feliz Kirk	1812-1862	375	465	800	NE, SL, USHR, SDS-2-3X

Union Generals of The Civil War

Abbreviations: AOP = Army of the Potomac , DPW = distinguished post-war career, ESPV = exhibits signifigant pricing variations, G = Governor/state, KIA = Killed in action, LA = Lincoln association, MW = Mexican War, NE = numerous engagements, PM - Postmaster, PU = pricing undetermined, SALS = Signifigant autograph letter signed, SL = state legislature, WP = West Point, USHR = United States House of Representatives, USS = United States Senate

Name	DB/DD	SIG	LS/DS	ALS	Comments
Abercrombie, John J.	1798-1877	65	100	250	Seven Pines, NE, MW, SALS-2X
Allen, Robert	1811-1886	45	55	110	Quartermaster duties, MW
Alvord, Benjamin	1813-1884	35	50	75	WP, MW, researcher & writer
Ames, Adelbert	1835-1933	50	80	250	NE, Gettysburg,USS, G/ Miss.
Ammen, Jacob	1806-1894	25	40	100	Shiloh, Corinth College professor
Anderson, Robert	1805-1871	150	300	300	Charleston Harbor, MW
Andrews, Christopher C.	1829-1922	30	50	225	Murfreesboro, Arkansas, writer, diplomat
Andrews, George L.	1828-1899	40	60	100	Cedar Mt., WP, professor, US marshall
Arnold, Lewis G.	1817-1871	40	80	200	Fort Pickens, MW
Arnold, Richard	1828-1882	50	80	150	First Manassas, NE, WP, Son of RI Gov.
Asboth, Alexander S.	1811-1868	55	140		Elkhorn Tavern, Marianna, diplomat
Augur, Christopher C.	1821-1898	60	110	150	Penninsular, Cedar Mt., NE, MW, WP
Averill, William Woods	1832-1900	75	140	200	First Manassas, NE, WP, inventor
Ayres, Romeyn Beck	1825-1888	50	100	200	First Manassas, AOP, WP, MW
Bailey, Joseph	1825-1867	110	200		Red River, civil engineer, sheriff
Baird, Absalom	1824-1905	40	65	145	First Manassas, NE, WP, inspector gen.
Baker, Edward D.	1811-1861	120	150	250	Ball's Bluff (Leesburg),USHR, MW, USS
Baker, La Fayette C.	1826-1868	150	175	250	Spy, provost marshal
Banks, Nathaniel P.	1816-1894	100	165	200	NE, SL, USHR, G/Mass., U.S. marshal
Barlow, Francis C.	1834-1896	50	75	250	Peninsular, NE, Sec. of state N.Y.
Barnard, John Gross	1815-1882	35	50	180	Chief engineer AOP, WP, writer
Barnes, James	1801-1869	60	100	150	AOP, Gettysburg, WP, civil engineer
Barnes, Joseph K.	1817-1883	165	400		Surgeon General, MW, LA
Barnum, Henry A.	1833-1892	50	100	175	First Manassas, Gettysburg, Lookout Mt.
Barry, William F.	1818-1879	70	140	175	First Manassas, AOP, WP, MW, writer
Bartlett, Joseph J.	1834-1893	40	80	160	AOP, Second Man.,U.S. minister
Bartlett, William F.	1840-1876	60	115	175	Peninsular, Wilderness
Baxter, Henry	1821-1873	30	80	175	NE, Gettysburg, businessman, diplomat
Bayard, George Dashiell	1835-1862	225	300	600	NE, Valley, WP, KIA, SALS-2X
Beal, George Lafayette	1825-1896	35	75	150	NE, Book-binder, adj.general of ME
Beatty, John	1828-1914	35	60	115	NE, banker, USHR, historian
Beatty, Samuel	1820-1885	40	65	120	Shiloh, Corinth, NE,MW, sheriff, farmer
Belknap, William Worth	1829-1890	50	125	150	Shiloh, SL, Sec. of War - Grant
Benham, Henry W.	1813-1884	36	60	110	Corps of Engineers, AOP, WP, MW
Benton, William P.	1828-1867	135	200	300	W. Virginia, Vicksburg, MW, lawyer, DA

Name	DB/DD	SIG	LS/DS	ALS	Comments
Berry, Hiram Gregory	1824-1863	400	600	1150	First Manassas, AOP, SL, mayor, KIA
Bidwell, Daniel David	1819-1864	300	675	1000	Peninsular, Gettysburg *KIA, SALS-2X
Birge, Henry Warner	1825-1888	45	130		Vicksburg, Red River, merchant
Birney, David Bell	1825-1864	250	375	1000	Peninsular, Seven Pines, AOP
Birney, William	1819-1907	30	50	110	AOP, prolific writer, U.S. att. Wash. D.C.
Blair, Jr., Francis P.	1821-1875	40	60	100	Georgia, Carolinas, MW, attor. gen., USS
Blenker, Louis (Ludwig)	1812-1863	130	300	600	First Manassas, Cross Keys,SLS/DS-2X
Blunt, James G.	1826-1881	40	60	120	Indian Territory
Bohlen, Henry	1810-1862	150	400	575	Cross Keys, Cedar Mountain, MW, KIA
Bowen, James	1808-1886	40	75	145	New Orleans provost,Erie Railroad pres.
Boyle, Jeremiah Tilford	1818-1871	45	100	245	Shiloh, controversial
Bradley, Luther P.	1822-1910	40	100	200	Murfreesboro, Chickamauga, Atlanta
Bragg, Edward S.	1827-1912	55	100	200	NE, AOP, Congress, diplomat, politician
Brannan, John M.	1819-1892	50	100	200	Chickamauga, Chattanooga, MW
Brayman, Mason	1813-1895	40	100	165	Belmont, editor, lawyer, gov. Idaho Terr.
Briggs, Henry S.	1824-1887	50	85	160	Peninsular, Seven Pines, SL, judge
Brisbin, James S.	1837-1892	60	125	200	First Manassas, Gettysburg, author
Brooke, John R.	1838-1926	50	75	200	Peninsular, military gov. Puerto Rico
Brooks, William T.H.	1821-1870	60	100	140	Peninsular, Seven Days, WP, MW
Brown, Egbert B.	1816-1902	25	40		Springfield, mayor, pension agent
Buchanan, Robert C.	1811-1878	50	125		Seven Days, Second Manassas, MW
Buckingham, Catha. P.	1808-1888	30	75	125	WP, teacher, company president,ESPV
Buckland, Ralph P.	1812-1892	100	175	270	Shiloh, Vicksburg, mayor, SL, Congress
Buell, Don C.	1818-1898	100	150	260	AOP, Shiloh, Corinth, WP, MW
Buford, John	1826-1863	850	2200	5000	AOP, Second Manassas, WP
Buford, Napoleon B.	1807-1883	50	130	350	Belmont, Island No.10, Vicksburg
Burbridge, Stephen G.	1831-1894	35	65		Shiloh, Vicksburg, farmer
Burnham, Hiram	1814 -1864	110	220		Peninsular, Fredericksburg, KIA
Burns, William W.	1825-1892	35	60	100	West Virginia, Peninsular, MW
Burnside, Ambrose E.	1824-1881	125	300	440	SP - $875AOP, MW,USS, SALS - 2-3X
Bussey, Cyrus	1833-1915	30	50		Elkhorn Tavern, western Arkansas, SL
Busteed, Richard	1822-1898	25	60	125	Fort Monroe
Butler, Benjamin F.	1818-1893	250	500	600	NE, USHR, SLS/DS & SALS - 5X
Butterfield, Daniel	1831-1901	125	300	400	Penins., NE, "Taps" composer, SDS-2X
Cadwalader, George	1806-1879	40	100	140	Advisor, MW
Caldwell, John C.	1833-1912	50	100	175	Peninsular, Gettysburg, diplomat
Cameron, Robert A.	1828-1894	50	100	200	Island No. 10, Vicksburg, Red River
Campbell, Charles T.	1823-1895	45	100	200	Seven Pines, Peninsular, MW, SL
Campbell, William B.	1807-1867	50	75	100	Congress, MW, G/(TN
Canby, Edward R. S.	1817-1873	100	225	300	New Mexico, Mobile, MW
Carleton, James H.	1814-1873	50	75	150	"California col.", MW, f. H. G. Carleton
Carlin, William P.	1829-1903	50	100	165	Chickamauga, Chattanooga, Atlanta,WP
Carr, Eugene A.	1830-1910	100	260	650	Texas, WP, Indian fighter, SALS 2.5 - 3X
Carr, Joseph B.	1828-1895	45	100	170	Big Bethel, NE,Sec.of State for NY
Carrington, Henry B.	1824-1912	50	100	215	Dakota Territory, western Virginia
Carroll, Samuel S.	1832-1893	60	100	200	Cedar Mt., Fredericksburg, Gettysburg
Carter, Samuel P.	1819-1891				NE, Major general (army) & rear adm., PU
Casey, Silas	1807-1882	65	125	250	MW, "Infantry Tactics" author SALS - 2X
Catterson, Robert F.	1835-1914	45	80	150	Shenandoah, Carolinas,NE, mayor
Chamberlain, Joshua L.	1828-1914	750	1400	2000	Gettysburg, G/ME, SALS- 1.5 - 2X
Chambers, Alexander	1832-1888	55	125	200	Shiloh, Vicksburg, WP

Name	DB/DD	SIG	LS/DS	ALS	Comments
Champlin, Stephen G.	1827-1864	275	550		Peninsular, Seven Pines
Chapin, Edward P.	1831-1863				Peninsular, KIA, PU, scarce
Chapman, George H.	1832-1882	50	100	175	Second Manassas, Publisher, judge, SL
Chetlain, Augustus L.	1824-1914	40	100	165	Shiloh, Iuka, Corinth, Pres. CSE
Chrysler, Morgan H.	1822-1890	100	200		Peninsular, milit. governor,
Clark, William T.	1831-1905	40	100	150	Atlanta Lawyer, USHR (expelled)
Clay, Cassius M.	1810-1903	100	250	500	MW, Diplomat, controversial late in life.
Clayton, Powell	1833-1914	25	50	100	Missouri, Arkansas, G/AK, USS,
Cluseret, Gustave P.	1823-1900				Cross Keys, Shenandoah, PU
Cochrane, John	1813-1898	40	100	160	NE, USHR, attor. gen. (NY), SALS- 2X
Conner, Patrick E.	1820-1891	50	120	150	Fort Douglas, Fort Connor, writer
Conner, Selden	1839-1917	60	145	260	Gettysburg, NE, G/ME, at 25 brig. gen.
Cook, John	1825-1910	35	90	160	Fort Donelson, mayor, sheriff, SL, LA
Cooke, Philip St. Geo.	1809-1895	55	125	200	Washington, Peninsular WP, MW, author
Cooper, James	1810-1863	165	250	500	Valley, Camp Chase, USHR, SL, USS
Cooper, Joseph	1823-1910	40	100	200	Wild Cat Mt., Murfreesboro, Atlanta, NE
Copeland, Joseph T.	1813-1893	35	90	150	Washington, Annapolis Junction, judge
Corcoran, Michael	1827-1863	575	1200	2000	Washington, Manassas, clerk, ESPV
Corse, John M.	1835-1893	40	80	200	Corinth, Chattanooga, ESPV-LS/DS
Couch, Darius N.	1822-1897	75	100	160	Peninsular, Sharpsburg, NE, WP, MW
Cowdin, Robert	1805-1874	200	400		First Manassas, Peninsular, Fair Oaks
Cox, Jacob D.	1828-1900	30	65	120	NE, SL, G/OH, Sec. of Int., USHR
Craig, James	1817-1888	40	60	120	District of Nebraska, MW, state senator
Crawford, Samuel W.	1829-1892	60	100	240	AOP, Sharpsburg, Gettysburg
Crittenden, Thomas L.	1819-1893	125	250	400	Shiloh, Tullahoma, MW, ESPV
Crittenden, Thomas T.	1825-1905	75	160	300	Western Virginia, Shiloh, Murfreesboro
Crocker, Marcellus M.	1830-1865	350	700		Shiloh, Corinth, Vicksburg, WP, lawyer
Crook, George	1828-1890	200	450	575	Western Virginia, NE, WP, frotiersman
Croxton, John T.	1836-1874	175	220	315	Mill Springs, Tullahoma, NE, diplomat
Cruft, Charles	1826-1883	65	125	200	Fort Donelson, Corinth, NE
Cullum, George W.	1809-1892	50	100	150	C.o.s.Gen. H. Halleck, WP, "Bio. Reg."
Curtis, Newton M.	1835-1910	50	100	175	Cold Harbor, Petersburg,SL, Congress,
Curtis, Samuel R.	1805-1866	60	75	250	Pea Ridge, WP, MW, mayor, Congress
Custer, George A.	1839-1876	4000	11000	15000	SP - $10000, AOP, Gettysburg WP
Cutler, Lysander	1807-1866	120	175	300	Second Manassas, Fredericksburg, SL
Dana, Napoleon J.T.	1822-1905	40	80	175	Sharpsburg, MW, ESPV - DS/LS
Davidson, John W.	1824-1881	75	150	300	Penninsular, Missouri, WP, SALS-2X
Davies, Henry E.	1836-1894	60	100	200	Second Manassas, Gettysburg
Davies, Thomas A.	1809-1899	45	110	165	Corinth, Washington, WP, writer
Davis, Edmund J.	1827-1883	40	75	140	G/TX
Davis, Jefferson C.	1828-1879	60	125	150	Fort Sumter, NE, MW, not CSA Pres.
Deitzler, George W.	1826-1884	35	65	115	Wilson's Creek, mayor
Delafield, Richard	1798-1873	45	80	125	Governors Island, Sandy Hook, WP
Dennis, Elias S.	1812-1894	55	100	230	Fort Donelson, Vicksburg, SL, sheriff
Dent, Frederick T.	1820-1892	50	115	245	Pres. Grant's military sec., WP, MW
Denver, James W.	1817-1892	100	200	365	Corinth, Shiloh, MW, state senator
De Russy, Gustavus A.	1818-1891	100	200	300	Peninsular, Malvern Hill, WP, MW
De Trobriand, Phil. R. D.	1816-1897	80	200	350	Chancellorsville, Gettysburg, author
Devens, Charles, Jr.	1820-1891	50	100	200	NE, Gettysburg, SL, USAG
Devin, Thomas C.	1822-1878	55	100	200	Maryland, Fredericksburg, Gettysburg
Dewey, Joel A.	1840-1873				Iuka, Corinth, Atlanta, AG/TN, PU

Name	DB/DD	SIG	LS/DS	ALS	Comments
Dix, John A.	1798-1879	100	250	300	Garrison duties, G/NY, USS, S/Treasury
Dodge, Charles C.	1841-1910	50	100	200	Suffolk, Virginia Phelps Dodge Corp.
Dodge, Grenville M.	1831-1916	60	125	185	Atlanta, Elkhorn, USHR
Doolittle, Charles C.	1832-1903	50	100	200	Penninsula, Seven Days
Doubleday, Abner	1819-1893	500	2250	1500	NE, Gettysburg, WP, baseball folklore
Dow, Neal	1804-1897	50	100	175	District of Florida, Port Hudson, mayor
Duffie, Alfred N.A.	1835-1880	75	150	200	Second Manassas, Chancellorsville
Dumont, Ebenezer	1814-1871	50	120	200	West Virginia, MW, USHR, G/IT
Duryee, Abram	1815-1890	75	150	225	Big Bethel, Second Manassas
Duval, Isaac H.	1824-1902	35	75	165	West Virginia, USHR, SL
Dwight, William	1831-1888	60	125	180	Williamsburg, Red River, NE, WP
Dyer, Alexander B.	1815-1874	100	160	285	Ordinance officer,WP, MW"Dyer shell"
Eaton, Amos B.	1806-1877	40	55	125	Comm. gen. U.S. Army, WP, MW
Edwards, John	1815-1894	40	65	130	Army of the Southwest, SL, congress
Edwards, Oliver	1835-1904	50	100	150	NE, Gettysburg postmaster,
Egan, Thomas W.	1834-1887	55	120		Seven Pines, Peninsular, AOTP
Ellet, Alfred W.	1820-1895	40	75	150	Dept. of MS, Marine Brig., Vicksburg
Elliott, Washington L.	1825-1888	50	100	200	Wilson's Creek, Springfield, Corinth, WP
Emory, William H.	1811-1887	75	150	300	NE, WP, writer,relatedB.Franklin
Estey (Este), George P.	1829-1881	40	85	170	Laurel Hill, Mill Springs, Tullahoma
Eustis, Henry L.	1819-1885	75	150	260	NE, Gettysburg, WP, author
Ewing, Charles	1835-1883	50	100	200	Vicksburg, Chattanooga, Atlanta
Ewing, Hugh B.	1826-1905	45	115	225	South Mountain, Sharpsburg, author
Ewing, Thomas Jr.	1829-1896	60	110	200	Cane Hill, NE, USHR, sec. Z. Taylor
Fairchild, Lucius	1831-1896	35	80	125	Falling Waters, Second Manassas,G/WI
Farnsworth, Elom J.	1837-1863				Gettysburg, KIA, PU
Farnsworth, John F.	1820-1897	50	100	160	Peninsular, Maryland, Congress
Ferrero, Edward	1831-1899	55	130	250	Second Manassas,NE, WP, SDS-2X
Ferry, Orris S.	1823-1875	50	130	200	Shenandoah Valley, SL, USS
Fessenden, Francis	1839-1906	60	140	200	Red River, Shiloh, Pleasant Hill
Fessenden, James D.	1833-1882	40	75	100	Carolina coast, Atlanta, SL
Fisk, Clinton B.	1828-1890	60	100	200	Missouri, Arkansas
Force, Manning	1824-1899	50	100	175	Shiloh, Vicksburg, Atlanta, Carolina
Forsyth, James W.	1835-1906	50	125	200	Peninsular, Maryland,WP, cmdr. WK
Foster, John G.	1823-1874	50	100	200	Fort Sumter, North Carolina,WP, MW
Foster, Robert S.	1834-1903	50	100	200	Rich Mountain, Suffolk, LA
Franklin, William	1823-1903	100	200	260	First Manassas, Maryland, WP, MW
Fremont, John C.	1813-1890	250	750	1450	California, USS, TG/AZ, SALS-4-5X
French, William H.	1815-1881	75	150	300	Peninsular, Gettysburg, WP, MW
Fry, James B.	1827-1894	40	80	125	Washington, staff service,WP, writer
Fry, Speed S.	1817-1892	50	100	150	Fishing Creek, Shiloh, Stone's River
Fuller, John W.	1827-1891	60	125	200	Iuka, Corinth, Carolinas, Atlanta
Gamble, William	1818-1866	140	200	300	Warrenton, VA, Malvern Hill, Gettysburg
Garfield, James A.	(see Presidents of the United States)				
Garrard, Kenner	1827-1879	100	200	300	Gettysburg, WP, SDS/LS & SALS - 2X
Garrard, Theophilus T.	1812-1902	50	100		Wild Cat Mt., Baker's Creek, MW
Geary, John W.	1819-1873	100	200	500	Harper's Ferry, Gettysburg, G/PA, ESPV
Getty, George W.	1819-1901	50	100	200	WP, MW, insp. gen. AOTP, SALS-3-4X

Name	DB/DD	SIG	LS/DS	ALS	Comments
Gibbon, John	1827-1896	115	200	340	NE, Gettysburg, WP, MW, author
Gibbs, Alfred	1823-1868	100	200	300	Cook's Spring, WP, MW, SALS-2X
Gilbert, Charles C.	1822-1903	40	100	150	Wilson's Creek, AOK, WP, MW
Gilbert, James I.	1823-1884	50	100		Red River, Nashville, Mobile
Gillem, Alvan C.	1830-1875	50	125	230	Western North Carolina, WP, AG/TN
Gillmore, Quincy A.	1825-1888	40	100	150	Fort Sumter, Washington, WP
Gordon, George H.	1823-1886	50	100	125	Upper Potomac, NE, WP, MW, author
Gorman, Willis A.	1816-1876	115	200	400	First Manassas, SL,Congress, TG/MN
Graham, Charles K.	1824-1889	125	165	300	Peninsular, Seven Pines, Gettysburg
Graham, Lawrence P.	1815-1905	50	100	200	Yorktown, WP, MW
Granger, Gordon	1822-1876	100	200	250	Wilson's Creek, New Madrid, WP, MW
Granger, Robert S.	1816-1894	40	100	145	Kentucky, Tennessee, N. Alabama
Grant, Lewis A.	1828-1918	50	100	200	Peninsular, NE, Asst. S/War
Grant, Ulysses Simpson (see Presidents of the United States)					
Greene, George S.	1801-1899	50	125	200	Cedar Mountain, Sharpsburg, WP
Gregg, David M.	1833-1916	65	135	200	Maryland,Gettysburg, WP, SALS-2X
Gresham, Walter Q.	1832-1895	50	100	150	Vicksburg, Atlanta, SL, SALS-2X
Grierson, Benjamin H.	1826-1911	60	150	300	Tennessee, SDS/LS & SALS-2X
Griffin, Charles	1825-1867	150	200	300	First Manassas, Peninsular, WP, MW
Griffin, Simon G.	1824-1902	50	100	200	First and Second Manassas,NE, SL
Grose, William	1812-1900	40	100	175	Shiloh, Army of the Cumberland, SL
Grover, Cuvier	1828-1885	40	80	150	Second Manassas, Peninsular, WP
Hackleman, Pleasant	1814-1862	300	445		Ball's Bluff, Corinth, KIA, ESPV
Halleck, Henry W.	1815-1872	150	500	1000	WP, controversial, SALS-4-5X
Hamblin, Joseph E.	1828-1870	120	200		Peninsular, Maryland, Gettysburg
Hamilton, Andrew J.	1815-1875	50	100	200	New Orleans, Congress
Hamilton, Charles S.	1822-1891	60	125	250	Iuka, Corinth, Shenandoah, WP, MW
Hamilton, Schuyler	1822-1903	40	80	150	Island No. 10, Corinth, WP, MW
Hamlin, Cyrus	1839-1867	150	200	300	Cross Keys, s. H. Hamlin (VP)
Hammond, William A.	1828-1900	75	150	340	Surgeon Gen. U.S. Army, author
Hancock, Winfield	1824-1886	300	700	1500	Gettysburg, NE,WP, MW, ESPV
Hardie, James A.	1823-1876	85	175	300	Maryland, Sharpsburg, WP, MW,
Hardin, Martin D.	1837-1923	100	150	375	Peninsular, Gettysburg, WP, writer
Harding, Abner C.	1807-1874	50	100	200	Monmouth, Fort Donelson, Congress
Harker, Charles Garrison	1835-1864				Shiloh, Perryville, Atlanta, WP, KIA, PU
Harland, Edward	1832-1915	40	80	170	Sharpsburg, First Manassas, NE, SL
Harney, William S.	1800-1889	75	150	300	Department of the West, MW, ESPV
Harris, Thomas M.	1817-1906	35	80	155	Shenandoah Valley, SL, LA
Harrow, William	1822-1872	100	200	300	Mine Run, Atlanta, Gettysburg
Hartranft, John F.	1830-1889	85	175	350	Bull Run, G/PA, SALS - 2 - 3 X, LA
Hartsuff, George L.	1830-1871	50	100	200	West Virginia, Second Manassas, WP
Hascall, Milo S.	1829-1904	40	100	180	Atlanta, Corinth, Murfreesboro, WP
Haskin, Joseph A.	1818-1874	50	100	200	Washington, Ft. Independ., WP, MW
Hatch, Edward	1832-1889	60	125	200	Corinth, Central Mississippi, Nashville
Hatch, John P.	1822-1901	40	100	200	Shenandoah, WP, MW, ESPV-LS/DS
Haupt, Herman	1817-1905	55	115	225	Chief/construction, WP, SALS-2X
Hawkins, John P.	1830-1914	35	75	150	Commisary Department, WP
Hawley, Joseph R.	1826-1905	50	100	150	First Manassas, Flordia, G/CT, USS
Hayes, Joseph	1835-1912	125	200	400	Sharpsburg, Gettysburg, reclusive
Hayes, Rutherford B.	(see Presidents of the United States)				
Haynie, Isham N.	1824-1868	135	200	325	Fort Henry, Fort Donelson, SL, MW

Name	DB/DD	SIG	LS/DS	ALS	Comments
Hays, Alexander	1819-1864	300	675	1000	Peninsular, Gettysburg WP, MW, KIA
Hays, William	1819-1875	45	100	185	Peninsular, Gettysburg, WP
Hazen, William B.	1830-1887	80	150	200	Shiloh, Perryville, Atlanta, WP
Heintzelman, Samuel P.	1805-1880	50	100	175	First Manassas, Yorktown, WP
Herron, Francis J.	1837-1902	50	100	200	Wilson's Creek, Elkhorn Tavern
Hincks, Edward W.	1830-1894	100	200	300	Ball's Bluff, Peninsular, Maryland, SL
Hitchcock, Ethan A.	1798-1870	100	200	300	Com. General of prisoners, WP, MW
Hobson, Edward H.	1825-1901	40	80	120	Kentucky, Buffington's Island, MW
Holt, Joseph	1807-1894	80	175	350	Judge adv. gen., S/War, PM, SALS-2X
Hooker, Joseph	1814-1879	300	1000	2250	AOTP, WP, MW, controversial, SALS-2X
Hovey, Alvin P.	1821-1891	60	125	200	Vicksburg, Shiloh, MW, Congress, G/IN
Hovey, Charles E.	1827-1897	40	75	140	Arkansas Post
Howard, Oliver O.	1830-1909	150	300	365	First Manassas, Peninsula, Seven Pines
Howe, Albion P.	1818-1897	50	100	200	Harper's Ferry, WP, SALS-2-3X
Howell, Joshua B.	1806-1864	275	500		Peninsula, Goldsboro
Humphreys, Andrew A.	1810-1883	100	200	250	Maryland, Gettysburg, WP
Hunt, Henry J.	1819-1889	75	150	200	First Manassas, Malvern Hill, WP, MW
Hunt, Lewis C.	1824-1886	50	100	200	Peninsular, Seven Pines, WP, MW
Hunter, David	1802-1886	85	175	200	First Manassas, WP, SALS-2X
Hurlbut, Stephen A.	1815-1882	100	200	400	Shiloh,SL, congress, SALS-5-6X
Ingalls, Rufus	1818-1893	60	125	250	AOTP /qm, WP, MW, SALS-2X
Jackson, Conrad	1813-1862				Dranesville, MW, KIA, PU
Jackson, James S.	1823-1862	300	600	1200	AOK, MW, Congress, KIA
Jackson, Nathaniel J.	1818-1892	40	75	150	Gaines's Mill, S. Mountain,Sharpsburg
Jackson, Richard H.	1830-1892	35	70	135	Fort Pickens, Army of the James
Jameson, Charles D.	1827-1862				First Manassas, Peninsular, PU
Johnson, Andrew	(see Presidents of the United States)				
Johnson, Richard W.	1827-1897	50	100	175	Murfreesboro, Chickamauga, WP
Jones, Patrick H.	1830-1900	100	200	300	Peninsular, Second Bull Run, Atlanta
Judah, Henry M.	1821-1866	300	500	850	Washington, Corinth, WP, MW, ESPV
Kane, Thomas L.	1822-1883	100	225	360	Dranesville, Gettysburg, SALS-2-3X
Kautz, August V.	1828-1895	50	100	150	Peninsular, LA, MW, WP
Kearny, Philip	1815-1862	400	650	940	Peninsular, "Kearny patch", KIA
Keim, William H.	1813-1862				Shenandoah Valley, PU
Kelley, Benjamin F.	1807-1891	50	75	150	West Virginia, Maryland
Kenly, John R.	1818-1891	75	150	250	Shenandoah Valley, AOTP
Ketcham, John H.	1832-1906	75	150	300	Gettysburg, Resaca,SL, USHR
Ketchum, William S.	1813-1871	40	90	125	War and Treasury departments, WP
Keyes, Erasmus D.	1810-1895	75	200	350	First Manassas, Peninsular, WP
Kiernan, James L.	1837-1869				Pea Ridge, practiced medicine, PU
Kilpatrick, Hugh J.	1836-1881	150	300	500	AOTP, Gettysburg, WP, ESPV-AF
Kimball, Nathan	1822-1898	50	100	200	NE, Kernstown, Atlanta, MW, SL
King, John H.	1820-1888	60	125	200	Shilo, Murfreesboro, Atlanta, MW
King, Rufus	1814-1876	40	80	150	WP, worked in newspaper business
Kirby, Edmund	1840-1863				First Manassas, NE, WP, PU
Kirk, Edward N.	1828-1863	365	550		Shiloh, Murfreesboro
Knipe, Joseph F.	1823-1901	55	100	200	Shenandoah, Cedar Mountain, MW
Krzyzanowski, Wladimir	1824-1887	75	150	250	Washington, Cross Keys, S. Manassas

Name	DB/DD	SIG	LS/DS	ALS	Comments
Lander, Frederick W.	1821-1862	200	300	600	Edwards Ferry, Rich Mountain,SALS-2X
Lauman, Jacob G.	1813-1867	100	200	300	Missouri, Belmont, Fort Donelson
Lawler, Michael K.	1814-1882	45	100	175	Ft.Donelson, Vicksburg, MW, SALS-2X
Ledlie, James H.	1832-1882	75	150	230	Spotsylvania, AOTP
Lee, Albert L.	1834-1907	50	100	200	Vicksburg, Big Black River, Red River
Leggett, Mortimer D.	1821-1896	65	125	150	West.Virginia, Atlanta, Carolinas. ESPV
Lightburn, Joseph A. J.	1824-1901	60	120	200	Chattanooga, Atlanta, West Virginia, WP
Lockwood, Henry H.	1814-1899	50	100	200	Maryland, Virginia, Gettysburg, MW
Logan, John A.	1826-1886	100	200	300	Corinth, Atlanta, MW, SL, USHR, USS
Long, Eli	1837-1903	50	100	200	Murfreesboro, Tullahoma, Atlanta
Lowell, Charles R.	1835-c.1864				Peninsular, Sharpsburg, PU
Lucas, Thomas J.	1826-1908	50	100	200	Ball's Bluff, Vicksburg, Red River, MW
Lyon, Nathaniel	1818-1861				Missouri, Wilson's Creek, WP, MW, PU
Lytle, William H.'	1826-1863	350	550		Carnifex Ferry, Alabama, MW. SL
McArthur, John	1826-1906	60	150	300	Fort Henry, Shiloh, Vicksburg, Atlanta
McCall, George A.	1802-1868	100	150	250	Peninsular, MW, inspectors general
McClellan, George B.	1826-1885	300	400	875	AOTP, WP, MW, G/NJ, (NJ), SALS-2-3X
McClernand, John A.	1812-1890	60	130	200	Vicksburg, Louisiana, Texas, Congress
McCook, Alexander M.	1831-1903	50	100	225	First Manassas, AOO, Shiloh, WP
McCook, Daniel	1834-1864				Wilson's Creek, Perryville,PU
McCook, Edward M.	1833-1909	50	100	230	Chickamauga, Perryville, TG/CO
McCook, Robert L.	1827-1862	365	650		West Virginia, Carnifix Ferry, Mill Springs
McDowell, Irvin	1818-1885	100	200	300	AOTP, WP, MW, SALS-2X
McGinnis, George F.	1826-1910	50	100	220	Fort Donelson, Shiloh, Vicksburg, MW
McIntosh, John B.	1829-1888	125	200		Peninsular, Maryland, AOTP, MW
Mckean, Thomas J.	1810-1870	60	120	250	Missouri, Corinth, WP, MW
Mackenzie, Ranald S.	1840-1889	125	250	350	Second Manassas, Gettyburg, WP
McKinstry, Justus	1814-1897	40	80	150	Dept. /West, WP, MW, controversial
McLean, Nathaniel C.	1815-1905	75	115	200	Chancellorsville, Atlanta,s. J. McLean
McMillan, James W.	1825-1903	50	100	200	New Orleans, Red River, Cedar Creek
McNeil, John	1813-1891	50	100		Missouri, SL, sheriff, commissioner
McPherson, James B.	1828-1864	550	1200	2400	Fort Henry, Ft. Donelson, Shiloh, WP
Maltby, Jasper A.	1826-1867	125	200	300	Vicksburg, mayor, MW
Mansfield, Joseph K. F.	1803-1862	200	375	600	Washington, , WP, MW, KIA, SALS-4-5X
Manson, Mahlon D.	1820-1895	50	100	150	Rich Mountain, SL, Congress
Marcy, Randolph B.	1812-1887	50	100	200	Michigan, Wisconsin, WP, MW, ESPV
Marston, Gilman	1811-1890	40	80	150	Peninsular, SL, Congress, USS
Martindale, John H.	1815-1881	50	100	180	Peninsular, Milt. Gov. (Wash., D.C.) WP
Mason, John S.	1824-1897	50	120	215	Fredericksburg, California, WP, MW
Matthies, Charles L.	1824-1868	150	260		Island No. 10, Corinth, Iuka, SL
Meade, George G.	1815-1972	500	750	1500	NE, Gettysburg,SDS - 2-3X, SALS-2X
Meagher, Thomas F.	1823-1867	150	300	600	AOTP, ESPV, SLS/DS-2-3X, SALS-2X
Meigs, Montgomery C.	1816-1892	50	150	200	Quartermaster general, WP
Meredith, Solomon	1810-1875	230	375	500	Second Manassas, Gettysburg, SL
Meredith, Sullivan A.	1816-1874	80	175	320	First & Second Manassas'
Merritt, Wesley	1834-1910	60	125	230	AOTP, Gettysburg, WP,
Miles, Nelson A.	1839-1925	150	300	400	Seven Pines, Sharpsburg
Miller, John F.	1831-1886	40	75	115	Murfreesboro, Tullahoma, SL, USS
Miller, Stephen	1816-1881	100	200	300	Shenandoah, Seven Pines, G/MN
Milroy, Robert H.	1816-1890	45	120	240	Western Virginia, Shenandoah Valley

Name	DB/DD	SIG	LS/DS	ALS	Comments
Mitchel, Ormsby	1809-1862				Department of the Ohio WP, PU
Mitchell, John G.	1838-1894	50	100	200	Tennessee, Chickamauga, Carolinas
Mitchell, Robert B.	1823-1882	80	150	275	Wilson's Creek, Perryville, MW, TG/NM
Montgomery, William R.	1801-1871	40	100	180	First Manassas, Annapolis, WP, MW
Morell, George W.	1815-1883	50	100	245	Peninsular, Seven Days, WP, MW
Morgan, Charles H.	1834-1875	50	125	250	Fort Monroe, Washington, AOTP
Morgan Edwin D.	1811-1883	40	70	100	Dept. NY, G/NY, USS, SL
Morgan, George W.	1820-1893	75	150	300	MW, Congress, ESPV, SALS-5X
Morgan, James D.	1810-1896	50	100	175	Island No. 10, Corinth, Atlanta, Carolina
Morris, William H.	1827-1900	75	150	250	Gettysburg, Wilderness, Spotsylvania
Morton, James S.	1829-1864				Ft. Deleware, Ft. Hancock, WP, KIA, PU
Mott, Gershom	1822-1884	40	100	150	AOTP, Seven Pines, MW, ESPV
Mower, Joseph A.	1827-1870	55	115	225	Iuka, Corinth, Vicksburg, Red River, MW
Nagle, James	1822-1866				South Mountain, Sharpsburg, MW, PU
Naglee, Henry M.	1815-1886	40	75	150	Washington, Peninsular, MW, SDS-5X
Negley, James Scott	1826-1901	50	100	150	Murfreesboro, MW, Congress
Neill, Thomas H.	1826-1885	50	100	150	Frontier, Salem Church, Mine Run, WP
Nelson, William	1824-1862	425	630	1200	Shiloh, Corinth, popular w/collectors
Newton, John	1822-1895	100	200	365	Washington, Gettysburg, Congress
Nickerson, Franklin S.	1826-1917	40	75	100	Baton Rouge, Louisiana, Red River
Oglesby, Richard J.	1824-1899	50	100	130	Fort Henry, MW, SL, USS, G/IL
Oliver, John M.	1828-1872	50	125	235	Shiloh, Corinth, Atlanta, Carolina
Opdycke, Emerson	1830-1884	50	100˙		Shiloh, Chickamauga, Chattanooga
Ord, Edward O.	1818-1883	100	200	400	Corinth, Vicksburg, WP, MW
Orme, William W.	1832-1866				Prairie Grove, Vicksburg, LA, PU
Osborn, Thomas O.	1832-1904	50	100	150	Drewry's Bluff, Fort Gregg, diplomat
Osterhaus, Peter J.	1823-1917	50	100	150	Wilson's Creek, Elkhorn Tavern, NE
Owen, Joshua T.	1821-1887	50	100	165	AOTP, SL
Paine, Charles J.	1833-1916	100	175	275	Washington, "America's Cup" defender
Paine, Eleazer A.	1815-1882	60	125	200	Paducah, KY, Corinth, WP, LA
Paine, Halbert E.	1826-1905	50	100	200	Washington, Congress, Author
Palmer, Innis N.	1824-1900	50	100	200	First Manassas, Peninsular, WP, MW
Palmer, John M.	1817-1900	100	150	250	New Madrid, Island, G/IL, USS, PC
Parke, John G.	1827-1900	100	200	400	Maryland, Fredericksburg, Knoxville, WP
Parsons, Lewis	1818-1907	75	150	300	Dept. of the Mississippi
Patrick, Marsena R.	1811-1888	50	100	150	Second Manassas, AOTP - provost, WP
Patterson, Francis E.	1821-1862				Wiliamsburg, Seven Pines, scarce, PU
Paul, Gabriel R.	1813-1886				NE, Gettysburg, WP, MW, PU
Peck, John James	1821-1878	100	175	350	Peninsular, Suffolk, WP, MW, Congress
Pennypacker, Galusha	1844-1916	100	200	260	Petersburg, Fort Fisher
Penrose, William Henry	1832-1903	50	125	250	Second Manassas, Gettysburg
Phelps, John S.	1814-1886	40	100	150	Pea Ridge, Congress, G/MI
Phelps, John W.	1813-1885	50	150	200	Newport News, WP, MW, writer
Piatt, Abram S.	1821-1908	50	100	200	West Virginia, Second Manassas, NE
Pierce, Byron R.	1829-1924	40	80	160	First Manassas, Gettysburg, dentist,
Pile, William A.	1829-1889	50	100	150	Benton Barracks, congress,TG/NM
Pitcher, Thomas G.	1824-1895	50	100	150	Cedar Mountain, S.Manassas, WP, MW
Pleasonton, Alfred	1824-1897	50	100	200	Washington, Peninsular, WP, MW
Plummer, Joseph B.	1816-1862				Wilson's Creek, WP, MW, PU

Name	DB/DD	SIG	LS/DS	ALS	Comments
Poe, Orlando M.	1832-1895	55	120	200	Peninsular, Second Manassas, WP
Pope, John	1822-1892	100	150	300	Island No. 10, AOV, WP, MW
Porter, Andrew	1820-1872	100	200	475	First Manassas, AOP, WP, MW, LA
Porter, Fitz J.	1822-1901	100	200	400	Peninsular, WP, MW, SALS-2X
Porter, Edward	1823-1889	50	100	150	Chief of staff - Foster
Potter, Joseph H.	1822-1892	50	100	200	New Mexico, Chancellorsville,WP, MW
Potter, Robert B.	1829-1887	80	150	300	Cedar Mountain, Maryland, Vicksburg
Potts, Benjamin F.	1836-1887	75	150	260	West Virginia, Cross Keys, Vicksburg
Powell, William H.	1825-1904	50	100	150	Shenandoah, Cedar Creek
Pratt, Calvin E.	1828-1896	75	150	275	Peninsular, Mechanicsville
Prentiss, Benjamin M.	1919-1901	50	100	160	Shiloh, Dist. of Eastern Arkansas, MW
Prince, Henry	1811-1892	40	75	125	Cedar Mountain, Rapidan,MW, SALS-5X
Quinby, Issac F.	1821-1891	60	125	200	First Manassas, Dist of Mississippi, WP
Ramsay, George D.	1802-1882	40	75	150	Washington, Ordanance Dept., WP
Ransom, Thomas E.	1834-1864				Shiloh, Vicksburg, Red River , PU
Raum, Green B.	1829-1909	35	70	135	Corinth, Chattanooga, Atlanta, congress
Rawlins, John A.	1831-1869	75	150	300	U.S. Grant staff Lawyer, S/War
Reid, Hugh T.	1811-1874	80	160	225	Shiloh, Corinth, Vicksburg
Reilly, James W.	1828-1905	50	100	200	Knoxville, Atlanta, Franklin, SL
Reno, Jesse L.	1823-1862				Second Manassas, WP, KIA, PU
Revere, Joseph W.	1812-1880	100	200	400	Seven Days, Fredericksburg
Reynolds, John F.	1820-1863	500	1500		Maryland, Fredericksburg, WP, MW, KIA
Reynolds, Joseph J.	1822-1899	65	150	200	Cheat Mountain, Chickamauga, WP
Rice, Americus V.	1835-1904	50	100	200	Shiloh, Atlanta, Vicksburg, congress
Rice, Elliott W.	1835-1887	100	150	275	Belmont, Shiloh, Atlanta, Carolinas
Rice, James C.	1829-1864	400	600	1200	Peninsular, Gettysburg
Rice, Samuel A.	1828-1864				Missouri, Arkansas, Jenkin's Ferry, PU
Richardson, Israel	1815-1862				First Manassas, WP, MW. KIA, PU
Ricketts, James B.	1817-1887	75	150	275	First & Second Manassas, WP, MW
Ripley, James W.	1794-1870	50	175	200	Ordanance Department, WP
Roberts, Benjamin S.	1810-1875	45	100	225	Second Manassas, WP, MW
Robinson, James S.	1827-1892	75	150	260	Shenandoah, Gettysburg, congress
Robinson, James C.	1817-1897	120	220	300	NE, Gettysburg, AOP, WP, MW
Rodman, Isaac P.	1822-1862				Carolinas, Sharpsburg, SL, KIA, PU
Rosecrans, William S.	1819-1898	130	275	400	Western VA.,WP,congress, SALS-3X
Ross, Leonard F.	1823-1901	50	100	155	Corinth, Vicksburg, MW
Rousseau, Lovell H.	1818-1869	60	125	225	Shiloh, Murfreesboro,MW, SL, congress
Rowley, Thomas A.	1808-1892	60	125	200	Yorktown, Williamsburg, NE, MW
Rucker, Daniel H.	1812-1910	30	75	100	Quartermaster's Department, MW
Ruger, Thomas H.	1833-1907	40	100	135	Maryland, Gettysburg, Carolina , WP
Russell, David A.	1820-1864				Peninsular, Maryland, WP, MW, KIA, PU
Saloman, Friedrich	1826-1897	40	80	150	Missouri, Arkansas, Surveyor, Surveyor
Sanborn, John B.	1826-1904	50	100	200	Iuka, Vicksburg, SL, USHR, USS
Sanders, William P.	1833-1863				Washington, Kentucky,WP, KIA, PU
Saxton, Rufus	1824-1908	40	80	115	Harper's Ferry, McClellan's staff, WP
Scammon, Eliakim P.	1816-1894	45	90	175	Carnifix Ferry, Maryland, WP, MW,
Schenck, Robert C.	1809-1890	35	60	120	First & Second Manassas, congress, SL
Schimmelfenning, Alex.	1824-1865				Second Manassas, Gettysburg, PU
Schoepf, Albin F.	1822-1886	50	100	165	Fishing Creek, Perryville, Fort Delaware

Name	DB/DD	SIG	LS/DS	ALS	Comments
Schofield, John M.	1831-1906	65	120	200	Atlanta, Tenn., S/War, WP, SALS-2X
Schurz, Carl	1829-1906	75	150	200	Shenandoah, Gettysburg, USS, editor
Scott, Robert	1826-1900	65	140	175	Vicksburg, Atlanta, S.Carolina, G/SC
Scott, Winfield	1786-1866	250	500	850	CIC army, MW,Presidential nominee
Sedgwick, John	1813-1864	200	400	800	Sharpsburg, WP, MW, KIA
Seward, William H., Jr.	1839-1920	65	100	200	New York Heavy Artillery, Washington
Seymour, Truman	1824-1891	75	150	250	Fort Sumter, AOP, WP, MW
Shackelford, James M.	1827-1909	50	100	200	Fort Donelson, Cumberland Gap
Shaler, Alexander	1827-1911	45	80	150	Washington, AOP, Wilderness
Shepard, Isaac F.	1816-1889	50	100	135	Arkansas Post, SL, editor, diplomat
Shepley, George F.	1819-1878	45	90	125	New Orleans, , Milt. Gov. (LA), judge
Sheridan, Philip H.	1831-1888	350	900	2100	SP -2250, AOP, WP, SDS-7 SALS-2X
Sherman, Francis T.	1825-1905	50	100	200	Murfreesboro, Atlanta, Five Forks, SL
Sherman, Thomas W.	1813-1879	40	80	120	Port Hudson, New Orleans, WP, MW
Sherman, William T.	1820-1891	500	1200	2500	SB - $2750, ESPV, SALS- 2-20X
Shields, James	1810-1879	75	120	150	Shenandoah Valley, SL, USS
Sibley, Henry H.	1811-1891	100	200	400	Gen. U.S. Volunteers, G/MN, SL, ESPV
Sickles, Daniel E.	1819-1914	125	250	275	NE, Gettysburg,SL, Congress, diplomat
Sigel, Franz	1824-1902	80	150	200	Carthage, Elkhorn Tavern
Sill, Joshua W.	1831-1862				Murfreesboro, Georgia, WP, KIA, PU
Slack, James R.	1818-1881	75	150	200	Vicksburg, Island No. 10, SL
Slemmer, Adam J.	1829-1868	140	215	300	Corinth, Kentucky, Murfreesboro, WP
Slocum, Henry W.	1827-1894	100	150	200	Peninsular, Second Manassas, WP, SL
Slough, John P.	1829-1867	200			Military Gov. of Alexandria, SL
Smith, Andrew J.	1815-1897	50	125	200	Vicksburg, Chickasaw Bluffs, WP
Smith, Charle F.	1807-1862	250	500		Dept. of Utah, Fort Donelson, WP, MW
Smith, Giles A.	1829-1876	85	175	260	Shiloh, Corinth, Vicksburg, Atlanta
Smith, Green C.	1826-1895	50	75	150	Lebanon, TN, TG/Mont, MW, Congress,
Smith, Gustavus A.	1820-1885	200	425	875	Fort Sumter, ESPV, SLS/DS-5-6X
Smith, John E.	1816-1897	75	150		Shiloh, Vicksburg, Atlanta, Carolinas
Smith, Morgan L.	1821-1874	100	200	260	Shiloh, Chattanooga, Atlanta, diplomat
Smith, Thomas C. H.	1819-1897	35	70	120	Aide-de-camp Gen. Pope, controversial
Smith, Thomas K.	1820-1887	60	115	200	Vicksburg, Red River, diplomat
Smith, William F.	1824-1903	50	100	175	First Manassas, Maryland, WP, historian
Smith, William S.	1830-1916	50	100	225	West Virginia, Shiloh, Perryville, WP
Smyth, Thomas A.	1832-1865				Gettysburg, Appomattox , PU
Spears, James G.	1816-1869	125	240	300	Wild Cat Mountain, Mill Springs, C. Gap
Spinola, Francis B.	1821- ?				Manassas Gap, SL, congress, PU
Sprague, John W.	1817-1893	50	100	175	New Madrid, Island No. 10, Corinth
Stahel, Julius	1825-1912	55	100	200	Second Manassas, Shenandoah
Stanley, David S.	1828-1902	50	100	200	Missouri, WP, ESPV, SALS-3-4X
Stannard, George J.	1820-1886	50	100	200	Fort Harrison, F. Manassas, Gettysburg
Starkweather, John C.	1830-1890	60	150	200	Perryville, Murfreesboro, Chattanooga
Steedman, James B.	1817-1883	80	155	275	Philippi, Perrysville, MW., SL, printer
Steele, Frederick	1819-1868	115	225	330	Arkansas, Vicksburg, W.Creek, WP, MW
Stevens, Isaac I.	1818-1862				Port Royal, WP, MW, congress, KIA, PU
Stevenson, John D.	1821-1897	75	150	200	Corinth, Vicksburg, Chickamauga, SL
Stevenson, Thomas G.	1836-1864				Roanoke Island, New Bern,KIA, PU
Stokes, James H.	1815-1890	75	150	300	Every fight of the western army, WP
Stolbrand, Charles J.	1821-1894	50	100	165	Vicksburg, Chattanooga, Atlanta
Stone, Charles P.	1824-1887	65	125	200	First Bull Run, WP, MW, controversial
Stoneman, George	1822-1894	50	150	200	West Virginia, AOP, WP, MW, G/CA

Name	DB/DD	SIG	LS/DS	ALS	Comments
Stoughton, Edwin H.	1838-1868				Peninsular, WP, PU
Strong, George C.	1832-1863				First Manassas, WP, KIA, PU
Strong, William	1805-1867				District of St. Louis, paralyzed later, PU
Stuart, David	1816-1868	100	175	250	Shiloh, Chickasaw Bluffs, congress
Stumbaugh, Fred. S.	1817-1897	50	100	150	Shiloh, Kentucky
Sturgis, Samuel D.	1822-1889	50	100	200	Fort Smith, Wilson's Creek, WP, MW
Sullivan, Jeremiah C.	1830-1890	40	75	150	Philippi, Shenandoah Valley, Iuka
Sully, Alfred	1820-1879	65	140	175	Peninsular, Sharpsburg, WP, MW,
Sumner, Edwin V.	1797-1863	265	525		Peninsular, Seven Pines, Sharpsburg
Swayne, Wager	1834-1902	40	75	130	Corinth, Tennessee, Kenesaw
Sweeny, Thomas W.	1820-1892	60	125	200	Wilson's Creek, Fort Donelson, Shiloh
Sykes, George	1822-1880	75	150	220	First Manassas, Gettysburg, WP, MW
Taylor, George W.	1808-1862				Seven Days, Manassas, KIA, PU
Taylor, Joseph P.	1796-1864	75	200	245	Commissary general, MW, b. Z. Taylor
Taylor, Nelson	1821-1894	60	125	200	Virginia Peninsula, MW, congress
Terrill, William R.	1834-1862				Kentucky, Shiloh, Corinth, WP, PU
Terry, Alfred H.	1827-1890	125	250	300	First Manassas, SLS/DS-2X, SALS - 2X
Terry, Henry D.	1812-1869	75	150	200	Washington, Peneinsular, AOP
Thayer, John M.	1820-1906	50	100	200	Fort Donelson, USS, G/NE
Thomas, John H.	1816-1870	135	250	425	Mill Springs, Perryville, WP, ESPV
Thomas, Henry G.	1837-1897	75	150	225	First Manassas, Overland
Thomas, Lorenzo	1804-1875	100	150	300	Adjutant general of the army, WP, MW
Thomas, Stephens	1809-1903	50	100	150	Washington, Cedar Crk. SL, USS
Thruston, Charles M.	1798-1873	50	100	135	Protected railways, WP, mayor
Tibbits, William B.	1837-1880	75	150	300	Peninsular, Big Bethel, Sec. Manassas
Tillson, Davis	1830-1895	50	115	150	Cedar Mountain, Second Manassas, SL
Todd, John B. S.	1814-1872	50	100	200	Army of the Tenn. WP, MW, congress
Torbert, Alfred T. A.	1833-1880	110	200	300	Second Manassas, Gettysburg, WP
Totten, Joseph G.	1788-1864	75	150	200	Chief engineer of the army, MW, WP
Tower, Zealous B.	1819-1900	30	60	110	Fort Pickens, Sec. Manassas, WP, MW
Turchin, John B.	1822-1901	50	125	250	Huntsville, Athens, Chickamauga
Turner, John W.	1833-1899	60	125	200	Petersburg, District of Henrico, WP
Tuttle, James M.	1823-1892	50	100		Fort Donelson, Shiloh, Vicksburg, SL
Tyler, Daniel	1799-1882	50	100	150	First Manassas, Corinth, Harper's Ferry
Tyler, Erastus B.	1822-1891	40	80	150	Fredericksville, Chancellorsville
Tyler, Robert O.	1831-1874	100	200	300	Peninsular, Gettysburg, WP
Tyndale, Hector	1821-1880	50	75	100	Front Royal, Cedar Mt., Sec. Manassas
Ullmann, Daniel	1810-1892	40	80	150	Second Manassas, Cedar Mountain
Underwood, Adin B.	1828-1888	50	75	150	Shenandoah Valley, Chancellorsville
Upton, Emory	1839-1881	100	150	200	Spotsylvania, WP, SDS-2-3X
Van Alen, James H.	1819-1886	60	125	200	Washington, Peninsular, Hooker's adc
Van Cleve, Horatio P.	1809-1891	50	100	165	Fishing Creek, Corinth, Murfreesboro
Van Derveer, Ferdinand	1823-1892	50	90	180	Corinth, Perryville, Atlanata, MW
Vandever, William	1817-1893	40	75	150	Pea Ridge, Arkansas Post, congress
Van Vliet, Stewart	1815-1901	50	100	150	AOP, WP, MW, SALS-2X
Van Wyck, Charles H.	1824-1895	40	75	100	S.Carolina, congress, USS
Veatch, James C.	1819-1895	50	100	175	Fort Donelson, Shiloh, Corinth, SL
Viele, Egbert L.	1825-1902	35	75	100	WP, MW, eng. N.Y. Cen. Park, congress
Vincent, Strong	1837-1863				Yorktown, Gettysburg, KIA, PU

Name	DB/DD	SIG	LS/DS	ALS	Comments
Vinton, Francis L.	1835-1879				Virginia Pen., Fredericksburg, WP, PU
Vogdes, Israel	1816-1889	50	100	150	Fort Pickens, Charleston, Norfolk, WP
von Steinwehr, Adolph	1822-1877	75	150	230	First & Second Manassas, Gettysburg
Wade, Melancthon S.	1802-1868				Camp Dennison, businessman, PU
Wadsworth, James S,	1807-1864	50	100	200	Military G/DC, Gettysburg
Wagner, George D.	1829-1869				Murfressboro, Chickamauga, SL, PU
Walcutt, Charles C.	1838-1898	50	100	175	Shiloh, Vicksburg, Jackson, Atlanta
Wallace, Lewis "Lew"	1827-1905	175	325	500	NE, MW, SL, TG/NM, author "Ben Hur"
Wallace, William H. L.	1821-1862				Fort Donelson, Shiloh, MW, KIA, PU
Ward, John H. H.	1823-1903	50	100	125	First & Second Manassas, Peninsular
Ward, William T.	1808-1878	50	100	175	Kentucky, Atlanta, MW, SL, congress,
Warner, James Meech	1836-1897	40	75	150	Washington, Spotsylvania, WP
Warren, Fitz-Henry	1816-1878	40	80	145	Dept. of the Gulf, Red River, diplomat
Warren, Gouverneur K.	1830-1882	125	250	500	Bethel Chur., WP, SLS/DS & SALS - 2X
Washburn, Cadwallad.C.	1818-1882	60	125	150	Missouri, congress, G/WI
Watkins, Louis D.	1833-1868				Peninsular, Gaine's Mill, Kentucky, PU
Webb, Alexander S.	1835-1911	40	100	175	Peninsular, Fort Pickens, Gettysburg
Weber, Max (Von)	1824-1901	50	100	150	Sharpsburg, Washington, Harpers Ferry
Webster, Joseph D.	1811-1876	100	200	250	Grant's and Sherman's chief of staff. MW
Weed, Stephen H.	1831-1863				Peninsular,Gettysburg, WP, KIA, PU
Weitzel, Godfrey	1835-1884	50	100	200	Fort Fisher, Appomattox, WP
Wells, William	1837-1892	75	150	225	Shenandoah Valley, Second Bull Run
Welsh, Thomas	1824-1863				Charleston Harbor, AOP, MW, PU
Wessells, Henry W.	1809-1889	50	100	230	Missouri, AOTP, Peninsular, WP, MW
West, Joseph R.	1822-1898	50	100	150	Arizona, Red River, MW, USS
Wheaton, Frank	1833-1903	65	120		First Manassas, Williamsburg, VA
Whipple, Amiel W.	1816-1863	150	250	400	First Manassas, Washington, WP, KIA
Whipple, William D.	1826-1902	40	75	100	First Manassas, WP, adc W.T. Sherman
Whitaker, Walter C.	1823-1887	50	100	165	Shiloh, Murfreesboro, Atlanta , MW, SL
White, Julius	1816-1890	35	75	150	Elkhorn Tavern, Harper's Ferry, SL
Wild, Edward A.	1825-1891	100	175	250	First Bull Run, Peninsular, Seven Pines
Willcox, Orlando B.	1823-1907	100	200	360	Sharpsburg, First Manassas, WP, MW
Williams, Alpheus S.	1810-1878	100	175	330	AOP, Gettysburg, Atlanta , MW, USHR
Williams, David H.	1819-1891	40	100	165	Seven Pines, Malvern Hill, Maryland
Williams, Nelson	1823-1897	40	75	120	Missouri, Shiloh, Businessman
Williams, Seth	1822-1866	50	100	150	Adj.gen dept., AOTP, WP, SLS/DS-2X
Williams, Thomas	1815-1862				North Carolina, WP, MW, KIA, PU
Williamson, James A.	1829-1902	80	175	300	Elkhorn Tavern, NE, Vicksburg, ESPV
Willich, August (von)	1810-1878				Shiloh, Perryville, Murfreesboro, PU
Wilson, James H.	1837-1925	100	200	400	South Mt., Vicksburg, Washington, WP
Wistar, Issac	1827-1905	40	100	140	Ball's Bluff, Peninsular, Sharpsburg
Wood, Thomas J.	1823-1906	50	100	150	Shiloh, Perryville, WP, MW, ESPV-ALS
Woodbury, Daniel P.	1812-1864				Fort Jefferson, Fort Taylor,WP, PU
Woods, Charles	1827-1885	40	75	125	Fort Donelson, Shiloh, Carolinas, WP
Woods, William B.	(see United States Supreme Court)				
Wool, John E.	1784-1869	125	250	475	Dept.East, MW, SALS-2X
Wright, George	1801-1865				Virtually no involvement WP, MW, PU
Wright, Horatio	1820-1899	75	150	235	Florida, First Manassas,WP, engineer
Zook, Samuel	1821-1863				Anapolis, First Manassas, KIA, PU

ENTERTAINMENT

WHAT YOU NEED TO KNOW

* A very popular area of autograph collecting is acquiring the signatures of prominent individuals in the area of the performing arts.

* Understanding the impact of the performing arts on our society, and even that of certain entertainers in pivotal roles, will help you gage the demand for, and value of certain autographs.

* Individuals active in the performing arts are often associated with their key performances. Thus key items, such as depictions of them in such a role, often command greater value.

* The signed photograph is by far the most popular form of collecting in this niche.

* Vintage signed photographs from many pioneers of television and motion pictures command premium value (Often 2X listed price)

* Handwritten letters from modern-day entertainers rarely enter the market, however short notes are common with many.

* Due to its popularity, collecting in this area has many pitfalls. Facsimile signatures in many forms exist, including printed, secretarial, ghost-signed and machine-signed.

* Just because an entertainer charges for their signature, does not mean that that amount then becomes the value of their autograph.

MARKET FACTS

* This market is very dynamic, so much so that my research rates it as unstable.

* The market has shown significant price variations- a sign of unfamiliarity by both dealers and collectors.

* Prices are driven by screen legends and those stars who are currently popular.

* Forgery is common, particularly with popular new stars and established legends.

* Obtaining a full set of signatures of Academy Award recipients remains popular with collectors in this niche.

TRENDS

* Collecting autographed cast photographs, from popular television shows, movies, or plays, remains popular with collectors. When autographed cast photographs are unavailable, collectors often opt for assemblages in numerous forms, such as index cards, canceled checks, album pages, etc. as an alternative and often impressive substitute.

* The use of fan mail services to answer autograph requests continues to be popular with actors.

* Popular entertainers, in current roles, continue to command inflated prices when compared to the overall market.

Notes:

* The selected entries in the list below reflect those of greatest interest to collectors and signatures that are actively offered in the market place.

* The list below is not intended to be comprehensive.

* ALS value listings are for handwritten letters of fundamental content.

Abbreviations: $ = charges for autographs, ALS = autographed latter signed, CF = controversial figure, DS/LS = document signed/letter signed, ES = elusive signer, FA = forgery/facsimile alert, GWTW = Gone With the Wind, IAWL = It's A Wonderful Life, RS = responsive signer, Sig. = signature, SP = signed photograph, WOO = Wizard of Oz,

Name	db/dd	Sig.	DS/LS	ALS	SP	Comments
Aames, Willie	1960 -	5	15		15	"Eight Is Enough" - TV
Abbott, Bud	1895 - 1974	225	365		450	Comedian, "Buck Privates"
Abbott, George	1887 - 1995	35	60	80	125	Producer,"Damn Yankees"
Abel, Walter	1898- 1987	20	30	45	25	"Raintree County"
Abraham, F. M.	1939 -	25	40	50	35	"Amadeus," elusive signer
Abrahams, Jim	1944-	5	10		15	"Airplane!," producer, director
Acquanetta	1920-?	30			40	Cheyenne Indian actress
Adams, Brooke	1949 -	5	10	15	12	"Invasion of the Body ..."
Adams, Don	1926 -	15	30		25	"Get Smart" - TV
Adams, Edie	1929 -	5	10	15	10	"The Ernie Kovacs Show"
Adjani, Isabelle	1955 -	15	25	50	20	"Camille Claudel"
Adler, Luther	1903-1984	15	20	30	25	"The Last Angry Man"
Affleck, Ben	1972-	15	45		40	"Good Will Hunting"
Agar, John	1921 - 2002	15	30	55	30	"The Sands of Iwo Jima," RS
Agutter, Jenny	1952 -	5	10	15	10	"Logan's Run"
Aherne, Brian	1902-1986	20	30	40	45	"Juarez"
Aiello, Danny	1933 -	10	25	30	25	"Moonstruck," writer, RS

Name	DB/DD	Sig.DS/LS	ALS	SP	Comments
Aimee, Anouk	1932 -	5	10	15	10	"A Man and a Woman"
Alba, Jessica	1981-	5	10		15	"Dark Angel"
Alberghetti, A.M	1936 -	5	15	30	12	Fifties sex symbol, sig. illegible
Albert, Eddie	1908 -	15	30	50	40	"Green Acres" - TV, $
Albert, Edward	1951 -	5	10	15	10	"Midway," son of Eddie
Albertson, Fr.	1909-1964	25	35	45	30	"Psycho," "IAWL," "Alice ..."
Albright, Lola	1925-	10	20	30	20	"Champion," "Kid Galahad"
Alda, Alan	1936 -	15	35		40	"M * A * S * H" - TV, writer, FA
Alda, Robert	1914-1986	10	15	25	20	"Rhapsody in Blue," stage actor
Alexander, Ben	1911-1969	55	60	65	110	"All Quiet on the Western Front"
Alexander, Jane	1939 -	5	10	15	10	"All The President's Men"
Alexander, Jas.	1959 -	15	25	40	25	"Seinfeld" - TV
Allan, Elizabeth	1908-1990	20	25	35	25	"David Copperfield," "Camille"
Allen, Debbie	1950 -	5	10	15	10	"Fame," choreog., s. P. Rashad
Allen, Gracie	1902-1964	80	200		150	TV star w/George Burns
Allen, Joan	1956 -	5	10	15	10	"Comromising Positions"
Allen, Karen	1951 -	10	20	30	20	"Raiders of the Lost Ark"
Allen, Nancy	1950 -	5	10	15	10	"Robocop"
Allen, Rex	1922-	15	20	25	25	"The Legend of Lobo," TV actor
Allen, Steve	1921 -2000	15	30	65	40	"The Steve Allen Show," writer
Allen, Tim	1953 -	15	30	75	50	"Home Improvement" - TV, FA
Allen, Woody	1935 -	20	40	65	40	"Annie Hall," director, writer, RS
Alley, Kirstie	1955 -	20	45	60	50	"Cheers," often elusive
Allgood, Sara	1883-1950	20	30	40	45	"How Green Was My ..."
Allyson, June	1917 -	15	25	35	25	"The Glenn Miller Story"
Alonso, Maria C.	1957 -	5	10	15	10	"The Running Man,"RS
Alt, Carol	1960 -	10	20	25	15	Supermodel
Altman, Robert	1925 -	10	20	30	20	"The Player," director, writer
Alvarado, Trini	1969 -	5	10	15	10	"Rich Kids"
Ameche, Don	1908 -1993	25	45	50	50	"Swanee River," RS
Ames, Adrienne	1909 -1947	25	40	65	45	"The Avenger," rare in SP
Ames, Leon	1903-1993	25	30	40	30	Character actor, "Little Women"
Amis, Suzy	1961 -	5	10	15	10	"Blown Away"
Amos, John	1941 -	10	15	20	15	"Good Times"
Anderson, Ed.	1905-1977	55	200	235	170	GWTW, assoc. w/J.Benny
Anderson, Gillian	1968 -	25	50	75	50	"The X-Files" - TV, often elusive
Anderson, Harry	1952 -	5	10	15	10	"Night Court"
Anderson, Judith	1898 - 1992	25	45	60	50	"The Ten Commandments"
Anderson, Kevin	1960 -	5	10	15	10	"Sleeping with the Enemy"
Anderson, Loni	1946 -	10	20	30	25	"WKRP in Cincinnati," FA
Anderson, M.S.	1962 -	10	15	25	20	"Little House on the Prairie"
Anderson, Melody	1955 -	5	10	15	10	"Flash Gordon"
Anderson, Pamela	1967-	15	40		50	"V.I.P."
Anderson, Richard	1926 -	5	10	15	10	"The Six Million Dollar Man"
Anderson, R.Dean	1950 -	5	10	15	15	"MacGyver"
Andersson, Bibi	1935 -	5	10	15	15	"The Seventh Seal"
Andress, Ursula	1936 -	15	30		50	"Dr. No"
Andrews, Anthony	1948 -	5	10	15	10	"Brideshead Revisited"
Andrews, Dana	1909 -1992	20	35	60	40	"The Best Years of Our Lives"
Andrews, Julie	1934 -	35	45	75	50	"Mary Poppins," FA
Angel, Heather	1909-1986	20	25	30	40	"The Informer," "Lifeboat"
Angeli, Pier	1932-1971	65	80	215	125	"Teresa," distinctive signature

Name	DB/DD	Sig.DS/LS	ALS	SP	Comments
Aniston, Jennifer	1969 -	25	50	65	50	"Friends" - TV, evasive, FA
Ankers, Evelyn	1918-1985	20	35	60	40	"Queen of the Horror Movies"
Ann-Margret	1941 -	15	30	45	35	"Viva Las Vegas"
Annabella	1909 -	20	30	40	45	"Wings of the Morning"
Annaud, J.J.	1943 -	5	10	15	10	"Quest for Fire"; "The Lover"
Anspach, Susan	1945 -	5	10	15	10	"Five Easy Pieces"
Anton, Susan	1950 -	10	20	30	25	"Goldengirl," actor, singer
Anwar, Gabrielle	1970 -	15	25	30	35	"Scent of a Woman"
Applegate, Christina	1972 -	10	20	30	35	"Married ... with Children"
Arbuckle, M.D.	1897-1975	65	125	230	115	m. "Fatty," comic leading lady
Arbuckle, Fatty	1887-1933	380	445	795	825	Comic actor of the silent screen
Archer, Anne	1947 -	10	20	30	15	"Fatal Attraction"
Arden, Eve	1912 - 1990	20	35	40	50	"Mildred Pierce," "Our Miss..."
Arenholz, Steph	1969 -	5	10	15	10	Actor
Arkin, Alan	1934 -	5	10	20	15	"The In-Laws," actor, director
Arlen, Richard	1899 - 1976	25	45	80	45	"Wings," pilot
Arliss, Florence	1871- 1950	25	40	50	45	Brit. character actress
Arliss, George	1868 - 1946	35	60	70	45	"House of Rothshild," illegible
Armetta, Henry	1888 - 1945	25	35	45	75	"A Farewell to Arms,"
Armstrong, Bess	1953 -	5	10	15	10	"On Our Own"
Armstrong, Lou	1900 - 1971					(see jazz)
Armstrong, Rob	1890-1973	70	80	100	225	"King Kong," "Son of Kong"
Arnaz, Desi	1917 - 1986	45	115	80	200	TV, a.leaf w/Lucy - $200
Arnaz, Desi, Jr.	1953 -	5	10	15	10	"Here's Lucy," singer
Arnaz, Lucie	1951 -	5	10	15	10	"Here's Lucy"
Arness, James	1923 -	25	75	75	60	"Gunsmoke," b. Peter Graves
Arno, Sig	1895-1975	15	25	40	25	German comedian, "Up in Arms"
Arnold, Edward	1890-1956	45	50		80	"Diamond Jim," "Meet Nero..."
Arnold, Tom	1959 -	20	40	60	40	"Roseanne" - TV, FA
Arquette, Patricia	1968 -	5	10	15	20	"True Romance,"s.Rosanna
Arquette, Rosanna	1959 -	15	25	40	30	"Desperately Seeking Susan"
Arthur, Beatrice	1926 -	5	15	25	15	"Maude"
Arthur, Jean	1905 - 1991	65	120	200	150	"Mr. Smith Goes to Washington"
Ashley, Elizabeth	1939 -	5	10	20	15	"Evening Shade"
Asner, Edward	1929 -	5	10	15	10	"Lou Grant," RS
Assante, Armand	1949 -	20	40	75	40	"The Doctors"
Astaire, Fred	1899 - 1987	75	200	285	200	"Top Hat," part.Ginger Rogers
Astin, John	1930 -	10	20	30	25	"The Addams Family," f.S.Astin
Astin, Sean	1971-	10	25		30	"Encino Man"
Astor, Mary	1905-1987	50	100	225	150	"Beau Brummel," "Don Juan"
Ates, Roscoe	1892-1962	35	40	70	70	"The Champ," "GWTW"
Atkins, Christopher	1946 -	5	10	15	10	"The Blue Lagoon"
Atkinson, Rowan	1955-					"Mr. Bean," PU
Attenborough, Richard	1923 -	30	50	70	60	"Ghandi," producer, director
Atwill, Lionel	1885 - 1946	100	265	425	200	Horror film star
Auberjonois, Rene	1940 -	5	10	15	10	"Deep Space Nine"
Auer, Mischa	1905 - 1967	20	40	50	45	"My Man Godfrey"
Auermann, Nadja	1971 -	5	10	15	15	Supermodel
Aumont, Jean-Pierre	1909 - 2001	20	40	50	65	"Assingnment in Brittany," Fr.
Autry, Alan	1952 -	5	10	15	10	"In the Heat of the Night"
Autry, Gene	1907 - 1998	35	100	155	75	Singing cowboy, songwriter
Avalon, Frankie	1939 -	15	25	35	30	Fifties teen idol, "Venus"

Name	DB/DD	Sig.DS/LS	ALS	SP	Comments
Axton, Hoyt	1938 - 1999				(SEE MUSIC SECTION)
Aykroyd, Dan	1952 -	20	30	50	35	"Ghostbusters," SNL - TV, RS
Ayres, Lew	1908 -	15	20	40	30	"All Quiet on the Western Front"
Azaria, Hank	1964-					"The Simpsons," PU

Abbott (Bud) & Costello (Lou)

* In-person only, are most likely the only authentic form.

* Signatures in all forms are highly sought.

* Watch out for secretarial signatures – both signatures often signed by the same person.

* Highly sought by collectors are signed publicity photographs from Universal Pictures.

* Abbott's signature was typically very large, sometimes twice the size of Costello's.

Name	DB/DD	Sig.DS/LS	ALS	SP	Comments
Bacall, Lauren	1924 -	20	40	60	35	"To Have and Have Not," RS
Bach, Barbara	1947 -	5	10	15	10	"The Spy Who ...," Mrs. R.Starr
Bacon, Kevin	1958 -	20	40	50	45	"Footloose," "Apollo 13," FA
Bailey, Pearl	1918 - 1990	20	35	45	40	"Porgy and Bess"
Bain, Barbara	1934 -	5	10	15	10	"Mission Impossible"
Bainter, Fay	1892 - 1968	60	80	125	120	"Jezebel,"scarce in vintage SP
Baio, Scott	1961 -	5	10	15	10	"Happy Days," RS
Baker, Aaron	1958-	15	20	30	25	'Lord of the Rings'"
Baker, Carroll	1931 -	10	20	30	20	"Kindergarten Cop"
Baker, Liz	1968-	10	15	20	20	"Titanic"
Baker, Joe Don	1936 -	5	10	15	10	"Walking Tall"
Baker, Josephine	1906 - 1975	175	350	400	575	Music hall diva,seductress
Baker, Kathy	1950 -	5	10	15	15	"Picket Fences"
Baker, Rebecca	1909-	15	20	25	30	"Wizard of Oz"
Bakshi, Ralph	1938 -	5	10	15	10	"Fritz the Cat," animator, director
Bakula, Scott	1955 -	5	10	20	35	"Quantum Leap," RS
Balaban, Bob	1945 -	5	10	15	10	"Midnight Cowboy"
Baldwin, Adam	1962 -	10	15	20	15	"My Bodyguard"
Baldwin, Alec	1958 -	20	40	50	45	"The Hunt for Red October," ES
Baldwin, Stephen	1966 -	15	30	45	40	"Threesome"
Baldwin, William	1963 -	15	30	45	40	"Backdraft"
Bale, Christian	1974-	10	20		20	"American Psycho"
Ball, Lucille	1911 -1989	150	400	750	500	"I Love Lucy," ES, sig. variations
Ball, Suzan	1933-1955	175	325	400	345	"Untamed Frontier"
Ballard, Kaye	1926 -	10	20	30	20	Actor, singer
Balsam, Martin	1919 -1996	25	45	50	40	"A Thousand Clowns"
Bancroft, Anne	1931 -	10	20	30	20	"The Graduate," m. Mel Brooks
Banderas, Antonio	1960 -	25	50	80	60	"Philadelphia," "Evita," ES
Bankhead, Tallulah	1903 - 1968	65	130	200	210	"Lifeboat"
Banks, Tyra	1973-	10	20	25	30	Model, actor, FA
Bara, Theda	1890-1955	200	375	425	300	Silent era "vamp," "Under ..."
Baranski, Christine	1952 -	10	20	30	20	"Cybill," "The Real Thing"
Barbeau, Adrienne	1945 -	10	20	25	20	"Maude," RS
Bardem, Javier	1969-	10	20		15	"Before Night Falls"
Bardot, Bridgitte	1934 -	35	50	65	70	"And God Created Woman," RS

Name	DB/DD	Sig.DS/LS	ALS	SP	Comments
Bari, Lynn	1913-1989	5 10	20	15	"The Bridge of San Luis Rey"
Barker, Bob	1923-	5 10		15	"The Price is Right"
Barker, Lex	1919 - 1973	75 100	165	130	"Tarzan" film series
Barkin, Ellen	1954 -	5 10	20	15	"Sea of Love"
Barnes, Binnie	1905-1998	10 20	30	20	"The Private Life of Henry VIII"
Barnett, Vince	1902-1977	20 30	40	40	Character actor, "Scarface"
Barrett, Rona	1936-	5 10		15	Columnist
Barrie, Wendy	1912 - 1978	30 50	60	50	"The Private Life of Henry VIII"
Barrymore, Diana	1921 - 1960	45 50	60	50	"Eagle Squadron," d. John
Barrymore, Drew	1975 -	25 50	60	50	"E.T., the Extra-Terrestrial"
Barrymore, Ethel	1878 - 1959	100 170	350	200	"None But the Lonely Heart"
Barrymore, John	1882 - 1942	185 275	325	500	"Grand Hotel," stage actor
Barrymore, John D.	1932 -	20 35	45	35	Actor, f. Drew
Barrymore, Lionel	1878 -1954	100 200	300	200	IAWL, " Key Largo"
Bartel, Paul	1938 - 2000	10 20	30	20	"Eating Raoul," director, writer
Bartholomew, Fred.	1924 - 1992	35 45	50	70	"David Copperfield," child star
Bartiromo, Maria	1967-	5	10	15	TV financial journalist
Barty, Billie	1925-	10 15	20	15	"Footlight Parade," "Roman..."
Baryshnikov, Mikhail	1948 -	80 100	200	175	"White Nights," ES
Basehart, Richard	1914-1984	10 20	25	15	"He Walked By Night," TV actor
Basinger,Kim	1953 -	15 25	45	40	" 9 1/2 Weeks," RS
Basquette, Lina	1907-1994	20 30	45	30	"Ziegfeld Follies" star
Bassett, Angela	1958 -	15 25	35	25	"Misery"
Bateman, Jason	1969 -	10 20	30	25	"The Hogan Family"
Bateman, Justine	1966 -	10 20	30	20	"Family Ties"
Bates, Alan	1934 -	5 10	15	10	"An Unmarried Woman"
Bates, Barbara	1925-1969	150 260	325	275	"All Ablut Eve," "The Caddy"
Bates, Kathy	1948-	20 50		35	"Misery," RS
Bauer, Steven	1956 -	5 10	15	10	"Wiseguy"
Baxter, Anne	1923 - 1985	25 40	55	50	"The Razor's Edge"
Baxter, Keith	1933 -	5 10	15	10	Actor
Baxter, Meredith	1947 -	5 10	15	10	"Family Ties"
Baxter, Warner	1889 - 1951	30 55	75	65	"In Old Arizona"
Bay, Willow	1963-	5 15		20	Model
Beacham, Stephanie	1947 -	5 10	15	10	"The Colbys"
Beals, Jennifer	1963 -	15 25	30	25	"Flashdance," ES
Beasley, Allyce	1954 -	5 10	15	10	"Moonlighting"
Beatty, Ned	1937 -	10 15	20	15	"Deliverance"
Beatty, Warren	1937 -	35 100	225	45	"Shampoo," "Reds," ES
Beavers, Louise	1902-1962	95 200	285	180	"Beulah" - TV series
Beck, John	1943 -	5 10	15	10	"Dallas"
Beck, Michael	1949 -	5 10	15	10	"Xanadu"
Beckett, Scotty	1929-1968	65 130	200	125	Child actor, "Our Gang" member
Beckinsale, Kate	1973-	10 25		25	"Pearl Harbor"
Bedelia, Bonnie	1946 -	5 10	15	10	"Presumed Innocent"
Beery, Noah, Sr.	1884 - 1946	85 150	250	170	"Don Juan," silent film. scarce
Beery, Wallace	1885 - 1949	110 175	350	275	"The Champ," "Grand Hotel"
Begley, Ed, Jr.	1949 -	5 10	15	10	"St. Elsewhere"
Bel Geddes, Barbara	1922 -	20 40	50	30	"Vertigo," "I Remember Mama"
Belafonte, Harry	1927 -	20 40	65	40	"Island in the Sun," singer, ES
Belafonte, Shari	1954 -	5 10	15	10	"Hotel"
Bell, Jamie	1986-	10 20		20	"Billy Elliott"

Name	DB/DD	Sig.DS/LS	ALS	SP	Comments
Bellamy, Madge	1900-1990	15	25	45	30	"The Most Beautiful Girl ..."
Bellamy, Ralph	1904 - 1991	17	25	35	45	"The Awful Truth"
Bellows, Gil	1967-	10	20		20	"Ally McBeal"
Belmondo, Jean - Paul	1933 -	60	100	150	75	"Breathless," tough signature
Belushi, Jim	1954 -	5	10	15	15	"K-9"
Belushi, John	1942-1982	200	500		500	SNL
Benchley, Robert	1889-1945	55	95	180	80	Critic, "How to Sleep"
Bendix, William	1906 - 1964	50	75	125	150	"The Babe Ruth Story"
Benedict, Dirk	1945 -	5	10	15	10	"The A-Team"
Benigni, Roberto	1952-	15	35		35	"Life Is Beautiful"
Bening, Annette	1958 -	20	40	85	50	"The Grifters," Mrs. W. Beatty
Benjamin, Richard	1938 -	5	10	15	10	"Love at First Bite"
Bennett, Bruce	1909-	20	25	30	40	Herman Brix, "Tarzan"
Bennett, Constance	1904-1964	40	65	125	75	"Three Faces East," silent star
Bennett, Joan	1910 - 1990	20	35	40	40	"Little Women," "Father of ..."
Benny, Jack	1894 - 1974	100	275	400	175	"Charley's Aunt," radio & TV pio.
Benson, Bobby	1956 -	5	10	15	12	"Ice Castles," "Beauty and ..."
Berenger, Tom	1950 -	20	30	40	50	"Platoon"
Berenson, Marisa	1947 -	10	15	20	20	"Barry Lyndon"
Bergen, Candice	1946 -	15	20	30	40	"Murphy Brown" - TV, elusive
Bergen, Edgar	1903 - 1978	75	100	145	150	Partner "C. McCarthy"
Bergen, Polly	1930 -	10	20	30	40	"The Winds of War"
Bergman, Ingmar	1918 -	40	50	60	100	"The Silence," writer, director
Bergman, Ingrid	1913 - 1982	150	200	300	400	"Gaslight," "Anastasia"
Bergner, Elizabeth	1898 - 1986	15	30	45	30	"Escape Me Never," sig.illegible
Berkeley, Busby	1895 - 1976	150	200	275	300	"42nd Street," "Go Into ..."
Berle, Milton	1908 - 2002	30	75		50	"Always Leave Them Laughing"
Berlin, Irving	1888 - 1989					(see Music section)
Bernardi, Herschel	1923 - 1986	35	70	130	75	"Fiddler on the Roof"
Bernhard, Sandra	1955 -	5	10	15	10	"Roseanne"
Bernsen, Corbin	1954 -	15	20	40	35	"L.A. Law"
Berri, Claude	1934 -	10	20	30	20	Actor, director, producer
Berry, Halle	1968 -	25	50		40	"Boomerang," FA
Bertinelli, Valerie	1960 -	10	20	25	20	"One Day at a Time"
Best, Edna	1900-1974	25	30	40	50	British stage actress, "Escape"
Best, Willie	1913-1962	65	125	200	130	"Sleep 'n Eat" Best, TV actor
Bialik, Mayim	1975 -	5	10	15	10	"Blossom"
Bickford, Charles	1889-1967	55	110	125	100	"Anna Christie," "The Song ..."
Biehn, Michael	1956 -	10	15	25	45	"The Terminator"
Biel, Jessica	1982-	10	20		25	"7th Heaven"
Biggs, Jason	1978-	10	25		20	"American Pie"
Billingsley, Barbara	1922 -	5	10	15	10	"Leave it to Beaver"
Billingsley, Peter	1972 -	5	10	15	10	"A Christmas Story"
Bing, Herman	1889-1947	32	55	100	60	"Dinner at Eight," "The Merry..."
Binoche, Juliette	1964 -	20	60	75	60	"The English Patient"
Birney, David	1939 -	5	10	15	10	"ST. Elsewhere"
Bishop, Joey	1918 -	10	20	35	20	"The Joey Bishop Show," RS
Bissell, Whit	1919-1981	12	20	30	25	Character actor, "Destination.."
Bisset, Jacqueline	1944 -	10	20	30	20	"The Deep"
Bisset, Josie	1969 -	15	30	40	45	"Melrose Place"
Bixby, Bill	1934-1993	40	75		75	"My Favorite Martian"
Black, Jack	1969-	15	30		40	"High Fidelity"

Name	DB/DD	Sig.DS/LS	ALS	SP	Comments
Black, Karen	1942 -	5	10	15	15	"Easy Rider"
Black, Lisa Hartman	1956-	5	10		15	"Knot's Landing"
Blackmer, Sidney	1895 -1973	20	30	35	40	"Little Caesar," "Heidi"
Blades, Ruben	1948 -	5	10	15	10	"The Milagro Beanfield War"
Blaine, David	1973-	15	40		40	Magician
Blaine, Vivian	1921 - 1995	10	20	30	25	"State Fair," "Guys and Dolls"
Blair, Janet	1921 -	15	20	25	25	"My Sister Eileen"
Blair, Linda	1959 -	10	20	25	30	"The Exorcist"
Blake, Robert	1933 -	20	40		45	"Baretta," charged w/murder
Blakely, Susan	1950 -	5	10	15	10	"Rich Man, Poor Man"
Blanc, Mel	1908 -1989	70	150	200	275	Voice of Warner Bros. car. char.
Blanchett, Cate	1969-	15	30		40	"Elizabeth"
Blandick, Clara	1880-1962	500	1000			"WOO," "Tom Sawyer," ESPV
Blane, Sally	1910-	10	15	20	20	"The Vagabond Lover"
Blanks, Billy	1955-	10	25		25	Tae-Bo fitness program
Bledsoe, Tempestt	1973 -	5	10	15	10	"The Cosby Show"
Bleeth, Yasmine	1968-	15	25		45	"Baywatch"
Blondell, Joan	1909 - 1979	35	45	75	65	"The Blue Veil," "Stage Struck"
Bloom, Claire	1931 -	10	15	20	15	"Richard III"
Blore, Eric	1887-1959	33	40	75	60	"The Lady Eve"
Blue, Ben	1901-1975	35	40	65	60	Vaudevillian, "For Me and My..."
Blue, Monte	1890-1963	35	45	60	70	Silent star, "Dodge City"
Blyth, Ann	1928 -	10	20	30	15	"Mildred Pierce," singer, RS
Blyth, Betty	1893-1972	45	75	100	150	"Queen of Sheba," silent star
Bochco, Steven	1943 -	5	10	20	10	"NYPD Blue," producer, RS
Bogarde, Dirk	1921 - 199	10	20	30	20	"Death in Venice"
Bogart, Humphrey	1899 - 1957	1000	1650		2240	FA, numerous secretarial
Bogart, Mayo M.	1904-1951	30	50	65	50	"Marked Woman," a.H.Bogart
Bogosian, Eric	1953 -	5	10	15	10	"Talk radio"
Boland, Mary	1880 - 1965	20	45	90	55	"Ruggles of Red Gap"
Boles, John	1895 - 1969	25	35	60	50	"Stella Dallas," "Only Yesterday"
Bolger, Ray	1904 - 1987	75	135	300	225	WOO, SP - WOO role 1-2X
Bologna, Joseph	1938 -	5	10	15	10	"Chapter Two," ES
Bonaduce, Danny	1959 -	5	10	15	10	"The Partridge Family," RS
Bonanova, Fortunio	1893-1969	25	45	65	50	"Citizen Kane," "For Whom ..."
Bond, Ward	1903-1960	125	155	200	250	Western film star, GWTW
Bondi, Beulah	1904 - 1987	25	40	50	45	"Gorgeous Hussey," IAWL
Bonet, Lisa	1967 -	5	10	12	10	"The Cosby Show," RS
Bonham-Carter, Helena	1966 -	10	20		15	"A Room with a View"
Bonner, Frank	1942 -	5	10	15	10	"WKRP in Cincinnati"
Bono, Sonny	1935 - 1998	35	75	150	75	"The Sonny and Cher...," USHR
Bonsall, Brian	1982 -	5	10	15	10	"Family Ties"
Boone, Pat	1934 -	5	10	15	10	"The Pat Boone Show," RS
Booth, Shirley	1898 - 1992	25	50	65	50	"Hazel" - TV, "Come Back..."
Boothe, Powers	1949 -	5	10	15	10	"Guyana Tragedy: The Story..."
Bordoni, Irene	1895 - 1953	25	35	45	55	"Louisianna Purchase,"com.
Boreanaz, David	1971-	10	20		15	"Angel"
Borgnine, Ernest	1915 -	15	25	30	25	"Marty," "From Here To Eternity"
Borzage, Frank	1893-1962	45	100	225	165	"the great romanticist" director
Bosson, Barbara	1939 -	5	10	15	10	"Hill Street Blues"
Bostwick, Barry	1945 -	10	15	20	20	"The Rocky Horror ..."
Bottoms, Joseph	1954 -	5	10	15	10	"The Black Hole"

Name	DB/DD	Sig.DS/LS	ALS	SP	Comments
Bottoms, Sam	1955 -	5	10	15	10	"Apocalypse Now"
Bottoms, Timothy	1951 -	5	10	15	15	"Johnny Got His Gun," RS
Boxleitner, Bruce	1950 -	5	10	15	10	"Scarecrow and Mrs. King," RS
Boyd, William	1895 - 1972	185	300	425	375	Hopalong Cassidy, sig. var.
Boyer, Charles	1897 - 1978	35	50	85	110	"Gaslight," French actor
Boyle, Lara Flynn	1970 -	10	15	20	15	"Twin Peaks"
Boyle, Peter	1933 -	5	10	15	10	"Young Frankenstein"
Bracco, Lorraine	1955 -	5	10	20	15	"GoodFellas"
Bracken, Eddie	1920-2002	10	25		20	"The Miracle of Morgan's..."
Brackett, Charles	1892-1969	25	50	75	60	Drama critic, producer
Bradna, Olympe	1920 -	15	45	75	30	"Souls at Sea," French actress
Brady, Alice	1892 - 1939	80	150	230	160	"In Old Chicago," "Young Mr..."
Brady, Scott	1924-1985	20	45	50	35	"Canon City," "Johnny Guitar"
Branagh, Ken	1960 -	10	20		25	"Henry V"
Brand, Neville	1921-1992	90	120		125	Decorated G.I., "D.O.A."
Brandauer, Klaus Maria	1944 -	15	25	50	30	"Out of Africa"
Brando, Marlon	1924 -	225	565		600	"On The Waterfront," C, ES
Brasselle, Keefe	1923-1981	25	50		45	"The Eddie Cantor Story"
Bratt, Benjamin	1963-	10	25	50	20	"Law & Order"
Breen, Bobby	1927-	15	20	30	25	"Make a Wish," "Hawaii Calls"
Brendel, El	1890-1964	25				"Sunny Side Up"
Brennan, Eileen	1935 -	5	10	30	15	"Private Benjamin"
Brennan, Walter	1894 - 1974	100	165	250	175	First actor to win 3 AA, TV actor
Brenneman, Amy	1964 -	10	20	50	15	"NYPD Blue"
Brenner, David	1945 -	10	20		20	"Nightlife," comedian
Brent, George	1904-1979	35	40		50	"Jezebel," "42nd Street"
Brian, Mary	1908-	12	25	50	25	"Peter Pan," "Beau Geste"
Brice, Fanny	1891-1951	150	225	300	300	"Ziegfeld Follies" star
Bridges, Beau	1941 -	10	25		15	"The Fabulous Baker Boys"
Bridges, Jeff	1949 -	15	30		30	"The Fabulous Baker Boys"
Bridges, Lloyd	1913 - 1998	20	50	100	45	"Sea Hunt"
Bridges, Todd	1966 -	5	10		10	"Diff'rent Strokes"
Brimley, Wilford	1920 -	15	30	60	25	"Cocoon"
Brinkley, Christie	1954 -	10	25		30	Supermodel
Brinkley, David	1920-2003	20	40	110	40	News anchor
Britt, May	1933 -	20	40		30	"Murder, Inc.," Swedish actress
Brittany, Morgan	1951 -	10	25		30	"Dallas"
Britton, Barbara	1919-1980	15	30		30	"Captain Kidd," The Revlon..."
Broderick, Helen	1891-1959	35	65		60	"Top Hat," "Swing Time"
Broderick, Matthew	1962 -	15	30	70	25	"Ferris Bueller's Day Off"
Brokaw, Tom	1940-	12	35	75	25	"NBC Nightly News," author
Brolin, James	1940 -	20	45	75	40	"Marcus Welby, M.D."
Bronson, Charles	1921 - 2003	25	50	100	50	"Death Wish"
Brook, Clive	1887 - 1974	45	75		100	"Sherlock Holmes"
Brooke, Hillary	1914-	15	30	60	25	"Jane Eyre," "My Little Margie"
Brooks, Albert	1947 -	10	25	50	25	"Defending Your Life," director
Brooks, Geraldine	1925-1977	20	35	80	35	"Possessed," "Cry Wolf"
Brooks, James L.	1940 -	15	30		20	"Mary Tyler Moore Show" - cre.
Brooks, Mel	1926 -	15	35	70	30	"Blazing Saddles," director, FA
Brooks, Phyllis	1914-	10	20		20	"The Unseen," "High Powered"
Brosnan, Pierce	1952 -	20	50	100	40	"Remington Steele"
Brown, Blair	1948 -	10	20		15	"The Days and Nights Molly..."

Name	DB/DD	Sig.DS/LS	ALS	SP	Comments
Brown, Bryan	1947 -	10	20		15	Actor, married to Rachel Ward.
Brown, George	1943 -	10	20		15	"Colossus: The Forbin Project"
Brown, Joe E.	1892-1973	42	50	110	75	"Show Boat," "Some Like It Hot"
Brown, Johnny M.	1904-1974	60	110		150	"Billy the Kid," "B" movie star
Brown, Joy	1950-	5	10	20	10	On-air psychologist
Brown, Vanessa	1928-	15	30	40	40	"Margie," "The Ghost and ..."
Bruce, Nigel	1895 - 1953	165	300	325	300	"Sherlock Holmes" - Dr. Watson
Bruce, Virginia	1910-1982	25	45		35	"Jane Eyre," "Born to Dance"
Bryan, Jane	1918-	10	25	50	25	"Kid Galahad," "The Old Maid"
Brynner, Yul	1915 - 1985	50	100	200	125	"The King and I," sig. illegible
Buchanan, Edgar	1903-1979	40	75		100	"Move Over, Darling!"
Buck, Frank	1888 - 1950	30	65	120	70	"Bring 'Em Back Alive," hunter
Buckley, Betty	1947 -	10	20	35	15	"Eight is Enough," RS
Bujold, Genevieve	1942 -	10	20		20	"Dead Ringers"
Bullock, Sandra	1967 -	10	25		35	"Speed"
Bundchen, Gisele	1980-	15	35		35	Model
Burghoff, Gary	1943 -	12	25	40	30	"M * A * S * H"
Burke, Billie	1885 - 1970	130	250	425	225	WOO, "Merrily We Live"
Burke, Delta	1956 -	10	20	30	25	"Designing Women"
Burnett, Carol	1933 -	15	30	50	30	"The Carol Burnett Show"
Burnette, "Smiley"	1911-1967	40	60		65	"Frog Millhouse," westerns
Burns, Ed	1968 -	20	45		30	"The Brothers McMullen"
Burns, George	1896 - 1996	30	75	150	60	TV pio., w/Gracie - $175 - a. leaf
Burr, Raymond	1917 -1993	40	75	150	70	"Rear Window," "Perry Mason"
Burrows, Darren E.	1966 -	5	10		15	"Northern Exposure"
Burstyn, Ellen	1932 -	15	35	65	30	"Alice Doesn't Live ..."
Burton, Levar	1957 -	20	55	110	50	"Star Trek: The Next Gen..."
Burton, Richard	1925 - 1984	125	225	300	210	"Beckett," "Who's Afraid ..."
Burton, Tim	1958-	15	30	65	40	"Edward Scissorhands," director
Buscemi, Steve	1957-	15	30		20	"Fargo".
Busey, Gary	1944 -	15	30	60	25	"The Buddy Holly Story"
Busfield, Timothy	1957 -	12	20	40	25	"thirtysomething"
Bushman, Francis X.	1883-1966	60	100	125	125	"Ben Hur," "Romeo and Juliet"
Butler, Brett	1958 -	5	10		10	"Grace Under Fire," comedian
Buttons, Red	1918 -	15	30	65	25	"Sayonara," TV and club comic
Buttram, Pat	1917-1994	30	50		60	"The Gene Autry Show"
Buzzi, Ruth	1936 -	5	10	25	10	"Laugh-In," RS
Byington, Spring	1893-1971	30	60		45	"Little Women"
Byrne, Gabriel	1950-	15	25		20	"Miller's Crossing"

Bogart, Humphrey

* In-person only, are most likely the only authentic form.

* Signatures in all forms are highly sought.

* Watch out for secretarial signatures!

* Highly forged due to strong demand and limited supply.

* This is an example where collectors should consult an expert before buying or selling his signature.

Name	DB/DD	Sig.DS/LS	ALS	SP	Comments

Brando, Marlon

* In-person autographs, are most likely the only authentic forms of his signature.

* Signatures in all forms are highly sought.

* He would reluctantly sign items early in his career. In later years however, signing was limited to rare occassions on his current movie set.

* A recluse, Brando opts to live on his own island and shun all public attention.

* Brando's siganture is highly forged due to strong demand and limited supply.

* Of the authentic items finding there way to the market, and there are few, most are of unusual form such as menus, receipts, etc.

Name	DB/DD	Sig.DS/LS	ALS	SP	Comments
Caan, James	1939-	15	30	50	30	"The Godfather," RS
Cabot, Bruce	1904 - 1972	70	85	100	150	"King Kong," "Dodge City"
Cabot, Sebastian	1918-1977	40	50	120	80	Brit.char. actor, "Family Affair"
Caesar, Sid	1922-	15	25	40	30	"Your Show of Shows"
Cage, Nicolas	1964-	15	40	80	30	"Raising Arizona," RS
Cagney, James	1899 - 1986	85	175	225	250	"Yankee Doodle Dandy," RS
Cagney, Jeanne	1919-1984	25	40	50	40	"Yankee Doodle Dandy"
Cain, Dean	1966-	20	40	75	45	"Lois & Clark" - TV, FA
Caine, Michael	1933-	20	40	80	45	"The Cider House Rules," RS
Calabro, Thomas	1959-	5	10	15	10	"Melrose Place" - TV
Calhern, Louis	1895 - 1956	40	50	65	50	"Duck Soup," "Notorious"
Calhoun, Rory	1922- 1999	20	40	50	30	"The Spoliers," "The Texan"
Callow, Simon	1949-	5	10	15	10	"A Room with a View"
Calvet, Corinne	1925-	10	15	20	15	"La Part de l'Ombre"
Cameron, James	1954-	15	30	55	25	"Titanic," director
Cameron, Kirk	1970-	10	20	30	20	"Growing Pains"
Camp, Colleen	1953-	10	20	25	20	"Dallas"
Campbell, Bill	1960-	5	10	15	10	"The Rocketeer"
Campbell, Billy	1959-	5	10		15	"Once and Again"
Campbell, Bruce	1958-	5	10	15	10	"The Adventures of Briscoe..."
Campbell, Naomi	1970-	20	35	40	40	Supermodel
Campbell, Neve	1973-	15	25	45	40	"Party of Five"
Campbell, Tisha	1970-	5	10	15	10	"Martin"
Campion, Jane	1954-	10	20	25	20	"The Piano," director
Candy, John	1950-1994	50	100		100	"Stripes"
Cannon, Dyan	1937-	10	15	20	25	"Bob & Carol & Ted & Alice"
Canova, Judy	1916-1983	20	30	35	30	"In Caliente," "Chatterbox"
Cantinflas	1911-1994	55	75	115	100	Mexican actor, "Around the ..."
Cantor, Eddie	1892 - 1964	70	145	215	230	Vaudeville and radio star
Capra, Frank	1897 - 1991	45	150	285	90	Famed director, IAWL, RS
Capshaw, Kate	1953-	5	10	15	20	"Indiana Jones and the ..."
Cara, Irene	1959-	5	10	15	10	"Fame," singer
Caray, Harry	1921-1998	30	55	65	50	Announcer for the Chi. Cubs
Cardinale, Caludia	1959-	5	10	15	10	"The Pink Panther"
Carey, Drew	1958-	10	20	25	20	"The Drew Carey Show," RS
Carey, Harry	1878-1947	140	175	200	275	Pioneer of westerns

Name	DB/DD	Sig.DS/LS	ALS	SP	Comments
Carey, MacDonald	1913-1994	15	30	60	30	"Dream Girl," "The Great Gatsby"
Carlin, George	1937-	10	25	40	25	"Seven Dirty Words"
Carlisle, Kitty	1914-	10	15	20	15	"A Night at the Opera," TV guest
Carlisle, Mary	1912-	10	15	25	20	"College Humor," "Double or ..."
Carlson, Richard	1912-1977	30	50	60	60	"It Came From Outer Space"
Carne, Judy	1939-	5	10	15	10	"Laugh-In"
Carney, Art	1918-2003	25	50	80	45	"The Honeymooners," RS
Caron, Leslie	1931-	10	20	30	20	"Lili"
Carpenter, John	1948-	10	20	45	25	"Halloween," director, writer
Carradine, David	1936-	5	10	15	10	"Kung Fu"
Carradine, John	1906-1988	75	100	150	150	"Stagecoach," "The Grapes..."
Carradine, Keith	1949-	5	10	15	10	"The Will Rogers Follies"
Carradine, Robert	1954-	5	10	15	10	"Revenge of the Nerds"
Carrera, Barbara	1951-	5	10	15	25	Model, "Dallas"
Carrey, Jim	1962-	40	100	200	65	"Ace Ventura: Pet Detective"
Carrillo, Leo	1880-1961	60	100	175	175	Pancho in "Cisco Kid" films. TV
Carroll, Diahann	1935-	10	20	45	20	"I Know Why the Caged Bird..."
Carroll, Leo G.	1892 - 1972	45	80		75	"Wuthering Heights"
Carroll, Madeline	1906-1987	30	75	150	65	"The 39 Steps," "Secret Agent"
Carroll, Nancy	1904-1965	20	25	30	40	"The Shopworn Angel"
Carry, Julius		5	10	15	10	"Murphy Brown"
Carson, Jack	1910-1963	20	30	40	40	"Mildred Pierce," "Cat on a ..."
Carson, Johnny	1925-	20	40	75	40	"The Tonight Show," ES
Carter, Dixie	1939-	5	10	15	10	"Designing Women"
Carter, Lynda	1951-	5	10	20	20	"Wonder Woman"
Carter, Nell	1948-2003	10	20	35	20	"Gimmie a Break," singer
Carteris, Gabrielle	1961-	10	20	30	20	"Beverly Hills 90210"
Cartwright, Veronica	1950-	5	10	15	10	"Alien"
Caruso, David	1956-	10	20	30	20	"NYPD Blue"
Carvey, Dana	1955-	10	25	30	30	"Wayne's World," SNL
Cass, Peggy (Mary M.)	1924-1999	10	20	35	20	"To Tell the Truth"
Cassidy, David	1950-	15	40		40	"The Partridge Family"
Cassidy, Jack	1927-1976	30	75		45	Entertainer
Cassidy, Joanna	1944-	5	10	20	15	"Buffalo Bill"
Cates, Phoebe	1963-	10	15	25	20	"Fast Times at Ridgemont High"
Catlett, Walter	1889-1960	15	25	30	30	Vaudeville and stage comedian
Cattrall, Kim	1956-	5	10	15	10	"The Bonfire of the Vanities"
Caulfield, Joan	1922-1991	15	25	35	30	"Blue Skies," "Dear Ruth"
Cavett, Dick	1936-	10	20	30	20	"The Dick Cavett Show," RS
Chabert, Lacey	1982-	5	10		15	"Party of Five"
Chamberlain, Richard	1935-	10	20	30	25	"Dr. Kildare"
Chan, Jackie	1954-	20	40		45	"Rumble in the Bronx"
Chandler, Helen	1906-1965	40	50	65	80	"Outward Bound," "The Last ..."
Chandler, Jeff	1918-1961	60	75	150	120	"Broken Arrow," westerns
Chaney, Lon	1883-1930	1200	3500	3250	2000	"The Man of a Thousand ..."
Chaney, Lon, Jr.	1906-1973	350	825	700	700	"Of Mice and Men"
Channing, Carol	1921 -	10	25	30	20	"Thoroughly Modern Mille"
Channing, Stockard	1944-	5	10	15	10	"Grease"
Chao, Rosalind		5	10	15	10	M*A*S*H*
Chaplin, Charlie	1889-1977	350	775	800	850	Screen legend, ES, FA
Chaplin, Geraldine	1944-	10	20	30	25	"Dr. Zhivago"
Chaplin, Lita Grey	1909-1995	30	35	50	40	m. Charlie Chaplin

Name	DB/DD	Sig.DS/LS	ALS	SP	Comments
Chaplin, Sydney	1885-1965	20	25	40	40	"Charley's Aunt," b. Charlie
Charisse, Cyd	1922-	5	10	15	25	"Brigadoon"
Charo	1951-	5	10	15	15	"The Love Boat," singer
Charters, Spencer	1875-1943	25	40	45	50	"Whoopee," "Tobacco Road"
Chase, Chevy	1943-	10	20	30	20	SNL, "The Blues Brothers"
Chatterton, Ruth	1893-1961	20	25	35	50	"Madame X," "Sarah and Son"
Cheadle, Don	1964-	10	20		15	"Devil in a Blue Dress"
Cher (Cherilyn La Piere)	1946 -	35	50	50	70	"Moonstruck," "Sonny & Cher"
Chevalier, Maurice	1888-1961	70	150	175	150	Popular Frenchman
Child, Julia	1912-	10	20	35	20	"Mastering the Art ...," chef
Chiles, Lois	1950-	5	10	15	20	"The Way We Were," model
Chong, Rae Dawn	1962-	5	10	15	15	"The Color Purple," d. T.Chong
Chong, Thomas	1938-	10	20	25	20	"Up in Smoke," partner C. Marin
Christensen, Hayden	1981-	10	25		20	"Star Wars: Episode..."
Christian, Linda	1923-	10	20	25	20	"Battle Zone," "Athena"
Christie, Julie	1941-	30	40	40	65	"Dr. Zhivago"
Christopher, William	1932-	10	20	35	20	"M*A*S*H," RS
Chung, Connie	1946-	5	10		15	TV journalist, RS
Churchill, Marguerite	1909-	20	40	55	30	"The Big Trail," "The Valiant"
Churchill, Sarah	1914-1982	25	40	45	45	"Royal Wedding," d. Winston
Chyna (J.Laurer)	1969-	10	25		25	WWF
Ciannelli, Eduardo	1887-1969	30	35	40	55	"Reunion in Vienna"
Clark, Dane	1913-1998	10	20	30	25	"Whiplash," "Moonrise," RS
Clark, Dick	1929-	10	25	35	25	"American Bandstand"
Clark, Fred	1914-1968	30	40	50	60	"A Place in the Sun"
Clark, Petula	1932-	10	25	35	20	"Downtown," singer, actor
Clark, Roy	1933-	5	10	15	10	"Hee Haw," responsive signer
Clay, Andrew Dice	1958-	5	10	15	10	"The Adventures of Ford..."
Clayburgh, Jill	1944-	10	15	20	20	"An Unmarried Woman"
Cleese, John	1939-	15	30	40	30	"Monty Pyhon's Flying Circus"
Clift, Montgomery	1920-1966	250	375	600	725	Talented actor, FHTE, FA
Clooney, George	1961-	25	50	65	70	"ER," elusive signer - illegible
Clooney, Nick	1935-	5	10		15	"American Movie Classics"
Clooney, Rosemary	1928 - 2002	10	25	35	25	"White Christmas," TV star
Close, Glenn	1947-	20	45	60	70	"Fatal Attraction," FA
Clute, Chester	1891-1956	20	35	40	35	"Yankee Doodle Dandy"
Clyde, Andy	1892-1967	60	100	125	155	"Annie Oakley," "The Green..."
Cobb, Joe	1917-	15	30	35	35	"Our Gang" member
Cobb, Lee J.	1911-1976	60	75	100	120	"On The Waterfront"
Coburn, Charles	1877-1961	45	100	120	130	"The More the Merrier"
Coburn, James	1928-2002	25	50		50	"The Magnificent Seven"
Coca, Imogene	1908-2001	15	30	35	30	"Your Show of Shows"
Cody, Iron Eyes	1904-1999	25	50		50	"the crying Indian"
Coen, Ethan	1958-	5	10	15	10	"Raising Arizona," director
Coen, Joel	1955-	5	10	15	10	"Raising Arizona," b. Ethan
Cohan, George M.	1878-1942					(See Music Section)
Colasanto, Nick	1924-1985	40	100		75	"Cheers"
Colbert, Claudette	1905-1996	40	150	200	100	"It Happened One Night"
Cole, Nat King	1919-1965					(See Music Section)
Coleman, Dabney	1932-	10	20	20	15	"Buffalo Bill"
Coleman, Gary	1968-	5	10	20	15	"Diff'rent Strokes," FA
Coleman, Nancy	1917-	10	20	30	15	"Kings Row," "Edge of ...," RS

Name	DB/DD	Sig.DS/LS	ALS	SP	Comments
Collins, Cora Sue	1927-	5	10	10	10	Child star, "Treasuer Island"
Collins, Gary	1938-	5	10	10	10	"Home"
Collins, Joan	1933-	25	30	35	50	"The Girl in the Red Swing"
Collins, Stephen	1947-	5	10	10	10	"Tales of the Gold Monkey"
Collyer, June	1907-1968	15	20	25	30	"The Trouble With Father" - TV
Colman, Ronald	1891-1958	65	150	150	170	"A Double Life," "Lost Horizon"
Colonna, Jerry	1903-1986	15	25	25	30	"Road to Singapore"
Columbo, Russ	1908-1934	60	100	175	155	"Dynamite," "Moulin Rouge"
Columbus, Chris	1958-	10	20	20	10	"Home Alone," director
Compson, Betty	1897-1974	20	25	45	60	"The Miracle Man," "The Barker"
Conaway, Jeff	1950-	5	10	10	10	"Taxi"
Conklin, "Heinie"	1880-1959	45	60	65	75	"All Quiet on the Western Front"
Conklin, Chester	1888-1971	115	125	225	250	"Modern Times," "The Great ..."
Conlin, Jimmy	1884-1962	25	35	45	40	"Sharps and Flats"
Connelly, Jennifer	1970-	10	20	30	35	"A Beautiful Mind"
Connery, Sean	1930-	80	165	325	130	"James Bond" series - SP -2X
Connolly, Walter	1887-1940	80	100	100	115	"It Happened One Night"
Connors, Mike	1925-	10	20	25	20	"Mannix"
Conried, Hans	1917-1982	20	25	30	40	"The 5,000 Fingers of Dr. T"
Conroy, Kevin	1955-	5	10	10	10	Actor, voice "Batman:..."
Constantine, Michael	1927-	10	15	20	15	"Room 222"
Conte, Richard	1911-1975	15	20	25	20	"Guadalcanal Diary"
Conti, Tom	1941-	5	10	10	10	"Reuben Reuben"
Conway, Kevin	1942-	5	10	10	15	"Slaughterhouse Five"
Conway, Tim	1933-	5	10	10	15	"The Carol Burnett Show," RS
Conway, Tom	1904-1967	60	120	150	150	"Sky Murder," "Lady Be Good"
Coogan, Jackie	1914-1984	30	45	50	60	Silent child star
Cook, Elisha, Jr.	1906-1995	20	30	45	65	"The Maltese Falcon"
Cooper, Gary	1901-1961	255	500	500	765	Screen legend, "High Noon"
Cooper, Gladys	1888-1971	40	50	75	65	British actress, "Rebecca"
Cooper, Jackie	1921-	20	30	40	50	"Our Gang" series, "Skippy"
Coote, Robert	1909-1982	20	35	45	45	British actor, "Gunga Din"
Copperfield, David	1956-	5	10	15	20	Magician, RS
Coppola, Francis Ford	1939-	40	100	100	75	"The Godfather"
Coppola, Bernadette	1966-	10	20		20	"A Beautiful Mind"
Corbin, Barry	1940-	5	10	15	10	"Northern Exposure"
Corday, Mara	1932-	5	10	20	10	"Sea Tiger," "The Naked Gun"
Corey, Wendell	1914-1968	40	55	75	80	"Rear Window"
Corley, Pat	1930-	5	10	10	10	"Murphy Brown"
Cort, Bud	1950-	5	10	10	10	"Harold and Maude"
Cortez, Ricardo	1899-1977	30	40	40	45	"The Torrent," "The Maltese..."
Cosby, Bill	1937-	10	15	25	25	"The Cosby Show" - TV, RS
Costas, Bob	1952-	10	20	35	15	Sportscaster
Costello, Delores	1905-1979	30	35	55	60	"The Sea Beast"
Costello, Lou	1906-1959	265	550	600	500	"Abbott & ", sheet w/BA - $600
Costner, Kevin	1955-	40	100	200	75	"The Untouchables," FA, ES
Cotten, Joseph	1905 - 1994	25	35	60	45	"Citizen Cane," "Gaslight"
Coulier, David		5	10	15	10	"Full House"
Couric, Katie	1957-	5	10	15	10	"Today"
Cowan, Jerome	1897-1972	60	120		100	"The Maltese Falcon"
Coward, Noel	1899-1973	175	250	400	350	"In Which ...," SB - $200
Cox, Courtney	1964-	20	45	65	50	"Friends," ES, FA

Name	DB/DD	Sig.DS/LS	ALS	SP	Comments
Cox, Ronny	1938-	5	10	10	10	"Beverly Hills Cop"
Coyote, Peter	1942-	5	10	15	10	"Jagged Edge"
Crabbe, Buster	1907 - 1983	40	75	65	80	"Tarzan," 1932 Olympics
Crain, Jeanne	1925 -	20	25	35	50	"Pinky," "State Fair," "Margie"
Crane, Bob	1928-1978	150	250		300	"Hogan's Heroes"
Craven, Wes	1939-	10	20	25	20	"Nightmare on Elm Street"
Crawford, Broderick	1910-1986	40	145	145	100	"All The King's Men"
Crawford, Cindy	1964-	5	20	30	40	Supermodel, "House of Style"
Crawford, Joan	1904-1977	65	175	175	200	"Mildred Pierce," "Sudden..."
Crawford, Michael	1942-	25	40	45	75	"The Phantom of the Opera"
Cregar, Laird	1916-1944	110	125	250	300	Character actor, "Charley's..."
Crenna, Richard	1927-2003	20	30	75	40	"Rambo: First Blood Part Ii"
Crews, Laura Hope	1880-1942	200	350	375	400	GWTW - Aunt Pittypat, scarce
Crisp, Donald	1880-1974	75	100	125	150	"How Green Was... Valley"
Cristal, Linda	1936-	15	20	25	25	"The Alamo," "The High .."
Cromwell, Richard	1910-1960	20	25	30	35	"Jezebel," "Young Mr. Lincoln"
Cronkite, Walter	1916-	15	30		25	"CBS Evening News," RS
Cronyn, Hume	1911-2003	20	40	65	45	"The Seventh Cross"
Crosby, Bing	1901-1977	70	300	400	175	"Going My Way," "Hoilday Inn"
Crosby, Cathy Lee	1949-	5	10	15	20	"That's Incredible!"
Crosby, Denise	1958-	5	10	15	20	"Star Trek: The Next ..."
Cross, Ben	1948-	10	25		20	"Chariots of Fire"
Crouse, Lindsay	1948-	5	10	10	10	"The Verdict"
Crowe, Russell	1964-	25	50		50	"Gladiator"
Cruise, Tom	1962-	60	200		115	"Top Gun," "Jerry Maguire"
Cruz, Penelope	1974-	15	30		35	"All About My Mother"
Cryer, Jon	1965-	5	10	10	10	"The Famous Teddy Z"
Crystal, Billy	1947-	20	40	75	40	"When Harry Met Sally...," RS
Cugat, Xavier	1900-1990	35	50	75	125	bandleader, "Rhumba King"
Culkin, Macauly	1980-	25	35	35	50	"Home Alone," elusive signer
Cullum, John	1930-	5	10	10	10	"Northern Exposure"
Culp, Robert	1930-	10	15	20	25	"I Spy"
Cummings, Irving	1888-1959	40	65	55	80	Director, "Curly Top"
Cummings, Robert	1908-1990	20	35	40	40	"King's Row"
Curry, Tim	1946-	25	35	45	50	"The Rocky Horror ..."
Curtin, Jane	1947-	10	20	25	20	"Kate & Allie," SNL
Curtis, Jamie Lee	1958-	30	45	50	75	"A Fish Called Wanda"
Curtis, Tony	1924-	20	40	75	55	"Some Like It Hot," f. Jamie L.
Cusack, Cyril	1910-	5	10	15	10	"Farenheit 451"
Cusack, Joan	1962-	5	10	10	10	"Working Girl"
Cusack, John	1966-	20	30	40	45	"Say Anything"
Cusack, Sinead	1948-	5	10	15	10	Actor, m. Jeremy Irons

Cagney, James

* He was an elusive signer in-person, however many had success writing him during retirement.

* Signatures in all forms have a consistent demand, especially those associated with key roles.

* Typical responses included a small signed photograph, a typed letter or one of his postcards.

* The common form of his signature is "J.Cagney" which has a striking resemblance to that of his sister Jeanne.

Name	DB/DD	Sig.DS/LS	ALS	SP	Comments
D'Abo, Olivia	1969-	5	10		10	"The Wonder Years"
D'Angelo, Beverly	1954-	5	10	15	10	"Hair"
D'Arbanville, Patti	1951-	10	20		20	Actress
D'Arcy, Alexander	1908-	10	15	20	15	"Fifth Avenue Girl"
D'Eipocio, Nick	1961-	10	20		25	"Life is Beautiful"
D'Ononfrio, Vincent	1959-	5	10		15	"The Newton Boys"
D'Orsay, Fifi	1904-1983	20	25	30	30	"They Had to See Paris"
DaCosta, Morton	1914-1989	20	25	35	30	"The Music Man," director
Dafoe, Willem	1955-	10	15	30	25	"Mississippi Burning"
Dahl, Arlene	1924-	10	20	35	20	"Life With Father"
Dailey, Dan	1914-1978	20	30	50	40	"The Best Things ..."
Daley, Rosie	1961-	5	10	10	10	"In the Kitchen with Rosie"
Dall, John	1918-1971	25	30	45	40	"The Corn is Green," "Rope"
Dalton, Timothy	1944-	10	20	30	25	"The Living Daylights"
Daly, Carson	1973-	10	20		20	MTV veejay
Daly, Timothy	1956-	20	40	70	50	"Wings"
Daly, Tyne	1946-	5	10	15	10	"Cagney & Lacey"
Damita, Lily	1901-	45	75	100	75	French actress, Mrs. Errol Flynn
Damon, Matt	1970-	20	40	65	45	"Good Will Hunting"
Dana, Viola	1897-1987	15	20	30	25	Silent era star, "Two Sisters"
Dance, Charles	1946-	5	10	10	10	"The Jewel in the Crown"
Dandridge, Dorothy	1923-1965	60	140		270	"A Day at the Races"
Danes, Claire	1979-	20	35	65	50	"My So-Called Life"
Dangerfield, Rodney	1921-	10	25	40	25	"Back to School"
Daniels, Bebe	1901-1971	25	30	65	60	Silent era star, "Rio Rita"
Daniels, Jeff	1955-	15	25	40	50	"The Purple Rose of Cairo"
Daniels, William	1927-	10	20	30	20	"St. Elsewhere"
Danner, Blythe	1943-	5	10	15	10	"The Prince of Tides"
Danson, Ted	1947-	25	40	50	60	"Cheers" - TV, ES
Dante, Michael	1935-	5	10	10	10	"Custer"
Danza, Tony	1951-	10	20	25	20	"Who's the Boss?"
Darnell, Linda	1921-1965	50	150		200	"Song of Bernadette"
Darrieux, Danielle	1917-	10	15	15	20	"Mayerling," "The Rage of Paris"
Davenport, Harry	1866-1949	160	275		265	GWTW, "The Hunchback ..."
Davidovich, Lolita	1961-	5	10	10	10	"Blaze"
Davidson, Jaye	1967-	5	10	15	10	"The Crying Game"
Davidson, John	1941-	5	10	10	15	"Hollywood Squares," host
Davies, Marion	1897-1961	45	75	175	150	"The Patsy," "Show People"
Davis, Bette	1908-1989	65	180	315	200	SP from "Jezebel" - $325
Davis, Clifton	1945-	5	10	10	10	"Never Can Say Goodbye"
Davis, Geena	1957-	10	45	50	45	"Thelma and Louise"
Davis, Joan	1907-1961	30	60	50	60	"I Married Joan" - TV
Davis, Kristin	1965-	10	25	45	30	"Sex and the City"
Davis, Nancy	(See First Ladies)					"Hellcats of the Navy"
Davis, Ossie	1917-	10	15	20	20	"Evening Shade"
Davis, Sammy, Jr.	1925-1990	50	80	125	160	"Porgy and Bess," ES, FA
Dawber, Pam	1950-	5	10		10	"Mork and Mindy," RS
Day, Doris	1924-	10	50	65	35	"The Doris Day Show," SDS-6X
Day, Laraine	1917-	15	30		35	"Dr. Kildare" series
Day-Lewis, Daniel	1957-	25	60		80	"My Left Foot," "The Boxer"
Dean, James	1931-1955	2270	7000		5650	"Rebel Without a Cause"
Dean, Jimmy	1928-	5	10	15	15	"The Jimmy Dean Show"

Name	DB/DD	Sig.DS/LS	ALS	SP	Comments
DeCamp, Rosemary	1914-	10	25	35	20	"Yankee Doodle Dandy," RS
DeCarlo, Yvonne	1922-	10	25	35	30	"Slave Girl," "The Munsters" - TV
DeCordoba, Pedro	1881-1950	30	50		50	"For Whom the Bell Tolls"
Dee, Francis	1907-	10	15	20	20	"Playboy of Paris," "Little ..."
Dee, Ruby	1924-	10	15	30	20	"Do the Right Thing"
Dee, Sandra	1942-	5	10	10	15	"Gidget"
Deforest, Calvert	1923-	5	10	10	10	Actor, Larry "Bud" Melamn
DeGeneres, Ellen	1958-	15	35	60	30	"Ellen," controversial
DeHaven, Gloria	1924-1993	10	15	20	25	"Best Foot Forward"
DeHavilland, Olivia	1916-	40	125		75	STLS/ALS, inc.GWTW -X2
Dekker, Albert	1904-1968	15	20	25	25	"The Killers," "East of Eden"
Del Rio, Dolores	1905-1983	35	45	60	70	"Madame Du Barry"
Delaney, Kim	1961-	10	20		25	"NYPD Blue"
Delany, Dana	1956-	10	20	25	25	"China Beach,"RS
DeLaurentis, Dino	1919-	15	35	55	35	"King Kong," producer
Dell, Gabriel	1919-1988	20	25	30	35	"Dead End Kids" member
Delon, Alain	1935-	5	10	10	10	"Is Paris Burning?"
Del Toro, Bemicio	1967-	15	30	60	30	"Traffic"
Deluise, Dom	1933-	5	10	10	10	"The Dom Deluise Show," RS
Deluise, Peter	1967-	5	10	10	10	"21 Jump Street"
Demarest, William	1892-1983	20	35	30	40	"The Jolson Story"
DeMille, Cecil B.	1881-1959	80	225	425	300	"The Ten Commandments"
Demme, Jonathan	1944-	10	25	30	25	The Silence of the Lambs"
Demornay, Rebecca	1962-	20	35	50	50	"The Hand That Rocks the..."
Dempsey, Patrick	1966-	10	15	15	15	"Loverboy"
Dench, Judy	1934-	20	45		50	"Shakespeare in Love"
Deneuve, Catherine	1943-	20	35	50	60	"Belle de Jour"
DeNiro, Robert	1943-	25	40	75	60	"Taxi Driver," "Raging Bull," RS
Dennehy, Brian	1939-	10	20	40	25	"Death of a Salesman"
Denning, Richard	1914-1998	10	15	20	20	"Union Pacific," "Hawaii Five-O"
Denny, Regginald	1891-1967	20	25	25	30	"Private Lives," "Love Letters"
Denver, Bob	1935-	10	25	40	25	"Gilligan's Island"
Depardieu, Gerard	1948-	10	20	25	30	"Green Card"
Depp, Johnny	1963-	25	55	75	70	"21 Jump Street"
Derek, Bo	1956-	15	25	30	35	"10" SP - 2X, m. John Derek
Derek, John	1926-1998	25	50	100	50	"The Ten Commandments"
Dern, Bruce	1936-	10	15	20	20	"Coming Home"
Dern, Laura	1967-	15	25	35	50	"Jurassic Park," d. Bruce Dern
De Rossi, Portia	1973-	15	35		35	"Ally McBeal"
Devane, William	1937-	5	10	10	15	"Knots Landing"
Devine, Andy	1905-1977	50	100		130	"A Star is Born," "Stagecoach"
Devito, Danny	1944-	15	25	35	25	"Taxi," "Batman" SP - 2-3X
Dewhurst, Colleen	1926-1991	15	25	35	35	"The Nun's Story," m. G.C. Scott
Dexter, Anthony	1919-	10	15	10	10	"Valentino"
Dey, Susan	1952-	10	20	25	25	"L.A. Law"
Deyoung, Cliff	1945-	5	10	15	10	"The Hunger"
Diaz, Cameron	1972-	15	25	35	50	"The Mask," model
DiCaprio, Leonardo	1975-	50	100	250	125	"Titanic" SP w/Winslet - $265
Dickinson, Angie	1932-	5	15	20	15	"Police Woman,"RS
Diesel, Vin	1967-	10	30		25	"Fast and the Furious"
Dietrich, Marlene	1901-1992	60	160	275	175	"Morocco," "The Blue Angel"
Diggs, Taye	1971-	10	20		20	"How Stella..."

Name	DB/DD	Sig.DS/LS	ALS	SP	Comments
Diller, Phyllis	1917 -	5	10	10	10	"The Phyllis Diller Show," RS
Dillon, Kevin	1965-	5	10	15	10	"The Doors"
Dillon, Matt	1964-	10	25	25	30	"The Outsiders"
Disney, Walt	(See Cartoonists)					Animator, "Snow White"
Divine	1945-1988	50	100		100	"Hairspray"
Dix, Richard	1894-1949	30	45	55	75	Silent film star, "Cimarron"
Dixon, Donna	1957-	10	15	20	20	"Bosom Buddies"
Dobson, Kevin	1943-	5	10	15	15	"Knots Landing"
Doherty, Shannen	1971-	20	40	50	50	"Beverly Hills 90210"
Donahue, Heather	1973-	10	20		20	"The Blair Witch Project"
Donahue, Phil	1935-	15	30	50	30	Talk show host, reluctant signer
Donahue, Troy	1936-2001	15	30	50	35	"Hawaiian Eye"
Donaldson, Sam	1934-	5	10		10	"Prime Time Live," RS
Donat, Robert	1905-1958	70	100	135	250	SP ,"Goodbye...Chips" - $600
Donlevy, Brian	1899-1972	35	75	100	75	"Beau Geste," "Destry Rides..."
Donnelly, Ruth	1896-1982	15	25	35	30	"The Snake Pit"
Donovan, Jason	1968-	5	10	10	10	Singer, actor
Doran, Ann	1911-	10	20	25	20	"Blondie," character actress, RS
Dorn, Philip	1905-1975	20	30	30	35	"I Remember Mama"
Dorsey, Jimmy	1904-1957	(See Music Section)				
Dorsey, Tommy	1905-1956	(See Music Section)				
Douglas, Donna	1935-	5	10	15	15	"The Beverly Hillbillies," RS
Douglas, Illeana	1965-	10	20	35	20	"To Die For"
Douglas, Kirk	1916-	25	55	70	50	"The Bad and the Beautiful"
Douglas, Melvyn	1901-1981	25	55	100	55	"Hud," "Mr. Blandings Builds ..."
Douglas, Michael	1944-	20	40	35	50	"Wall Street," "Fatal Attraction"
Douglas, Paul	1907-1959	15	25	35	40	"Born Yesterday"
Dow, Peggy	1928-	10	15	15	20	"Undertow," "Harvey"
Dow, Tony	1945-	5	10	15	15	"Leave It to Beaver"
Down, Lesley-Ann	1954-	5	10	15	15	"Dallas"
Downey, Morton	1933-2001	15	30		30	Controversial talk show host
Downey, Robert, Jr.	1965-	25	40	55	60	"Chaplin"
Downey, Roma	1963-	20	30	35	45	"Touched by an Angel"
Downs, Hugh	1921-	10	20	25	25	"20/20," RS
Downs, Johnny	1913-1994	35	60		65	"Our Gang" series
Drake, Tom	1918-1982	5	10	10	10	"Meet Me in St. Louis"
Drescher, Fran	1957-	20	40	50	55	"The Nanny"
Dresser, Louise	1880-1965	40	50	65	70	"The Eagle," "Mammy"
Dressler, Marie	1869-1934	120	200	300	250	"Min and Bill," character actress
Drew, Ellen (Terry Ray)	1915-	5	10	15	10	"Christmas in July"
Dreyfuss, Richard	1947-	15	40	80	45	"Mr. Holland's Opus"
Driscoll, Bobby	1937-1968	150	175	200	340	Child star, "Song of the South"
Driver, Minnie	1970-	10	25	30	20	"Good Will Hunting," RS
Dru, Joanne	1923-	10	20	25	20	"All the King's Men," Red River"
Drudge, Matt	1966-	5	15		10	Cybercolumnist
Duchovny, David	1960-	45	100	265	115	"The X-Files"
Dudikoff, Michael	1954-	5	10	15	10	"American Ninja"
Duff, Howard	1917-1990	20	25	30	40	"Naked City," m. Ida Lupino
Duffy, Julia	1950-	5	10	10	10	"Newhart"
Duffy, Karen	1961-	5	10		10	"MTV" personality
Duffy, Patrick	1949-	10	20	20	20	"Dallas"
Dukakis, Olympia	1931-	20	35	50	45	"Moonstruck"

Name	DB/DD	Sig.DS/LS	ALS	SP	Comments
Duke, Patty	1946-	15	20	25	25	"The Miracle Worker," child star
Dukes, David	1945-	5	10	10	10	"Sisters"
Dullea, Keir	1936-	10	15	20	25	"2001: A Space Odyssey"
Dumont, Margaret	1889-1965	210	300	340	400	Work w/Marx Bros, tough sig.
Dunaway, Faye	1941-	10	25	40	35	"Mommie Dearest"
Dunbar, Dixie	1919-1991	10	15	15	20	"Rebecca of Sunnybrook Farm"
Duncan, Sandy	1946-	5	10	10	15	"Funny Face"
Dunn, James	1905-1967	65	100	125	130	"A Tree Grows in Brooklyn"
Dunn, Josephine	1906-1983	20	30	35	40	"The Singing Fool," "Big Time"
Dunne, Griffin	1955-	5	10	15	10	"After Hours"
Dunne, Irene	1901-1990	30	25	50	60	Popular actress, nom. for 5 AA
Dunnock, Mildred	1904-1991	15	20	25	30	"Cat On A Hot Tin Roof"
Dunst, Kirsten	1982-	15	30		25	"Spiderman"
Duprez, June	1918-1984	25	35	35	45	"The Four Feathers"
Durante, Jimmy	1893-1980	30	75	120	75	Com., "Little Miss Broadway"
Durbin, Deanna	1921-	20	25	45	35	"That Certain Age"
Durning, Charles	1933-	10	15	15	20	"Evening Shade"
Duryea, Dan	1907-1968	20	25	35	40	"Scarlet Street"
Dutton, Charles	1951-	5	10	10	10	"Roc"
Duvall, Robert	1931-	25	50	75	60	"Tender Mercies"
Duvall, Shelly	1949-	10	15	20	20	"The Shining"
Dysart, Richard	1929-	10	20	30	20	"L.A. Law"

Dean, James

* A Hollywood legend after only three films – "East of Eden," "Rebel Without a Cause" and "Giant"

* Signatures in all forms are in demand.

* Some checks and documents have entered the market in recent years.

* Any signed photographs of Dean in character, should be questioned.

Name	DB/DD	Sig.DS/LS	ALS	SP	Comments
Eastwood, Clint	1930-	30	125		60	"Unforgiven," RS, SDS-2X
Ebert, Roger	1942-	5	10	20	10	Film critic
Ebsen, Buddy	1908-2003	25	75	100	50	"Breakfast at Tiffany's"
Eddy, Nelson	1901-1967	55	150	150	130	"Naughty Marietta," singer
Eden, Barbara	1934-	15	25	30	35	"I Dream of Jeannie"
Edwards, Anthony	1963-	15	45	60	60	"ER"
Edwards, Blake	1922-	15	15	30	30	The "Pink Panther" series
Edwards, Cliff	1895-1971	60	75	125	135	GWTW, Pinocchio"
Edwards, Vince	1928-1996	15	30	40	30	"Ben Casey" - TV
Eggar, Samantha	1939-	5	10	15	10	"The Collector"
Eikenberry, Jill	1947-	10	15	15	15	"L.A. Law"
Eilers, Sally	1908-1978	20	25	30	40	"Bad Girl," "State Fair"
Ekberg, Anita	1931-	10	15	20	25	"La Dolce Vita"
Ekland, Britt	1942-	10	15	20	30	"After the Fox"
Electra, Carmen	1972-	20	50		45	"Baywatch"
Elfman, Jenna	1971-	10	25	30	30	"Dharma & Greg"
Elizondo, Hector	1936-	5	10	10	10	"Freebie and the Bean"
Ellerbee, Linda	1944-	5	10		15	"Our World"
Elliott, Chris	1960-	5	10	10	10	"Get a Life," comedy writer, actor

Name	DB/DD	Sig.DS/LS	ALS	SP	Comments
Elliott, Gordon	1903-1965	55	100	125	150	"The Great ...Wild Bill Hickok"
Elliott, Sam	1944 -	15	30	50	40	"Tombstone"
Ellis, Patricia	1916-1970	40	65	65	100	"42nd Street"
Eltz, Theodore von	1894-1964	50	65	70	100	character actor, "The Big Sleep"
Elvira (C. Peterson)	1951-	10	15	25	30	Horror film hostess
Elwes, Cary	1962-	5	10	15	10	"The Princess Bride"
Emerson, Hope	1897-1960	20	30	35	40	"Caged"
Englund, Robert	1949-	10	20	40	30	"Nightmare on Elm Street"
Ephron, Nora	1941-	15	20	25	25	"Sleepless in Seattle"
Erickson, Leif	1911-1986	25	30	45	50	"Conquest," "On the ..."
Errol, Leon	1881-1951	50	70	75	90	Vaudeville star, comedy shorts
Erwin, Stuart	1903-1967	25	35	45	50	"Pigskin Parade," TV star
Esmond, Jill	1908-1990	45	65	75	90	"The White Cliffs of Dover"
Esposito, Giancarlo	1958-	5	10	10	10	"Do the Right Thing"
Estevez, Emilio	1962-	10	20	25	25	"Repo Man," writer
Estrada, Erik	1949-	5	10	10	10	"CHiPS" - TV
Evangelista, Linda	1965-	10	20	25	30	Supermodel
Evans, Dale	1912-2001	30	55	75	55	"The Yellow Rose of Texas"
Evans, Linda	1942-	10	20	30	40	"Dynasty," RS
Evans, Madge	1909-1981	20	25	30	45	"David Copperfield," child star
Evans, Maurice	1901-1989	25	30	40	50	"Scrooge," "Planet of the Apes"
Evans, Mike	1949-	5	10	10	10	"The Jeffersons" - TV
Everett, Chad	1936-	10	15	25	25	"Medical Center"
Everett, Rupert	1959-	10	20	30	15	"My Best Friend's Wedding"
Evigan, Greg	1953-	5	10	10	10	"B.J. and the Bear," RS
Ewell, Tom	1909-1994	25	30	30	40	"The Seven Year Itch"
Eythe, William	1918-1957	25	45		50	"Special Agent," died at 38

Eastwood, Clint

* While he has been responsive to requests in-person, most of his fan mail is allegedly ghost signed.

* Early in his career his signature was legible and he often took time to personalize requests.

* Today, his siganture has been abbreviated to "Cl Eastwood" with the "E" crossing the "t" in his last name.

* He is currently responding to most mail requests with a facsimile-signed photograph.

Name	DB/DD	Sig.DS/LS	ALS	SP	Comments
Fabares, Shelley	1944-	10	15	15	20	Actor, m. Mike Farrell
Fabio (Fabio Lanzoni)	1961-	20	50	60	55	"I Can't Believe It's Not Butter"
Fabray, Nanette	1920-	5	10	15	20	"One Day at a Time"
Fairbanks, Douglas	1883-1939	165	325	400	365	Screen legend
Fairbanks, Douglas, Jr.	1909-2000	25	60	100	50	"Little Caesar," "Gunga Din"
Fairchild, Morgan	1950-	10	15	25	30	"Falcon Crest"
Falco, Edie	1963-	10	25	30	25	"The Sopranos"
Falk, Peter	1927-	10	25	35	20	"Columbo"
Falkenburg, Jinx	1919-2003	10	25	30	30	Model, "Meet Me on Broadway"
Fallon, Jimmy	1974-	10	20	30	20	SNL
Farantino, James	1938-	10	15	20	25	"Dynasty"
Farina, Dennis	1944-	10	15	25	20	"Crime Story"
Farley, Chris	1964-1997	30	60	85	75	SNL, Wayne's World, FA

Name	DB/DD	Sig.DS/LS	ALS	SP	Comments
Farmer, Francis	1914-1970	165	200	275	435	"Ebb Tide," SSP-2X
Farnsworth, Richard	1920-2000	20	50		40	"The Natural"
Farr, Jamie	1934-	5	10	25	20	"M*A*S*H" SP-2X, RS
Farrell, Charles	1901-1990	20	30	35	45	"My Little Margie" - TV
Farrell, Colin	1976-	10	20	30	20	"Minority Report"
Farrell, Glenda	1904-1971	30	40	65	75	"I Am a Fugitive From a ..."
Farrell, Mike	1939 -	5	10	25	20	"M*A*S*H,"RS
Farrow, Mia	1945-	15	30	25	30	"Rosemary's Baby"
Favreau, Jon	1966-	10	20	30	20	"Swingers"
Fawcett, Farrah	1947-	15	25	45	40	"Charlie's Angels"
Fay, Frank	1894-1961	25	35	35	50	"Harvey" - Broadway
Faye, Alice	1912-1998	25	45	55	50	"Alexander's Ragtime Band"
Fazenda, Louise	1889-1962	35	70	75	80	"Alice in Wonderland"
Feld, Fritz	1900-1993	12	15	25	25	Character actor, "At the Circus"
Feldman, Corey	1971-	10	20	25	25	"Stand By Me"
Feldon, Barbara	1941-	5	10	10	20	"Get Smart," RS
Feldshuh, Tovah	1953-	5	10	15	10	"The Idolmaker"
Fell, Norman	1924-1998	10	20	30	20	"Three's Company"
Fenn, Sherilyn	1965-	15	20	15	30	"Twin Peaks"
Ferrell, Will	1967-	15	30	40	40	SNL
Ferrer, Jose	1912-1992	30	50	75	60	"Cyrano de Bergerac"
Ferrer, Mel	1912-	5	10	20	15	"Falcon Crest," producer
Ferrer, Miguel	1954-	5	10	15	15	"Twin Peaks"
Ferrigno, Lou	1952-	10	15	40	25	"The Incredible Hulk"
Ferris, Barbara	1940-	5	10	10	10	"The Strauss Family"
Fetchit, Stepin	1902-1985	40	85	150	175	"In Old Kentucky"
Fidler, Jimmie	1900-1988	10	20	25	20	Hollywood gossip reporter
Field, Betty	1918-1973	20	35	35	40	"What a Life!," "Of Mice and..."
Field, Sally	1946-	15	30	45	35	"The Flying Nun," FA,ES
Field, Virginia	1917-1992	10	15	20	20	"Waterloo Bridge"
Fields, Gracie	1898-1979	25	35	50	70	"Molly and Me," singer, comedy
Fields, Kim	1969-	5	10	10	10	"The Facts of Life"
Fields, Stanley	1883-1941	30	45	50	55	"Little Caesar," "Show Boat"
Fields, W.C.	1879-1946	400	1000	1250	1500	Screen legend, SSP- .5 - 1X
Fiennes, Joseph	1970-	10	20	30	20	"Shakespeare in Love"
Fiennes, Ralph	1962-	20	35	50	55	"Schindler's List," "Hamlet"
Fierstein, Harvey	1954-	5	10	15	10	"Mrs. Doubtfire"
Finney, Albert	1936-	10	20	25	20	"Shoot the Moon"
Fiorentino, Linda	1960-	15	25	35	60	"The Last Seduction"
Firth, Colin	1960-	5	10	15	10	"Another Country"
Fishburne, Laurence	1961-	15	25	40	40	"Boyz N the Hood," "Tribeca"
Fisher, Carrie	1956-	10	25	30	30	"Star Wars," d. D. Reynolds
Fisher, Eddie	1928-	10	15	25	20	"The Eddie Fisher Show"
Fisher, Joely	1967-	5	10		10	"Ellen"
Fitzgerald, Barry	1888-1961	140	165	225	275	"Going My Way," "Ebb Tide"
Fitzgerald, Geraldine	1912-1992	20	40	65	50	"Wuthering Heights"
Flagstad, Kirsten	1895-1962	100	185	250	275	"The Big Broadcast of 1938"
Flatley, Michael	1958-	10	25		25	"Lord of the Dance"
Fleming, Rhonda	1922-	15	25	30	45	"Spellbound," "Gunfight at ..."
Fletcher, Bramwell	1904-1988	40	50	65	80	"The Mummy," "The Scarlet..."
Fletcher, Louise	1934-	10	20	25	20	"One Flew over the ..."
Flockhart, Calista	1964-	20	40	75	45	"Ally McBeal"

Name	DB/DD	Sig.DS/LS	ALS	SP	Comments
Flynn, Errol	1909-1959	350 675	800	740	Screen legend, FA
Foch, Nina	1924-	10 15	12	10	"Executive Suite"
Foley, Mick	1965-	20 40	75	40	WWF, Mankind
Follows, Megan	1968-	5 10	15	10	"Anne of Green Gables"
Fonda, Bridget	1964-	15 30	40	30	"Singles," d. Peter Fonda
Fonda, Henry	1905-1982	60 155	200	150	Screen legend, "The Grapes..."
Fonda, Jane	1937-	10 55	40	35	"Barbella," "On Golden Pond"
Fonda, Peter	1939-	10 40	45	50	"Easy Rider," s. Henry Fonda
Fontaine, Joan	1917-	10 15	35	25	"Suspicion"
Foran, Dick	1910-1979	20 25	40	40	"Stand Up and Cheer"
Ford, Faith	1964-	5 10	15	15	"Murphy Brown"
Ford, Glenn	1916-	40 70	100	85	"The Blackboard Jungle"
Ford, Harrison	1942-	60 175	300	140	"Indiana Jones" SP-2X, ES
Ford, Wallace	1898-1966	25 35	40	50	"Possessed," "Freaks"
Forlani, Clare	1971-	10 20	30	25	"Meet Joe Black"
Forster, Robert	1941-	5 10	10	10	"Banyon"
Forsythe, John	1918-	20 30	35	35	"In Cold Blood,""Dynasty"
Foster, Jodie	1962-	45 125	250	80	"The Silence of the Lambs"
Foster, Meg	1948-	10 25	25	20	"Cagney and Lacey"
Foster, Preston	1901-1970	25 60	65	60	"My Friend Flicka"
Fox, James	1939-	5 10	10	10	"The Loneliness of ..."
Fox, Matthew	1966-	10 15	25	20	"Party of Five"
Fox, Michael J.	1961-	20 30	40	40	"Family Ties"
Fox, Vivica A.	1964-	15 30	45	30	"Independence Day"
Foxworth, Robert	1941-	5 10	10	10	"Falcon Crest"
Foxworthy, Jeff	1958-	5 10	25	20	"You Might Be a Redneck If..."
Foxx, Redd	1922-1991	30 50		50	"Sanford and Son"
Foy, Eddie, Jr.	1905-1983	25 30	35	50	"Yankee Doodle Dandy"
Foy, Eddie, Sr.	1854-1928	30 45	50	60	
Frakes, Jonathan	1952-	10 15	20	25	"Star Trek: The Next..."
Franciosa, Anthony	1928-	5 10	10	15	"The Long Hot Summer"
Francis, Anne	1930-	5 10	15	15	Former child model, actor
Francis, Genie	1962-	5 10		15	"General Hospital"
Francis, Kay	1903-1968	30 40	60	75	"Living On Velvet," "Stranded"
Franken, Al	1951-	5 10		10	Actor, author
Franklin, Bonnie	1944-	5 10		15	"One Day At A Time"
Franz, Dennis	1944-	20 30	35	45	"NYPD Blue"
Fraser, Brendan	1967-	15 25		25	"The Mummy"
Frawley, William	1887-1966	300 400	450	500	"I Love Lucy" - TV
Freeman, Kathleen	1919-	10 15	20	20	"Singin' in the Rain"
Freeman, Morgan	1937-	25 85	75	55	"Driving Miss Daisy"
Freeman, Nora	1926-	10 20	30	20	"Black Beauty," "Dear Ruth"
Frewer, Matt	1958-	5 10	15	10	"Max Headroom"
Fricker, Brenda	1945-	15 30	45	60	"My Left Foot"
Funicello, Annette	1942-	15 30		35	"Beach Blanket Bingo," var. sig.
Funt, Allen	1914-1999	20 35		40	"Candid Camera," ES
Furness, Betty	1916-1994	20 25	30	40	TV commercial queen

Name	DB/DD	Sig.DS/LS	ALS	SP	Comments

Flynn, Errol

* He was an obliging signer in-person but allegedly paid little, if any, time responding to his fan mail.

* His signature is often flamboyant, with the "E" the largest character.

* The signature breaks in his last name are often inconsistent, as is the formation of the "F."

* Authentic signed photographs are scarce and when they do surface in the market are typically large (11" x 14") black & white portraits or possibly a still from one of his movies.

* He often added an underline beneath his signature.

* Common salutations: "All my good wishes," "Very kindest regards"

Name	DB/DD	Sig.DS/LS	ALS	SP	Comments
Gabin, Jean	1904-1976	25	35	40	50	French actor, "Grand Illusion"
Gable, Clark	1901-1960	375	450		900	GWTW, FA, SP w/CL - $1200
Gable, John Clark	1961-	10	15	20	15	Actor, s. Clark Gable
Gabor, Eva	1921-1995	30	35	50	50	"A Royal Scandal"
Gabor, Zsa Zsa	1917-	10	15	25	20	"Moulin Rouge"
Gail, Maxwell	1943-	5	10	15	10	"Barney Miller"
Gallagher, Peter	1955 -	5	10	10	10	"sex, lies and videotape"
Gandolfini, James	1961-	20	40		40	"The Sopranos"
Garbo, Greta	1905-1990	1785	3500		9350	Screen legend, reclusive, FA
Garcia, Andy	1956-	10	20	25	35	"The Godfather Part III"
Gardiner, Reginald	1903-1980	20	35	30	40	Brit. actor, "A Yank in the RAF"
Gardner, Ava	1922-1990	60	135	150	150	"Mogambo," "The Barefoot ..."
Garfield, John	1913-1952	85	120		400	"Body and Soul"
Gargan, William	1905-1979	20	30	40	45	"They Knew What They ..."
Garland, Beverly	1930-	5	10	10	10	"My Three Sons"
Garland, Judy	1922-1969	435	900		900	TWOO, FA, autograph var.
Garner, James	1928-	15	25	50	30	"The Rockford Files"
Garner, Jennifer	1972-	10	20		20	"Alias"
Garofalo, Janeane	1964-	15	25	35	40	"The Truth About Cats ..."
Garr, Teri	1949-	15	25	30	45	"Tootsie"
Garrett, Betty	1919-	10	15	15	20	"All In The Family"
Garson, Greer	1908-1996	30	130	160	80	"Mrs. Miniver," "Madame Curie"
Garth, Jennie	1972-	20	30	50	40	"Beverly Hills 90210," FA
Gaynor, Janet	1906-1984	35	85	125	115	One first Oscar for best actress
Gaynor, Mitzi	1930-	10	15	20	15	"South Pacific," $5 for SP
Gazzara, Ben	1930-	5	10	15	15	"Inchon," RS
Geary, Anthony	1947-	10	15	15	25	"General Hospital," FA, ES
Geary, Cynthia	1966-	5	10	10	15	"Northern Exposure"
Gellar, Sarah Michelle	1977-	10	25		30	"Buffy the Vampire Slayer"
George, Gladys	1900-1954	50	65	75	75	"The Maltese Falcon," scarce
Gerard, Gil	1943-	10	15	20	25	"Buck Rogers in the 25th ..."
Gere, Richard	1948-	25	125	150	60	"An Officer and a Gentleman
Gertz, Jami	1965-	5	10	10	10	"Less Than Zero"
Getty, Balthazar	1975-	5	10	10	10	"Where the Day Takes You"
Getty, Estelle	1923-	5	10	15	15	"The Golden Girls," RS
Ghostley, Alice	1926-	5	10	10	15	"Bewitched"
Giannini, Giancarlo	1942-	20	30	45	40	"Seven Beauties"

Name	DB/DD	Sig.DS/LS	ALS	SP	Comments
Gibbons, Leeza	1957-	5	10	15	10	"Entertainment Tonight," FA
Gibbs, Marla	1933-	5	10	10	10	"The Jeffersons"
Gibson, Henry	1935-	5	10	10	10	"Laugh-In"
Gibson, Hoot	1892-1962	140	175	225	250	Cowboy, silent and sound star
Gibson, Mel	1956-	45	150	275	125	"Lethal Weapon," ES, FA
Gielgud, John	1904-2000	40	75	130	80	British stage actor
Gifford, Frances	1920-1994	10	15	15	15	"Jungle Girl," "The Glass Key"
Gifford, Kathie Lee	1953-	5	10	15	10	"Live with Regis and ..."
Gilbert, Billy	1894-1971	25	35	45	50	"Snow White and the ..."
Gilbert, Melissa	1964-	5	10	15	35	"Little House on the Prairie"
Gilbert, Sara	1975-	10	15	20	20	"Roseanne," s. Melissa Gilbert
Gilchrist, Connie	1901-1985	10	20	25	20	"Barnacle Bill," "A Letter to ..."
Gillette, William	1855-1937	65	200	225	150	"Sherlock Holmes"
Gilliam, Terry	1940-	5	10	10	10	"Monty Python and the ..."
Gillis, Ann	1927-	10	15	20	25	Child actress, "Little Orphan..."
Ginty, Robert	1948-	5	10	10	10	"Baa Baa Black Sheep"
Gilpin, Peri	1961-	5	10		10	"Frasier"
Girardot, Etienne	1856-1939	45	85	115	100	"Go West, Young Man"
Gish, Dorothy	1898-1968	70	100	125	130	Best remembered blue jeans!
Gish, Lillian	1896-1993	30	75	140	75	"Duel in the Sun"
Givens, Robin	1964-	5	10	10	15	"Head of the Class"
Glaser, Paul Michael	1943-	5	10	15	20	"Starsky and Hutch"
Glass, Ron	1945-	5	10	10	10	"Barney Miller"
Gleason, Jackie	1916-1987	85	200	275	225	"The Honeymooners" - TV
Gleason, James	1882-1959	50	75	75	80	"Meet John Doe," "Suddenly"
Gleason, Joanna	1950-	5	10	10	15	"Into the Woods," d. M. Hall
Glenn, Scott	1942-	25	55	65	50	"The Right Stuff"
Gless, Sharon	1943-	10	15	20	25	"Cagney and Lacey"
Glover, Crispin	1964-	5	10	10	10	"Back to the Future"
Glover, Danny	1947-	10	25	45	30	"Lethal Weapon"
Glover, John	1944-	10	15	20	20	"Shamus"
Glover, Savion	1973-	10	20	25	30	"The Tap Dance Kid"
Goddard, Paulette	1911-1990	30	65	130	110	"So Proudly We Hail," author
Gold, Tracey	1969-	5	10	15	15	"Growing Pains"
Goldberg, (Bill)	1966-	15	30	40	30	Wrestler
Goldberg, Whoopi	1949-	10	20	30	30	"Ghost," responsive signer
Goldblum, Jeff	1952-	15	30	40	35	"The Big Chill," reluctant signer
Goldthwait, Bobcat	1962-	5	10	10	10	"Police Academy"
Goldwyn, Tony	1960-	5	10	10	10	"Ghost"RS
Golino, Valeria	1966-	10	20	25	35	"Rain Man"
Gomez, Thomas	1905-1971	30	40	50	60	"Ride The Pink Horse"
Gooding Jr., Cuba	1968-	15	30	45	40	"Jerry Maguire"
Goodman, John	1952-	15	25	35	45	"Roseanne"
Gorcey, Leo	1915-1969	130	150	200	175	"Dead End Kids," "Bowery ..."
Gordon, Bert	1922-	25	35	40	45	Horror film star, "Cyclops"
Gordon, Ruth	1896-1985	20	25	30	40	"Rosemary's Baby"
Gorshin, Frank	1933-	10	20	25	50	"Batman" SP - 2X
Gossett, Louis Jr.	1936-	15	25	45	30	"An Officer and a Gentleman"
Gould, Elliott	1938-	10	15	20	20	"Bob & Carol & Ted & Alice"
Goulet, Robert	1933-	5	10	20	15	"Blue Light"
Grable, Betty	1916-1973	110	150	225	285	World War II pin-up
Graham, Heather	1970-	15	25		30	"Boogie Nights"

Name	DB/DD	Sig.DS/LS	ALS	SP	Comments
Grahame, Gloria	1925-1981	60	120	200	165	IAWL, "Crossfire," 'The Bad ..."
Grammer, Kelsey	1955-	15	25	50	45	"Frasier," reluctant signer, FA
Grandy, Fred	1948-	5	10	10	10	"The Love Boat"
Granger, Farley	1925-	5	10	15	20	"Rope," "Strangers on a Train"
Granger, Stewart	1913-1993	30	55	60	60	"Waterloo Road," "Captain ..."
Grant, Cary	1904-1986	265	450	540	425	Screen icon, "Topper"
Grant, Hugh	1960-	25	40	55	65	"Four Weddings and a Funeral"
Grant, Lee	1927-	10	20	30	30	"Peyton Place"
Granville, Bonita	1923-1988	20	25	30	40	"These Three," "Lassie" - TV
Grapewin, Charley	1875-1956	275	525		450	"The Petrified Forest"
Grauman, Sid	1879-1950	50	60	100	100	Theater owner, "Star Dust"
Graves, Peter	1926-	10	15	20	20	"Mission: Impossible"
Graves, Ralph	1900-1977	25	30	40	45	"Sporting Life," "Out of Luck"
Gray, Coleen	1922-	15	25	40	35	"Kiss of Death," "Red River"
Gray, Gilda	1901-1959	55	110	125	150	Polish dancer, "Cabaret"
Gray, Linda	1940-	10	20	20	25	"Dallas"
Gray, Spalding	1941-	10	20	25	20	"The Killing Fields," writer
Grayson, Kathryn	1922-	10	15	20	15	"Show Boat," "Kiss Me, ...," RS
Green, Brian Austin	1973-	10	20		20	"Beverly Hills, 90210"
Green, Mitzi	1920-1969	25	35	35	45	"Tom Sawyer," child star
Green, Tom	1971-	10	25		25	"Tom Green Show"
Greenaway, Peter	1942-	5	10	15	10	"The Cook, the Thief, His ..."
Greene, Richard	1914-1985	20	35	65	45	"The Hound of the Baskervilles"
Greenstreet, Sydney	1879-1954	235	450	500	650	"The Maltese Falcon," C, scarce
Greenwood, Joan	1921-1987	25	40	40	45	"Tom Jones," "Stage Struck"
Greer, Jane	1924-2001	20	40	45	30	"Out of the Past," "Against ..."
Grey, Jennifer	1960-	10	25	35	50	"Dirty Dancing," d. Joel Gray
Grey, Joel (Joel Katz)	1932-	10	20	25	20	"Cabaret," RS
Grey, Nan	1918-1993	10	15	20	20	"Three Smart Girls," "Margie"
Grey, Virginia	1917-	10	15	15	20	"The Women," "Wyoming"
Grier, David Alan	1955-	10	15	15	15	"In Living Color"
Grier, Pam	1949-	5	10		10	"Jackie Brown"
Griffith, Andy	1926-	25	50	75	50	"The Andy Griffith Show"
Griffith, Corinne	1894-1979	40	60	100	110	Silent era star, "Black Oxen"
Griffith, Melanie	1957-	25	40	50	65	"Working Girl"
Grodin, Charles	1935-	5	10	15	15	"Midnight Run," RS
Gross, Mary	1953-	10	20	25	15	SNL, s. Michael Gross
Gross, Michael	1947-	10	15	15	15	"Family Ties," b. Mary Gross
Guardino, Harry	1925-	10	15	15	20	"Dirty Harry"
Guest, Christopher	1948-	5	10	10	10	"This Is Spinal Tap," writer
Guest, Lance	1960-	5	10	10	10	"Knots Landing"
Guillame, Robert	1937-	5	10	10	10	"Soap"
Guiness, Alec	1914-2000	50	75	130	75	"Bridge on the River Kwai"
Gulager, Clu	1928-	5	10	15	15	"The Last Picture Show"
Gumbel, Bryant	1948-	10	20	25	20	"Today," RS
Gustafson, Karin	1959-	5	10	10	10	"Taps"
Guttenberg, Steve	1958-	10	15	20	25	"Three Men and a Baby," RS
Guy, Jasmine	1964-	10	15	20	25	"A Different World"
Gwenn, Edmund	1875-1959	85	150	175	200	"Miracle on 34th Street" - SP-7X
Gwynne, Fred	1926-1993	75	150		225	"The Munsters"

Garland, Judy

* Her signature is always in demand.

* She was a responsive signer in-person, but many mail requests for her signature often went unanswered.

* Her signature varied dramatically during her lifetime and can be very difficult to authenticate.

* Although "The Wizard of Oz" items related items are in demand, she signed very few from her classic role. During the filming of the movie, she did sign some black & white photographs (portraits) for those who asked.

* She also responded to some requests with MGM studio portraits, most of which are larger in size (11" x 14").

* Common salutations: "kindest wishes," "sincerely"

Garbo, Greta

* Intensely private, her catch phrase became "I want to be alone" and she did exactly that becoming a recluse in retirement.

* She signed autographs rarely and only during the height of her Hollywood fame.

* Garbo never responded to autograph requests by mail.

* A few documents and personal checks have entered the market, but they are also very scarce and expensive.

* She hasn't been a target of forgers, because most collectors realize that she never signed anything she didn't have to.

Name	DB/DD	Sig.DS/LS	ALS	SP	Comments
Haas, Lukas	1976-	5	10	10	10	"Witness"
Hack, Shelley	1952-	5	10	15	20	"Charle's Angels" - TV
Hackett, Buddy	1924-2003	20	40		35	"The Love Bug," RS
Hackman, Gene	1930-	30	75		55	"The French Connection"
Haden, Sara	1897-1981	15	25	25	30	"Spitfire," "Andy Hardy" series
Hagerty, Julie	1955-	5	10	10	10	"Airplane!"
Hagman, Larry	1931-	15	30	50	35	"Dallas," s. Mary Marrtin
Haid, Charles	1943-	5	10	10	10	"Hill Street Blues," director
Haim, Corey	1972-	10	15	15	20	"The Lost Boys"
Haines, William	1900-1973	20	30	35	40	"The Tower of Lies"
Hale, Alan	1892-1950	60	65	100	115	"Robin Hood," "The Sea Hawk"
Hale, Alan, Jr.	1918-1990	45	65	80	115	The Skipper,"Gilligan's Island"
Hale, Barbara	1922-	15	30		30	"Perry Mason" - TV, RS
Haley, Jack	1899-1979	125	150	300	265	TWOO, "Rebecca of ..."
Hall, Anthony Michael	1968-	5	10	10	10	"Sixteen Candles"
Hall, Arsenio	1959-	5	10	15	15	Actor, talk show host
Hall, Bridget	1977-	10	15	20	40	Supermodel
Hall, Deidre	1947-	5	10	10	15	"Days of Our Lives," RS
Hall, Huntz	1920-1999	15	20	25	45	"Dead End Kids"

Name	DB/DD	Sig.DS/LS	ALS	SP	Comments
Hall, Jerry	1956-	10	25		25	Model
Hall, Jon	1913-1979	40	50	75	60	"Ramar of the Jungle" - TV
Hall, Juanita	1901-1968	80	125		130	"South Pacific"
Hall, Monty	1924-	5	10	10	10	"Let's Make a Deal"
Hall, Porter	1888-1953	25	35	30	40	"The Plainsman," "His Girl ..."
Hamel, Veronica	1943-	10	35	25	25	"Hill Street Blues"
Hamill, Mark	1952-	5	10	20	25	"Star Wars" trilogy SP-2X
Hamilton, George	1939-	5	10	10	10	"Love at First Bite"
Hamilton, Linda	1956-	20	30	25	55	"The Terminator"
Hamilton, Margaret	1902-1985	120	275	435	300	TWOO, RS
Hamlin, Harry	1951-	10	15	20	20	"L.A. Law"
Hammond, Darrell	1955-	15	25		30	SNL
Hampshire, Susan	1941-	5	10	10	10	"The Forsythe Saga"
Hanks, Tom	1956-	45	150		100	"Forrest Gump," "Apollo 13"
Hannah, Daryl	1960-	10	30	45	60	"Splash"
Harden, Marcia Gay	1959-	15	30		30	"Pollock"
Harding, Ann	1902-1981	20	25	30	35	"Holiday," "The Animal ..."
Hardison, Kadeem	1966-	5	10	10	10	"A Different World"
Hardwicke, Cedric	1893-1964	40	70	100	110	"The Ten Commandments"
Hardy, Oliver	1892-1957	310	355	555	610	"Laurel & ", SP w/Hardy - $1475
Harewood, Dorain	1950-	5	10	10	10	"Roots - The Next Generation"
Hargitay, Mariska	1964-	10	20		20	"Law & Order:..."
Harlow, Jean	1911-1937	1200	1750	3365	2675	30's screen star, scrace, FA
Harmon, Angie	1972-	15	30		30	"Law & Order"
Harmon, Mark	1951-	10	15	20	25	"St. Elsewhere"
Harper, Jessica	1949-	5	10	10	10	Actor
Harper, Tess	1950-	10	15	20	20	"Crimes of the Heart"
Harper, Valerie	1940-	5	10	15	15	"The Mary Tyler Moore Show"
Harrelson, Woody	1961-	20	40	50	60	"Cheers" - TV, ES
Harrington, Pat	1929-	5	10	10	10	"One Day at a Time"
Harris, Barbara	1935-	5	10	10	15	"Family Plot"
Harris, Ed	1950-	15	30	40	45	"Apollo 13," "The Right Stuff"
Harris, Julie	1925-	5	10	15	15	"Knots Landing"
Harris, Mel	1957-	5	10	10	15	"thirtysomething"
Harris, Richard	1930-2002	25	50	70	55	"A Man Called Horse"
Harris, Thomas	1940-	15	25		25	"Silence ...Lambs," reclusive
Harrison, Gregory	1950-	5	10	15	15	"Trapper John, MD"
Harrison, Jenilee	1959-	5	10	10	15	"Dallas"
Harrison, Noel	1935-	5	10	12	15	"The Girl from U.N.C.L.E."
Harrison, Rex	1908-1990	45	75	100	80	"Dr. Doolittle" - SP - 2X
Hart, John	?	20	25	35	40	The first Lone Ranger
Hart, Mary	1944-	5	10	15	20	"Entertainment Tonight"
Hart, Melissa Joan	1976-	25	40	50	60	"Sabrina, the Teenage Witch"
Hart, Moss	1904-1961					(see Authors section)
Hart, Richard	1915-1951	25	35	50	60	"B.F.'s Daughter"
Hart, William S.	1870-1946	150	225		415	Early western star
Hartley, Mariette	1940-	5	10	15	15	"Peyton Place"
Hartman, David	1935-	5	10	15	10	"Good Morning America"
Hartman, Phil	1948-1998	50	100		100	SNL, writer, "Talk Radio"
Hartnett, Josh	1978-	10	20		20	"Pearl Harbor"
Harvey, Steve	1960-	15	25		30	"The Steve Harvey Show"
Hasselhoff, David	1952-	20	50	50	50	"Baywatch"

Name	DB/DD	Sig.DS/LS	ALS	SP	Comments
Hasso, Signe	1910-	10	15	15	20	"Karriar," "The Story of Dr..."
Hatcher, Teri	1964-	25	50	60	75	"Lois & Clark: The New ..."
Hathaway, Anne	1982-	10	20		20	"The Princess Diaries"
Hauer, Rutger	1944-	10	15	20	35	"Blade Runner"
Haver, June	1926-	5	10	10	15	"The Dolly Sisters," RS
Havoc, June	1916-	10	15	15	20	"Four Jacks and a Jill"
Hawke, Ethan	1970-	20	40		45	"Dead Poets Society"
Hawkins, Jack	1910-1973	50	80	75	120	"The Fallen Idol," "Ben Hur"
Hawn, Goldie	1945-	20	40	45	50	"Private Benjamin"
Hayakawa, Sessue	1889-1973	150	200	200	265	"The Bridge on the River Kwai"
Hayden, Russell	1912-1981	30	50	60	80	"Hopalong Rides Again"
Hayden, Sterling	1916-1986	35	50		60	"The Asphalt Jungle," "Dr..."
Hayek, Selma	1966-	20	40	50	45	"Desperado"
Hayes, Gabby	1885-1969	140	175		475	Western film sidekick
Hayes, Helen	1900-1994	25	50	60	75	"Airport," SB - $40
Hayes, Sean	1970-	15	30		30	"Will & Grace"
Hays, Robert	1947-	5	10	10	10	"Airplane!"
Hayward, Louis	1909-1985	15	25	40	50	"The Man in the Iron Mask"
Hayward, Susan	1918-1975	180	315	500	475	"I Want To Live," FA
Hayworth, Rita	1918-1987	165	335		375	"Only Angels Have Wings," FA
Head, Edith	1907-1981	35	70	130	145	Hollywood costume designer
Headly, Glenne	1955-	5	10	10	10	"Dirty Rotten Scoundrels"
Healy, Ted	1896-1937	40	50	50	75	"Soup to Nuts," "Bombshell"
Heard, John	1946-	5	10	10	10	"Home Alone"
Heaton, Patricia	1958-	15	30		30	"Everybody Loves Raymond"
Heche, Ann	1969-	10	20		20	"Volcano"
Heckart, Eileen	1919-2001	15	40	45	30	"The Bad Seed"
Hedren, Tippi	1935-	15	25	30	35	"The Birds," $25 donation
Heflin, Van	1910-1971	40	80	75	80	"Johnny Eager," "Santa Fe Trail"
Heiss, Carol	1940-	15	30	30	30	Olympic skater, "Snow White..."
Helgenberger, Marg	1958-	10	20		15	"CSI: Crime Scene..."
Hemingway, Margaux	1955-1996	20	45		35	Model
Hemingway, Mariel	1961-	20	55	40	40	"Manhattan"
Hemsley, Sherman	1938-	5	10	10	10	"The Jeffersons"
Henderson, Florence	1934-	5	10	10	10	"The Brady Bunch"
Henie, Sonja	1910-1969					(see Misc. Sports section)
Hennessy, Jill	1968-	10	20		20	"Crossing Jordan"
Henner, Marilu	1952-	15	25	30	40	"Taxi"
Henreid, Paul	1908-1992	30	70		80	"Casablanca," "Goodbye, Mr..."
Henriksen, Lance	1940-	5	10	10	10	"Aliens"
Henry, Buck	1930-	5	10	10	10	"Get Smart"
Henry, Justin	1971-	5	10	10	10	"Kramer vs. Kramer"
Hensley, Pamela	1950-	5	10	10	15	"Matt Houston"
Henson, Jim	1936-1990	75	150		225	"The Muppet Show"
Henstridge, Natasha	1974-	10	20		30	"Species"
Hepburn, Audrey	1929-1993	125	400	500	270	"Roman Holiday," "Sabrina"
Hepburn, Katharine	1907-2003	200	400	500	400	SSP -2X, SP- $375, FA
Herbert, Hugh	1887-1952	15	20	35	30	"Footlight Parade"
Herman, Pee-Wee	1952-	10	15	25	20	"Pee-Wee's Playhouse"
Herrmann, Edward	1943-	5	10	10	10	"The Paper Chase"
Hershey, Barbara	1948-	10	20	25	25	"Hannah and Her Sisters"
Hersholt, Jean	1886-1956	25	35	80	55	"Greed," "Emma"

Name	DB/DD	Sig.DS/LS	ALS	SP	Comments
Hervey, Jason	1972-	5	10	10	10	"The Wonder Years"
Hesseman, Howard	1940-	5	10	15	10	"WKRP in Cincinnati"
Heston, Charlton	1924-	10	30	50	30	"Ben Hur," RS
Hewitt, Jennifer Love	1979-	10	20	30	25	"Party of Five," autograph col.
Heydt, Louis Jean	1905-1960	45	80	135	85	"Test Pilot," GWTW
Hickman, Darryl	1931-	5	10	10	15	Child star, "If I Were King"
Hickman, Dwayne	1934-	10	20	20	20	"The Many ... Dobie Gillis," $
Hicks, Catherine	1951-	5	10	15	15	"Peggy-Sue Got Married"
Hill, Arthur	1922-	5	10	10	10	"Owen Marshall, Counsellor..."
Hill, Benny	1925-1992	30	75		60	"The Benny Hill Show"
Hill, Steven	1922-	5	10	10	15	"Law and Order"
Hiller, Wendy	1912-2003	25	40	50	35	"Separate Tables," "Pygmalion"
Hillerman, John	1932-	5	10	15	20	"Magnum P.I."
Hilliard, Harriet	1914-	20	25	25	35	"The Adventures of Ozzie ..."
Hines, Gregory	1946-2003	25	40		50	"The Cotton Club," dancer
Hingle, Pat	1923-	5	10	10	15	"Gunsmoke"
Hirsch, Judd	1935-	5	10	20	20	"Taxi"
Hitchcock, Alfred	1899-1980	275	550	620	650	Director, "The Birds," FA
Hodge, Patricia	1946-	5	10	10	10	"The Elephant Man"
Hodges, Eddie		25	35	40	45	Child star, "A Hole In The Head"
Hodiak, John	1914-1955	25	35	40	50	"Lifeboat," "The Harvey Girls"
Hoey, Dennis	1893-1960	80	175	200	210	British actor, "Sherlock Holmes"
Hoffman, Dustin	1937-	35	80	125	65	"The Graduate," "Rain Man," FA
Hogan, Hulk	1953-	15	30		35	WWF, actor
Hogan, Paul	1939-	10	20	25	20	"Crocodile Dundee"
Holbrook, Hal	1925-	10	20	25	25	"All The President's Men"
Holden, Fay	1895-1973	25	45	45	50	"Andy Hardy" fim series
Holden, Gloria	1908-1991	20	40	35	45	"Dracula," "Dodge City"
Holden, William	1918-1981	50	100	200	175	"Stalag 17," "Sunset Boulevard"
Holliday, Judy	1922-1965	135	300	400	350	"Born Yesterday," rare all forms
Holliman, Earl	1928-	5	10	10	10	"Police Woman"
Holloway, Sterling	1905-1992	30	50	55	60	Voice of cartoon characters
Holly, Lauren	1966-	20	45	75	65	"Picket Fences"
Holm, Celeste	1919-	10	15	20	25	"Gentleman's Agreement"
Holmes, Katie	1978-	10	20	30	15	"Dawson's Creek"
Holmes, Phillips	1909-1942	75	150	325	175	"Nana," "The Man I Killed," KIA
Hooks, Jan	1957-	5	10	10	15	"Designing Women"
Hope, Bob	1903-2003	50	175		125	Screen leg.,"Road" series, FA
Hopkins, Anthony	1937-	30	55	125	65	"Silence of the Lambs," FA
Hopkins, Miriam	1902-1972	40	100	125	125	"Becky Sharp," "Dr. Jekyll ..."
Hopper, Dennis	1936-	25	40	75	50	"Easy Rider"
Hopper, Hedda	1890-1966	25	50	30	45	"Topper," "Sunset Boulevard"
Horne, Lena	1917-	15	25	25	30	"Stormy Weather," "Ziegfeld..."
Horton, Edward Everett	1886-1970	30	45	65	70	"Top Hat," "Lost Horizon"
Hoskins, Bob	1942-	5	10	10	15	"Who Framed Roger Rabbit"
Howard, Arliss	1955-	5	10	10	15	"Full Metal Jacket"
Howard, John	1913-	10	20	30	35	"Lost Horizon"
Howard, Ken	1944-	5	10	10	10	"The White Shadow"
Howard, Leslie	1893-1943	300	600	1125	615	"Berkeley Square," GWTW
Howard, Ron	1954-	25	50		55	"Apollo 13," director, ES
Howard, Sidney	1891-1939	55	125	240	100	Hollywood screenplay author
Howard, William K.	1899-1954	55	115	175	100	"Sherlock Holmes," director

Name	DB/DD	Sig.DS/LS	ALS	SP	Comments
Howe, James Wong	1899-1976	45	50	60	75	"The Thin Man"
Howlin, Olin	1896-1959	50	100	235	110	"So Big," GWTW
Hudlin, Reginald	1961-	5	10	10	10	"House Party"
Hudlin, Warrington	1952-	5	10	10	10	"House Party," b. R. Hudlin
Hudson, Kate	1979-	10	20		15	"Almost Famous"
Hudson, Rochelle	1914-1972	35	40	50	50	"Rebel Without a Cause"
Hudson, Rock	1925-1985	65	145	300	125	"Giant," "Pillow Talk," FA
Hughes, Mary Beth	1919-	10	15	10	15	"The Great Profile"
Hughley, D.L.	1963-	10	20		25	"The Hughleys"
Hulce, Tom	1953-	10	15	20	25	"Amadeus"
Hull, Henry	1890-1977	65	100	115	120	"Werewolf of London"
Hull, Warren	1903-1974	30	40	55	60	"The Spider," "The Green ..."
Hung, Sammo	1952-	15	30		25	"Martial Law," director
Hunt, Helen	1963-	25	50	60	75	"Mad About You," "Twister"
Hunt, Linda	1945-	10	15	15	20	"The Year of Living ..."
Hunt, Marsha	1917-	10	15	15	20	"Lost Angel"
Hunter, Holly	1958-	25	50	75	75	"Broadcast News"
Hunter, Jeffrey	1925-1969	50	100		70	"The True Story of Jesse ..."
Hunter, Kim	1922-2002	20	40	65	40	"A Streetcar Named Desire"
Hunter, Tab	1931-	10	15	20	25	"Damn Yankees"
Huppert, Isabelle	1955-	5	10	10	10	"Entre Nous"
Hurley, Elizabeth	1965-	20	40	50	75	Actor, model
Hurt, John	1940-	10	20	20	25	"The Elephant Man"
Hurt, Mary Beth	1948-	5	10	10	10	"The World According to Garp"
Hurt, William	1950-	25	50	75	65	"Children of a Lesser God"
Hussey, Ruth	1914-	10	20	20	25	"The Philadelphia Story"
Huston, Anjelica	1951-	10	25	40	30	"Prizzi's Honor"
Huston, John	1906-1987	45	100	100	100	Legendary director,"Jezebel"
Huston, Walter	1884-1950	115	200	175	230	Character actor, "Dodsworth"
Hutton, Betty	1921-	10	15	20	25	"The Greatest Show on Earth"
Hutton, Lauren	1943-	5	10	15	25	"American Gigolo," model, RS
Hutton, Timothy	1960-	15	30	45	40	"Ordinary People"
Hyer, Martha	1929-	10	15	20	30	"Some Came Running"

Hamilton, Margaret

* A gifted character actress, Hamilton was nothing short of unforgettable as the Wicked Witch of the West (WWW) in "The Wizard of Oz"

* What surprises many is that she was one of the warmest and most caring individuals you would ever want to meet, just extraordinary!

* She was extremely responsive to her fans throughout her entire life.

* During the last years of her life, Hamilton often responded to requests with black & white still photographs from "Oz" or a black & white portrait. The "Oz" photos often included "WWW" underneath her signature exemplifying how proud she was of her work.

* All "Oz" related signed items are in demand and have exhibited considerable value increases in recent years.

Hanks, Tom

* One of the few stars to make a successful transition form television to motion pictures.

* With his film resume now including some of the biggest films of all-time – "Forrest Gump," "Philadelphia," "Apollo 13," he has become nothing short of a megastar.

* Hanks is a reluctant but obliguing signer in-person, however getting a signature from a mail request is nearly impossible.

* Because supply has not met demand, Hanks is now a target of forgers. Unfortunately, most of what appears in the market is fake.

* Most of the authentic Hanks items that do appear in the market are not represenative of him in an Oscar winning role.

Name	DB/DD	Sig.DS/LS	ALS	SP	Comments
Ice Cube	1969-	10	20	25	30	"Boyz N the Hood," rap artist
Ice-T (Tracy Morrow)	1958-	10	20	25	35	"New Jack City," rap artist
Idle, Eric	1943-	10	20	25	30	"Monty Python's Flying Circus"
Iman	1955-	10	20	25	30	Model, m. David Bowie
Imus, Don	1940-	5	10	15	10	"Imus in the Morning," radio host
Ingels, Marty	1936-	5	10	10	10	"The Pruitts of Southhampton"
Ingram, Rex	1895-1969	140	250	300	340	"The Green Pastures"
Ireland, John	1914-1992	15	25	25	30	"All the King's Men"
Ireland, Kathy	1963-	10	20	25	30	Model
Irons, Jeremy	1948-	15	25	40	40	"The French Lieutenant's..."
Irving, Amy	1953-	5	10	10	15	"Yentl"
Irwin, Bill	1950-	5	10	10	15	"Eight Men Out"
Ives, Burl	1909 -1995	30	55	75	50	"The Big Country," ballad singer
Ivey, Judith	1951-	5	10	15	15	"Designing Women"
Ivory, James	1928-	10	15	25	20	"Howard's End," director

Jolson, Al

* Forever linked to the film "The Jazz Singer"— the world's first feature talkie, Jolson appeared in many films.

* Jolson was extremely popular with his fans and often spent considerable time signing autographs.

* His often single stroke signature has remained popular with collectors for years, most of which prefer it on a photograph.

* Signed photographs from "The Jazz Singer" command the highest prices, however they are scarce.

Name	DB/DD	Sig.DS/LS	ALS	SP	Comments
Jackee (Jackee Harry)	1956-	5	10	10	15	"227"
Jackman, Hugh	1968-	20	40		40	"X-Men"
Jackson, Glenda	1936-	10	20	20	20	"Women in Love"
Jackson, Joshua	1978-	10	20		20	"Dawson's Creek"
Jackson, Kate	1948-	10	25	25	50	"Charlie's Angels"
Jackson, Samuel L.	1949-	20	45	50	70	"Pulp Fiction"
Jackson, Victoria	1958-	10	15	20	15	SNL
Jacobi, Derek	1938-	10	15	20	15	"The Day of the Jackal"

Name	DB/DD	Sig.DS/LS	ALS	SP	Comments
Jacobi, Lou	1913-	10	20	30	20	"Irma La Douce"
Jaffe, Sam	1893-1984	25	35	40	50	"The Asphalt Jungle"
Jagger, Bianca	1945-	10	25		20	Actor
Jagger, Dean	1903-1991	20	25	30	40	"Twelve O'Clock High"
James, Clifton	1925-	10	15	20	15	"Cool Hand Luke," RS
Janis, Conrad	1928-	5	10	20	15	"Mork and Mindy," RS
Janney, Allison	1959-	10	20		25	"The West Wing"
Jason, Sybil	1929-	10	15	15	15	"The Singing Kid"
Jean, Gloria	1928-	5	10	15	20	"Never Give a Sucker ...," RS
Jeffries, Lionel	1926-	5	10	10	10	"The Water Babies"
Jenkins, Allen	1900-1974	30	40	45	50	"42nd Street," "Dead End"
Jennings, Peter	1938-	15	30	50	25	"ABC's World News Tonight"
Jessel, George	1898-1981	35	75	80	100	"The Jazz Singer," TV host
Jeter, Michael	1952-2003	10	20	30	15	"Evening Shade"
Jewell, Isabel	1909-1972	55	70	100	100	"Blessed Event," GWTW
Jillian, Anne	1951-	5	10	10	20	"It's a Living"
Johansen, David	1950-	10	15	20	20	"Scrooged"
Johns, Glynis	1923-	10	15	25	30	"Glynis"
Johnson, Artie	1929-	5	10	10	15	"Laugh-In"
Johnson, Beverly	1952-	5	10	15	15	Model, actor
Johnson, Don	1949-	15	25	45	50	"Miami Vice" - TV
Johnson, Kay	1904-1975	35	45	45	50	"thirteen Women," "White ..."
Johnson, Van	1916-	10	20	25	25	"The Caine Mutiny," "Battle..."
Johnston, Eric	1896-1962	10	20	25	25	Pres. Motion Picture Assoc.
Jolie, Angelina	1975-	15	30	45	35	"Girl Interrupted"
Jolson, Al	1886-1950	150	375	500	360	"The Jazz Singer" SP-.5X
Jones, Allan	1908-1992	15	20	30	40	"A Night At The Opera"
Jones, Buck	1889-1942	185	255		370	"Riders of Death Valley"
Jones, Carolyn	1929-1983	60	125	100	100	"The Bachelor Party"
Jones, Dean	1931-	5	10	10	15	"The Shaggy D.A."
Jones, Grace	1952-	20	30	35	40	"A View to Kill"
Jones, James Earl	1931-	10	25	30	25	"The Great White Hope," FA
Jones, Jeffrey	1947-	5	10	10	10	"Ferris Bueller's Day Off"
Jones, Jennifer	1919-	135	260	300	300	"Song of Bernadette," ES
Jones, Marcia Mae	1924-	5	10	10	15	"These Three," "The Champ"
Jones, Sam J.	1954-	5	10	10	15	"Falsh Gordon"
Jones, Shirley	1934-	5	15	25	20	"The Partridge Family"
Jones, Spike	1911-1965	30	50	60	65	"Bring On the Girls," bandleader
Jones, Star	1962-	5	10		10	"The View"
Jones, Terry	1942-	10	15	15	20	"Monty Python's Life of Brian"
Jones, Tommy Lee	1946-	45	85	75	50	"The Fugitive," ES
Jory, Victor	1902-1982	60	125	225	165	GWTW, "The ...Tom Sawyer"
Jourdan, Louis	1919-1993	30	55	125	75	"Three Coins in the Fountain"
Jovovich, Milla	1975-	10	20		20	"The Fifth Element"
Joy, Leatrice	1896-1985	15	25	40	35	"Ten Commandments"
Joyce, Brenda	1915-	25	40	40	45	"Tarzan," retired at age 34
Judd, Ashley	1968-	15	30		25	""Double Jeopardy"
Judge, Arlene	1912-1974	20	25	35	40	"Are These Our Children?"
Jump, Gordon	1932-2003	10	20	30	20	"WKRP in Cincinnati," RS
Justin, John	1917-	40	50	50	75	"Thief of Baghdad," RAF pilot

Kelly, Gene

* Charming character actor, dancer and choreographer, Kelly appeared in numerous films including "For Me And My Gal," "An American in Paris" and "Singin in the Rain".

* Kelly was an obliguing signer in-person however utilized a variety of methods to answer his fan mail including facsimile and ghost signed photographs.

* Kelly did answer some requests personally, however it was far less than many sources claim.

* A signed still photograph from his classic number in "Singin in the Rain" is by far the most popular form sought by collectors.

Name	DB/DD	DB/DD	Sig.DS/LS	ALS	SP	Comments
Kaczmarek, Jane	1955-	10	20		20	"Malcolm in the Middle"
Kahn, Madeline	1942-1999	15	30	40	35	"Blazing Saddles"
Kanakaredus, Melina	1967-	10	20		20	"Providence"
Kane, Carol	1952-	5	10	10	15	"Taxi"
Kane, Helen	1903-1966	30	45	50	75	"Good Boy," "Sweetie"
Kanin, Garson	1912-1999	15	20	25	30	"The True Glory," director, RS
Kaprisky, Valerie	1963-	5	10	10	15	"Breathless"
Karloff, Boris	1887-1969	315	500	600	575	Horror ALS - 2-3X, SP - 2X
Katt, William	1955-	5	10	10	10	"The Greatest American Hero"
Kaufman, Andy	1949-1984	75	150		175	SNL
Kaufman, George	1889-1961	40	80	160	65	"Animal Crackers," screenwriter
Kavner, Julie	1951-	5	10	10	15	M. Simpson, "Rhoda" SP-2X
Kaye, Danny	1913-1987	75	125	200	135	"The Secret Life of Walter Mitty"
Kaye, Stubby	1918-1997	10	20	30	25	"Guys and Dolls"
Kazurinsky, Tim	1950-	5	10	15	15	SNL
Keach, Stacy	1941-	10	20	25	20	"M.Spillane's Mike Hammer"
Keaton, Buster	1895-1966	235	375		590	Silent film, "Sunset Boulevard"
Keaton, Diane	1946-	20	40	50	60	"Annie Hall"
Keaton, Michael	1951-	25	40	75	65	"Batman" SP-$75
Keel, Howard	1917-	10	15	20	20	"Dallas," unresponsive via mail
Keeler, Ruby	1909-1993	30	40	50	60	"Forty Second Street"
Keene, Tom	1896-1963	30	45	50	55	"Sundown Trail," "Our Daily..."
Keener, Catherine	1959-	10	20	30	20	"Being John Malkovich"
Keeshan, Bob	1927-	15	30		30	"Captain Kangaroo"
Keighley, William	1889-1984	20	40	50	40	Director, "G-Men"
Keitel, Harvey	1939-	15	30		30	"The Paino"
Keith, David Lemuel	1954-	5	10	10	10	"An Officer and a Gentleman"
Kellaway, Cecil	1893-1973	30	50	75	80	"The Luck of the Irish," "Harvey"
Keller, Marthe	1945-	5	10	10	10	"Marathon Man"
Kellerman, Sally	1937-	10	15	20	25	"M*A*S*H"
Kelley, David E.	1956-	10	25		20	"Ally McBeal"
Kelley, Deforest	1920-	15	30	55	40	"Star Trek"
Kelly, Gene	1912-1996	50	225	200	100	"Singin' in the Rain"
Kelly, Grace (Monaco)	1928-1982	265	740	845	530	"High Noon," ESPV-SP
Kelly, Moira	1968-	10	20	25	30	"The Cutting Edge"
Kelly, Nancy	1921-	10	20	25	20	"The Bad Seed," "Jesse James"
Kennedy, Arthur	1914-1990	35	45	75	70	"Champion," "Bright Victory"
Kennedy, Edgar	1890-1948	140	250	250	265	Keystone Kop, "San Francisco"
Kennedy, George	1925-	10	20	25	35	"Cool Hand Luke," FA

Name	DB/DD	Sig.DS/LS		ALS	SP	Comments
Kennedy, Madge	1891-1987	15	25	30	35	"Poppy," "Lust for Life"
Kensit, Patsy	1968-	15	20	30	50	"Lethal Weapon 2"
Kerns, Joanna	1953-	5	10	10	15	"Growing Pains," FA
Kerr, Deborah	1921-	20	25	25	30	"From Here To Eternity"
Keyes, Evelyn	1919-	20	50	40	50	GWTW, "The Jolson Story"
Kibibble, Ish	1908-	10	15	20	20	Merwyn Bogue, Trumpeter
Kidder, Margot	1948-	10	15	20	25	"Superman"
Kidman, Nicole	1967-	25	50	75	65	"Moulin Rouge"
Kiel, Richard	1939-	10	15	25	25	"The Spy Who Loved Me"
Kietel, Harvey	1939-	15	20	25	35	"Bad Lieutenant"
Kilborn, Craig	1962-	5	10		10	"The Daily Show"
Kilbride, Percy	1888-1964	130	250		325	"Ma and Pa Kettle"
Kilburn, Terry	1926-	10	15	20	20	"A Christmas Carol"
Kiley, Richard	1922-1999	15	35	45	30	"Man of La Moncha"
Kilmer, Val	1959-	40	100	200	100	"Batman Forever," "The Doors"
King, Alan	1927-	5	10	15	15	"The Anderson Tapes"
King, Henry	1888-1982	35	50	60	70	Director, "Tol'able David"
King, Larry	1933-	10	20	35	15	"Larry King Live," RS
King, Perry	1948 -	5	10	15	15	"Riptide"
Kingsley, Ben	1943-	15	25	50	40	"Gandhi"
Kinison, Sam	1953-1992	40	75		75	Comedian
Kinnear, Greg	1964-	10	20	25	20	"As Good As It Gets"
Kinski, Nastassja	1960-	15	45	40	50	"Cat People"
Kirby, Bruno (Bruce)	1949-	10	20	30	15	"City Slickers"
Kirk, Phyllis	1926-	15	30	35	40	"The Thin Man" - TV
Kirkland, Sally	1944-	5	10	10	15	"Anna"
Kitt, Eartha	1928-	10	20	30	25	"The Mark of the Hawk," singer
Klein, Robert	1942-	5	10	15	15	"Comedy Tonight"
Klemperer, Werner	1920-2000	25	40	50	40	"Hogan's Heroes," RS
Kline, Kevin	1947-	15	25	40	40	"The Big Chill," m. P.Cates
Klugman, Jack	1922-	15	25		25	"The Odd Couple" - TV
Klum, Heidi	1973-	10	25		30	Model
Knight, "Fuzzy"	1901-1976	65	115	125	150	"She Done Him Wrong"
Knight, Michael E.	1959-	5	10	10	15	"All My Children"
Knight, Ted	1923-1986	30	50		65	"Mary Tyler Moore Show"
Knight, Shirley	1936-	10	15	20	20	"The Dark at the Top of…"
Knotts, Don	1924-	15	25	30	30	"The Andy Griffith Show"
Knowles, Patric	1911-	10	20	20	25	"How Green Was My Valley"
Knox, Alexander	1907-	15	20	25	30	"The Sea Wolf"
Knoxvolle, Johnny	1971-	10	20		15	"Jackass"
Koenig, Walter	1936-	15	30	40	35	"Star Trek," writer, director
Kolb, Clarence	1875-1964	30	40	45	55	"My Little Margie" - TV
Koppel, Ted	1940-	10	20		20	"Nightline," ES
Kopell, Bernie	1933-	5	10	20	10	"The Love Boat"
Korda, Alexander	1893-1956	55	70	100	100	"The Private Life of Henry VIII"
Korman, Harvey	1927-	5	10	15	20	"The Carol Burnett Show"
Kotto, Yaphet	1937-	5	10	10	15	"Live and Let Die"
Kournikova, Anna	1981-	20	40	50	40	Former tennis player, FA
Krabbe, Jeroen	1944-	10	15	15	20	"The Fugitive"
Krakowski, Jane	1968-	10	25		30	"Ally McBeal"
Krige, Alice	1955-	5	10	10	10	"Chariots of Fire"
Kruger, Otto	1885-1974	35	45	50	85	"High Noon," "Dracula's …"

Name	DB/DD	Sig.DS/LS	ALS	SP	Comments
Kruschen, Jack	1922-	10	20	25	20	"The Apartment," "Cape Fear"
Kubrick, Stanley	1928-1999	40	65	125	115	"2001:A Space Odyssey"
Kudrow, Lisa	1963-	20	40	45	50	"Friends"
Kuralt, Charles	1934-1997	30	65	115	50	"On the Road"
Kurtz, Swoosie	1944-	5	10	15	22	"Sisters," RS
Kutcher, Ashton	1978-	10	20		25	"That 70's Show"
Kwan, Nancy	1939-	10	15	35	40	"The World of Suzie Wong"

Laurel and Hardy

* During the pinnacle of their success they used just about every method known to handle the enormous amounts of fan mail. From facsimile signatures to ghost signers, you name it they probably tried it.

* The most common form entering the hobby is on autograph album pages where both signatures appear.

* If photographs are encountered that have both signatures often it is a posed black & white studio portrait, often 11" x 14". Independently, they used other sized photographs to sign also.

* Typically inscriptions were handled by Stan, who often printed something appropriate such as "Our Best Wishes Always."

* Later in life, Laurel did answer some fan mail but it was sporadic. Often his letters are signed simply "Stan" rather than in full.

Name	DB/DD	Sig.DS/LS	ALS	SP	Comments
La Rue, Jack	1900-1984	15	20	25	30	"A Farewell to Arms"
Ladd, Alan	1913-1964	80	110	175	200	"This Gun For Hire," "Shane"
Ladd, Cheryl	1951-	10	15	25	45	"Charlie's Angels"
Ladd, Diane	1932-	5	10	10	15	"Alice Doesn't Live Here..."
Lagasse, Emeril	1959-	5	10		15	Chef, TV host
Lahr, Bert	1895-1967	320	500		565	TWOO, "Always Leave ...
Lahti, Christine	1950-	5	10	15	15	"Swing Shift"
Lake, Arthur	1905-1987	40	65		55	"Blondie" film series
Lake, Ricki	1968-	10	20	25	25	"Hairspray," talk show host, RS
Lake, Veronica	1919-1973	145	300	180	275	"Star-Spangled Rhythm"
Lamarr, Hedy	1913-2000	40	80	130	115	"Ecstacy," "Samson and Delilah"
Lamas, Fernando	1915-1982	25	35	45	50	"Rich, Young and Pretty"
Lamas, Lorenzo	1958-	10	15	20	25	"Falcon Crest"
Lambert, Christopher	1957-	15	25	30	40	"Greystroke: The ... Tarzan"
Lamour, Dorothy	1914-1996	25	40	70	50	"Road" series w/Hope & Crosby
Lancaster, Burt	1913-1994	65	150	265	100	"Elmer Gantry,"
Lanchester, Elsa	1902-1986	35	70		70	"Come to the Stable"
Landau, Martin	1931-	15	30	35	40	"Mission:Impossible"
Landers, Audrey	1959-	5	10	10	15	"Dallas"
Landesberg, Steve	1945-	5	10	10	15	"Barney Miller"
Landi, Elissa	1904-1948	50	70	75	80	"The Count of Monte Cristo"
Landis, Carole	1919-1948	135	300	350	235	"A Day at the Races"
Landis, Jessie R.	1904-1972	35	55	60	75	"North By Northwest"
Landis, John	1950-	15	25	30	30	"Twilight Zone - The Movie"
Landon, Michael	1936-1991	100	200		200	"Bonanza," FA
Lane, Abbe	1935-	10	20	20	20	"Xavier Cugat Show," m. Xavier
Lane, Charles	1953-	10	15	15	20	"Sidewalk Stories," director

Name	DB/DD	Sig.DS/LS	ALS	SP	Comments
Lane, Diane	1965-	10	15	15	15	"Rumble Fish"
Lane, Lola	1906-1981	20	25	25	30	"Four Daughters"
Lane, Nathan	1956-	20	35	40	50	"The Birdcage," FA
Lane, Rosemary	1914-1974	20	25	30	35	"Four Wives," Lane sisters
Lang, Fritz	1890-1976	75	230		160	Director, "Metropolis," "M"
Lang, June	1915-	15	20	25	20	"Wee Willie Winkie"
Langdon, Harry	1884-1944	125	250	300	250	"Tramp, Tramp, Tramp"
Lange, Hope	1931-	5	15	25	25	"The Ghost and Mrs. Muir"
Lange, Jessica	1949-	20	40	50	75	"Frances," "Tootsie"
Lange, Ted	1947-	5	10	10	10	"The Love Boat"
Langella, Frank	1940-	15	25	35	25	"Dracula" - SP - 2X
Langford, Frances	1914-	15	25	35	30	"The Glenn Miller Story"
Lansbury, Angela	1925-	10	25	40	45	"Murder She Wrote" - TV, RS
Lansing, Robert	1929-	5	10	10	10	"The Man Who Never Was"
Lanza, Mario	1921-1959	175	410	500	700	"The Great Caruso,"
Larroquette, John	1947-	10	20	20	25	"Night Court"
Lasalle, Eriq	1962-	10	25		25	"ER"
Lasser, Louise	1939-	5	10	15	15	"Bananas"
Latifah, Queen	1970-	15	20	25	40	"Jungle Fever," rap artist
Lauer, Matt	1957-	10	20	25	20	"Today," RS
Laughton, Charles	1899-1962	100	200	250	250	"The Private Life of Henry VIII"
Laurel, Stan	1890-1965	200	350	475	400	SP w/OH - $900
Laurie, Piper	1932-	5	10	10	15	"Carrie"
Lavin, Linda	1937-	5	10	10	15	"Alice," singer
Law, Jude	1972-	10	25		20	"The Talented Mr. Ripley"
Lawford, Peter	1923-1984	35	75		100	"Mrs. Miniver," "The White ..."
Lawless, Lucy	1968-	20	40	50	75	"Xena: Warrior Princess," FA
Lawrence, Carol	1935-	5	10	15	15	"West Side Story," singer
Lawrence, Gertrude	1898-1952	25	50	50	50	"The Glass Menagerie"
Lawrence, Joey	1976-	5	10	15	15	"Blossom"
Lawrence, Martin	1965-	10	10	15	20	"Martin"
Lawrence, Vicki	1949-	5	10	10	15	"Mama's Family"
Lawson, Leigh	1945-	5	10	10	15	"Tess"
Leach, Robin	1941-	5	10	10	10	"Lifestyles...Rich and Famous"
Leachman, Cloris	1930-	10	20	25	20	"The Mary Tyler Moore Show"
Lear, Norman	1922-	10	30	50	25	"All in the Family," producer
Leary, Denis	1957-	10	20		15	"Dennis Leary: Lock 'n' Load"
Learned, Michael	1939-	5	10	10	10	"The Waltons," RS
Leblanc, Matt	1967-	15	25	35	40	"Friends" - TV
Lebrock, Kelly	1960-	10	25		25	"Weird Science"
Lederer, Francis	1906-	15	20	25	25	"Pandora's Box," "Midnight"
Ledger, Heath	1979-	10	20		15	"The Patriot"
Ledoyen, Virginie	1956-	10	20		20	"The Beach"
Lee, Brandon	1965-1993	265	685		600	"The Crow"
Lee, Bruce	1940-1973	425	850	1750	1100	"Enter the Dragon"
Lee, Christopher	1922-	30	60	150	100	Horror film legend.
Lee, Gypsy Rose	1913-1970	75	150	225	265	Burlesque SP - 2X
Lee, Jason Scott	1966-	10	20	20	20	"Dragon: The Bruce Lee Story"
Lee, Michele	1942-	5	10	10	15	"Knots Landing"
Lee, Pamela	1967-	15	25	35	40	"Baywatch," sexy SP - 2X
Lee, Spike (Shelton)	1957-	10	25	30	20	"Do the Right Thing," director
Leeds, Andrea	1914-1984	10	15	15	25	"Stage Door," "Come and Get It"

Name	DB/DD	Sig.DS/LS	ALS	SP	Comments
Leeves, Jane	1963-	5	10	15	15	"Frasier"
Leguizamo, John	1965-	5	10	15	20	"Carlito's Way"
Leibman, Ron	1937-	5	10	10	10	"Kaz," RS
Leifer, Carol	1956-	5	10		10	"Alright Already," comic
Leigh, Janet	1927-	5	15	20	15	"Psycho," RS
Leigh, Jennifer Jason	1962-	15	20	30	45	"Fast Times At Ridgemont High"
Leigh, Vivien	1913-1967	400	600	750	600	GWTW, SP - 2X, "A Street..."
Leighton, Laura	1968-	15	25	30	40	"Melrose Place"
Leisen, Mitchell	1898-1972	35	55	60	65	"Hands Across the Table"
Leitch, Donovan	1968-	5	10	10	10	Actor, son of folk singer
Lemat, Paul	1952-	5	10	10	15	"American Graffiti"
Lemmon, Chris	1954-	5	10	10	15	"Swing Shift," s. Jack Lemon
Lemmon, Jack	1925- 2001	25	50	75	50	"Some Like It Hot," "Missing"
Leno, Jay (James Leno)	1950-	10	25	25	40	"The Tonight Show," FA
Leonard, Robert Sean	1969-	5	10	10	15	"Dead Poets Society"
Leonard, Robert Z.	1889-1968	30	45	40	55	Director, "Ziegfeld Girl"
Leonard, Sheldon	1907-1997	15	30	50	30	"Guys and Dolls," IAWL
Leoni, Tea	1966-	15	25	35	45	"The Naked Truth"
Lerner, Michael	1941-	5	10	10	10	"Barton Fink"
Leslie, Joan	1925-	5	10	10	15	"High Sierra," "Sergeant York"
Letterman, David	1947-	25	45	50	50	"Late Show w/D.Letterman," ES
Levy, Eugene	1946-	5	10	10	10	"SCTV," writer
Lewis, Al	1910-	10	20	20	25	"The Munsters"
Lewis, Emmanuel	1971-	5	10	10	10	"Webster"
Lewis, Jerry	1926-	20	25	45	30	"My Friend Irma," RS
Lewis, Juliette	1973-	20	35	40	45	"Cape Fear"
Lewis, Richard	1947-	5	10		10	Comic
Li, Jet	1963-	15	30		30	"Romeo Must Die"
Light, Judith	1949-	5	10	10	15	"Who's the Boss?," RS
Lillie, Beatrice	1898-1989	30	40	50	40	"Thoroughly Modern Millie"
Limbaugh, Rush	1951-	10	20	30	25	"The Rush Limbaugh Show"
Lincoln, Abbey	1930-	5	10	10	15	"For Love of Ivy"
Lincoln, Elmo	1889-1952	420	650		1200	"The Birth of a Nation," "Tarzan"
Linden, Hal	1931-	10	20	20	20	"Barney Miller"
Lindsay, Margaret	1910-1981	20	40	50	45	"Cavalcade," "Ellery Queen"
Linkletter, Art	1912-	10	20	25	20	"People Are Funny"
Linn-Baker, Mark	1954-	5	10	15	15	"Perfect Strangers"
Linney, Laura	1964-	10	25		25	"The Truman Show"
Linville, Larry	1939-2000	20	45	55	35	"M*A*S*H"
Liotta, Ray	1955-	20	30	50	45	"GoodFellas"
Lipnicki, Jonathan	1990-	10	15		10	"Jerry Maguire"
Lithgow, John	1945-	10	20	35	25	"3rd Rock from the Sun," RS
Littlefield, Lucien	1895-1960	30	40	40	45	"The Torrent," "Henry Aldrich"
Liu, Lucy	1967-	15	30		30	"Ally McBeal"
Lloyd, Christopher	1938-	15	25	25	30	"Taxi"
Lloyd, Emily	1970-	10	15	20	25	"Wish you Were Here"
Lloyd, Harold	1893-1971	185	235	500	365	"Safety Last," "The Freshman"
Locke, Sondra	1947-	10	20	20	20	"The Gauntlet"
Lockhart, Gene	1891-1957	30	45	50	60	"Algiers," "Going My way"
Lockhart, June	1925-	10	20	25	20	"Meet Me in St. Louis," $
Locklear, Heather	1961-	20	40	50	55	"Dynasty," FA
Lockwood, Gary	1937-	10	15	15	15	"2001: A Space Odyssey"

Name	DB/DD	Sig.DS/LS	ALS	SP	Comments
Lockwood, Harold A.	1887-1918				"The House...Thousand...," PU
Lockwood, Margaret	1916-1990	20	40	50	45	"The Lady Vanishes"
Logan, Joshua	1908-1988	30	45	40	50	"Picnic," "Bus Stop," director
Loggia, Robert	1930-	5	10	10	15	"Mancuso, FBI"
Lollobrigida, Gina	1927-	10	20	25	30	"Solomon and Sheba"
Lom, Herbert	1917-	15	30	40	35	"Spartacus"
Lombard, Carole	1908-1942	315	775	1000	775	"My Man Godfrey"
Long, Shelley	1949-	15	35	60	40	"Cheers"
Loos, Anita	1893-1981	25	40	65	40	Playwright, novelist
Lopez, Jennifer	1969-	20	40		40	"The Cell"
Lord, Jack	1930-1998	30	60	75	50	"Hawaii Five-O," FA
Lord, Pauline	1890-1950	30	55	75	65	"Anna Christie"
Lords, Traci	1968-	5	15	25	30	"MP," porn star SP - 2-4.5X
Loren, Sophia	1934-	25	40	50	50	"Two Women," RS
Lorre, Peter	1904-1964	200	365		365	"The Maltese Falcon" SP-2X, C
Louis-Dreyfus, Julia	1961-	15	30	35	40	"Seinfeld," FA
Louise, Anita	1915-1970	20	30	35	40	"My Friend Flicka"
Louise, Tina (Blacker)	1934-	10	20	25	25	"Gilligan's Island"
Lovitz, Jon	1957-	10	20	30	25	SNL
Lowe, Chad	1968-	5	10	10	10	"Life Goes On," b. Rob Lowe
Lowe, Edmund	1890-1971	25	40	65	50	"The Cisco Kid"
Lowe, Rob	1964-	20	30	35	40	"The West Wing"
Loy, Myrna	1905-1993	25	50	50	70	"The Thin Man"
Lucas, George	1944-	40	125		60	"Star Wars" SP-2X, director, FA
Lucci, Susan	1950-	10	20	25	30	"All My Children," FA
Luckinbill, Laurence	1934-	5	10	10	15	"The Boys in the Band"
Luft, Lorna	1952-	5	10	10	10	"Where the Boys Are"
Lugosi, Bela	1882-1956	365	1775		1500	Horror film star, "Dracula," FA
Lukas, Paul	1895-1971	50	85	120	100	"Watch on the Rine," "Little..."
Luke, Keye	1904-1991	20	35	50	45	"Kung Fu" - TV
Lumet, Sidney	1924-	15	30	35	30	"Twelve Angry Men," director
Lund, John	1911-1992	10	15	20	20	"High Society"
Lunden, Joan	1950-	5	10	10	10	"Good Morning America"
Lundgren, Dolph	1959-	10	20		30	"Rocky IV"
Lunt, Alfred	1892-1977	35	50	75	60	Sigs. w/L. Fontanne - $40
Lupino, Ida	1914-1995	25	65	100	70	"The Adv...Sherlock Holmes"
Lupone, Patti	1949-	5	10	10	10	"Life Goes On," RS
Lupus, Peter	1937-	10	20	20	20	"Mission: Impossible"
Lyndon, Jimmy	1923-	25	40	40	50	Known for char.Henry Aldrich
Lynn, Diana	1926-1971	35	40	40	50	"Bedtime for Bonzo"
Lynn, Jeffrey	1909-	10	15	20	20	"Four Wives"
Lytell, Bert	1885-1954	40	50	100	75	"The First Legion" - stage

Marvin, Lee

* Talented actor who appeared in many popular films includingg "Cat Ballou," "The Dirty Dozen" and "Paint Your Wagon".

* Throughout his life he was a very difficult person to get a signature out of and never answered his fan mail.

* His signature is not only tough to find, but expensive.

* He is buried alongside Joe Louis in Arlington Cemetary.

Name	DB/DD	Sig.DS/LS	ALS	SP	Comments
Mac, Bernie	1957-	10	20		20	"The Bernie Mac Show"
MacArthur, James	1937-	15	25		30	"Hawaii Five-O," RS
Macchio, Ralph	1962-	5	10	10	10	"The Karate Kid"
MacCorkindale, Simon	1952-	5	10	10	10	"Falcon Crest"
MacDonald, Jeanette	1901-1965	75	175	300	150	"The Merry Widow"
MacDonald, Norm	1962-	10	25		20	SNL
MacDowell, Andie	1958-	10	20	15	30	"sex, lies and videotape"
MacGraw, Ali	1938-	5	10	15	25	"Love Story"
Mack, Helen	1913-1986	15	30	45	30	"King Kong," radio producer
MacLachlan, Kyle	1959-	10	20	25	20	"Twin Peaks"
MacLaine, Shirley	1934-	15	30	50	35	"Terms of Endearment," RS
MacMurray, Fred	1907-1991	40	80	165	65	"My Three Sons"
MacNaughton, Robert	1966-	5	10	10	20	"E.T., the Extra-Terrestrial"
MacNee, Patrick	1922-	15	20	35	35	"The Avengers"
MacNeil, Robert	1931-	5	15		15	"MacNeil/Lehrer Report"
MacNichol, Peter	1958-	10	20		25	"Ally McBeal"
MacPherson, Elle	1965-	10	20	25	35	Supermodel, actor, RS
MacRae, Gordon	1921-1986	20	50	100	45	"Oklahoma," singer
Macy, William H.	1950-	15	25		20	"Fargo"
Maddona (M. Ciccone)	1958-					(See Music)
Madigan, Amy	1951-	10	15	20	20	"Places in the Heart"
Madsen, Michael	1959-	10	15	20	30	"Reservoir Dogs"
Madsen, Virginia	1963-	5	10	15	15	"Electric dreams"
Magnani, Anna	1907-1973	275	445	500	475	"The Rose Tattoo," "Open City"
Magnuson, Ann	1956-	5	10	10	10	"Anything but Love"
Maguire, Tobey	1975-	15	30		40	"Spiderman"
Maher, Bill	1956-	10	20	25	25	"Politically Incorrect" - TV
Mahoney, John	1940-	5	10	10	20	"Cheers," "Frasier"
Majors, Lee (H. L. Yeary)	1940-	5	10	15	15	"The Six Million Dollar Man"
Makepeace, Chris	1964-	5	10	10	10	"My Bodyguard"
Mako (Makoto Iwamatsu)	1933-	5	10	15	20	"The Sand Pebbles"
Malden, Karl	1914-	10	20	30	25	"The Sts.of San Francisco," RS
Malkovich, John	1953-	15	30	30	45	"Dangerous Liaisons"
Malone, Dorothy	1925-	30	55	110	60	"Written on the Wind"
Maloney, Janel	1969-	10	20		25	"The West Wing"
Maltin, Leonard	1950-	5	10		10	"Entertainment Tonight"
Mamet. David	1947-	5	10	15	25	"Glengarry Glen Ross," RS
Mandel, Howie	1955-	5	10	20	25	"St. Elsewhere"
Manetti, Larry	1947-	5	10	10	10	"Magnum P.I."
Manheim, Camryn	1961-	10	20	30	20	"The Practice," auto. collector
Mann, Terrence	1945-	5	10	15	15	"Les Miserables"
Manners, David	1901-	30	60	120	60	"Dracula," horror film hero
Mannoff, Dinah	1958-	5	10	15	15	"Empty Nest"
Mansfield, Jayne	1932-1967	165	400		450	"Will Success Spoil Rock..."
Mantegna, Joe	1947-	10	15	20	200	"The Godfather, Part III"
Marceau, Marcel	1923-	25	60	200	100	Pantomimist, "Bip"
March, Frederic	1897-1975	50	125	185	110	"Dr. Jekyll and Mr. Hyde"
Marchand, Nancy	1928-2000	10	20	30	20	"Lou Grant," RS
Marcovicci, Andrea	1948-	5	10	10	10	"Trapper John, MD"
Margo	1917-1985	20	30	35	40	"Lost Horizon," m. E. Albert
Marguiles, Julianna	1966-	15	25	30	35	"ER"
Marin, Cheech (R.Marin)	1946-	5	15	15	20	"Up in Smoke"

Name	DB/DD	Sig.DS/LS	ALS	SP	Comments
Marinaro, Ed	1950-	10	20	30	20	"Hill Street Blues"
Markey, Enid	1890-1981	125				"Tarzan," the first screen "Jane"
Marlowe, Hugh	1911-1982	30	50	75	55	"All About Eve," "Monkey Bus."
Marsh, Mae	1895-1968	40	50	75	70	"The Birth of a Nation," TGOW
Marshall, Brenda	1915-1992	15	30	30	35	"The Sea Hawk," m. W. Holden
Marshall, E.G.	1910-1998	20	45	70	40	"Twelve Angry Men"
Marshall, Herbert	1890-1966	30	75	160	70	"The Letter," "The Little Foxes"
Marshall, Penny	1942-	15	30		30	"Laverne and Shirley"
Marshall, Peter	1930-	10	20	30	30	"The Hollywood Squares"
Martin, Andrea	1947-	5	10	10	12	"SCTV"
Martin, Dean	1917-1995	35	150		115	"Bells Are Ringing," FA
Martin, Dick	1923-	5	25	20	20	"Laugh-In"
Martin, Mary	1913-1990	40	75	100	65	"Birth of the Blues," "Night ..."
Martin, Pamela Sue	1953-	10	15	20	25	"Dynasty"
Martin, Steve	1945-	15	20	45	35	"A Wild and Crazy Guy"
Martindale, Wink	1934-	5	10	10	10	"Tic Tac Dough"
Marvin, Lee	1924-1987	100	175		200	"The Dirty Dozen"
Marx, Chico	1886-1961	175	250	350	375	"Animal Crackers," Marx Bros
Marx, Groucho	1890-1977	260	425		300	Marx Bros, FDC, all sigs. - $1825
Marx, Harpo	1888-1964	400	750		665	Marx Bros, often adds drawing
Marx, Zeppo	1901-1979	85	120	150	125	"Marx Brothers," "Duck Soup"
Mason, Jackie	1934-	5	10	10	10	"Chicken Soup"
Mason, James	1909-1984	35	65	75	75	"A Star Is Born," "The Desert..."
Mason, Marsha	1942-	5	10	10	20	"The Goodbye Girl," RS
Massey, Ilona	1912-1974	30	40	35	40	"Northwest Outpost"
Massey, Raymond	1896-1983	40	75	145	70	"Abe Lincoln in ...," "Dr. Kildare"
Masterson, Mary Stuart	1966-	5	10	10	25	"Fried Green Tomatoes"
Masterson, Peter	1934-	5	10	10	15	"The Exorcist"
Mastrantonio, Mary Eliz.	1958-	15	40	50	60	"The Color of Money"
Masur, Richard	1948-	5	10	15	15	"One Day at a Time"
Mathers, Jerry	1948-	10	20	30	25	"Leave It to Beaver," $
Matheson, Tim	1947-	5	10	20	15	"N. Lampoon's Animal House"
Mathews, Denise	1963-	5	10	10	10	"The Last Dragon"
Matthau, Walter	1920-2000	25	50		40	"The Odd Couple"
Mature, Victor	1915-1999	20	40		45	"Samson and Delilah"
Maxwell, Marilyn	1921-1972	15	25	30	30	"Summer Holiday," singer
May, Elaine	1932-	5	10	10	15	"Ishtar," director, writer
Maynard, Ken	1895-1973	100	125	150	150	"Texas Gunfighter"
Mayo, Virginia	1920-	10	20	25	25	"The Best Years of Our Lives"
Mazar, Debi	1964-	5	10	10	15	"Civil Wars: L.A. Law"
Mazursky, Paul	1930-	5	10	15	15	"Down and Out in Beverly Hills"
McCallum, David	1933-	10	15	20	20	"The Great Escape"
McCambridge, Merc.	1918-	50	60	70	60	"All the King's Men"
McCarey, Leo	1898-1969	50	100	100	75	Director, "Duck Soup"
McCarthy, Andrew	1962-	5	10	10	10	"Less Than Zero"
McCarthy, Jenny	1972-	25	45	50	60	"Singled Out"
McCarthy, Kevin	1914-	10	20	25	20	"Invasion of the Body ..."
McClanahan, Rue	1934-	5	10	20	15	"The Golden Girls," RS
McClurg, Edie	1950-	5	10	10	10	"The Hogan Family"
McConaughey, Matthew	1970-	20	40	55	65	"A Time To Kill"
McCormack, Eric	1963-	15	25	40	30	"Will & Grace"
McCormick, Myron	1907-1962	30	50	55	60	"Jolson Sings Again"

Name	DB/DD	Sig.DS/LS	ALS	SP	Comments
McCoy, Tim	1891-1978	60	100	130	125	"The Indians Are Coming"
McCrea, Joel	1905-1990	20	40	40	40	"Dead End," "Bird of Paradise"
McDaniel, Hattie	1895-1952	620	1100	2000	2120	GWTW, "Beulah," FA
McDermott, Dylan	1961-	15	30		35	"The Practice"
McDonald, Marie	1923-1965	45	60	75	90	"It Started With Eve," model
McDonnell, Mary	1952-	10	20	35	30	"Dances with Wolves," RS
McDormand, Frances	1957-	15	30		30	"Fargo"
McDowall, Roddy	1928-1998	25	45	75	50	"How Green Was My Valley"
McDowell, Malcolm	1943-	10	25	40	30	"A Clockwork Orange"
McFadden, Cynthia	1956-	5	10		10	Television journalist
McFarland, G. "Spanky"	1928-1993	30	45	50	55	Child star, "Our Gang" series
McGavin, Darren	1922-	20	40	35	40	"The Court Martial of Billy Mit."
McGillis, Kelly	1957-	10	20	30	40	"Witness"
McGovern, Elizabeth	1961-	5	10	20	20	"Ragtime"
McGregor, Ewan	1971-	20	35		40	"Star Wars..."
McGuire, Dorothy	1918-2001	25	40	55	40	"Gentleman's Agreement"
McHugh, Frank	1899-1981	25	50	50	60	"The Crowd Roars," GMW
McKean, Michael	1947-	5	10	10	10	"Laverne & Shirley"
McKellar, Danica	1975-	5	10	10	10	"The Wonder Years"
McKellen, Ian	1939-	15	30		30	"The Lord of the Rings"
Mckeon, Nancy	1966-	5	10	15	20	"The Facts of Life"
McLaglen, Victor	1886-1959	140	240	250	280	"The Informer," "Gunga Din"
McMahon, Ed	1923-	10	25		20	"The Tonight Show"
McNichol, Kristy	1962-	5	10	15	20	"Empty Nest"
McQueen, Butterfly	1911-1995	60	120	150	115	GWTW, "Mildred Pierce"
McQueen, Steve	1930-1980	200	500	540	400	"Bullitt," FA, elusive signer!
McRaney, Gerald	1948-	5	10	10	15	"Major Dad," FA
McTeer, Janet	1961-	12	25		30	"Tumbleweeds"
Meadows, Audrey	1924-1996	25	50	60	55	"The Honeymooners"
Meadows, Jayne	1920-	5	10	10	10	Actor, quiz show regular
Meaney, Colm	1953-	15	25	25	30	"Star Trek: The Next ..."
Meara, Anne	1929-	5	10	10	15	"The Out-of-Towners"
Medina, Patricia	1919-	5	10	15	15	"The Foxes of Harrow"
Meek, Donald	1880-1946	45	75	85	80	"Stagecoach," "State Fair"
Meeker, Ralph	1920-1988	30	40	45	50	"Picnic" - stage, "Kiss Me ..."
Melchior, Lauritz	1890-1973	40	85	135	165	"Thrill of a Romance"
Menjou, Adolphe	1890-1963	25	50	60	70	"The Front Page," SB - $40
Meredith, Burgess	1908-1997	25	40	50	50	"Of Mice and Men," "Batman"
Merkel, Una	1903-1986	20	30	30	35	"Destry Rides Again"
Merman, Ethel	1909-1984	40	100		175	"There's No Business Like..."
Merrick, David	1911-2000	45	70	140	75	"The Great Gatsby"
Merrill, Gary	1914-1990	20	30	40	40	"Young Dr. Kildare" - TV
Messing, Debra	1968-	15	30		30	"Will & Grace"
Metcalf, Laurie	1955-	5	10	15	20	"Roseanne"
Methot, Mayo	1904-1951	25	40	50	45	"Mr. Deed Goes to Town"
Meyers, Ari	1970-	5	10	10	10	"Kate & Allie"
Michaels, Lorne	1944-	20	35	40	40	SNL, producer, writer
Middler, Bette	1945-	25	50	75	60	"The Rose"
Mifune, Toshiro	1920-1997	25	35	50	45	"Throne of Blood"
Milano, Alyssa	1972-	20	35	40	55	"Who's the Boss?"
Miles, Sarah	1941-	10	15	25	20	"Ryan's Daughter"
Miles, Sylvia	1934-	5	10	25	20	"Midnight Cowboy"

Name	DB/DD	Sig.DS/LS	ALS	SP	Comments
Miles, Vera	1929-	5	10	15	15	"Psycho," RS
Milland, Ray	1905-1986	35	60	70	75	"The Lost Weekend"
Miller, Ann	1923-	15	25	40	30	"On the Town"
Miller, Dennis	1953-	10	15	25	20	SNL
Miller, Patsy Ruth	1905-	30	40	50	50	"The Hunchback of Notre..."
Miller, Penelope Ann	1964-	15	30	40	40	"Carlito's Way"
Mills, Hayley	1946-	10	15	20	20	"The Parent Trap"
Mills, John	1908-	15	25	35	30	"Ryan's Daughter"
Mills, Juliet	1941-	5	10	15	10	"Nanny and the Professor"
Mills, Stephanie	1957-	5	10	15	15	"The Wiz"
Mimiuex, Yvette	1939-	5	10	10	15	"The Black Hole"
Mineo, Sal	1939-1976	200	250		300	"Rebel Without a Cause"
Minnelli, Liza	1946-	20	35	45	35	"Cabaret," often signs "Liza"
Minter, Mary Miles	1902-1984	100	150	175	200	Leading silent film star
Miou-Miou	1950-	5	10	10	10	"Going Places"
Miranda, Carmen	1909-1955	120	200	300	400	"The Brazilian Bombshell"
Mirren, Helen	1945-	5	10		20	"Prime Suspect"
Mitchell, Cameron	1918-1994	10	25	30	30	"Death of a Salesman"
Mitchell, Grant	1874-1957	45	80	75	80	TGOW, "Tobacco Road"
Mitchell, Thomas	1892-1962	250	500	500	525	"Stagecoach," GWTW, IAWL
Mitchum, James	1941-	5	10	10	10	"Thunder Road"
Mitchum, Robert	1917-1997	25	50	75	55	"The Story of G.I. Joe," FA
Mix, Tom	1880-1940	100	200	325	400	"Sky High," "Desert Love"
Modine, Matthew	1959-	15	25		30	"Vision Quest"
Moffat, Donald	1930-	5	10	10	15	"Clear and Present Danger"
Mohr, Jay	1971-	12	25		25	"Jerry Maguire," SNL
Moll, Richard	1942-	10	15	20	20	"Night Court"
Monroe, Marilyn	1926-1962	1850	3000	6250	5575	DS "NJD" - $7400, TBC-$3000
Montalban, Ricardo	1920-	15	30		30	"Sayonara," "Fantasy Island"
Montez, Maria	1920-1951	55	85		125	"Arabian Nights," "Cobra ..."
Montgomery, Elizabeth	1933-1995	50	75		100	"Bewitched," check - $40
Montgomery, George	1916-2000	5	10	15	15	"Riders of the Purple Sage"
Montgomery, Robert	1904-1981	20	30	30	30	"Night Must Fall," sig. illegible
Moore, Clayton	1908-1999	15	30	65	50	"Lone Ranger," RS
Moore, Colleen	1900-1988	12	25	30	35	Silent star,"So Big," "Sally"
Moore, Demi (D.Guynes)	1962-	55			145	"Ghost," elusive
Moore, Dickie	1925-	10	15	20	20	"Oliver Twist," "Miss Annie..."
Moore, Dudley	1935-2002	25	50		50	"Arthur," FA
Moore, Grace	1901-1947	75	140	230	150	"One Night of Love"
Moore, Julianne	1960-	10	25		20	"Boogie Nights"
Moore, Mary Tyler	1936-	15	30	50	35	"The M.Tyler Moore Show," FA
Moore, Roger	1927-	25	80	150	75	"Live and Let Die"
Moore, Terry	1929-	10	15	15	25	"Mighty Joe Young," "Peyton..."
Moore, Victor	1876-1962	30	50	60	60	"Make Way for Tomorrow"
Moran, Erin	1961-	5	10	10	10	"Happy Days"
Moran, Jackie	1923-1990	30	60	60	50	GWTW
Moranis, Rick	1954-	5	10	15	20	"Honey, I Shrunk the Kids"
Moreau, Jeanne	1928-	5	10	10	15	"Jules et Jim"
Moreno, Rita	1931-	5	10	15	20	"West Side Story"
Morgan, Dennis	1910-	10	15	15	15	"Kitty Foyle," "In This Our Life"
Morgan, Frank	1890-1949	400	685	1120	625	TWOO - hardest to obtain
Morgan, Harry	1915-	10	20	25	25	"Dragnet" - TV, "M*A*S*H" - TV

Name	DB/DD	Sig.DS/LS	ALS	SP	Comments
Morgan, Helen	1900-1941	60	150	265	200	"Show Boat," "Applause"
Morgan, Michele	1920-	15	25	25	30	French actress, "Joan of Paris"
Morgan, Ralph	1882-1956	40	55	60	70	"The Power and the Glory"
Moriarity, Cathy	1960-	5	10	15	20	"Raging Bull"
Moriarity, Michael	1941-	10	20	25	30	"Law and Order"
Morita, Noriyuki "Pat"	1932-	5	10	10	15	"The Karate Kid"
Morley, Robert	1908-1992	40	65	70	75	"Marie A.," "The African Queen"
Morris, Chester	1901-1970	40	50	60	70	"Alibi," "Boston Blackie"
Morrow, Rob	1962-	20	30	40	40	"Northern Exposure"
Morse, David	1953-	5	10	15	10	"St. Elsewhere"
Morton, Joe	1947-	5	10	12	15	"Terminator 2: Judgement Day"
Moss, Kate	1974-	10	20	15	25	Supermodel
Most, Donny	1953-	5	10	10	10	"Happy Days"
Mostel, Josh	1946-	5	10	10	10	"City Slickers"
Mostel, Zero	1915-1977	85	140	250	175	"Fiddler on the Roof"
Movita (M.Castenada)	1915-	10	20	20	20	"Mutiny on the Bounty"
Mowbray, Alan	1896-1969	50	65	70	85	"Becky Sharp," "The King..."
Moyers, Bill	1934-	5	10		10	"Bill Moyer's Journal"
Muldaur, Diana	1938-	10	15	15	30	"Star Trek:Voyager"
Mulgrew, Kate	1955-	10	20		25	"Ryan's Hope," "Star Trek:..."
Mulhall, Jack	1887-1979	30	50	55	60	"The Three Musketeers"
Mulhern, Matt	1960-	5	10	10	10	"Major Dad"
Mull, Martin	1943-	5	10	12	15	"Mary Hartman, Mary Hartman"
Mullaly, Megan	1958-	10	25		25	"Will & Grace"
Mulligan, Richard	1932-2000	10	20	30	30	"Empty Nest"
Mumy, Billy	1954-	10	20		20	"Lost in Space"
Muni, Paul	1895-1967	70	100	135	185	"The Story of Louis Pasteur"
Muniz, Frankie	1985-	12	25		25	"Malcolm in the Middle"
Munsel, Patrice	1925-	20	30	50	45	"Melba," operatic soprano
Munson, Ona	1906-1955	155	215	265	240	GWTW, "The Shanghai..."
Murphy, Audie	1924-1971	140	200	415	300	"To Hell and Back," war hero
Murphy, Eddie	1961-	15	25	45	40	"Beverly Hills Cop," SNL
Murphy, George	1902-1992	20	30	30	30	"Show Business," "Step Lively"
Murphy, Michael	1938-	5	10	10	10	"Manhattan"
Murray, Bill	1950-	15	30	50	40	"Ghostbusters," SNL
Murray, Ken	1903-1988	10	10	15	20	"The Man Who Shot Liberty ..."
Murray, Mae	1885-1965	40	50	60	70	Silent star, "The Merry Widow"
Music, Lorenzo	1937-	5	10	10	10	"Rhoda"
Murrow, Edward R.	1908-1965	125	300		255	Broadcast journalist
Myers, Mike	1963-	20	35	50	40	SNL, "Austin Powers"

The Marx Brothers

* The original Marx Brothrs consisted of Chico (1886-1961), Groucho (1890-1977), Harpo (1888-1964), Gummo (1897-1977) and Zeppo (1901-1979). The latter two brothers would essentially step aside before the trios film career would begin, although Zeppo was in their first five films.

* Incredibly popular, all were asked for their autographs often, and always complied.

* Of the trio, Harpo's signature appears less and can command a greater value.

* If a single item was signed by all of them, it was commonly first names only, the exception being those

Name	DB/DD	Sig.DS/LS	ALS	SP	Comments

penned early in their career.

* The most prolific in all forms was Groucho, whom I corresponded with many times during the last years of his life. He often answered autograph requests with a studio portrait black & white photograph. Most of these were personalized.

Name	DB/DD	Sig.DS	/LS	ALS	SP	Comments
Nabors, Jim	1932-	15	25		25	"Gomer Pyle," RS, check - $10
Nagel, Anne	1912-1966	30	55	50	60	"The Green Hornet" series
Nagel, Conrad	1897-1970	25	40	50	80	"Dangerous Corner"
Naish, J. Carrol	1897-1973	30	55	60	75	"Sahara," "A Medal for Benny"
Naldi, Nita	1899-1961	32	55	50	60	"Blood and Sand," reclusive
Nash, Clarence	1904-1985	120	170	150	175	Voice of Donald Duck
Natwick, Mildred	1908-	15	25	30	25	"Barefoot in the Park"
Naughton, David	1951-	5	10	15	20	"An American Werewolf ...," RS
Naughton, James	1945-	5	10	10	10	"The Good Mother"
Nazimova, Alla	1879-1945	50	80	90	110	"Blood and Sand," AQS - $80
Neagle, Anna	1904-1986	15	25	30	35	"Victoria the Great," "E. Cavell"
Neal, Patricia	1926-	20	40	50	45	"Breakfast at Tiffany's"
Neeson, Liam	1952-	25	50		50	"Schindler's List," FA
Neff, Hildegard	1925-	25	35	40	45	"The Snows of Kilimanjaro"
Negri, Pola	1894-1987	35	65	75	100	Silent film star
Neill, Sam	1947-	20	35	40	40	"Jurassic Park"
Nelligan, Kate	1951-	10	15	20	20	"The Prince of Tides"
Nelson, Craig	1946-	10	15	20	25	"Coach"
Nelson, David	1936-	10	20	25	25	"The Adventures of Ozzie ..."
Nelson, Gene	1920-1996	20	50	60	75	"Oklahoma!," director
Nelson, Harriet Hilliard	1914-1994	30	50	65	55	Both sigs.(w/O) on a. leaf - $95
Nelson, Judd	1959-	5	10	10	10	"The Breakfast Club"
Nelson, Ozzie	1906-1975	40	65	70	80	"Here Come the Nelsons"
Newhart, Bob	1929-	5	15	15	20	"The Bob Newhart Show"
Newley, Anthony	1931-1999	10	20	25	25	"The Candy Man"
Newman, Paul	1925-	100	200		250	"The Sting," ES, FA
Newton, Robert	1905-1956	50	75	145	100	'Treasure Island," "Oliver Twist"
Newton, Thandie	1972-	10	20		20	"Beloved"
Nguyen, Dustin	1962-	5	10	10	10	"21 Jump Street"
Nicholson, Jack	1937-	25	150		50	"One Flew Over ...," RS
Nielsen, Leslie	1926-	10	20	25	25	"The Naked Gun," FA
Nielsen, Brigitte	1963-	5	10	15	25	"Red Sonja"
Nilsson, Anna Q.	1888-1974	20	30	40	40	"Sunset Boulevard"
Nimoy, Leonard	1931-	30	75		65	"Star Trek," ES, FA
Niven, David	1909-1993	40	85	150	80	"Wuthering Heights"
Nixon, Cynthia	1966-	10	25		25	"Sex and the City"
Noiret, Philippe	1931-	5	10	10	10	"Cinema Paradiso"
Nolan, Lloyd	1902-1985	25	65	115	50	"Peyton Place"
Nolte, Nick	1940-	10	25	40	40	"48 Hrs."
Noonan, Tommy	1922-1968	50	75	100	85	"Gentlemen Prefer Blondes"
Normand, Mabel	1894-1930	190	325	600	435	"Tillie's Punctured Romance"
Norris, Chuck	1940-	10	25	50	40	"Good Guys Wear Black"
Norton, Edward	1969-	15	25	30	35	"Primal Fear"
Nouri, Michael	1945-	10	15	15	20	"Flashdance"
Novak, Kim	1933-	15	40	50	75	"Picnic," "Vertigo"
Novarro, Ramon	1899-1968	30	60	75	100	"Mati Hari"

Name	DB/DD	Sig.DS/LS	ALS	SP	Comments
Novello, Don	1943-	10	20		25	"Father Guido Sarducci - SNL"
Nugent, Elliott	1899-1980	15	25	25	25	Playwright, "The Male Animal"
Nuyen, France	1939-	10	20	20	22	"South Pacific"
O'Brian, Hugh	1925-	20	30	55	50	"Wyatt Earp" - TV, RS
O'Brien, Conan	1963-	5	10	15	15	"NBC's Late Night with ..."
O'Brien, Edmond	1915-1985	25	45	60	50	"War of the Worlds"
O'Brien, George	1900-1985	25	40	50	55	Boxer, "Fort Apache," "Sunrise"
O'Brien, Margaret	1937-	20	40	35	40	"Jane Eyre," Sig. (child) - 2X
O'Brien, Pat	1899-1983	40	125	200	100	"Angels With Dirty Faces"
O'Brien, Virginia	1922-	10	20	20	15	"Miss Red Hot Frozen Face"
O'Connor, Carroll	1924-2001	25	45		45	"All in the Family"
O'Connor, Donald	1925-2003	25	40		40	"Singin' in the Rain," SSP - 2X
O'Conner, Hugh	1962-1995	20	40		30	"In the Heat of the Night"
O'Connor, Una	1880-1959	45	100	160	90	"Cavalcade," "The Informer"
O'Donnell, Cathy	1923-1970	40	65		75	"The Best Years of Our Lives"
O'Donnell, Chris	1970-	20	50	70	55	"Scent of a Woman,"SSP-$75
O'Donnell, Rosie	1962-	10	20	45	25	"The Rosie ... Show," FA
O'Hara, Catherine	1954-	5	10	10	12	"Home Alone"
O'Hara, Maureen	1920-	15	30	45	30	"How Green Was My Valley"
O'Keefe, Dennis	1908-1968	10	15	20	20	"B" picture star
O'Neal, Ryan (Patrick)	1941-	10	20	30	30	"Love Story"
O'Neal, Tatum	1963-	10	15	25	25	"Paper Moon"
O'Neil, Barbara	1908-1980	175	340		320	"All This and ...," GWTW
O'Neill, Ed	1946-	5	10	15	15	"Married ...with Children"
O'Neill, Jennifer	1949-	5	10	20	15	"Summer of '42"
O'Reilly, Bill	1949-	5	15		20	"The... Factor"
O'Shea, Milo	1926-	5	10	10	10	"The Verdict," RS
O'Sullivan, Maureen	1911-1998	20	35	50	40	"Tarzan" movies
O'Toole, Annette	1953-	5	20	15	20	"Superman III"
O'Toole, Peter	1932-	30	75	125	65	"Lawrence of Arabia"
Oakie, Jack	1903-1978	20	60	115	45	"The Great Dictator"
Oberon, Merle	1911-1979	50	100	175	85	" Wuthering Heights"
Odets, Clifford	1903-1963	60	115	200	125	"None But the Lonely Heart"
Oland, Warner	1880-1938	175	325		330	"The Jazz Singer," C.Chan films
Oldman, Gary	1958-	15	30	35	45	"B.Stoker's Dracula" SP - $55
Olin, Ken	1954-	5	10	10	10	"thirtysomething"
Olin, Lena	1955-	15	25	25	30	"Havana"
Oliver, Edna May	1883-1942	50	100	165	110	"Drums Along the Mohawk"
Oliver, Vic	1898-1964	25	50	65	50	"Room For Two," comedian
Olivier, Laurence	1907-1989	45	150	175	200	Stage legend, "Hamlet"
Olmos, Edward James	1947-	5	10	15	15	"Miami Vice," slow - RS
Olsen, Ashley	1986-	5	15		20	"Full House," FA, Both SP - $35
Olsen, Mary-Kate	1986-	5	15		20	"Full House," FA
Olsen, Moroni	1889-1954	40	80	145	85	"Mildred Pierce"
Olsen, Ole	1892-1963	20	40	40	50	"Hellzapoppin'," vaudeville act
Olson, Nancy	1928-	10	15	20	25	"Sunset Boulevard," "Airport"
Ontkean, Michael	1946-	5	10	10	15	"Twin Peaks"
Opatoshu, David	1918-	10	15	25	20	"The Naked City," "Exodus"
Oppenheimer, Alan	1930-	5	10	10	10	"Murphy Brown"
Orbach, Jerry	1935-	10	20	30	30	"Law and Order"
Orman, Suze	1951-	5	10		15	Author, popular TV guest

Name	DB/DD	Sig.DS/LS	ALS	SP	Comments
Ormond, Julia	1965-	20	50	75	65	"Legends of the Fall"
Osgood, Charles	1933-	5	10		15	Broadcast journalist
Otis, Carre	1968-	5	10	15	20	Model, actor
Ouspenskaya, Maria	1876-1949	160			340	Russian actress, "Love Affair"
Overman, Lynne	1887-1943	25	50	65	50	"Little Miss Marker"
Ovitz, Michael	1946-	10	20	45	25	Studio executive
Owen, Reginald	1887-1972	35	50	60	65	"Sherlock Holmes"
Oxenberg, Catherine	1961-	15	25	25	30	"Dynasty"
Oz, Frank	1944-	10	25		40	"The Muppet Show"

O'Connor, Carroll

* His role as Archie Bunker on "All in the Family" solidified his reputation as one of the finest television actors ever.

* In his early years, O'Connor was very obliguing to autograph requests.

* During O'Connor's years on "All in the Family" his popularity necessitated the use of a fan mail service to answer requests for his signatures with facsimile signed photographs.

* Later in his life, depending upon what address you contacted him through, he complied willingly to all autograph requests.

* The tragic death of his son took a severe toll on O'Connor in his later years. Throughout all of his anguish he remained true to his fans and committed to his beliefs. He remains incredibly popular not only for his acting ability but for his convictions.

* A number of his signed checks have been in the market and are typically offered for about $35.

Price, Vincent

* A gifted character actor, Price became known for his work in horror films, such as "House of Wax," "The Fly" and "Return of the Fly."

* He was an obliging signer in-person, however mail requests were often unanswered.

* Price later turned to television work and even played a villain on the series "Batman."

* Fortunately for collectors many Price signed documents, most in check form, have entered the market making it easy to acquire his signature for your collection.

* A number of his signed checks have appeared in the market for about $35.

Name	DB/DD	Sig.DS/LS	ALS	SP	Comments
Pacino, Al	1940-	25			65	"The Godfather," DS - $475
Pacula, Joanna	1957-	10	15	20	20	"Gorky Park"
Page, Geraldine	1924-1987	25	55	80	65	"The Trip to Bountiful," "Hondo"
Paget, Debra	1933-	25	40	35	55	"Broken Arrow"
Paige, Janis	1922-	10	15	15	15	"Pajama Game," "Trapper ..."
Palance, Jack	1920-	30	60		75	"City Slickers"
Palin, Michael	1943-	10	20	25	25	"Monty Python's Flying Circus"
Pallette, Eugene	1889-1954	70	110	160	115	"The Three Musketeers"
Palmer, Betsy	1926-	5	10	10	10	"I've Got a Secret," RS

Name	DB/DD	Sig.DS/LS	ALS	SP	Comments
Palmer, Lilli	1911-1986	20	45	50	60	"Secret Agent"
Palminteri, Chazz	1951-	10	20	20	20	"A Bronx Tale," playwright
Paltrow, Gwyneth	1973-	25	45	50	65	"Shakespeare..."
Pangborn, Franklin	1893-1958	60	75	80	80	"A Star is Born," "My Man ..."
Paquin, Anna	1982-	50	60		80	"The Piano," RS, ESPV
Pare, Michael	1959-	5	10	10	15	"Eddie and the Cruisers"
Parillaud, Anne	1961-	10	15	20	20	"La Femme Nikita"
Parker, Cecilia	1915-1993	25	40	40	45	"Andy Hardy" films
Parker, Dorothy	1893-1967	40	65	100	55	"A Star Is Born," screenwriter
Parker, Eleanor	1922-	5	10	15	15	"Caged,""Interrupted ...," RS
Parker, Fess	1925-	10	25	30	30	"Daniel Boone"
Parker, Jameson	1947-	5	10	10	15	"Simon and Simon"
Parker, Jean	1912-	20	30	35	35	"Little Women," "Sequoia"
Parker, Mary-Louise	1964-	10	30		30	"Proof"
Parker, Sarah Jessica	1965-	15	35		40	"Sex and the City""
Parks, Larry	1914-1975	35	65		75	"The Jolson Story"
Parsons, Estelle	1927-	5	10	15	15	"Roseanne"
Parsons, Louella	1893-1972	25	35	65	50	Gossip columnist, actor
Parton, Dolly	1946-	5	20	30	25	"9 to 5," RS
Pascal, Gabriel	1894-1954	50	70	100	85	"Pgymalion," "Major Barbara"
Pastorelli, Robert	1954-	5	10		10	"Murphy Brown"
Patinkin, Mandy	1952-	25	40	45	45	"Yentl"
Patric, Jason	1966-	5	10	15	15	"Rush"
Patrick, Gail	1911-1980	12	20	20	25	"Stage Door," "Love Crazy"
Patrick, Lee	1911-1982	25	45	55	50	"The Maltese Falcon"
Patrick, Robert	1959-	10	15	20	20	"Terminator 2: ...," SP - $25
Patterson, Elizabeth	1874-1966	30	40	45	55	"Tobacco Road," "Little ..."
Patterson, Lorna	1957-	5	10	10	10	"Private Benjamin"
Patterson, Melody	1947-	5	10	15	10	"F Troop," SP - $15
Patton, Will	1954-	5	10	10	10	"No Way out"
Pauley, Jane	1950-	5	10	15	15	"Dateline NBC," m. G. Trudeau
Paxton, Bill	1955-	20	50	50	55	"Twister"
Payne, John	1912-1989	25	40	50	65	"Miracle on 34th Street"
Pays, Amanda	1959-	5	10	15	15	"The Flash"
Pearce, Alice	1913-1966	25	40	40	45	"On The Town," "Bewitched"
Pearl, Jack	1895-1982	15	25	25	25	"The Jack Pearl Show" - radio
Peary, Harold	1908-1985	25	40	45	50	"The Great Gildersleeve"
Peck, Gregory	1916-2003	35	150		75	"To Kill A Mockingbird," SSP-2X
Peet, Amanda	1972-	10	20		20	"The Whole Nine Yards"
Pena, Elizabeth	1961-	5	10	10	15	"La Bamba"
Pendleton, Austin	1940-	5	10	10	10	"What's Up Doc?," RS
Pendleton, Nat	1895-1967	40	50	55	50	"At the Circus," "Dr. Kildare"
Penn, Robin Wright	1966-	10	20		25	"Forrest Gump," m. S. Penn
Penn, Sean	1960-	25	50		50	"Dead Man Walking"
Penny, Joe	1956-	5	10	10	10	"Jake and the Fatman"
Peppard, George	1929-1994	25	45		50	"Breakfast at Tiffany's"
Perez, Rosie	1964-	10	25	30	35	"Do the Right Thing"
Perkins, Anthony	1932-1992	50	75	100	65	"Friendly Pers....," SP - $210
Perkins, Elizabeth	1961-	5	10	10	10	"Big"
Perlman, Rhea	1948-	10	15	20	25	"Cheers," m. Danny DeVito
Perlman, Ron	1950-	5	10	15	15	"Beauty and the Beast"
Perreau, Gigi	1941-	5	10	15	10	"Bonzo Goes to College"

Name	DB/DD	Sig.DS/LS	ALS	SP	Comments
Perrine, Valerie	1943-	5	10	15	20	"Beverly Hills 90210"
Perry, Matthew	1969-	25	50	55	60	"Friends," FA, RS
Pesci, Joe	1943-	20	45		45	"My Cousin Vinny," RS
Pescow, Donna	1954-	5	10	10	10	"Saturday ... Fever," SP - $20
Peters, Bernadette	1948-	10	20		30	"Pennies from Heaven"
Peters, Brock	1927-	5	10	15	15	"To Kill a Mockingbird"
Peters, Jean	1926-2000	65	100	100	100	"Captain from Castile"
Peters, Susan	1921-1952	100	130	150	125	"Random Harvest"
Petersen, William	1953-	5	10	10	10	""To Live and Let Die in L.A."
Petty, Lori		5	10	10	10	"A League of Their Own"
Pfeiffer, Michelle	1957-	25	60		80	"The Fabulous Baker Boys"
Philbin, Regis	1933-	5	15		15	"Live With Regis and Kelly," RS
Phillippe, Ryan	1974-	10	20		25	"54"
Phillips, Bijou	1980-	10	20		25	"Black and White"
Phillips, Lou Diamond	1962-	10	20	25	25	"La Bamba"
Phillips, Mackenzie	1959-	10	20	25	30	"One Day at a Time"
Phillips, Michelle	1944-	15	30	35	40	"Knots Landing," (See Music)
Phoenix, Joaquin	1974-	10	25		25	"Gladiator"
Phoenix, River	1971-1993	210	445		420	"Stand By Me," tragic death
Pichel, Irving	1891-1954	55	80	75	100	"An ... Tragedy," "Cleopatra"
Pickens, Slim	1919-1983	85	165	175	195	"Dr. Strangelove," "Blazzing..."
Pickford, Mary	1893-1979	65	150	280	170	Silent legend, "Coquette"
Picon, Molly	1898-1992	20	30	40	60	"Fiddler On The Roof"
Pidgeon, Walter	1897-1984	25	50	75	75	"Mr. Miniver," "Madame Curie"
Pierce, David Hyde	1959-	10	20	25	35	"Frasier"
Pinchot, Bronson	1959-	5	10	10	10	"Perfect Strangers"
Pinkett, Jada	1971-	10	20	25	25	"The Nutty Professor"
Pinza, Ezio	1893-1957	60	125	200	165	"Tonight We Sing"
Piscopo, Joe	1951-	10	25	25	30	SNL
Pitt, Brad	1964-	40	225		85	"Legends of the Fall," ES
Pitts, ZaSu	1898-1963	40	60	70	85	"Oh,Susannah" - TV
Place, Mary Kay	1947-	5	10	15	15	"The Big Chill"
Plato, Dana	1964-1999	20	40		30	"Diff'rent Strokes"
Pleshette, John	1942-	5	10	10	15	"Knots Landing"
Pleshette, Suzanne	1937-	5	10	15	15	"The Bob Newhart Show"
Plowwright, Joan	1929-	10	15	20	20	"Enchanted April"
Plumb, Eve	1958-	5	10	10	15	"The Brady Bunch"
Plummer, Amanda	1957-	10	15	20	20	"The Fisher King"
Plummer, Christopher	1927-	10	15	20	25	"The Sound of Music"
Poitier, Sidney	1927-	25	55		65	"Guess Who's Coming ..."
Polanski, Roman	1933-	35	70	130	100	"Rosemary's Baby," director
Pollack, Sydney	1934-	15	30	35	30	"The Way We Were," director
Pollan, Tracy	1960-	10	20	25	30	"Family Ties"
Polley, Sara	1979-	10	20		15	"The Sweet Hereafter"
Pons, Lily	1904-1976	50	110	150	165	"That Girl From Paris"
Portman, Natalie	1981-	20	35		40	"Star Wars:...," sig. var.
Posey, Parker	1968-	10	20		15	"House of Yes"
Post, Markie	1950-	5	10	10	10	"Night Court,"RS
Potter, Carol	1948-	10	15	20	20	"Beverly Hills 90210"
Potts, Annie	1952-	10	15	20	25	"Designing Women"
Poundstone, Paula	1960-	5	10	10	15	Actor, comedian
Povich, Maury	1939-	5	10	10	15	"A Current Affair," m. C.Chung

Name	DB/DD	Sig.DS/LS	ALS	SP	Comments
Powell, Dick	1904-1963	30	45	60	75	"42nd Street," "Murder My ..."
Powell, Eleanor	1910-1982	15	20	40	50	"Born to Dance," tap dancer
Powell, William	1892-1984	65	75	100	120	"My Man Godfrey," "The Thin..."
Power, Tyrone	1913-1958	115	215		280	"In Old Chicago," "The ... Zorro"
Powers, Mala	1931-	5	10	10	10	"Rose of Cimarron," RS
Powers, Stephanie	1942-	10	15	20	25	"Hart to Hart," FA
Powter, Susan	1957-	5	10	10	10	"Stop the Insanity!"
Preisser, June	1923-1984	20	25	30	35	"Babes in Arms," "Strike Up ..."
Preminger, Otto	1906-1986	60	100	125	120	"The Man ... Golden Arm," dir.
Prentis, Paula	1939-	5	10	15	15	"What's New Pussycat?"
Presley, Priscilla	1945-	10	25		35	m. Elvis Presley
Preston, Kelly	1962-	10	20	25	25	"52 Pick-Up," m. John Travolta
Preston, Robert	1918-1987	45	100	150	100	TMMSP- $125
Price, Vincent	1911-1994	40	100		125	SBC-$120, SC - $35
Priestley, Jason	1969-	20	30	35	40	"Beverly Hills 90210"
Principal, Victoria	1950-	10	15	25	35	"Dallas"
Pringle, Aileen	1895-1989	20	25	30	30	Silent era star, "Three Weeks"
Prinze, Freddie	1954-1981	75	100		150	"Chico and the Man"
Prinze, Freddie, Jr.	1976-	15	30		25	"She's All That"
Probst, Jeff	1961-	5	10		10	"Survivor"
Pryce, Jonathan	1947-	5	10	10	10	"Miss Saigon"
Pryor, Nicholas	1935-	5	10	10	10	"Risky Business"
Pryor, Richard	1940-	10	25	60	30	"Stir Crazy," sig. var.
Pullman, Bill	1954-	25	40	50	65	"While You Were Sleeping"
Purcell, Sarah	1948-	5	10	10	10	"Real People"
Purdom, Edmund	1924-	10	20	20	20	"The Student Prince"
Pyle, Denver	1920-1997	15	30	50	30	RS

Pitt, Brad

* Pitt made his mark in hollywood by appearing in "A River Runs Through It," "Interview with a Vampire" and "Legends of the Fall."

* As a "Hollywood Hearthrob" he attracts considerable attention both from fans and tabloids. His marriage to Jennifer Aniston in 2000 virtually guaranteed him that his image would never be off the newstand.

* He is nearly impossible to acquire in-person and even if you get a response from a mail request, which is rare, it will be a ghost signature.

* Adding to the complexity of acquiring a real autograph is the lack of consistency in his signature, which is often illegible and abbreviated.

* Unfortunately, most signed photographs being offered in the market are fake. If you need his signature be patient as eventually documents will surface in the market.

Name	DB/DD	Sig.DS/LS	ALS	SP	Comments
Quaid, Dennis	1954-	20	30	40	45	"The Big Easy"
Quaid, Randy	1950-	10	20	25	25	"The Last Picture Show"
Qualen, John	1899-1987	20	25	30	35	Character actor, "His Girl Friday"
Quillan, Eddie	1907-1990	25	50	55	50	"Mutiny on the Bounty"
Quinlan, Kathleen	1954-	10	20		20	"Family Law"
Quinn, Aidan	1959-	5	10	10	10	"The Playboys"

Name	DB/DD	Sig.DS/LS	ALS	SP	Comments
Quinn, Anthony	1915-2001	25	50		60	"Viva Zapata," "Lust For Life"
Quivers, Robin	1953-	5	10	10	15	"The Howard Stern Show"
Radcliffe, Daniel	1989-	15	30		30	"Harry Potter," SSP-2X
Radner, Gilda	1946-1989	75	150		150	SNL
Raffin, Deborah	1953-	5	10	10	15	"Once Is Not Enough"
Raft, George	1895-1980	60	135	150	150	"Scarface"
Rainer, Louise	1909-1993	25	35	45	50	"The Great Ziegfeld"
Raines, Ella	1921-1988	10	15	20	20	"Corvette K-225," "Phantom..."
Rains, Claude	1889-1967	140	285		255	"Mr. Smith Goes to Wash...."
Ralph, Sheryl Lee	1956-	5	10	10	15	"The Distinguished Gentleman"
Ralston, Esther	1902-1994	12	20	45	40	"American Venus" of silent films
Ralston, Vera	1921-	10	15	25	25	Olympics, "Ice Capades," RS
Rambeau, Marjorie	1889-1970	30	35	50	50	"Primrose Path," "Torch Song"
Ramis, Herald	1944-	5	10	10	15	"Ghostbusters," SP - $20
Rampling, Charlotte	1946-	5	10	15	20	"The Verdict"
Rand, Sally	1903-1979	50	80		75	Fan dance queen
Randall, Tony	1920-	5	10	20	25	"The Odd Couple," RS
Raphael, Sally Jessy	1943-	5	10	10	10	"Sally Jesse Raphael"
Rasche, David	1944-	5	10	10	10	"Sledge Hammer"
Rashad, Phylicia	1948-	5	10	10	15	"The Cosby Show"
Rathbone, Basil	1892-1967	255	500		500	"Sherlock Holmes," SP - $500
Rather, Dan	1931-	12	25		25	"CBS Evening News..."
Ratzenberger, John	1947-	5	10	20	20	"Cheers"
Rawlinson, Herbert	1885-1953	25	30	55	75	Screen idol, "The Sea Wolf"
Raye, Martha	1916-1994	20	60	50	50	"Hellzapoppin'"
Raymond, Gene	1908-	10	15	20	25	"B" star, "Smilin' Through"
Reagan, Ronald, Jr.	1958-	5	10	10	10	s.of Ronald Reagan
Reason, Rex	1928-	10	15	20	20	"This Island Earth"
Reasoner, Harry	1923-1991	30	60	125	40	CBS broadcast journalist
Redford, Robert	1937-	60	200	400	135	"B. Cassidy ...Sundance Kid"
Redgrave, Corin	1939-	5	10	10	10	"A Man for All Seasons"
Redgrave, Lynn	1943-	5	15	15	20	"House Calls"
Redgrave, Michael	1908-1985	25	50	50	60	"Mourning Becomes Electra"
Redgrave, Vanessa	1937-	15	30	50	60	"Playing for Time"
Reed, Donna	1921-1986	50	75	225	185	"The Donna Reed Show" - TV
Reed, Oliver	1938-1999	20	35		40	"The Three Musketeers"
Reed, Pamela	1953-	5	10	10	15	"The Right Stuff"
Reed, Robert	1932-1992	50	75		100	"The Brady Bunch"
Reems, Harry	1947-	20	40	50	50	"Deep Throat"
Reeve, Christopher	1952-	55	150	265	135	"Superman"
Reeves, George	1914-1959	900	4000		1250	DS GWTW - $6000, FA
Reeves, Keanu	1964-	20	50	50	65	"The Matrix"
Reeves, Steve	1926-2000	25	45	60	50	"Hercules," $
Regalbuto, Joe		5	10	10	10	"Murphy Brown"
Regan, Phil	1906-	15	50	30	30	"Singing Policeman"
Reid, Tim	1944-	5	10	10	10	"WKRP in Cincinnati"
Reid, W. Wallace	1891-1923	225	540		600	"The King...Paramount," BOAN
Reiner, Carl	1922-	10	10		30	"The Dick Van Dyke Show"
Reiner, Rob	1945-	5	10	25	25	"All in the Family," SP - $30
Reinhold, Judge	1957-	5	10	15	20	"Beverly Hills Cop"
Reinking, Ann	1949-	5	10	15	20	"Annie," dancer

Name	DB/DD	Sig.DS/LS	ALS	SP	Comments
Reiser, Paul	1957-	10 20	30	30	"Mad About You"
Reitman, Ivan	1946-	5 10	15	15	"Ghostbusters," director
Remick, Lee	1935-1991	40 50	60	75	"Days of Wine and Roses"
Renaldo, Duncan	1904-1980	30 100	125	150	"Cisco Kid"
Rennie, Michael	1909-1971	100 145	165	200	"The Day the Earth Stood Still"
Reuben, Gloria	1965-	10 20		20	"ER"
Revere, Anne	1903-1990	20 35	35	40	"National Velvet"
Reynolds, Bert	1936-	15 30		40	"Smokey and the Bandit"
Reynolds, Debbie	1932-	10 30	50	25	"Singin' In The Rain," SP - $50
Reynolds, Gene	1925-	5 10	10	15	"Dianna," "Heidi," RS
Reynolds, Marjorie	1923-1997	15 25	30	25	"Holiday Inn"
Rhames, Ving	1959-	5 10		15	"Only in America:..."
Rhodes, Erik	1906-1990	25 35	35	50	Radio comedian, "Top Hat"
Ribeiro, Alfonso	1971-	5 10	10	10	"Fresh Prince of Bel Air," dancer
Ricci, Christina	1980-	15 30	40	50	"The Opposite of Sex," FA
Rich, Adam	1968-	5 10	10	10	"Eight Is Enough"
Rich, Irene	1891-1988	10 15	20	20	"Craig's Wife," "The Certain..."
Richards, Denise	1971-	10 20		20	"Wild Things," m.C. Sheen
Richards, Michael	1949-	15 25	30	30	"Seinfeld"
Richardson, Miranda	1958-	20 40	40	50	"The Crying Game"
Richardson, Natasha	1963-	20 35	40	50	"The Handmaid's Tale"
Richardson, Ralph	1902-1993	35 45	50	60	Brit. stage actor, "The Heiress"
Richardson, Susan	1952-	5 10	10	10	"Eight Is Enough"
Richter, Andy	1966-	5 10		15	"Late Show... O'Brien"
Rickles, Don	1926-	5 10	15	15	"The Don Rickles Show"
Rickman, Alan	1946-	15 30		30	"Die Hard"
Riegert, Peter	1947-	5 10	10	10	"Crossing Delancey"
Rigby, Cathy	1952-	5 10	15	20	Actor, gymnast
Rigg, Diana	1938-	10 25	35	40	"The Avengers"
Ringwald, Molly	1968-	20 40	50	50	"Sixteen Candles"
Ripa, Kelly	1970-	10 20		20	"Live with Regis..."
Ritter, John	1948-2003	20 45		40	"Three's Company"
Ritter, Tex	1907-1974	100 200	325	265	Recording star, actor, cowboy
Ritter, Thelma	1905-1969	50 100	200	140	"Rear Window," "Pillow Talk"
Rivera, Geraldo	1943-	10 20	25	20	"Geraldo," FA
Rivers, Joan	1937-	5 10	20	20	"Can we talk..."
Roach, Hal	1892-1992	125 300		175	Industry comedy pioneer
Roach, Hal, Jr.	1921-1972	15 25	45	25	Producer, "Of Mice and Men"
Robards, Jason Jr.	1922-2000	25 50	70	50	"All The President's Men"
Robbins, Jerome	1918-1998	60 100	130	100	"Fiddler on the Roof," chore.
Robbins, Tim	1958-	20 40	50	45	"The Player"
Roberts, Eric	1956-	10 20	25	25	"The Pope of Greenwich..."
Roberts, Julia	1967-	45 200	250	110	"Pretty Woman"
Roberts, Tanya	1955-	5 10	15	25	"Charlie's Angels"
Roberts, Tony	1939-	5 10	15	15	"Play It Again, Sam"
Robertson, Cliff	1925-	5 10	25	25	"Charly"
Robeson, Paul	1898-1976	140 245	300	500	"Ol' Man River," singer
Robinson, Anne	1944-	5 10		10	"The Weakest Link"
Robinson, "Bojangles"	1878-1949	115 225	500	450	"The Little Colonel"
Robinson, Edward G.	1893-1973	65 175	165	225	"Little Caesar," BC - $80
Robinson, Jay	1930-	5 10	10	15	"The Robe"
Robson, Flora	1902-1984	30 50	75	85	Stage actress, "Saratoga Trunk"

Name	DB/DD	Sig.DS/LS	ALS	SP	Comments
Robson, May	1858-1942	50	85	125	90	"Lady For A Day," "A Star Is…"
Rock, Chris	1966-	15	25	30	35	"The Chris Rock Show," "LW4"
Rock, The (D. Johnson)	1972-	20	40		45	"The Scorpion Knig," WWF
Roddenberry, Gene	1921-1991	100	175		200	"Star Trek"
Rogers, Chas."Buddy"	1904-1999	25	45		60	"America's Boy Friend"
Rogers, Fred "Mr."	1928-2003	10	25		30	"It's a beautiful day…"
Rogers, Ginger	1911-1995	45	160	300	170	Fred Astaire's dance partner
Rogers, Mimi	1956-	10	15	20	25	"Someone To Watch Over Me"
Rogers, Roy	1912-1998	50	140	250	100	"Under Western Skies," singer
Rogers, Wayne	1933-	5	10	10	10	"M*A*S*H," RS
Rogers, Will	1879-1935	300	1000	1250	1150	"State Fair," comedian
Rogers, Will Jr.	1912-	10	20	25	25	"The Story of Will Rogers"
Roker, Al	1954-	5	10		10	"Today," RS
Roland, Gilbert	1905-1994	25	30	40	45	"Camille," fourth "Cisco Kid"
Rolle, Esther	1922-1998	10	20	35	20	Driving Miss Daisy," RS
Roman, Ruth	1924-1999	20	35	45	40	"The Long Hot Summer"
Romano, Ray	1957-	10	25		30	"Everybody Loves Raymond"
Romberg, Sigmund	1887-1951	110	225	340	250	Composer, "The Desert Song"
Romero, Cesar	1907-1993	30	50	100	75	"Cisco Kid," "Batman" - TV
Romlin-Stamos, Reb.	1972-	10	25		45	Model
Rooney, Andy	1919-	10	20		25	"60 Minutes"
Rooney, Mickey	1920-	20	80	100	30	"Boys Town," "Babes in Arms"
Roseanne	1953-	15	30	35	40	"Roseanne," FA
Ross, Katharine	1943-	15	25	30	35	"The Graduate"
Ross, Marion	1928-	5	10	10	15	"Happy Days"
Ross, Shirley	1909-1975	25	40	45	50	"The Big Broadcast of 1938"
Rossellini, Isabella	1952-	10	20	30	40	"Blue Velvet"
Roth, Lillian	1910-1980	40	65	80	100	"The Love Parade," "Animal…"
Roth, Tim	1961-	5	10	10	15	"Reservoir Dogs"
Roundtree, Richard	1942-	5	10	15	15	"Shaft"
Rourke, Mickey	1953-	15	30	30	40	"9 1/2 Weeks"
Rowlands, Gena	1934-	5	10	10	15	"Gloria," RS
Rudner, Rita	1955-	5	15	10	15	Actor, cemedian
Ruehl, Mercedes	1948-	20	35	40	40	"Lost in Yonkers"
Ruggles, Charles	1886-1970	50	65	75	80	"It Happened on Fifth Avenue"
Ruggles, Wesley	1889-1972	25	30	50	50	"Silk Stockings," "I'm No Angel"
Rush, Barbara	1927-	5	10	10	15	"Bigger Than Life," "It Came…"
Rush, Geoffrey	1951-	10	20	25	30	"Shine"
Russell, Harold	1914-2002	25	35	45	35	"The Best Years of Our Lives"
Russell, Jane	1921-	10	15	25	30	"Gentlemen Prefer Blondes"
Russell, Keri	1976-	10	20		35	"Felicity"
Russell, Kurt	1951-	15	25	35	40	"Stargate"
Russell, Nipsey	1924-	5	10	10	10	"Car 54, Where Are You?"
Russell, Rosalind	1908-1976	45	70	100	115	"My Sister Eileen," "Auntie…"
Russell, Theresa	1957-	10	15	20	20	"Black Widow"
Russo, Rene	1954-	15	30	45	45	"Lethal Weapon 3"
Rutherford, Ann	1917-	15	25	30	45	"Andy Hardy" series, GWTW
Rutherford, Margaret	1892-1972	60	145	200	200	"The VIPs," "Murder She Said"
Ruttan, Susan	1948-	5	10	10	15	"L.A. Law"
Ryan, Jeri	1968-	15	30		40	"Star Trek:…"
Ryan, Meg	1961-	30	50	100	75	"When Harry Met Sally…"
Ryan, Peggy	1924-	10	15	30	30	Dancer, D. O'Connor's partner

Name	DB/DD	Sig.DS/LS	ALS	SP	Comments
Ryan, Robert	1909-1973	25	40	75	75	"Crossfire," "Setup"
Ryder, Winona	1971-	25	50	100	85	"Beetlejuice"

Redford, Robert

* An established force in hollywood, Refdord is typically associated with his acting roles alongside Paul Newman in films such as "Butch Cassidy and the Sundance Kid" and "The Sting."

* His directing prowess earned him in Oscar for Best Director in 1980 for "Ordinary People."

* Redford founded the nonprofit Sundance Institute in Park City, Utah, which sponsors an annual film festival and provides support for independent film production. It is during this event that collectors are most likely to obtain an in-person autograph.

* Redford made his stage debut in 1959 ("Tall Story") and his film debut in 1969 ("War Hunt"). During his early years he was a reluctant but obliging signer.

* Any autographed item acquired indirectly after1970 is likely to be ghost signed.

* Redford has utilized a variety of fan mail services for years, most of which apply a ghost signature to whatever items are sent or answer requests with a facsimile signed photograph or postcard.

Reeves, George

* A talented character actor, Reeves is often associated with his television role as Superman in the popular hit series "Adventures of Superman."

* Reeves signature is constantly in demand not only for his role as Superman but for his appearances in many movies including "Gone With the Wind."

* He was very obliguing to autograph requests and had a genuine appreciation for his fans.

* Reeves popularity as Superman led to his employment of services to answer his fan mail.

* Some photographs of him in costume have surafced signed simply "Best Wishes, Superman" and are not as appealing as those signed with his full name.

Name	DB/DD	Sig.DS/LS	ALS	SP	Comments
Sabu	1924-1963	90	165	400	210	"Elephant Boy," "Jungle Book"
Sagal, Katey	1956-	5	10	10	15	"Married ...with Children"
Saget, Bob	1956-	5	10	10	10	"Full House"
Saint James, Susan	1946-	10	15	20	20	"Kate & Allie"
Saint, Eva Marie	1924-	15	20	25	30	"On The Waterfront," RS
Sajak, Pat	1946-	5	10	10	10	"Wheel of Fortune, RS
Sales, Soupy	1930-	5	10	10	10	"The Soupy Sales Show"
Salt, Jennifer	1944-	5	10	10	15	"Midnight Cowboy"
Samms, Emma	1960-	10	20	25	30	"Dynasty"
San Giacomo, Laura	1961-	10	15	20	30	"sex, lies and videotape"
Sanders, George	1906-1972	75	120	150	160	"The Saint," "The Falcon"
Sanders, Richard	1940-	5	10	10	10	"WKRP in Cincinnati"
Sandler, Adam	1966-	10	20	25	30	SNL, FA
Sands, Julian	1958-	5	10	10	10	"A Room with a View"
Sandy, Gary	1946-	5	10	10	10	"WKRP in Cincinnati"

Name	DB/DD	Sig.DS/LS	ALS	SP	Comments
Sanford, Isabel	1917-	5 10	10	12	"The Jeffersons"
Sarandon, Chris	1942-	5 10	10	12	"Dog Day Afternoon"
Sarandon, Susan	1946-	20 50	125	65	"Thelma and Louise"
Savage, Fred	1976-	5 10	10	15	"The Wonder Years," FA
Savage, John	1949-	5 10	10	10	"The Deer Hunter"
Savalas, Telly	1924-1994	30 60		55	
Savant, Doug	1964-	5 10	10	15	"Melrose Place"
Savitch, Jessica	1947-1983	75 150		150	Broadcast journalist
Sawyer, Diane	1945-	5 10		15	"Primetime Live"
Scacchi, Greta	1960-	5 10	15	30	"Presumed Innocent"
Scalia, Jack	1951-	5 10	15	20	"Wolf"
Scarpelli, Glenn	1968-	5 10	10	12	"One Day at a Time"
Schary, Dore	1905-1980	20 25	30	35	"Boy's Town," writer, producer
Scheider, Roy	1935-	10 20	20	25	"Jaws"
Schell, Maximilian	1930-	10 20	25	30	"Judgement at Nuremberg"
Schiffer, Claudia	1971-	10 25	30	35	Supermodel
Schildkraut, Joseph	1895-1964	70 150	150	175	"The Life of Emile Zola"
Schlessinger, Laura	1947-	5 10		10	"Dr. Laura"
Schneider, Maria	1952-	5 10	15	20	"Last Tango in Paris"
Schorr, Daniel	1916-	5 10		10	Broadcast journalist
Schroder, Rick	1970-	10 25	25	30	"Lonesome Dove"
Schultz, Dwight	1947-	5 10	10	10	"The A-Team"
Schwarzenegger, Arn.	1947-	25 100	240	75	"The Terminator," SSP -$125
Schwimmer, David	1966-	20 45	75	55	"Friends"
Schygulla, Hanna	1943-	5 10	10	10	"Dead Again"
Sciorra, Annabella	1964-	10 15	20	25	"The Hand that Rocks ..."
Scofield, Paul	1922-	10 25	60	25	"A Man For All Seasons"
Scolari, Peter	1954-	5 10	10	10	"Bosom Buddies"
Scorsese, Martin	1942-	30 175	230	60	"Taxi Driver"
Scott, George C.	1926-1999	40 140		90	"Patton," refused AA, ES
Scott, Gordon	1927-	15 30	25	30	"Trazan's Hidden Jungle"
Scott, Lizabeth	1922-	10 15	15	20	"You Came Along," "Desert..."
Scott, Martha	1914-2003	10 25	30	30	"Our Town," "Ben Hur," RS
Scott, Randolph	1898-1987	55 100	115	130	"Jesse James," "Virginia City"
Scott, Ridley	1937-	10 15	15	20	"Thelma and Louise," director
Scott, Willard	1934-	5 10	10	10	"Today," weatherman
Scott, Zachary	1914-1965	30 50	110	60	"Mildred Pierce"
Seagal, Steven	1952-	20 50	75	45	"Under Seige"
Seal, Elizabeth	1933-	5 10	10	15	L"Irma La Douce"
Sedgwick, Kyra	1965-	15 35	35	40	Actor, m. Kevin Bacon
Segal, George	1934-	5 10	15	20	"Look Who's Talking"
Seinfeld, Jerry	1955-	25 75	140	60	"Seinfeld," FA
Sellecca, Connie	1955-	10 20	25	25	"Hotel," m. John Tesh
Selleck, Tom	1945-	15 25	65	35	"Magnum, P.I.," FA, RS
Sellers, Peter	1925-1980	120 200		200	"Inspector Clouseau" -PP
Serling, Rod	1924-1975	150 300	400	400	"The Twilight Zone"
Sessions, Almira	1888-1974	20 35	40	40	"Little Nellie Kelly"
Sevigny, Chloe	1974-	10 20		15	"Boys Don't Cry"
Seymour, Jane	1951-	15 30	40	45	"Dr. Quinn, Medicine ...," FA
Seymour, Stephanie	1968-	15 25	35	45	Supermodel
Shaffer, Paul	1949-	5 10		10	"Late Show with D.Letterman"
Shalit, Gene	1932-	5 10	10	10	"Today," film critic

Name	DB/DD	Sig.DS/LS	ALS	SP	Comments
Shandling, Garry	1949-	15	25	35	40	"Larry Sanders Show"
Sharif, Omar	1932-	20	50	70	75	"Dr. Zhivago"
Shatner, William	1931-	25	50	75	65	"Star Trek"
Shaughnessy, Mickey	1920-1985	20	40	40	45	"From Here To Eternity"
Shaver, Helen	1951-	10	15	15	20	"The Amityville Horror"
Shawn, Dick	1928-1987	55	100	150	125	"The Producers"
Shawn, Wallace	1943-	10	15	15	15	"My Dinner with Andre"
Shea, John	1949-	5	10	10	10	"Lois & Clark"
Shean, Al	1868-1949	65	120	110	125	"San Francisco," p.w/Gallagher
Shearer, Harry	1943-	5	10	10	10	"This Is Spinal Tap"
Shearer, Moira	1926-	30	50	50	65	"The Red Shoes," ballet dancer
Shearer, Norma	1900-1983	100	300	350	265	"The Divorcee," nomi. 6 AA
Sheedy, Ally	1962-	5	10	10	10	"WarGames"
Sheen, Charlie	1965-	15	25	25	25	"Platoon," FA
Sheen, Martin	1940-	12	25	30	30	"Apocalypse Now,"RS
Sheindlin, Judith	1942-	5	10		10	"Judge Judy"
Shelley, Carole	1939-	5	10	10	10	"The Elephant Man"
Shepard, Cybill	1950-	20	35	40	50	"Cybill"
Sheridan, Ann	1915-1967	60	115	100	125	"King's Row," "Shine On ..."
Sheridan, Jim	1949-	10	15	20	20	"My Left Foot," director
Sheridan, Nicollette	1963-	10	25	25	30	"The Sure Thing"
Sherriff, R.C.	1896-1975	40	110	150	100	"Goodbye Mr. Chips"
Sherwood, Robert E.	1896-1955	45	60	70	70	Critic, editor, "The Best Years..."
Shields, Brooke	1965-	20	40	50	50	"Pretty Baby"
Shire, Talia (T.Coppola)	1946-	25	75	100	50	"Rocky I-V," SDS - 2X, ES
Shirley, Anne	1918-1993	20	25	40	40	"Stella Dallas"
Shoemaker, Ann	1891-1978	20	35	35	40	"Sunrise at Campobello"
Shore, Dinah	1917-1994	25	50	100	60	"Thank Your Lucky Stars"
Shore, Pauly	1968-	5	10		10	"The Weez"
Short, Martin	1950-	10	20	25	25	SNL
Show, Grant	1962-	20	35	35	45	"Melrose Place"
Showalter, Max	1917-	5	10	10	10	"Leave It to Beaver,"RS
Shriver, Maria	1955-	10	25		20	Broadcast journalist
Shue, Andrew	1967-	15	30	30	40	"Melrose Place"
Shue, Elisabeth	1963-	20	40	50	65	"Leaving Las Vegas"
Sidney, Sylvia	1910-1999	20	30	45	30	"City Streets," "Summer ..."
Sigler, Jamie-Lynn	1981-	10	20		25	"The Sopranos"
Sikking, James B.	1934-	5	10	10	15	"Hill Street Blues"
Silva, Henry	1928-	10	15	15	15	"Johnny Cool," "Green ..."
Silver, Ron	1946-	15	25	25	30	"Reversal of Fortune"
Silverheels, Jay	1919-1980	160	350		380	"Tonto" in "The Lone Ranger"
Silverman, Jonathan	1966-	5	10	10	10	"The Single Guy," RS
Silvers, Phil	1912-1985	50	100	215	185	"You'll Never Get Rich"
Silverstone, Alicia	1976-	25	55	75	80	"Clueless"
Simmons, Jean	1929-	15	20	25	30	"Hamlet," "The Happy Ending"
Simmons, Richard	1948-	5	10	10	10	"Sweatin' to the Oldies"
Simms, Larry	1934-	5	10	10	15	""Blondie" film series
Simon, Neil	1927-	25	50		55	Playwright
Simon, Simone	1910-	20	40	45	45	"Cat People"
Simpson, Russell	1880-1959	65	120	150	130	TGOW, "Billy the Kid"
Sinatra, Frank	1915-1998	240	675		325	
Sinbad (David Adkins)	1956-	10	15	20	25	"A Different World"

Name	DB/DD	Sig.DS/LS	ALS	SP	Comments
Sinise, Gary	1955-	10	25		30	"Forrest Gump"
Singer, Lori	1962-	5	10	10	12	"Fame"
Singleton, John	1968-	10	15	15	20	"Boyz N the Hood"
Singleton, Penny	1908-	12	15	20	20	"Good News," "Boy Meets Girl"
Siskel, Gene	1946-1999	15	25		25	"Siskel & Ebert & The Movies"
Skelton, Red	1910-1997	50	100	155	115	"Whistling in the Dark"
Skerritt, Tom	1933-	10	15	25	25	"Picket Fences," "Top Gun"
Skye, Ione	1971-	5	10	10	10	"Say Anything"
Slater, Christian	1969-	15	25	30	45	"Heathers"
Slater, Helen	1965-	10	20	20	30	"Supergirl"
Sloane, Everett	1909-1965	30	50	50	60	"Citizen Kane"
Smirnoff, Yakov	1951-	5	10	10	10	"What a Country!"
Smith, Alexis	1921-1993	20	50	40	40	"Dive Bomber," "Rhapsody..."
Smith, Bob	1917-1998	25	35	50	50	"Howdy Doody," RS
Smith, C. Aubrey	1863-1948	40	80	130	80	Brit. actor, "Queen Christina"
Smith, Charles Martin	1953-	10	20	20	25	"American Graffiti"
Smith, Jaclyn	1947-	5	15	20	25	"Charlie's Angels"
Smith, Jeff	1939-	5	10	10	10	"The Frugal Gourmet"
Smith, Kate	1909-1986	50	200	175	130	"This Is The Army," singer
Smith, Liz	1923-	5	10	15	10	Gossip columnist
Smith, Maggie	1934-	10	20	25	25	"Sister Act"
Smith, Will	1968-	30			75	"Independence Day," rap artist
Smits, Jimmy	1955-	10	25	30	30	"L.A. Law," RS
Smothers, Dick	1939-	10	20		20	"The S. Brothers Comedy Hour"
Smothers, Tom	1937-	10	20		20	SP both - $35
Snipes, Wesley	1962-	20	120	175	70	"New Jack City"
Snodgrass, Carrie	1946-	5	10	10	12	"Diary of a Mad Housewife," RS
Snyder, Tom	1936-	5	10	10	10	"Late Late Show with...," RS
Sobieski, Leelee	1982-	10	20		15	"Joan of Arc"
Somers, Suzanne	1946-	10	20	30	30	"Three's Company"
Sommer, Elke	1940-	5	10	10	15	"A Shot in the Dark,"RS
Sondergaard, Gale	1899-1985	35	60	60	70	"The Life of Emile Zola"
Sorbo, Kevin	1958-	25	50	130	65	"Hercules"
Sorvino, Mira	1969-	20	40	50	65	"Mighty Aphrodite"
Sorvino, Paul	1939-	15	30	40	40	"GoodFellas"
Sothern, Ann	1909-2001	25	45	60	55	"Ann Sothern Show," "Maisie"
Soul, David	1943-	10	20		15	"Starsky and Hutch," SP - $15
Spacek, Sissy	1949-	20	40	50	50	"Coal Miner's Daughter"
Spacey, Kevin	1959-	15	30	40	45	"American Beauty," RS
Spade, David	1954-	10	20		20	"Just Shoot Me," SNL
Spader, James	1960-	5	10	10	10	"sex, lies, and videotape"
Spano, Joe	1946-	5	15	15	15	"Hill Street Blues"
Spano, Vincent	1962-	5	10	10	10	"Rumble Fish"
Sparks, Ned	1883-1957	30	35	55	65	"42nd Street," "Magic Town"
Spelling, Aaron	1923-	10	15	25	25	"Beverly Hills, 90210"
Spelling, Tori	1973-	15	30	40	55	"Beverly Hills, 90210"
Spielberg, Steven	1947-	65	200		100	"Schindler's List," director, FA
Springer, Jerry	1944-	10	20		20	TV shock host, mayor
St. John, Jill	1940-	10	15	20	25	"Diamonds Are Forever"
Stack, Robert	1919-2003	20	30	40	35	"Written on the Wind"
Stallone, Sylvester	1946-	32	150	300	85	"Rocky," reluctant signer
Stamos, John	1963-	10	15	15	20	"Full House"

Name	DB/DD	Sig.DS/LS		ALS	SP	Comments
Stamp, Terence	1939-	10	20	20	25	"Superman II"
Stander, Lionel	1908-1994	15	25		30	"Mr. Deeds Goes to Town"
Standings, Guy	1873-1937	35	100		75	"Brit. actor, "Death Takes..."
Stang, Arnold	1925-	5	10	15	20	"The Man With The Golden Arm"
Stanton, Harry Dean	1926-	5	10	10	10	"Paris, Texas"
Stanwyck, Barbara	1907-1990	35	85	125	100	"Ball of Fire," television star
Stapleton, Jean	1923-	5	10	20	20	"All in the Family," RS
Stapleton, Maureen	1925-	10	20	25	25	"Lonely Hearts," "Airport"
Steele, Bob	1906-1988	28	35	50	60	"Of Mice and Men," "F Troop"
Steenburgen, Mary	1953-	15	40	40	40	"Parenthood"
Steiger, Rod	1925-2002	15	30		35	"In the Heat of the Night"
Steinberg, David	1942-	10	20	20	25	"Paternity," director
Sten, Anna	1908-1993	20	25	35	40	"Nana," "We Live Again"
Sterling, Jan	1923-	10	20	25	25	"Caged," "The High ... Mighty"
Sterling, Robert	1917-	10	20	25	25	"Only Angels...Wings"
Stern, Daniel	1957-	10	20	20	25	"The Wonder Years"
Stern, Howard	1954-	15			30	Radio shock-jock
Sternhagen, Frances	1930-	5	10	15	10	"Driving Miss Daisy," RS
Stevens, Andrew	1955-	5	10	15	15	"Dallas"
Stevens, Connie	1938-	5	10	20	20	"Hawaiian Eye"
Stevens, Craig	1918-2000	15	25	30	25	"Peter Gunn" - TV
Stevens, Fisher	1963-	5	10	10	10	"Short Circuit"
Stevens, K.T.	1919-	5	10	10	10	"Kitty Foyle," "Vice Squad"
Stevens, Ray	1939-	5	10	10	10	"Andy Williams ... Ray Stevens"
Stevens, Rise	1908-	15	30	35	40	"Going My Way," opera singer
Stevens, Stella	1936-	5	10	15	15	"Santa Barbara"
Stevenson, Parker	1952-	5	10	10	15	"Falcon Crest"
Stewart, James	1908-1997	45	200		150	"Harvey" sk.- $375, BC - $200
Stewart, Jon	1962-	10	20		20	"The Jon Stewart Show"
Stewart, Martha	1941-	5	10		10	"Martha Stewart Living, RS
Stewart, Martha	1922-	5	10	10	15	"Holocaust"
Stewart, Patrick	1940-	25	50	130	70	"Star Trek: ...Generation"
Stiers, David Ogden	1942-	40	100		85	"M*A*S*H," reluctant signer
Stiles, Julia	1981-	10	20		20	"10 Things I Hate About You"
Stiller, Ben	1966-	10	20	25	30	"Reality Bites"
Stiller, Jerry	1931-	5	10	15	15	Actor, f. Ben Stiller
Stockwell, Dean	1935-	10	20	20	25	"Quantum Leap"
Stockwell, John	1961-	5	10	10	10	"My Science Project"
Stolz, Eric	1961-	10	20	25	25	"Mask"
Stone, Dee Wallace	1948-	5	10	10	12	"E.T., the Extra-Terrestrial"
Stone, George E.	1904-1967	25	50	50	50	"Seventh Heaven"
Stone, Lewis	1878-1953	40	50	75	75	"Andy Hardy" film series
Stone, Oliver	1946-	25	65	50	40	"Platoon," RS
Stone, Sharon	1958-	30	100	180	60	"Basic Instinct," FA
Stooges, Three:						
Moe Howard	1897-1975					
Larry Fine	1911-1974					Larry sig. $130
Curly Howard	1906-1952	1350	4000		3375	Final lineup SP - $650
Storch, Larry	1923-	5	10	15	15	"F Troop"
Storm, Gale	1922-	5	10	15	20	"My Little Margie"
Stossel, John	1947-	5	10		10	"20/20"
Stowe, Madeleine	1958-	15	25	30	40	"The Last of the Mohicans"

Name	DB/DD	Sig.DS/LS	ALS	SP	Comments
Strassman, Marcia	1948-	5	10	10	10	"Welcome Back Kotter"
Strathairn, David	1949-	5	10	10	10	"Matewan"
Strauss, Peter	1947-	10	20	25	30	"The Jericho Mile"
Strauss, Robert	1913-1975	32	50	50	60	"Stalag 17"
Streep, Meryl	1949-	25	50	60	65	"Sophie's Choice"
Streisand, Barbra	1942-					(see Music section)
Stringfield, Sherry	1967-	15	25	30	35	"ER"
Stritch, Elaine	1925-	5	10	10	10	"September"
Stroheim, Erich von	1885-1957	195	400		475	"Greed," "Sunset Boulevard"
Struthers, Sally	1948-	5	10	15	15	"All in the Family"
Stuart, Gloria	1909-	15	30	30	30	"Titanic," "Time Out For Murder"
Sturges, Preston	1898-1959	30	55	50	60	"The Great McGinty," "Palm..."
Styne, Jule	1905-1994	30	50	60	55	"It's Magic," composer, pianist
Sullavan, Margaret	1911-1960	55	100	200	165	"Three Comrades"
Sullivan, Ed	1901-1974	35	100		150	"The Ed Sullivan Show"
Sullivan, Barry	1912-1994	15	25	40	30	"Lady in the Dark"
Sullivan, Susan	1944-	5	10	15	15	"Falcon Crest"
Sullivan, Tom	1947-	5	10	10	10	Actor, singer
Sutherland, Donald	1934-	10	20	25	25	"Ordinary People"
Sutherland, Kiefer	1966-	10	25	25	30	"24"
Sutton, Grady	1908-	10	20	20	20	Character actor, "Alice Adams"
Suvari, Mena	1979-	10	25		25	"American Beauty"
Suzman, Janet	1939-	5	10	10	12	"Nicholas and Alexandra"
Svenson, Bo	1941-	5	10	10	10	"Walking Tall"
Swain, Dominique	1980-	5	10		15	"Lolita"
Swank, Hilary	1974-	15	30		35	"Boys Don't Cry"
Swanson, Gloria	1897-1983	50	200		150	"Sunset Boulevard," RS
Swarthout, Gladys	1904-1969	30	65	70	70	"Champagne Waltz," opera
Swayze, Patrick	1952-	20	50	50	65	"Dirty Dancing"
Sweeney, D.B.	1961-	10	15	15	25	"The Cutting Edge"
Sweet, Blanche	1895-1986	30	45	40	50	"The Lonedale Operator"
Swenson, Inga	1932-	5	10	10	10	"Benson"
Swit, Loretta	1937-	10	20	25	30	"M*A*S*H"
Switzer, Carl "Alfalfa"	1927-1959	340			700	"Our Gang" member

The Three Stooges

* The biggest issue surrounding signatures of The Three Stooges is understanding the lineup so that material can be dated and valued properly.

* Originally formed in 1925, The Three Stooges consisted of Moe Howard (1897-1975), his brother Shemp Howard (1895-1955) and Larry Fine (1902-1975). In 1932, Shemp was then replaced by his brother Curly Howard (1903-1952). When health problems forced Curly to leave the group, Shemp rejoined in 1946. When Shemp died in 1955, Joe Besser (1907-1988) replaced him. Joe DeRita ('Curly Joe," 1909-1993) then replaced Besser in 1959.

* The most sought after iteration of the group is Moe, Larry and Curly Howard and it is also the most expensive even when they signed only their first names, which was common.

* Individually, the signature of Curly Howard is worth more than that of both Moe and Larry's combined.

* When each member signed separately, they often used their last name.

Taylor, Elizabeth

* A gifted actress, Taylor established an impressive film resume including "Cat On A Hot Tin Roof," "Cleopatra," "Butterfield 8" and "Who's Afraid of Virginia Woolf."

* She was responsive to autograph requests early in her career, however as her popularity grew the chances of acquiring an authentic signature diminished.

* Once her personal life became front-page tabloid news she, along with whomever she was with at the time - often Richard Burton, became reclusive.

* Throughout her career she has used various methods to respond to her fan mail including stamped signatures, facsimile signed photographs and even ghost signers.

* While documents that include her signature are often expensive, they may be your only alternative for acquiring an authentic autograph.

Name	DB/DD	Sig.DS/LS	ALS	SP	Comments
T, Mr. (Lawrence Tero)	1952-	5	10	10	15	"The A-Team"
Takei, George	1939-	15	20	25	25	"Star Trek"
Talbot, Lyle	1904-1994	20	40	40	50	"The Bob Cummings Show"
Talmadge, Constance	1898-1973	40	60	75	80	Actor
Talmadge, Norma	1893-1957	60	175	260	150	"Secrets," "Camille"
Tamblyn, Russ	1934-	5	10	20	20	"West Side Story"
Tambor, Jeffrey	1944-	5	10	10	15	"Hill Street Blues"
Tamiroff, Akim	1899-1972	40	50	75	80	"The Genral Died at Dawn"
Tandy, Jessica	1909-1994	40	50	65	75	SP w/m.Cronyn - $115
Tarantino, Quentin	1963-	25	50	75	60	"Pulp Fiction," director, writer
Tate, Sharon	1943-1969	275	500		750	"Valley of the Dolls"
Taylor, Deems	1886-1966	45	80	75	90	"Fantasia" narrator, journalist
Taylor, Elizabeth	1932-	185			425	FA, sec. sig. are common
Taylor, Estelle	1899-1958	20	30	45	50	"The Ten Commandments"
Taylor, Lili	1967-	5	10	10	10	"Mystic Pizza"
Taylor, Robert	1911-1969	40	150		175	"Magnificent Obsession"
Taylor, Rod	1929-	5	15	20	15	"The Time Machine," RS
Temple, Shirley	1928-	25	50	75	65	Early 1936 FDC - $275
Tennant, Victoria	1950-	10	20	20	25	"L.A. Story"
Thalberg, Irving	1899-1936	300	500	750	525	MGM artistic dir., scarce
Theron, Charlize	1975-	10	20		25	"The Cider House Rules"
Thicke, Alan	1947-	5	10	10	10	"Growing Pains," RS
Thiessen, Tiffany Amber	1974-	20	40	35	50	
Thomas, Betty	1948-	5	10	10	15	"Hill Street Blues," RS
Thomas, Danny	1914-1991	25	50		60	"The Jazz Singer," TV actor
Thomas, Dave	1949-	5	10	10	12	"SCTV"
Thomas, Henry	1972-	5	10	10	15	"E.T., the Extra-Terrestrial"
Thomas, Jay	1948-	5	10	10	15	"Murphy Brown"
Thomas, Jonathan T.	1981-	25	50	50	50	"Home Improvement"
Thomas, Kristin Scott	1960-	20	40	40	45	"The English Patient"
Thomas, Marlo	1938-	5	10	20	20	"That Girl"
Thomas, Philip Michael	1949-	20	35	30	40	"Miami Vice"
Thomas, Richard	1951-	5	10	20	20	"The Waltons"
Thomas, William T.	1931-1980	60	150	200	125	"Our Gang," "Buckwheat"
Thompson, Emma	1959-	20	50	45	65	"Howards End,"RS

Name	DB/DD	Sig.DS/LS	ALS	SP	Comments
Thompson, Lea	1951-	5	10	15	15	"Back to the Future"
Thompson, Sada	1929-	5	10	10	10	"Family"
Thorne-Smith, Court.	1968-	15	30	30	35	"Melrose Place"
Thornton, Billy Bob	1955-	30	60	135	75	"Sling Blade," screenwriter
Thurman, Uma	1970-	25	60	50	60	"Dangerous Liaisons"
Tibbett, Lawrence	1896-1960	40	125	150	130	"The Rogue Song," opera
Tiegs, Cheryl	1947-	10	15	20	25	Model, RS
Tierney, Gene	1920-1991	25	45	50	50	"Tobacco Road"
Tierney, Lawrence	1919-	10	20	25	25	"Dillinger," "Born to Kill"
Tiermey, Maura	1965-	10	20		20	"ER"
Tilly, Meg	1960-	10	15	15	20	"The Big Chill"
Tilton, Charlene	1958-	10	20	25	30	"Dallas"
Tobias, George	1901-1980	60	130	185	145	"Sergeant York," "Mildred..."
Tobin, Genevieve	1901-	15	30	30	30	"Easy to Love," "Zaza"
Todd, Ann	1909-1993	25	40	45	45	"The Seventh Veil," "Daybreak"
Todd, Richard	1919-	80	125	220	150	"The Hasty Heart," "The Dam..."
Todd, Thelma	1905-1935	200	275	400	500	"Monkey Business"
Tolkan, James	1931-	5	10	10	12	"Back to the Future"
Tomei, Marisa	1964-	20	40	40	45	"My Cousin Vinny"
Tomlin, Lily	1939-	10	20	25	25	"Rowan & Martin's Laugh-In"
Tone, Franchot	1905-1968	35	100	100	75	"Mutiny on the Bounty"
Toomey, Regis	1898-1991	20	40	40	45	"G-Men," "Dive Bomber"
Torn, Rip	1931-	15	25	20	25	"Sweet Bird of Youth"
Totter, Audrey	1918-	10	20	20	20	"The Girl With ... Voices"
Toumanova, Tamara	1917-	30	80	125	125	"Torn Curtain," Russian ballerina
Townsend, Robert	1957-	10	20	25	25	"Hollywood Shuffle"
Tracy, Lee	1898-1968	18	30	35	35	"The Best Man," "Bombshell"
Tracy, Spencer	1900-1967	175	425		350	Sig. w/ Hepburn - $800
Traubel, Helen	1899-1972	45	90	100	110	"Deep in my Heart"
Travanti, Daniel J.	1940-	5	10	15	20	"Hill Street Blues"
Travers, Bill	1922-	5	10	10	10	"Born Free"
Travers, Henry	1874-1965	200	375	545	400	"Mrs. Miniver," IAWL
Travis, Nancy	1961-	5	10		10	"Three Men and a Baby"
Travolta, John	1954-	35	125		75	"Saturday Night Fever," RS, FA
Treacher, Arthur	1894-1975	25	45	50	60	"Mary Poppins," TV sidekick
Trebek, Alex	1940-	5	10	10	10	"Jeopardy!," RS
Trevor, Claire	1909-	30	60		75	"Key Largo," "Dead End"
Tripplehorn, Jeanne	1959-	20	35	40	50	"The Firm"
Trump, Marla Maples	1963-	5	10	15	25	"The Will Rogers Follies"
Tucker, Chris	1971-	15	25		30	"Rush Hour"
Tucker, Forrest	1919-1986	30	45	50	50	"The Yearling," "F Troop" - TV
Tucker, Michael	1944-	5	10	10	15	"L.A. Law"
Tucker, Sophie	1884-1966	40	75	75	75	"Honky Tonk"
Tune, Tommy	1939-	10	15	15	30	Actor, director, dancer, RS
Turlington, Christy	1969-	5	10	15	25	Supermodel
Turner, Janine	1963-	20	40	50	50	"Northern Exposure"
Turner, Kathleen	1954-	10	25	30	40	"Romancing the Stone"
Turner, Lana	1920-1995	40	100	125	100	"Peyton Place"
Turturro, John	1957-	5	10	10	10	"Barton Fink"
Twiggy (Lesley Hornby)	1949-	20	25	30	35	"The Boy Friend"
Tyler, Liv	1977-	25	50	50	70	"Stealing Beauty"
Tyson, Cicely	1933-	10	15	20	20	"The Auto... Miss Jane Pittman"

Temple, Shirley

* A child actor of the thirties, Shirley Temple captured our hearts in numerous films including "The Little Colonel," "Curly Top"and "The Little Princess."

* She has always been an obliguing signer until recently when she decided to discontinue the practice.

* Since her 1950 marriage to Charles Black, she has always signed "Shirley Temple Black."

* Most sought by collectors are early examples of her signature - just "Shirley Temple," especially on vintage photographs.

* She has not only had an incredible film career, but also a prestigious public service role as an Ambassador for this country.

Travolta, John

* Travolta languished for nearly a decade in forgettable and unpopular films until "Pulp Fiction" catapulted him into the spotlight once again.

* He made his stage debut with "Who Will Save the Plow" in 1966 and his film debut in "The Devil's Rain" in 1975.

* Travolta's response to his fans is extraordinary, always taking the time to talk with them and to sign autographs.

* Prior to "911," it was reported that he has used ghost signers to handle much of his mail, but after seeing him in-person those claims can be dismissed.

* As America fights terrorism, Travolta – like many stars, has turned to a fan mail service to screen his mail.

Name	Date	DB/DD	Sig.DS/LS	ALS	SP	Comments
Uggams, Leslie	1943-	5	10	15	15	"Roots," singer
Ullman, Tracey	1959-	10	20	25	30	"The Tracey Ullman Show"
Ullmann, Liv	1939-	5	10	25	30	"Persona," RS
Umeki, Miyoshi	1929-	250			400	"Sayonara," "Flower Drum..."
Underwood, Blair	1964-	10	15	20	20	"L.A. Law"
Urich, Robert	1946-2002	25	50		50	"Spenser: For Hire"
Ustinov, Peter	1921-	35	100	65	70	"Spartacus," "Topkapi"
Vaccaro, Brenda	1939-	5	10	10	12	"Midnight Cowboy," RS
Vadim, Roger	1928-	15	25	30	35	Movie director
Valentine, Scott	1958-	5	10	10	10	"Family Ties"
Valentino, Rudolph	1895-1926	800	2465	1750	1830	Silent film legend
Vallee, Rudy	1901-1986	20	40	40	40	"The Bachelor," singer
Valli, Alida	1921-	25	40	45	50	"The Third Man," signs "Valli"
Vallone, Raf	1918-	5	10	10	10	"Obsession"
Van Ark, Joan	1943-	5	10	10	10	"Knots Landing"
Van Damme, J.-Claude	1960-	25	130	215	60	"Kickboxer," FA
Van Der Beek, James	1977-	10	20		25	"Dawson's Creek"
Van Devere, Trish	1945-	5	10	10	10	"The Day of the Dolphin"
Van Doren, Mamie	1931-	15	20	25	35	"Girls School"

Name	DB/DD	Sig.DS/LS	ALS	SP	Comments
Van Dyke, Dick	1925-	10	20	25	25	"The Dick Van Dyke Show," RS
Van Dyke, Jerry	1931-	5	10	15	20	"Coach"
Van Fleet, Jo	1919-1996	10	20	35	40	"East of Eden"
Van Patten, Dick	1928-	5	10	10	10	"Eight Is Enough," RS
Van Peebles, Mario	1957-	5	10	15	15	"Posse," s. of Melvin
Van Peebles, Melvin	1932-	5	10	15	15	Actor, writer, composer
Van Susteren, Greta	1954-	5	10		15	CNN
Van, Bobby	1930-1980	35	60	65	65	TV actor, "Kiss Me, Kate"
Vance, Vivian	1913-1979	200	225		350	"I Love Lucy"
Varney, Jim	1949-2000	15	25	35	30	"Ernest Goes..."
Vaughn, Robert	1932-	10	15	15	15	"The Man From U.N.C.L.E." - TV
Vaughn, Vince	1970-	10	20		20	"Swingers"
Veidt, Conrad	1893-1943	100	150	150	300	"Casablanca"
Velez, Eddie	1958-	5	10	10	10	"Extremities"
Velez, Lupe	1908-1944	80	140	165	200	"Mexican Spitfire"
Velijohnson, Reginald	1952-	5	10	10	10	"Family Matters"
Vendela (Kirsebom)	1967-	10	20	20	25	Supermodel
Vera, Ellen	1926-1981	25	40	40	50	"On the Town," "Three Little..."
Verdon, Gwen	1925-2000	15	25	30	30	"Damn Yankees"
Vereen, Ben	1946-	10	20	30	20	"Roots"
Veruschka	1943-	5	10	15	25	"Blow Up," model
Villechaize, Herve	1943-1993	45	75		75	"Fantasy Island"
Vincent, Jan-Michael	1944-	5	10	15	15	"The Mechanic"
Vinson, Helen	1907-	15	25	35	40	"Torrid Zone," "Private Words"
Visnuc, Goran	1972-	10	20		20	"ER"
Voight, Jon	1938-	20	40	40	50	"Midnight Cowboy"
Von Stroheim, Erich	1885-1957	165	350	450	500	"Sunset Boulevard," director
Von Sydow, Max	1929-	15	25	35	30	"The Exorcist"

Wayne, John

* "The Duke" was a screen icon and gave many brilliant performances in films such as "Stagecoach," "Sands of Iwo Jima" and "True Grit."

* His prolific career attracted the attention of many, forcing him to use a variety of methods to handle his fan mail.

* Wayne was often unpredictable in-person to autograph requests and could comply or simply walk away depending upon his mood at the time.

* He was more obliguing to requests later in his life than earlier in his career.

* Collectors should look for two things in an original Wayne signature. First, the double backed formation of the "o" in John, which is often cited by autograph collectors, and the "yn" combination in Wayne. The creation of the latter often finds the "n" dipping below the signature baseline.

Name	DB/DD	Sig.DS/LS	ALS	SP	Comments
Waggoner, Lyle	1935-	5	10	10	10	"Wonder Woman"
Wagner, Jack	1959-	5	10	10	15	"General Hospital"
Wagner, Lindsay	1949-	10	15	20	20	"The Bionic Woman," FA
Wagner, Robert	1930-	15	20	25	30	"The Longest Day"
Wahl, Ken	1956-	5	10	10	10	"Wiseguy"
Walburn, Raymond	1887-1969	15	20	25	30	"State of the Union"

Name	DB/DD	Sig.DS/LS	ALS	SP	Comments
Walken, Christopher	1943-	15	30		40	"The Deer Hunter"
Walker, Clint	1927-	5	10	10	15	"Cheyenne"
Walker, Helen	1920-1968	20	35	40	40	"Nightmare Alley," "Impact"
Walker, Jimmie	1948-	5	10	10	10	"Good Times"
Walker, Robert	1918-1951	50	100	175	150	"Strangers on a Train"
Wallace, Mike	1918-	20	40		25	"60 Minutes"
Wallach, Eli	1915-	10	20		25	"The Good, the Bad and..."
Walsh, M.Emmet	1935-	5	10	15	15	"Blood Simple," RS
Walston, Ray	1917-2001	20	35		35	"My Favorite Martian"
Walter, Jessica	1940-	5	10	10	15	"Play Misty for Me"
Walter, Tracey		10	15	15	20	"Batman"
Walters, Barbara	1931-	10	20		25	"20/20," RS
Wanamaker, Sam	1919-	15	30	35	35	"Death on the Nile"
Wanger, Walter	1894-1968	40	130	125	125	"The Trail of the Lonesome..."
Ward, Burt	1946-	15	25	30	30	"Batman"
Ward, Fred	1942-	5	10	10	10	"Henry and June"
Ward, Rachel	1957-	10	20	25	30	"Against All Odds"
Ward, Sela	1956-	15	30	45	65	"Sisters"
Warden, Jack	1920-	5	10	15	20	"Crazy Like a Fox"
Warfield, Marsha	1955-	5	10	15	20	"Night Court"
Warner, David	1941-	5	10	10	10	"The Omen"
Warner, H.B.	1876-1958	35	70	135	105	"Lost Horizon," IAWL
Warner, Julie	1965-	5	10	10	10	"Doc Hollywood"
Warner, Malcolm-Jamal	1970-	10	20	20	20	"The Cosby Show"
Warren, Estella	1978-	10	25		40	Model, "Planet of the Apes"
Warren, Lesley Ann	1946-	5	10	15	20	"Mission: Impossible"
Warrick, Ruth	1915-	15	20	25	25	"Citizen Kane"
Warwick, Robert	1878-1964	25	50	50	55	Silent era actor, "The Sea Hawk"
Washington, Denzel	1954-	25	145	150	65	"Malcolm X," FA
Waters, Ethel	1896-1977	55	110	125	170	"Pinky," singer
Waters, John	1946-	10	20	20	25	"Hairspray," director, writer
Waterson, Sam	1940-	10	15	15	20	"The Killing Fields"
Watson, Emily	1967-	10	20		25	"Breaking the Waves"
Waxman, Al	1934-2001	10	15	25	15	"Cagney and Lacey"
Wayans, Damon	1961-	10	25	25	25	"In Living Color"
Wayne, David	1914-1995	10	20	25	25	"The Three Faces of Eve"
Wayne, John	1907-1979	425	900	960	725	"True Grit," FA, SDS-2X
Wayne, Patrick	1939-	5	10	10	15	"McClintock"
Weathers, Carl	1948-	10	15	20	20	"Rocky"
Weaver, Dennis	1925-	10	15	25	25	"McCloud"
Weaver, Fritz	1926-	5	10	10	10	"Marathon Man"
Weaver, Sigourney	1949-	15	30	40	50	"Alien," "Ghostbusters"
Webb, Clifton	1891-1966	35	50	60	70	"The Razor's Edge"
Webb, Jack	1920-1982	50	100	130	100	"Dragnet," FA
Webb, Veronica	1965-	10	20		20	"Veronica Webb Sight"
Weidler, Virginia	1927-1968	25	40	40	50	"The Philadelphia Story"
Weissmuller, Johnny	1904-1984	150	245		300	"Tarzan,"SP - $265, SDS - $500
Weisz, Rachel	1971-	10	25		25	"The Mummy"
Weitz, Bruce	1943-	5	10	10	15	"Hill Street Blues"
Welch, Raquel (Tejada)	1940-	10	25	25	50	"One Million Years B.C."
Weld, Tuesday	1943-	10	15	20	25	"Looking for Mr. Goodbar"
Welk, Lawrence	1903-1992	25	50		35	"The Lawrence Welk Show"

Name	DB/DD	Sig.DS/LS	ALS	SP	Comments
Weller, Paul	1947-	5	10	10	15	"Robocop"
Welles, Orson	1915-1985	100	500		275	"Citizen Kane," SP - $325
Wellman, William	1896-1975	40	75	75	80	"Wings," "Battleground"
Wendt, George	1948-	10	20	25	30	"Cheers"
West, Adam	1929-	10	25	30	30	"Batman"
West, Mae	1892-1980	75	150	300	250	"My Little Chickadee," FA
Westheimer, Ruth	1928-	5	10	15	10	"Ask Dr. Ruth"
Westley, Helen	1875-1942	50	125	175	100	"Dimples," "Heidi"
Whalen, Michael	1902-1974	20	35	35	40	"Ten Little Indians," "Country..."
Whaley, Frank	1963-	10	15	15	15	"The Doors"
Whalley, Joanne	1964-	5	10	10	12	"Willow"
Wheeler, Bert	1895-1968	30	60	100	75	"Ziegfeld" star, comedy team
Whelan, Arleen	1915-1993	12	25	25	25	"Kidnapped," "Dear Wife"
Whelchel, Lisa	1963-	5	10	10	10	"The Facts of Life"
Whitaker, Forest	1961-	10	20	10	20	"The Crying Game"
Whitaker, Johnny	1959-	5	10	10	15	"Family Affair"
White, Betty	1922-	10	15	20	25	"The Golden Girls"
White, Jaleel	1976-	5	20		20	"Family Matters"
White, Jesse	1918-1997	15	25	30	30	Maytag repair man, "Harvey"
White, Vanna	1957-	5	10	10	15	"Wheel of Fortune"
Whitelaw, Billie	1932-	10	15	15	20	"Charlie Bubbles"
Whitford, Bradley	1959-	10	25		25	"The West Wing"
Whitman, Stuart	1926-	10	15	20	15	"The Mark," "Cimarron Strip"
Whitmore, James	1921-	10	15	15	20	"Battleground"
Whitney, Eleanor	1917-	5	10	10	15	"Millions in the Air"
Whitty, May	1865-1948	40	60	75	80	"Night Must Fall"
Whorf, Richard	1906-1966	20	35	40	40	"Yankee Doddle Dandy"
Widmark, Richard	1914-	10	25	25	25	"Kiss of Death," "The Alamo"
Wiest, Dianne	1948-	10	20	25	35	"Hannah and Her Sisters"
Wilbur, Crane	1889-1973	30	50	60	75	"The Perils of Pauline"
Wilcox, Larry	1947-	5	10	10	10	"CHiPS"
Wilcoxon, Henry	1905-1984	25	35	40	50	"Cleopatra," assoc. producer
Wilde, Cornel	1915-1989	20	30	35	40	"A Song To Remember"
Wilder, Billy	1906-2002	25	65		55	"The Lost Weekend"
Wilder, Gene	1935-	10	25	40	25	"Young Frankenstein"
Williams, Barry	1954-	5	10	10	12	"The Brady Bunch"
Williams, Billy Dee	1937-	10	20	25	25	"Lady Sings the Blues"
Williams, Cindy	1947-	5	10	15	15	"Laverne & Shirley"
Williams, Clarence III	1939-	5	10	10	15	"The Mod Squad"
Williams, Esther	1923-	10	20	25	25	"Bathing Beauty"
Williams, Jobeth	1953-	10	15	15	20	"The Big Chill"
Williams, Michele	1980-	10	20		20	"Dawson's Creek"
Williams, Montel	1956-	5	10	15	15	"The Montel Williams Show"
Williams, Rhys	1892-1969	25	45	40	45	"The Bells of St. Mary"
Williams, Robin	1952-	25	225	250	65	"Mork and Mindy," RS
Williams, Treat	1951-	5	10	15	15	"Prince of the City"
Williams, Vanessa	1963-	20	40	50	50	"Kiss of the Spider Woman"
Williamson, Kevin	1965-	10	25		20	Screenwriter
Williamson, Nicol	1938-	5	10	10	15	"Excalibur"
Willis, Bruce	1955-	45	150		75	"Die Hard," FA
Wills, Chill	1903-1978	60	75	85	100	"The Alamo," voice of "Francis"
Wilson, August (F. Kittel)	1945-	20	30		30	Playwright, "The Piano Lesson"

Name	DB/DD	Sig.DS/LS	ALS	SP	Comments
Wilson, Demond	1946-	10 15	20	25	"Sanford and Son"
Wilson, Don		10 15	15	15	"The Jack Benny Show"
Wilson, Flip	1933-1998	20 40		40	"The Flip Wilson Show"
Wilson, Luke	1971-	10 20		20	"The Royal Tenenbaums"
Wilson, Marie	1916-1972	20 40	50	65	"Boy Meets Girl"
Wilson, Owen	1968-	10 20		20	"Bottle Rocket"
Winchell, Paul	1922-	15 30	35	40	"The Paul Winchell... Show"
Windom, William	1923-	5 10	15	15	"Murder She Wrote"
Windsor, Claire	1897-1972	15 20	25	25	"Rich Men's Wives," "Money..."
Windsor, Marie	1922-	5 10	15	20	"B" movie star, "Force of Evil"
Winfield, Paul	1940-	5 10	15	15	"Sounder"
Winfrey, Oprah	1954-	20 50		50	"The Oprah Winfrey Show," FA
Wing, Toby	1915-	10 20	25	30	Singer, dancer, "42nd Street"
Winger, Debra	1955-	15 100	30	35	"Terms of Endearment"
Winkler, Henry	1945-	5 10	20	25	"Happy Days"
Winninger, Charles	1884-1969	35 70	60	70	"Show Boat," "Destry Rides..."
Winningham, Mare	1959-	5 10	20	30	"St. Elmo's Fire," RS
Winslet, Kate	1975-	55 150		125	"Titanic," FA, ES
Winters, Jonathan	1925-	10 15	20	20	"The Jonathan Winters Show"
Winters, Shelley	1922-	10 25	25	25	"The Diary of Ann Frank"
Winwood, Estelle	1883-1984	20 40	40	50	British stage actor, "The Swan"
Withers, Jane	1926-	10 15	20	25	Actor
Witherspoon, Reese	1976-	10 25		30	"The Man in the Moon"
Wolf, Scott	1968-	15 30	40	40	"Party of Five"
Wong, Anna May	1907-1961	100 175	175	200	"The Shanghai Express"
Wong, B.D.	1962-	5 10	10	12	"M. Butterfly"
Wood, Elijah	1981-	15 25		30	"The War"
Wood, Natalie	1938-1991	125		350	"Miracle on 34th Street," RS
Woodard, Alfre	1953-	5 10	10	10	"Cross Creek"
Woods, James	1947-	15 25	35	50	"Ghosts of Mississippi"
Woodward, Edward	1930-	10 15	15	15	"The Equalizer"
Woodward, Joanne	1930-	20 75	70	35	"The Three Faces of Eve"
Woolley, Monty	1888-1963	40 115		120	"The Man Who Came to ..."
Woollsey, Robert	1889-1938	35 50	50	70	"Rio Rita" - stage, "High Flyers"
Worley, Jo Anne	1937-	5 10	10	10	"Laugh-In"
Wray, Fay	1907-	30 60	125	65	"King Kong"
Wright, Max	1943-	5 10	10	10	"ALF"
Wright, Steven	1955-	5 10	10	15	Comedian
Wright, Teresa	1918-	25 50	75	65	"The Pride of the Yankees"
Wuhl, Robert	1951-	5 10	10	15	"Bull Durham"
Wyatt, Jane	1911-	5 10	15	15	"Lost Horizon"
Wycherly, Margaret	1881-1956	30 50	60	60	"White Heat," stage actress
Wyle, Noah	1971-	20 40	40	45	"ER"
Wyman, Jane	1914-	20 100		55	"Johnny Belinda," SB - $45
Wynn, Ed	1886-1966	75 155		150	"The Diary of Anne Frank"
Wynn, Keenan	1916-1986	20 30	40	40	"Kiss Me Kate," s. of Ed Wynn
Wynter, Dana	1930-	10 15	15	15	"Invasion of ... Snatchers"

Willis, Bruce

* Willis made his stage debut in the 1977 production of "Heaven and Earth."

* He and his family live in the once quiet town of Hailey, Idaho, in the Rockies. Perpetuating the theory "if you build it they will come," Willis owns nearly every building on Main Street. It is there and only there that you may get an authentic signature, but don't hold your breath.

* Most often associated with the "Die Hard" film series, Willis hates signing autographs and will go out of his way to avoid the task.

* All of his mail is handled by a fan mail service that responds with a facsimile signed photograph.

* Because Willis doesn't sign, forgers sign for him and the market is littered with fake material. Collectors should exercise extreme caution when purchasing any item supposedly signed by Willis, especially photographs in key roles.

Wood, Natalie

* A brilliant actress who appeared in film such as "Miracle on 34th Street," "Rebel Without a Cause," "West Side Story" and "Splendor in the Grass."

* She was very responsive to her fans and signed autographs both in-person and through mail requests.

* Her signature is highly sought by collectors and continues to reach new price levels each year.

Name	DB/DD	Sig.DS/LS	ALS	SP	Comments
York, Michael	1942-	10	15	20	20	"Logan's Run," illegible sig.
Young, Carlton	1907-1971	15	30		30	"Wyatt Earp" - TV
Young, Clara Kimball	1890-1960	50	100	150	85	"Camille," "Trilby"
Young, Gig	1913-1978	35	65	125	75	"They Shoot Horses..."
Young, Loretta	1913-2000	30	60	100	70	"The Farmer's Daughter"
Young, Robert	1907-1998	25	40	65	50	"Marcus Welby, M.D."
Young, Roland	1887-1953	20	40	45	50	"Topper"
Young, Sean	1959-	5	10		20	"No Way Out," RS
Youngman, Henny	1906-1998	15	25	40	30	Actor, comedian
Yurka, Blanche	1887-1974	30	50	75	55	"A Night to Remember," opera
Zadora, Pia	1956-	5	10	15	20	"Naked Gun 33 1/3"
Zahn, Paula	1956-	5	10		10	"CBS This Morning"
Zal, Roxana	1969-	5	10	10	15	"Something About Amelia"
Zanuck, Darryl F.	1902-1979	60	275		100	"The Grapes of Wrath"
Zellweger, Renee	1969-	15	35		60	"Jerry Maguire"
Zemeckis, Robert	1951-	15	30		30	"Forrest Gump"
Zeta-Jones, Catherine	1969-	20	40		50	"The Mask of Zorro"
Ziering, Ian	1964-	15	30	30	30	"Beverly Hills 90210"
Zimbalist, Efrem, Jr.	1923-	10	15	20	25	"77 Sunset Strip," "The F.B.I."
Zimbalist, Stephanie	1956-	10	20	25	25	"Remington Steele"
Zimbalist, Jason	1959-	10	20		25	"Night Court"
Zmed, Adrian	1954-	5	10	15	15	"T.J. Hooker"
Zorina, Vera	1917-	20	35	35	45	"Follow the Boys," opera
Zukor, Adolph	1873-1976	75	155	220	165	Pioneer movie executive
Zuniga, Daphne	1962-	15	30	45	55	"Melrose Place," FA

FIRST LADIES OF THE UNITED STATES

WHAT YOU NEED TO KNOW

* Similar to the Presidents, the popularity of the First Lady varies with each administration, as does her signing habits.

* Not all presidential widows were granted the franking privilege, in fact Mrs. Lincoln was so disliked by Congress, that it took her years for approval. On December 18, 1973 Congress finally permitted every living presidential widow to have the franking privilege.

* Similar to their husbands, many First Ladies utilized the services of machines to sign their name. Both Betty Ford and Pat Nixon were notorious for having their correspondence machine signed.

MARKET FACTS

* The signatures (Sig.) of these distinguished women have out paced the autographs of the Presidency by nearly two fold. As an entity in the autograph market, signatures of the First Ladies have out paced all but four popular areas of collecting.

* It is nearly impossible to form a complete set of First Lady autographs.

MARKET TRENDS

* Administration dated autograph material has only genuinely impacted the value of Jacqueline Kennedy (two fold) and Eleanor Roosevelt correspondence. Whether or not this slow trend will continue, or migrate into other administrations, remains to be seen.

A Brief Overview of First Ladies

Washington, Martha Dandridge Custis

* Martha was a widow of a prominent planter Daniel Parke Custis. By him she had four children, two of whom survived childhood.

* She was a gracious hostess and first lady.

* The Mount Vernon Ladies Association purchased many of her letters that have

appeared in the market.

db/dd	Sig.	(married), state of origin, sons and daughters
1731-1802	8650	(1759), VA, No sons or daughters

Adams, Abigail Smith

* A prolific writer, Abigail corresponded often with her husband during the Revolution.

* Abigail was an early heroine of the women's liberation movement.

* Her health seemed to always be in question. She returned to Massachusetts in 1801.

* As the First Lady she was the first to preside over the White House.

* During her later years she renewed correspondence with Thomas Jefferson.

db/dd	Sig.	DS/LS	ALS	
1744-1818	525	1825	7000	(1772), MA, S-3, D-2

Jefferson, Martha Wayles Skelton

* Few written examples exist.

* Her signature in any form is considered extremely rare.

* She died 19 years before her husband's term as president.

db/dd	Sig.	DS/LS	ALS	
1748-1782				VA, D-2, PU

Madison, Dorothea "Dolly" Payne Todd

* Charming and vivacious, she occasionally served as official hostess during the Jefferson administration.

* After her husband's death at Montpelier, she returned to Washington and its social circuit.

* To pay her creditors she sold Madison's papers to Congress.

* She loved poetry and its not unusual for an unsigned handwritten piece to enter the market.

db/dd	Sig.	DS/LS	ALS	
1768-1849	775	1850	3945	(1794), NC, No sons or daughters

Monroe, Elizabeth Kortright

* Elizabeth Kortright was the daughter of an officer in the British army.

* As First Lady she suffered from an unidentified chronic ailment that forced her into seclusion.

* Her elder daughter, Eliza often acted for her as official hostess.

* Elizabeth, in stark contrast to Dolley Madison, did nothing to cultivate the Washington social circuit, and as such was unpopular and reclusive.

* Her writings, in any form, are considered extremely rare.

db/dd	Sig.	DS/LS	ALS	
1768-1830				(1786), NY, S-0, D-2, also dec. infant, PU

Adams, Louisa Catherine

* Louisa Adams, the only foreign-born First Lady, suffered from numerous physical problems including migraine headaches and bouts with depression.

* Similar to her predecessor she became withdrawn and reclusive.

* Although she was a prolific journal writer, she seemed to correspond only to close friends.

db/dd	Sig.	DS/LS	ALS	
1775-1852	240	500	1250	(1797), MD, b. London, S-3, D-1

Jackson, Rachel Donelson Robards

* Rachel Jackson was a controversial, popular, and dynamic women.

* She suffered from heart trouble and her sudden death in 1828 seemed to have been brought about by battles with the press over her controversial past.

* Much of her correspondence was dictated and seldom signed in her hand.

db/dd	Sig.	DS/LS	ALS	
1767-1828	575	2025	6750	(1791), VA, No sons or daughters, n. adopted

Van Buren, Hannah Hoes

* Shy, and occasionally withdrawn, Hannah Hoes Van Buren contracted tuberculosis and died at the young age of 35.

* Her writings in any form are considered extremely scarce, if not unobtainable.

db/dd	Sig.	DS/LS	ALS	
1783-1819				(1807), NY, S-4, extremely scarce!, PU

Harrison, Anna Tuthill Symmes

* Anna Harrison was the only woman to be both the wife of one president and the grandmother of another.

* Because of her husband's sudden death she never occupied the White House.

* She became the first recipient of a president's widow pension.

db/dd	Sig.	DS/LS	ALS	
1775-1864	700	1100	2450	(1795), NJ, S-5, D-4, FF - $975

Tyler, Letitia Christian

* Devoted to her family, Letitia Tyler was quiet, shy and often withdrawn.

* She suffered a paralytic stroke in 1839 that left her an invalid.

* Her First Lady duties were confined to the upstairs quarters of the White House where she remained a recluse.

db/dd	Sig.	DS/LS	ALS	
1790-1842)				(1813), VA, S-3, D-4, plus a deceased infant, PU

Tyler, Julia Gardiner

* Julia Tyler, in stark contrast to her predecessor, was a young and vivacious First Lady who adored her social role in Washington.

db/dd	Sig.	DS/LS	ALS	
1820-1889	200	500	650	(1844), NY, S-5, D-2

Polk, Sarah Childress

* Charming, intelligent, yet conservative, Sarah Polk welcomed her role as First Lady.

* In her role, Sarah hosted the first Thanksgiving dinner at the White House.

db/dd	Sig.	DS/LS	ALS	SP	
1803-1891	425	650	1100	1200	(1824), TN, No sons or daughters

Taylor, Margaret Mackall Smith

* A reclusive First Lady, "Peggy" Taylor was a semi invalid who found solace in the confines of the second floor of the White House.

* Her daughter Mrs. Betty Bliss attended to the role of official hostess.

* Perhaps the scarcest of all First Lady signatures, less than a handful are known to exist.

db/dd	Sig.	DS/LS	ALS	SP	
1788-1852					(1810), MD, S-1, D-3, only 1 exists, PU

Fillmore, Abigail Powers

* Abigail Fillmore was a teacher and former instructor of her husband.

* The Fillmores shared a love for books and were responsible for the establishment of the first permanent library at the White House.

*Susceptible to sickness, her role as First Lady was often filled by her daughter.

* Surprisingly little autographed material of hers has found its way into the market.

db/dd	Sig.	DS/LS	ALS	
1798-1853				(1826), NY, S-1, D-1, PU

Fillmore, Caroline McIntosh

* Caroline Fillmore was the widow of a prominent businessman.

* She married and settled with the former President in Buffalo, New York.

db/dd	Sig.	DS/LS	ALS	
1813-1881	540	800	925	(1858), NJ, No sons or daughters

Pierce, Jane Means Appleton

* Shy and somewhat melancholy, Jane Pierce became depressed and reclusive following the death of her son Bennie in 1853.

* Resentful at husband's ambition, the two were often at odds with one another.

* She withdrew from the role of First Lady and opted for the seclusion of the upstairs quarters at the White House for nearly two years.

db/dd	Sig.	DS/LS	ALS	
1806-1863	230	475	1000	(1834), NH, S-3

(Buchanan) Lane (Johnston), Harriet

* President Buchanan did not marry, and the role of the First Lady was given to his orphaned niece Harriet Lane.

db/dd	Sig.	DS/LS	ALS	SP	
1830-1906	125	250	350	275	Buchanan did not marry, Lane was his niece.

Lincoln, Mary Todd

* Although she was personable, popular and articulate (spoke French fluently), Mary Lincoln suffered mental instability throughout her life.

* Her irrational behavior, no doubt enhanced by the death of two of her sons, led to hallucinations and commitment to a mental institution.

db/dd	Sig.	DS/LS	ALS	SP	
1818-1882	325	1100	9000	3000	(1842), KY, S-4, FF $4,000, ALS - $16500

Johnson, Eliza McCardle

* Marrying at a younger age than any other First Lady, Eliza Johnson became a semi-invalid in middle age.

* Too ill to handle the role of First Lady, she joined her husband at the White House, but remained in a room on the second floor. She would appear publicly on only two occasions.

db/dd	Sig.	DS/LS	
1810-1876	650	1275	(1827), TN, S-3, D-2

Grant, Julia Boggs Dent

* Julia Grant loved the role of First Lady and entertained lavishly at the White House.

db/dd	Sig.	DS/LS	ALS	SP	
1826-1902	150	400	750	500	(1848), MO, S-3, D-1, ALS content - $1500

Hayes, Lucy Ware Webb

* An extremely active First Lady, Lucy Hayes was the first in her position to have graduated from college.

* "Lemonade Lucy" was active in the temperance movement and instituted the customary White House Easter egg roll.

db/dd	Sig.	DS/LS	ALS	SP	
1831-1889	250	300	400	675	(1852), OH, S-7, D-1

Garfield, Lucretia Rudolph

* Lucretia "Crete" Garfield was a teacher whose appetite for knowledge seemed endless.

* Her intention of restoring the White House and its furnishings was ended when she contracted malaria.

* She became withdrawn following her husband's assassination.

db/dd	Sig.	DS/LS	ALS	SP	
1832-1918	125	175	200	200	(1858), OH, S-4, D-1

Arthur, Ellen Lewis Herndon

* Ellen "Nell" Arthur, daughter of a distinguished naval officer, had a passion for music that was hampered often by her poor health.

* She died of pneumonia at the young age of 42.

* She didn't live long enough to see her husband become President.

* Her autographed material in any form is virtually unobtainable.

db/dd	Sig.	DS/LS	ALS	
1837-1880	600	1000	1200	(1859), VA, S-2, D-1

Cleveland, Frances Folsom

* Frances Cleveland was the only First Lady married in the White House.

* The youngest ever in her role, Frances was the only First Lady to preside during two nonconsecutive administrations.

* She was the first presidential widow to remarry.

* Among First Ladies, she is perhaps the most common of all to be found in check form.

db/dd	Sig.	DS/LS	ALS	SP	
1864-1947	60	100	275	225	(1886), NY, S-2, D-3

Harrison, Caroline Lavina Scott

* Caroline Harrison renovated the White House, installed electricity and even put up the first Christmas tree in her new residence.

db/dd	Sig.	DS/LS	ALS	SP	
1832-1892	175	275	1180	750	(1853), OH, S-1, D-1

Harrison, Mary Scott Lord

* A widow, Mary Harrison married the former President and survived him by nearly a half century.

db/dd	Sig.	DS/LS	ALS	SP	
1858-1948	75	140	180	125	(1896), PA, D-1

McKinley, Ida Saxton

* Polished and charming, Ida McKinley tragically developed epilepsy and became fully dependent upon her husband.

* As an invalid she passed time by sewing. Her First Lady role fell to that of the wife of the vice president, Mrs. Garret Hobart.

db/dd	Sig.	DS/LS	ALS	SP	
1847-1907	400	625	975	450	(1871), OH, D-2

Roosevelt, Alice Hathaway Lee

* Intelligent and charming, Alice Roosevelt died from Bright's disease and childbirth complications at the young age of 22.

* Her signature in any form is incredibly scarce.

db/dd	Sig.	DS/LS	ALS	SP	
1861-1884					(1880), MA, D-1, very scarce, PU

Roosevelt, Edith Kermit Carow

* Edith Roosevelt, had a gift for organization and used it to remodel the White House.

db/dd	Sig.	DS/LS	ALS	SP	
1861-1948	55	250	365	400	(1886), CT, S-4, D-1

Taft, Helen Herron

* Helen "Nellie" Taft was the first wife of a President to ride alongside him down Pennsylvania Avenue on Inauguration Day.

* The Washington Tidal Basin is also a monument to her memory as it is she who arranged for the planting of 3,000 Japanese cherry trees.

* Two months into the Taft's term, she suffered a stroke that greatly impaired her speech.

* She is the only woman to be the wife of both a President and Supreme Court Justice

db/dd	Sig.	DS/LS	ALS	SP	
1861-1943	125	230	575	1000	(1886), OH, S-2, D-1

Wilson, Ellen Louise Axson

* Cultured in the fine arts, Ellen Wilson spent many hours in an art studio set up on the third floor of the White House.

* She succumbed to Bright's disease at the White House in 1914.

db/dd	Sig.	DS/LS	ALS	SP	
1860-1914	125	375	600	400	(1885), GA, D-3

Wilson, Edith Bolling Galt

* A gallant example during World War I, Edith Wilson was a respected and active First Lady.

* Following the president's stroke in 1919, she became pivotal in his recovery and essential as his "office manager" – she screened his work.

db/dd	Sig.	DS/LS	ALS	SP	
1872-1961	85	225	280	200	(1915), VA, No children, FF - $100

Harding, Florence King De Wolfe

* Florence "Flossie" Harding, with her somewhat "rough edges", managed to be an effective circulation manager for her husband's successful newspaper.

* As First Lady she hosted elegant parties and felt comfortable mingling with guests, all while living through a rough marriage.

db/dd	Sig.	DS/LS	ALS	SP	
1860-1924	75	200	325	200	(1891), OH, No sons or daughters, WHC - $85

Coolidge, Grace Anna Goodhue

* Well-educated and charming, Grace Coolidge was a popular hostess, effective First Lady and altruistic in her crusading on behalf of the deaf and the Red Cross.

db/dd	Sig.	DS/LS	ALS	SP	
1879-1957	75	230	250	150	(1905), VT, S-2

Hoover, Lou Henry

* Multilingual, intelligent, charming and often spontaneous, Lou Hoover was an effective First Lady.

* She was always gracious to autograph collectors.

db/dd	Sig.	DS/LS	ALS	SP	
1875-1944	115	175	250	200	(1899), IA, S-2, WHC - $125

Roosevelt, Anna Eleanor Roosevelt

* One of the most loved and respected First Ladies, Eleanor Roosevelt was well-educated, articulate and extremely active in government affairs.

* When her husband was stricken with polio, she became the cornerstone to his recovery.

* She transformed the function of First Lady to a role of substance over distinction.

* Her signature in numerous forms – especially TLS, is abundant in the autograph market.

db/dd	Sig.	DS/LS	ALS	SP	
1884-1962	65	250	450	225	(1905), NY, S-4, D-1, WHC - $150

Truman, Elizabeth Virginia "Bess"

* Reluctantly accepting the role of First Lady, during a time when we were at war and the White House was under repair, Bess Truman toned down much of the activities held in tradition by previous administrations.

* When she died at the age of 97, she was the longest living First Lady.

* She was always extremely gracious to autograph collectors.

db/dd	Sig.	DS/LS	ALS	SP	
1885-1982	75	135	240	160	(1919), MO, D-1

Eisenhower, Mamie Geneva Doud

* Private, gracious and conforming, Mamie Eisenhower effectively carried out the role of First Lady.

* She was guarded and occasionally reluctant to autograph requests.

db/dd	Sig.	DS/LS	ALS	SP	
1896-1979	60	125	235	50	(1916), IA, S-1, plus a deceased infant

---

Kennedy, Jacqueline Lee Bouvier

* Intelligent, graceful, sophisticated and articulate, Jacqueline Kennedy was one of the most popular First Ladies.

* She remodeled the White House, became a fashion trendsetter and created the "Camelot" ambiance and legacy of the Kennedy administration.

* As her popularity transcended all the previous bounds for her position, she was hounded by the media and in particular the tabloid photographers.

* Since her death everything she owned, touched, gave away or wrote has become collectible.

* She often wrote brief handwritten notes of appreciation to acquaintances, many of which have found there way into the autograph market.

db/dd	Sig.	DS/LS	ALS	SP	
1929-1994	375	1200	2150	2250	(1953), NY, S-1, D-1, SB - $795, ESPV

Johnson, Claudia "Lady Bird" Alta Taylor

* A very active and intelligent First Lady, Lady Bird Johnson campaigned on behalf of the beautification of America.

* She fought gallantly against poverty and numerous other issues while creating "an island of peace" at the White House.

* Although subdued in her later years, she spent much of her life happily complying to requests for her signature.

db/dd	Sig.	DS/LS	ALS	SP	
1912-	40	100	200	100	(1934), TX, D-2

Nixon, Thelma Catherine Patricia Ryan

* A gifted actor and teacher, Pat Nixon promoted certain issues as First Lady, but for the most part avoided publicity.

* Although not reluctant, she was somewhat elusive toward autograph requests.

* Most authentic signed material appears as "Pat Nixon," versus her full name.

db/dd	Sig.	DS/LS	ALS	SP	
1912-1993	50	100	280	200	(1940), NV, D-2, WHC - $75 - $130

Ford, Elizabeth Bloomer Warren "Betty"

* A gifted dancer and model, Betty Ford tackled many issues as First Lady. From the liberalization of abortion laws to the Equal Rights Amendment, she was always direct and candid with her feelings.

* Forever linked to the Betty Ford Clinic, the premier chemical dependency recovery center, she is certainly one of the most outspoken of all the First Ladies.

* She is approachable and extremely warm to autograph requests.

db/dd	Sig.	DS/LS	ALS	SP	
1918-	30	130	50	40	(1948), IL, S-3, D-1

Carter, Rosalynn Smith

* From interior decorating to keeping the books for the peanut business, Rosalynn Carter was an intelligent and active voice for the President.

* She testified before Congress on behalf of improved funding for mental health programs and fought alongside her husband on numerous humanitarian issues.

* In recent years, her patience toward autograph seekers has worn thin.

db/dd	Sig.	DS/LS	ALS	SP	
1927-	25	100	130	40	(1946), GA, S-3, D-1

Reagan, Anne Frances "Nancy" R. Davis

* A gifted actress, Nancy Reagan returned opulence to the White House, while playing an pivotal but subdued role as First Lady.

* Her flair for fashion and formality, while in contrast to her predecessors, became a distinct part of her legacy.

* She has always been reluctant and elusive toward autograph seekers.

db/dd	Sig.	DS/LS	ALS	SP	
1921-	45	150	215	110	(1952), NY, S-1, D-1

Bush, Barbara Pierce

* Intellectual, candid, organized and energetic, Barbara Bush turned attention away from the First Lady and toward the issues.

* Literacy and the plight of the homeless became the key benefactors from her role as First Lady.

* She remains a prolific writer and is extremely warm to autograph requests.

* She is both a wife and mother to a former President of the United States.

db/dd	Sig.	DS/LS	ALS	SP	
1925-	50	160	185	95	(1945), NY, S-4, D-2

Clinton, Hillary Rodham

* The first lawyer to become First Lady, Hillary Clinton is a strategic thinker of tremendously high intellect.

* She has been active in campaigning for the rights of America's children, while also fighting for other issues, such as national health reform.

* She has been somewhat guarded and elusive to autograph requests.

* Hillary Clinton is the first former First Lady to be elected to the United States Senate (NY).

* As Senator, Mrs. Clinton has her staff handle autograph requests, most of which are machine-signed.

* Senator Clinton, a leader in the Democratic party, has often been mentioned as a possible Presidential candidate.

db/dd	Sig.	DS/LS	ALS	SP	
1947-	40	125	165	50	(1975), IL, D-1

Bush, Laura Welch

* Laura Bush, a former Texas schoolteacher, has been active in numerous education and literacy campaigns.

* She launched the first National Book Festival on September 8, 2001.

* She became the first First Lady in history to record a full presidential radio address.

* As First Lady, she has maintained a low-profile with the media.

db/dd	Sig.	DS/LS	ALS	SP	
1946-	30	110	150	40	(1977), TX, D-2

FOOTBALL

WHAT YOU NEED TO KNOW

* Similar to other sports, the advent of a legitimate Hall of Fame gives collectors a finite group of individuals to concentrate their autograph pursuit upon.

* The Pro Football Hall of Fame in Canton, Ohio provides collectors with unique access to its living members. Typically, the annual induction ceremony brings together more living inductees than any other sport.

* Generally speaking, most participants in this area are compliant to autograph requests.

MARKET FACTS

* Upon induction, a members signature will spike in value until demand is meant.

* The market has shown significant price variations in form for non-playing Hall of Fame members - coaches, owners, commissioners, etc.

* Demand for the signatures of the sports early stars remains strong.

* The market is driven by the signatures of many popular stars such as Jim Brown, Dick Butkus, Larry Csonka, Eric Dickerson, Frank Gifford, Joe Namath, Gale Sayers, and Lawrence Taylor.

* Forgeries do exist, but have dissipated in recent years.

* Obtaining a full set of signatures from every member of the Hall of Fame is difficult but achievable.

TRENDS

* New forms, such as postcards, vintage equipment, artwork, etc. have added to the interest in this area of autograph collecting.

* Signature values for key participants in this area have exhibited greater consistency over the last few years.

Abbreviations: MH = mini-helmet, RS = responsive signer, Sig = signature/index card, SGLA = signed Goal Line Art, SP = signed photograph, SSF = single-signed football

Name	Sig.	SP	MH	SGLA	SSF	Comments
Adderley, Herb	5	15	50	15	75	HOF 1980
Aikman, Troy	15	35	70		200	
Allen, Marcus	15	30	60		150	Elusive signer
Alworth, Lance	8	20	50	25	100	HOF 1978
Alzado, Lyle	100	200	375		525	
Ameche, Alan	100	200				
Arington, Lavar	10	25	50		100	
Atkins, Doug	5	12	40	15	55	HOF 1982, RS
Badgro, Red	15	25	55	25	80	HOF 1982, baseball demand
Barber, Tiki	10	20	40		70	
Barney, Lem	5	15	40	15	60	HOF 1992, RS
Battles, Cliff	60	210				
Baugh, Sammy	20	45		55	200	HOF 1963, RS
Bednarik, Chuck	10	20	40	25	70	HOF 1967, RS, adds stamp
Bell, Bert						HOF 1963, PU
Bell, Bobby	5	15	40	20	65	HOF 1983
Berry, Raymond	5	15	40	20	65	HOF 1973
Bidwill, Charles						HOF 1967, PU
Biletnikoff, Fred	10	15	40	30	70	HOF 1988
Blanda, George	10	17	40	26	65	HOF 1981
Bledsoe, Drew	10	30	50		60	RS
Blount, Mel	5	12	40	25	60	HOF 1989
Bradshaw, Terry	10	28	45	40	150	HOF 1989, RS
Brady, Tom	15	30	55		100	
Brees, Drew	10	20	40		100	RS
Brown, Jim	25	50	100	40	155	HOF 1971, reluctant signer
Brown, Paul	35	50		100	200	HOF 1967
Brown, Roosevelt	5	12	40	27	60	HOF 1975
Brown, Willie	5	15	40	25	60	HOF 1984
Bryant, Paul "Bear"	100	220				
Buchanan, Buck	30	60			250	HOF 1990
Buoniconti, Nick	10	20	45		75	HOF 2001, RS
Butkus, Dick	15	30	60	35	140	HOF 1979
Campbell, Earl	10	20	40	35	110	HOF 1991, RS
Canadeo, Tony	10	20	40	20	70	HOF 1974, RS
Carr, Joe						HOF 1963, PU
Carter, Chris	15	30	60		120	
Chamberlin, Guy						HOF 1965, PU
Christiansen, Jack	50	100	200			HOF 1970
Clark, Dutch	75	200				HOF 1963
Connor, George	10	20	40	25	75	HOF 1975, RS
Conzelman, Jimmy	185					HOF 1964
Couch, Tim	15	30		60	120	
Creekmur, Lou	10	20	40	30	70	HOF 1996, RS
Csonka, Larry	20	40	75	40	125	HOF 1987, FA
Davis, Al	50	125	250	450	250	HOF 1992, elusive signer
Davis, Terrell	15	40	75		160	
Davis, Willie	10	20	40	30	75	HOF 1981
Dawson, Len	10	25	65	25	100	HOF 1987

Name	Sig.	SP	MH	SGLA	SSF	Comments
DeLamielleure, Joe	10	20	40	20	70	HOF 2003
Dickerson, Eric	20	40	80		150	HOF 1999
Dierdorf, Dan	10	20	40	25	75	HOF 1996
Ditka, Mike	15	30	60	35	100	HOF 1988
Donovan, Art	10	20	40	30	75	HOF 1968
Dorsett, Tony	20	40	75	40	130	HOF 1994
Driscoll, Paddy						HOF 1965, PU
Dudley, Bill	10	20	40	30	70	HOF 1966
Dunn, Warrick	10	25	45		85	
Edwards, Turk	150	300	3x5	125		HOF 1969
Elway, John	15	40	75		175	Elusive signer!
Esiason, Boomer	10	25	50		100	
Ewbank, Weeb	15	30	60	35	110	HOF 1978, RS
Faulk, Marshall	15	30	75		150	
Favre, Brett	20	50	100		200	$, available in all forms
Fears, Tom	10	20	40	30	75	HOF 1970
Finks, Jim	100	200				HOF 1995
Flaherty, Ray	20	50			125	HOF 1976
Ford, Len	175	300				HOF 1976
Fortmann, Dan	35	75				HOF 1965
Fouts, Dan	15	30	60	35	115	HOF 1993
Gannon, Rich	15	40	75		125	
Garner, Charlie	10	20	40		80	
Gatski, Frank	10	20	40	25	75	HOF 1985, RS
George, Bill	100	200				HOF 1974
Gibbs, Joe	15	30	60	50	125	HOF 1996, catch him at the track
Gifford, Frank	15	40	75	35	125	HOF 1977
Gillman, Sid	10	20	40	25	75	HOF 1983, RS
Graham, Otto	15	30	65	40	125	HOF 1965, $
Grange, Red	60	150		150	600	HOF 1963
Grant, Bud	15	30	60	35	120	HOF 1994
Greene, Joe	15	30	55	35	125	HOF 1987
Gregg, Forrest	10	20	50	25	75	HOF 1977
Griese, Bob	15	30	65	40	125	HOF 1990
Groza, Lou	10	20	45	35	80	HOF 1974
Guyon, Joe	160	300				HOF 1966
Halas, George	75	150				HOF 1963
Ham, Jack	15	30	55	30	75	HOF 1988
Hampton, Dan	10	25	50		85	HOF 2002
Hannah, John	10	20	40	25	75	HOF 1991
Harris, Franco	20	40	80	40	125	HOF 1990, FA
Harrington, Joey	15	30	55		115	
Harrison, Marvin	15	30	60		125	
Haynes, Mike	10	20	40	25	75	HOF 1997
Hein, Mel	20	50			165	HOF 1963
Hendricks, Ted	10	20	45	30	75	HOF 1990
Henry, Pete						HOF 1963, PU
Herber, Arnie	100	200				HOF 1966

Name	Sig.	SP	MH	SGLA	SSF	Comments
Hewitt, Bill						HOF 1971, PU
Hirsch, Elroy	10	20	40	30	75	HOF 1968, RS
Holmes, Priest	15	30	60		100	
Hornung, Paul	25	30	65	40	150	HOF 1986, $
Houston, Ken	10	20	40	25	75	HOF 1986
Hubbard, Cal						HOF 1963, (see baseball)
Huff, Sam	15	30	60	35	100	HOF 1982
Hunt, Lamar	10	25	50	25	80	HOF 1972
Hutson, Don	30	50	80	75	155	HOF 1963
Irvin, Michael	15	30	60		120	
Jackson, Tom	10	20	35		60	
James, Edgerrin	15	30	70		150	
Johnson, Jimmy	10	20	40	25	75	HOF 1994
Johnson, Willie	10	20	40		65	RS
Joinier, Charlie	10	20	40	30	75	HOF 1996
Jones, Deacon	10	25	50	30	90	HOF 1980
Jones, Stan	10	20	40	25	70	HOF 1991
Jordan, Henry	300	550				HOF 1995
Jurgensen, Sonny	10	25	50	30	80	HOF 1983
Karras, Alex	10	25	50		75	
Kearse, Jevon	10	25	50		80	
Kelly, Jim	15	35	75		150	HOF 2002
Kelly, Leroy	10	25	50	25	80	HOF 1994, $
Kemp, Jack	15	30	65		100	USS, FA
Kiesling, Walt						HOF 1966, PU
Kinard, Frank "Bruiser"	100	200				HOF 1971
Krause, Paul	10	25	45	30	75	HOF 1998
Lambeau, Curly						HOF 1963, PU
Lambert, Jack	10	25	50	30	120	HOF 1990
Landry, Tom	15	30	70	35	125	HOF 1990, RS
Lane, Dick	10	25	50	30	80	HOF 1974, $
Langer, Jim	10	20	40	30	70	HOF 1987
Lanier, Willie	10	20	40	25	70	HOF 1986, RS
Largent, Steve	15	30	60	35	125	HOF 1995, USHR
Lary, Yale	10	20	40	25	70	HOF 1979, RS
Lavelli, Dante	10	20	40	25	65	HOF 1975, RS
Layne, Bobby	75	150				HOF 1967
Leemans, Tuffy	175					HOF 1978
Levy, Marv	15	30	55	25	80	HOF 2001, FA
Lewis, Jamal	20	40	75		150	RS
Lewis, Ray	15	30	60		120	
Lilly, Bob	10	25	50	30	85	HOF 1980
Little, Larry	10	20	40	25	70	HOF 1993
Lofton, James	15	30	60	30	80	HOF 2003
Lombardi, Vince	225	500				HOF 1971, checks plentiful
Long, Howie	15	35	75	40	125	HOF 2000
Lott, Ronnie	15	30	50	30	100	HOF 2000
Luckman, Sid	25	50	65	60	125	HOF 1965

Name	Sig.	SP	MH	SGLA	SSF	Comments
Lyman, Link	100	200				HOF 1964
Lynch, John	15	30	60		120	
Mackey, John	15	25	50	25	75	HOF 1992
Manning, Peyton	25	50	75		159	
Mara, Tim						HOF 1963. PU
Mara, Wellington	15	35	65	50	80	HOF 1997, RS
Marchetti, Gino	10	25	50	25	75	HOF 1972, RS
Marshall, George						HOF 1963, PU
Matson, Ollie	10	20	40	25	70	HOF 1972, RS
Matuszek, John	50	120			300	
Maynard, Don	15	25	50	25	75	HOF 1987
McAfee, George	10	25	50	25	75	HOF 1966
McCormack, Mike	12	25	50	25	75	HOF 1984
McDonald, Tommy	10	20	45	25	75	HOF 1998
McElhenny, Hugh	15	30	60	30	85	HOF 1970
McMahon, Jim	15	30	50		85	
McNabb, Donovan	20	40	75		175	
McNair, Steve	15	30	55		100	
McNally, Johnny						HOF 1963, PU
Meredith, Don	20	50	75		200	
Michalske, Mike	45	110				HOF 1964
Millner, Wayne	100	200				HOF 1968
Mitchell, Bobby	10	20	40	25	70	HOF 1983
Mix, Ron	10	25	50	25	75	HOF 1979
Monk, Art	15	30	60		120	
Montana, Joe	25	55	125		200	
Moon, Warren	15	30	60		100	
Moore, Lenny	10	20	40	25	70	HOF 1975
Moss, Randy	20	50	100		200	
Motley, Marion	15	30	60	35	100	HOF 1968
Munchak, Mike	10	25	50	25	75	HOF 2001
Munoz, Anthony	15	30	60	35	75	
Musso, George	10	20	40	25	75	HOF 1982
Nagurski, Bronko	50	100	175		350	HOF 1963
Namath, Joe	35	70	115	60	200	HOF 1985
Neale, Greasy						HOF 1969, PU
Nevers, Ernie	75	150				HOF 1963
Newsome, Ozzie	10	20	40		75	HOF 1999
Nitschke, Ray	30	50	85	60	130	HOF 1978
Noll, Chuck	10	25	50	35	75	HOF 1993
Nomellini, Leo	10	25	50	25	75	HOF 1969
Olsen, Merlin	15	30	60	40	100	HOF 1982
Otto, Jim	15	25	50	30	80	HOF 1980
Owen, Steve						HOF 1966. PU
Owens, Terrell	15	30	55		100	
Page, Alan	15	30	60	30	100	HOF 1988
Palmer, Carson	15	30	55		100	RS
Parcells, Bill	20	45	75		130	FA

Name	Sig.	SP	MH	SGLA	SSF	Comments
Parker, Clarence	10	20	40	25	75	HOF 1972
Parker, Jim	10	20	40	25	75	HOF 1973
Paterno, Joe	25	50	100		200	FA
Payton, Walter	50	115	225	100	275	HOF 1993
Pennington, Chad	15	30	60		100	
Perry, Joe	15	30	60	35	80	HOF 1969
Piccolo, Brian	250	565				
Pihos, Pete	15	30	60	35	80	HOF 1970
Plunkett, Jim	15	30	50		100	
Rashad, Ahmad	15	30	60		100	
Ray, Shorty						HOF 1966, PU
Reeves, Dan						HOF 1967, PU
Renfro, Mel	10	20	40	25	75	HOF 1996
Rice, Jerry	25	50	100		200	$
Riggins, John	25	50	100		150	HOF 1992, elusive signer
Ringo, Jim	10	20	40	30	75	HOF 1981, RS
Robustelli, Andy	15	25	50	30	80	HOF 1971
Rockne, Knute	700	2500				
Rooney, Art	50	100			335	HOF 1964, RS
Rooney, Dan	15	35	75		100	HOF 2000, RS
Rozelle, Pete	20	40			150	HOF 1985, RS
Sanders, Barry	25	65	125		225	
Sanders, Deion	15	30	60		125	Sig. variations
Sapp, Warren	20	40	75		150	
Sayers, Gale	25	45	80	45	130	HOF 1977, RS
Schmidt, Joe	10	20	45	25	80	HOF 1973
Schramm, Tex	15	30	60	30	100	HOF 1991, RS
Seau, Junior	15	30	65		100	
Sehorn, Jason	10	20	40		75	
Selmon, Lee Roy	10	25	50	30	75	HOF 1995, RS
Sharpe, Shannon	10	20	40		115	
Sharpe, Sterling	15	30	50		120	
Shaw, Billy	10	25	45		75	HOF 1999
Shell, Art	15	30	60	35	100	HOF 1989
Shula, Don	15	30	65	40	110	HOF 1997, RS
Simms, Phil	10	25	50		100	
Simpson, O.J.	30	50	75	75	200	HOF 1985, controversial
Singletary, Mike	10	25	60	35	100	HOF 1998, RS
Slater, Jackie	10	25	50	25	75	HOF 2001
Smith, Bruce	15	30	60		100	
Smith, Emmitt	25	50	100		200	
Smith, Jackie	10	20	40	25	85	HOF 1994
St.Clair, Bob	15	25	45	35	80	HOF 1990
Stabler, Ken	15	25	50		100	
Stallworth, John	10	25	50		80	HOF 2002
Starr, Bart	15	40	75	35	150	HOF 1977
Staubach, Roger	20	40	75	40	150	HOF 1985
Stautner, Ernie	10	20	40	25	75	HOF 1969, RS
Stenerud, Jan	10	20	40	25	75	HOF 1991, RS, $
Strahan, Michael	15	30	50		100	

Name	Sig.	SP	MH	SGLA	SSF	Comments
Strong, Ken	75	150				HOF 1967
Stydahar, Joe	60	150				HOF 1967
Summerall, Pat	15	30	60		100	
Swann, Lynn	15	35	60	35	85	HOF 2001
Tarkenton, Fran	15	35	75	40	150	HOF 1986, $
Taylor, Charley	10	20	40	25	80	HOF 1984
Taylor, Jim	10	20	45	30	80	HOF 1976
Taylor, Lawrence	25	50	75		150	HOF 1999
Testaverde, Vinny	10	25	50		80	
Theismann, Joe	10	25	50		85	
Thomas, Thurman	10	25	50		100	
Thorpe, Jim	625	1450				HOF 1963
Tittle, Y.A.	15	30	60	30	100	HOF 1971
Trafton, George	120	250				HOF 1964
Trippi, Charley	10	20	40	25	75	HOF 1968
Tunnell, Emlen	80	150				HOF 1967
Turner, Clyde	20	40	75	75	150	HOF 1966
Unitas, Johnny	25	50	75	40	150	HOF 1979, RS
Upshaw, Gene	10	20	40	25	80	HOF 1987
Urlacher, Brain	15	25	75		150	
VanBrocklin, Norm	75	150				HOF 1971
VanBuren, Steve	10	20	40	25	80	HOF 1965
Vick, Michael	20	40	75		150	
Walker, Doak	20	35	50	50	130	HOF 1986, RS
Walsh, Bill	15	30	60	40	125	HOF 1993
Warfield, Paul	10	20	45	30	90	HOF 1983. RS
Warner, Kurt	20	40	75		175	
Waterfield, Bob	65	135			375	HOF 1965
Webster, Mike	10	25	40	30	70	HOF 1997
Weinmeister, Arnie	10	20	40	25	75	HOF 1984
White, Randy	10	25	45	30	80	HOF 1994
White, Reggie	20	45	75		150	
Wilcox. Dave	10	20	40		75	HOF 2000
Williams, Ricky	15	40	75		200	
Willis, Bill	10	20	40	25	75	HOF 1977
Wilson, Larry	10	20	40	30	80	HOF 1978
Winslow, Kellen	10	25	50	30	100	HOF 1995
Wojciechowicz, Alex	20	40	80		200	HOF 1968
Wood, Willie	10	20	40	30	75	HOF 1989
Yary, Ron	10	20	40	30	75	HOF 2001
Young, Steve	20	40	75		150	
Youngblood, Jack	15	30	50	30	75	hOF 2001

HOCKEY

WHAT YOU NEED TO KNOW

* Similar to other sports, the advent of a legitimate Hall of Fame (Toronto, Canada) gives collectors a finite group of individuals to concentrate their autograph pursuit upon.

* The National Hockey League was formed in 1970.

* The league started with six franchises, and nearly went bankrupt in the Seventies due to waning interest and financial mismanagement.

* Striking national television broadcast deals and expansion to warm-weather locations such as San Jose, and Tampa Bay, revitalized the league in the Nineties.

* The number of teams now in the league is thirty.

* Of all the four major sports, hockey players are the most responsive to autograph requests.

MARKET FACTS

* Upon induction into the Hall of Fame, a members signature will spike in value until demand is meant.

* Demand for the signatures of the sports early stars remains strong, with pricing often erratic in various forms.

* The market is driven by the signatures of many popular stars such as Wayne Gretzky, Gordie Howe, Marcel Dionne, Mark Messier, Phil Esposito, Mario Lemieux and Bobby Hull.

* Forgeries do exist, but they are not as common as those encountered in other sports.

* While the sport is popular in the United States, it still can't rival the interest in Canada. Because of this pricing can vary significantly above the border.

TRENDS

* New forms, such as postcards, vintage equipment, artwork, etc. have added to the interest in this area of autograph collecting.

* Hockey autograph values continue to lag that of the other major four sports.

* Continued league expansion enhances interest in this area of collecting.

Abbreviations: Sig. - signature, SP = signed photograph, Puck = autographed puck, PU = pricing undetermined

Name	Sig.	SP	Puck	Comments
Abel, Sid	10	40	50	HOF 1969
Amonte, Tony	10	25	30	
Adams, Jack				HOF 1959, PU
Apps, Sr., Syl				HOF 1961, PU
Arbour, Al	7	15	20	
Armstrong, George	30			HOF 1975
Bailey, Ace	50	125	200	HOF 1975
Bain, Dan	100			HOF 1945
Baker, Hobey	350			HOF 1945
Barber, Bill	10	20	25	HOF 1990
Barry, Marty	60	120		HOF 1965
Bathgate, Andy	10	20	25	HOF 1978
Belfour, Ed	20	55	60	
Bauer, Bobby	100			HOF 1978
Beliveau, Jean	10	25	30	HOF 1972
Benedict, Clint	50	150		HOF 1965
Bentley, Doug	60	130		HOF 1964
Bentley, Max	55	130		HOF 1966
Blake, Toe	50	110		HOF 1966
Boivin, Leo	10	25	30	HOF 1986
Boon, Dickie	100			HOF 1952
Bossy, Mike	10	25	30	HOF 1991
Bouchard, Butch	10	20	35	HOF 1966
Boucher, Frank	125	250		HOF 1958
Boucher, George	80	225		HOF 1960
Bourque, Ray	20	50	60	
Bower, Johnny	10	20	25	HOF 1976
Bower, Dubbie	140			HOF 1945
Bowman, Scotty	15	30	45	HOF 1991
Brimsek, Frank	35	80	100	HOF 1966
Broadbent, Punch	75	150		HOF 1962
Brodeur, Martin	25	50	70	
Broda, Turk	115	375		HOF 1967
Bucyk, John	10	20	25	HOF 1981
Bure, Pavel	15	35	45	
Burch, Billy	125	250		HOF 1974
Cameron, Harry	120	265		HOF 1962
Cheevers, Gerry	10	20	25	HOF 1985
Chelios, Chris	10	30	50	RS
Cherry, Don	15	30	40	
Clancy, King	50	100		HOF 1958
Clapper, Dit	50	150		HOF 1947

Name	Sig.	SP	Puck	Comments
Clarke, Bobby	15	25	40	HOF 1987
Coffey, Paul	10	25	30	
Cleghorn, Sprague	125	250		HOF 1987
Colville, Neil	40	110		HOF 1967
Conacher, Charlie	100	225		HOF 1961
Cook, Bill	50	130		HOF 1952
Coulter, Art	30	110		HOF 1974
Cournoyer, Yvan	10	20	25	HOF 1982
Cowley, Bill	40	115		HOF 1968
Crawford, Rusty	65			HOF 1962
Day, Hap	50	150		HOF 1961
Delvecchio, Alex	10	20	25	HOF 1977
Denneny, Cy	70	180		HOF 1959
Dionne, Marcel	10	20	25	HOF 1992
Drillon, Gordie	40	110		HOF 1975
Drinkwater, Graham	215			HOF 1950
Dryden, Ken	35	100		HOF 1983
Dumart, Woody	10	25	30	HOF 1992
Dunderdale, Tommy	135			HOF 1974
Duman, Bill	100	235		HOF 1964
Dutton, Red	40	100		HOF 1958
Dye, Babe	115	225		HOF 1970
Esposito, Phil	15	30	35	HOF 1984
Esposito, Tony	10	25	30	HOF 1988
Federov, Sergei	15	40	60	
Fesitov, Slava	15	35	50	HOF 2001
Flaman, Fern	10	20	25	HOF 1990
Forsberg, Peter	20	45	60	
Foyston, Frank	60	125		HOF 1958
Frederickson, Frank	50	165		HOF 1958
Gadsby, Bill	10	15	25	HOF 1970
Gainey, Bob	15	35	40	HOF 1992
Gardiner, Herb	60	165		HOF 1958
Garner, Jimmy	265			HOF 1962
Geoffrion, Boom Boom	10	20	30	HOF 1972
Gerard, Eddie	260			HOF 1945
Giacomin, Eddie	10	25	30	HOF 1987
Gilbert, Red	10	25	30	HOF 1982
Gilmour, Billy	130			HOF 1962
Goheen, Moose	60			HOF 1952
Goodfellow, Ebbie	35	100		HOF 1963
Grant, Mike	130			HOF 1950
Green, Shorty	110			HOF 1962
Gretzky, Wayne	100	200	250	HOF 1999
Griffis, Si	130			HOF 1950
Hainsworth, George	115	320		HOF 1961
Hall, Glenn	10	20	30	HOF 1975

Name	Sig.	SP	Puck	Comments
Harvey, Doug	95			HOF 1973
Hasek, Dominik	25	55	100	
Hawerchuk, Dale	10	20	30	HOF 2001
Hay, George	75			HOF 1958
Hern, Riley	300			HOF 1962
Hextall, Bryan	50	125		HOF 1969
Holmes, Hap	170			HOF 1972
Hooper, Tom	120			HOF 1962
Horton, Tim	100	300		HOF 1977
Howe, Gordie	20	50	75	HOF 1972
Howe, Syd	50	100		HOF 1965
Howell, Harry	10	20	30	HOF 1979
Hull, Bobby	15	40	50	HOF 1983
Hull, Brett	25	55	89	
Hutton, Bouse	120			HOF 1962
Hyland, Harry	120			HOF 1962
Irvin, Dick	110	225		HOF 1958
Jackson, Busher	75	150		HOF 1971
Jagr, Jaromir	20	50	75	
Johnson, Ching	100	250		HOF 1958
Johnson, Ernie	150			HOF 1952
Johnson, Tom	10	20	25	HOF 1970
Joliat, Aurel	100	200		HOF 1947
Joseph, Curtis	15	30	50	
Kariya, Paul	10	25	50	
Keats, Duke	75	160		HOF 1958
Kelly, Red	10	20	25	HOF 1969
Kennedy, Teeder	10	20	30	HOF 1966
Keon, Dave	10	25	30	HOF 1986
Konstantinov, Vladimir	25	50	60	
Kurri, Jari	10	20	25	
Lach, Elmer	10	20	25	HOF 1966
Lafleur, Guy	10	20	30	HOF 1988
Lalonde, Newsy	125			HOF 1950
Laperriere, Jacques	10	20	25	HOF 1987
Lapointe, Guy	10	20	25	HOF 1993
Laprade, Edgar	10	20	25	HOF 1993
Leetch, Brian	15	35	45	
Lemaire, Jacques	10	20	30	HOF 1984
Lemieux, Mario	50	100	150	HOF 1997
LeSueur, Percy	150			HOF 1961
Lindros, Eric	20	40	50	
Lindsay, Ted	10	20	25	HOF 1966
Lumley, Harry	15	30	40	HOF 1980
MacKay, Mickey	120			HOF 1952
Mahovlich, Frank	10	20	25	HOF 1981
Malone, Joe	125			HOF 1950

Name	Sig.	SP	Puck	Comments
Mantha, Sylvio	60	130		HOF 1960
Marshall, Jack	100			HOF 1965
Maxwell, Steamer	110			HOF 1962
McDonald, Lanny	10	20	25	HOF 1992
Messier, Mark	25	75	100	
McGee, Frank	300			HOF 1945
McGimsie, Billy	115			HOF 1962
McNamara, George	125			HOF 1958
Mikita, Stan	10	25	35	HOF 1983
Modano, Mike	15	35	45	
Moore, Dickie	10	20	25	HOF 1974
Moran, Paddy	125			HOF 1958
Morenz, Howie	450			HOF 1945
Mosienko, Bill	40	130		HOF 1965
Mullen, Joe	10	20	25	HOF 2000
Neely, Cam	15	30	35	
Nighbor, Frank	100	200		HOF 1947
Noble, Reg	100			HOF 1962
O'Connor, Buddy	160	125		HOF 1988
Oliver, Harry	30	125		HOF 1967
Olmstead, Bert	10	25	35	HOF 1985
Orr, Bobby	25	65	100	HOF 1979
Parent, Bernie	19	20	30	HOF 1984
Park, Brad	10	20	25	HOF 1988
Perreault, Gil	10	20	25	HOF 1990
Phillips, Tommy	325			HOF 1945
Pilote, Pierre	10	20	25	HOF 1975
Pitre, Didier	265			HOF 1962
Plante, Jacques	69	170	250	HOF 1978
Potvin, Denis	10	20	25	HOF 1991
Primeau, Joe	115	235		HOF 1963
Pronovost, Marcel	10	20	25	HOF 1978
Pulford, Bob	10	25	30	HOF 1991
Pulford, Harry	165			HOF 1945
Quackenbush, Bill	35	100		HOF 1976
Rankin, Frank	215			HOF 1961
Ratelle, Jean	25	50	100	HOF 1985
Rayner, Chuck	10	20	25	HOF 1973
Reardon, Ken	10	20	30	HOF 1966
Richard, Henri	10	20	30	HOF 1979
Richard, Maurice	25	55	100	HOF 1961
Richter, Mike	20	40	75	
Richardson, George	365			HOF 1950
Roberts, Gordon	60	150		HOF 1971
Ross, Art	100	250		HOF 1945
Roy, Patrick	20	50	75	
Russell, Blair	85			HOF 1965

Name	Sig.	SP	Puck	Comments
Russell, Ernie	75	150		HOF 1965
Ruttan, Jack	65	125		HOF 1962
Sakic, Joe	10	30	40	
Savard, Denis	10	20	30	HOF 2000
Savard, Serge	10	20	25	HOF 1986
Sawchuk, Terry	150	375		HOF 1971
Schmidt, Milt	10	20	25	HOF 1961
Schriner, Sweeney	45	100		HOF 1962
Seibert, Earl	35	115		HOF 1963
Seibert, Oliver	165			HOF 1961
Shore, Eddie	100	275		HOF 1947
Shutt, Steve	10	20	25	HOF 1993
Siebert, Babe	325			HOF 1964
Simpson, Joe	60	150		HOF 1962
Sittler, Darryl	10	25	30	HOF 1989
Smith, Al	115	280		HOF 1962
Smith, Billy	10	20	25	HOF 1993
Smith, Clint	10	20	25	HOF 1991
Smith, Hooley	80	175		HOF 1972
Smith, Tommy	60			HOF 1973
Stanley, Allan	10	20	25	HOF 1981
Stanley, Barney	70			HOF 1962
Stevens, Scott	20	40	65	
Stewart, Jack	75	135		HOF 1964
Stewart, Nels	170	250		HOF 1962
Stuart, Bruce	165			HOF 1961
Stuart, Hod	575			HOF 1945
Taylor, Cyclone	165			HOF 1947
Thompson, Tiny	135			HOF 1959
Tretiak, Vladislav	15	25	40	HOF 1989
Trihey, Harry J.	235			HOF 1950
Trottier, Bryan	10	25	30	HOF 1997
Ullman, Norm	10	20	25	HOF 1982
Walker, Jack	170			HOF 1960
Watson, Harry E.	130			HOF 1962
Watson, Harry	10	20	25	HOF 1994
Weiland, Cooney	65	175		HOF 1971
Westwick, Harry	160			HOF 1962
Whitcroft, Fred	265			HOF 1962
Wilson, Phat	100	220		HOF 1962
Worsley, Gump	10	20	25	HOF 1980
Yzerman Steve	15	55	80	

MISCELLANEOUS SPORTS -
Selected Entries

WHAT YOU NEED TO KNOW

* Entire books have been written about collectibles, including autographs, in some of these areas.

* Although some of the sports listed here are extremely popular with fans, the autographs of key participants and pioneers attract the most interest with collectors.

* Many of the participants listed in this area are very responsive to fans requests for their signature.

MARKET FACTS

* The value of autographs for most of the participants in this area trail that of the four major sports.

* Forgeries, although encountered with a few participants in these areas, are infrequent and not a key concern for most collectors.

* Current popular Olympic athletes attract far greater attention than their predeccessors.

TRENDS

* Sports marketing has improved considerably over the past few decades in sports such as NASCAR and golf. Because of this a greater variety of autographed material is now available to collectors.

* The advent of many new stars in golf, tennis and NASCAR continues to draw fans to these sports.

* Achievements, such as Lance Armstrong in cycling, continue to inspire fans and add interest to the hobby of autograph collecting.

Notes:
Abbreviations: GB = golf ball signed, Sig = signature, SP = signed photograph, TB = tennis ball signed

Name	Sig.	SP	Comments:

Bowling

Anthony, Earl	25	50	Bowling, (1938-2001)

Cycling

Armstrong, Lance	30	75	Cyclist
Lemond, Greg	25	50	Cyclist

Golf

Alcott, Amy	15	25	GHOF
Berg, Patty	25	40	GHOF
Casper, Billy	10	20	
Hagen, Walter	400	1250	(1892-1969)
Hogan, Ben	125	300	(1912-1997), GB-$150
Inkster, Julie	10	20	Golfer
Jones, Bobby	500	2000	(1902-1971), GB-$N/A
Lopez, Nancy	10	25	GHOF
Nelson, Byron	20	50	Golfer, GB-$75
Nicklaus, Jack	25	50	Golfer, GB-$60
Norman, Greg	10	30	Golfer, GB-$40
Palmer, Arnold	25	50	Golfer, GB-$60
Sarazan, Gene	10	25	Golfer, GB-$40, RS
Sheehan, Patty	15	25	HOF
Snead, Sam	20	50	Golfer, GB-$40 (1912-2002)
Sorenstam, Annika	15	30	FA
Trevino, Lee	10	25	Golfer, GB-$40, FA
Watson, Tom	10	25	Golfer, GB-$35, RS
Webb, Karrie	10	20	Austrailian golfer
Whitworth, Kathy	15	30	7-time LPGA POY
Woods, Tiger	35	75	Golfer, GB-$100
Zaharias, Babe D.			Golfer, GB-$N/A, ESPV, PU

Horse Racing

Arcaro, Eddie	25	50	Jockey, (1916-97)
Cordero, Angel	15	30	Jockey, 3 Derby wins
Hartack, Bill	20	40	Jockey, 5 Derby wins
Krone, Julie	15	30	Jockey - female
Pincay, Laffit, Jr.	15	25	Jockey
Shoemaker, Willie	40	80	(1931-2003), jockey

Olympics/Track & Field/

Ashford, Evelyn	15	30	Sprinter
Bannister, Roger	25	50	Physician, SSP-2X
Beamon, Bob	10	20	Long jumper, RS
Bikila, Abebe			Ethiopian runner, (1932-73), PU
Biondi, Matt	10	15	Swimmer

Name	Sig.	SP	Comments:
Blair, Bonnie	10	25	Speed skater
Blanker-koen, Fanny			Track, PU
Bubka, Sergei	10	25	Ukrainian pole vaulter
Button, Dick	10	25	Figure skater
Caulkins, Tracy	10	25	Swimmer
Coe, Sebastian	15	30	British runner
Comaneci, Nadia	15	35	Romanian gymnast
Daehlie, Bjoern	15	30	Norwegian X-country skier
Decker Slaney, Mary	10	20	Runner
de Verona, Donna	10	20	Swimmer, RS
Devers, Gail	10	20	Runner
Ederle, Gertrude			Swimmer, 1st. E. Channel, PU
Edwards, Theresa	10	25	Basketball, Olympian
El Guerrouj, Hicham	15	35	Moroccan runner
Evans, Janet	10	25	Swimmer
Evans, Lee	15	30	Runner
Ewry, Ray			(1873-1937), run., PU, scarce
Fleming, Peggy	15	30	Figure skater, FA
Fosbury, Dick	15	40	High jumper
Gebrselassie, Haile	20	40	Ethiopian runner
Gibson, Althea	30	70	(1927-2003)
Giardelli, Marc	20	40	Skier, 5 - W. Cups
Griffith, Joyner, Flo.	25	50	(1959-1998), sprinter
Hamill, Dorothy	15	30	Figure skater
Hamilton, Scott	15	35	Figure skater, RS, FA
Hamm, Mia	15	30	Soccer player, RS
Heiden, Eric	25	45	Speed skater
Henie, Sonja	70	175	Figure skater
Hughes, Sarah	15	30	Figure skater
Jenner, Bruce	10	25	Decathlon, RS
Jennings, Lynn	10	20	Runner
Johnson, Michael	20	45	Runner
Jones, Marion	10	20	Runner, long jumper
Joyner-Kersee, Jackie	15	30	Heptathlon, long jumper
Killy, Jean Claude	20	40	Skier, RS
Korbut, Olga	15	30	Gymnast, RS
Kristiansen, Ingrid	15	25	Norwegian runner
Kwan, Michelle	10	25	Figure skater
Lewis, Carl	10	20	Sprinter, long jumper, RS
Lipinski, Tara	10	20	Figure skater, RS
Louganis, Greg	10	20	Diver, RS
Mathias, Bob	10	25	Decathlon, RS
McKinney, Tamara	10	20	Alpine skier
Meagher, Mary	10	20	Swimmer
Meyer, Debbie	10	25	Swimmer
Mills, Billy	10	25	Runner, RS
Moses, Edwin	15	30	Hurdler
Newby-Fraser, Paula	15	30	Ironman Triathlon Champ
Nurmi, Paavo			(1897-1973) , dis. runner, PU
Oerter, Al	15	30	Discus thrower
Owens, Jesse	100	225	(1913-1980), runner
Prefontaine, Steve			Runner, scarce, PU, (1951-75)

Name	Sig.	SP	Comments:
Radcliffe, Paula	10	20	Marathon runner
Retton, Mary Lou	10	25	Gymnast, RS
Rodgers, Bill	10	20	Runner
Rudolph, Wilma	30	75	(1940-1994), runner
Samuelson, Joan Ben.	10	20	Marathon runner
Shorter, Frank	15	30	Runner
Spitz, Mark	30	75	Swimmer, elusive
Street, Picabo	15	30	Skier
Thompson, Jenny	15	40	Swimmer
Thompson, Daley	15	30	Decathlete
Tomba, Alberto	30	75	Alpine skier
Tyus, Wyomia	15	25	Runner
Van Dyken, Amy	20	35	Swimmer
Viren, Lasse	15	30	Finish runner
Waitz, Grete	20	40	Marathon runner
Witt, Katarina	20	45	German figure skater
Yamaguchi, Kristi	15	30	Figure skater
Zatopek, Emil			(1922-2000), Czech runner, PU

Tennis

Name	Sig.	SP	Comments:
Agassi, Andre	10	30	Tennis player, TB-$40
Ashe, Arthur	25	75	(1943-1993), TB-$100
Borg, Bjorn	10	30	Tennis player, TB-$40
Bueno, Maria	10	25	4 U.S. Titles
Capriati, Jennifer	10	25	Tennis player, TB - $40
Conners, Jimmy	10	30	Tennis player, TB-$40
Connolly, Maureen	125	250	(1934-69)
Court, Margaret	10	30	Tennis player, TB-$N/A
Davenport, Lindsay	10	20	Tennis player, TB - $40
Edberg, Stefan	15	30	Tennis player, TB - $45
Evert, Chris	10	30	Tennis player, TB-$40
Gibson, Athea	15	50	Tennis player, TB-$N/A
Graf, Steffi	10	30	Tennis player, TB-$45
Hingis, Martina	10	30	Tennis player, TB-$40
King, Billie Jean	10	25	Tennis player, TB-$35
Laver, Rod	10	25	Tennis player, TB - $40
Lendl, Ivan	10	20	Tennis player, TB - $40
McEnroe, John	15	30	Tennis player, TB-$40
Navratilova, Martina	25	50	Tennis player, TB-$45
Newcombe, John	15	30	Tennis player, TB - $45
Sabatini, Gabriela	10	30	Tennis player, TB-$40, FA
Sampras, Pete	15	35	Tennis player, TB-$50, RS
Seles, Monica	10	35	Tennis player, TB-$45
Tilden, Bill	150	350	Tennis player, TB-$N/A
Williams, Serena	25	55	Tennis player, TB -$55
Williams, Venus	25	50	Tennis player, TB - $50
Wills, Helen	40	80	Tennis player, TB-$N/A

Name	Sig.	SP	Comments:

Automobile Racing

Name	Sig.	SP	Comments:
Andretti, Mario	10	25	Auto Racing
Earnhardt, Dale	50	125	(1951-2001), Auto Racing
Earnhardt, Dale, Jr.	25	50	Auto Racing
Elliot, Bill	15	30	Auto Racing
Fangio, Juan			Argentinian, 5-G. Prix wins, PU
Foyt, A.J.	10	25	Auto Racing
Gordon, Jeff	20	40	Auto Racing
Guthrie, Janet	10	25	1st woman in Indy 500
Jarrett, Ned	10	25	Auto Racing
Johnson, Junior	10	25	Auto Racing
Luyendyk, Arie	10	20	Auto Racing
Muldowney, Shirley	10	25	Dragster
Oldfield, Barney			Auto racing pioneer, PU
Parsons, Benny	10	20	Auto Racing
Petty, Lee	20	65	Auto Racing
Petty, Richard	10	25	Auto Racing
Rahal, Bobby	10	25	Auto Racing
Rutherford, Johnny	10	20	Auto Racing
Schumacher, Michael	25	50	Auto Racing, FA
Stewart, Jackie	15	30	Auto Racing
Unser, Al	15	30	Auto Racing
Unser, Al, Jr.	15	25	Auto Racing
Unser, Bobby	10	20	Auto Racing
Wallace, Rusty	10	25	Auto Racing

Soccer

Name	Sig.	SP	Comments:
Beckham, David	50	125	English soccer star, ESPV
Pele	40	80	Brazilian soccer star

Women's basketball

Name	Sig.	SP	Comments:
Cooper, Cynthia	15	25	4-time MVP WNBA

MUSIC

CLASSICAL MUSIC AUTOGRAPHS AND MANUSCRIPTS

WHAT YOU NEED TO KNOW

* Always popular among autograph collectors has been those signatures and manuscripts of the worlds premier composers. However material is not only scarce, but beyond the price level of the average collector.

* Many attribute the interest in this area to musics universal appeal. An individual need not speak Russian to appreciate the talent of many of the country's finest composers.

* Many composers are also music collectors themselves.

MARKET FACTS

* This niche of the market continues to drive the value of manuscripts to all-time highs. Most collectors remember the 1977 Christies sale of an autographed letter from Mozart to his wife Constanze for an astounding $25,500.

* The market is driven by the popularity of its masters, Johann Sebastian Bach, Wolfgand A. Mozart, Joseph Hayden, and Ludwig van Beethoven.

* Institutional libraries and museums continue to dominate this area of collecting.

TRENDS

* Highly sought forms in this area of the hobby include: original musical compositions - in all forms from initial sketch to a final version, AMQS - attractive for display and commonly given out by composers, ALS (Autograph Letter Signed) - as with all niches content is paramount, followed by scarcity, condition and length, SP (Signed Photograph) and all other forms - tickets, programs, etc.

* Although interest in this area peaks at the Beethoven, Bach and Mozart level, many collectors can still enjoy autographed items from American composers at reasonable prices. Irving Berlin, Leonard Bernstein and Aaron Copland are still at affordable levels, as are many others.

* From orchestra conductors to soundtrack composers, this area is filled with treasures. Many composers are more than willing to accommodate an autograph request with an AMQS.

Abbreviations: AMQS = autograph musical quotation signed, ANS = autograph note signed, ESPV = exhibits significant pricing variations, PU = pricing undetermined

Name	db/dd	Sig.	DS/LS	ALS	SP	Comments/Assoc.
Bach, Carl P. E.	1714-1788					German, PU
Bach, Johann Christian	1735-1782					German, PU
Bach, Johann Sebastian	1685-1750	2750	24650	37600		German, ESPV, all forms rare
Barber, Samuel	1910-1981	50	250	300	100	U.S., "Vanessa"
Bartok, Bela	1881-1945	400	750	2000	1500	Hungarian, strong demand Inst.
Beach, Amy	1867-1944	60	150	460	200	U.S.
Beethoven, Ludwig van	1770-1827	10100	25460	40000		German, scarce music. sketches
Bellini, Vincenzo	1801-1835	500	2500			Italian, rare in letters
Berg, Alban	1885-1935	150	375	1275		Austrian, "Lulu"
Beriloz, Hector	1803-1869	225	500	525		French, AMQS-$3900
Bernstein, Leonard	1918-1990	120	350	600	225	U.S., "Mass," RS, SCC-$75
Bizet, Georges	1838-1875	500	1250	2440		French, scarce in letters
Bloch, Ernest	1880-1959	75	155	300	100	Swiss/U.S., "Macbeth"
Boccherini, Luigi	1743-1805	150	325			Italian, chamber music
Borodin, Alexander	1833-1887	260	500	1000		Russian
Boulez, Pierre	1925-	35	60	80	30	French,
Brahms, Johannes	1833-1897	1250	1875	3500		AMQS-$7500, scarce forms, AU
Britten, Benjamin	1913-1976	125	380	450	225	British, very popular
Bruckner, Anton	1824-1896	1400	2800	5000	2750	Austrian
Buxtehude, Dietrich	1637-1707					Danish, PU
Cage, John	1912-1992	50	130	175	75	U.S.
Chabrier, Emmanuel	1841-1894	100	200	400		French
Charpentier, Gustave	1860-1956	100	200	300	250	French
Chopin, Frederic	1810-1849	2000	4000			Polish, ANS-$24800, AU
Copland, Aaron	1900-1990	75	200	550	165	U.S., "Appalachian Spring," RS
Debussy, Claude	1862-1918	500	1150	1675	2250	French, AMQS-$4250 - rare
Donizetti, Gaetano	1797-1848	600	1200	1850		Italian
Dukas, Paul	1865-1935	70	150	300	150	French
Dvorak, Antonin	1841-1904	500	1000	2000		Czech, AQMS - rare
Elgar, Edward	1857-1934	150	300	750	500	British, scarce in AQMS, SP
Falla, Manuel de	1876-1946	200	400	725		Spanish, "The Three-Cor. Hat"
Faure, Gabriel	1845-1924	125	250	250	500	French
Franck, Cesar	1822-1890	425	1200	1495		Belgian, SALS-2-3X
Gershwin, George	1898-1937	840	1675		3475	U.S., "Rhapsody in Blue"
Glass, Phillip	1937-	25	50	100	45	U.S. , "The Voyage," RS
Glinka, Mikhail	1804-1857					Russian, PU
Gluck, Christoph W.	1714-1787	825	2450	4250		German, "Alceste"
Goldsmith, Jerry		10	25	50	20	U.S., movie soundtracks
Gounod, Charles	1818-1893	175	400	1200	500	French, "Romeo and Juliet"
Grieg, Edvard	1843-1907	475	925	1840		Norwegian, available
Handel, George Fred.	1685-1759	1250	6500			German/british, "Messiah"
Hanson, Howard	1896-1981	25	50	100	50	U.S.
Harris, Roy	1898-1979	60	125		75	U.S.
Haydn, Franz Joseph	1732-1809					Austrian, PU
Heifetz, Jascha	1901-1987	130	275			Russin-born American, available

Name	db/dd	Sig.	DS/LS	ALS	SP	Comments/Assoc.
Herbert, Victor	1859-1924	100	200	300	300	AQNS - common
Hindemith, Paul	1895-1963	125	250	500	175	U.S.
Holst, Gustav	1874-1934	50	150	300	200	British, "The Planets"
Honegger, Arthur	1892-1955	60	155	325	60	French
Horner, James		15	30	55	25	U.S., movie soundtracks
Horowitz, Vladimir	1903-1989	130	275		160	Piano virtuoso
Hovhaness, Alan	1911-	40	100	225	100	U.S.
Humperdinck, Engelbert	1854-1921	100	210	400	225	German, "Hansel and Gretel"
Ives, Charles	1874-1954	225	800	1750	450	U.S., rare
Khachaturian, Aram	1903-1978	150	300	550	600	Russian
Kodaly, Zoltan	1882-1967	150	300	500	375	Hungarian
Kreisler, Fritz	1875-1962	125	225	300	250	Austrian, available
Laio, Edouard	1823-1892					French, PU
Lehar, Franz	1870-1948	100	200	500	300	Hungary, available
Leinsdorf, Erich						Conductor, PU
Leoncavallo, Ruggero	1857-1919	200	425		500	Italian, generally available
Levine, James						Conductor, MOO. PU
Liszt, Franz	1811-1886	500	1175			Hungarian, AMQS - scarce
MacDowell, Edward	1861-1908	175	300	600	375	U.S., "To a Wild Rose," rare
Mahler, Gustav	1860-1911	600	1350	3200		Austrian, ALS - scarce
Mariner, Neville						Conductor, PU
Mascagni, Pietro	1863-1945	175	355	710	575	Italian, available
Massenet, Jules	1842-1912	75	150	300	300	French, available all forms
Mendelssohn, Felix	1809-1847	850	2250	4750		German, "A Midsummer Night..."
Menotti, Gian-Carlo	1911-	125	250		300	Italian/U.S., "The Medium".
Montevardi, Claudio	1567-1643					Italian, PU
Moussorgsky, Modest	1839-1881					Russian, "Pictures at ...," PU
Mozart, Wolfgang Amad.	1756-1791					Austrian, scarce in all forms, PU
Munch, Charles		15	35		70	Conductor, BSO
Nelson, John						Conductor, ESO, PU
Offenbach, Jacques	1819-1880	150	300	575		French, strong recent demand
Pachelbel, Johann	1653-1706					German, PU
Paderewski, Ignacy	1860-1941	200	450	600	500	Polish also prime minister
Paganini, Niccolo	1782-1840	415				Italian, scarce in some forms
Pendercki, Krzystof	1933-	25	50	100	50	Polish
Perlman, Itzhak		20	50		40	Violinist
Poulenc, Francis	1899-1963	150	300	500	300	French
Prokofieff, Sergi	1891-1953	475	1150		1200	Russian, AMQS-$2900
Puccini, Giacomo	1858-1924	500	1000	2000	1000	Ita., AMQS-$1950, ALS-$775
Purcell, Henry	1659-1695					English, PU
Rachmaninoff, Sergei	1873-1943	265	700		500	Russian, available and popular
Ravel, Maurice	1875-1937	550	1500	2490	1600	French, "Bolero," AQMS - rare
Rimsky-Korsakov, Nik.	1844-1908	500	1800		1725	Russian, AMQS-$5800
Rossini, Gioacchino	1792-1868	640	1500	3000		Italian, "William Tell"
Rubinstein, Artur	1887-1982	50	140	250		Pianist
Saint-Saens, Camille	1835-1921	150	300	500	400	French, strong demand Inst.
Scarlatti, Alessandro	1660-1725		7250	15000		Italian, rare
Scarlatti, Domenico	1685-1757					Italian, PU
Schoenberg, Arnold	1874-1951	350	1275	2500	600	Austrian, uncommon
Schubert, Franz	1797-1828	2850	6500	12750		Austrian, rare ALS
Schumann, Robert	1810-1856	1000	2000	4000		German, ALS music con. scarce
Shostakovich, Dimitri	1906-1975	365	725	1765		Russian, scarce outside Russia

Name	db/dd	Sig.	DS/LS	ALS	SP	Comments/Assoc.
Sibellus, Jean	1865-1957	450	1100	2250	1100	Finnish
Smetana, Bedrich	1824-1884	2000		10000		Czech
Solti, Sir Georg	1912-1997	40	75		75	Conductor
Stockhausen, Karlheinz	1928-	35	70		40	German
Strauss, Richard	1864-1949	275	600	800	750	German, AMQS - scarce
Stravinsky, Igor	1882-1971	350	600		750	Russian
Sullivan, Arthur	1842-1900	200	400	600		England
Takemitsu, Toru	1930-1996	35	75		50	Japanese
Tchalkovsky, Peter I.	1840-1893	2500	4000	7000		Russian, "Nutcracker," rare
Thomas, Michael Tilson		20	45		45	Conductor, SSO
Thomson, Virgil	1896-1989	50	100	150	125	U.S.
Verdi, Giuseppe	1813-1901	1275	2000	3465		Italian, AMQS-$8500
Villa-Lobos, Heitor	1887-1959	125	250	900	250	Brazilian
Vivaldi, Antonio	1678-1741					Italian, PU
Wagner, Richard	1813-1883	1275	1950	3575		German, "Rienzi," SP- rare
Weber, Karl Maria von	1786-1826	325	1015	1340		German, rare DS
Williams, Ralph Vaugh.	1872-1958					English, common, PU
Wolf, Hugo	1860-1903	275				Austrian
Yo-Yo Ma	1955-	25	50		40	Violincello

NOTABLE BLUES AND JAZZ ARTISTS

WHAT YOU NEED TO KNOW

* At the turn of the 20th century a new form of polyphonic syncopated music developed, and it was called jazz. Characterized by solo virtuosic improvisation, jazz was initially a form of dance music, but as it evolved it grew increasingly intricate and even experimental.

* Various distinct forms of jazz quickly emerged. Pioneered by many seminal musicians such as Charlie Parker, Louis Armstrong, and John Coltrane, jazz not only gained the respect of musics toughest critics, but grew into a respected art form.

* Rooted in black American and other popular forms of music, jazz styles originated from many places across this country. Cities such as New Orleans, where Dixieland jazz was born, became increasingly popular and slowly migrated up the Mississippi River. Noted disciples of this form of music included King Oliver and Jelly Roll Morton. While popular among jazz enthusiasts, both Oliver and Morton were not household names, therefore autograph requests didn't flood their mail boxes.

* Autograph collectors were common in the Thirties and it wasn't unusual to find numerous fans lingering outside jazz halls such as the Savoy Ballroom in Harlem. Signatures were easily obtained from jazz legends such as Count Basie, Billie

Holiday and Duke Ellington. Fortunately for collectors some autograph albums from this time period have found there way into the market, with many containing very scarce signatures. While autographs from Jimmie Lunceford, Ivie Anderson and Chick Webb are highly desirable and scarce, other individuals are even more difficult to find.

* Blues was a form of African-American music that originated from the rural South in the late 19th Century. Characterized by a 12-bar construction and free form lyrics, blues became popular with many of the war-torn regions of the former Confederacy. The pioneers of early blues were common folk who entertained and vented their emotions to those around them. While obscurity surrounds both the roots of these early musicians and the origination of many of their songs, no one can argue about the tremendous influence blues has had on American music. For example, the legendary bluesman of the Twenties, Blind Lemon Jefferson has influenced all the greats who have followed, including Joe Williams, T-Bone Walker and even B.B. King. Similar to jazz, the signatures of the pioneers of this music form are extremely scarce.

Name	db/dd	Sig.LS/DS	ALS	SP	Comments/Assoc.
Adderley, Julian "Cannonball"	1928-1975	40	65		75	Alto sax player
Armstrong, Louis "Satchmo"	1900-1971	265	500	725	500	Singer, trumpet player
Bailey, Mildred	1907-1951					Blues singer, PU
Baker, Chet	1929-1988	30	65		60	Trumpet player
Basie, Count	1904-1984	80	225		250	Orchestra leader,
Bechet, Sidney	1897-1959	135	600		200	Soprano sax player
Beiderbecke, Bix	1903-1931	5500				Composer, cornet,
Benford, Tommy	1906-1994	20	50		40	Drummer
Berigan, Bunny	1909-1942					Trumpet player, singer
Bigard, Barney	1906-1980	70	135		170	Clarinet player
Blackwell, Ed	1929-1992	25	40		40	Drummer
Blanton, Jimmy	1921-1942					Bass, PU
Bolden, Charles "Buddy"	1868-1931					Cornet player, PU
Broonzy, Big Bll	1893-1958	40	55		65	Blues singer, guitar
Brown, Clifford	1930-1956					Trumpet player, PU
Byas, Don	1912-1972	25	45		45	Tenor sax
Calloway, Cab	1907-1994	35	50	75	150	Band leader
Carney, Harry	1910-1974	30	70		60	Baritone sax
Catlett, Sidney	1910-1951					Drummer, PU
Cheatham, Doc	1905-1997	15	30		30	Big band trumpeter
Cherry, Don	1937-1995	20	40		45	Lyrical jazz trumpeter
Christian, Charlie	1919-1942					Guitar player, PU
Clarke, Kenny	1914-1985	30	60		60	Modern drum pioneer
Clayton, Buck	1911-1991	30	55		50	Trumpet player,
Cleveland, James	1931-1991	25	40		45	Gospel singer
Cohn, Al	1925-1988	25	50		45	Tenor sax player
Cole, Cozy	1909-1981	20	40		35	Drummer
Coltrane, John	1926-1967	350	700		1250	Innovative tenor sax
Condon, Eddie	1904-1973	45	100		75	Band leader, guitar
Dameron, Tadd	1917-1965	35	60		60	Piano player, composer

Name	db/dd	Sig.	DS/LS	ALS	SP	Comments/Assoc.
Davis, Eddie "Lockjaw"	1921-1986	30	50		50	Tenor sax player
Davis, Miles	1926-1991	175	350		500	Trumpet player, pioneer
Davison, Wild Bill	1906-1989	40	100		85	Cornet player, pioneer
Desmond, Paul	1924-1977	35	50		60	Alto sax player
Dickenson, Vic	1906-1984	30	50		50	Trombone player,
Dixon, Willie	(See Rock 'n' Roll)					
Dodds, Johnny	1892-1940	50	80		75	Clarinet player
Dodds, Warren "Baby"	1898-1959	40	50		50	Drummer
Dorsey, Jimmy	1904-1957	40	150	300	270	Band leader, clarinet
Dorsey, Tommy	1905-1956	50	150	250	150	Band leader, trombone
Eldridge,Roy	1911-1989	30	60		75	Trumpet player,
Ellington, Duke	1899-1974	225	500	1000	500	Band leader, composer,
Evans, Bill	1929-1980	25	50		45	Piano player
Evans, Gil	1912-1988	20	45		40	Composer, arranger
Fitzgerald, Ella	1918-1996	50	75	125	100	Jazz vocalist, elusive
Garland, "Red"	1923-1984	25	50		35	Piano player
Garner, Erroll	1921-1977	85	150		165	Piano, composer
Getz, Stan	1927-1991	100	200		250	Tenor sax player
Gillespie, Dizzy	1917-1993	75	100	250	125	Composer, trumpet
Goodman, Benny	1909-1986	75	175	265	185	Band leader, clarinet
Gordon, Dexter	1923-1990	30	50		60	Tenor sax player
Hackett, Bobby	1915-1976	30	50		60	Trumpet and cornet
Handy, W.C.	1873-1958	300	500		800	Composer,
Hawkins, Coleman	1904-1969	150	250		265	Tenor sax player
Henderson, Fletcher	1898-1952	25	50		45	Orchestra leader,
Herman, Woody	1913-1987	25	100		75	Band leader, clarinet
Higginbotham, Jay C.	1906-1973	40	50		60	Trombone player
Hines, Earl "Fatha"	1905-1983	140	250		275	Piano player
Hodges, Johnny	1906-1970	40	60		55	Alto sax player
Holiday, Billie	1915-1959	750	1200		2000	Blues singer,
Hooker, John Lee	1917-	40	100		125	Guitarist and blues
Hopkins, Sam "Lightnin"	1912-1982	40	75		125	Guitarist, singer
Howlin' Wolf	1910-1976	300	500		850	Guitarist, harmonica
Jackson, Mahaila	1911-1972	100	200		185	Gospel singer
Jefferson, Blind Lemon	1897-1930	1250	2500		2500	Guitarist, blues singer
John, Little Willie	(see Rock 'n' Roll)					
Johnson, Bunk	1879-1949	225	450		600	Cornet and trumpet
Johnson, James P.	1891-1955	140	500		225	Composer, piano player
Johnson, Robert	1912-1938					Guitarist, singer,
Jones, Jo	1911-1985	30	50		50	Drummer
Jones, Philly Joe	1923-1985	25	40		40	Drummer
Jones, Thad	1923-1986	25	40	75	60	Trumpet and cornet
Joplin, Scott	1868-1917	700	1000	2250		Ragtime composer
Jordan, Louis	1908-1975	35	70		70	Singer, alto sax player
Kenton, Stan	1912-1979	50	100		125	Orchestra leader
King, Albert	1923-1992	20	50		50	Blues guitarist
Krupa, Gene	1909-1973	50	200		120	Band and combo leader
LaFaro, Scott	1936-1961					Bass player, PU
Ledbetter,						
Huddie "Leadbelly"	1888-1949				5000	Guitarist, blues singer
Lewis, Mel	1929-1990	20	40	75	55	Orchestra leader
Lunceford, Jimmie	1902-1947	45	100		150	Band leader, sax player

Name	db/dd	Sig.	DS/LS	ALS	SP	Comments/Assoc.
Marsalis, Wynton	1961-					Trumpeter
McClellan, William "Scrugs"	1907-1931	75	150		200	Guitar player
McPartland, Jimmy	1907-1991	30	50		55	Trumpet player
McRae, Carmen	1920-1994	20	35		45	Jazz singer
Miller, Glen	1904-1944	200	750	500	450	Band leader, Trombone
Mingus, Charles	1922-1979	135	250		225	Composer, bass player
Monk, Thelonius	1920-1982	100	200		200	Piano player,
Montgomery, Wes	1925-1968	40	60		50	Guitarist
Morton, "Jelly Roll"	1885-1941	500	750			Composer, singer,
Moten, Bennie	1894-1935					Piano player, PU
Mulligan, Gerry	1927-1996	20	40	50	35	Baritone sax player
Murphy, Turk	1915-1987	25	40	50	65	Band leader, trombone
Navarro, Theodore "Fats"	1923-1950					Trumpet player. PU
Nichols, Red	1905-1965	40	70		75	Cornet player
Oliver, King	1885-1938	400	800			Cornet player
Oliver, Sy	1910-1988	35	70		80	Composer, conductor
Ory, Kid	1886-1973	125	250		230	Trombone player
Parker, Charlie	1920-1955	375	1200		3250	Composer, alto sax
Pass, Joe	1929-1994	20	35		45	Guitarist
Pepper, Art	1925-1982	35	50		70	Alto sax player
Pettiford, Oscar	1922-1960	45	75		60	Bop bassist
Powell, Bud	1924-1966	100	200		200	Piano player
Pullen, Don	1942-1995	20	40		40	Percussive piano player
Ra, Sun	c.1915-1993	25	50		60	Bandleader, composer
Rainey, Gertrude "Ma"	1886-1939	475	1275			Blues singer
Redmon, Don	1900-1964	20	30		60	Composer, arranger
Reinhardt, Django	1910-1953	65	125		125	European guitarist
Rich, Buddy	1917-1987	40	75		150	Band leader, drummer
Rodney, Red	1928-1994	20	35		40	Trumpeter
Rosolino, Frank	1926-1978	25	40		40	Trombone player
Rowles, Jimmy	1918-1996	15	25		30	Composer, accompanist
Rushing, Jimmy	1903-1972	30	60		50	Blues singer
Russell, Pee Wee	1906-1969	25	50		50	Clarinet player
Sims, Zoot	1925-1985	30	50		60	Tenor, alto sax , clarinet
Singleton, Zutty	1898-1975	25	45		40	Drummer
Smith, Bessie	1894-1937	550	1150		2000	Blues singer
Smith, Clarence "Pinetop"	1904-1929					Boogie Woogie, PU
Smith, Willie "The Lion"	1897-1973	85	150		140	Stride pianist
Spanier, Muggsy	1906-1967	40	75		65	Band leader, coronet
Stitt, Sonny	1924-1982	20	40		30	Alto, tenor sax player
Strayhorn, Billy	1915-1967	40	80		65	Composer, piano player
Tatum, Art	1910-1956					Piano player, PU
Taylor, Art	1929-1995	20	40		35	Bandleader, drummer
Teagarden, Jack	1905-1964	75	100		135	Trombone player
Tough, David	1908-1948					Drummer, PU
Tristano, Lennie	1919-1978	30	55		50	Piano player, composer
Turner, Joe	1911-1985	50	120		150	Blues singer
Vaughan, Sarah	1924-1990	50	100	275	150	Singer
Venuti, Joe	1904-1978	55	125		100	Pioneer jazz violinist
Walker, T-Bone	1910-1975	50	125		100	Electric guitar pioneer
Waller, Thomas "Fats"	1904-1943	350	400	800	600	Piano player, composer

Name	db/dd	Sig.	DS/LS	ALS	SP	Comments/Assoc.
Washington, Dinah	1924-1963	140	200		225	Singer
Waters, Ethel	1896-1977	50	135	175	175	Jazz and blues singer
Waters, Muddy	(See Rock 'n' Roll section)					
Watson, Johnny	1935-1996	25	50	125	60	Guitarist (R&B)
Webb, Chick	1902-1939					Band leader, drum., PU
Webster, Ben	1909-1973	140	250			Tenor sax player
Whiteman, Paul	1890-1967	70	150		240	Orchestra leader
Williams, Charles "Cootie"	1908-1985					Band leader, PU
Williams, Mary Lou	1914-1981					Composer, piano, PU
Wilson, Cassandra	1955-					Singer, composer
Wilson, Teddy	1912-1986	50	100	125	100	Composer, piano player
Winding, Kal	1922-1983					Composer, PU
Yancey, Jimmy	1894-1951					Piano player, PU
Young, Lester "Pres"	1909-1959	90	80	160	175	Composer

OPERA

WHAT YOU NEED TO KNOW

* An opera is a dramatic musical work in which singing takes the place of speech. Music, dancing and spectacular stage interact and are of paramount importance.

* Opera originated in the late 16th-century Florence when the musical declamation, lyrical monologues and choruses of Classical Greek drama were reproduced in current form.

* An operetta is a light form of opera. It includes music, dance and spoken dialogue. While it can employ many elements, it is often romantic or sentimental. Its origins lie in the 19th-centuriy and became an amusing departure from opera. A familiar example is Gilbert and Sullivan's "Pirates of Penzance" (1879).

* While not as popular now as other forms of music, opera singers often became the most popular singers of their time, such as Enrico Caruso and Maria Callas.

MARKET FACTS

* The most popular form is an autographed photograph from a performer in a key role.

* Participants in this niche are generally very responsive to autograph requests.

TRENDS

* While this is not an extremely popular area of collecting, its values have exhibited consistent appreciation.

Name	db/dd	Sig.	DS/LS	ALS	SP	Comments/Assoc.
Alda, Frances	1883-1952	30	60	125	80	Soprano
Althouse, Paul	1889-1954	35	75	150	100	Tenor
Amato, Pasquale	1878-1942	45	100	200	130	Baritone
Anderson, Marion	1902-1993	175	220	275	365	Contralto
Bjorling, Jussi	1911-1960	520	675	1000	950	Tenor
Bocelli, Andrea	1958-	25	75		50	
Bori, Lucrezia	1887-1960	45	100	125	100	Soprano
Callas, Maria	1923-1977	325	875	900	1200	Soprano
Calve, Emma	1858-1942	65	125	200	475	Soprano
Carreras, Jose		20	50		50	Tenor
Caruso, Enrico	1873-1921	300	575	700	1100	Tenor, self-caricatures
Challapin, Feodor	1873-1938	225	275	525	575	Bass
Christoff, Boris	1914-1993	25	60	125	80	Bass
Crooks, Richard	1900-1972	25	50	60	75	Tenor
De Luca, Giuseppe	1876-1950	45	85	120	110	Baritone
De Reszke, Edouard	1853-1917	150	225	250	275	Bass
De Reszke, Jean	1850-1925	130	200	225	250	Tenor
Destinn, Emmy	1878-1930	125	185	225	230	Soprano
Domingo, Placido		30	80		65	Tenor
Eames, Emma	1865-1952	40	75	120	85	Soprano
Farrar, Geraldine	1882-1967	75	120	125	125	Soprano
Flagstad, Kirsten	1895-1962	100	180	225	245	Soprano
Fremstad, Olive	1871-1951	110	200	350	400	Soprano
Galli-Curci, Amelita	1882-1963	75	150	300	250	Soprano
Garden, Mary	1874-1967	40	70	100	150	Soprano
Gigli, Benjamino	1890-1957	110	225	275	300	Tenor
Gobbi, Tito	1913-1984	35	70	100	125	Baritone
Hempel, Frieda	1885-1955	30	75	100	100	Soprano
Jeritza, Maria	1887-1982	25	50	75	100	Soprano
Kipnis, Alexander	1891-1978	50	100	125	125	Bass
Lehmann, Lilli	1848-1929	75	175	325	200	Soprano
Lehmann, Lotte	1888-1976	35	75	150	150	Soprano
Lind, Jenny	1820-1887	100	200	300		Soprano
McCormack, John	1884-1945	55	175	335	200	Tenor
Marchesi, Bianche	1863-1940	60	150	175	200	Soprano
Melba, Nellie	1861-1931	100	200	325	500	Soprano
Melchior, Lauritz	1890-1973	50	125	200	200	Tenor
Milanov, Zinka	1906-1989	30	75	125	125	Soprano
Nordica, Lillian	1857-1914	75	150	230	275	Soprano
Patti, Adelina	1843-1919	125	250	350	500	Soprano
Pavarotti, Luciano	1935-	45	100		75	Tenor
Pears, Peter	1910-1986	25	50	60	60	Tenor
Peerce, Jan	1904-1984	25	50	75	70	Tenor
Pinza, Ezio	1892-1957	75	150	300	225	Bass
Pons, Lily	1898-1976	50	100	200	150	Soprano
Ponselle, Rosa	1897-1981	50	75	125	300	Soprano
Sembrich, Marcella	1858-1935	100	200	275	275	Soprano
Steber, Eleanor	1916-1990	25	50	100	85	Soprano
Tetrazzini, Luisa	1871-1940	100	150	250	250	Soprano
Tibbett, Lawrence	1896-1960	60	125	125	150	Baritone
Tucker, Richard	1913-1975	50	50	100	125	Tenor
Viardot, Pauline	1821-1910	50	125	200	150	Mezzo-soprano

Name	db/dd	Sig.	DS/LS	ALS	SP	Comments/Assoc.
Warren, Leonard	1911-1960	100	200	225	250	Baritone

POPULAR

WHAT YOU NEED TO KNOW

* Popular music has always meant popular autograph subjects and this is not likely to change.

* Similar to rock 'n' roll stars, subjects can be elusive especially recent stars.

MARKET FACTS

* The most encountered form is the signed photograph.

* Similar to classical and extremely popular with collectors in this niche is the AMQS - autograph musical quotation signed.

* Alternatives in form include sheet music, contracts, programs, playbills, posters, albums, singles, compact discs, and even tour programs.

Notes: See also rock 'n' roll section.

Name	db/dd	Sig.	DS/LS	ALS	SP	Comments/Assoc.
Adler, Richard	1921-	20	40	75	35	U.S., "Damn Yankees"
Ager, Milton	1893-1979	25	40	50	40	U.S., "Ain't She Sweet?"
Altman, Arthur	1910-1994	20	30	40	35	U.S. "All or Nothing at All"
Anderson, Leroy	1908-1975	30	75	150	50	U.S. "Syncopated Clock"
Anka, Paul	1941-	5	15	25	20	"My Way,"RS!
Arlen, Harold	1905-1986	60	100	150	75	U.S. "Stormy Weather"
Ashman, Howard	1950-1991	50	100	130	80	U.S. lyricist, "The Little Mermaid"
Bacharach, Burt	1928-	20	40	50	35	U.S., "Raindrops Keep..."
Ball, Ernest	1878-1927					U.S., "When Irish Eyes..., PU
Berlin, Irving	1888-1989	200	1100	2000	1150	U.S., "White Christmas"
Blake, Eubie	1883-1983	65	200	180	100	U.S., "I'm Just Wild About Harry"
Bock, Jerry	1928-	35	50	75	60	U.S., "Fiddler on the Roof"
Bond, Carrie Jacobs	1862-1946	40	100	145	50	U.S., I Love You Truly"
Brown, Nacio Herb	1896-1964	50	125	150	75	U.S., "Singing in the Rain"
Burke, Johnny	1908-1984	25	65	100	50	U.S. lyricist, "Misty"
Caesar, Irving	1895-1996	25	60	100	50	U.S. lyricist, "Just a Gigolo"
Cahn, Sammy	1913-1993	20	75	100	50	U.S. lyricist, "High Hopes," RS
Carmichael, Hoagy	1899-1981	50	175	300	225	U.S., "Stardust," AMQS- $325
Church, Charlotte	1986-	15	40		30	Wales, classical, "Voice of..."
Cohan, George M.	1878-1942	125	200	350	275	U.S., "Give My Regards to ..."
Cohen, Leonard	1934-	15	25	50	30	U.S. lyricist, "Suzanne"
Coleman, Cy	1929-	10	20	30	25	U.S., "Sweet Charity," RS
Comden, Betty &						

Name	db/dd	Sig.	DS/LS	ALS	SP	Comments/Assoc.
Green, Adolph	1919-, 1915-	20	40	65	40	U.S. lyricist, "New York, NY"
Coots, John Frederick	1897-?	40	65	135	50	U.S., "For All We Know"
Coward, Noel	1899-1973	175	250	375	350	British, "Bitter Sweet"
David, Hal	1921-	15	30	75	40	U.S. lyricist, "What the ...," RS
De Sylva, Buddy	1895-1950	60	100	145	100	U.S. lyricist, ""April Showers"
Diamond, Neil	1941-	30	100	150	75	U.S., "I'm a Believer"
Dietz, Howard	1896-1983	25	65	80	50	U.S. lyricist, "Dancing in ..."
Donaldson, Walter	1893-1947	75	150	250	150	U.S., "Main' Whoopee"
Dubin, Al	1891-1945	40	75	75	65	U.S. lyricist, "Tiptoe Through..."
Duke, Vernon	1903-1969	35	50	60	50	U.S., "April in Paris"
Dylan, Bob	1941-	200	450		450	U.S., "Blowin' in the Wind"
Ebb, Fred	1936-	10	25	40	25	U.S. lyricist, "Cabaret," RS
Edwards, Gus	1879-1945	50	125	150	100	U.S., "School Days"
Edwards, Sherman	1919-1981	30	50	70	60	U.S., "See You In September"
Ellington, Duke	(see Blues & Jazz)					
Fain, Sammy	1902-1989	20	40	45	40	U.S., "I'll Be Seeing You"
Fields, Dorothy	1905-1974	25	60	75	50	U.S. lyricist, "Don't Blame Me"
Fisher, Fred	1875-1942	60	115	150	125	U.S., "Chicago"
Foster, Stephen Collins	1826-1864	1150	3000			U.S., "My Old Kentucky Home"
Frimi, Rudolf	1879-1972	125	250	350	250	Czech./U.S. "The Firefly"
Gay, John	1685-1732					British, "The Beg...Opera," PU
Gershwin, George	1898-1937	860	1750	5000	3100	U.S., "I've Got a Crush on You"
Gershwin, Ira	1896-1983	100	200	300	200	U.S. lyricist, "Embraceable You"
Gilbert, William S.	1836-1911	200	400	750	650	British, "H.M.S. Pinafore"
Goffin, Gerry	1939-	15	40	50	30	U.S. lyricist, "Up on the Roof"
Gordon, Mack	1905-1959	40	65	125	50	U.S. lyricist, "You'll Never Know"
Gould, Morton	1913-1996	25	50	75	50	U.S., "Fall River Suite"
Grofe, Ferde	1892-1972	125	230	275	125	U.S., "Grand Canyon Suite"
Hamilsch, Marvin	1944-	10	25	50	20	U.S., "The Way We Were"
Hammerstein, Oscar II	1895-1960	165	300		275	U.S. lyricist, "Ol' Man River"
Harburg, E.Y. (Yip)	1898-1981	175	300		250	U.S. lyricist, "Over the Rainbow"
Hart, Lorenz	1895-1943	500				U.S. lyricist, "Blue Moon"
Henderson, Ray	1896-1970	30	50	60	45	U.S., "Five Foot Two Eyes ..."
Herbert, Victor	1859-1924	100	200	400	350	Irish/U.S., "Babes in Toyland"
Herman, Jerry	1933-	10	30	45	25	U.S., "Hello Dolly," RS
Heyward, DuBose	1885-1940	150	400	300	275	U.S. lyricist, "Summertime"
Holland, B., Dozier, L., Holland, E.	1941-, 1941-, 1939-	125				U.S., "Heat Wave," "Stop! In..."
Jobim, Antonio Carlos	1927-1994	25	40	75	50	Brazil, "One Note Samba"
Joel, Billy	1949-	25	50	145	70	U.S., "Piano Man," FA
Joplin, Scott	1868-1917	700	1125	2210		U.S., "Treemonisha"
Kahn, Gus	1886-1941	55	70	80	75	U.S. lyricist, "Memories"
Kander, John	1927-	10	20	40	20	U.S., "Cabaret," RS
Kern, Jerome	1885-1945	300	825	2000	2000	U.S., "Show Boat"
King, Carole	1942-	15	50	60	25	U.S., "Up on the Roof," RS
Lane, Burton	1912-1997	15	25	30	25	U.S., "Finian's Rainbow"
Lehar, Franz	1870-1948	100	200	475	300	Hung., "Merry Widow"
Leiber, J. & Stoller, M.	1933-, 1933-	150				U.S., " Hound Dog,"
Leigh, Mitch	1928-	20	30	40	35	U.S., "Man of La Mancha"
Lennon, John	1940-1980	600	2500		1100	British, "The Beatles"
Lerner, Alan J.	1918-1986	50	100	235	185	U.S. lyricist, "My Fair lady"
Loesser, Frank	1910-1969	125	200	375	225	U.S., "Guys and Dolls"

Name	db/dd	Sig.	DS/LS	ALS	SP	Comments/Assoc.
Loewe, Frederick	1901-1988	50	80	150	75	U.S./Austrian, "My Fair Lady"
Mancini, Henry	1924-1994	25	100	125	75	U.S., "Moon River," RS
Mann, Barry & Weil, Cynthia	1939-, 1937 -	50			75	U.S., "You've Lost That..."
McCartney, Paul	1942-	200	550		300	British, "The Beatles"
McHugh, Jimmy	1894-1969	30	60	120	60	U.S., "Don't Blame Me"
Menken, Alan	1950-	20	50	55	40	U.S., "Beauty and the Beast"
Mercer, Johnny	1909-1976	50	125	200	125	U.S. lyricist, "That Old Black..."
Merrill, Bob	1921-	10	20	35	25	U.S. lyricist, "People"
Meyer, Joseph	1894-1987	25	50	60	50	U.S., "If You Knew Susie"
Norworth, Jack	1879-1959	150	275	250	250	U.S. lyricist, "Shine On..."
Olcott, Chauncey	1858-1932	50	75	125	100	U.S., "Mother Machree"
Parish, Mitchell	1901-1993	25	40	75	50	U.S. lyricist, "Stardust"
Pomus, Jerome "Doc"	1925-1991	20	40	50	40	U.S., "A Teenager in Love"
Porter, Cole	1893-1964	275	600		1000	U.S., "Anything Goes"
Razaf, Andy	1895-1973	50	100	200	100	U.S. lyricist, "Honeysuckle..."
Robin, Leo	1900-1984	25	45	50	40	U.S. lyricist, "Diamonds are..."
Robinson, Smokey	1940-	30	125	225	60	U.S., "Shop Around"
Rogers, Richard	1902-1979	100	300	475	200	U.S., , "Oklahoma!," RS
Romberg, Sigmund	1887-1951	150	250	375	250	Hungarian, "Maytime"
Rome, Harold	1908-1993	20	50	100	40	U.S., "Pins and Needles"
Rose, Vincent	1880-1944	50	75	150	115	U.S., "Blueberry Hill"
Ruby, Harry	1895-1974	25	100	200	50	U.S., "Who's Sorry Now?"
Schwartz, Arthur	1900-1984	40	100	250	75	U.S., "That's Entertainment"
Sedaka, Neil	1939-	10	25	30	20	U.S., "Breaking Up is...," RS
Simon, Paul	1942-	25	100	200	75	U.S., "Sounds of Silence"
Sondheim, Stephen	1930-	25	100	200	100	U.S., "A Little Night Music"
Sousa, John Phillip	1854-1932	175	300	500	1000	U.S., "Stars and Stripes..."
Straus, Oskar	1870-1954	150	225	250	225	Austrian, "Chocolate Soldier"
Strauss, Johann	1825-1899	500	1500	2000	4000	Austrian, "Blue Danube"
Strouse, Charles	1928-	20	50	100	40	U.S., "Bye Bye Birdie"
Styne, Jule	1905-1994	30	75	135	60	British/U.S., "Funny Girl"
Sullivan, Arthur S.	1842-1900	200	400	750	1000	British, "Pirates of Penzance"
Taylor, Deems	1885-1966	25	75	100	50	U.S., "Peter Ibbetson"
Tobias, Harry	1905-1994	20	40	60	45	U.S., "I'll Keep the Lovelight..."
Van Alstyne, Egbert	1882-1951	45	90	120	75	U.S., "Pretty Baby"
Van Heusen, Jimmy	1913-1990	75	125	200	115	U.S., "Love and Marriage"
von Tilzer, Albert	1878-1956	50	100	200	75	U.S., "Take Me ...Ball Game"
von Tilzer, Harry	1872-1946	40	100	150	60	U.S., "On a Sunday Afternoon"
Waller, Fats	(see Blues & Jazz)					
Warren, Harry	1893-1981	35	75	150	50	U.S., "We're in the Money"
Webb, Jimmy	1946-	25	50	100	50	U.S., "Up, Up and Away"
Webber, Andrew Lloyd	1948-	75	250		425	British, "Cats," very elusive !
Webster, Paul F.	1907-1984	25	50	75	50	U.S. lyricist, "Secret Love"
Weill, Kurt	1900-1950	250	700	1150	400	German/U.S., "Threepenny..."
Wenrich, Percy	1887-1952	60	125	240	130	U.S., "Moonlight Bay"
Whiting, Richard A.	1891-1938	50	100	150	100	U.S., "Beyond the Blue ..."
Williams, John	1932-	25	50	100	50	U.S., "Star Wars" series
Wilson, Meredith	1902-1984	30	60	100	60	U.S., "The Music Man"
Wonder, Stevie	(see Rock 'n' Roll)					
Yellen, Jack	1892-1991	15	35	50	30	U.S. lyricist, "Happy Days ..."
Youmans, Vincent	1898-1946	60	150	275	150	U.S., "No, No, Nanette"

ROCK 'N' ROLL

WHAT YOU NEED TO KNOW

* Popular with many collectors, rock 'n' roll signatures can command significant prices.

* Response rates to indirect autograph requests are very low in this niche.

* In many cases, limited artist availability greatly reduces the opportunity to acquire an authentic signature.

* When possible, collectors prefer to acquire signatures in-person to guarantee authenticity.

* Illegible, hastily signed or unusual variations of authentic autographed material is common in this niche and serves only to add increased complications to the authentication process.

MARKET FACTS

* This market is driven by the most popular entertainers, such as Elvis Presley and The Beatles.

* Forgeries are encountered and can be difficult to determine as such because of the lack of viable facsimiles for comparison.

* Popular forms include photographs, albums, programs, compact discs, guitars, and posters.

* Most collectors prefer the signatures of original group members over latter variations. In unique cases, such as The Temptations, this can differ.

TRENDS

* Other than legends, the most popular current entertainers are in greatest demand.

* With the passing of each generation, many older performers have become more accessible to collectors.

* Unlike Elvis, The Beatles and Kiss, memorabilia marketing has played a limited role with most bands during the last few decades.

Abbreviations: KS = key signature(s), RS = responsive signers

Name	Sig.	LS/DS	SP	Comments,/Notes
AC/DC	125	225	300	Bon Scott (KS),, "Highway To Hell"
Adams, Bryan	25	45	65	"Cuts Like a Knife," "Have You Ever Really..."
Aerosmith	150	275	400	"Sweet Emotion," "Dream On," RS
Aguilera, Christina	20	40	50	"What a Girl Wants"
The Allman Brothers Band	125	240	300	(1995), D. Allman (KS), B. Oakley (KS)- $400
Amos, Tori	25	50	60	"Crucify"
The Animals	200	350	400	(1994), E. Burden (KS), C. Chandler (KS)
Anthony, Marc	17	30	45	"Contra la Corriente"
Apple, Fiona	10	25	40	"Criminal"
Arie, India	15	30	40	"Video"
The Association	20	35	50	"Cherish," "Windy," "Never My Love"
Avalon, Frankie	10	15	25	"Venus," 'Why," "Ginger Bread"
Badu, Erykah	15	30	25	"Baduizm," real name Erica Wright
Baker, LaVern	20	25	45	(1991), "I Cried a Tear," "Jim Dandy"
Hank Ballard ... Midnighters	40	75	150	(1990), a scarce signature, "Work With Me..."
The Band	225	300	270	(1994), R. Manuel (KS), "The Weight"
Bass, Lance				NSYNC, PU
The Beach Boys	250	450	500	(1988), B. Wilson (KS), D. Wilson (KS,)
Beastie Boys	25	35	50	"(You Gotta) Fight for Your Right (to Party)"
The Beatles	1750		3500	(1988), "Penny Lane," "Let It Be," FA
Beck	20	30	40	"Loser", real name Beck Hansen
Beckham, Victoria				Posh Spice, PU
The Bee Gees	35	70	100	(1997), "Stayin' Alive"
Benatar, Pat	15	30	50	"Hit Me With Your Best Shot," "We Belong"
Berry, Chuck	50	100	150	1986),elusive, "Johnny B. Goode"
The Big Bopper (J.P. Richardson)	275	350	450	"Chantilly Lace", K. w/B. Holly
Bjork	25	50	35	"Post," real name Bjork Gudmundsdottir
Black, Clint	20	40	30	"Killin' Time," FA
Black Sabbath	55	125	175	"Paranoid," Catch them at a reunion concert!
Bland, Bobby "Blue"	25	60	75	(1992), reclusive and evasive signer!
Bilge, Mary J.	10	15	20	"Real Love," "Be Happy"
Blind Faith	200	400	500	Grech (1946-90, KS)"Can't Find My Way Home"
Blind Melon	50	65	75	Shannon Hoon (1967-1995, KS)
Blondie	30	60	75	"Heart of Glass"
Blood, Sweat and Tears	30	55	85	D.C. Thomas (KS), "Spinning Wheel"
Bolton, Michael	20	40	25	"How Am I Supposed..."
Bonds, Gary U.S.	10	15	25	"Quarter to Three," "School Is Out!," RS
Bon Jovi	55	125	175	J. Bon Jovi (KS), "Livin' on a Prayer"
Booker T. and the MG's	50	115	125	(1992), Booker T. Jones (KS), A. Jackson (KS)
Bostic, Earl	15	35	45	(1913-1965), "Flamingo," "Sleep"
Bowie, David (David Jones)	100	150	180	(1996), "Space Oddity," "Fame"
Boyz II Men	60	125	150	"I'll Make Love to You"
Brandy	25	50	35	"The Boy is Mine," real name Brandy Norwood
Braxton, Toni	20	40	60	"Un-Break My Heart"
Brooks, Garth	25	60	60	"Ropin' the Wind," RS
Brown, James	20	45	65	(1986), RS, "Papa's Got a Brand New Bag"
Brown, Melanie				Scary Spice, PU
Brown, Ruth	20	35	50	(1993), "Lucky Lips," "This Little Girl..."
Browne, Jackson	15	30	45	"Doctor My Eyes," "Stay"
Buffalo Springfield	85	125	175	(1997), N. Young (KS), S. Stills (KS)

Name	Sig.	LS/DS	SP	Comments,/Notes
Buffet, Jimmy	25	55	60	"Margaritaville"
Bunton, Emma				Baby Spice, PU
Bush	35	50	65	"Glycerine"
The Byrds	300	575	600	(1991), G. Clark (1941-1991) "Turn! Turn! Turn!"
Carey, Mariah	30	75	65	"Vision of Love," "Honey," "Fantasy," FA
Carpenter, Mary Chapin	15	40	25	"He Thinks He'll Keep Her"
The Cars	40	50	55	R. Ocasek (KS), "Shake It Up"
Carter, Nick				Backstreet Boys, PU
Cash, Johnny	50	110	100	(1992,)"I Walk the Line," FA (1932-2003)
Cash, Rosanne	30	60	50	"I Don't Know Why You..."
Charles, Ray	65	150	175	(1986), DS-$300, "Georgia on My Mind," RS
Chasez, J.C.				NSYNC, PU
Cheap Trick	40	60	75	"Surrender," "The Flame," RS
Checker, Chubby	10	25	30	"The Twist," RS
Chesney, Kenny	15	40	30	"You Had Me from Hello," RS
Chicago	85	150	175	T. Kath (1946-1978), P. Cetera (KS)
Chisholm, Melanie				Sporty Spice, PU
Clapton, Eric	50	60	75	"Layla, RS
The Clash	40	100	120	"Rock the Casbah," "Train in Vain..."
The Coasters	50	125	150	(1987), "Yakety Yak"
Cochran, Eddie	350	700	800	(1987), (1938-1960), "Summertime Blues"
Cocker, Joe	20	30	35	"With a Little Help From My Friends," FA
Cole, Paula	15	25	30	"Where Have All the Cowboys Gone?"
Collins, Phil	20	30	50	"Against All Odds," RS - in-person
Colvin, Shawn	15	25	30	"Sunny Came Home"
Combs, Sean "Puff Daddy"	15	35	40	"I'll Be Missing You," "P.Diddy"
Connick, Harry, Jr.	20	40	25	Crooner
Cooke, Sam	300	600	650	(1986), (1935-1964), "You Send Me," "Shake"
Coolio	15	25	40	"Gansta's Paradise"
Cooper, Alice	20	40	75	"Elected," "School's Out," "You and Me"
Costello, Elvis	10	25	35	"Alison," RS
Cream	150	150	300	(1993), E. Clapton (KS), "Sunshine of ..."
Creedence Clearwater Revival	175	325	350	(1993), T. Fogerty (1941-1990)
Crosby, Stills and Nash	50	150	175	(1997), "Suite: Judy Blue Eyes"
Crow, Sheryl	15	25	50	"All I Want to Do"
The Cure	40	60	80	"Love Song," "Friday I'm in Love"
The Crystals	50	75	80	"Da Doo Ron Ron," "Then He Kissed Me"
Cypress Hill	20	30	35	"Insane in the Brain"
D'Angelo	15	30	25	"Voodoo"
Danny and the Juniors	25	50	65	D. Rapp (KS), "At the Hop," "
Darin, Bobby	55	100	125	(1990), (1936-1973), "Splish Splash"
Spencer Davis Group	40	100	125	S.Winwood (KS), "Gimme Some Lovin"
Deep Purple	50	80	125	"Smoke on the Water,"
Def Leppard	75	150	175	S. Clark (1960-1991), "Photograph"
Depeche Mode	40	50	65	"Enjoy the Silence"
Didley, Bo	25	40	50	(1987), "Who Do You Love"
Dion and the Belmonts	25	40	60	(1989), "Runaround Sue"
Dion, Celine	30	65	75	"My Heart Will ..."
Dire Straits	30	65	80	M. Knopfler (KS), "Money For Nothing"
Domino, Fats	25	40	50	(1986), "Blueberry Hill," "Blue Monday," RS

Name	Sig.	LS/DS	SP	Comments,/Notes
Donovan	15	20	35	"Mellow Yellow"
The Doobie Brothers	45	75	85	"What a Fool Believes," "China Grove"
The Doors	1750	2500	3000	(1993), J.Morrison - $700 - $1,500
Dorough, Howie				Backstreet Boys, PU
The Drifters	500	800	1000	Four key lineups, all various prices
Duran Duran	45	100	135	"Hungry Like the Wolf," "The Reflex"
Dylan, Jakob	30	60	55	The Wallflowers
The Eagles	150	200	250	"Hotel California," some RS
Earth, Wind and Fire	30	60	75	"Shining Star"
Eddy, Duane	30	60	65	(1994), "Rebel-Rouser"
Edmonds, Kenneth "Babyface"	20	50	40	Singer, producer
Elliott, Missy	15	30	35	"Supa Dupa Fly"
Emerson, Lake and Plamer	100	150	200	"Lucky Man," have done private signings
Eminem	30	70	55	"The Real Slim Shady," Marshall Mathers III
En Vogue	25	40	50	"Hold On"
Etheridge, Melissa	15	30	25	Singer, songwriter
Epstein, Brian				(1934-1967), The Beatles, scarce, PU
The Eurythmics	50	75	100	"Sweet Dreams (Are Made of This)"
The Everly Brothers	50	75	100	(1986), "Wake Up, Little Susie"
Fatone, Joey				NSYNC, PU
The Five Satins	20	40	55	"In the Still of the Night," "Shadows"
Fleetwood Mac	175	250	300	"Dreams," Rumours lineup key
The Four Seasons	40	100	115	(1990), F. Valli (KS) - $20-$50
The Four Tops	60	125	150	(1990), "I Can't Help Myself ..."
Franklin, Aretha	25	50	55	(1987), "Respect"
Gabriel, Peter	20	40	50	Former member of Genesis, "Red Rain"
Gaye, Marvin	150	300	300	(1939-1984), Sheet music - $350
Genesis	75	100	125	"Genesis Live" lineup; P. Collins (KS)
Gill, Vince	20	40	35	"When I Call Your Name," RS
Grand Funk Railroad	30	75	100	"We're an American Band"
Grand Master Flash and ...	10	25	30	"The Message"
Grant, Amy	10	25	20	"Baby, Baby," RS
The Grateful Dead	300	550	700	J. Garcia (KS), Mckernan - $100-325 - scarce
Gray, Macy	20	45	30	"I Try"
Green, Al	15	35	40	(1995), RS, "Let's Stay Together"
Guns N' Roses	150	175	200	"Sweet Child o' Mine"
Bille Haley and the Comets	400	725	750	(1987), B. Haley was an elusive signer!
Hall and Oates	40	50	55	"Kiss on My List," "Maneater," "Out of Touch"
Halliwell, Geri				Ginger Spice, PU
Harrison, George	250	500	400	(1943-2001), The Beatles
Haughton, Aaliyah	65	100	80	(1979-2001)
Heart	30	55	60	Ann & Nancy Wilson (KS), "Barracuda"
Hendrix, Jimi	850	2000	2250	(1992), FA, "Purple Haze"
Herman's Hermits	30	75	100	P. Noone (KS), "Mrs. Brown, You've Got ..."
Hill, Faith	15	30	35	"The Kiss"
Hill, Lauryn	20	40	40	"The Miseducation of..."
Buddy Holly and the Crickets	875	1250	1650	(1986), B. Holly (KS), "That'll Be the Day"

Name	Sig.	LS/DS	SP	Comments,/Notes
Hooker, John Lee	50	120	150	(1991), "Boogie Chillun"
Hootie and the Blowfish	35	80	110	D. Rucker (KS), "Hold My Hand," "Let Her Cry"
Houston, Whitney	35	75	100	"I Will Always Love You," elusive
Ice Cube	20	50	35	Rap artist, actor
Iglesias, Enrique	15	35	30	Singer
Imbruglia, Natalie	20	40	40	"Torn"
The Impressions	30	75	100	(1991), C. Mayfield (KS), "For Your Precious ..."
INXS	60	120	175	D. Hutchence (KS), "Need You Tonight"
Isaak, Chris	25	60	45	"Wicked Game," FA
The Isley Brothers	30	100	125	(1992), values without J. Hendrix
The Jackson Five	275	350	400	(1997), M. Jackson (KS), "ABC," "I'll Be There"
Jackson, Alan	25	100	50	"Neon Rainbow"
Jackson, Janet	25	60	75	"Control," "When I Think of You"
Jackson, Michael	200	300	350	"Rock With You," "Billie Jean," "Thriller," RS
James, Etta	20	40	45	(1993), "Roll With Me, Henry," "At Last," RS
Tommy James / the Shondells	45	70	100	T. James (KS), "Crimson and Clover"
Jay and the Americans	25	50	65	"This Magic Moment," "Cara Mia," "She Cried"
Jay - Z	20	35	25	"Money Ain't a Thang," real name Shawn Carter
Jean, Wyclef	15	30	20	"The Fugees"
Jefferson Airplane	125	200	250	(1996), "White Rabbit," RS
Jethro Tull	40	60	80	I.Anderson (KS) $15-$30, "Thick as a Brick"
Jewel	15	50	55	"You Were Meant for Me"
Jett, Joan	15	20	35	"I Love Rock 'n' Roll"
John, Elton	50	85	125	(1994), "Candle in the Wind," "Crocodile Rock"
John, Little Willie	225	500		(1996), died in prison, "Sleep," "Fever"
Jones, Quincy	35	80	50	Producer, FA
Joplin, Janis	725	2000	2250	(1995), "Me and Bobby McGee"
K.C. and the Sunshine Band	25	35	40	"Get Down Tonight," "I'm Your Boogie Man"
Keyes, Alicia	20	40	35	"Fallin'," real name Alicia Augello-Cook
Kid Rock	25	60	45	"Devil Without...," real name Robert Ritchie
King, B.B.	20	50	50	(1987), "The Thrill is Gone," RS
King, Carole	15	20	25	"it's Too Late," "Jazzman," RS
The Kinks	75	125	150	(1990), "You Really Got Me," "Lola"
Kirkpatrick, Chris				NSYNC, PU
Kiss	130	150	175	"Rock 'n' Roll All Night," Values for original lineup
Gladys Knight and the Pips	25	55	70	(1996), G. Knight (KS, "Midnight Train ..."
Knowles, Beyonce				Destiny's Child, PU
Krall, Diana	20	45	30	"Peel Me a Grape"
Kravitz, Lenny	15	30	20	"It Ain't Over..."
Lang. k.d.	15	35	25	"Constant Craving"
Led Zeppelin	750	1200	1250	(1995), J. Bonham (KS, "Stairway to Heaven")
Lee, Brenda	10	20	30	"I'm Sorry"
Lennon, John	700	1750	1100	(1940-1980), "Imagine," FA
Lewis, Jerry Lee	35	50	85	(1986), "Whole Lotta Shakin' Going On"
(LIL) Bow Wow	15	25	20	Rapper, real name Shad Moss
Little Anthony and the Imperials	30	50	55	"Tears on My Pillow"
Little Richard	65	125	150	(1986), an elusive signer, "Tutti Frutti"
Littrell, Brian				Backstreet Boys, PU

Name	Sig.	LS/DS	SP	Comments,/Notes
Live	25	30	45	E. Kowalczyk (KS), "Lightning Crashes"
L.L. Cool J	20	30	40	"Mama Said Knock You Out," (James T. Smith)
Lovett, Lyle	10	25	20	Singer, songwriter
The Lovin' Spoonful	35	65	75	"Summer in the City," "Do You ... Magic"
Frankie Lymon ... Teenagers	450	600	700	"Why Do Fools Fall in Love?," (1993), ESPV
Lynn, Loretta	10	30	25	"Coal Miner's Daughter," RS
Lynne, Shelby				Singer, PU
Lynyrd Skynyrd	250	300	300	Values for original lineup, R. Van Zant (KS)
Madonna	150	300	375	"Live To Tell," a very elusive signer, FA
The Mamas and the Papas	400	500	600	C. Elliott (KS) - $150, "Monday, Monday"
Mann, Aimee				Singer, songwriter, PU
Manson, Marilyn	30	75	65	Brian Warner (KS),
Manson, Shirley				Version 2.0, PU
Marley, Bob and the Wailers	1250	2250	3000	(1994). B. Marley (KS) - $1000, "Exodus"
Martha and the Vandellas	25	65	75	(1995), M. Reeves (KS), "Dancin' in the Streets"
Martin, Ricky	20	45	35	"Livin' La Vida Loca"
The Marvelettes	35	60	75	G. Dobbins (KS), "Please, Mr. Postman"
Master P	15	35	25	"No Limit," real name Percy Miller"
Matchbox 20	30	75	60	R.Thomas (KS)
Mathews, Dave	25	60	30	Singer, songwriter, RS
McCartney, Paul	150	400	350	"Jet," "Band on the Run," "Maybe I'm ..."
McEntire, Reba	10	25	20	"Is There Life Out There?"
McGraw, Tim	20	50	30	"Not a Moment Too Soon," RS
McLachlan, Sarah	15	30	25	"Touch"
McLean, A.J.				Backstreet Boys, PU
McLean, Don	10	15	15	"American Pie," "Vincent," "Crying"
McPhatter, Clyde	600	1150	1275	(1987), (1932-1972), "A Lover's Question"
Meatloaf	15	25	35	"Paradise by the Dashboard Light," RS
Mellencamp, John (Cougar)	20	35	50	"Jack and Diane," "Hurts So Good"
Men at Work	15	25	30	"Who Can It Be Now?," "Down Under"
Merchant, Natalie	15	40	30	10,000 Maniacs
Metallica	75	160	200	J. Hetfield (KS), C. Burton (1962-1986)
Michael, George	25	50	65	"Faith," "Father Figure," "One More Try"
Midler, Bette	25	50	30	"Wind Beneath my Wings," actor
Mitchell, Joni	25	50	75	(1997),"Big Yellow Taxi," RS
Monica	15	35	25	"The Boy Is Mine," real name Monica Arnold
The Monkees	150	200	225	M. Nesmith (KS) - $35-$55, "I'm a Believer"
Moody Blues	100	175	200	Scarce with D. Laine (vintage)
Moore, Mandy	15	35	25	"Candy"
Morissette, Alanis	50	75	100	An elusive signer!, "Ironic"
Morrison, Van	45	75	125	(1993), "Brown-Eyed Girl," elusive signer
Nelson, Ricky	130	225	300	(1987), "Hello, Mary Lou," "Travelin' Man," RS
Nelson, Willie	20	45	30	Singer, songwriter
Nine Inch Nails (NIN)	35	50	65	(Trent Reznor), "Closer"
Nirvana	300	500	400	K. Cobain (KS), "Smells Like Teen Spirit"
No Doubt	40	75	65	G. Stefani (KS)
The Notorious B.I.G.	15	30	25	"Mo Money Mo Problems"
Oasis	50	120	135	Liam & Noel Gallagher (KS), "Wonderwall"
Orbison, Roy	125	250	250	(1987), "Oh, Pretty Woman," "Crying"

Name	Sig.	LS/DS	SP	Comments,/Notes
Osbourne, Ozzy	30	60	55	Former member of Black Sabbath, "Crazy Train"
Osmond, Donny	15	30	25	"One Bad Apple"
Osmond, Marie	10	25	20	"Paper Roses"
Parliament Funkadelics	60	125	150	(1997), "One Nation Under a Groove"
Parton, Dolly	10	30	25	"9 to 5," actor, RS
Pearl Jam	150	275	350	E.Vedder (KS), "Jeremy," "Go"
Perkins, Carl	25	50	100	(1987), "Blue Suede Shoes," "Matchbox," RS
Peter, Paul & Mary	25	50	60	"Leavin' on a Jet Plane," "Puff the Magic..."
Tom Petty ...Heartbreakers	40	70	110	T. Petty (KS), "Refugee"
Phlower	30	45	50	"Jingle Your Bells," "Trying to Find the ...
Pickett, Wilson	20	45	50	(1991), "Land of 1,000 Dances," "In the ..."
Pink	10	25	20	"Lady Marmalade," real name Alecia Moore
Pink Floyd	150	300	325	(1996), original lineup - $600 - $700
The Platters	100	200	275	(1990), D. Lynch & T. Williams(KS)
The Police	50	85	115	Sting (KS), "Every Breath You Take," "Roxanne"
Poco	25	40	60	"Crazy Love," "Heart of the Night"
Pop, Iggy	15	30	40	"Lust for Life"
Presley, Elvis	575	1500	1200	(1986), SP - $600 - $3500, FA
Presley, Lisa Marie	25	50	40	Singer, d. Elvis, PU
The Pretenders	50	150	200	Values for original lineup, C. Hynde (KS)
Price, Lloyd	10	35	45	"Stagger Lee," "Lawdy Miss Clawdy"
Prince (Symbol)	100	175	225	"Purple Rain," "7," "U Got the Look"
Procol Harum	40	60	75	"A Whiter Shade of Pale," "Conquistador"
Public Enemy	35	45	50	"Fight the Power," "Can't Truss It"
Queen	400	600	750	F. Mercury (KS) - $225 - $650, "Bohemian..."
Queen Latifah	20	50	30	Rap artist, actor, real name Dana Owens
Raitt, Bonnie	10	25	15	"Something To Talk About," RS
The Ramones	80	130	200	"Blitzkrieg Bop"
Redding, Otis	375	750	800	(1989), a scarce signature, "(Sittin' on) The ..."
Red Hot Chilli Peppers	45	100	110	H. Slovak (scarce), "Brass in Pocket"
Reed, Jimmy	25	50	100	(1991), (1925-1976), "Honey I Do"
Reed, Lou	25	40	55	"Walk on the Wild Side"
R.E.M.	150	180	175	M. Stipe (KS) - an elusive signer, original lineup
Rhymes, Busta	20	45	30	"Woo Hah!...," real name Trevor Smith
Richardson, Kevin				Backstreet Boys, PU
The Righteous Brothers	70	130	225	"You've Lost That Lovin' Feelin'," "Ebb Tide"
Rimes, Leann	15	30	20	"Blue"
Rios, Chris "Big Pun"	35	70	70	(1971-2000), "Capital Punishment"
Rivers, Johnny	10	20	25	"Poor Side of Town," "Memphis"
Smokey Robinson ...Miracles	30	55	65	(1987), S. Robinson (KS), DS - $150
The Rolling Stones	500	1250	1300	(1989), values for original lineup, Jones (KS)
The Ronettes	30	40	50	R. Spector (KS), "Be My Baby"
Ronstadt, Linda	25	30	45	"You're No Good," "Blue Bayou"
Ross, Diana				(The Supremes)
Run-D.M.C.	30	45	50	"Walk This Way," "Sun City"
Salt-N-Pepa	25	35	50	"Shoop," "Whatta Man," "Let's Talk About..."
Sam and Dave	100	150	175	(1992), D. Prater (1937-1988)
Santana/Carlos Santana	35	40	50	"Black Magic Woman," "Oye Como Va"

Name	Sig.	LS/DS	SP	Comments./Notes
Seal	15	25	30	(Sealhenry Samuel), "Kiss From a Rose"
Selena	40	120	125	(1971-1995), "Amor Prohibidio"
The Sex Pistols	550	800	900	Values for original lineup, S. Vicious (KS)
Tupac Shakur	100	200	150	(1971-1996), "How Do U Want IT"
Shaggy	15	30	25	"It Wasn't Me," real name Orville Burrell
Shakira	15	40	35	"Whenever, ...," real name Shakira I.M. Ripoll
Shannon, Del	45	75	85	(1939-1990), "Runaway," "Hats Off to Larry"
The Shirelles	40	110	125	(1996), A. Harris (1940-1982), "Soldier Boy"
Simon, Carly	20	35	50	"You're So Vain," author
Simon and Garfunkel	65	150	175	(1990), "Bridge Over Troubled Water"
Simpson, Jessica	15	30	25	"I Wanna Love You..."
Sisqo	15	30	20	"Thong Song," real name Mark Andtrews
Sly and the Family Stone	85	175	200	(1993), S. Stone (KS), "Everyday People"
Smashing Pumpkins	40	80	115	B. Corgan (KS), "Today"
Smith, Patti	35	75	110	"Horses," "Because the Night," "Gloria"
Snoop Dogg	15	40	25	Rap artist, real name Calvin Broadus
Soundgarden	35	70	80	C. Cornell (KS), "Outshined"
Spears, Britney	30	75	70	"(Hit Me)...Baby One More Time"
Spice Girls	70	150	175	G. Spice (KS), "Wannabe"
Springsteen, Bruce	50	100	125	"Born to Run," RS
Squeeze	25	35	55	P. Carrack (KS), "Tempted," "Hourglass"
Steely Dan	75	125	150	"Do It Again," elusive signers
Steppenwolf	35	65	75	"Born to Be Wild," "Magic Carpet Ride"
Stewart, Rod	35	60	75	(1994),"Maggie Mae," RS
Sting	25	60	75	"If You Love Somebody, Set Them Free"
Strait, George	20	50	30	"Carrying Your Love..."
The Sugar Hill Gang	10	15	20	"Rapper's Delight"
Summer, Donna	15	20	25	"Bad Girls"
The Supremes	250	500	600	(1988), D. Ross (KS), F. Ballard (1943-1976)
Sutcliffe, Stuart				(1940-1962) The Beatles, rare, PU
Talking Heads	40	80	90	D.Byrne (KS), "Psycho Killer," "Burning ..."
Taylor, James	30	50	75	"You've Got a Friend," "Fire and Rain," RS
The Temptations	200	300	350	(1989), varies by lineup, E. Kendricks (KS)
Thomas, Rozonda				(See TLC)
Three Dog Night	45	100	125	"Joy to the World," "Liar," "Eli's Coming"
Timberlake, Justin				NSYNC, PU
TLC	30	45	50	"Waterfalls"
T. Rex	150	400	450	(Marc Bolan), "Bang a Gong (Get It On)"
Tucker, Tanya	10	25	20	"Delta Dawn"
Turner, Big Joe	100	200	225	(1987), (1911-1985), "Shake, Rattle & Roll"
Ike and Tina Turner	50	125	175	(1991), "Proud Mary"
Turner, Tina	25	50	60	(1991), "What's Love Got to Do With It?"
The Turtles	40	65	75	Volman & Kaylan (KS), "Happy Together"
Twain, Shania	25	70	50	"Come On Over"
U2	100	225	200	"(Pride) In the Name of Love," "One"
Usher	20	40	30	"My Way" , real name Usher Raymond IV
Valens, Ritchie	450	700	750	High school yearbook - $2,500 - $3,000
Vandross, Luther	25	50	35	"Here and Now"
Van Halen	80	150	140	E. Van Halen (KS), "Dreams," "Panama"

Name	Sig.	LS/DS	SP	Comments,/Notes
Vaughan, Stevie Ray	200	300	350	"Crossfire"
The Velvet Underground	150	250	275	(1996), original lineup
Wallace, Christopher	30	50	60	(1972-1997), Notorious B.I.G."
Warwick, Dionne	10	15	20	"I Say a Little Prayer," "Love Power"
Waters, Muddy	150	300	350	(1987), "I Can't Be Satisfied"
Watkins, Tionne				TLC, PU
Wells, Mary	25	35	45	(1943-1992), "My Guy," "Two Lovers"
White, Barry	30	55	60	(1944-2003)
The Who	600	1000	1250	(1990), K. Moon (KS) - $200 - $250
Williams, Lucinda	15	25	20	"Car Wheels on a Gravel Road"
Wilson, Jackie	275	400	325	(1987), (1934-1984), ESPV
Wonder, Stevie	200			(1989), Uses a thumbprint signature!
Wright, Eroc "Eazy-E"	35	60	60	(1963-1995), NWA
Wyonna	25	50	30	"The Judds"
Yanni	20	45	30	Pianist
The Yardbirds	200	275	300	(1992), values vary by lineup
Yes	150	250	300	Values for original lineup or (8/71-7/72) group
Young, Neil	40	75	100	(1995), "Down by the River," "Heart of Gold"
The Young Rascals/The Rascals	45	100	125	(1997), F. Cavaliere (KS), "Good Lovin'"
Zappa, Frank/The Mothers ...	150	225	300	(1995), (1940-1993), "Dancin' Fool"
ZZ Top	60	100	125	"Legs," "Sleeping Bag," "Velcro Fly," RS

FREE Autographs
& Much More!

THE NEWSMAKERS
The Innocent, The Guilty, The controversial, The Legendary

WHAT YOU NEED TO KNOW

* Controversial is an adjective which means "of, relating to, or arousing controversy"; a public figure.

* Controversy sells, as do the autographs of the controversial.

* Fundamental issues in collecting controversial individuals or the infamous are authenticity, availability and even risk.

* Few authentic examples of many infamous people are even known to exist, while others are so rare that they seldom enter the market.

* The signature of a controversial figure, such as one accused of murder, can be worth more than their victim. For example, a comparable letter from Lee Harvey Oswald can command twice as much as President John F. Kennedy.

* Many controversial figures are in the spotlight only briefly, therefore the demand for their signature can have radical fluctuations.

* Complicating collecting the signatures of certain controversial individuals has been the signing habits of those incarcerated. While a few of the infamous are prolific, most are not. Individuals such as the serial killer Jeffrey Dahmer rarely, if at all, answered mail.

* Collectors are advised to exercise caution when pursing subjects and materials in this area.

MARKET FACTS

* Pricing in this area continues to be highly subjective. Many major dealers differ in opinion regarding the scarcity of certain autographed items.

* This niche of the market is often impacted by the influx of a quanity of material, such as checks signed by syndicate gangster Carlo Gambino. Because of this pricing will often radically fluctuate until demand has been meant.

* Common forms include: Sig., LS, DS, ALS, sketches and unusual forms. Authentic signed photographs are not typically encountered.

TRENDS

* The one consistent trend in this niche is that "current newsmakers" are always in demand.

* Current newsmakers seldom have lasting public appeal therfore speculating on autographed material of certain individuals can be dangerous.

Abbreviations:

Assorted Selected Entries

Name	db/dd	Sig.	LS/DS	ALS	Comments
Abbott, Jack Henry	1944-	20	45	80	Writer
Anastasia, Albert	1903-1957				Mafia chief, PU
Atlas, Charles	1893-1972	30	75		SP - $125, muscle developer
Bailey, Harvey	1889-1979				"Old Harve," Bankrobber, PU
Barker, "Ma"	1872-1935	1275			Gangleader
Barrow, Clyde	1909-1934	2000	4500		Murderer, Robber
Bass, Sam	1851-1878				Stagerobber, trainrobber, PU
Becker, Charles	1869-1915				Police lieutenant, murderer, PU
Bembenek, Lawrencia	1959-	25	50	125	"Bambi," murderer
Berkowitz, David,	1953-	50	100	200	"Son of Sam" serial killer, RS
Bianchi, Kenneth	1952-	40	80	150	"The Hillside Strangler"
Blake, Robert	1933-	(See Entertainment)			
Bonanno, Joseph	1905-				Mafia Family Chief, "Bananas," PU
Bonney, W.H.	c.1859-1881			17000	"Billy the Kid," outlaw
Booth, John Wilkes	1838-1865	3000	10000		Lincoln assassin, ESPV
Borden, Lizzie	1860-1927				Alleged ax murder, ESPV, PU,
Bruce, Lenny	1925-1966	250	500		Comedian, controversial
Buchalter, Louis	1897-1944				"Lepke," racketeer, murderer, PU
Bundy, Theodore	1947-1989	125	250		Serial killer
Buttafuoco, Joey	1956-	5	20	30	Mechanic
Capone, Al	1899-1947	3000	11500	4250	Chicago gangster, "Scarface"
Carter, Billy	1937-1988	35	70		SP - $75, Peanut farmer
Cassidy, "Butch"	1866-?				"Robert Parker," bankrobber, PU
Chapman, Mark David	1955-	100	175		Shot John Lennon
Chavez, Cesar	1927-1993	50	100	200	United Farm Workers
Chessman, Caryl	1921-1960	225	450	500	American criminal
Colombo, Joseph, Sr.	1914-1978	75	150	300	Mafia boss
Colosimo, James	1877-1920				Gangster, PU
Condit, Gary		20	45		USHR
Cody, William	1846-1917	750	1500	2000	SP - $4500, "Buffalo Bill"
Corona, Juan V.	1933-				Serial killer, PU
Costello, Frank	1893-1973	1565			Mafia boss
Cunanan, Andrew	? - 1997	80	150		Murderer, Gianni Versace
Czolgosz, Leon	1873-1901		20000		Assassin of William McKinley

Name	db/dd	Sig.	LS/DS	ALS	Comments
Dahmer, Jeffrey	1960-1994	600	800	3250	Serial killer
Dalton, Emmett	1871-1937	750	2000	4500	American outlaw, SP - $2750
Dalton, Grat	1862-1892	1000	5000	3000	American outlaw
Dalton, Robert	1867-1892	1000	5000	3000	American outlaw
Dalton, William	1873-1893				American outlaw, PU
Daniel, Jack	1850-1911	100	200		Whiskey maker
DeSalvo, Albert	1931-1973	100	200	450	"The Boston Strangler"
Diamond, John "Legs"	1896-1931				Racketeer, PU
Dillinger, John	1903-1934	3750	7500	15000	Bankrobber
Duke, Doris	1912-1993	30	70		"the poor little rich girl"
Escobar, Pablo					Columbian drug lord, PU
Evers, Medgar	1925-1963	200	400		MI NAACP secretary, ESPV
Fisher, Amy	1974-	25		150	Shot M.J. Buttafuoco
Fixx, Jim	1932-1984	20	50		SB-$70, runner
Fleiss, Heidi		10	25	50	Hollywood Madame, SP - $30
Floyd, Charles A.	1901-1934				"Pretty Boy," bankrobber, PU
Ford, Robert					Killed Jesse James, PU
Foster, Vince					Pres. Clinton friend, PU
Fox, Terry	1958-1981	115	200		'Marathon of Hope," inspiration
Fromme, Lyn."Squeaky"	1952-	60	150	275	Manson family member, SP - $100
Gacy, John Wayne	1942-1992	75	150	225	Serial killer, SP - $200
Gambino, Carlo	1902-1976	70	140	275	Syndicate gangster
Genovese, Vito	1897-1969	125			Mafia chief
Giancana, Sam	1908-1975	100	200		Syndicate gangster
Gilmore, Gary	1940-1977	25	50	100	SP - $75
Goetz, Bernhard		20	40	50	Subway shooter
Gotti, John	1940-2002	100	300	150	ALS - $1,750, SP - $100, ESPV
Gravanno, Sammy		40	80		"The Bull," murderer, informant
Graves, L.C.	1918-1995	25	50		SP - $50, policeman, JFK association.
Guiteau, Charles J.	1844-1882	500	1000	6500	Garfield assassin
Hardin, John W.	1853-1895	2000	4000		Murderer
Harding, Tonya	1970-	10	20		Figure skater
Harris, Mrs. Jean	1923-	35	70	150	Scarsdale diet killer, SP - $75
Hauptmann, Bruno R.	1899-1936	600	1250		Lindbergh baby kidnapper
Hearst, Patricia	1955-	50	100		"Tania," robber
Henning, Doug	1947-2000	25	50	100	SP - $50, "The Magic Show"
Hinckley, John W.	1956-	40	125	200	Reagan assassin
Hoffman, Abbie	1936-1989	40	100		"Chicago Seven"
Holmes, John	1944-1988	125	250		"The Devil In Miss Jones," actor
Houdini, Harry	1874-1926	1000	2000	4500	SP - $3000, Magician
Hussein, Saddam	1937-				Iraq president, PU
James, Frank	1844-1915	1200	2250	4500	Outlaw
James, Jesse	1847-1882				American outlaw, PU
Jennings, Al	1863-1961	325		400	Trainrobber
Jones, Paula		20	40		Pres. Clinton accusser
Karpis, Alvin	1908-1979	100	200		Bankrobber, burglar

Name	db/dd	Sig.	LS/DS	ALS	Comments
Kaczynski, Ted		50	100		"Unabomber"
Keating, Charles H.	1924-	25	50		Swindler
Kelly, George R.	1897-1954				"Machine Gun," bootlegger, kidnapper
Kevorkian, Dr. Jack		30	50	100	Assisted suicide doctor, controversial
Kidd, Captain William	c.1645-1701				British pirate, PU
King, Rodney G.		15	30		Riot victim
Kopechne, MaryJo	1940-1969				Drowning victim, PU
Koresh, David	? - 1993				Cult leader, PU
Laffite, Jean	c.1780-c.1826				French pirate, PU
Lansky, Meyer	1902-1983	1000	2500		Mobster, signed check $2750
Leary, Timothy	1920-1996	40	80		SP - $75, RS, 1960s activist
Leopold, Nathan	1906-1971	130	400	600	Loeb & Leopold case
Lewinsky, Monica	1973-	25	50	100	Intern, designer
Liberace	1919-1987	75	150		SP - $150, showman
Loeb, Richard	1907-1936				Murderer, kidnapper, PU
Lucas, Henry Lee	1937-	45	125		Serial killer
Luciano, Char. "Lucky"	1897-1962	150			Crime syndicate chief
McGurn, Jack	1904-1936				"Machine Gun"
Manson, Charles	1934-	125	250		Hippie cult leader, SP - $200
McVeigh, Timothy		100	200		Oklahoma City bomber
Menendez, Eric		15	30	100	Family killer
Menendez, Lyle		15	30	100	Family killer
Milk, Harvey	1930-1978	35	100		SFCBS, victim
Moore, Sara Jane		45	75	250	Shot at Gerald Ford, SP - $100
Moran, George "Bugs"	1893-1957				Bootlegger, PU
Nelson, George	1908-1934				"Baby Face," murderer, PU
Ness, Eliot	1903-1957	400	800		Rare-ALS & SP, Federal agent
Nichols, Terry		50	100		Oklahoma City bomber
Noriega, Manuel		10	25	60	Panamanian dictator, RS
O'Bannion, Charles	1892-1924				"Deanie," bootlegger, PU
Oswald, Lee Harvey	1939-1963	2000	8500	11000	J.F.K. assassin
Purvis, Melvin	1900-1960	50	100		FBI agent
Pusser, Buford	1937-1974	125	250	450	Sheriff, "Walking Tall"
Ramirez, Richard	1960-	50	125		"The Night Stalker"
Ray, James Earl	1928-	50	175	350	Martin Luther King assassin, SP - $200
Retz, Gilles de	1404-1440				French soldier, PU
Rosenberg, Ethel	1915-1953				Convicted espionage, PU
Rosenberg, Julius	1918-1953				Convicted espionage, PU
Rothstein, Arnold	1882-1928				Gambler, PU
Rubin, Jerry	1938-1994	30	75	150	"Chicago Seven"
Ruby, Jack	1911-1967	265	500	5500	Shot Lee Harvey Oswald
Rudolph, Eric Robert	1966-	30	75		Alleged bomber
Sade, Marquis de	1740-1814	265	700	2150	French writer
Schindler, Oskar	1908-1974				Manufacturer, "Schindlerjuden," PU
Schultz, Dutch	1902-1935				Bootlegger. PU

Name	db/dd	Sig.	LS/DS	ALS	Comments
Sedgwick, Edie	1943-1971	100	175		SP - $200, model
Sheppard, Marilyn	1923-1954				Victim, PU
Sheppard, Sam	1924-1970	125	250		"The Fugitive," doctor
Siegel, Benjamin	1906-1947				"Bugsy," syndicate gangster, PU
Simpson, O.J.	(See football)				
Sirhan Sirhan	1946-	225	400		Shot Robert F. Kennedy
Skakel, Michael		25	50		Murderer
Smith, Robert	1879-1950	100	200		AA founder
Smith, Susan	1971-	20	40		Murderer
Speck, Richard	1941-1991	30	75		Murderer
Starr, Belle	1848-1889				Horse thief, PU
Stroud, Robert F.	1887-1963	225	500		"The Birdman of Alcatraz"
Suratt, John H.	1844-?				Alleged A. Lincoln conspirator, PU
Sutton, Willie	1901-1982	65		325	Bank robber, SP - $100
Tiny Tim	1932-1996	25	40	60	SP - $50, Entertainer
Tippit, J.D.	1924-1963				Policeman, killed by L.H. Oswald, PU
Tranower, Herman	1910-1980	50	100	200	Author
Torrio, John	1882-1957				Gangster, syndicate chief, PU
Touhy, Roger	1898-1959				Bootlegger, PU
Valachi, Joseph	1904-1971				Syndicate gangster, PU
Watson, "Tex"		25	45		Manson family member
Wilson, Bill	1895-1971	40	100		AA founder
Younger, Bob		2650			American desperado
Younger, Cole	1844-1916	2250			American desperado
Younger, James		2500			American desperado
Zangara, Joseph	1902-1933				FDR assassin, PU

PHILOSOPHERS & RELIGIOUS LEADERS/CLERGY

WHAT YOU NEED TO KNOW

* Religion is a code of belief or philosophy, which often involves the worship of a God or gods. Belief in a supernatural power is not essential (absent in Buddhism & Confucianism), but faithful adherence is typically viewed as rewarding.

* Chief religions:
  Ancient & Pantheist: Babylonia, Assyria, Egypt, Greece and Rome.
  Book religions: Judaism, Christianity (Roman Catholic, Eastern Orthodox, Protestant), Islam (Sunni & Shiite)
  Combined derivations: Baha'ism, the Unification Church and Mormonism.
  Oriental: Hinduism, Buddhiem, Jainism, Parseeism, Confucianism, Taoism, and Shinto.

* Since the existence of mankind as a civilization, religion has played a paramount role. While the definition of a "religious" manuscript or autograph is often vague, as it could include parchment, papyrus, cloth, paper and even stone, most tend to limit the term to our modern era.

* As many of our earliest religious texts are considered sacred, most have found permanent homes in museums, (Vatican, the British Library, the Boodleian, etc.) shrines, or institutions. It is highly unlikely that they would ever find solace in a public sale.

* While documents such as the Dead Sea Scrolls, found in 1947, are not likely to face the autograph market, the letters of popes, saints, cardinals and numerous other eminent religious personages do.

MARKET FACTS

* Renaissance popes have enjoyed some level of interest, as have many popular modern day religious leaders.

* Most autographed material of the Popes of the Roman Catholic Church is very rare prior to the sixteenth century. The most desireable pieces are those signed while pope under the papal name.

* There has been numerous forged documents in this area, many of which have

been uncovered by document experts.

TRENDS

* While the appreciation in value of signatures of religious leaders and figures has been significant, it has trailed other areas.

* Autographed material of the Popes of the Roman Catholic Church remain very inconsistent in pricing.

Abbreviations: POTRCC - Pope of the Roman Catholic Church. PU - prices undetermined

Name	Dates	Sig.	DS	ALS	SP	Comments
Abbott, Grace	1878-1939					Social worker, PU
Abbott,Lyman	1835-1922	30	55	80	50	U.S. clergyman, reformer
Adler, Felix	1851-1933					Fndr. Ethical Culture Soc., PU
Alexander VII	1599-1667					POTRCC - 1655, PU
Alexander VIII	1610-1691	1200	2500			POTRCC - 1689
Allen, Richard	1760-1831					Religious leader, PU
Austin, J.L.	1911-1960					British philosopher, PU
Ayer, A.J.	1910-1989					British philosopher, PU
Bahaullah	1817-1892					Founder of Bahai faith, PU
Barth, Karl	1886-1968	45	110	140	80	Swiss theologian
Beecher, Henry W.	1813-1887	75	150	225	200	Religious leader
Benedict XIII	1649-1730					POTRCC - 1724, PU
Benedict XIV	1675-1758	1000	2000			POTRCC - 1740
Benedict XV	1854-1922	150	300	500		POTRCC - 1914
Bentham, Jeremy	1748-1832	100	225	450		British philosopher, reformer
Bergson, Henri	1859-1941					French philosopher, author, PU
Berkeley, George	1685-1753					Philosopher, idealist,PU
Biddle, John	1615-1662					Fdr. English Unitarianism, PU.
Boehme, Jakob	1575-1624					German theosophist, mystic, PU
Bonhoeffer, Dietrich	1906-1945					Ttheologian, killed by Nazis
Brewster, William	1567-1644					Pilgrim leader, PU
Brunner, Emil	1889-1966					Swiss protestant theologian, PU
Bruno, Giordano	1548-1600					Italian philosopher,PU
Buber, Martin	1878-1965					Jewish philosopher
Calvin, John	1509-1564	8000	16000			Fr. theologian, P.Reform., PU
Carnap, Rudolph	1891-1970					German-born philosopher, PU
Channing, William E.	1780-1842	50	100	150		Religious leader, PU
Clement IX	1600-1669					POTRCC - 1667, PU
Clement X	1590-1676					POTRCC - 1670, PU
Clement XI	1649-1721					POTRCC - 1700, LS - $325
Clement XII	1652-1740					POTRCC - 1730, PU
Clement XIII	1693-1769					POTRCC - 1758, LS - $995
Clement XIV	1705-1774					POTRCC - 1769, PU

Name	Dates	Sig.	DS	ALS	SP	Comments
Comte, Auguste	1798-1857					French philosopher, PU
Cotton, John	1585-1652					Puritan theologian, PU
Coughlin, Charles E.	1891-1979	25	45	60	30	Religious leader
Descartes, Rene	1596-1650		18500			Fr. philos., mathem., ESPV
Dewey, John	1859-1952	50	150	225	75	U.S. philosopher
Diderot, Denis	1713-1784					French philosopher, PU
Dwight, Timothy	1752-1817	50	100	150		Religious leader, writer
Eddy, Mary Baker	1821-1910	1500	2750	3750		Fdr. Christian Sci., SB-$2750
Edwards, Jonathan	1703-1758	150	300	375		U.S. preacher, theologian
Eliot, John	1604-1690					Religious leader, PU
Fichte, Johann	1762-1814					Ger. idealist, philosopher, PU
Finney, Charles G.	1792-1875	40	75	125		Religious leader
Fox, George	1624-1691					Founder Society of Friends, PU
Gibbons, James	1834-1921	60	150		150	Religious leader
Gladden, Solomon W.	1836-1918					Religious leader, PU
Graham, William "Billy"	1918-		30	100	150	50	Religious leader
Gregory XV	1554-1623	1650	3275			POTRCC - 1621
Gregory XVI	1765-1846	300	500			POTRCC - 1831, ALS - $225
Hegel, Georg W.F.	1770-1831	1000	2000			German idealist, philosopher
Heidegger, Martin	1889-1976					Ger. existentialist, PU
Herder, Johann G.	1744-1803					German philosopher, PU
Hobbs, Thomas	1588-1679					English phil., theorist, PU
Hooker, Thomas	1586-1647					Religious leader, PU
Hume, David	1711-1776					Empiricist philosopher
Husseri, Edmund	1859-1938					German philosopher, PU
Hutchinson, Anne M.	1591-1643					Religious leader, PU
Huxley, Thomas	1825-1895	60	150	250		British philosopher, educator
Inge, William	1860-1954	40	80	160		British theologian
Innocent X	1574-1655					POTRCC- 1644, PU
Innocent XI	1611-1689					POTRCC - 1676, LS - $995
Innocent XII	1615-1700					POTRCC - 1691, PU
Innocent XIII	1655-1724					POTRCC - 1721, PU
James, William	1842-1910	100	200	400	150	U.S. philosopher, SDS-2X
Jaspers, Karl	1883-1969					German exitentialist phil. , PU
John Paul I	1912-1978	600	1250			POTRCC - 1978, reign. 34 days.
John Paul II	1920-					POTRCC - 1978, ESPV, PU
John XXIII	1881-1963	500	1100			POTRCC - 1958
Kent, Immanuel	1724-1804					German philosopher, PU
Kierkegaard, Soren	1813-1855					Dan. religious philosopher, PU
Knox, John	1505-1572					Ldr. of Prot. Reform. in Scotland
Lee, Ann	1736-1784					Religious leader, PU
Leibniz, Gottfried von	1646-1716					Ger. philosopher, logician, PU
Leo XI	1535-1605					POTRCC - 1605, PU

Name	Dates	Sig.	DS	ALS	SP	Comments
Leo XII	1760-1829					POTRCC - 1823, PU
Leo XIII	1810-1903					POTRCC - 1878, notable, PU
Locke, John	1632-1704	1000	2000			Eng. political theorist, SDS-5-6X
Marcel, Gabriel	1889-1973					Exitentialist, philosopher, PU
Maritain, Jacques	1882-1973	25	50	100		Neo-Thomist philosopher
Mather, Cotton	1663-1728	850	2250	3000		Orthodox Pur., SADS-$4500
Mather, Increase	1639-1723					Religious leader, PU
Merieau-Ponty, Maurice	1908-1961					Fr. exitentialist philosopher, PU
Merton, Thomas	1915-1968	350	825			Trappist monk, spiritualist, PU
Mill, John Stuart	1806-1873	125	350	700		British philosopher
Moody, Dwight	1837-1899	75	150	225	150	U.S. evangelist
Moore, George.E.	1873-1958	65	200	250	150	British philosopher, professor
Muhammad, Elijah	1897-1975	150	400	650	250	Religious leader
Muhlenberg, Henry M.	1711-1787					Lutheran Church in America, PU
Newman, John H.	1801-1890	200	400	500	500	R. Catholic convert, cardinal
Niebuhr, Reinhold	1892-1971	75	150	200	100	Protestant theologian
Nietzsche, Friedrich	1844-1900	900	1500	4000		Philosopher, poet, SALS-2X
Pascal, Blaise	1623-1662					Fr. philosopher, scientist, PU
Paul V	1552-1621	2400				POTRCC - 1605
Paul VI	1897-1978	280	370			POTRCC - 1963, Sig. - $195
Peale, Norman Vincent	1898-1993	30	75	150	50	U.S. religious leader, RS
Peirce, C.S.	1839-1914					U.S. philosopher, pragmatist, PU
Pius IX	1792-1878	120	200	400		POTRCC - 1846
Pius VI	1717-1799	350	750			POTRCC - 1775, DS - $495
Pius VII	1742-1823	1250	2000			POTRCC - 1800
Pius VIII	1761-1830	1000				POTRCC - 1829, ESPV
Pius X	1835-1910	250	500			POTRCC - 1903
Pius XI	1857-1939	400	1000		1000	POTRCC - 1922
Pius XII	1876-1958	350	750		700	POTRCC - 1939, ESPV
Rauschenbusch, Walter	1861-1918					Religious leader, author, PU
Royce, Josiah	1855-1916					U.S. idealist philosopher, PU
Russell, Bertrand	1872-1970	100	250	500	275	British philosopher, logician
Russell, Charles T.	1852-1916					Fdr. Jehovah's Witnesses, PU
Ryan, John A.	1869-1945					Religious leader, reformer, PU
Santayana, George	1863-1952	75	200	400	150	U.S. philosopher, poet
Sarte, Jean-Paul	1905-1980	150	300	500	250	French philosopher
Schelling, Friedrich von	1775-1854					German philosopher, PU
Schleiermacher, Fried.	1768-1834					Protestant theolog., author, PU
Schopenhauer, Arthur	1788-1860	1000	3000	6000		German philosopher, author
Schweitzer, Albert	1875-1965	225	500	1000	750	German theologian
Seabury, Samuel	1729-1796					Religious leader, loyalist, PU
Serra, Junipero	1713-1784					Religious leader, missionary. PU
Smith, Joseph	1805-1844	750	1500	9500		"The Book of Mormon", ESPV
Spellman, Francis J.	1889-1967	25	50	100	60	Religious leader, prolific writer
Spencer, Herbert	1820-1903	75	150	250	125	British evolutionary philosopher
Spinoza, Baruch de	1632-1677					Dutch philosopher, PU
Strong, Josiah	1847-1916	40	75	135	80	Religious leader, "Our Country"

Name	Dates	Sig.	DS	ALS	SP	Comments
Sunday, Billy	1862-1935	100	200	300	400	U.S. evangelist, baseball player
Suzuki, Daisetz Teitaro	1870-1966					Buddhist scholar, editor, PU
Swedenborg, Emanuel	1688-1772	1250	3575	9500		Philosopher, scientist, ESPV
Tellhard de Chardin, P.	1881-1955					French Jesuit priest, PU
Tillich, Paul	1886-1965	50	100	150		U.S. philosopher, theologian
Turner, Henry M.	1834-1915					Religious leader, PU
Urban VIII	1568-1644	1725	3500			POTRCC - 1623
Ward, Lillian D.	1867-1940	50	75	145		Social worker
Wesley, John	1703-1791	350	1000	2000		British theologian, priest
Whitefield, George	1714-1770					Religious leader, evangelist, PU
Whitehead, Alfred North	1861-1947	100	250	550	250	British philosopher, author
Williams, Roger	c.1603-1683	4200	15750			Founder Rhode Island
Wise, Isaac M.	1819-1900	75	150	200		Religious leader, rabbi
Wise, Stephen S.	1874-1949	50	75	125	50	Religious leader, rabbi, editor
Wittgenstein, Ludwig	1889-1951	50	100	200	75	Austrian philosopher, professor
Young, Brigham	1801-1877	400	1500	4000	3000	SDS-5-6X, SALS-2-3X

THESE MEN LIVED BY THEIR REPUTATION

SO DO WE

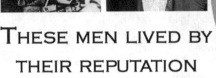

Signature House

SINCE 1994

In ten years we have grown in quality, integrity and our willingness to please our customers.

We have built our name on reliability. Our bidders receive a lifetime guarantee of authenticity plus our exclusive Golden Guarantee. Consignors receive current market information and free appraisals plus the most competitive rates available.

Would you rather sell your collectibles now? Whether you have one autograph or a collection, you can have your check tomorrow.

Contact us for a catalog.

Gil & Karen Griggs
407 Liberty Avenue
Bridgeport, WV 26330
Phone: (304) 842-3386   Fax: (304) 842-3001
email: editor@signaturehouse.net
website: www.signaturehouse.net

POLITICIANS, EDUCATORS, REFORMERS, LAWYERS & LABOR LEADERS

WHAT YOU NEED TO KNOW

* An awkward title for a very unstable, yet intriguing area of collecting in the autograph market.

* In the area of politicians, considerable speculation has always revolved around individuals who may be future Presidents of the United States.

* With the exception of reformers, there is an abundance of most material in this niche.

* With the advent of television and certainly Court TV, the names of numerous prominent attorneys are becoming household words and even celebrities. From F. Lee Bailey and Melvin Belli, to Robert Shapiro and Gloria Allred, we have become intrigued with these legal participants.

* Ironically, as a labor leader you don't always have to come up missing, in order to have your autograph worth something, in fact this area has done very well over the past two decades. As with the other fields, content and relevance means everything to the appreciation of an autographed item.

* The advent of word processing brought with it office inovation that radically altered correspondence. In this area of collecting it is common to encounter form letters, rich in content, but of limited value.

* Machine-signed documents – where relevant, are common in this niche.

MARKET FACTS

* Autograph value tends to migrate toward very key contributors to their fields, such as Clarence Darrow of the legal profession, and Susan B. Anthony in the area of temperance, anti-slavery and women suffrage movements.

* Content-rich form letters, often imperceptible to the owner, routinely enter the market.

TRENDS

* Women and minority contributors to these fields have shown significant appreciation and interest within the hobby. This area should continue to exhibit

significant and consistent price gains over the next decade.

Abbreviations: PC = Presidential canidate, PU = pricing undetermined

Name	db/dd	Sig.	DS	ALS	SP	Comments
Abbott, Grace	1878-1939					Social worker, PU
Acheson, Dean	1893-1971	20	60	110	50	U.S. S/State, SP-$150, ESPV
Ackerman, Amos T.	1821-1880	25	50	100		AG, UG
Adams, Brooks	1848-1927	75	130	220	100	U.S. historian
Adams, Charles F.	1866-1954	20	40		25	S/Navy, HH
Adams, Charles Francis	1807-1886	40	130	200		Diplomat, s. J.Q. Adams
Adams, Henry	1838-1918	125	250	350	150	U.S. historian, STLS - 1.5 - 2X
Addams, Jane	1860-1935	75	175	325	275	Cofounder of Hull House
Agnew, Spiro Theodore	1918-1996	30	150	260	75	Political leader, VP, FA
Aldrich, Nelson W.	1841-1915	15	20	40	20	Political leader
Alger, Russell A.	(See Civil War - Union Generals)					S/War, WM
Allison, William B.	1829-1908	15	25	40	20	Political leader, USS
Altgeld, John P.	1847-1902	10	40	50	20	Political leader, Governor (IL)
Anderson, Clinton P.	1895-1975	10	20		20	S/Agriculture, HT
Anderson, John B.	1922-	10	20		20	PC, RS
Anderson, Robert B.	1910-1989	10	25		25	S/Treasury, DE
Anthony, Susan B.	1820-1906	200	1225	1750	1500	U.S. temperance, ESPV
Armstrong, John	1758-1843	100	225	450		S/War, JM, scarce
Ashley, William Henry	1778-1838	25	40	65		Political leader, USHR
Austin, Stephen F.	1793-1836	1000	2500	7000		Pol. leader, Texas, MDS-$1800
Bacon, Francis	1561-1626	2000	4000	10000		English philosopher, statesman
Bacon, Robert	1860-1919	30	45	110		S/State, TR
Badger, George	1795-1866	20	40	75		S/Navy, WH
Baker, James A., III	1930-	5	15	30	20	White House chief of staff
Baker, Newton D.	1871-1937	15	60	85	40	Political leader, S/War, WW
Baker, Ray S.	1870-1946	15	30	50	20	Journalist, reformer, "Wilson: ..."
Ballinger, Richard A.	1858-1922	20	40	75		S/Interior, WT
Bancroft, George	1800-1891	30	75	130		U.S. historian, S/Navy, JP
Barbour, James	1775-1842	35	70	120		S/War, JQA
Barkley, Alben	1877-1956	30	75	150	50	VP/Truman
Barnard, Henry	1811-1900	20	50	110		U.S. public school reformer
Barnardo, Thomas	1845-1905	30				British social reformer
Barry, William	1785-1835	20	45	60		PG, AJ
Barton, Clara	1821-1912	150	525	750	675	Red Cross, SALS-$700-$975
Baruch, Bernard M.	1870-1965	20	135	200	100	U.S. financier, TLS-$150
Bates, Edward	1793-1869	40	100	250		AG, AL
Bayard, Thomas F.	1828-1898	25	50	120		S/State, GC
Beard, Charles A.	1874-1948	15	40	75	20	U.S. historian, author
Beard, Mary R.	1876-1958	40	85	125	50	Reformer, historian
Beecher, Henry Ward	1813-1887	60	125	200	200	U.S. clergyman, abolitionist
Belknap, William W.	(See Civil War - Union Generals)					S/War, UG
Bell, John	1797-1869	100	150	195		S/War, WH, scarce
Bellamy, Edward	1850-1898	30	60	165		Reformer, writer
Benedict, Ruth	1887-1948	40	80	140		U.S. anthropologist

Name	db/dd	Sig.	DS	ALS	SP	Comments
Benjamin, Judah P.	(See Civil War - CSA Generals)					
Benson, Ezra T.	1899-	10	22		20	S/Agriculture, DE
Benton, Thomas Hart	1782-1858	65	100	200		U.S. Missouri senator
Berger, Victor Louis	1860-1929	55	100	160	75	Political leader, newpaper editor
Berle, Adolf A, Jr.	1895-1971	30	75	140	45	Lawyer
Berrien, John M.	1781-1856	35	60	125		AG, AJ
Bethune, Mary M.	1875-1955	140	300	600	200	Educator
Betttleheim, Bruno	1903-1990	50	100	200	100	Aust./U.S. psychoanalyst
Beveridge, Albert J.	1862-1927	10	25	50	25	Political leader, historian
Bibb, George	1776-1859	30	60	120		S/Treasury, JT
Biddle, Francis	1886-1968	20	40	80	30	AG, FDR
Birney, James G.	1792-1857	55	100	200		Reformer, antislavery movement
Bissell, Wilson S.	1847-1903	25	50	115		PG, GC
Black, Jeremiah S.	1810-1883	30	60	120		AG, JB
Blaine, James G.	1830-1893	30	50	130	50	U.S. , S/State, JG
Blair, Montgomery	1813-1883	100	200	500		PG, AL
Blanc, Louis	1811-1882	50	100	200		French socialist leader, historian
Blanding, Sarah G.	1899-1985	10	20	35	25	U.S.Vassar College, 1946-1964
Bliss, Cornelius N.	1833-1911	20	40	80		S/Interior, WM
Bloomer, Amelia	1818-1894	300	350	550		U.S. suffragette, social reformer
Bloomfield, Leonard	1887-1949	20	75	150	45	U.S. linguist
Blount, Winton M.	1921-	10	20		20	PG, RN
Bonaparte, Charles J.	1851-1921	25	50	110		AG, TR
Booth, William	1829-1912	150	200	375	200	British Salvation Army founder
Borah, William E.	1865-1940	15	25	50	25	U.S. senator, isolationist
Borie, Adolph E.	1809-1880	25	50	100		S/Navy, UG
Boutwell, George S.	1818-1905	20	40	90		S/Treasury, UG
Bowers, Claude G.	1878-1958	30	65	120	50	Historian, diplomat, author
Boyd, Alan S.	1922-	10	20	45	20	S/Transportation, LBJ
Bradford, William	1755-1795					AG, GW, scarce
Branch, John	1782-1863	25	65	150		S/Navy, AJ
Brannan, Charles F.	1903-	15	30		25	S/Agriculture, HT
Breckinridge, John	1760-1806					AG, TJ
Breckinridge, John C.	1821-1875	(See Civil War - CSA Generals)				
Breckinridge, Soph.P.	1866-1948	50	125	200	80	Social worker, educator
Brennan, Peter J.	1918-	10	20		25	S/Labor, RN
Brewster, Benjamin H.	1816-1888	30	60	120		AG, CA
Bridges, Harry R.	1901-1990	50	150	220	150	Labor leader
Brinegar, Claude S.	1926-	10	20		25	S/Transportation, RN
Bristow, Benjamin	1832-1896	(See Civil War - Union Generals)			S/Treasury, UG	
Brooks, Van Wyck	1886-1963	25	65	115	35	U.S. historian, author
Browder, Earl R.	1891-1973	15	30	60	20	PC
Brown, Aaron W.	1795-1859	40	100			PG, JB
Brown, John	1800-1859	875	2150	4500		SALS-2X,SBC-$2800
Brown, Moses		(See Revolutionary War)				
Brown, Walter F.	1869-1961	10	30	50	20	PG, HH
Brown, William W.	c.1815-1884	15	35	45		Writer, reformer
Brownell, Herbert Jr.	1904-	15	30	50	25	AG, DE
Browning, Orville	1806-1881	35	70	135		S/Interior, AJ
Bruce, Blanche K.	1841-1898	375	650	1175		Political leader, USS
Bryan, William Jennings	1860-1925	110	350	350	440	SC-$125, ANS-$225, S/State
Bullitt, William C.	1891-1967	15	25	50	30	U.S. diplomat, first amb. USSR

Name	db/dd	Sig.	DS	ALS	SP	Comments
Bunche, Ralph	1904-1971	60	150	250	125	Founder of United Nations
Bundy, McGeorge	1919-	10	25	50	20	Educator, JFK administration
Burke, Edmund	1729-1797					British political philosopher, PU
Burleson, Albert S.	1803-1937	10	25	50		PG, WW
Butler, Benjamin F.	1818-1893 (See Civil War - Union Generals)					S/War, AJ
Butler, Nicholas Murray	1862-1947	15	40	125	45	U.S. educator
Butz, Earl L.	1909-	12	25	45	25	S/Agriculture, RN
Byrnes, James F.	1879-1972 (See Supreme Court Justices)					S/State, HT
Cabrini, Frances X.	1850-1917					Nun, first American saint, PU
Calhoun, John C.	1782-1850	150	300	450	350	States' rights adv., S/War, JM
Cameron, James D.	1833-1918	30	55	70		S/War, UG
Cameron, Simon	1799-1889	100	150	200	225	USS, S/War, AL
Campbell, George	1769-1848					S/Treasury, JM, scarce, PU
Campbell, James	1812-1893	20	40	85		PG, FP
Campbell, Joseph	1904-1987	20	45	65	30	U.S. author, editor, teacher
Cannon, Joseph G..	1836-1926	25	45	100	40	Political leader, USS
Carlisle, John G.	1835-1910	20	40	80		S/Treasury, GC
Carlyle, Thomas	1795-1881	100	200	400		Historian, critic
Carson, Rachel L.	1907-1964	100	200	300	250	Reformer, SALS- 5X
Cass, Lewis	1782-1866	45	80	140		S/War, AJ, S/State, JB
Catt, Carrie Chapman	1859-1947	75	150	275	200	U.S. suffragette
Celebrezze, Anthony J.	1910-	10	25	50	30	S/HE&W, JFK
Chandler, William E.	1835-1917	20	40	75		S/Navy, CA
Chandler, Zachariah	1813-1879	25	40	75		S/Interior, UG
Channing, Edward	1856-1931	35	60	100	50	U.S. Historian
Chapin, Roy D.	1880-1936	15	30	55	20	S/Commerce, HH
Chapman, Oscar L.	1896-1978	15	25	35	25	S/Interior, HT
Chase, Salmon P.	1808-1873 (See Supreme Court Justices)					S/Treasury, AL
Chavez, Cesar	1927-1993	50	125		125	U.S. labor leader, U.F.W.A., RS
Cheney, Richard B.	1941-	15	30		25	S/Defense, VP
Clark, Ramsey	1927-	10	25	40	20	AG, LBJ
Clark, Tom C.	1899-1977 (See Supreme Court Justices)					AG, HT
Clay, Henry	1777-1852	125	400	650		FF-$150,SALS-$7500, S/State
Clayton, John M.	1796-1856	30	65	135		S/State, ZT
Clifford, Clark	1906-	12	25		25	S/Defense, LBJ
Clifford, Nathan	1803-1881 (See Supreme Court Justices)					AG, JP
Clinton, DeWitt	1769-1828	70	250	2340		Erie Canal advocate
Clinton, George M.	1792-1864	125	225	365		VP, scarce ALS, died in office
Cobb, Howell	1815-1868 (See Civil War - CSA Generals)					S/Treasury, JB
Cohen, Wilbur J.	1913-1987	10	20		20	S/HE&W, LBJ
Colby, Bainbridge	1869-1950	20	40	65	35	S/State, WW
Coleman, William T.	1920-	10	20		25	S/Transportation, GF
Colfax, Schuyler	1823-1885	60	120	250		VP
Collamer, Jacob	1791-1865	30	60	100		PG, ZT
Collier, John	1884-1968	30	75	125	60	Reformer,educator, author
Colman, Norman J.	1827-1911	25	45	80		S/Agriculture (first), GC
Commons, John R.	1862-1945	30	75	115	40	U.S. economist, labor historian
Conkling, Roscoe	1829-1888	25	35	50	40	Political leader, USS
Connally, John B.	1917-	25	50	115	50	S/Treasury, RN, JFK association
Connor, John T.	1914-	12	25		20	S/Commerce, LBJ
Conrad, Charles	1804-1878	40	50	150		S/War, MF

Name	db/dd	Sig.	DS	ALS	SP	Comments
Cortelyou, George B.	1862-1940	20	40	75		S/Treasury, TR
Corwin, Thomas	1794-1861	30	60	100		S/Treasury, MF
Couzens, James	1872-1936	15	35	50	30	Political leader, automobile mfr.
Cox, Jacob D.	1828-1900	(See Civil War - Union Generals)				S/Interior, UG
Cox, James G.	1870-1957					PC
Coxey, Jacob S.	1854-1951	30	50	160	45	Reformer
Crawford, George	1798-1872	35	50	115		S/War, ZT
Crawford, William	1772-1834	50	150	250		S/Treasury, JM, PC, scarce
Creel, George	1876-1953	25	55	90	35	Political leader, journalist
Creswell, John A.J.	1828-1891	25	50	70		PG, UG
Crittenden, John J.	1787-1863	25	55	115		AG, WH
Croce, Benedetto	1866-1952	30	45	75	40	Italian philosopher, statesman
Crowninshield, Ben.	1772-1891	35	80	175		S/Navy, JM
Cummings, Homer S.	1870-1956	20	40	80		AG, FDR
Curley, James M.	1874-1958	20	40	50	30	Political leader, USHR, Gov. MA
Curtis, Charles	1860-1936	50	100	200	85	VP
Curtis, George William	1824-1892	50	100	125		Editor, reformer
Cushing, Caleb	1800-1879	25	50	110		AG, FP
Daley, Richard J.	1902-1976	25	55	100	45	Political leader
Dallas, Alexander	1759-1817	50	115	200		S/Treasury, JM
Dallas, George	1792-1864	100	200	300		VP, Dallas, Texas
Dana, Richard H.	1815-1882	60	175	225		Writer, lawyer, reformer
Daniels, Josephus	1862-1948	20	35	135	40	Political leader, S/Navy, WW
Darrow, Clarence	1857-1938	400	1550	2500	1500	ANS-$650, LS-$3500
Daugherty, Harry M.	1860-1941	20	40	75	45	Political leader, AG, WH
Davis, Dwight F.	1879-1945	25	60	130	55	S/War, CC
Davis, James J.	1873-1947	20	40	80		S/Labor, WH
Davis, Jefferson	1808-1889	600	2000	2340	2500	S/War, FP, CSA President
Davis, John W.	1873-1955	20	40	75	30	PC
Dawes, Charles G.	1865-1951	40	125	275	250	U.S. statesman, PC
Day, Dorothy	1897-1980	25	50	130	50	U.S. fdr .Catholic Worker move.
Day, J. Edward	1914-	15	30	70	25	PG, JFK
Day, William R.	1849-1923	(See Supreme Court Justices)				S/State, WM
De Leon, Daniel	1852-1914	35	70	125		Reformer
De Voto, Bernard A.	1897-1955	35	75	125	50	U.S. historian
Dearborn, Henry	1751-1829	125	325	500		S/War, TJ, ESPV
Debs, Eugene V.	1855-1926	75	200	250	100	U.S. labor leader, PC, scarce
Delano, Columbus	1809-1896	30	55	100		S/Interior, UG
Delany, Martin R.	1812-1885	225	600	2350		Reformer
Denby, Edwin	1870-1929	20	40	85		S/Navy, WH
Dennison, William	1815-1882	125	225	420		PG, AL
Dent, Frederick B.	1922-	10	20		20	S/Commerce, RN
Dern, George H.	1872-1936	40	100	130		S/War, FDR
Devens, Charles	1820-1891	(See Civil War - Union Generals)				AG, RH
Dewey, Melvil	1851-1931	50	80	125	65	Library book decimal system
Dewey, Thomas E.	1902-1971	45	80	150	125	G/NY, PC,
Dexter, Samuel	1761-1816					S/Treasury, JA, scarce, PU
Dickerson, Mahlon	1770-1853	25	65	130		S/Navy, AJ
Dickinson, Don M.	1846-1917	15	30	60		PG, GC
Dickinson, Jacob M.	1851-1928	25	50	100		S/War, WT
Dillon, C. Douglas	1909-	20	40		30	S/Treasury, JFK, RS

Name	db/dd	Sig.	DS	ALS	SP	Comments
Dirksen, Everett M.	1896-1969	25	75	135	60	Senate Republican min. ldr.
Dix, Dorothea	1802-1887	50	175	525		U.S. crusader for the mentally ill.
Dix, John A.	1798-1879 (See Civil War - Union Generals)					S/Treasury, JB
Doak, William N.	1882-1933	15	30	55	20	S/Labor, HH
Dobbin, James C.	1814-1857	35	70	140		S/Navy, FP
Dole, Robert	1923-	10	25	75	40	Political leader, USS, FA, PC
Dole, Sanford B.	1844-1926	50	225	400	125	Political leader, jurist
Donaldson, Jesse M.	1885-1970	15	30	45	20	PG, HT
Donnelly, Ignatius	1831-1901	30	60	80		Political leader, SL, USHR
Donovan, William J.	1883-1959	100	200	300	125	Attorney, Government official
Dooley, Thomas	1927-1961	100	200	400	150	"Jungle doctor"
Douglas, Stephen A.	1813-1861	220	325	775	300	Democratic leader, PC
Douglass, Frederick	1817-1895	300	800	3000		Reformer, SDS & SALS - 2X
Dow, Neal	(See Civil War - Union Generals)					
Drexel, Katharine M.	1858-1955	40	100	200		Reformer
Du Bois, William E.B.	1868-1963	40	100	150	65	Reformer, writer,NAACP
Duane, William	1780-1865	30	60	120		S/Treasury, AJ
Dubinsky, David	1892-1982	25	60	100	75	Labor leader
Dukakis, Michael	1933-	10	25		20	PC
Dulles, John Foster	1888-1959	35	80	140	60	S/State, DEt
Dunlop, John T.	1914-	10	20		15	S/Labor, GF
Durant, Ariel	1896-1981	70	120			
Durant, Will	1885-1981	75			125	U.S. historians, RS
Durkheim, Emile	1858-1917					Fr. fdr.of modern sociology, PU
Durkin, Martin P.	1894-1955	20	40		25	S/Labor, DE
Eaton, John	1790-1856	25	50	100		S/War, AJ
Edison, Charles	1890-1969	20	40		25	S/Navy, FDR
Eliot, Charles W.	1834-1926	20	35	60	50	Educator
Elkins, Stephen B.	1841-1911	20	40	75		S/War, BH
Endicott, William C.	1826-1900	25	40	65	40	S/War, GC
Engels, Friedrich	1820-1895					German political writer, PU
Erikson, Erik	1902-1994	25	50	70	30	U.S. psychoanalyst, author
Eustis, William	1753-1825					S/War, JM, scarce, PU
Evarts, William M.	1818-1901	20	40	80		AG, AJ
Everett, Edward	1794-1865	75	150	200		S/State, MF
Ewing, Thomas	1789-1871	40	100	200		S/Treasury, WH
Fairbanks, Charles W.	1852-1918	50	100	250	125	VP
Fairfield, Charles S.	1842-1924	20	40	75		S/Treasury, GC
Fall, Albert B.	1861-1944	25	60	100	40	S/Interior, WH, USS
Farley, James A.	1888-1976	10	30	55	20	PG, FDR
Ferraro, Geraldine	1935-	10	20	45	15	Politician, journalist
Fessenden, William P.	1806-1869	45	70	165		S/Treasury, AL
Finch, Robert H.	1925-	10	20	40	15	S/HE&W, RN
Fish, Hamilton	1808-1893	25	75	100		S/State, UG
Fisher, Irving	1867-1947	30	60	75	40	U.S. economist
Fisher, Walter	1862-1935	25	50	100		S/Interior, WT
Fiske, John	1842-1901	40	80	135		U.S. historian, lecturer
Flemming, Arthur S.	1905-	20	40		30	S/HE&W, DE
Flexner, Abraham	1866-1959	40	100	150	50	Educator
Floyd, John B.	1806-1863 (See Civil War - CSA Generals)					S/War, JB

Name	db/dd	Sig.	DS	ALS	SP	Comments
Folger, Charles J.	1818-1884	25	50	100		S/Treasury, CA
Folks, Homer	1867-1963	25	65	115	30	Reformer
Folsom, Marion B.	1893-1976	15	30		20	S/HE&W, DE
Forrestal, James V.	1892-1949	50	100	145	40	S/Navy, FDR
Forsyth, John	1780-1841	30	60	150		S/State, AJ
Forten, James	1766-1842	75	150	240		Reformer
Forward, Walter	1786-1852	25	50	100		S/Treasury, JT
Foster, Charles	1828-1904	30	60	100	45	S/Treasury, BH
Foster, John W.	1836-1917	30	65	115	50	S/State, BH
Foster, William Z.	1881-1961	20	35		25	PC
Fourier, Charles	1772-1837					French utopian socialist, PU
Fowler, Henry H.	1908-	10	25		25	S/Treasury, LBJ, RS
Francis, David R.	1850-1927	25	50	120		S/Interior, GC
Frazer, Sir James G.	1854-1941	40	100		50	British anthropologist
Freeman, Orville	1918-		10	25	50	30	S/Agriculture, JFK
Freemont, John C.	1813-1890	(See Civil War - Union Generals)				
Frelinghuysen, F.T.	1817-1885	25	50	125		S/State, CA
Friedan, Betty G.	1921-	10	20	30	15	Reformer
Fulbright, J. William	1905-1995	15	30	75	30	U.S. senator
Fuller, Sarah M.	1810-1850	75	150	250		Reformer, writer
Gage, Lyman J.	1836-1927	25	50	115		S/Treasury, WM
Gallatin, Albert	1761-1849	80	275	400		S/Treasury, TJ
Gardner, John W.	1912-	12	25		20	S/HE&W, LBJ
Garfield, James R.	1865-1950	15	35	70	30	S/Interior, TR
Garland, Augustus	1832-1899	60	130	200		AG, GC
Garner, John N.	1868-1967	40	145	200	150	Political leader, USHR, VP
Garrison, Lindley M.	1864-1932	30	70	150	45	S/War, WW
Garrison, William Lloyd	1805-1879	110	150	300		U.S. abolitionist
Gary, James	1833-1920	15	30	55		PG, WM
Gates, Thomas S. Jr.	1906-1983	15	35	60	25	S/Defense, DE
Genet, Edmond C.	1763-1834	70	160	400		Diplomat, SALS-2X
Gentile, Giovanni	1875-1944	50	150			Italian philosopher, educator
George, Henry	1839-1897	35	125	175		Journalist, reformer
Gerry, Elbridge	1744-1814	(See Revolutionary War)			VP, Signer	
Gibbon, Edward	1737-1794					British historian
Gilman, Daniel C.	1831-1908	50	100	175		Educator
Gilmer, Thomas	1802-1844	50	100	160		S/Navy, JT
Gilpin, Henry D.	1801-1860	30	60	110		AG, MVB
Gingrich, Newt	1943-	10	15	40	15	Political leader
Glass, Carter	1858-1946	20	40	50	30	Political leader, S/Treasury, WW
Goff, Nathan Jr.	1843-1919	25	50	80		S/Navy, RH
Goldberg, Arthur J.	1908-1990	(See Supreme Court Justices)		S/Labor, JFK		
Goldman, Emma	1869-1940	100	250	500	130	U.S. anarchist, birth-control adv.
Goldmark, Josephine	1877-1950	35	75	150	40	Reformer
Goldwater, Barry	1909-1998	15	35	65	40	Political leader, USS
Gompers, Samuel	1850-1924	125	150	300		U.S. labor leader
Good, James W.	1866-1929	20	45	55		S/War, HH
Gore, Albert, Jr.	1948-	20	50		40	VP, Clinton
Gore, Howard M.	1887-1947	15	30	50	25	S/Agriculture, CC
Graham, George	1772-1830	25	60	100		S/War, JM
Graham, William A.	1804-1875	20	40	60		S/Navy, MF

Name	db/dd	Sig.	DS	ALS	SP	Comments
Granger, Francis	1792-1868	20	35	55		PG, WH
Granger, Gideon	1767-1822	60	125	220		PG, TJ
Greeley, Horace	1811-1872	55	200	300		PC
Gregory, Thomas W.	1861-1933	20	40	55		AG, WW
Gresham, Walter Q.	1832-1895	(See Civil War - Union Generals)				PG, CA, S/State, GC, S/Treas.
Grew, Joseph C.	1880-1965	10	30	50	25	Diplomat
Griggs, John W.	1849-1927	15	40	80		AG, WM
Grimke, Angelina E.	1805-1879	100	150	300		Reformer, pioneer feminist
Grimke, Sarah Moore	1792-1873	75	150	300		Reformer, pioneer feminist
Gronlund, Laurence	1846-1899	25	75	150		Reformer
Gronouski, John A.	1919-	10	25		25	PG, JFK
Grundy, Felix	1777-1840	30	60	115		AG, MVB
Guthrie, James	1792-1869	25	40	80		S/Treasury, FP
Habersham, Joseph	1751-1815	(See Revolutionary War)				PG, GW, scarce
Hall, Granville S.	1846-1924	60	150	250	75	Social scientist, educator
Hall, Nathan	1810-1874	20	40	80		PG, MF
Hamilton, Alexander	1757-1804	(See Revolutionary War)				S/Treasury, GW
Hamilton, Paul	1762-1816	40	80	140		S/Navy, JM, scarce
Hamlin, Hannibal	1809-1891	100	200	300		VP
Hammond, James H.	1807-1864	25	50	75		Political leader
Hancock, Winfield	1824-1886	(See Civil War - Union Generals)				
Hand, Learned B.	1872-1961	75	150	300	130	Jurist
Hanna, Marcus A.	1837-1904	30	150	215	40	Political leader, manu., SDS-2X
Hannegan, Robert E.	1903-1949	25	50		45	PG, HT
Hardin, Clifford M.	1915-	10	20		20	S/Agriculture, RN
Harlan, James	1820-1899	30	55	110		S/Interior, AJ
Harmon, James	1846-1927	30	60	120		AG, GC
Harper, William R.	1856-1906	50	100	200		Educator
Harriman, William Averell	1891-1986	30	60	125	50	S/Commerce, HT
Harrington, E. Michael	1928-1989	20	45	75	30	Exposed U.S. poverty
Harris, Townsend	1804-1878	30	75	125		Diplomat, educator
Harris, William T.	1835-1909	35	125	250		Educator
Hastie, William H.	1904-1976	20	40	65	30	Jurist
Hathaway, Stanley K.	1924-	10	20		15	S/Interior, GF
Hatton, Frank	1846-1894	20	35	70		PG, CA
Hay, John	1838-1905	65	130	200	100	S/State, WM
Hays, Will H.	1879-1954	15	25	45		PG, WH
Haywood, William D.	1869-1928	35	100	165		Labor leader, controversial
Hearst, George	1820-1891	225	300	400		Political leader, businessman
Hendricks, Thomas A.	1819-1885	50	110	200		VP, SDS-2X, died in office
Henry, George	1839-1897					U.S. economist, reformer. PU
Henshaw, David	1791-1852	20	50	100		S/Navy, JT
Herbert, Hilary A.	1834-1919	15	25	50		S/Navy, GC
Herter, Christian A.	1895-1966	25	45		35	S/State, DE
Hewitt, Abram S.	1822-1903	35	50	60		Political leader, manufacturer
Hickel, Walter J.	1919-	10	25		20	S/Interior, RN
Hillman, Sidney	1887-1946	40	60	150	100	U.S. labor leader
Hills, Carla A.	1934-	10	25		20	S/H&UD, GF
Hiss, Alger	1904-	50	75	200		Diplomat
Hitchcock, Ethan A.	1835-1909	35	70	135		S/Interior, WM
Hitchcock, Frank H.	1869-1935	20	40	70		PG, WT

Name	db/dd	Sig.	DS	ALS	SP	Comments
Hoar, Ebenezer	1816-1895	35	60	130		AG, UG
Hoar, George Frisbie	1826-1904	15	25	25	20	Political leader, USHR, SS
Hobart, Garret A.	1844-1899					VP, scarce, PU
Hobbes, Thomas	1588-1679					English philosopher, poli., PU
Hobby, Oveta Culp	1905-	12	25		25	S/HE&W, DE
Hodges, Luther H.	1898-1974	15	30		25	S/Commerce, JFK
Hodgson, James D.	1915-	10	20		15	S/Labor, RN
Hoffa, James	1913-1975	300	365	600	425	Union leader
Hofstadter, Richard	1916-1970	25	50	65	30	U.S. historian
Holt, John	1924-1985	25	50	75	40	U.S. educator and author
Holt, Joseph	1807-1894	(See Civil War - Union Generals)				S/War, JB
Hoover, John Edgar	1895-1972	50	175	250	200	Government official, FBI
Hopkins, Harry Lloyd	1890-1946	20	40	75	30	Reformer, S/Comm., FDR
House, Edward M.	1858-1938	30	125	250	50	U.S. diplomat, advisor
Houston, David F.	1866-1940	15	30		25	S/Treasury, WW
Houston, Sam	1793-1863	750	2250	3500		President Texas Republic
Howe, Samuel G.	1801-1876	20	40	75		U.S. social reformer
Howe, Timothy O.	1816-1883	15	30	45		PG, CA
Hubbard, Sam D.	1799-1855	25	50	85		PG, MF
Hughes, Charles E.	1862-1948	(See Supreme Court Justices)				S/State, WH
Hull, Cordell	1871-1955	50	125	200	100	S/State, FDR
Humphrey, George M.	1890-1970	15	30		25	S/Treasury, DE
Humphrey, Hubert H.	1911-1978	30	150	265	50	USS, PC, VP
Hunt, William H.	1823-1884	15	30	70		S/Navy, JG
Hurley, Patrick J.	1883-1963	20	40		30	S/War, HH
Hutchins, Robert M.	1899-	20	45	75	25	Educator
Hyde, Arthur M.	1877-1947	15	30		30	S/Agriculture, HH
Ickes, Harold L.	1874-1952	25	50	90	35	S/interior, FDR, STLS- 17X
Ingham, Samuel	1779-1860	30	75	140		S/Treasury, AJ
Jackson, Helen	1830-1885	20	40	65	40	Writer, reformer
Jackson, Jesse L.	1941-	15	35	75	25	Political leader, reformer, RS
Jackson, Robert H.	1892-1954	(See Supreme Court Justices)				AG, FDR
James, Thomas L.	1831-1916	15	25	55		PG, JG
Jardine, William M.	1879-1955	15	30	50	20	S/Agriculture, CC
Jewell, Marshall	1825-1883	35	70	140		PG, UG
Johnson, Alvin	1874-1971	10	25	50	25	Educator
Johnson, Cave	1793-1866	30	80	150		PG, JP
Johnson, Hiram	1866-1945	20	45	55	25	Political leader, USS
Johnson, James W.	1871-1938	40	125	250	80	Writer, reformer
Johnson, Louis A.	1891-1966	20	40		30	S/Defense, HT
Johnson, Reverdy	1796-1876	25	65	100		AG, ZT
Johnson, Richard M.	1780-1850	70	150	300		VP
Jones, Jesse	1874-1956	15	30		25	S/Commerce, FDR
Jones, Mary H. "Mother"	1830-1930	70	200	450	225	Labor leader
Jones, William						S/Navy, JM, scarce, PU
Katzenbach, Nicholas	1922-	10	25		20	AG, LBJ
Kefauver, Carey Estes	1903-1963	15	30	45	20	Political leader, USS
Keller, Helen	1880-1968	225	475	2250	1000	Crusader,FA,SDS-2X
Kelley, Florence	1859-1932	55	110	225	80	Reformer

Name	db/dd	Sig.	DS	ALS	SP	Comments
Kellogg, Frank B.	1856-1937	30	80	125	40	S/State, SDS & ALS - 2X
Kendall, Amos	1789-1869	25	50	110		PoG, AJ, journalist
Kennan, George F.	1904-	10	35	50	20	Diplomat
Kennedy, David M..	1905-	10	25		20	S/Treasury, RN
Kennedy, Edward M.	1932-	12	25		25	USS, RS
Kennedy, John P.	1795-1870	25	50	85		S/Navy, MF
Kennedy, Joseph P.	1888-1969	100	200		200	Diplomat
Kennedy, Robert F.	1925-1968	225	700	2750	700	AG, JFK, USS, FA, SDS-2X
Kent, James	1763-1847	70	110	200		Jurist
Key, David M.	1824-1900	25	45	90		PG, RH
Keynes, John Maynard	1883-1946	125	800		250	British economist
King, Horatio	1811-1897	40	85			PG, JB, SDS-2X
King, Martin Luther	1929-1968	2100	4200		3500	S. program - $3000, SB-$2500
King, Rufus	1755-1827		(See Revolutionary War)			
King, William R.	1786-1853					VP, died in office, scarce, PU
Kirk, Russell	1918-1994	20	40	50	25	U.S. social philosopher
Kirkwood, Samuel J.	1813-1894	20	45	70		S/Interior, JG
Kissinger, Henry A.	1923-	50	250	400	100	S/State, RN, FA, SB-$100
Kleindienst, Richard G.	1923-	15	25		25	AG, RN
Kleppe, Thomas	1919-	10	20		20	S/Interior, GF
Knebel, John A.	1936-	10	20		20	S/Agriculture, GF
Knox, Frank	1874-1944	30	65	110		S/Navy, FDR
Knox, Henry	1750-1806		(See Revolutionary War)			S/War, GW
Knox, Philander	1853-1921	30	60	115	50	AG, WM
Kroeber, Alfred L.	1876-1960	35	70	125	45	U.S. cultural anthropologist
Krug, Julius A.	1907-1970	20	40		30	S/Interior, HT
Kuhn, Maggie	1905-1995	15	35	45	25	Gray Panthers founder
Kunstler, William	1919-1995	25	50	125	35	Attorney, SDS & ALS - 2-3X
La Follette, Robert Jr.	1895-1953	15	25	35	25	Political leader, USS
LaFollette, Robert M.	1855-1925	25	65	100	35	U.S. Wisconsin public official
LaGuardia, Fiorello H.	1882-1947	25	75	150	150	Political leader, mayorr NYC
Laird, Melvin R.	1922-	10	25		20	S/Defense, RN
Lamar, Lucius Q.C.	1825-1893	(See Supreme Court Justices)				S/Interior, GC
Lamont, Daniel S.	1851-1905	20	40	75		S/War, GC
Lamont, Robert P.	1867-1948	15	30		25	S/Commerce, HH
Landon, Alf	1887-1987	20	60	100	55	Political leader, G/KS
Lane, Franklin K.	1864-1921	20	45	80	30	S/Interior, WW
Lansing, Robert	1864-1929	30	75	140	50	S/State, WW
Lasch, Christopher	1932-1994	15	25	30	20	U.S. social critic, historian
Laughlin, James L.	1850-1933					U.S. economist, PU
Lee, Charles	1758-1815					AG, GW, AG. JA, PU, scarce
Legare, Hugh S.	1797-1843	35	70	125		AG, JT
Levi, Edward	1911-	10	25		20	AG, GF
Levy-Bruhl, Lucien	1857-1939					French philosopher, PU
Lewin, Kurt	1890-1947					U.S. German-born psy., PU
Lewis, John L.	1880-1969	50	75	215	80	U.S. labor leader, UMW
Lieber, Francis	1800-1872	50	125	175		Political scientist
Lilienthal, David E.	1899-1981	20	40	60	30	Administrator
Lincoln, Levi	1749-1820					AG, TJ, PU
Lincoln, Robert T.	1843-1926	100	200	300		S/War, JG
Lindsey, Benjamin B.	1869-1943	20	40	50	30	Reformer

Name	db/dd	Sig.	DS	ALS	SP	Comments
Livingston, Edward	1764-1836	30	65	120		S/State, AJ
Lloyd, Henry D.	1847-1903	45	90	140		Publicist, reformer
Locke, John	1632-1704	1000	2000			English philosopher, ESPV
Lockwood, Belva	1830-1917					PC, scarce, PU
Lodge, Henry Cabot	1850-1924	45	100	225	100	U.S. Republican senator
Logan, George	1753-1821	40	100	130		Political leader, USS
Long, Huey P.	1893-1924	100	160	245	140	Louisiana political czar, gov.
Long, John D.	1838-1915	20	40	65		S/Navy, WM
Lorenz, Konrad	1904-1989					Austrian ethologist, PU
Lovejoy, Elijah P.	1802-1837					Reformer, PU
Lovett, Robert A.	1895-1986	12	25		20	S/Defense, HT
Lowell, Abbott L.	1856-1943	20	55	120	75	Educator
Luce, Claire Booth	1903-1987	40	125	200	75	Writer, diplomat, USHR
Lundy, Benjamin	1789-1839	60	120	240		Reformer, priv. papers burned!
Lyon, James T.	1923-	10	20		15	S/H&UD, RN
Lyon, Mary Mason	1797-1849	70	150	300		Educator
Macaulay, Thomas B.	1800-1859	50	100	150		British historian, statesman
Macdonald, Dwight	1906-1982	20	45	100	30	Critic, political activist
MacVeagh, Franklin	1837-1934	15	25	55	25	S/Treasury, WT
MacVeagh, Wayne	1833-1917	40	70	130		AG, JG
Malcolm X (M. Little)	1925-1965	1000	4000	5000		Reformer, STLS & ALS - 3X
Malinowski, Bronislaw	1884-1942					Social anthropology, PU
Malthus, Thomas R.	1766-1834	500	1000	2000		British economist
Mann, Horace	1796-1859	50	150	275		Pioneered public school system
Mannheim, Karl	1893-1947					Hungarian sociologist, his. PU
Manning, Daniel	1831-1887	15	30	65		S/Treasury, GC
Marcuse, Herbert	1898-1979	45	100	200	75	Philosopher, writer, educator
Marcy, William L.	1786-1851	40	100	200		S/War, JP
Marsh, George P.	1801-1882	40	100	125		Diplomat, scientist, USHR
Marshall, George C.	1880-1959	200	300	500	400	S/Defense, HT, S/State, HT
Marshall, James W.	1822-1910	25	50	100		PG, UG
Marshall, John	1755-1835	(See Supreme Court Justices)				S/State, JA
Marshall, Thomas R.	1854-1925	55	135		125	VP, somewhat scarce
Marx, Karl	1818-1883	1000	2000			German pol. philosopher, ESPV
Mason, John Y.	1799-1859	25	50	100		S/Navy, JT
Mathews, Forrest D.	1935-	10	20		15	S/HE&W, GF
Maynard, Horace	1814-1882	25	50	75		PG, RH
Mazzini, Giuseppe	1805-1872	130	360	750		Italian pol. philosopher, ESPV
McAdoo, William G.	1863-1941	30	60	115	40	S/Treasury, WW
McCarthy, Joseph R.	1908-1957	40	125	250	110	USS, Communist hunter
McClellan, George	1826-1885	(See Civil War - Union Generals)				PC
McClelland, Robert	1807-1880	35	70	130		S/Interior, FP
McCrary, George W.	1835-1890	30	75	140		S/War, RH
McCulloch, Hugh	1808-1895	50	130	165		S/Treasury, AL & CA
McElroy, Neil H.	1904-1972	15	25		20	S/Defense, DE
McGovern, George	1922-	12	25		20	PC
McGranery, James P.	1895-1954	20	40		25	AG, HT
McGrath, J. Howard	1903-1966	15	35		20	AG, HT
McGuffey, William H.	1800-1873	125	475	800		U.S. public educator
McHenry, James	1753-1816	(See Revolutionary War)				S/War, GW, scarce
McKay, Douglas	1893-1959	25	50	100	25	S/Interior, DE

Name	db/dd	Sig.	DS	ALS	SP	Comments
McKenna, Joseph	1843—1926	(See Supreme Court Justices)				AG, WM
McKennan, Thomas	1794-1852	30	60	110		S/Interior, MF
McLane, Louis	1786-1857	20	45	70		S/State, AJ
McLean, John	1785-1861	(See Supreme Court Justices)				PG, JM
McNamara, Robert S.	1916-	10	40	75	20	Businessman,S/Defense, JFK
McReynolds, James C.	1862-1946	(See Supreme Court Justices)				AG, WW
Mead, George H.	1863-1931					U.S. phil., soc. psyc., PU
Mead, Margaret	1901-1978	100	150	200		U.S. cultural anthropologist
Meany, George	1894-1980	20	35	80	100	Labor leader, AFL-CIO, RS
Meigs, Return	1764-1824	70	160	200		PG, JM, ESPV-ALS
Meiklejohn, Alexander	1872-1964	20	40	50	25	British-born educator
Mellon, Andrew	1855-1937	225	450	965	400	S/Treasury, WH, SDS-2X
Menninger, Karl	1893-1990	40	100	150	75	Founded Menninger Clinic
Meredith, Edwin T.	1876-1928	25	50	110		S/Agriculture, WW
Meredith, William	1799-1873	25	50			S/Treasury, ZT
Merriam, Charles E.	1874-1953	10	30	75	25	Political scientist
Metcalf, Victor H.	1853-1936	20	40	75		S/Navy, TR
Meyer, George von L.	1858-1918	15	30	60		PG, TR
Mill, James	1773-1836	100	250	500		Philosopher, historian
Miller, Kelly	1863-1939	40	100	150	65	Educator, sociologist
Miller, Perry G.	1905-1963					U.S. historian, PU
Miller, William H.H.	1840-1917	20	40	80		AG, BH
Mills, Ogden L.	1884-1937	15	35	70		S/Treasury, HH
Mitchell, James P.	1900-1964	15	30	65	20	S/Labor, DE
Mitchell, John	1870-1919	45	100		75	Labor leader
Mitchell, John N.	1913-1988					AG, RN, PU, ESPV
Mitchell, William D.	1874-1955	20	40	80	25	AG, HH
Mommsen, Theodor	1817-1903					German historian, PU
Mondale, Walter	1928-	15	30		30	VP, PC
Montessori, Maria	1870-1952	325	750	1100		Italian educator, physician
Moody, William H.	1853-1917	(See Supreme Court Justices)				AG, TR
Morgenthau, Henry Jr.	1891-1967	40	80	130	50	S/Treasury, FDR
Morison, Samuel Eliot	1887-1976	15	35			U.S. historian
Morrill, Justin S.	1810-1898	40	65	100		Political leader, USS
Morrill, Lot M.	1812-1883	25	50	85		S/Treasury, UG
Morris, Gouverneur		(See Revolutionary War)				
Morton, Julius S.	1832-1902	25	50	75		S/Agriculture, GC
Morton, Levi P.	1824-1920	50	100	200		VP, ESPV - SP
Morton, Paul	1857-1911	20	40	70		S/Navy, TR
Morton, Rogers	1914-1979	15	30	60	25	S/Interior, RN
Moses, Robert	1888-1981	20	40	50	50	Government official
Mott, Lucretia	1793-1880	100	150	400	300	U.S. reformer, feminist pioneer
Mueller, Frederick H.	1893-1976	10	25	50	15	S/Commerce, DE
Mumford, Lewis	1895-1990	25	50	100	50	Writer, reformer, educator
Murphy, Frank	1890-1949	(See Supreme Court Justices)				AG, FDR
Murray, Philip	1886-1952	30	40	55	40	Labor leader
Myrdal, Gunnar	1898-1987					Swedish economist, PU
Nader, Ralph	1934-	10	25	50	25	Reformer, PC
Nagel, Charles	1849-1940	15	30	50		S/L&C, TR
Needham, Joseph	1900-1995					British scientific historian, PU
Nelson, John	1794-1860	20	40	85		AG, JT

Name	db/dd	Sig.	DS	ALS	SP	Comments
Nevins, Allan	1890-1971	25	50	80	50	U.S. historian, biographer
New, Harry S.	1858-1937	20	35	60		PG, WH
Newberry, Truman H.	1864-1945	20	40	75	30	S/Navy, TR
Nightingale, Florence	1820-1910	400	900	1325		Brit. fdr. mod. nursing, SB-$395
Niles, John M.	1787-1856	25	45	65		PG, MVB
Noble, John W.	1831-1912	(See Civil War - Union Generals)				S/Interior, BH
Norris, George W.	1861-1944	15	30	55	45	Political leader, USS
Noyes, John H.	1811-1886	35	80	135		Reformer
Nye, Gerald P.	1892-1971	10	25	30	15	Political leader, USS
O'Brien, Lawrence F.	1917-	15	30		25	PG, LBJ
O'Neill, Thomas P. "Tip"	1912-1994	15	35	55	40	USHR
O'Reilly, John B.	1844-1890	30	55	125	50	Reformer
Olney, Richard	1835-1917	30	55	120		S/State, GC
Ortega y Gasset, Jose	1883-1955					Spanish philosopher, PU
Osgood, Samuel	1748-1813	(See Revolutionary War)				PG, GW, scarce
Owen, Robert	1771-1858	75	200	300		British political philosopher
Page, Walter	1855-1918	45	90	150		Writer, diplomat
Paine, Thomas	1737-1809	4000				U.S. political theorist
Palmer, Alexander	1872-1936	15	25	40	25	USHR, AG, WW
Pankhurst, Emmeline	1858-1928	50	150	300		British woman suffragist
Pareto, Vilfredo	1848-1923					Italian econ., sociologist, PU
Parker, Alton B.	1852-1926					PC, scarce, PU
Parker, Theodore	1810-1860	60	110	200		Reformer
Parkman, Francis	1823-1893	50	100	200		U.S. historian
Patterson, Robert P.	1891-1952	20	45		30	S/War, HT
Paul, Alice	1885-1977	30	100	150	65	Reformer
Paulding, James	1778-1860	30	70	145		S/Navy, MVB
Payne, Henry C.	1843-1904	15	30	60		PG, TR
Payne, John B.	1855-1935	25	45	60		S/Interior, WW
Peabody, Elizabeth P.	1804-1894	125				Education pioneer
Perkins, Frances	1880-1965	20	40	80	30	Reformer. S/Labor, FDR
Peterson, Peter G.	1926-	10	20		15	S/Commerce, RN
Phillips, Wendell	1811-1884	50	75	150		Reformer
Pickering, Timothy	1745-1829	(See Revolutionary War)				S/State, GW
Pierrepont, Edwards	1817-1892	20	40	65		AG, UG
Pinchot, Gifford	1865-1946	40	100	150	60	Political leader, G/PA
Pinckney, Charles C.	1746-1836	(See Revolutionary War)				
Pinckney, Thomas	1750-1828	(See Revolutionary War)				PC
Pinkney, William	1764-1822					AG, JM, scarce, PU
Poinsett, Joel	1779-1851	50	150	215		S/War, MVB
Porter, James M.	1793-1862	30	70	125		S/War, JT
Porter, Peter	1773-1844	60	120	145		S/War, JQA
Powderly, Terence V.	1849-1924	40	75	130	50	Labor leader
Powell, Adam Clay., Jr.	1908-1972	40	55	75	45	Political leader
Prescott, William	1796-1859	50	100	200		Early American historian
Preston, William	1805-1862	30	75	135		S/Navy, ZT
Proctor, Redfield	1831-1908	25	45	100		S/War, BH
Proudhon, Pierre J.	1809-1865					Fr. social theorist, anarchist, PU
Quayle, Dan	1947-	10	20		15	VP, RS

Name	db/dd	Sig.	DS	ALS	SP	Comments
Quesnay, Francois	1694-1774					French economic theorist, PU
Ramsey, Alex	1815-1903	25	50	110		S/War, RH
Randall, Alexander	1819-1872	20	40	75		PG, AJ
Randolph, Asa P.	1889-1979	50	125	235	100	Labor leader
Randolph, Edmund	1753-1813	(See Revolutionary War)				S/State, GW
Randolph, John	1773-1833	125	250	500		U.S. , advocate states' rights
Rankin, Jeannette	1880-1973	100	200	300	150	First woman member USHR
Rawlins, John A.	1831-1869	(See Civil War - Union Generals)				S/War, UG
Rayburn, Sam	1882-1961	45	60	115	65	U.S. Democratic leader
Redfield, William C.	1789-1932	20	40	55		S/Commerce, WW
Reed, Thomas B.	1839-1902	20	40	50		Political leader, SL, USHR
Reid, Whitelaw	1837-1912	35	70	100	50	Journalist, diplomat
Reuther, Walter	1907-1970	30	50	100	45	U.S. labor leader, headed UAW
Ribicoff, Abraham A.	1910-	10	25		20	S/HE&W, JFK
Ricardo, David	1772-1823					British economic theorist, PU
Richardson, Elliot L.	1920-	10	30		25	AG, S/Def., RN, S/Com., GF
Richardson, William	1821-1896	20	40	75		S/Treasury, UG
Riis, Jacob A.	1849-1914	25	60	120	45	Reformer, journalist
Robeson, George M.	1829-1987	20	40	70		S/Navy, UG
Robinson, James H.	1863-1936					U.S. historian, educator, PU
Rock, John	1825-1866	30	70	120		Lawyer, physician
Rockefeller, Nelson	1908-1979	20	75	150	40	U.S.G/NY, VP
Rockhill, William W.	1853-1914	45	115	150	50	Diplomat
Rogers, Carl	1902-1987					U.S. psychotherapist, PU
Rogers, William P.	1913-	15	30		25	AG, DE, S/State, RN
Romney, George W.	1907-1995	10	25	45	15	G/Mich., S/H&UD, RN
Root, Elihu	1845-1937	75	150	225	150	U.S. lawyer, S/War, WM
Roper, Daniel C.	1867-1943	15	40		25	S/Commerce, FDR
Rousseau, J.-Jacques	1712-1778	500	1500	3000		French social philosopher
Royall, Kenneth C.	1894-1971	15	40		25	S/War, HT
Rumsfeld, Donald	1932-	10	25		20	S/Defense, GF
Rush, Richard	1780-1859	60	120	215		AG, JM
Rusk, Dean	1909-1995	15	45	75	25	S/State, JFK
Rusk, Jeremiah M.	1830-1893	(See Civil War - Union Generals)				S/Agriculture, BH
Russell, Richard B.	1897-1971	12	25	50	20	Political leader, G/GA, USS
Rustin, Bayard	1910-1987	25	45	100	30	Reformer
Salk, Lee	1926-1992					U.S. child psychologist, PU
Sanger, Margaret	1883-1966	75	180	275	90	U.S. social reformer
Sapir, Edward	1884-1939					German/U.S. anthropologist, PU
Sargent, John G.	1860-1939	15	30	50	25	AG, CC
Saussure, Ferdinand de	1857-1913					Swiss, linguistics, PU
Sawyer, Charles W.	1887-1979	15	25		20	S/Commerce, HT
Saxbe, William B.	1916-	10	20		15	AG, RN
Schacht, Hjalmar	1877-1970	100	200	300		German economist
Schlesinger, James R.	1929-	10	20		15	S/Defense, RN
Schofield, John M.	1831-1906	(See Civil War - Union Generals)				S/War, AJ
Schumpeter, Joseph	1883-1950					Czech./U.S. economist, PU
Schurz, Carl	1829-1906	(See Civil War - Union Generals				
Schwellenbach, Lewis	1894-1948	15	25		20	S/Labor, HT
Scott, Emmett J.	1873-1957	25	100	125	55	Educator

Name	db/dd	Sig.	DS	ALS	SP	Comments
Scott, Winfield	1786-1866	(See Civil War - Union Generals)				PC
Seaton, Fred A.	1909-1974	15	30		20	S/Interior, DE
Seton, Elizabeth	1774-1821					First nat-born Amer. saint, PU
Seward, William H.	1801-1872	100	200	325		S/State, AL assain. related-10X
Seymour, Horatio	1810-1886					PC, scarce, PU
Shaftesbury, Earl of	1801-1885	40	80	150		British social reformer
Shaw, Leslie M.	1848-1932	20	50	65		S/Treasury, TR
Shaw, Robert G.	1837-1863					Reformer, civil war colonel, PU
Shays, Daniel	1747-1825					Reformer, PU
Sherman, James S.	1855-1912					VP, died in office, scarce, PU
Sherman, John	1823-1900	60	200			S/State, WM, S/Treasury, RH
Shultz, George P.	1920-	10	25		20	S/Treasury, S/Labor, RN
Simmel, George	1858-1918					German sociologist, phil., PU
Simon, William E.	1927-	10	25		20	S/Treasury, RN
Skinner, B.F.	1904-1989	30	50	75	60	U.S. psychologist, RS
Smith, Adam	1723-1790					British economist, PU
Smith, Alfred E.	1873-1944	40	85	175	100	G/NY, PC
Smith, Caleb B.	1808-1864	50	150	250		S/Interior, AL
Smith, Charles E.	1842-1908	15	25			PG, WM
Smith, Cyrus R.	1899-	12	25		15	S/Commerce, LBJ
Smith, Gerald L.K.	1898-1976					PC, scarce, PU
Smith, Hoke	1855-1931	12	30		25	S/Interior, GC
Smith, Margaret Chase	1897-1995	10	25	65	20	USHR, elected both houses
Smith, Robert	1757-1842	50	150	300		S/Navy, TJ
Snyder, John W.	1896-1985	15	25		25	S/Treasury, HT
Southard, Samuel	1787-1842					S/Navy, JM, PU
Sparks, Jared	1789-1866	25	50	75		U.S. historian, educator
Speed, James	1812-1887	60	100	135		AG, AL, rare, ESPV
Spencer, John C.	1788-1855	25	50	100		S/War, S/Treasury, JT
Spengler, Oswald	1880-1936					German philosopher, hist., PU
Spingarn, Joel E.	1875-1939	40	100	150	60	Educator, reformer
Spreckels, Rudolph	1872-1958	30	45	75	50	Reformer, Mfr., s. of Claus
Stanbery, Henry	1803-1881	25	45	130		AG, AJ
Stans, Maurice	1908-	10	20		15	S/Commerce, RN
Stanton, Edwin M.	1814-1869	170	225	500	200	AG, JB, war dated - 2-3X
Stanton, Elizabeth Cady	1815-1902	175	250	500		U.S. woman suffrage pioneer
Steffens, Jos.Lincoln	1866-1936	65	125	215	100	Journalist, reformer
Steinem, Gloria	1934-	10	15	40	15	Reformer,RS
Stephens, Alexander H.	1812-1883	200	345	500		USHR, G/GA, VP CSA
Stettinius, Edward R., Jr.	1900-1949	30	75	150	40	U.S. industrialists, S/State, FDR
Stevens, Thaddeus	1792-1868	40	100	200		Political leader, USHR
Stevenson, Adlai E.	1835-1914					VP, scarce, PU
Stevenson, Adlai E.	1900-1965	50	75	150	100	U.S. Democratic leader,PC
Steward, Ira	1831-1883	40	100	160		Labor leader
Stimson, Henry L.	1867-1950	30	100	175	40	U.S. statesman, S/War, WT
Stoddert, Benjamin	1751-1813	100	220			S/Navy, JA, scarce
Stone, Harlan F.	1872-1946	(See Supreme Court Justices)				AG, CC
Stone, Lucy	1818-1893	125	250	350	340	U.S. feminist, SDS-2-3X
Storey, Moorfield	1845-1929	65	130	245		Lawyer, reformer
Stowe, Harriet E. B.	1811-1896	275	350	700		Writer, reformer
Straus, Oscar S.	1850-1926	20	40	65		S/L&C, TR
Strauss, Lewis L.	1896-1974	15	25		25	S/Commerce, DE

Name	db/dd	Sig.	DS	ALS	SP	Comments
Stuart, Alexander	1807-1891	25	50	80		S/Interior, MF
Summerfield, Arthur E.	1807-1891	25	50	80		PG, DE
Sumner, William G.	1840-1910					U.S. social scientist, econ., PU
Swanson, Claude A.	1862-1939	20	40		30	S/Navy, FDR
Taft, Alphonso	1810-1891	25	50	120		S/War, UG
Taft, Robert A.	1889-1953	25	45	75	35	U.S. conservative Senate leader
Taine, Hippolyte	1828-1893					French historian, PU
Taney, Roger B.	1777-1864	(See Supreme Court Justices)				S/Treasury, AJ
Taussig, Frank W.	1859-1940	20	50	65	50	U.S. economist, educator
Taylor, A.J.P.	1906-1989					British historian, PU
Teller, Henry M.	1820-1914	20	40	75	30	S/Interior, CA
Teresa, Mother, of Cal.	1910-1997	250	400	600	350	Rom. Catholic nun, fndr. MOC
Thomas, Lorenzo	1804-1875	(See Civil War - Union Generals)				
Thomas, M. (Martha) C.	1857-1935	60	125	250	100	Educator
Thomas, Norman M.	1884-1968	40	80	145	50	U.S. social reformer, PC
Thomas, Phillip	1810-1890	25	50	100		S/Treasury, JB
Thompson, Jacob	1810-1885					S/Interior, JB, PU
Thompson, Richard W.	1809-1900	20	40	60		S/Navy, RH
Thompson, Smith	1768-1843	(See Supreme Court Justices)				S/Navy, JM
Thurmond, Strom	1902-	15	25		20	USS, PC
Tilden, Samuel J.	1814-1886	60	125	225		Political leader, PC
Tinbergen, Nikolaas	1907-1988					Dutch/British ethologist, PU
Tobin, Maurice J.	1901-1953	15	30		25	S/Labor, HT
Tocqueville, Alexis de	1805-1859	100	200	400		French political scientist
Tompkins, Daniel D.	1774-1825	65	120	175		VP
Toucey, Isaac	1792-1869	25	65	120		AG, JP
Townsend, Francis E.	1867-1960	50	100	175	125	U.S. pension reformist of 1933
Toynbee, Arnold	1889-1975	25	50	80	50	British historian
Tracy, Benjamin F.	1830-1915	20	40	65		S/Navy, BH
Treitschke, Heinrich von	1834-1896					German historian, PU
Trevelyan, George	1838-1926	25	50	100	70	British historian, statesman
Trowbridge, Alex. B.	1929-	10	20		15	S/Commerce, LBJ
Tubman, Harriet R.	1821-1913					Reformer, PU
Tuchman, Barbara	1912-1989	50	150	275	75	U.S. history author
Turner, Frederick J.	1861-1932	55	125	250	100	U.S. historian
Tweed, William M.	1823-1878	150	250	425		U.S. politician leader
Tyner, James N.	1826-1904	20	40	60		PG, UG
Udall, Stewart L.	1920-	10	20		20	S/Interior, JFK
Upshur, Abel P.	1791-1844					S/State, JT, scarce, PU
Usery, W.J.	1923-	10	20		15	S/Labor, GF
Usher, John P.	1816-1889	40	80	150		S/Interior, AL
Vallandigham, Clement	1820-1871	115	200	300		Political leader, USHR
Vandenberg, Arthur H.	1884-1951	15	45	65	25	U.S. senator
Vebien, Thorstein B.	1857-1929					U.S. econ., social phil., PU
Vera Cruz, Phillip	1905-1994	25	55	75	40	United Farm Workers Union
Vico, Giovanni	1668-1744					Ita. historian, philosopher, PU
Vilas, William F.	1840-1908	15	25	40		PG, GC
Villard, Oswald G.	1872-1949	45	90	135	75	Journalist, reformer
Vinson, Fred M.	1890-1953	(See Supreme Court Justices)				S/Treasury, HT

304 The Official AUTOGRAPH™ Price Guide

Name	db/dd	Sig.	DS	ALS	SP	Comments
Volpe, John A.	1908-	10	20		15	S/Transportation, RN
Von Neumann, John	1903-1957					Educator, mathematician, PU
Wade, Benjamin	1800-1878	30	65	125		Political leader, USS
Wagner, Robert F.	1877-1953	25	85	175	35	Political leader, USS
Walker, Frank C.	1886-1959	10	20		15	PG, FDR
Walker, Robert J.	1801-1869	20	50	75		S/Treasury, JP, USS
Wallace, George C.	1919-	10	35	75	25	Political leader, governor, RS
Wallace, Henry	1888-1965	50	125	250	100	S/Agriculture, FDR, PC, VP
Walton, Izaak	1593-1683					English biographer, PU
Wanamaker, John	1838-1922	50	75	150	125	Merchant, PG, BH
Washburne, Elihu B.	1816-1887	25	50	100		S/State, UG
Washington, Booker T.	1856-1915	225	300	900	1200	Educator, SLS-2-3X, ESPV
Watson, Marvin	1924-	10	20		15	PG, LBJ
Watson, Thomas E.	1856-1922	20	45	55	30	Political leader, USHR
Weaver, James B.	1833-1912					PC, rare
Weaver, Robert C.	1907-	20	50	80	45	S/H&UD, LBJ
Webb, Sidney J.	1859-1947	40		100	165	Fabian Society and Labor Party
Webb, Beatrice	1858-1943	45		100	200	Fabian Society and Labor Party
Webb, Walter P.	1888-1963					U.S. historian, PU
Weber, Max	1864-1920					German sociologist, PU
Webster, Daniel	1782-1852	150	500	560		USHR, USS, SLS-$1750. PC
Webster, Noah	1758-1843	500	800	1540		Lexicographer, SC-$500
Weed, Thurlow	1797-1882	20	30	40		Political leader, journalist
Weeks, John W.	1860-1926	15	30	60		S/War, WH
Weeks, Sinclair	1893-1972	15	25		20	S/Commerce, DE
Weinberger, Caspar W.	1917-	10	20		15	S/HE&W, RN
Weld, Theodore D.	1803-1895	35	70	100		Reformer
Welles, Gideon	1802-1878	125	250	300	700	S/Navy, AL, LS-$295
Wells-Barnett, Ida B.	1862-1931	120	275	575		Reformer
West, Roy O.	1868-1958	15	25		20	S/Interior, CC
Wheeler, William A.	1819-1887	100	200			VP
White, Alfred T.	1846-1921	40	75	125		Reformer
White, Andrew D.	1832-1918	25	100	150	75	Educator, diplomat
White, Hugh L.	1773-1840					PC, rare, PU
Whitehead, Alfred N.	1861-1947	70	200	365	125	Educator, philosopher
Whiting, William F.	1864-1936	20	40	65		S/Commerce, CC
Whitney, William C.	1841-1904	20	30	50	30	Financier, S/Navy, GC
Wickard, Claude R.	1893-1967	10	20		20	S/Agriculture, FDR
Wickersham, George W.	1858-1936	15	30		25	AG, WT
Wickliffe, Charles	1788-1869	25	45			PG, JT
Wilberforce, William	1759-1833	60	150	300		British social reformer
Wilbur, Curtis D.	1867-1954	10	20		20	S/Navy, CC
Wilbur, Ray L..	1875-1949	15	25		25	S/Interior, HH
Wiley, Harvey W.	1844-1930	100	200	300	150	Reformer, chemist
Wilkie, Wendell	1892-1944	35	70		50	PC
Wilkens, William	1779-1865	30	60	100		S/War, JT
Wilkins, Roy	1901-1981	15	30	100	20	Reformer, NAACP, RS
Willard, Emma Hart	1787-1870	50	115	175		Pio. higher education women
Willard, Francis E.	1839-1898	55	75	200		U.S. temperance
Williams, G.H.	1820-1910	15	40			AG, UG
Willkie, Wendell L.	1892-1944	20	60	150	100	Political leader

Name	db/dd	Sig.	DS	ALS	SP	Comments
Wilmot, David	1814-1868	70	150	225		Political leader
Wilson, Charles E.	1890-1961	15	30		25	S/Defense, DE
Wilson, Henry	1812-1875	80	150			VP, scarce
Wilson, James	1836-1920	15	35			S/Agriculture, WM
Wilson, William B.	1862-1939	15	30		20	S/Labor, WW
Wilson, William L.	1843-1900	15	30			PG, GC
Windom, William	1827-1891	20	40			S/Treasury, JG
Wirt, William	1772-1834	50	100	135		AG, JM, scarce
Wirtz, W. Willard	1912-	10	20		15	S/Labor, JFK
Wolcott, Oliver	1760-1833	(See Revolutionary War)				S/Treasury, GW
Wollstonecraft, Mary	1759-1797					Brit. women's rights author, PU
Wood, Robert C.	1923-	10	20		15	S/H&UD, LBJ
Woodbury, Levi	1789-1851	60	125	250		S/Treasury, AJ
Woodhull, Victoria	1838-1927	130	225	500		Reformer, PC
Woodin, William H.	1868-1934	15	35		25	S/Treasury, FDR
Woodring, Henry A.	1890-1967	25	50		30	S/War, FDR
Woodward, Calvin M.	1837-1914	25	50	80		Educator
Work, Hubert	1860-1942	20	40		25	PG, WH
Wright, Luke E.	1846-1922	25	50	75		S/War, TR
Wright, Silas	1795-1847	15	40	75		Political leader, USHR
Wynne, Robert J.	1851-1922	20	35		25	PG, TR
Young, Whitney M.	1921-1971	15	30	55	20	Reformer

PRESIDENTS OF THE UNITED STATES

WHAT YOU NEED TO KNOW

* One of the most popular, and perhaps logical, areas of autograph collecting in America.

* While the choice of what particular form to collect will most often be determined by your finances, an individual entering this niche must have a clear understanding of what types of items were available to the subject and at what particular period.

* United States Presidents have very diverse backgrounds.

* A premium is added to material dated during an administration. For example, William Henry Harrison held the prestigious office for only about a month. While Harrison presidential material is scarce, other mementos of his life are not.

* Like many areas of collecting certain forms are common such as clipped signatures, autographed album pages, index cards, postcards, free franks, business cards, canceled checks, etc. while others may be unique to the office such as ship's papers, land grants, pardons, military discharges and appointments. Naturally not all forms were available to all the Presidents of the United States.

Document Overview

* Presidential Appointments & Commissions - come in various sizes and typographical layouts depending upon the position.

* Military Commissions - often ornate with attractive military vignettes appearing at the top and bottom of the parchment. Earlier versions have straight text for "PRESIDENT of the United States of AMERICA" (circa Jefferson) while the more common later variation has curved text (circa Lincoln). There are some seal variations. As one might expect, naval commissions are not as common as those issued for the army.

* Land Grants - common from Jefferson to the first term of A. Jackson. There are three common types encountered - two horizontal formatted and one vertical format. The most common is the horizontal formatted version that does not include a vignette.

* Ship's Papers or Sea Letters - common in four languages English, French, Spanish and Dutch, although earlier versions have only three. Used on foreign voyages, this document was to insure safe passage when presented. These papers typically exhibit extreme wear due to folding.

* Sea Passports - often ornate with dual engravings appearing at the top of the document. A scalloped top edge acts as a puzzle piece to verify its authenticity. These documents were used in the Mediterranean as part of an agreement to guarantee safe passage.

* Affix the Seal - a document, signed by the President, authorizing the Secretary of State to affix the seal of the United States.

* Patents - these scarce and ornate documents provide details regarding an invention.

---

* In recent years it has been customary for an administrations papers to be housed in a Presidential library upon completion of term. In earlier years however most were donated to a university or institution such as the National Archives.

MARKET FACTS

* As a collection, investing in a complete set of Presidential signatures is like buying a lot of "blue chip" stock - limited volatility, with a strong basis of fundamentals.

* Popular among collectors has been forms such as "The Executive Mansion" card (2 3/4" x 4 1/4"), which bore the title in the upper right-hand corner and offered the subject a quick and inexpensive solution to a note or autograph request. While this card was introduced by by President Grant, it was later accompanied by a similar card bearing "White House," "Washington" (3 5/8" x 4 3/4") originated by Theodore Roosevelt.

* Machine signed, or "Autopenned," signatures have been prevalent since the Kennedy administration. Ironically it was John F. Kennedy, also an autograph collector, who introduced a whole new element of intrigue into the oval office.

* Facsimile signatures, in the form of machine-generated, printed or "ghost" signed, are commonly available in the market.

* Forgeries of Presidential signatures have been common and even well-documented for years in the hobby.

* Obtaining a full set of authentic signatures from every United States President is extremely costly, difficult and time consuming. It may even require the outside services of well-known experts.

TRENDS

* Earlier Presidential material has decreased exponentially to the increased participation in the market.

* The advent of technology has created numerous correspondence options - machine-generated handwriting, signatures, etc., for the President.

* There has been an increased influx of repaired Presidential documents in the market over the past few years.

* Exercise caution when evaluating the pertinence of a particular form of Presidential memorabilia. In recent years there has been a tendency to over exaggerate the relevance of certain documents.

* The sophistication of many hobby organizations has led to monumental research in this area.

* The greatest appreciation (25 years) in autographed material from a United States President: U.S. Grant.

* The least appreciation (25 years) in autographed material from a United States President: G. Ford.

Abbreviations: ALS = autographed letter signed, ANS = autographed note signed, APT = appointment, db/dd = date of birth/date of death, DS = document signed, ENG = engraving signed, ESPV = exhibits significant pricing variations, FF = Free Frank, LG = land grant, MA = military appointment, NC = note card, SB = signed book, Sig. = signature, SHP = ships papers, SP = signed photograph, TLS = typed letter signed, WH/EMC = White House card/Executive Mansion card, WHCC = White House Christmas Card

Presidential Overviews

John Adams Overview

* Prolific and insightful, the letters of John Adams typically exemplify an asymmetric quality to his calligraphy. His early handwriting is often small and in great contrast to term examples.

* Size and character formations vary regularly, with his signature decreasing in proportion and legibility with age.

* Considered by many to be the rarest of the early Presidents, term dated material is scarce and certainly attributable to his single term in office.

* His hands shook with palsy by the time he became president. The transformation in his signature, to nearly illegible prior to his death, has led to much confusion among collectors.

* Adams was a voracious reader and often added handwritten notes in the margins of his books.

* He was also a prolific writer and diarist, recording the many details of the people he met and the places he visited.

* Common forms: "John Adams," "J. Adams"

Adams, John

db/dd	Sig.	FF	DS	MA	ALS
1735-1826	1850	3350	6000	2900	17500

Note: First Pres. to live in the White House; his common name lends itself to identity confusion.
Recent Offerings: ALS, 1802, strong content - $32,900; LS, 1 p, 1821, good content - $26,900

John Quincy Adams Overview

* Similar to his father, Adams handwriting transformed with age due to illness.

* While his early correspondence is consistent, insightful, small and legible, the latter was in stark contrast.

* Adams was also a poet, and while an occasional manuscript poem may be unearthed, it is uncommon.

* A single term president, lends itself to the rarity of associated material, although alternatives are certainly available to collectors in the form of documents, such as land grants and even an occasional frank.

* Daniel Brent was Adams' secretary and his handwriting bore a stark similarity to the president, thus determining an ALS from a DS might provide collectors with a research challenge.

* Adams was proficient in a number of languages including Latin, Greek, Dutch, French and somewhat with Spanish.

* He was also the only former president to serve as a U.S. representative.

* Most common form of his signature appears on land grants.

* Common forms: "John Quincy Adams," "J.Q. Adams" and later "J.Q.A"

Adams, John Quincy

db/dd	Sig.	FF	DS	LG	ALS	ENG
1767-1848	375		1450	825	2650	5500

Notes: SALS 7x - 9X
Recent Offerings: Cut signature - $200; ALS, 2 pp, 1822, signed as S/State - $2395; ALS, 2 pp, 1827, as President, good content - $9,900

Chester A. Arthur Overview

* Perhaps the easiest of all presidential handwriting to identify, Chester Arthur was not an advocate of lifting his pen off the paper once he began writing, therefore most of his words are connected.

* Non-presidential Arthur material is common, with many handwritten letters found on "Custom House, New York, Collector Office" letterhead or "Law Offices of Arthur, Phelps, Knevals & Ransom" stationary.

* Of the scarce presidential items collectors are likely to encounter, military appointments seem to hit the market occasionally, along with a signed manuscript letter or card. The latter being the engraved depiction of the White House which he introduced in a convenient card format. These cards were in addition to the already used "Executive Mansion" version.

* Worth noting is that Arthur was the first president to utilize a typewriter as part of his daily routine (1881-1885).

* He was bedridden in his final months and during this time he directed that all of his public and private papers, in his possession, were to be burned.

* Common forms: "C. A. Arthur," "Chester A. Arthur"

Arthur, Chester Alan

db/dd	Sig.	FF	DS	MA	ALS	WH/EMC	SP
1830-1886	350		925	750	1800	425	700

Notes: ALS (term) - $3750
Recent Offerings: ALS, 2 pp, on Executive Mansion letterhead, 1884 - $3195

James Buchanan Overview

* With his ornate calligraphy, Buchanan rivaled only Washington for the most attractive, yet precise handwriting of any President.

* Buchanan's signature varied little over his life, with perhaps the most notable example the increase in his signature's size as he grew in prominence.

* His typical single page correspondences have been offered for years in the autograph market and although examples have been exemplary of most of the periods of his life - with the slight exception being his term, interest has been generally moderate or below average.

* Now considered slightly controversial, as greater details of his personal life have been unearthed over the years, one can now anticipate some additional interest.

* During his retirement he was a very prolific writer.

* Common form: "James Buchanan"

Buchanan, James

db/dd	Sig.	FF	DS	MA	ALS	SP	Add. comments
1791-1868	375	500	865	650	1750	1350	Only Pres. never married.

Recent Offerings: ALS, 2 pp, average content - $1700; FF, 1863, envelope - $275, DS, 1860, as President, 1 p. - $1950; ALS, 1 p, 1846, good association - $2995

George Bush

* Before joining Reagan on the successful Republican ticket in 1980, Bush served in the House of Representatives (1966), as American Ambassador to the United Nations (1971-73), Republican National Chairman (1973-74), special envoy to China (1974-75), then Director of the CIA (1976).

* While Bush is common in authentic post-presidential forms, many of his pre-presidential signatures are secretarial or autopenned.

* As President all authentic forms are scarce.

* Bush seems to have always had a passion for note cards and as President even introduced a new form.

* Since leaving office he has even done private signings for dealers, thus his material is readily available to collectors.

* Common forms: "George Bush," "George"

Bush, George Herbert Walker

db/dd	Sig.	DS	ALS	SP	WHCC	WH/EMC	SB
1924-	75	310	500	200	625	550	

Notes: 2X as President
Recent Offerings: Presidential library print, signed - $450; TLS, on Bush letterhead, 1 p, 1987, "thank you" note - $795

George Bush

* Similar to John Quincy Adams, Bush became the only other son of a president to win the White House.

* Because he lost the popular vote and didn't capture a majority in the Electoral College until five weeks after the election, material (Bush v. Gore) surrounding his accent to the White House is sought by both historians and collectors.

* Bush attended Yale University and the Harvard Business School.

* His first bid for public office, a 1978 campaign for a Congressional seat, ended in defeat.

* Bush left the oil business and headed for Washington, D.C. in 1987 to work for his father's presidential campaign.

* Bush, along with a family friend, purchased the Texas Rangers baseball team in 1987. He routinely accommodated fans by signing autographs, especially baseballs, at the ballpark.

* In 1998 Bush became the first Texas governor elected to a second consecutive four-year term.

* Common forms: "George Bush," "George"

Bush, George Walker

db/dd	Sig.	DS	ALS	SP	WHCC	WH/EMCSB	BB
1946-	50	225	500	150			

Notes: As is the case with any current President, it will take years before their signing habits at the White House are completely understood.
Recent Offerings: SP, 8" x 10" , lot includes a few minor items- $895

Jimmy Carter Overview

* By the time Jimmy Carter was elected to office, machines were being created that could reproduce an entire handwritten letter. Both machine generated and secretarial facsimiles of Carter's signature are commonly found in the market.

* Carter remains scarce in authentic handwritten letters, which typically began with a "To" salutation.

* Carter, who has become an outstanding humanitarian and prolific author, is probably best to obtain in a signed book form to complete a collection.

* Common forms: "Jimmy," "Jimmy Carter," "J. Carter" - later Carter, James Earl "Jimmy"

db/dd	Sig.	DS	ALS	SP	WHCC
1924-	95	325	850	175	650

Notes: SDS & SASLS - 2-3X; winner of the Nobel Peace Prize; other than books ,a reluctant signer
Recent Offerings: WHCC, 1977 - $495;

Grover Cleveland Overview

* Both the 22nd and 24th President of the United States, Grover Cleveland was also an Assistant District Attorney, Sheriff, Mayor and Governor.

* Although he wrote so small that many of his letters were difficult to read, he was always insightful, formal, polite and often charming.

* Abundant in many forms, collectors can anticipate finding signed appointments, handwritten letters and even photographs - the most prevalent being the profile bust cabinet photo by Gutekunst of Philadelphia.

* As president he also used "Executive Mansion" cards, which required a stamp since he never had franking privilege.

* Cleveland was said to answered all of his mail personally into his final years, a statement confirmed by the numerous examples I have seen over the years.

* Cleveland also authored numerous articles for the Saturday Evening Post from 1900-1906.

* Common form: "Grover Cleveland"

Cleveland, Stephen Grover

db/dd	Sig.	DS	APT	ALS	SP	WH/EMC
1837-1908	265	650	525	1100	900	350

Notes: Only Pres. to serve 2 inconsecutive terms
Recent Offerings: DS, as Mayor of Buffalo, 1882, bond issue - $350; ALS, as President, on Executive Mansion letterhead, 3 pp, with envelope - $2695

Bill Clinton Overview

* Despite the adversity encountered during his administration, William Jefferson Clinton remains incredibly popular.

* In-person he has always been charismatic, charming and even warm to autograph requests, however by mail it is a completely different picture. During his administration he averaged about 15,000 letters per week.

* Clinton has always made excellent use of machine-signed signatures.

* Like most modern Presidents it will take a years out of office before a variety of material will surface in the marketplace.

* Clinton often added holograph personalizations to a TLS. For example, a typed formal salutation to a Senator Kennedy, would entice the President to write "Ted" over it. Additionally, short expressions of gratitude are common.

* Common forms: "Bill Clinton," "Bill"

Clinton, William Jefferson

db/dd	Sig.	DS	ALS	TLS	SP	WH/EMC	SB
1946 -	240	525	2125	1000	400		

Note: Presidential material, much which has not entered the market, has made it difficult to establish accurate pricing.
Recent Offerings: TLS, as Governor AK, 1983, routine content, typical Clinton TLS markings - $395; SP, spectacular panoramic photograph of inauguration - $2995

Calvin Coolidge

* Coolidge was a man who believed that if you don't have anything good to say, well, why bother saying or even writing anything at all.

* Certainly one of the least profound and insightful presidents, his autographed material has been relatively common and in little demand.

* He had a knack for filling a page, even if it was far from necessary. His handwritten letters are scarce, as is term authored documents.

* Coolidge did have secretaries signing his name, although most are easily distinguished as such.

* During his retirement he wrote numerous articles for many national magazines.

* Common form: "Calvin Coolidge"

Coolidge, John Calvin

db/dd	Sig.	DS	ALS	TLS	SP	WH/EMC	SB
1872-1933	200	700	1200	800	600	350	

Recent Offerings: White House card - $200; TLS, as Lt. Gov., 1916, good content - $995; TLS, as President, on White House letterhead, 1 p, 1925 - $1995

Dwight D. Eisenhower Overview

* An extremely popular American General and the 34th President of the United States, Dwight Eisenhower has always been a favorite with autograph collectors.

* While dictated letters and typed letters signed have been generally available, those handwritten by "Ike" have not - the only exception an occasional letter he wrote to his wife.

* Signed photographs, particularly those of him in uniform, seem never to fill the demand, while routine presidential poses meet with less appeal.

* Eisenhower was the first president to introduce facsimile signatures on "White House" cards and thankfully they were identified as such on the back of the card.

* Many war dated correspondence bear secretarial signatures, so collectors beware!

* Beginning in 1946, Eisenhower's (machine) signature patterns are seen on letters, photographs, and countless souvenir items.

* Common form: Dwight D. Eisenhower," "D.E." - to friends, "Ike" very rare other than to his wife.

* "The Eisenhower Files, An In-Depth Philographic Study" by Paul K. Carr (UACC) is a must purchase for any Ike collector.

Eisenhower, Dwight David

db/dd	Sig.	DS	ALS	TLS	SP	WH/EMC	SB
1890-1969	300	800	3400	625	600	525	

Notes: TLS - 2 - 3X, ALS content - 1.5 X - 5X
Recent Offerings: TLS, as President (1953) w/handwritten postscript - $1850, DS - "Certificate of Merit" - $1200; TLS, 2 pp, 1951, good content, signed "Ike" - $895; TLS, 1 p,1965, good content —$2995; SP, inscribed - $495; SP, in uniform, inscribed -$895; SP, 1942, in uniform, inscribed - $1695

Millard Fillmore Overview

* Upon Zachary Taylor's death in 1850, Whig party member and vice-president Millard Fillmore became our 13th President.

* A prolific person who penned precise, prudent and prosaic communications, his lack of available presidential autographed materials is countered in the market by numerous non-presidential examples.

* Partly printed signed documents are perhaps the most common form offered, many of which relate to his days practicing law in Buffalo, New York. Fillmore also served in the House of Representatives (1833-35, 1837-43) and became the New York State Comptroller in 1848.

* Although other Presidents had been photographed, even John Quincy Adams, Fillmore marks the first president to become familiar with the task of inscribing his name to a carte de viste.

* Common forms: "Millard Fillmore"

Fillmore, Millard

db/dd	Sig.	FF	DS	ALS	SP
1800-1874	330	450	1035	1560	200

Notes: ESPV - ALS
Recent Offerings: ALS, good content, 1848 - $2000, DS; signed twice, as NY comptroller - $650; ALS, as President, 2 pp, 1852, -$1195

Gerald R. Ford Overview

* Following the resignation of Vice President Spiro Agnew in October 1973, Ford was appointed as his replacement. Ford then became President in August of 1974, when Nixon resigned. Gerald R. Ford had previously been a member of the House of Representatives (1949-73), becoming Minority Leader in 1965.

* Like all modern presidents, Ford made extensive use of the Autopen and secretarial signatures.

* While he is considered scarce in handwritten letters, a few do occasionally enter the market.

* Collectors will most likely run across authentic signed index cards, photographs or books before any other forms.

* Common forms: "Gerald R. Ford," "Gerald Ford," and "Jerry" or "Jerry Ford" to friends.

Ford, Gerald Rudolph

db/dd SB	Sig.	FF	DS	ALS	TLS	SP	WH/EMC
1913-	65		365	675	750	75	125

Notes: Only Pres. serve w/o being elected VP & P, STLS -2X, he has always been a responsive signer!
Recent Offerings: SP, large (10 1/2" x 13"), inscribed - $495

James A. Garfield Overview

* Having been assassinated just four months after taking office, Garfield's term related letters and documents are extremely scarce.

* Fortunately for collectors his pre-presidential material is quite common in many forms.

* Numerous fine manuscript signed letters, on House of Representatives letterhead, have found there way into the market, as have a few franks.

* Garfield did employ a secretary by the name of J. Stanley Brown, during the year prior to his election, whose handwriting bore a stark resemblance to the presidents. Collectors purchasing handwritten material from this era should exercise caution.

* Garfield is scarce on "Executive Mansion" cards, as well as all other examples

authored during his term.

* Common forms: "J.A. Garfield"

Garfield, James Abram

db/dd	Sig.	FF	DS	ALS	TLS	SP
1831-1881	300		1035	1755		2000

Notes: Died in office; scarce in all presidential material, ESPV-ALS
Recent Offerings: ALS, 1858, limited content - $1000; AQS, scarce, no date, 1 p., -$1995; ALS, on USHR letterhead, 1878 - $995

Ulysses S. Grant Overview

* The 18th President of the United States, Ulysses S. Grant, formerly "Cadet U.H. Grant," changed his name early in life.

* Grant's finest handwritten letters were authored during his war years, and as such have remained in demand for decades.

* A weak cabinet, disorganized policies and corrupt intimate associates scared much of his presidential legacy.

* Common in all forms, collectors are most likely to first encounter handwritten letters and signed documents.

* Although Grant introduced the formal "Executive Mansion" card, no doubt for short and expedient notes, ironically only few examples with signature are known to exist.

* Signed Grant photographs, both cabinets and c.d.v.'s, also occasionally surface in the market.

* Near the end of his life he lost his voice and was forced to communicate by notes.

* Common form: "U.S. Grant"

Grant, Ulysses Simpson

db/dd	Sig.	FF	DS	APT	ALS	SP
1822-1885	625		1500	1200	1500	3000

Recent Offerings: ALS as President, 1869, 1 1/2 pp, good content - $3000; ALS,

1885, 2 pp, good content - $2000; ALS, 1863, 1p, to Admiral porter - $7900; LS, no date, 1 p., "regrets unable to attend," -$2995; ALS, as President, 3 pp, 1871, good content - $11,900; ALS, 2 pp, 1863, good association - $15,900

Warren G. Harding Overview

* An interest in journalism led Warren Harding to purchase the Marion Star and as its editor, the paper prospered. A prolific Harding quickly caught the attention of Republican politicians. As a Lieutenant Governor (1904-06), then Senator (1914), he honed his political skills, before becoming his party's dark-horse nominee. While he was easily elected to the Presidency, the infrastructure of his Cabinet was filled with ineptness and corruption.

* During his rise to prominence his handwriting varied significantly, loosing considerable legibility.

* While his autographed material is uncommon and even scarce in some forms, the demand for such items has been weak over the past decades.

* Harding did use a rubber stamp to answer correspondence and even employed a secretary who mimicked his handwriting.

* After Harding died unexpectedly in San Francisco, his wife burned his papers, adding much speculation to her reasoning.

* Common forms: "W.G. Harding" - almost always connected, "Warren G. Harding"

Harding, Warren Gamaliel

db/dd	Sig.	FF	DS	ALS	TLS	SP	WH/EMC	SB
1865-1923	150		550	1575		1000	600	

Notes: Died in office;
Recent Offerings: DS, 1901, signed three times, 2 pp - $875; Last Will and Testament - $21,900; SP - $1495; ALS, USS, 1916, strong association - $3995; ALS, 2 pp, 1918, good content - $6995

Benjamin Harrison Overview

* Grandson of William Henry Harrison, Benjamin Harrison's pro-protection platform won him election as the 23rd President of the United States. Harrison served in the Union army, was active in Grant's Presidential campaign, involved in state politics and elected U.S. Senator for Indiana.

* His handwriting varied significantly over his lifetime, losing much of its legibility in his later years.

* Handwritten letters of Harrison are fairly scarce with most pre-presidential on "Porter, Harrison & Fishback, Attorneys at Law" letterhead and signed "Benja. Harrison".

* Some pre-presidential personal checks drawn from "Fletcher's Bank" in Indianapolis, IN have also found there way to the autograph market over the past decade.

* Unlike Cleveland, signed photographs of Harrison are scarce and may command a significant price.

* Much of his post-presidential material is in TLS or LS form on his personal stationary: "BENJAMIN HARRISON, 874 NORTH DELAWARE STREET, INDIANAPOLIS, IND." During his retirement he also penned numerous articles for national magazines.

* Common form: "Benj. Harrison"

Harrison, Benjamin

db/dd	Sig.	FF	DS	ALS	TLS	SP	WH/EMC
1833-1901	245		470	845		2250	500

Recent Offerings: Individual cabinet photographs signed by the President and Firts Lady - $3000; ALS, as President on Executive Mansion letterhead, 1 p, with envelope - $6995

William Henry Harrison Overview

* The most difficult signature to obtain on material authored while he was in the oval office, William Henry Harrison reflects a dichotomy of sorts as his non-presidential autographs are fairly common. He was aide-de-camp to General Anthony Wayne during his Indian fighting days.

* Harrison's handwriting evolved during his life and reached its pinnacle in form and substance during his quest for the presidency.

* Common forms: "Wm. H. Harrison," "Willm. Henry Harrison" and "W.H. Harrison"

Harrison, William Henry

db/dd	Sig.	FF	DS	ALS	TLS	SP	WH/EMC	SB
1773-1841	600		1650	3500				

Notes: Shortest Pres. term - 31 days, died in office, estimates place the number of documents signed in all forms at approximately thirty.
Recent Offerings: LS, 2 pp, 1812, orders as Commander of the Army - $13,900; ALS, 1 p, 1821 - $2995

Rutherford B. Hayes Overview

* Although much of his material has found its way into the hands of institutions, the autographed material of Rutherford B. Hayes has never been overly popular with collectors. Some of the institutional draw to artifacts of the Hayes administration has been attributed to interest in his economic recovery, civil service reform, and conciliation of the Southern states.

* Hayes handwritten letters typically fill the page, with some variations in legibility. Hayes was also prone to an occasional underline to emphasize a particular point.

* Collectors are more apt to encounter the president's signature on handwritten letters or commissions over many other forms.

* Hayes did occasionally make use of "Executive Mansion" cards for brief notes.

* Common forms: "R.B.Hayes," "Rutherford B. Hayes"

Hayes, Rutherford Birchard

db/dd	Sig.	FF	DS	NC	ALS	WH/EMC
1822-1893	240		800	700	800	500

Recent Offerings: DS, pardon warrant, 1 p, 1878-$495; ALS, 1 p,1876, "Private" correspondence, quotes Lincoln, strong content - $15,900

Herbert Hoover Overview

* Common in numerous autographed forms, particularly signed typed letters, Herbert Hoover will no doubt be one of the first signatures in your Presidential collection.

* Handwritten letters are nearly impossible to acquire as,even according to Hoover himself, he wrote very, very few.

* While his letters in general were far from interesting, he was a prolific writer who authored many intriguing books.

* Hoover did authorize his secretary to sign his name, therefore causing some confusion for collectors who often confuse the facsimile with an authentic signature.

* "White House" cards are attainable, but not common.

* Franks are even more difficult to encounter.

* Printed material, commonly in the form of "Thank you" notes, mimic his handwriting.

* In his final years he resided often at the Waldorf-Astoria Hotel in New York and was virtually deaf and blind.

* Common form: Herbert Hoover

Hoover, Herbert Clark

db/dd	Sig.	FF	DS	ALS	TLS	SP	WH/EMC	SB
1874-1964	165		385	3200	1100	415	500	500

Notes: ALS - ESPV, scarce
Recent Offerings: Signed book, 1934, first edition - $475; TLS, 1945, limited content - $100; Signed speech (copy) - $250, SP - $275; TLS, 1934, 1 p. - $495, SP, * 1/2" x 11" - $395; TLS, as President,1 p, fair content - $1195; TLS, on American Relief Administration letterhead, 1 p, 1920 - $1495

Andrew Jackson Overview

* Although the eloquence of his letters is far cry from his predecessors, Andrew Jackson's bold and succinct correspondence with its large signature are attractive to collectors.

* A truly charismatic figure, Jackson's candid letters often contained a fair share of spelling and grammatical errors, however few could claim it detracted from his message.

* While his handwriting and typical full signature changed little throughout his life, he did much to alter the signing habits of the presidency. Jackson discontinued signing land grants during his second term and bequeathed much of his signatory power to liberate himself from administrative details. Andrew Jackson Donelson, the president's nephew and secretary, handled many of these tasks that over time have led to much identification confusion in the autograph market.

From bank checks to land grants, Donelson adequately adorned the signature of his uncle as needed.

* Collectors are advised to exercise caution when purchasing any Jackson autographed second term items.

* Common form: "Andrew Jackson" - bold

Jackson, Andrew

db/dd	Sig.	FF	DS	LG	MA	APT	ANS	ALS
1767-1845	650	1400	1825	1450	2100	1600	1250	3430

Recent Offerings: DS, 1836, w/L. Cass, military commission - $3000; FF, good condition -$900, LS, 1830, "thank you" note - $3000; ADS, 1833, appointment - $6995; ALS, 1 p, 1811 - $2995

Thomas Jefferson Overview

* Consistent and often fascinating in content, the letters of Thomas Jefferson are highly sought by both collectors and institutions.

* While his handwriting varied little over his life, his bold signature often casts confusion in determining an ALS from a DS.

* Similar to Washington, authentic clipped signatures remain scarce and enter the market typically when collections are upgraded.

* Forgeries are common especially with regard to signatures and handwritten letters.

* Many of the Jefferson documents that appear in the market are land grants or ships' papers, some of which also bear the signature of James Madison.

* Although Jefferson also wrote in French - he also knew Greek and Latin, examples are scarce.

* He was a meticulous record keeper and an avid book collector. In fact a library of his books was sold to the government after the British destroyed the Library of Congress.

* Perfect copies of much of Jefferson's correspondence were created through the use of a polygraph that reproduced precisely the hand movements of a writer.

* Common form: "Th. Jefferson"

Jefferson, Thomas

db/dd	Sig.	FF	DS	ALS	SHP
1743-1826	3660	6200	7000	10,345	7000

Notes: SALS - 5-10X

Recent Offerings: DS, as President, w/H. Dearborn, 1802, military commission - $8500,; ALS, as President, w/FF, very good condition - $14, 500; ALS, as S/State, good content, 1793 - $28, 900; ALS, as President, 1 p., 1802, Monticello association - $16, 900; ALS, 1 p, 1826, strong content - $69,900; ALS, as President, 1 p, 1802 - $49,900; DS, as President with Madison as Secretary of State, four language ship's passport - $4995

Andrew Johnson Overview

* Johnson assumed the office following the death of Abraham Lincoln. Although Johnson believed in the former president's policies, he lacked the efficiency and skills to fulfill them. His conflict with radical Republicans led to his impeachment, that fell short by only a single vote. Following his term in office he was again elected to the Senate, which he had previously served in from 1957 to 1862. Johnson was also a former member of the House of Representatives (1843-54) and Governor of Tennessee (1853-57).

* Johnson's handwritten letters are typically routine and short in length, due to his lack of education and bad right arm, but nevertheless in demand because of there scarcity.

* He also used secretaries, his son and even a rubber stamp to fulfill the demand for his signature.

* Commissions, pardons and land grants typically enter the market and are good sources for an authentic example.

* While Johnson photographs (c.d.v's) are not common, they have occasionally appeared in the market with an appropriate hefty price tag.

* Collectors should familiarize themselves with all of Johnson's facsimile signatures before attempting to purchase an authentic example. Some forms, such as franks, were often signed by his son and can be tricky to identify.

* Common forms: "Andrew Johnson," and occasionally "A. Johnson" or "And. Johnson"

Johnson, Andrew

db/dd	Sig.	FF	DS	MA	ALS	SP
1808-1875	525	1600	1450	3000	Scarce	2825

Notes: ALS content - 2X-3X, ESPV - ALS, sig. pt. speech - $3000
Recent Offerings: LS, as President, limited content - $2500; DS, as President, military appointment, 1865, w/Stanton - $3295; ALS, 3 pp, 1869, strong content - $6995

Lyndon B. Johnson Overview

* Following Kennedy's assassination, Johnson carried out many of JFK's policies including his philosophy on correspondence. Secretarial, machine signed and facsimile examples of Johnson's signature are common in the market.

* Authentic Johnson signatures are scarcer than what collectors first thought.

* Post-presidential items found in the market are often dictated letters signed by "LBJ."

* Collectors wishing to purchase an authentic Johnson example may best to turn to signed books or photographs.

* The lack of interest in his autographed material over the past two decades seems to be dissipating somewhat as more information regarding his administration becomes declassified. Johnson's image has as been enhanced greatly by the release of many of his taped phone conversations.

* Common forms: "Lyndon B. Johnson," "Lyndon," "LBJ"

Johnson, Lyndon Baines

db/dd	Sig.	FF	DS	ALS	TLS	SP	WH/EMC	SB
1908-1973	225		670	3400	1400	525		

Recent Offerings:TLS, White House letterhead, 1 p. (small), 1965, -$1395

John F. Kennedy Overview

* Books have been written about the holograph habits of John F. Kennedy, who is by far the most unpredictable signature in history. (See "John F. Kennedy, Autographs from the Presidency, 1961-1963 ", By Paul K. Carr, UACC)

* The irony, of course, is that Kennedy himself was an autograph collector. His signature was unpredictable, inconsistent in slant, character formation, signature breaks, etc.

* The only consistent element to his signature have been the numerous machine signed patterns, secretarial facsimiles and forgeries.

* Because the demand for authentic Kennedy material has always been high and the variables in his signature numerous, he has constantly been a forgery target. Even the finest handwriting experts in the country have been deceived by forgeries, therefore collectors are at an incredible risk when purchasing his material.

* Handwritten letters are scarce as are examples found on "Air Force One" stationary.

* Collectors will typically encounter typed letters signed, signed photographs, or a variety of examples signed while Kennedy was campaigning.

* While some pre-presidential material was dictated, JFK often felt obligated to add a handwritten postscript.

* His prolific use of the Autopen has frustrated many a collector. Those of you who wish further information on the device should also purchase a copy of Charles Hamilton's book "The Robot That Helped to Make a President."

* Doodles and notes from Kennedy have also found there way to the market, but they too are difficult to authenticate.

* Common forms: "John Kennedy"

Kennedy, John Fitzgerald

db/dd	Sig.	FF	DS	ALS	TLS	SP	WH/EMC	SB
1917-1963	1400		2420	5280	4000	2650		

Notes: Died in office, doodle ("J") - $1600, ESPV - all forms
Recent Offerings: TLS, 1935, as teenager - $3500; SP - color photograph, 1963, from his trip to Berlin, personally signed - $5,995; SP, inside program, 1957 - $1495

Abraham Lincoln Overview

* Insightful and succinct, yet gracious and charming, the letters of Abraham Lincoln are the most sought of nearly anyone in history.

* The demand for Lincoln material far exceeds the supply, as well as the demand for material from any other U.S. President.

* His pre-presidential material is also scarce as are his legal briefs, many signed with the firm's name.

* "Draft Calls" and "Military Appointments" (which include the signature of Edwin M. Stanton, Secretary of War), do surface in the market, but like all Lincoln material carry a hefty price tag.

* Full signatures appear on official documents and formal papers signed as President, ninety-nine percent of all others examples in this form should be questioned.

* Most experts believe that less than ten and as little as two, authentic signed photographs of Lincoln are known to exist. If you understand the man you can certainly believe this to be true.

* Unfortunately, demand and the lack of significant variation in his handwriting has led to numerous forgeries ever since his death.

* Abraham Lincoln was the first president to introduce "Executive Mansion" stationary (octavo sheets).

* Collectors are advised to consult an expert before making any Lincoln autograph purchases.

* Lincoln association items remain a cost-effective alternative for collectors.

* Common form: "A. Lincoln"

Lincoln, Abraham

db/dd	Sig.	FF	DS	ALS	MA	ANS	SP
1809-1865	3400	7000	5000	9750	6250	4500	50000

Notes: Died in office, ALS content 1.5X - 20X
Recent Offerings: DS, Presidential pardon, w/W. Seward, 1862 - $18, 500; Autograph endorsement signed, 1864, very good condition - $8500; ALS, good content, 1861, 1 p., - $22,900; DS, pardon, 2 pp, 1864 - $12,900; ALS, Springfield, IL, 1 p. (small 4to), 1858, good provenance, strong content - $39,900; ALS, as President, 1 p, small, 1864, on Executive Mansion letterhead, strong content - $29,900; DS, pardon, 1864 - $7900; DS, 2 pp, 1862, pardon, also signed by William Seward - $22,900

James Madison Overview

* The letters and documents of the "Father of the Constitution" are in great demand by both collectors and institutions.

* While insightful handwritten letters are rare, even his prolific and mundane correspondence is getting increasingly difficult to acquire.

* Tremulous later examples are common as an arthritic Madison fought valiantly against the disease.

* His wife Dolley authored many a letter for her suffering husband during the latter years, most which were adorned by his print like signature.

* Many ships' papers, bearing both Madison and Monroe signatures, have been available to collectors throughout the years, with even a few franks surfacing.

* Military commissions and land grants are two other viable alternatives for acquiring his authentic signature.

* Be wary of cuts and exercise all the typical cautions associated with such a purchase.

* Madison was crippled by rheumatism during the last six months of his life and confined to his room.

* Madison kept a comprehensive journal on the Constitutional Convention and was proficient in Latin.

* Common form: "J. Madison" (exception legal documents), rare as "James Madison, Jr."

Madison, James

db/dd	Sig.	FF	DS	SHP	LG	NC	MA	ALS
1751-1836	435	1000	1650	2120	1875	2000	1000	3275

Notes: Bank check - $2500, ALS content 2-3X
Recent Offerings: DS, 1816, w/J. Monroe, appointment - $2500; cut signature, mounted - $550; DS, patent, signed as President, w/C.Rodney, 1809, - $1500; ALS, appointment, 1814 - $22,900; DS, signed by Madison as President and Monroe as S/State, 1 p. (large folio), 1811, four language ship's passport - $2695; ALS, as President, 1 p, 1815, good content - $6995; DS, as President, 1 p, 1810, land grant - $1195

William McKinley

* McKinley served in Congress and was also Governor of Ohio, before becoming a Republican Presidential candidate.

* Although Cleveland and Harrison were no strangers to the typewriter, McKinley seemed to be the first president truly comfortable with the machine, therefore some pre-presidential TLSs have turned up in the market.

* Handwritten letters of William McKinley as president are scarce, although some examples before he took office have been available.

* Collectors will typically encounter authentic signatures of McKinley in document form in the market. These will range from military commissions and appointments to simple appointments as Marshall of the United States.

* "Executive Mansion" cards and signed photographs can also be found.

* Common forms: "William McKinley"

McKinley, William

db/dd	Sig.	FF	DS	MA	APT	ALS	WH/EMC
1843-1901	280		425	700	600	1885	765

Notes: Died in office;
Recent Offerings: SP - signed composite photograph - $1395; ANS, on calling card, 1889 - $495

James Monroe Overview

* Succinct and often routine, the letters of James Monroe, exhibit many handwriting variances over his lifetime.

* Examples of his authentic signature can still be found in many forms especially documents such as land grants. It was common for land to be transacted in lieu of cash during his era.

* Monroe had the uncommon proclivity of having his handwriting increase in size over the body of a correspondence and like many other Presidents his script lost legibility due to age.

* Unlike many presidents, his writings rarely mentioned his religious faith.

* Common form: "James Monroe," also "J. Monroe," rare in other forms.

Monroe, James

db/dd	Sig.	FF	DS	SHP	LG	NC	MA	ALS
1758-1831	420	550	1500		1000		1400	2785

Recent Offerings: DS, 1823, appointment - $1200; DS, as President, 1825, w/J.Q. Adams, appointment - $1800; DS, command, signed as S/State, 1812 - $1495

Richard M. Nixon

* Authentic letters from the first President to submit his resignation are scarce, with the few surfacing being from his later years.

* Secretarial and Autopen samples are common, particularly on "White House" cards.

* Most authentic signed pieces from his presidency have been with his initials.

* Collectors wishing to complete a presidential set, may want to turn to a signed book authored by Nixon after leaving office.

* Common forms: "R. Nixon" - early, "Richard Nixon," "R.N.," and "Dick" or "Dick Nixon" to friends.

Nixon, Richard Milhous

db/dd	Sig.	FF	DS	APT	ALS	TLS	SP	WH/EMC	SB
1913-1994	250		650	2750	4165		400		

Notes: Only Pres. to resign., sample resig. letter authentically signed - $2500. Recent Offerings: DS, signed as President, appointment - $2995; TLS, White House letterhead, 1969, 1 p, signed "RN" - $895

Franklin Pierce Overview

* Often illegible and seldom intriguing in content - with the exception of friends and relatives, the letters of Franklin Pierce were far from literary masterpieces.

* Collectors will find handwritten letters, naval commissions and even perhaps a "Warrant for a Pardon" before any other forms.

* Clipped signatures, franks and signed photographs have always been scarce.

* Because Pierce repealed the Missouri Compromise and passed the Kansas-

Nebraska Act - which ultimately fueled the Civil War, he was not particular popular after leaving office.

* Common forms: "Franklin Pierce," also "Frank Pierce," "F. Pierce" and "Fr. Pierce"

Pierce, Franklin

db/dd	Sig.	FF	DS	NC	ALS
1804-1869	425	525	840	1565	925

Notes:
Recent Offerings: ALS, 1861, 1 p., good content - $1195; ALS, 2pp, 1863 - $895

James Know Polk Overview

* The eleventh President of the United States, James K. Polk, a former House Speaker and Governor of Tennessee, is perhaps most commonly associated with his elaborate, distinctive and often embellished signature.

* While the demand for his autographed material is far from impressive, the lack of consistency in availability contributes to the volatility in value.

* Of the documents that have surfaced in the market, appointments which often include the signature of Secretary of State James Buchanan, have drawn interest.

* Handwritten letters as Speaker of the House, and Congressman have also surfaced, while term related pieces remain elusive.

* Dictated letters also elusive while a few impressive multiple page early legal documents have found themselves in the hands of collectors.

* Considered by many historians as the greatest one-term president, it remains a shock to many that his writings do not command a greater price in the autograph market.

* Common form: "James K. Polk"

Polk, James Knox

db/dd	Sig.	FF	DS	APT	ALS
1795-1849	500	1000	1700	2000	3500

Notes: SALS- $5500 - $6000
Recent Offerings: ALS, 1836, 2 pp, good content - $1995

Ronald Reagan

* Former television and film star, Ronald Reagan first became interested in politics while serving as President of the Screen Actors Guild (1947-52). As Governor of California (1966-1974) he became increasingly popular and it became of little surprise that he would have greater political aspirations.

* As both a film star and politician, Reagan utilized proxy signers - including his mother.

* As the 40th President of the United States he signed very little, opting instead for all the now accepted alternatives.

* Fortunately for collectors, Reagan was passionate about maintaining old relationships through handwritten correspondence, some of which have found there way into the autograph market. Most of these are warm and friendly in content and often signed "RR," "Ron" or "Dutch."

* A few of his handwritten drafts as Governor have also appeared in the market, typically they have a red slash drawn across the sheet to indicate that they have been typed in final form. Despite this alteration, a commonly accepted office procedure, these drafts are also extremely popular with collectors.

* Common forms: "Ronald Reagan"

Reagan, Ronald Wilson

db/dd	Sig.	FF	DS	ALS	TLS	SP	WH/EMC	SB
1911-	250		640	1250		350		

Notes: Oldest President leaving office, oldest living President
Recent Offerings: ALS, 1961, 1 p., good content - $6900; ALS, on embossed personal note card, 2 pp, small, 1992, good content - $7900

Franklin D. Roosevelt Overview

* Polite, yet platitudinous, amicable, yet aseptic, perhaps best characterizes Franklin Rooselevet's correspondence, with the only exception those letters he wrote to intimate friends and relatives.

* Handwritten letters, particularly as president, are difficult to come by and when you do find one it is typically pre-presidential.

* Roosevelt also often signed his correspondence with initials only, and since he used proxy signers, many facsimiles can be difficult to distinguish.

* Roosevelt, also an autograph collector, varied his signature often and even used a rubber stamp as Governor of New York. Although "White House" cards and even "New York Sate" cards were commonly found in the market, they too have dissipated somewhat with the increased interest in the hobby.

* Common forms: "FDR," "Franklin D. Roosevelt"

Roosevelt, Franklin Delano

db/dd	Sig.	FF	DS	ALS	TLS	SP	WH/EMC	SB
1882-1945	250		1200	1500	1100	1000	425	

Notes: Only Pres. to serve more than 2 terms, died in office.
Recent Offerings: DS, as Governor NY, testimonial - $3000; DS, as President, w/C. Hull, 1935, appointment - $6500; Book, bound and guilt-stamped, "Veto Message" , 1935 - $5000; TLS, as Governor NY, 1930, information request - $375; TLS, as Governor NY, 1929, faded, 1 p - $695; SP, inscribed - $3495; TLS, on White House letterhead, 1941, good content - $9995; TLS, on White House letterhead, 2pp, 1944, good content - $23,900; TLS, on NY letterhead, 1932, good content - $4995;

Theodore Roosevelt Overview

* Despite the lack of gracefulness to his script, this "Roughrider' wrote clear, crisp and forceful letters.

* A prolific writer, whose handwriting varied little over his lifetime, Roosevelt spent time in the New York Legislature (1884), was President of the New York Police Board (1895-97), Assistant Secretary of the Navy (1898), Governor of New York State (1898-1900) and Vice-President in 1901, before assuming the Presidential office after the assassination of McKinley.

* His signature habits included the use of a rubber stamp as Governor of New York , as well permitting his secretary to sign on his behalf - as Governor and vice-president.

* While obtainable in all forms, collectors will typically cross paths with his signatures first on typed letters and documents.

* As president he changed the format of the "Executive Mansion" cards, to "White House" in hopes of presenting a different image.

* He was the first president to be known popularly by his initials.

* During 1910-1914 he was associate editor of Outlook magazine.

* The demand for his material has remained strong over the years, while exhibiting some nice price appreciation.

* Common forms: Theodore Roosevelt," "T. Roosevelt"

Roosevelt, Theodore

db/dd	Sig.	FF	DS	MA	APT	ALS	TLS	SP	WH/EMC
1858-1919	275		1650	1450	1300	1500	1300	1000	550

Notes: Youngest President, SB - $750
Recent Offerings: TLS, 1894, 1 p., good content - $1500; TLS, 1895, as Police Commissioner (NYC), -$850; ALS, 1902, strong content. $4500; AQS, as President, strong quote, c.1905, w/W.Reid - $5395; ALS, 1891, 3 pp., good content - $2995; DS, appointment postmaster, 1907 - $425; TLS, 1 p., 1916, strong association - $4995; ALS, 2 pp, 1887, good content - $2995; TLS, on letterhead of "The Outlook" magazine, 1 p, 1911, strong, quotes Lincoln - $17,900

William Howard Taft Overview

* The 27th President of the United States, William Howard Taft is perhaps best remembered as the only man to serve time both in the oval office and also as the Chief Justice of the U.S, Supreme Court (1921-1930).

* A prolific man of letters, his material has been common in many forms for years, the only exception being handwritten letters as President and "White House" cards.

* Many signed photographs, which were initially thought to be scarce, have surfaced from private collections over the years. These signed photographs depict Taft as both President and Chief Justice.

* Ironically, many collectors find his correspondence as Chief Justice far more interesting and appealing.

* After leaving the oval office he accepted an appointment as Kent professor of law at Yale University (1913-1921).

* Common forms: "Wm. H. Taft," and to friends and relatives "Bill," "Bill Taft"

Taft, William Howard

db/dd	Sig.	FF	DS	MA	APT	ALS	TLS	SP	WH/EMC
1857-1930	180		525	500	1000			500	

Notes: Only President to serve in the United States Supreme Court, ALS, as President -2X
Recent Offerings: TLS, 1918, as law professor - $175; SP, inscribed, 1914 - $895; TLS, on personal letterhead, 1915, good content - $1995

Zachary Taylor Overview

* Serving only fifteen months in office before his death, Zachary Taylor presidential autographed material presents a significant acquisition challenge for the collector.

* Pre-presidential autographed material that has surfaced has been typically signed documents.

* Bold, clean, and attractive handwritten letters, particularly those substantive in content remain elusive and in demand.

* Taylor at his literary finest , is represented best in correspondence during his Indian-fighting days. "Old Rough and Ready" fought in the War of 1812, the Black Hawk War and the Seminole War.

* Taylor was a poor speller during his entire life.

* Common forms: "Z. Taylor"

Taylor, Zachary

db/dd	Sig.	FF	DS	ALS
1784-1850	750		3000	4000

Notes: Died in office, term-related material - 1.5 - 2X, ESPV - DS & ALS
Recent Offerings: LS, as Major Gen.. U.S. Army, 2 1/2 pp, good content - $3095; ALS, 1 p, 1848, unique content - $5995; DS, 1845, 2 pp, bond - $3995

Harry S. Truman

* If your just wild about Harry, it probably had little to do with the content of one his letters. Often formal, Truman rarely displayed his passionate feelings in written form, but when he did you knew he meant it.

* Handwritten letters are scarce and when they do hit the market can command a significant price.

* Post-presidential typed letters signed have been common for years, with the

demand increasing steadily over the past two decades.

* As Senator, Truman authorized secretaries to sign his letters so exercise caution when purchasing material from this era.

* After the Presidency, Truman dated nearly every autograph he signed, which can make for an interesting study on signature variations.

* Common forms: " Harry Truman," "Harry S. Truman," "HST" - presidential memorandums

Truman, Harry S.

db/dd	Sig.	FF	DS	ALS	TLS	SP	WH/EMC
1884-1972	200		600		1100	525	350

Notes: Presidential pardon - $2500, White House engraving - $350, he was a responsive signer!
Recent Offerings: TLS, as President, good content, 1951, 1 p. WH stationery - $1000; Signature on card, along with a signature on a card from his wife Bess - $250; ANS, short, 1947, w/FF - $2000; TLS, USS, 1942, 1 p., fair/good content - $1195; SP - &7" x 10" color, 1952, inscribed - $995; SP - "classic Dewey Defeats Truman - Chicago Daily Tribune newspaper" photograph - $4995; TLS on White House letterhead, 1952, 1 p, -$1995; SP, inscribed - $495; TLS, U.S. Senate letterhead, 1 p, 1936 - $195

John Tyler Overview

* Following the death of William Henry Harrison, John Tyler became the first vice-president to assume the oval office.

* Tyler brought to the office greater administrative control and took great comfort in handling most of his correspondence.

* Typically his letters varied in length, legibility and content due to both his attitude and writing materials

* His often succinct and forceful script is best exemplified with examples during his term in office, with the most revealing in content those to his friends and relatives.

* While both handwritten letters and franks are somewhat common, documents and signed letters can be more elusive.

* Characteristic of his signature is the addition of a decorative line to which a date is often added nearby.

* During his last years he served as chancellor of his alma mater, the College of William and Mary.

* Tyler was the only president to join the Confederacy.

* Common form: "J. Tyler"

Tyler, John

db/dd	Sig.	FF	DS	ALS
1790-1862	450	650	1100	1325

Notes: SALS - 7X-10X, Presidential pardon - $1200
Recent Offerings: ALS, signed as President, 1 p, 1843, good content - $6995

Martin Van Buren Overview

* Although the first president born an American citizen had the capability to fire of an insightful correspondence, Van Buren seldom utilized this talent. Instead he opted for politically correct and often mundane communications.

* His script also transformed from small and legible to large and often unintelligible with age.

* Unfortunately for collectors, examples of his signatures are scarce in many forms and will require some patience before certain items find there way into the market. Likely this will be a document signed by Van Buren as Andrew Jackson's Secretary of State.

* As a youth Van Buren studied at the law firm of Francis Sylvester and often had the duty of making copies of documents.

* Common forms: "M. Van Buren," "M.V.B." or "M.V. Buren"

Van Buren, Martin

db/dd	Sig.	FF	DS	APT	ALS
1782-1862	370	475	1000	1500	4000

Recent Offerings: ALS, as President, 1839, good content, 4 pp. - $3000; ALS, later in life, 1859, fair content - $500; LS, as Vice President, 2 pp., -$2295; ALS, as President, 3 pp, 1840, - $6900

George Washington Overview

* With his attractive calligraphy, prolific and insightful output, George Washington, who seldom signed his full name - opting instead for "Go. Washington," was a prolific President.

* Each individual letter from Washington will necessitate some research to accurately determine price.

* Not common in a clipped signature form.

* Washington was a surveyor during his late teenage years. Some manuscript surveys, signed with a taller variation of his well-known holograph, do occasionally surface in the market.

* Pre-Revolution material of any kind is scarce.

* Washington forgeries are common . Examples (especially passes and checks)done by Robert Spring (mid 1800s) or later those of Joseph Cosey have been well-documented.

* During the Revolutionary War, Washington dictated most of his letters.

* Alexander Hamilton acted as Washington's secretary during the Revolutionary War, therefore many LS examples found were actually penned by the gifted statesman (First S/Treasury).

* Washington did personally sign all war discharges, however finding an example in "investment" condition is difficult.

* Although the language of diplomacy during this era was French, Washington never learned the language and did not attend a university.

Washington, George

Form Overview:

ALS	Presidential and post-presidential written in his own hand
Books	Volumes from his library bear bookplate and signature
Certificates	Often membership in the Society of the Cincinnati..., often faded
Checks	Rare, often forged
Cut signatures	Rare, often forged
Discharges	Personally signed, typically badly worn
FF	Scarce
Land surveys	Scarce, (early years),popular with collectors
Legal forms	More common than other forms
Lottery tickets	Scarce

LS	During the war years, dictated to secretaries, signed by him
Orders	Scarce, often badly worn
Ship's papers	Often badly worn (folds)
War passes	Rare, often forged

db/dd	Sig.	FF	DS	MA	APT	ALS
1732-1799	5500	7500	11500			17,000

Notes: ALS - content dependent, ESPV
Recent Offerings: LS, as Commander-in-Chief, 1780, 2 pp., w/FF, good content - $35,000; LS. order, 1777, 1 p., good association - $26, 900; ALS, 1 p, 1799, near end of life -$36,900

Woodrow Wilson Overview

* A gifted wordsmith, who also happened to have legible handwriting, Wilson wrote magnificent letters, particularly early in his life.

* As his responsibilities increased, so did the demand on his correspondence. He began limiting himself to brief notes, while also finding solace behind a typewriter. His signed typed letters will be some of the first examples collectors will encounter in the market, followed by military appointments.

* As Governor of New Jersey and during his run for the office, Wilson resorted to the use of a rubber stamp on correspondence.

* Wilson signed photographs do occasionally appear in the market as have a couple scarce canceled checks from his days at Princeton.

* Signed "White House" cards are also scarce and the ones that have entered the market have been signed at the top of the card.

* Following his 1919 stroke, his signature picked up a few slight variations.

* He was virtually blind in his final years.

Common form: "Woodrow Wilson"

Wilson, Thomas Woodrow

db/dd	Sig.	FF	DS	NC	MA	ALS	TLS	SB
1856-1924	250		600	750	1100	1200	950	750

Notes: Very rare as ALS during term
Recent Offerings: TLS, as President, 1918, 1 p., White House stationery, good

content - $1850; signature on card - $350; SB, his first book "Congressional Government," 1885, first edition, family related - $4000; TLS, as President, 1916, fair content - $895; TLS, 1 p., 1922, "thank you" - $1395; SP, inscribed, 1914 - $1495; TLS, the White House, 1914, good content , unique- $13,900; TLS, as Governor- elect of New Jersey , 1910, good content - $1395

  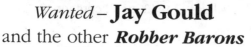 

COLONIAL AMERICA AND THE REVOLUTIONARY WAR

WHAT YOU NEED TO KNOW

* This period has been a viable area of collecting for decades.

* Over half of America's history took place before George Washington's inauguration.

* The colonial period of the United States culminated with the Revolutionary War.

* Understanding the signifigance of events during the colonial period - prior to the Revolution, requires a vast knowledge of early history.

* Not everyone knew how to read or write.

* Spelling variations exist with some names.

* Some records, land grants, ledgers, logs ... are inconsistent.

* A strong knowledge of the prominent families of this era, such as the Pinckney Family of SC - scion Charles and the Randolph Family of Virginia - Scion Wm: Randolph, will prove invaluable in building a comprehensive collection.

MARKET FACTS

* A wealth of written information, in various forms (letters, diaries, pay receipts, promisary notes, currency, etc.), document this period.

* Signatures of Revolutionary statesman, military leaders, Washington's generals, Signers of the Declaration of Independence and the Constitution, members of the Continental Congress and British military and political leaders dominated early autograph collections.

* The signifigance of Colonial period documents is less understood and thus susceptible to greater price fluctuations in a limited market segement.

TRENDS

* Historically signifigant letters and manuscripts of Revoltuionary leaders have always been and continue to be, highly desirable and expensive.

* Documents from this period continue to face restoration and preservation issues.

* While the demand from institutions (universities, historical societies, etc.) has remanied constant, private collectors have absorbed the bulk of quality material in recent years due to economic conditions.

* The migration of quality European manuscripts - often decendants of early American leaders, has disipated over the past few decades.

* Dealers continue to enjoy the majority participation in this market segment.

* While content is always preffered by both private collectors and institutions, the latter is more likely to absorb bulk collections.

* Documents in all forms from key leaders, such as Washington, Jefferson and Franklin, have grown beyond the budget of most collector's forcing many to pursue "association items" - often indirect correspondence .

* "Type collections" - items such as ledgers, bill of lading, etc. remain popular altrenatives for collectors.

Abbreviations: adc = aide-de-camp AO = American Officer, BM = British Museum, BO = British officer, CC = Continental Congress, CG = colonial general, CO = Cont'l officer, CW = colonial wars, DPW = distinguished post-war career, ESPV = exhibits signifigant pricing variations, f. = father, FIW = French and Indian War, G = Governor/state, IG = inspector general, k. = killed, KIA = Killed in action, LG = land grant, MG = Militia General, min = minister, MO = militia officer, n. = nephew, NE = numerous engagements, NYPL = New York Public Library, P = Parliament, PAHS = Pennsylvania historical society, PM - Postmaster, PU = pricing undetermined, SALS = Signifigant autograph letter signed, Signer = signer of the Declaration of Independence, SL = state legislature, Sur = surrendered, USHR = United States House of Representatives, USS = United States Senate, WA = George Washington association, WAb = Westminster Abbey

Name	DB/DD	SIG	LS/DS	ALS	Comment
Aachen, Treaty of	October 18, 1748 Ended War of the Austrian Succeession				
Abercromby, James	1706-1781				British officer, PU
Abercromby, James	? - 1775				British officer, PU
Abercromby, Sir Ralph	1734-1801				British officer, PU
Abercromby, Sir Robert	1740-1827				British officer, PU
Aboville, Francois M.,	1730-1817	240	513	1250	French officer, Yorktown
Acland, John Dyke	? - 1778				British politician/officer, PU
Adams, John	1735-1826				Second President of the US
Adams, Samuel	1722-1803	750	2025	9500	Signer, patriot, agitator, Gov.
Affleck, Edmund	1723?-1788				British commodore, PU
Agusta, GA	Various battles				
Alamance, Battle of the	May 16, 1771				

Name	DB/DD	SIG	LS/DS	ALS	Comment
Albany Convention and Plan	June 19 - July 10, 1754				
Alexander, "Stirling" W.	1726-1783	225	700	1600	Cont'l. general, papers in NYPL
Alfred-Glasgow Encounter	April 6, 1776				
Allen, Ethan	1738-1789	700	1750	3000	American officer; rare, author
Alliance-Sybille Engagement	January, 1783			Last naval action of the war.	
Alsop, John	? - 1794	190	375	875	Congressman, patriot
Amherst, Jeffery	1717 - 1797	525	1125	2226	British general, controversial
Amherst, Jeffrey	?-1815				British officer, PU
Andre, John	1751-1780	1750			British officer and spy, executed
Andrustown, New York	July 18, 1778				
Arbuthnot, Marriot	1711-1794	410	865	1550	British admiral, n.poet John
Archard de Bonvouloir	1749-1783				French secret agent, PU
Armand, Charles T.					General, extremely rare, PU
Armstrong, James					Cont'l officer (PA), PU
Armstrong, James					Cont'l officer (NC), PU
Armstrong, John	1758-1843	55	125	400	AO, USS, Sec. War, SALS-2X
Armstrong, John	1717-1795	220	360	800	Cont'l B.G., USHR, f.John
Arnold, Benedict	1741-1801	2175	6500	7800	Cont'l general, traitor, SALS-2X
Arnold, Peggy Shippen	1760-1804				Wife of Benedict, four sons, PU
Articles of Confederation	adopted: 11/15/77, ratified: 3/1/81				
Asgill, Charles	? - 1823				British officer, Huddy-Asgill, PU
Ashe, John	1720-1781	125	315	565	Patriot, politician and militia B.G.
Attucks, Crispus	1723-1770				Agitator, Boston "Massacre," PU
Baldwin, Jeduthan	1732-1788				Cont'l officer, Mass., FIW, PU
Baldwin, Loammi	1740-1807	300	655	1175	Civil engineer, Cont'l officer
Balfour, Nisbet	1743-1832	285	540	800	British officer, Parliament mem.
Bancroft, Edward (s)	1744-1820			1750	Double agent, writer & inventor
Barbe'-Marbois, Fran.	1745-1837				French politician, author, PU
Barras, Jacques-Melchior					French admiral, PU
Barre', Issac	1762-1802				British officer,Wilkes-Barre, PU
Barren Hill, PA	May 20, 1778				
Barry, John	1745-1803	1125	2250		Cont'l naval officer
Bartlett, Josiah	1729-1795	400	750	1210	Signer , CC, G/ NH, FF-$1050
Barton, William	1748-1831	300	600		Militia officer
Basking Ridge, NJ	December 13, 1776			Gen. Charles Lee's capture	
Baylor, George	1752-1784				CO, adc WA, rare, PU
Beaufort (Port Royal Island), SC	February 3, 1779				

Name	DB/DD	SIG	LS/DS	ALS	Comment
Beckwith, George (K.B.)	1753-1823	225	430		British officer, Gov. Bermuda, ...
Bedford, Gunning	1742-1797	575	1150		Cont'l. officer, Gov. (DE), USHR
Bedford, Gunning	1747-1812	235	400		Rev. states., USHR, SL, ESPV

Bedford-Fair Haven Raid, Mass.   September 5-6, 1778

| Belcher, Jonathan | 1682-1757 | 250 | 400 | 750 | Col. Gov. Mass. also NJ, |
| Belknap, Jeremy | 1744-1798 | | | | Clergyman, author ,historian, PU |

Bennington Raid   August 6-16, 1777   (Burgoyne's Offensive)

Bernard, Sir Francis	1712-1779	200	400	700	Royal Gov. NJ & Mass.
Berthier, Louis A.	1753-1815				French Lt., Marshal France, PU
Biddle, Nicholas	1750-1778				Cont'l naval officer, PU

Billingsport, NJ   October 2 & 9, 1777
Black Mingo Creek, SC   September 29, 1780
Blackstocks, SC   November 20, 1780

Blaine, Ephraim	? - 1804				Com. officer, PA, PU
Blanchard, Claude	1742-1802				Chief Commissary ,PU
Bland, Theodorick	1742-1790	200	375	750	CO, Pocahontas desc., USHR

Blue Licks, KY   August 19, 1782
Blue Mountain Valley, Sandy Hook, NJ   January 22-23, 1776
Blue Savannah, SC   September 4, 1780

| Boisbertrand, R.E. H. | 1746- ? | | | | French officer, PU |

Bonhomme Richard-Serapis Engagement   September 23, 1779

| Boone, Daniel | 1734-1820 | 7550 | 16000 | 35750 | Frontiersman |

Boston "Massacre"   March 5, 1770
Boston Campaign   April 19, 1775 - March 17, 1776
Boston Garrison   October 1, 1768 - March 17, 1776
Boston Siege   April 17, 1775 - March 17, 1776
Boston Tea Party   December 16, 1773

Botetourt, Nor. B. B..	1718 - 1770				Royal Gov. of VA, PU
Boudinot, Elias	1740-1821	310		800	Pres. Cont'l Cong. Dir. Mint
Bougainville, Louis A.	1729-1811				French explorer, admiral, PU

Bound Brook, NJ   April 13, 1777

Bouquet, Henry	1719-1765	345	720	1500	British general, papers BM
Bowler, Metcalf	1726-1789	75	150	300	Chief Justice of RI, informer
Boyd, Thomas	?-1779				Cont'l officer, tortured , PU
Braddock, Edward	1695-1755	420	925	1715	British general, WA adc of his

Bradstreets Capture of Ft. Frontenac   August 27, 1758
Brandywine, PA   September 11, 1777

Name	DB/DD	SIG	LS/DS	ALS	Comment
Brant, Joseph	1742-1807				Mohawk war chief, PU
Brant, Molly					Indian mistress ,PU
Braxton, Carter	1736-1797	425	800	2700	Signer of DOI, VA, SL
Briar Creek, GA	March 3, 1779				
Bristol, RI	October 7, 1775				
Brodhead's Expedition	August 11 - September 14, 1779				
Brodhead, Daniel	1736-1809				Cont'l officer, PA, very rare,PU
Brown, John "Pittsfield"	1744-1780				Patriot leader, PU
Brown, Thomas	? - 1825				Southern Tory leader, PU
Browne, Montfort	1774-1780				Gov. of New Providence, PU
Brunswick, NJ	June 22, 1777				
Bull's Ferry, N.J	July 20-21, 1780				
Bunker Hill, Mass.	June 17, 1775				
Burgoyne's Offensive	June - October, 1777				
Burgoyne, John	1722-1792	2165	3410	5120	British general, buried WAb
Burke, Edmund	1729-1797				British statesman, author, PU
Burke, Thomas	c.1747-1783	185	350		Congressman, Gov. NC
Burr, Aaron	1756-1836	375	900	1150	VP, ANS-$400, SALS-6-10X
Bushnell, David	c.1742-1824	300	675	1200	Inventor of submarine
Bushy Run, PA	August 5-6, 1763				
Bute, John Stuart	1713-1792	100	150	300	British prime minister
Butler, John	1725-1796	115	200	450	Loyalist leader, f.Walter
Butler, Percival	1760-1821				Cont'l officer, PU
Butler, Richard	1743-1791	160	275		Cont'l officer, Indian com.
Butler, Thomas	1754-1805	275			Cont'l officer, WA
Butler, Walter	1752? - 1781			800	Tory leader
Butler, William	?-1789				Cont'l officer, PU
Butler, Zebulon	1731-1795				Cont'l officer, PU
Byng, John	1704-1757				British admiral, PU
Byron, John	1723-1786	200	445		British admiral, Gov. Newfoundl.
Cadwalder, John	1742-1786	150	300		Militia general, SL (MD)
Cambray-Digny, L.A.J.	1751-1822				Cont'l officer, PU
Cambridge, Mass.	September 1, 1774				
Camden Campaign	July-August, 1780				
Campbell, Arch., (K.B.)	1739-1791	125	300	500	British officer, Gov. Jamaica
Campbell, John	?-1806				British general, PU
Campbell, John	1753-1784	325			British officer
Campbell, Lord William	?-1778	220	300		Royal Gov. of SC, N.Scotia P.
Campbell, William	1745-1781				Patriot ldr. at Kings Mt.,SL, PU
Can Creek, NC	September 12, 1780				
Canajoharie Settlements, NY	August 1-2, 1780				
Carleton, Christopher	?-1787				British off., a.d.c.Carleton, PU

Name	DB/DD	SIG	LS/DS	ALS	Comment
Carleton, Guy	1724-1808	600	1500		British general, Gov. of Canada
Carleton, Thomas	1736-1817	300			British officer, b.Guy
Carrington, Edward	1749-1810				Cont'l officer, USHR (VA), PU
Carroll, Char.of Carrollton	1737-1832	345	750	800	Signer, USS, BC-$550.
Carter, John Champe					Cont'l officer, PU
Caswell, Richard	1729-1789				Congressman, G/NC, PU
Cathcart, Sir William S.	1755-1843	125	250		British officer, ambassador

Caughnawaga (Fonda), NY	May 22, 1780, October 18, 1780
Cedars, The, Canada	May, 1776

Celoron de Blainville, P.	1753 - ?				Canadian volunteer, PU

Chambly, Canada	October 18, 1775

Champe, John	unknown				Cont'l soldier, kidnap Arnold, PU

Charleston Expedition	1776 and 1780
Charleston Raid of Prevost	May 11-12, 1779
Charleston, Mass	June 17, 1775, January 8, 1776
Charlotte, NC	September 26, 1780
Charlottesville Raid, VA	June 4, 1781

Chase, Samuel	1741-1811				See U.S. Supreme Court
Chastellux, Francois-J.	1734-1788	230	440		French officer, dignitary,writer
Chatham, William Pitt	1708-1778				English statesman, PU

Cherokee Expedition of James Grant	1761
Cherokee Ford, SC	February 14, 1779
Cherry Valley Massacre, NY	November 11, 1778
Chesapeake Bay	March 16, 1781 — Naval action
Chesapeake Capes	September 5, 1781

Choiseful, Etienne Fran.	1719-1785	155	325		French statesman
Church, Benjamin	1734?-1777	250	575		Informer, Mass.Indian fighter

Clapp's Mill, NC	March 2, 1781

Clark, Abraham	1726-1794	572	1430	4125	Signer of DOI (NJ), USHR
Clark, George Rogers	1752-1818	700	2600	3500	Conqueror of the Old Northwest
Clark, Thomas	? - 1792				Cont'l officer, very rare,PU
Clark, William	1770-1838	500	2100	2750	Lewis & Clark Expedition
Clarke, Alured	1745?-1832	220	400		British officer, Lt. G/Jamaica,
Clarke, Elijah (Clark)	1733-1799				Patriot, militia comdr., PU
Clerke, Sir FrancisC.					British officer, PU
Cleveland, Benjamin	1738-1806				Patriot leader (NC), PU

Clinton's Expedition, to Highlands	October 3-22, 1777

Clinton, George	1739-1812	150	250	400	First Gov. (NY), VP, SDS-2X
Clinton, Henry	1730-1795	500	1125	2450	British Comdr. in Chief, aristocrat
Clinton, James	1733-1812	250		650	Cont'l gen.(NY), SDS-2X

Name	DB/DD	SIG	LS/DS	ALS	Comment
Clymer, George	1739-1813	170	600	750	Signer DOI (PA), patriot, CC
Cochran, John	1730-1807	175	370		Last medical dir. Cont'l Army
Coffin, Issac, Sir	1759-1839				British admiral, PU
Coffin, John	1756-1838	200			Loyalist officer, b. Issac
Collier, George	1738-1795	200			British commodore, Parliament
Colomb, Pierre	1754-?				French volunteer, PU

Combahee Ferry, SC	August 27, 1782				
Congress-Savage Engagement	September 6, 1781				

Name	DB/DD	SIG	LS/DS	ALS	Comment
Connolly, John	c. 1750-?	225	470		Loyalist conspirator
Conway, Thomas	1733-1800?	75	140	250	Cont'l general, very rare
Conyngham, Gustavus	1747-1819				Amer. naval officer, PU

Cooch's Bridge (Iron Hill), DE	September 3, 1777

Name	DB/DD	SIG	LS/DS	ALS	Comment
Copley, John Singleton	1738-1815				American painter, see Artists
Corbin, Margaret C.	1751-1800				American heroine, PA, PU
Cornplanter	b.? - 1836				Seneca chief, PU
Cornstalk	c.1720-1777				Shawnee Chief, PU
Cornwallis, Charles	1738-1805	225	500	1430	British general, Gov. Gen.
Corny, Dominique-Louis	1736-1790				French commissary officer, PU

Cowan's Ford, NC	February 1, 1781
Cowpens, SC	January 17, 1781

Name	DB/DD	SIG	LS/DS	ALS	Comment
Craig, James Henry	1748-1812				British officer, G/Canada, PU
Craik, James	1730-1814				Chief physician,surgeon, PU
Crane, John	1744-1805				Cont'l officer, very rare,PU

Crawford's defeat	Sandusky & Olentangy, June 4-5, 1782

Name	DB/DD	SIG	LS/DS	ALS	Comment
Crawford, William	1732-1782	375			Frontiersman, Cont'l officer
Cresap, Michael	1742-1775				Border leader, Con.officer,PU
Cromot du Bourg, B.de					French officer, writer, PU

Crooked Billet, PA	May 1, 1778
Croton River, NY	May 14, 1781
Crown Point, NY	W. shore of Lake Champlain

Name	DB/DD	SIG	LS/DS	ALS	Comment
Cruger, John Harris	1738-1807				Tory officer, NY, scion of family
Cunningham, Bill	? - 1787	375			Tory partisan, Notorious leader
Cunningham, Robert	c.1739-1813	220	365		Tory leader
Cunningham, William	c.1717-1791	200			British provost marshall

Currytown, NY	July 9, 1781

Name	DB/DD	SIG	LS/DS	ALS	Comment
Dalling, John	? - 1798	300			British general, Gov. of Jamaica
Dalrymple, John	1749-1821				British officer, PU
Dalrymple, William	?-1807	210			British general

Danbury Raid, CN	April 23-28, 1777

Name	DB/DD	SIG	LS/DS	ALS	Comment
Dartmouth, William	1731-1801				British, Legge, 2d Earl of, PU
Davidson, George					Cont'l and militia officer, PU
Davidson, William Lee	1746-1781				Militia general, PU
Davie, William R.	1756-1820	175	350		Patriot officer, Gov. of NC
Dawes, William					Fellow courier of P. Revere, PU
Dayton, Elias	1737-1807	125	250	400	Cont'l general, SL, USHR, WA
Dayton, Jonathan	1760-1824	200	400	900	Cont'l officer, USHR, USS
De Haas, John Phillip	c. 1735-1786				Cont'l general, rare, PU
De Kalb, Johann					General, extremely rare, PU
De Lancey, Oliver	1718-1785				Sr. Loyalist officer in America,PU
De Lancey, Oliver	1749-1822				British, Gen. - Brit. Army, PU
De Peyster, Abraham	1753-c.1799				Loyalist officer, PU
De Peyster, Arent S.	1736-1832				Loyalist officer, PU
Deane, Silas	1737-1789	275	500		CC, first Amer. diplomat abroad
Dearborn, Henry	1751-1829	125	250	475	CC, Sec. of War, min/Portugal
Delaplace, William					British, sur.Ticonderoga, PU
Demont, William					American traitor, PU
Denison, Nathan	c.1740-1809	185			Militia officer
Despard, Edward M.	1751-1803	240	555		British naval officer
Despard, John	1745-1829	255			British officer
Destouches, Charles-R.					French admiral, PU
Dickinson, John	1732-1808	200	600	800	American theorist, SL, CC
Dickinson, Philemon	1739-1809	175			Militia general, USHR
Digby, Robert	1732-1814	230	475		British admiral
Donop, Carl Emil K.	1740-1777				Hessian officer, PU

Dorchester Heights, Mass.	March 2-27, 1776
Dorchester, SC	December 1, 1781

Name	DB/DD	SIG	LS/DS	ALS	Comment
Duane, James	1733-1797	160	350	700	Patriot statesman, mayor (NYC)
Dubuysson des Hays,	C.1752-1786				Cont'l officer, PU
Duche, Jacob	1738-1798				Chaplain of Cong., turncoat, PU
DuCoudray, Charles J.L.					General, nearly impossible, PU
Duer, William	1749-1799	150	345	700	USHR, militia officer, SALS-2X
Dulany, Daniel	1722-1797	130			Lawyer, political leader
Dundas, Thomas	1750-1794				British officer, PU
Dunmore, John Murray,	1732-1809				R.Gov./ VA, Gov. Bahamas, PU
Du Portail, Chevalier L.L.					General
Eden, Robert	1741-1784				Royal Gov. of MD, PU
Eden, William	1744-1814				British politician, Parliament,PU
Egleston, Joseph	1754-1811	150	300		Cont'l officer, SL, USHR
Elbert, Samuel	1743-1788				Cont'l general, Gov., rare, PU

Elizabethtown, NJ	January 6, 1777, Jan. 25 & June 6, 1780

Name	DB/DD	SIG	LS/DS	ALS	Comment
Ellery, William	1727-1820	180	360	700	Signer, CC, ESPV, DS-$185
Elliot, John	?-1808	200			British naval officer, Gov.,Par.
Ellis, Welbore	1713-1802				British , Par., Sec. at War, PU
Elphinstone, George K.	1746-1823	200			British off., first Viscount Keith
Enos, Roger	1729-1808	75	150		Cont'l officer, prominent VT
Erskine, Robert	1735-1780				Mapmaker Cont'l Army, PU
Erskine, William	1728-1795	200			British general

Name	DB/DD	SIG	LS/DS	ALS	Comment
Estaing, Charles H. T.	C.1729-1794	200	400		French admiral

| Eutaw Springs, SC | September 8, 1781 - The last major Southern engagement | | | | |

| Ewald, Johann von | 1744-1813 | | | | Hessian officer, author, PU |

| Fairfield, CT | July 8, 1779 | | | | |
| Falmouth (Portland), ME | October 18, 1775 | | | | |

Fanning, David	c.1755-1825				Tory partisan, PU
Fanning, Edmund	1739-1818				Tory leader, PU
Fanning, Nathaniel	1755-1805				American privateersman, PU
Febiger, Christian	1746-1796	175	350		Cont'l officer, Treas. of PA. rare
Feltman, William					Cont'l officer, diarist, PU
Ferguson, Patrick	1744-1780				British officer, inventor rifle, PU
Fermoy, Matthias Alexis.					Cont'l general, PU
Fersen, Hans Axel, C.	1755-1810				Swedish, controversial, PU

| Fishdam Ford, SC | November 9, 1780 | | | | |
| Fishing Creek, NC | August 18, 1780 | | | | |

Flower, Benjamin	1748-1781				Cont'l officer, PU
Flower, Samuel					Cont'l officer, PU
Floyd, William	1734-1821	575	1400	2000	Signer, CC, LS-$1950, ESPV
Fontanges, Vicomte de	1740-1822				French Maj. Gen., PU

| Fontenoy, Battle of | May 11, 1745 - Austrian Succession | | | | |

Fox, Charles James	1749-1806	40	100		British opposition politician
Francisco, Peter	c.1760-1836				War hero, PU
Franklin, Benjamin	1706-1790	3575	8800	16625	Signer, SALS-2X, SDS-3X
Franklin, William	1731-1813	175	400	775	Roy.Gov. NJ, Tory, s. B.Franklin
Franks, David S.					Maj. and a.d.c. Arnold, PU
Fraser, Simon	1738-1813				British officer, PU
Fraser, Simon	1729-1777				British general, k.Saratoga, PU
Fraser, Simon	1726-1782	325			Col. of Fraser Highlanders
Freneau, Philip Morin	1752-1832				First noted Amer. poet, PU
Frye, Joseph	1712-1794				Cont'l general, resigned,PU
Gadsden, Christopher	1724-1805				Cont'l gen., CC, Gov- dec., PU
Gage, Thomas	1719?-1787	275	900	1100	British Com. in Chief in America
Galloway, Joseph	c.1731-1803				Loyalist, SL, ESPV, PU
Galvez, Bernardo de	1746-1786	200			Gov. LA and FL
Galvin, William					French volunteer, PU
Gambier, James	1756-1833				British naval officer, PU
Gambier, James	1723-1789				British admiral, PU
Gansevoort, Peter	1749-1812				Cont'l officer, PU
Garth, George	? - 1819				British general, PU

| Gaspee affair | June 9, 1772 | | | | |

| Gates, Horatio | 1728-1806 | 275 | 500 | 1100 | Cont'l general, Wash. 's AG, |
| George III (see Royalty) | 1738-1820 | | | | King of Great Britain and Ireland |

Name	DB/DD	SIG	LS/DS	ALS	Comment
Georgetown, SC	11/15/80, 1/24/81 and 7/25/81 and 8/2/81				
Gerard, Conrad Alex.	1729-1790				First French Minister to U.S., PU
Germain(e), George S.	1716-1785				Brit. Sec. of State for Amer., PU
German Flats	(Herkimer) - September 13, 1778				
Germantown, PA, Battle of	October 4, 1777				
Gerry, Elbridge	1744-1814	475	900	2750	Signer & AOC,CC, Gov., VP, FF-$1000
Gibault, Pierre	1737-1804				Catholic missionary, PU
Gibson, George	1747-1791				Cont'l officer, PU
Gibson, John	1740-1822				Cont'l off., Sec.Indian Ter., PU
Gimat, Jean-Joseph S.					Cont'l off., adcLafay., Gov., PU
Girty, Simon	1741-1818				Renegade of the Old NW, PU
Gist, Christopher	c.1706-1759				Colonial explorer and scout, PU
Gist, Mordecai	1743-1792				Cont'l general, PU
Gist, Nathaniel	?-1796				Cont'l officer, PU
Gloucester, Cape Ann, Mass.	August 9, 1775				
Gloucester, NJ	November 25, 1777				
Gloucester, VA	October 3, 1781				
Glover, John	1732-1797	275	575	1500	Cont'l general, Del. River cros.
Gnadenhuetten Massacre, OH	March 7-8, 1782				
Golden Hill, Battle of	January 19, 1770				
Gordon, William	1728-1807				Historian, clergyman, PU
Gorham, Nathaniel	1738-1796	300	500	1445	Pres. Cont'l Cong., SL, ESPV
Gould, Paston	? - 1783				British Southern cmdr., PU
Gouvion, Jean Baptiste	1747-1792				French volunteer, PU
Grafton, Augustus H.F.	1735-1811				British politician, acting PM, PU
Graham , Joseph	1759-1836				American officer, writer, PU
Grant, James	1720-1806				British gen., Par., Gov/FL, PU
Grant, James					British officer, PU
Grasse, Francois J. P.	1722-1788				French admiral, PU
Graves, Samuel	1713-1787				British admiral, PU
Graves, Thomas	1725? - 1802				British admiral, PU
Great Brewster Island, Mass.	July 21 & 31, 1775				
Great Bridge, VA	December 9, 1775				
Great Savannah, SC	August 20, 1780				
Greaton, John	1741-1783				Cont'l gen., G. tavern, PU
Green Spring, SC	August 1, 1780				
Green Spring, VA	July 6, 1781				
Green, John	?- 1793				Cont'l officer, PU
Greene, Christopher	1737-1781				Cont'l officer, PU
Greene, Nathanael	1742-1786	1000	3000	3750	Cont'l general, SALS-2X
Grenville, George	1712-1770	225	700		British pre., Parl., Sec. of State

Name	DB/DD	SIG	LS/DS	ALS	Comment
Grey, Charles "No Flint"	1729-1807				British general, C in C Brit., PU
Gribeauval, Jean B.	1715-1789				French artillery general, PU
Gridley, Richard	1710-1796	200	400		First Amer. Chief of Engineers
Griffin, Cyrus	1748—1810	375	750		Pres. Cont'l Congress, SL
Guichen, Luc Urbain	1712-1790				French admiral, PU
Guilford Courthouse, NC	March 15, 1781				
Gunby, John					Cont'l officer, PU
Gwinnett, Button	c.1735-1777				Signer DOI, CC, 36 - 60 exist

War of Austriam Succession	1740 - 1748 - Background, key to officer developement				

Habersham, James	1712-1775				Colonial officer, merchant, PU
Habersham, John	1754-1799				Cont'l officer, Indian agent, PU
Habersham, Joseph	1751-1815	125	250	500	Patriot leader, USPM
Haldimand, Sir Frederick	1718-1791				British general, G/Can., PU
Hale, Nathan	1755-1776				"Martyr Spy,"CO, PU
Hale, Nathan	? - 1780				Cont'l officer, PU

Halfway Swamp, Singleton's, SC	December 12-13, 1780				

Hall, Lyman	1724-1790	1475	3210	4775	Signer DOI, CC, G/GA
Hamilton, Alexander	1757-1804	1325	4150	3350	CO, ADC GW, FF-$1500
Hamilton, Henry	? - 1796				Brit. officer, Gov. Ber., PU

Hampton, VA	October 24-25, 1775				

Hampton, Wade	c.1751 - 1835				Polit., soldier, USHR, PU
Hancock, John	1737-1793	2125	4910	9125	Signer, G/MA, rare -ALS, sig.

Hancok's Bridge, NJ	March 21, 1778				

Hand, Edward	1744-1802	175	400		Cont'l general, WA, AG
Hanger, George	c.1751-1824				Brit. officer, Clinton adc, PU

Hanging Rock, SC	August 6, 1780				

Hanson, John	1721-1783	2500			CC President, scarce in DS/ALS
Haraden, Jonathan	1744-1803				State Naval officer, PU

Harlem Cove (Manhattanville), NY	November 16, 1776				
Harlem Heights, NY	September 16, 1776				

Harmar, Josiah	1753-1813				Cont'l officer, Lt. Col., PU

Harpersfield, NY	April 2, 1780				

Harrison, Benjamin	c.1726-1791	500	1050	2500	Signer, CC, Gov., FF-$1250
Hart, John	c.1711-1779	325	500	1000	Signer, currency - $350
Hart, Nancy Morgan	?				Heroine, PU
Harvey, Edward					Acting C in C of British Army, PU
Haslet, John	? - 1777				CO, DE, killed in action, PU
Haussegger, Nicholas					Cont'l officer, turncoat, PU

Name	DB/DD	SIG	LS/DS	ALS	Comment
Haw River (Pyle's defeat), NC	**February 25, 1781**				
Hayne, Isaac	1745-1781				Militia officer, executed, PU
Hays, Mary Ludwig	1754-1832				Heroine, M. Pitcher legend, PU
Hazen, Moses	1733-1803				Cont'l officer, PU
Heath, William	1737-1814	175	1100	1500	Cont'l gen., SL, last Maj. Gen.
Heister, Leopold P.von	1707-1777				Hessian C in C, PU
Henry, John Joseph	1758-1811	50	100	200	Jurist, author
Henry, Patrick	1736-1799	1125	2500	5700	Patriot, LG- $2500, ESPV-ALS
Herkimer, Nicholas	1728-1777				MG, scarce in most forms, PU
Hewes, Joseph	1730-1779	2575	5750	11250	Signer, ESPV-ALS,one of five toughest!
Heyward, Thomas Jr.	1746-1809	475	1200	1500	Signer DOI, "Tho Heyward Jr"
Hillsboro Raid, NC	**Spetember 12, 1781**				
Hinrichs, Johann	? - 1834				Hessian officer, PU
Hobkirk's Hill (Camden), SC	**April 25, 1781**				
Hogun, James	?-1781				Cont'l general, rare, PU
Holker, Jean	1745-1822				French merchant, PU
Holtzendorff, Louis-Cas.	1728 - ?				Cont'l officer, PU
Hood, Samuel, 1st Vis.	1724-1816	50	100	150	British admiral, Parliament
Hood's Point (James River)	**January 3, 1781**				
Hooper, William	1742-1790	500	5150	6725	Signer DOI, DS-$3750, $6200
Hopkins, Esk	1718-1802	225	1200	1075	Navy, ESPV - LS/DS/ALS
Hopkins, John B.	1742-1796				Cont'l naval officer, PU
Hopkins, Stephen	1707-1785	200	500	1050	Signer DOI, scarce ALS, SALS-6X
Hopkinson, Francis	1737-1791	325	665	1385	Signer DOI, writer, artist, "F. Hopkinson"
Horry, Daniel Huger					American officer, PU
Horry, Hugh					American officer, PU
Horry, Peter					American officer, PU
Horseneck Landing (W. Greenwich), CN	**February 26, 1779**				
Hotham, William	1736-1813				British naval officer, PU
Houdin, Michel-Gabriel	? - 1802				Cont'l officer, PU
Howard, John Eager	1752-1827	145	315		CO, CC,G/MD, USS, S/War
Howe, George Augus.	1724-1758				British general, scarce, PU
Howe, Richard	1726-1799		900		British admiral, C in C, ESPV
Howe, Robert	1732-1796			750	Cont'l general, SL
Howe, William	1729-1814				British C in C, PU
Hubbardton, VT	**July 7, 1777**				
Huck, Christian					Loyalist officer, PU
Huger, Benjamin	1746-1779				Militia officer, PU
Huger, Daniel	1741-1799				Congressman, PU
Huger, Francis	1751-1811				Militia officer, PU
Huger, Issac	1743-1797	100	200	400	Cont'l general, PU

Name	DB/DD	SIG	LS/DS	ALS	Comment
Huger, John	1744-1804				Patriot leader, PU
Hull, William	1753-1825	175	400	800	Cont'l officer, BG in War 1812
Humpton, Richard	c.1733-1804				Cont'l officer, very rare,PU
Huntington, Jabez	1719-1786				Patriot, militia general, PU
Huntington, Jedediah	1743-1818	75	150	250	Cont'l general, PU
Huntington, Samuel	1731-1796	250	570	1840	Signer
Hutchinson, Thomas	1711-1780	200	400		Royal Gov. of Mass., historian

Hutchinson's Island (Savannah), GA	March 7, 1776

Name	DB/DD	SIG	LS/DS	ALS	Comment
Hyler, Adam					Whaleboat guerrilla, PU
Irvine, William	1741-1804	80	210	320	Cont'l general, SDS-2x
Izard, Ralph	1742-1804				US diplomat, USS, SL, PU
Jackson, Henry	1747-1809	70	135	230	Cont'l officer, PU
Jackson, Michael	1734-1801	65	120	225	Cont'l officer
Jackson, Robert	1750-1827				British medical officer, PU

Jamaica (Brookland), NY	August 28, 1776

Name	DB/DD	Comment
Jaquett, Peter	? - 1834	Cont'l officer, infor. varies, PU
Jasper, William	c. 1750-1779	Rev. hero, scarce, KIA, PU
Jay, John	(see U.S. Supreme Court)	

Johns Island, SC	December 28-19, 1781, November 4, 1782

Name	DB/DD	Comment
Johnson, Guy	c.1740-1788	Loyalist ldr., Indian Supt., SL,PU
Johnson, Henry	1748-1835	British officer, PU
Johnson, Sir John	1742-1830	Loyalist leader, PU
Johnson, Sir William	1715-1774	Supt. Indian Affairs, PU
Johnstone, George	1730-1787	British naval officer, P, PU

Johnstown, NY	October 25, 1781

Name	DB/DD	SIG	LS/DS	Comment
Jones, Allen	1739-1807			MG. politician, CC, PU
Jones, John Paul	1747-1792	5000	7500	Scarce, als-$45000, ESPV
Jones, Thomas	1731-1792			Loyalist historian, author, PU
Jones, Willie	c.1741-1801			Patriot leader, PU
Jumel, Stephen	c.1754-1832			Wine merchant, PU
Jungkenn, F. C.A.B	1732-1806			Minister of State, PU
Kachlein, Andrew				American officer, PU, sp. var.
Kachlein, Peter	? - 1789			MO, PU, sp. var.
Kalb, Johann	1721-1780			Cont'l gen., "Baron de Kalb,"PU

Kaskaskia, IL	July 4, 1778

Name	DB/DD	SIG	LS/DS	Comment
Kemble, Peter	1704-1789			Loyalist, PU
Kemble, Stephen	c.1730-1822			Brit.officer, adc to Gage, PU
Kenton, Simon	1755-1836	450	1475	Frontiersman

Kentucky Raid of Bird	April - June 1780
Kettle Creek, GA	February 14, 1779
Kings Mountain, SC	October 7, 1780

Name	DB/DD	SIG	LS/DS	ALS	Comment
Kingston (Esopus), NY	October 16, 1777				
Kip's Bay, NY	Spetember 15, 1776				
Kirkwood, Robert	1730-1791				Cont'l officer, KIA, PU
Klock's Field, NY	October 19, 1780				
Knowlton, Thomas	1740-1776				Cont'l officer, KIA, PU
Knox, Henry	1750-1806				Cont'l gen., S/War, PU, ESPV
Knyphausen, Wilhelm	1716-1800				German C in C, PU
Kosciuszko, Thaddeus	1746-1817	275			Cont'l officer
Lafayette, Marquis de	1757-1834	745	2235	3875	SALS-2-2.5X, ESPV-ALS
Lake George, NY	September 8, 1755 - One of first pitched battles US soil.				
Lamb, John	1735-1800				Cont'l Arty, Col., NY, PU
Landais, Pierre	1734-?				French naval officer, PU
Langdon, John	1741-1819	250	425	750	Patriot, USS, Gov. NH, SALS-2X
Langdon, Woodbury	c.1738-1805				Patriot, congressman, PU
Langlade, Charles M.	1729-c.1801				Indian leader, sp. var., PU
Laumoy, Jean Baptiste	1750-1832				Cont'l officer, very rare,PU
Laurance, John	1750-1810				Judge, SL, USS, PU
Laurens, Henry	1724-1792	1250	2225	3100	CC President, FF-$2000
Laurens, John	c.1754-1782				CO, GW vol. adc, PU
Lauzun, Armand Louis					French officer, PU
Lawson, Robert					American officer, PU
Learned, Ebenezer	1728-1801				Cont'l general, rare, PU
Lechmere Point (E. Cambridge), Mass.	November 9, 1775				
Lee, Arthur	1740-1792				Diplomat, troublemaker, PU
Lee, Charles	1731-1782	300	800	1850	Cont'l general, SALS-$3500
Lee, Charles	1758-1815	125	250	500	USAG., lawyer Burr, Chase
Lee, Francis Lightfoot	1734-1797	700	1250	4000	Congressman, Signer
Lee, Henry	1756-1818	225	600	700	Cavalry leader, G/VA, f. R.E. Lee
Lee, Richard Bland	1761-1827				Statesman, PU
Lee, Richard Henry	1732-1794	515	2250	3500	Signer, FF-$2000
Lee, William	1739-1795				Merchant, diplomat, PU
L'Enfant, Pierre Charles	1754-1825				Cont'l officer, PU
Lenud's (or Lanneau's) Ferry, SC	May 6, 1780				
L'Epine.					French volunteer, PU
Leslie, Alexander	c.1740-1794				British general, PU
Lewis, Andrew	1720-1781				Cont'l general, very rare,PU
Lewis, Francis	1713-1802	425	1500	2750	Signer DOI, CC, f. M. Lewis
Lewis, Morgan	1754-1844	60	110	140	Cont'l officer, G/NY
Lexington and Concord	April 19, 1775				
Liberty Affair	June 10, 1768				
Lillington, John					Militia officer, PU

Name	DB/DD	SIG	LS/DS	ALS	Comment
Lillington, Alexander	?-1786				MO, sig. "Alex Lillington," PU
Lincoln, Benjamin	1733-1810	110	200	400	Cont'l general, S/ War

| Little Egg Harbor, N.J. | | October 4-5, 1778 | | | |

Name	DB/DD	SIG	LS/DS	ALS	Comment
Livingston, Abraham					Cont'l officer, PU
Livingston, Henry B.	1750-1831				Cont'l officer, PU
Livingston, Henry B.	(see United States Supreme Court)				
Livingston, James	1747-1832				Cont'l officer, SL, PU
Livingston, Philip	1716-1778	325	1100	1250	Signer, "Phil Livingston"
Livingston, Richard					Cont'l officer, PU
Livingston, Robert R.	1746-1813	200	400	600	Aadm. oath GW., SALS-2X
Livingston, William	1723-1790	350	800	1500	Congressman, G/ NY
Livius, Peter	1729-1795				Canadian jurist, PU

Lloyd's Neck, Long Island, NY	September 5, 1779	
Lochry's Defeat, Ohio River	August 24, 25, 1781	
Long Island (Boston Harbor), Mass.	July 12, 1775	
Long Island, NY Battle of	August 27, 1776	
Long Island, NY	December 10, 1777	

Name	DB/DD	SIG	LS/DS	ALS	Comment
Loring, Joshua	1744-1789				Loyalist, commissary of prisoners, PU
Loudoun, John C.	1705-1782				Brit. C in C in America , PU
Louis XVI	(See Royalty/Heads of State)				
Lovell, James	1737-1814	100	200	300	Congressman, CC
Lovell, James (Jr.)	1758-1850				Cont'l officer, PU
Lovell, John	1710-1778				Loyalist, PU
(La) Luzerne, Chevalier					Second French Minister, PU
Lynch, Charles	1736-1796				MO, "founder of Lynch law," PU
Lynch, Thomas	1727-1776				Cont'l Congressman, PU
Lynch, Thomas Jr.	1749-1779				Signer, second tough. sig. form, auction item

| Machias, ME | | June 12, 1775 | | | |

Name	DB/DD	SIG	LS/DS	ALS	Comment
MacLean, Allan	1725-1797				British officer, var."Maclean," PU
MacLean, Francis	1718-1781				BO, G/Halifax, Canada, PU
Madison, James	(See Presidents of the US)				
Maham, Hezekiah	1739-1789				Militia officer, PU
Maitland, John	?-1779				British officer, PU
Malmady, Marquis de.					CO, sp. varaitions - Malmedy, PU

| Mamaroneck, NY, Raid of | | October 22, 1776 | | | |

Name	DB/DD	SIG	LS/DS	ALS	Comment
Manley, John	c.1734-1793				Amer. Naval officer, PU
Marion, Francis "S. Fox"	c.1732-1795				Southern partisan ldr., SL, PU
Marjoribanks, John	?-1781				British officer, PU
Marriner, William					Whaleboat guerrilla, PU
Marshall, John	(See United States Supreme Court)				

| Martha's Vineyard Raid | | c. September 8, 1778 | | | |

Name	DB/DD	SIG	LS/DS	ALS	Comment
Martin, Josiah	1737-1786				Royal G/NC, BO, PU
Mason, George	1725-1792				Statesman, constitutionalist, PU
Mathew, Edward	1729-1805	60	130		British general
Mathews, George	1739-1812	75	150		Cont'l officer, G/GA, USHR, rare

Matson's Ford, PA	December 11, 1777

Name	DB/DD	SIG	LS/DS	ALS	Comment
Maussac de La Marquisie, Bernard					French volunteer, PU
Mawhood, Charles	? - 1780				British officer, PU
Maxwell, William, "Scotch"	c.1733-1796				Cont'l general, PU
McAllister, Archibald	? - 1781				Cont'l officer, PU
McArthur, Archibald					British officer, PU
M(a)cDonald, Donald					British officer, PU
McDonald, Flora	1722-1790				Jacobite and Tory heroine, PU
McDougall, Alexander	1732-1786	100	200		CC, USS, USHR
McIntosh, John	1755-1826				Cont'l officer, PU
Mcintosh, Lachlan	1725-1806	500	950	1250	Cont'l general, duelled Gwinnett
McKean, Thomas	1734-1817	225	450	800	Signer, Congress, G/PA
McKinley, John	1721-1796	75	150		Pres. of DE
McLane, Allan	1746-1829				Cont'l officer, PU
Meigs, Return Jonathan	1740-1823	100	200	300	Cont'l officer, pioneer
Mercer, Hugh	c.1725-1777				Cont'l gen., respected,rare,PU
Middleton, Arthur	1742-1787	1250	3450	400	Signer
Middleton, Henry	1717-1784	3000			2nd Pres. Cont'l Congress
Mifflin, Thomas	1744-1800	175	350	800	Cont'l general, First Gov. of PA

Minden, Battle of	August 1, 1759
Mischianza, Philadelphia	May 18, 1778
Monick's Corner, SC	April 14, 1780 & October 16, 1781

Name	DB/DD	Comment
Monckton, Henry	1740-1778	British officer, PU
Monckton, Robert	1726-1782	BO, G/Nova Scotia & NY, PU
Moncrieff, James	1744-1793	BO, sp. variations, PU

Monmouth, NJ, Campaign	June 16 - July 5, 1778

Name	DB/DD	Comment
Monroe, James	(See Presidents of the United States)	
Montgomery, Richard	1738-1775	Cont'l general, very rare,PU

Montreal, Canada	September 25, 1775, November 13, 1775

Name	DB/DD	Comment
Montresor, James G.	1702-1776	Military engineer, PU
Montresor, John	1736-1799	British engineer, jwriter, PU
Moore, Alfred	(see United States Supreme Court)	
Moore, James	1737-1777	Cont'l general, very rare,PU
Moore, Maurice	1735-1777	Jurist and patriot, PU

Moores Creek Bridge, NC	February 27, 1776

Name	DB/DD	SIG	LS/DS	ALS	Comment
Morgan, Daniel	1736-1802				Frontiersman, CO, rare, PU
Morgan, John	1735-1789				Medical Dir. , PU
Morris, Gouverneur	1752-1816	225	600	715	Statesman, Congress, fin. writer

Name	DB/DD	SIG	LS/DS	ALS	Comment
Morris, Lewis	1726-1798	650	1000	2015	Signer, MG, ANS-$900
Morris, Robert	1734-1806	350	1500	2375	Signer, SC-$800, SDS-10-15X, ESPV-DS
Morris, Robert Hunter	c. 1700-1764				Chief Justice NJ, G/PA, PU
Morton, John	c. 1724-1777	450	800	1275	Signer, PA
Mottin de la Balme, Aug	1736-1780				Fr. cavalry trainer, sp. var., PU
Moultrie, John	1729-1798	200	400	500	Loyalist, Lt. Gov. of E. FL.
Moultrie, William	1730-1805	150	300		Cont'l general, SL, G/SC
Moylan, Stephen	1737-1811				Cont'l officer, PU
Muhlenberg, John P.G.	1746-1807	150	435		Lutheran clergyman, CG
Murphy, Timothy	1751-1818				Legendary marksman, PU
Musgrave, Thomas	1737-1812				British officer, PU
Musgrove's Mill, SC		August 18, 1780			
Nantasket Road, Mass.		May 17 & 19, 1776			
Nash, Abner	c.1740-1786				War Gov. NC, Congress, PU
Nash, Francis	c.1742-1777				Cont'l General, very rare,PU
Nassau (Providence), Bahamas	March 3-4, 1776				
Nelson, Horatio	1758-1805	675	3000	2900	British naval hero, ESPV
Nelson, Robert	1743-1818				Patriot, PU
Nelson, Thomas (Jr.)	1739-1789	550	1600	3000	Patriot, Signer DOI, militia general, Gov. VA
Nelson, William (Jr.)	c.1760-1813				Cont'l officer, PU
Neville, John	1731-1803				Cont'l officer, very rare, PU
Neville, Presley	1756-1818				Cont'l officer, PU
Newcastle, Thomas P.	1693-1768				English statesman, PU
Newport, RI		July 29-31 & August, 1778			
Newtown, NY		August 29, 1779			
New York		July 11-22, 1778			
Nicholas, Samuel					Senior Cont'l Marine officer
Nicola, Lewis	1717-1807				Cont'l officer, PU
Ninety-Six, SC		May, & June, 1781			
Nixon, John	1733-1808	150	300	450	Patriot, financier, first orator DOI
Norfolk, VA		January 1, 1776			
North, Sir Fred. "Lord"	1732-1792	100	350	500	British Prime Minister
O'Brien, Jeremiah	1744-1818				American naval officer, PU
Odell, Jonathan	1737-1818				Loyalist secret agent, satirist, PU
Odell, William					Tory officer, PU
Ogden, Aaron	1756-1839				CO, G/NJ, steam. pioneer, PU
Ogden, Matthias	1754-1791				Cont'l officer, PU
O'Hara, Charles	c.1740-1802				British guards general, PU
Orangeburg, SC		May 11, 1781			
Oriskany, NY, Ambush		August 6, 1777			

Name	DB/DD	SIG	LS/DS	ALS	Comment
Oswald, Eleazer	c.1755-1795				CO, journalist, PU
Oswald, Richard	1705-1784				British diplomat, PU
Otis, James	1725-1783	300	625	1465	Patriot, orator, scarce sig.
Otto, Bodo	1711-1787				Cont'l Army surgeon, PU
Paca, William	1740-1799	725	1900	2935	Signer, Gov. MD, jurist, "Wm Paca"
Paine, Robert Treat	1731-1814	275	500	1220	Signer DOI & OBP, Gov. CT, CC
Paine, Thomas	1737-1809	3200			Revolutionary writer

Paoli, PA	September 21, 1777
Parker's Ferry, SC	August 13, 1781

Name	DB/DD	SIG	LS/DS	ALS	Comment
Parker, John	1729-1775				Hero of Lexington, PU
Parker, Sir Hyde (Jr.)	1739-1807				British admiral, PU
Parker, Sir Hyde,	1714-1782				British admiral, "Old Vinegar,"PU
Parker, Sir Peter	1721-1811				British admiral, PU
Parsons, Samuel H.	1737-1789	230	475	525	Cont'l general, Indian commiss.
Paterson, James					BO, AG /Amer., sp. var - "tt," PU
Paterson, John	1744-1808				Cont'l general, PU
Pattison, James	1724-1805				BO, artillery officer, PU
Paulding, John	1758-1818				Captor of John Andre, PU

Paulus Hook, NJ	August 19, 1779

Peale, Charles Willson	(see Artists)

Peekskill Raid, NY	March 23, 1777
Pell's Point, NY	October 18, 1776

Name	DB/DD	SIG	LS/DS	ALS	Comment
Penn, John	1740-1788	1750	2400	3500	Signer DOI
Penn, William	1644-1718	1750	4500		Pennsylvania founder
Penot Lombart de Noirmont, Rene-Hippolyte	1750-1792				French volunteer, PU
Penot Lombart, Chevalier de La Neuville...	1744-c.1800				French volunteer, PU

Pensacola, FL	May 9, 1781

Name	DB/DD	SIG	LS/DS	ALS	Comment
Pepperrell, Sir William	1696-1759	100			Colonial merchant, MO
Percy, Hugh	1742-1817				BO, adc George III, PU

Petersburg, VA	April 23, 1781

Name	DB/DD	SIG	LS/DS	ALS	Comment
Phillips, William	c.1731-1781	200	400		BO, brilliant artilleryman, PU
Pickens, Andrew	1739-1817				MG, SL, Congress, PU
Pickering, Timothy	1745-1829	225	600	1400	S/War, SALS-$2800, ESPV
Pigot, Robert	1720-1796				British general, PU
Pinckney, Charles	1757-1824	250	600		G/SC, USS, PU, SDS-2X
Pinckney, Charles Cote.	1746-1825				CO, adc GW, SB-$1200
Pinckney, Thomas	1750-1828				CO, G/SC, adc Gates, PU

Piscataway, NJ	May 10, 1777

Name	DB/DD	SIG	LS/DS	ALS	Comment
Pitcairn, John	1722-1775				BO, immortalized Trumbull paint.
Point of Fork, VA	June 5, 1781				
Pollock, Oliver	c.1737-1823				Patriot supply agent, altruist
Pomeroy, Seth	1706-1777	200			Cont'l general, shadowy figure
Poor, Enoch	1736-1780	200			Cont'l general
Poundridge, NY	July 2, 1779				
Pownall, Thomas	1722-1805	175	350		Colonial Gov.
Prescott, Oliver	1731-1804	75	150		Physician and militia general
Prescott, Richard	1725-1788				British general, PU
Prescott, Robert	1725-1816				BO, G/Canada, PU
Prescott, Samuel	1751-c.1777				Physician, surgeon, PU
Prescott, William	1726-1795				MO, Bunker Hill hero, PU
Preudhomme de Borre, Philippe Hubert, Ch...	1717 - ?				Cont'l general, PU
Prevost, Augustine	1723-1786				British general, PU
Princeton, NJ	January 3, 1777				
Protector-Duff Engagement	June 9, 1780				
Pulaski, Casimir	c.1748-1779	465	960	2335	Cont'l leader, adc GW , extr. rare
Putnam, Isreal	1718-1790		2250		DS w/Z.Butler-$2600, very rare
Putnam, Rufus	1738-1824	200	400	800	CO, 1st Surv. Gen. of US
Quebec, Canada	December 31-January 1, 1776				
Quinby Bridge, SC	July 17, 1781				
Quinton's Bridge, NJ	March 18, 1778				
Rall, Johann Gottlieb	c.1720-1776				Hessian Col, Trenton, PU
Rams(a, o)eur's Mill, NC	June 20, 1780				
Ramsay, David	1749-1815				Historian, politician, PU
Ramsay, Nathaniel	1741-1817				CO, sp. var. "Ramsey," PU
Randolph, Peyton	c.1721-1775	450	1450		First Pres. CC, SDS-2X
Rankin, William					Tory, "Mr. Alexander," PU
Rastel, Philippe Francois, Sieur de Roch...					French veteran of Brit. Serv., PU
Rathbun, John Peck	1746-1823				CO, sp. var.: "(o)urne," PU
Rawdon-Hastings, F.	1754-1826	75	200	450	BO, adc King, statesman, ESPV
Read, Charles	1715-c.1780				American deserter, PU
Read, George	1733-1798	300	615	1175	Signer, lawyer, USS
Read, James	1743-1822				MO, naval commiss., PU
Read, Thomas	c.1740-1788				American naval officer, PU
Reed, James	1723-1807				Cont'l general, PU
Reed, Joseph	1741-1785	100	200		GW military sec., patriot
Reedy River, SC	December 22, 1775				

Name	DB/DD	SIG	LS/DS	ALS	Comment
Revere, Paul	1735-1818	4500	14500		Patriot, courier, ALS-$26000

Richmond, VA	January 5-7, 1781

Name	DB/DD	SIG	LS/DS	ALS	Comment
Riedesel, Baron Friedrich Adolphus	1738-1800				German general, PU
Ritzema, Rudolph					Cont'l officer, clergy, PU
Rivington, James	1724-1802	150	250		Journalist, printer, bookseller
Robinson, Beverley	1721-1792				Tory leader, PU
Rochambeau, Donatien Marie Jos. de Vimeur	1750-1813				French officer, G/Haiti
Rochambeau, Jean Baptiste Don. de Vimeur	1725-1807				Cmdr. Fr. army in America, PU
Rockingham, Charles Watson-Wentworth	1730-1782				Two time Brit. prime minister, PU

Rocky Mount, SC	August 1, 1780

Name	DB/DD	SIG	LS/DS	ALS	Comment
Rodney, Caesar	1728-1784	500	1525	1000	Signer, CC, ALS-2X, ESPV
Rodney, George B.	1719-1792				British admiral, P, PU
Rogers, Robert	1732-1795	300			Ranger hero, frontiersman
Rosenthal, Gustave H.	1753-1829				Cont'l off., sp. variations, PU
Ross, George	1730-1779	350	825	1150	Signer, jurist, lawyer Lan.PA, ESPV-DS
Rudolph, John	?-1782				Cont'l officer, PU
Rudolph, Michael					Cont'l officer, PU

Rugeley's Mill (Clermont), SC	December 4, 1780

Name	DB/DD	SIG	LS/DS	ALS	Comment
Rugeley, Col. Henry					Tory officer, PU
Rush, Benjamin	1746-1813	700	1350	2675	Signer, physician, SDS-$6900
Russell, William, (Sr.)	? - 1793				Cont'l officer, PU
Russell, William, Jr.	1758-1825				Militia officer, PU
Rutherford, Griffith	c.1731-c.1800				Southern patriot, PU
Rutledge, Edward (Ned)	1749-1800	375	725	1250	Signer, Congress, G/SC, SALS-2X
Rutledge, John	(see United States Supreme Court)				

Sag Harbor Raid, NY	May 23-24, 1777

Name	DB/DD	SIG	LS/DS	ALS	Comment
Saint-Simon Montblern, Claude Anne, Marq.					Fren. general ,PU
Saint-Simon, Claude Henri, Comte de	1760-1825				French officer, philosopher

Salem, Mass.	February 26, 1775

Name	DB/DD	SIG	LS/DS	ALS	Comment
Saltonstall, Dudley	1738-1796				CO, high ranking officer, PU
Sampson, Deborah	1760-1827				Cont'l heroine, PU
Sandwich, J. M., 4th Earl	1718-1792	175	400	600	First Lord of Admirality, S/State

Saratoga Battles, NY	September 19, 1777 & October 7, 1777
Savannah, GA	December 29, 1778 & October 9, 1779

Name	DB/DD	SIG	LS/DS	ALS	Comment
Scammell, Alexander	1747-1781			1500	CO, adc GW, AG to GW

Name	DB/DD	SIG	LS/DS	ALS	Comment
Schaffner, George					Cont'l officer, sp. variations

Schoharie Valley, NY	October 15-19, 1780				

Name	DB/DD	SIG	LS/DS	ALS	Comment
Schuyler, Phillip John	1733-1804	200	375		Cont'l general, SL, ESPV-DS
Scott, Charles	c.1739-1813	100	200	330	Cont'l general, SL, G/KY
Sears, Isaac	1730-1786				NYC mob leader, PU
Senter, Isaac	1755-1799				Army physician, diarist, PU
Serle, Ambrose					Civillian sec.to R. Howe, PU
Sevier, John	1745-1815	650	1125	800	MO, First Gov. TN, SL, SDS-3X

Sharon Springs Swamp, NY	July 10, 1781				

Name	DB/DD	SIG	LS/DS	ALS	Comment
Shaw, Samuel	1754-1794				CO, journal writer, PU

Shays's Rebellion	August 31, 1786 - February 4, 1787				

Name	DB/DD	SIG	LS/DS	ALS	Comment
Shays, Daniel	c. 1747-1825				CO, insurrectionist, PU
Shelby, Isaac	1750-1826		400		MO, First G/KY, SL, PU
Sheldon, Elisha					Col. of 2d Dragoons, rare, PU

Shell's Bush, NY	August 6, 1781				

Name	DB/DD	SIG	LS/DS	ALS	Comment
Shepard, William	1737-1817				Cont'l officer, rare, PU
Sherman, Roger	1722-1793	235	475	895	Signer, AOA, AOC & C
Shirley, William	1694-1771	200	400	800	Colonial Gov. of Mass, C in C

Short Hills (Metuchen), NJ	June 26, 1777				

Name	DB/DD	SIG	LS/DS	ALS	Comment
Shreve, Israel	?- 1799				Cont'l officer, PU
Silliman, Gold Selleck	1732-1790				MG, PU
Simcoe, John Graves	1752-1806				Brit.Cmdr., P, PU
Simitiere, Pierre-Eugene du (see Artists)					

SIGNERS OF THE DECLARATION OF INDEPENDENCE

Key:
Name, Date of birth, Date of death, Common signature forms, National Offices, State Offices, Profession, Distinctive characters, Comments; CC = Continental Congress, USHR = United States House of Represenatives, AOC = Articles of Confederation

Adams, John
1735-1826, full, 2nd Pres. U.S., 2nd. CC, (Mass.), "c," "C," "R," "f," "y," Rare in ALS

Adams, Samuel
1722 - 1803,"Sam Adams," CC (1774-75), SL, Lt. Gov. Mass (1789-94), Gov. (94-97),Tax collector, "C," "g," "F," ", 2nd cousin J. Adams.

Bartlett, Josiah

1729 - 1795, full, "J.B.," CC (1775-76, 78-79), SC of NH, Pres. NH, First Gov. NH, Physician, "C," very unique "d," "N," Rare in ALS.

Braxton, Carter

1736- 1797, full, CC (1775-76, 77-83, 85), VA delegate, "Br" combo, "th" combo, "d," Uncommon in ALS.

Carroll, Charles

1737-1832, "Ch. Carroll of Carrollton," CC (1776-78), MD delegate, USS (1789-92), MD con. (1776), "y," "Ch" combo, looping ending strokes,Last surviving Signer.

Chase, Samuel

1741-1811, full, CC (1774-78, 84, 85), USSC (1796-1811), Com. of Corr. (1774), American jurist, "d," "C', "p".

Clark, Abraham

1726-1794, "Abra: Clark," CC (1776-78, 79-83, 87-89), NJ delegate, US Congress (1791-94), American politician, "f," "p," very consistent character slant, Very rare in ALS.

Clymer, George

1739-1813, "Geo Clymer," CC (1776-78, 80-83), First Cong. (1789-91), American politician, Phil. merchant, "C," "d," "y," "N," smooth flowing, Rare in Revolutionary War dated material.

Ellery, William

1727- 1820, "Wm: Ellery," CC (1776-81, 83-85), RI delegate, American politician, "d," "f," "G," variations in "P," "t," some examples using lined paper.

Floyd, William

1734 - 1823, "Wm.Floyd," CC (1774-77, 78-83), NY delegate, USHR (1789-91), "d," "g," lower case descenders, Extremely rare in ALS.

Franklin, Benjamin

1706-1790, "B Franklin," diplomat, American patriot, inventor, writer/publisher, "C," "Th" combo, "p," "of" combo, Typically large attractive signature

Gerry, Elbridge

1744 - 1814, "E Gerry," CC (1776-81, 83-85) VP (1813-14), Gov. Mass. (1810-11), American politician, Both "y," "d" - especially at the end of a word, Signed both DOI & AOC.

Gwinnett, Button

1732 - 1777, full, CC (1776-77), Georgia delegate, Pres. GA (March-May 1777), American Revolutionary leader, "G". "tt" combination, Estimates of 51 - 60 signatures in existance.

Hall, Lyman

1724-1790, full, CC (1775-78), 1780), GA delegate, Gov. GA (1783), American Revolutionary leader, "H," Hall is rare in all forms.

Hancock, John

1737-1793, full, CC (1775-80, 85, 86), Mass. delegate, First Gov. Mass. (1780-85, 87-93), SL,

American Revolutionary politician, "C," "P," "d," "H," The first signer of the DOI.

Harrison, Benjamin
1726-1791, "Benj. Harrison," CC (1774-78), VA delegate, SL (1749-75), Gov. VA (1782-84), American Revolutionary leader, "B," "th" combo, Harrison is uncommon in ALS.

Hart, John
1711-1779, full, CC (1776), N.J. Provincial Assembly (1761-71), N.J. Council of Safety (1778-79), "C," "f".

Hewes, Joseph
1730-1779, full, decorative lines beneath sig., CC (1774-77, 1779), N.C. Senate (1763), American Revolutionary leader, "d," "D," consistent in slant, Hewes extremely scarce in any form.

Heyward, Thomas, Jr.
1746-1809, "Thos Heyward Junr," CC (1776-78), S.C. Provincial Congress (1774, 1775), American patriot, soldier, judge, "T," "H," "d".

Hooper, William
1742-1790, "Wm Hooper," CC (1774-77), All five N.C. Provincial Congresses, American Revolutionary leader, lawyer, judge,"f," "y," "ff" combination, One of the four rarest signers.

Hopkins, Stephen
1707-1785, "Step Hopkins," CC (1774-80), Gov. R.I. (1755, 56, 58-61, 63, 64, 67), American Colonial administrator, "P', "D," "d," "C".

Hopkinson, Francis
1737-1791, "Fran Hopkinson," CC (1776), Dist. judge (1789-90), American Revolutionary political leader, lawyer, writer, "D," "P," "H," Played a part in designing flag.

Huntington, Samuel
1731-1796, "S Huntington," CC (1776-84, as Pres. 1779-81, 83), Gov. C.T. (1786-96) , American Revolutionary politician, "I," "t"

Jefferson, Thomas, (See Presidents of the US)

Lee, Francis Lightfoot
1734-1797, full, CC (1775-79), Virginia House of Burgesses (1758-68, 69-78), American Revolutionary politician, "V', "d", Lee is rare in any form.

Lee, Richard Henry
1732-1794,"R.H. Lee," CC (1774-79), C (1784-89), USS (1789-92), Virginia House of Burgesses (1758-75), American Revolutionary statesman, "I," Signed both DOI & Con.

Lewis, Francis
1713-1803, full, adds decorative lines, CC (1774-79), NY, American merchant and patriot, "C," "F," "Th" combination.

Livingston, Philip
1716-1778, "Phil Livingston," CC (1774-78), American Revolutionary merchant and patriot, "P,"

"q," sig. often vertical slant   .

Lynch, Thomas, Jr.

1749-1779,"Lynch" - most samples cut from lib. books, CC (1776-77), American Revolutionary patriot, planter, Lost at sea, second rarest signer.(c. 1960, 81 auto., 2 ALS, 10 DS, 61 sigs.)

McKean, Thomas

1734-1817, "Tho M:Kean," CC & C of the Con. (1774-83), DE, Chief Jus. PA (1777-99), Gov. PA 1799-1801), American Revolutionary politician, jurist, "J", "D"

Middleton, Arthur

1742-1787, full, CC 1776-78, 81-83), S.C., American Revolutionary patriot, "ff" combination, "f," "d," One of the five rarest signers.

Morris, Lewis

1726-1789, full, CC (1775-77), N.Y., "L," "M," "T', "f"

Morris, Robert

1734-1806, "Robt Morris," CC (1775-78), Supt. Finance, USS (1789-95)   Bank of N. America (1782), Con. Con. (1787), American merchant, financier, politician, "th" combination, Imprisoned 1798-1801, died in poverty.

Morton, John

1724-1777, full, may add decorative lines, CC (1774-77), del. Stamp Act Con. (1765), PA Assem. (1756-76), American Revolutionary patriot, Sherriff, "d"

Nelson, Thomas, Jr.

1738-1787, "Thos Nelson Jr.," CC (1775-77, 79), VA, Gov. VA (1781), American Revolutionary politician, patriot, "th" and "of" combinations

Paca, William

1740-1799, "W. Paca," CC (1774-79), MD, Gov. MD (1782-85), Dist. Judge (1789-99) American Revolutionary leader, "th" and "to" combinations

Paine, Robert Treat

1731-1814, "R T Paine"   , CC (1774-78) MA, First At. Gen. MA (1777-90), MA Sup. Court American jurist, "y," Paine rare in ALS

Penn, John

1741-1788, "J Penn," CC (1775-80) NC, American Rev. leader, lawyer (VA/NC), "E," "y," "d" Penn is rare in any form

Read, George

1733-1798, "Geo: Read," CC (1774-77), DE, USS (1789-93), DE Con. Con. (1776), Con. Con. (1787), Just., American Revolutionary leader, lawyer, "f," crossing of "t"

Rodney, Cesar

1728-1784, full, CC 1774-76, 77, 78, Pres. of DE, American Revolutionary patriot, "th" and "of" combo, flamboyant sig.

Ross, George
1730-1779, "Geo: Ross," CC (1774-77), Judge of the Admirality (1779), American Revolutionary lawyer, jurist, patriot, "d," "C"

Rush, Benjmain
1745-1813, "Benj.n: Rush," "Dr. Rush," CC (1776, 77), Sur. Gen. Army (1797-1813), American Revolutionary physician, educator, "f," crossing of "t," Wrote num. medical books, scarce in ALS

Rutledge, John
1739-1800, Twice in CC, Sup. Ct. Justice (1790-91), First Pres. SC (1776-78), Gov. (1779-82), "C," "L" , Rare in ALS

Sherman, Roger
1721-1793, full, CC (1774-81, 83, 84), USHR, (1789-91), USS, SL, CT (1755, 56, 58-61, 64-66, 66-85) American Revolutionary leader, jurist, "D," "d," Only person to sign all four state papers.

Smith, James
1719-1806, "Ja.s Smith," CC, PA (1776-78), American Revolutionary leader, lawyer, "D," "f," "d," consistant in slant, may add "Atty for Def.d" on legal documents

Stockton, Richard
1730-1781, May add decorative lines, CC (1776), NJ Ex. Council , Assoc. Just (1774-76), American Revolutionary leader, lawyer, Very rare in ALS, rare in DS

Stone, Thomas
1743-1787, "T Stone," CC, MD (1775-78), Con. of Confed. (1784-85), American Revolutionary patriot and lawyer, "P," "th" combination, Very rare in ALS

Taylor, George
1716-1781, "Geo: Taylor," CC, PA (1776-77), PA member Com. of Correspondence American Revolutionary patriot, iron man, Very rare in any form

Thornton, Matthew
1714-1803, full, CC, NH (1776), American Revolutionary patriot, physician, "C', "f," "T," "t" Extremely rare in ALS

Walton, George
1741-1804, "Geo Walton," CC, GA (1776-79, 81), USS (1795-96), Gov. GA (1779-80, 89), C. Just. , judge, American Revolutionary politician, jurist, "Y," "y," Signed both DOI & AOC, rare in ALS

Whipple, William
1730-1785, "Wm. Whipple," CC, NH (1775-78), Asst. Just. Sup. Ct. of NH (1782-85), American Revolutionary leader, "th," "to" combos, crossing of "t"

Williams, William
1731-1811, " W Williams," CC, CT (1776-78, 83, 84), American Revolutionary politician, merchant,"C," "d," "t," Rare in ALS

Wilson, James

1742-1798, full, Con. (1774, 75-77), CC (1782, 83, 85-87), Ass. Just. US Sup Court (1789-98), delegate, American Revolutionary jurist, politician, "wh" combo, "D," , "f," "th" combo, Rare in war date ALS

Witherspoon, John

1723-1794, "Jn Witherspoon," CC, NJ (1776-79, 80-81, 82), College Pres. (Princeton) American Revolutionary patriot, clergyman, Many writing examples often very small, Rare in any form, leader Presbyterian church

Wolcott, Oliver

1726-1797, full, may add "judge," "O Wolcott," CC (1775-78, 80-84), Gov. CT (1796-97), Lt. Gov. (1787-96), American Revolutionary leader, patriot, "d," can be sloppy at times

Wythe, George

1726-1806, "G Wythe," flamboyant, CC, VA (1775-77), Judge VA High Ct, member Con. Con. American Revolutionary statesman, jurist, "f," "d," "y," well-formed letters, Very rare in ALS, rare in DS, taught Jefferson

Name	DB/DD	SIG	LS/DS	ALS	Comment
Skene, Phillip	1725-1810				Loyalist, PU
Skenesboro (Whitehall), NY	July 6, 1777				
Skinner, Corlandt	1728-1799	50	100	150	Tory officer
Smallwood, William	1732-1792				CG, Congress, G/ MD, PU
Smith, Francis	1723-1791				British officer, PU
Smith, James	c.1719-1806		2500	3500	Signer, nearly all papers destroyed in fire
Smith, Joshua Hett	1736-1818				Lawyer, NY, patriot, PU
Smith, William (I)	1697-1769				Colonial jurist, PU
Smith, William (II)	1728-1793				Jurist, writer, loyalist, PU
Somerset Courthouse (Millstone), NJ	January 20 and 22, 1777 & June 17, 1777				
Sower, Christopher	1754-1799				Loyalist, PA, sp. variations, PU
Spalding, Simon	1742-1814				Cont'l officer, CT, PA, PU
Spencer's Tavern	June 26, 1781				
Spencer, Joseph	1714-1789				Cont'l general, PU
Springfield, NJ, Raid of Knyphausen	June 7-23, 1780				
Springfield, NY	May 1778				
St. Clair, Arthur	1737-1818		500		CG, Congress, G/NW Ter.
St. Johns (St. Jean), Canada	May 14-18, 1775, Sept. 5 - November 2, 1775				
St. Louis, MO	May 26, 1780				
St. Luc de La Corne, Pierre					Fr. Canadian, sp. variations, PU

Name	DB/DD	SIG	LS/DS	ALS	Comment
St. Lucia captured by British	December 12-28, 1778				
Stansbury, Joseph	? - 1809				Loyalist secret agent, poet, PU
Stark, John	1728-1822	400	650	1375	Cont'l general, rare
Staten Island Expedition of Alexander	January 14-15, 1780				
Staten Island, NY, Sullivan's raid	August 22, 1777				
Stedman, Charles	c. 1745-1812				British officer, historian, PU
Stephen, Adam	1718-1791	75	150	300	Cont'l general
Steuben, Fried. W. A.	1730-1794	1275	2775		IG of the Cont'l Army
Stevens, Edward	1745-1820				Militia general, SL, VA, PU
Stewart, Alexander	c.1741-1794				British officer, PU
Stewart, Walter	c.1756-1796				Cont'l officer, PU
Stiles, Ezra	1727-1795				Patriot, Pres. Yale, PU
Stockton, Richard	1730-1781	525	975	2875	Signer , lawyer
Stone, Thomas	1743-1787	620	1100	2750	Signer, MD, few letters have survived
Stono Ferry, SC	June 20, 1779				
Stony Point, NY	July 16, 1779				
Stormont, David Murray					Viscount, PU
Stuart, John					British Supt. of Indian Affairs, PU
Suffren de saint Tropez,					
Pierre Andre de	1729-1788				French admiral, PU
Sullivan, John	1740-1795	165	400	600	Cont'l general, SL, G/NH
Sumner, Jethro	c.1735-1785				Cont'l general, PU
Sumter, Thomas	1734-1832	400	1150	2260	CO, SC, USS, Congress
Sunbury (Ft. Morris), GA	January 9, 1779				
Sutherland, William					BO, confusion over identity, PU
Swift, Henry					Cont'l officer, PU
Tallmadge, Benjamin (Jr.)	1754-1835	250	500	850	CO, secret service, Cong.
Tappan Massacre, NJ	September 28, 1778				
Tarleton's Viriginia Raid of	July 9 - 24, 1781				
Tarleton, Banastre	1754-1833			1200	British officer
Tarrant's Tavern, NC	February 1, 1781				
Taylor, George	1716-1781			35000	Signer DOI, Cont'l Congress, 4th toughest
Tearcoat Swamp, SC	October 25, 1780				
Ternay, Charles L.	1722-1780				French admiral, PU
Thacher, James	1754-1844		300		Cont'l surgeon, writer, historian
Thicketty Fort (Fort Anderson), SC	July 30, 1780				
Thomas, John	1724-1776				Cont'l general, rare, PU

Name	DB/DD	SIG	LS/DS	ALS	Comment
Thompson, Benjamin	1753-1814	250	500		Colonial adm., physicist, Loyalist
Thompson, William	1736-1781				Cont'l general, PU
Thornton, Matthew	c.1714-1803	650	1500	2000	Signer DOI, NH, SL, "M. Thornton" or full

Throg's Point (Neck), NY   October 12-18, 1776

Thruston, Charles Mynn	1738-1812				Cont'l officer, PU

Ticonderoga, NY   1755-1759, May 10, 1775, July 2-5, 1777

Tilghman, Tench	1744-1786				Adc and milt. sec. to GW, PU
Tonyn, Patrick	1725-1804				British officer, Gov. E. FL, PU
Townshend, Charles	1725-1767				Brit. pol., PU

Treadwell's Neck, LI, NY   October 10, 1781
Trenton, NJ   December 26, 1776

Trescott, Lemuel	? - 1826				Cont'l officer, PU

Trois Rivieres (Three Rivers), CanadaJune 8, 1776

Tronson de Coudray, P.	1738-1777				Cont'l general, PU
Trumbull, Benjamin	1735-1820				Clergyman and historian, PU
Trumbull, John	(see Artists)				
Trumbull, John	1710-1785	300	600	1100	G/ CN, the elder
Trumbull, John	(see Authors)				
Trumbull, John	1740-1809	140	320	600	Gov. CN, Congress, USS
Trumbull, Joseph	1738-1778				Commissary General Army, PU

Trumbull-Iris Engagement   August 8, 1781
Trumbull-Watt Engagement   June 2, 1780

Tryon, William	1729-1788	150	300	650	Royal Governor of NC & NY
Tuffin, Marquis de La R.	1750-1793				French vol., "Col. Armand," PU
Tupper, Benjamin	1738-1792				Cont'l officer, SL, rare, PU
Turnbull, George					Tory officer, PU

Unadilla, NY   October 6 - 8, 1778
Valcour Island (Lake Champlain) October 11-13, 1776
Valley Forge, PA   September 18, 1777
Valley Forge, PA, Winter Quarters December 19, 1777 - June 18, 1778

Van Cortlandt, Philip	1749-1831				Cont'l officer, sl, USHR, PU
Van Schaick, Gose	1736-1789				Cont'l officer, PU
Van wart, Isaac	1760-1828				Captor of John Andre, PU
Varick, Richard	1753-1831	100	200	300	CO, GW confidential secretary
Varnum, James Mitchell	1748-1789				Cont'l general, PU
Vaughan, John	? - 1795				British general, PU
Vence, Jean Gaspard	1747-1808				French privateer, admiral, PU
Vergennes, Charles G.	1717-1787				French foreign minister, PU
Vernier, Pierre-Francois	c.1737-1780				Vol., Maj., sp. variations, PU
Vernon, Edward	1684-1757				Brit. admiral, "Mt. Vernon," PU

Name	DB/DD	SIG	LS/DS	ALS	Comment
Vose, Joseph	1738-1816				Cont'l officer, very rare, PU
Wadsworth, Jeremiah	1743-1804	175	350	475	Commiss. gen.Army, Congress

Wahab's Plantation, NC September 21, 1780

Wallace, James	1731-1803				British naval officer, PU
Wallis, Samuel	?-1778				Loaylist secret agent, PU
Walpole, Horatio	1717-1797				English politician,writer, PU
Walpole, Robert	1676-1745	125	250	550	First Prime Minister
Walton, George	1741-1804	375	985	1250	Signer, ESPV-DS, $600-SDS-$2500
Ward, Artemas	1727-1800	375	1250		American politician and general
Ward, Samuel	1725-1776				G/RI, Congress, PU
Ward, Samuel (Jr.)	1756-1832				Cont'l officer, PU
Warner, Seth	1743-1784	250	700	1350	Militia officer, VT

Warren or White Horse Tavern, PA September 16, 1777

Warren, James	1726-1808	125	250	500	Politician leader
Warren, John	1753-1815				Cont'l surgeon, Mass., PU
Warren, Joseph	1741-1775	7000			Patriot leader killed at Bunker Hill
Washington, George	(see Presidents of the United States)				
Washington, William	1752-1810	100	200	300	Cont'l officer, relative of C in C.

Watereee Ferry, SC August 15, 1780

Watson, John W.T.	1748-1826				British officer, sp. variations, PU

Wawarsing, NY August 22, 1781
Waxhaws, SC May 29, 1780

Wayne, Anthony "Mad"	1745-1796	750	1750	3500	CG., papers PAHS, SDA-2X
Webb, Samuel B.	1753-1807	100	375	600	CO, adc/sec. to GW, SALS-2X
Webster, James	c.1743-1781				British officer, PU
Weedon, George	c.1730-1793				CG, act. AG GW, Joe Gourd, PU
Weems, Mason Locke	1759-1825				Clergyman, bookseller, PU
Wemyss, James					British officer, "most hated," PU
Wentworth, Paul	?-1793				Double spy, PU

Wetzell's Mills (or Mill) March 6, 1781
Wheeling, W. VA Sept. 1, 1777 and Sept. 11-13, 1782

Whipple, Abraham	1733-1819	250	600		CO, captured first British frigate
Whipple, William	1730-1785	700	1500	3000	Signer DOI, NH, "Wm: Whipple," DS-$2700
Whitcomb, John	1713-1785				Militia general, PU

White Plains, NY October 28, 1776

Whitefield, George	1714-1779				Evangelist, controversial, PU

Whitehaven, Engalnd April 27-18, 1778
Whitemarsh, PA December 5-8, 1777

Name	DB/DD	SIG	LS/DS	ALS	Comment
Wickes, Lambert	c.1742-1777				Cont'l naval officer, PU
Wilkes, John	1727-1797				British politician, PU
Wilkinson, James	1757-1825	150	375	450	Cont'l officer, scoundrel
Willett, Marinus	1740-1830	100	150	250	Cont'l officer
Williams, David	1754-1831				Captor of John Andre, PU
Williams, Otho Holland	1749-1794	150	300	640	Cont'l general, talented cmdr.
Williams, William	1731-1811	300	875	1175	Signer, CT, DS - $1450 (order), ESPV-DS

Williamson's Plantation, SC   July 12, 1780

Williamson, Andrew	c.1730-1786				Turncoat militia general, PU

Wilmington, NC   February 1 - November 18, 1781

Name	DB/DD	SIG	LS/DS	ALS	Comment
Wilmot, William					CO, last casualty of war?, PU
Wilson, James	(see United Staes Supreme Court)				
Witherspoon, John	1723-1794	750	2550	6500	Signer, clergyman, Col. Pres., scarce ALS
Woedtke, Frederick W.	c.1740-1776				Cont'l general, ext. rare, PU
Wolcott, Oliver	1726-1797	200	575	1200	Signer DOI, militia general, CT, SALS-2X
Wolfe, James	1727-1759				British general, PU
Woodford, William	1734-1780				Cont'l general, PU
Woodhull, Natahaniel	1722-1776				Militia general, PU
Wooster, David	1711-1777	250	740	2500	Cont'l general
Wright, Gov. Sir James	c.1714-1785				Royal Gov. GA, PU

Wyoming Valley "Massacre," PA July 3-4, 1778

Wyth, George Wythe"	1726-1806	600	1450	3000	Signer, VA, statesman, jurist, "G

Yorktown Campaign   May - October 1781
Young's House (Four Corners), NYFebruary 3, 1780

Zane, Ebenezer	1747-1812				Pioneer, VA, PU
Zane, Elizabeth	c.1759-c.1847				Heroine, PU
Zeisberger, David	1721-1808				Moravian missionary, PU

ROYALTY/HEADS OF STATE

WHAT YOU NEED TO KNOW

* If you can get past the language, cultural barriers, increased postage, and unique address formats, you may find yourself discovering this fascinating niche of the hobby.

* Similar to Presidents of the United States, the signatures of world leaders are preferred during their reign. A good example of the contrast in availability is Edward VII (England), Victoria's son, who is common as Prince of Wales, but scarce as King.

* Few prominent leaders, prior to the sixteenth century, learned to sign their names.

* Scribes were often used prior to the sixteenth century.

* Prior to the fourteenth century, most documents were not dated. An analysis of handwriting styles is how archivists determine dating.

TRENDS

* Quality photographs (popular by the mid-1850s) are the form of choice in this niche. Their price can vary significantly depending upon the subject.

* The most common form encountered is is a facsimile-signed photograph (often less than 8" x 10").

* Limited quality material in any form enters the market and when encountered is typically due to a particular dealer.

* Some dealers who specialize in this area often go overseas to make major purchases. Upon their arrival back to the United States often a large quantity of material is offered into the market. This is why quality material often enters the autograph market sporadically.

MARKET FACTS

* According to my research, only signed photographs from athletes and signatures of prominent women have had greater market appreciation during the last two and a half decades than the autographed pictures of world leaders and politicians.

* As a niche, including all forms minus SP, this area of the hobby out performed many including American authors, U.S. Presidents and even Scientists & doctors.

Abbreviations: b. = brother of, d. = daughter of, s. = son of, Sig = signature, LS/DS = letter signed/document signed, ST = used stamps (wood)

Name	db/dd	Sig.	LS/DS	ALS	Comments
Abdul-Hamid II	1842-1918	55	165		Last Sultan of Turkey
Abdullah Ibn Hussein	1882-1951				First King of Jordan, PU
Aberdeen, George G.	1784-1860	40			British statesman
Adenauer, Konrad	1876-1967	50	150	165	Chancellor, Germany, SP - $150
Albert, Prince	1819-1861	140	250	430	Husband of Queen Victoria
Albert I (Belgium)	1875-1934	40	125		
Alexander I (Russia)	1777-1825	1325			MLS-1400, sig. French & Rus.
Alexander II (Russia)	1818-1881	375	740		LS-$750
Alexander III	1845-1894	130	315	600	Tsar of Russia, controversial
Alfonso XIII	1886-1941	225	500	600	King of Spain, var. "Yo El Rey"
Anne	1665-1714	525	1125	2200	England, ALS - $2115
Anne, Princess		100	200		England, SP - $150
Anne Boleyn	1504-1536				Wife Henry VIII, PU
Anne of Austria	1601-1666				Queen Consort Louis XIII, PU
Anne of Cleves	1515-1557				Wife Henry VIII, PU
Asquith, Herbert H.	1852-1928	35	70	150	British statesman
Augereau, Pierre F.C.	1757-1816	135	325	500	French marshal
Augustus II of Poland	1670-1733	375			
Auriol, Vincent	1884-1966	35	100		President of France
Attlee, Clement	1883-1967	55	100		British Socialist statesman
Baldwin, Stanley	1867-1947	50	100	130	British statesman
Balfour, Arthur J.	1848-1930	60	125	150	British statesman, philosopher
Barras, Paul J. F N	1755-1829				French revolutionary, PU
Beaverbrook, William M.	1879-1964	25	60		Statesman
Benes, Eduard	1884-1948	65	100		Czechoslovak patriot, SP - $185
Ben-Gurion, David	1886-1973	310	525	1150	Israeli statesman, SP - $550
Bevin, Ernest	1881-1951	25	50	110	British Labour statesman
Bhutto, Zulfikar Ali	1928-	30	65		President of Pakistan
Bismarck, Otto	1815-1898	280	575	730	"The Iron Chancellor"
Bonaparte, Joseph	1768-1844	125	245		Spain, LS-$225
Boris III	1894-1943	65	120		King of Bulgaria, SP - $170
Brandt, Willy	1913-1992	30	140		German statesman, SP - $70
Brezhnev, Leonid	1906-	320	800		Soviet statesman, SP -$365
Briand, Aristide	1862-1932	40	80		French statesman
Bruce, Stanley	1883-1967	20	45		Australian statesman
Burke, Edmund	1729-1797				British statesman, PU
Bustamante, Sir W. Alex.	1884-1977				Jamaica, prime minister, PU

Dynasties of Europe - France (987-1848)
The dynasties of France are often divided into four branches: the Direct Capetians, the Valois Branch, the Bourbon Branch and the Restored Bourbons. The last three Valois produced no male Heirs so the

Name	db/dd	Sig.	LS/DS	ALS	Comments

throne passed to the victor of the Wars of Religion, Henry of Navarre - distant cousin Louis IX, who began the reign of the Bourbon branch of the Capetians. (After 1700, and despite interruptions, the Bourbon family became kings of Spain.) Reigns: The Bourbon Branch : Henry IV (1589-1610), Louis XIII (1610-43), Louis XIV (1643-1715), Louis XV (1715-74), Louis XVI (1774-92), French Revolution and Napoleon (1792-1814); Restored Bourbons: Louuis XVIII (1814-24), Charles X (1824-30), Louis Philippe (Bourbon-Orleans) (1830-48).

Name	db/dd	Sig.	LS/DS	ALS	Comments
Callaghan, James	1912-	35	70	140	British prime minister, SP - $50
Canning, George	1770-1827	50	100	150	British prime minister
Carlos I, King	1863-1908				Portugal King, assassinated, PU
Carlos III, King	1716-1788				King of Spain, "Yo el Rey" var.
Carlotta (Mexico)	1840-1927	350	700		
Casement, Roger	1864-1916				Irish nationalist, hanged, scarce
Catherine de Medicis	1519-1589				Queen of Henry II of France
Catherine II, the Great	1729-1796	750	1750		LS - $1500, $1250, Russia
Cavour, C. Camillo B. d.	1810-1861	300	500		Italian statesman
Cecil, William					First baron Burghley
Chamberlain, A. Neville	1869-1940	75	225		British prime minister, SP - $175
Charlemagne (France)					PU, extremely rare
Charles I (England)	1600-1649	800	2225	4000	s. James VI of Scotland
Charles II (England)	1630-1685	1000	2250		DS-$2750, s. Charles I
Charles IX(France)	1550-1574	435	1275		s. Henry II
Charles V (France)	1337-1422	600	1800		DS-$2300
Charles VI (France)	1368-1422	400	1200		"Charles the Mad"
Charles VII (France)	1403-1461				s. Charles VI, PU
Charles VIII (France)	1470-1498				"the Affable", scarce, PU
Charles XIV (Sweden)	1763-1844	150	500		DS-$450
Charles, Prince of Wales	1948-	750		1250	SP - $750
Chiang Kai-Shek	1887-1974	115	230	500	Chinese dictator
Chifley, Joseph B.	1885-1951				Australian statesman . PU
Christina (Sweden)	1626-1689	1500			d. Gustav II Adolphus
Christian V (Denmark)	1649-1699				PU
Churchill, Sir Winston	1874-1965	750	1500	3000	Br. prime minister, SP - $2650
Clarendon, Edward H.	1609-1674				English statesman, PU
Clemenceau, Georges	1841-1929	125	180	200	French statesman
Colbert, Jean B.	1619-1683				French statesman, PU
Collins, Michael	1890-1922				Irish nationalist, PU
Compton, Spencer	1673-1743				English statesman, PU
Cromwell, Oliver	1599-1658				"Oliver P" - protector, PU
Cromwell, Richard	1626-1712				s. Oliver (John Clarke), PU
Derby, Edward	1799-1869				British statesman, PU
DeValera, Eamon	1882-1975				Irish statesman, PU
Devereux, Robert	1566-1601				Second earl of Essex, PU
Devonshire, William C.	1720-1764				Br. prime minister, scarce, PU
Devonshire, Victor C.W.	1868-1938				Gov. - General of Canada, PU
Diana, Princess	1961-1997	1250		6750	SALS-$10000, CC-$7500, CC w/Char. $3500
Diaz, Porfirio	1830-1915	100	200	300	Mexican president
Disraeli, Benjamin	1804-1881	200	400	750	British prime minister

Name	db/dd	Sig.	LS/DS	ALS	Comments
Dolfuss, Engelbert	1892-1934				Austrian statesman, murdered
Douglas-Home, Sir Alec	1903-				British statesman, PU
Dubcek, Alexander	1921-	100	150	250	Czechoslovak statesman
Edward IV (England)	1442-1483				Scarce, PU
Edward V (England)	1470-1483				Excessively rare, PU
Edward VI (England)	1537-1553				ST, very rare, PU
Edward VII (England)	1841-1910	150	500		s. Queen Victoria, ST
Edward VIII (England)	1894-1972	1100	2300		DS-$2750, SB-$1200
Elizabeth I (England)	1533-1603	6000	12000		Scarce and in demand
Elizabeth II (England)	1926-	350	700		d. George VI
Espartero, Baldomero	1792-1879				Spanish statesman, PU
Essex, Robert D.	1566-1601				English nobleman, PU
Faisal (Bin Abdul Aziz)	1904-1975	50	100	165	King Saudi Arabia, assassinated
Farouk	1920-1965	35	110		King of Egypt, SP - $75
Ferdinand the Catholic	1452-1516				(Castile and Aragon), PU
Francis I (France)	1494-1547	600	1250		s. Charles, Count of Ang.
Francis II (France)	1544-1560				Excessively rare, PU
Francis Joseph	1830-1916				Austro-Hungarian emperor
Fraser, Peter	1884-1950	20	45		Prime minister New Zealand
Frederick II, the Great	1712-1786	500	1075	2425	DS-$975, (Prussia)
Gandhi, Indira	1917-1984	150	375	400	Prime minister India
George I (England)	1660-1727	300	1000	2500	s. Sophia
George II (England)	1683-1760	400	800	1250	s. George I
George III (England)	1738-1820	250	600	750	DS-$250, $475, $575SDS-2X
George IV (England)	1762-1830	130	400	700	s. George III
George V (England)	1865-1936	125	500	750	s. Edward VII, ST
George VI (England)	1895-1952	200	400		DS-$375, TDS-$195, s. Geo. V
Giscard D'EstainG, V	1926-	45	100		French president
Gladstone, William E.	1809-1898	75	150	300	British statesman
Goderich, F.J.R.	1782-1859	25	50	100	British statesman
Godolphin, Sidney	1645-1712	100	200	300	English statesman
Grafton, Augustus H. F.	1735-1811				English statesman, PU
Grenville, George	1712-1770	225	700		English statesman
Grenville, William W.	1759-1834	100	250	550	English statesman
Grey, Charles	1764-1845	50	100	180	British statesman
Grey, Lady Jane	1537-1554				Queen of England, 11 days, PU
Guizot, Francois P.	1787-1974				French statesman, PU
Gustav V	1907-1950				Sweden, PU
Gustav VI (Adolf)	1882-1973	140	275		Sweden
Gustavus Adolphus	1594-1632	165	300		s. Charles IX, Sweden
Haakon VII	1872-1957	125	210		First King of Norway
Haile Selassie	1891-1975	200	300	500	Emperor of Ehtiopia
Hardie, J Keir	1856-1915				Scotish politician, PU
Hastings, Warren	1732-1818	75	150	250	British administrator
Heath, Edward	1916-	50	100	125	British prime minister, SP - $50
Henry VII (England)	1457-1509	1250			s. E. Tudor, fin. DS available
Henry VIII (England)	1491-1547	4000			s. Henry VII, ST
Hertzog, James B.	1866-1942				S. African statesman, PU

Name	db/dd	Sig.	LS/DS	ALS	Comments
Hirohito, Emperor	1901-	2000			Emperor of Japan
Ho Chi-Minh	1892-1969	500	1150	2000	Vietnamese statesman
Hughes, William M.	1864-1952				Australian statesman, PU
Hussein I, King	1935-	100	165	280	King of Jordan

Dynasties of Europe - The Holy Roman Empire (962-1806)

The Habsburgs
The House of Habsburg - a version of the name of their castle, was one of the most eminent of the European dynasties. From the 15th century they became hereditary rulers of the Empire and through a series of marriages gained, by inheritance, the Netherlands, the Spanish kingdoms and Spain's empire in the New World, and Hungary and Bohemia. (From the reign of Francis I, the official family name is Habsburg-Lorraine). Reigns: Joseph I (1705-11), Charles VI (1711-40), Interregnum - 1740-42, Charles VII (1742-45), Francis I (1745-65), Joseph II (1765-90), Leopold II (1790-92), Francis II (1792-1806).

Name	db/dd	Sig.	LS/DS	ALS	Comments
Inonu, Ismet	1884-				Turkish statesman, PU
Isabella, the Catholic	1451-1504	1000	3400		(2)DS w/Ferdinand V - $6400
Ito, Hirobuni	1841-1909	75	150		Japanese statesman
Ivan IV, the Terrible	1530-1584				s. Vasily III, Russia, scarce, PU
James I (England)	1566-1625	700	1400	3650	s. Mary, Queen of Scots, ST
James II (England)	1633-1701	500	1650	1750	s. Charles I, scarce as King
James V (Scotland)	1512-1542				f. M. Queen of Scots, PU
Jinnah, Quaid-i-Azim	1876-1948				Gov. General Pakistan, PU
Josephine, Empress	1763-1814	750	1500	2650	w. Napoleon
Juan Carlos	1938-				King of Spain, PU
Juarez, Benito	1806-1872	500	1250	1650	Mexican patriot
Kalakaua, David	1836-1891	125	375	725	Hawaii
Kamehameha IV	1824-1863	1150	2500		Hawaii
Kaunda, Kenneth	1924-	35	70		Zambian statesman
Kaunitz, W. A.	1711-1794				Austrian statesman, PU
Kenyatta, Jomo	1889-	100	200		Kenyan national leader
Khama, Sir Seretse	1921-				Botswana national leader, PU
Khrushchev, Nikita	1894-1971	300	400	600	Soviet statesman
Kiesinger, Kurt G.	1904-				W. German statesman, PU
King, William L.	1874-1950	60	225		Canadian statesman
Kosygin, Alexei N.	1904-	250	500	1000	Soviet statesman
Kruger, Paul	1825-1904	100	285		S. African statesman
Laurier, Sir Wilfrid	1841-1919				Canadian prime minister, PU
Law, Andrew	1858-1923	40	80	140	British statesman
Lenin, Vladimir	1870-1924				Russian statesman, rare all forms
Leopold II of Belgium	1835-1909	125	400	600	s. Leopold I
Li Hung-Chang	1823-1901				Chinese statesman, PU
Liliuokalani	1838-1917	200	400	800	Queen of the Hawaiian Islands
Liverpool, Robert B.	1770-1828				British prime minister, PU
Loyd-George, David	1863-1945				British prime minister, PU
Louis XI (France)	1423-1483				s. Charles VII, PU
Louis XII (France)	1462-1515	800	1625		s. Charles
Louis XIII (France)	1601-1643	750	1500		s. Henry IV
Louis XIV (France)	1638-1715	500	1000		s. Louis XIII, numerous variations

Name	db/dd	Sig.	LS/DS	ALS	Comments
Louis XV (France)	1710-1774	700	1450	5000	s. Louis
Louis XVI (France)	1754-1793	350	1000		DS-$900
Louis XVII (France)	1785-1795				Rare signature, PU
Louis XVIII (France)	1755-1824	250	500	1200	
Ludwig I (Bavaria)	1786-1868	100	285	500	King of Bavaria
Maria Theresa (Austria)	1717-1780	200	575	850	Empress, available
Marie Antoinette	1755-1793	1500	5000		Queen, (France), sig. variations
Marie Louise	1791-1847				w. Napoleon, small sig.
Marie de Medici	1573-1642	500	1000		Queen
Mary Stuart (Q. of Scots)	1542-1587				Scarce LS/DS, PU
Mary I (England)	1516-1558	1000	3250	7000	d. Henry VIII, ST, Mary Tudor
Mary II	1662-1694	540	1250		
Masaryk, Thomas	1850-1937	80	160	300	President Czechoslovakia
Maximilian (Mexico)	1832-1867	275	550	1100	b. Francis Joseph
Maximilian I	1459-1519				Holy Roman Emperor, PU
Maximillian II	1527-1576	200	450	900	Holy Roman Emperor
Medici Cosmo I de	1389-1464	450	1250		Fdr. Medici dynasty
Meir, Golda	1898-1979	125	250	500	Israeli prime minister
Melbourne, William L.	1779-1848	40	80	150	British prime minister
Menzies, Sir Robert	1894-	25	50	100	Australian statesman
Metternich, Klemens W.	1773-1859	100	250	350	Austrian statesman
Mikoyan, Anastas I.	1895-				Soviet statesman, PU
Mongkut (Siam), Rama IV	1804-1868				King of Siam, PU
Mussolini, Benito	1883-1945	325	500	1150	Italian dictator
Napoleon I (France)	1769-1821	750	1625		LS-$1395, $2200
Napoleon II	1811-1832				King of Rome, rare, PU
Napoleon III (France)	1808-1873	125	465	550	DS-$500, MA (DS)-$600
Nasser, Gamal	1918-1970	100	375	400	Egyptian statesman
Nehru, Jawaharlal	1889-1964	150	300	675	Indian statesman
Newcastle, Thomas	1693-1768				English statesman, PU
Nicholas I	1796-1855	800	1500		Tsar of Russia
Nicholas II (Russia)	1868-1918	1250	2500		TDS-$3000, DS-$1800
Nyerere, Julius	1922-	15	30	75	Tanzania statesman
Olav V	1903-				King of Norway, PU
Paasikivi, Juo	1870-1956				Finnish statesman, PU
Pahlavi, Mohammed	1919-	125	200	300	Ruler of Iran
Palmerston, Henry J.	1784-1865	50	110	150	British prime minister
Papen, Franz von	1879-1969	75	150	225	German chancellor
Paul I	1754-1801	250	550	1500	Tsar of Russia
Pearson, Lester	1897-1972	30	70	135	Canadian prime minister
Pedro II (Brazil)	1798-1834	100	200	300	s. John VI of Portugal
Peel, Sir Robert	1788-1850	60	120	165	British prime minister
Pelham, Henry	1695-1754	50	135	250	British prime minister
Perceval, Spencer	1762-1812	130	270		Br. prime minister, assassinated
Peron, Juan	1895-1974	150	320	525	Argentinian dictator
Peter I, the Great (Russia)	1672-1725	1000	4000	8000	ADS-$4875
Philip, prince consort (England)					PU
Phillip II (Spain)	1527-1598	300	1650		LS-$2750

Name	db/dd	Sig.	LS/DS	ALS	Comments
Phillip IV	1605-1665	250	600	1000	King of Spain
Philip, Prince	1921-	125	200		Consort Elizabeth II
Pitt, William	1708-1778	165	325		Earl of Chatham, the Elder
Pitt, William	1759-1806	175	350		Youngest Brit. prime minister
Podgorny, Nikolay V.	1903-				Pres. USSR, scarce, PU
Poincare, Raymond	1860-1934	55	125	210	French prime minister
Pompadour, Jeanne A.	1721-1764	200	400	900	Mistress
Pompidou, Georges	1911-1974	25	45		French president
Portland, William H.	1738-1809	60	220		British prime minister

Dynasties of Europe - Romanov Dynasty (Russia)

Early in the 17th century, the national assembly elected Michael Romanov as czar in 1613. The dynasty died out in 1762 when at the death of czarina Elizabeth, her nephew Peter III briefly succeeded. His family ruled until the Russian Revolution. Their name was Holstein-Gottorp but ruled under the name Romanov. Reigns: Peter I, the Great, alone (1689-1725), Catherine I (1725-27), Peter II (1727-30), Anna (1730-40), Ivan VI (1740-41), Elizabeth (1741-62), Peter III (1762), Catherine II the Great (1762-96), Paul (1796-1801), Alexander I (1801-25), Nicholas I (1825-55), Alexander II (1855-81), Alexander III (1881-94), and Nicholas II (1894-1917).

Rainier III, Prince	1923-	100	200	300	Monaco ruler
Reading, Rufus D.	1860-1935	50	100	200	English statesman
Rhee, Syngman	1875-1965	155	260	825	Korean president
Richard III (England)	1452-1485				Scarce, PU
Rockingham, Charles	1730-1782	150	300	500	English statesman, ESPV-DS
Rosas, Juan M.	1793-1877	20	40	75	Dictator Argentina
Rosebery, Archibald P	1847-1929	30	65	120	British prime minister

Dynasties of Europe - Spain (1506- present)

Until 1808 there was no kingdom called Spain but a number of seperate entities of which Castile and Argon were the only principal ones. With the deaths of Isabella, then Ferdinand, the crowns passed to their grandson, the Habsburg Charles of Ghent; in the Empire he was Charles V, in the Spanish kingdoms Charles I. His Habsburg Dynasty ruled until 1700 when the line died out and was replaced by the Bourbon Dynasty which has ruled with numerous interruptions until today.

Habsburgs
Reigns: Charles I (Holy Roman Emperor as Charles V) (1506-56)
Phillip II (1556-98)
Phillip III (1598-1621)
Phillip IV (1621-65)
Charles II (1665-1700)

Bourbons
Reigns: Phillip V (1700-46)
Ferdinand VI (1746-59)
Charles III (1759-88)
Charles IV (1788-1808)
Joseph Bonaparte (1808-13)
Ferdinand VII (1814-33)
Isabella II (1833-68)
Interregnum (1868-70)
Amadeo (1870-73)
Republic (1873-75)
Alphonso XII (1875-85)

Name	db/dd	Sig.	LS/DS	ALS	Comments
	Alphonso XIII (1886-1931)				
	Republic (1931-36)				
	Civil War (1936-39)				
	Franco regime (1939-75)				
	Juan Carlos (1975-present)				
Sadat, Anwar	1918-1981	125	230	320	Egyptian statesman
Salisbury, Robert	1830-1903	45	90	175	English statesman
Schmidt, Helmut	1918-	25	40	70	German statesman
Shelburne, William	1737-1805	55	150		English statesman
Sidmouth, Henry A.	1757-1844	40	75	110	English statesman
Silhouette, Etienne de	1709-1767				French finance minister, PU
Simpson, Wallis	1896-1986	160	350	600	Popular
Smuts, Jan C.	1870-1950	65	125	250	S. African statesman
Stuart, P. Charles E.	1720-1788				g. James II, "Charles R", PU
Stuart, P. James E.	1688-1766				s. James II, "Jacques R", PU
Sun Yat-Sen	1866-1925	600	1125	1750	Chinese patriot

Dynasties of Europe - England (871-Present)

Stuarts

Elizabeth I never married and had no heirs, so the Tudor line died with her. Rule passed to Elizabeth's cousin James VI of Scotland who ruled in England as James I. Turbulence with the Puritans and Parliamnet twice turned the Stuarts from the throne: Charles I was beheaded and James II was betrayed by his daughters and the husband of one, William of Orange. Reigns: James I (1603-25), Charles I (1625-49), Interregnum - Oliver Cromwell (1649-58) and Richard Cromwell (1658-59), Charles II (1660-85), James II (1685-88), William III and Mary II (1689-94), William III (1694-1702), Anne (1702-14).

Hanoverians and Windsors

Queen Anne had 17 children but died without leaving an heir. Geneological and religious considerations brought to the throne the German House of Hanover. After the reign of Victoria (the family is Saxe-Coburg-Gotha) under political pressures (1917), George V changed the name to Windsor. Reigns: George I (1714-27), George II (1727-60), George III (1760-1820), George IV (1820-30), William IV (1830-37), Victoria (1837-1901), Edward VII (1901-10), George V (1910-36), Edward VIII (1936), George VI (1936-52) and Elizabeth II (1952- present)

Name	db/dd	Sig.	LS/DS	ALS	Comments
Talleyrand, Charles	1754-1838	60	165		French statesman
Tallien, Jean L.	1769-1820				French revolutionary, PU
Thatcher, Margaret	1925-	50	150	240	English politician
Thiers, Louis	1797-1877	40	80	170	French statesman
Trudeau, Pierre	1919-	25	50	125	Canadian statesman
Turgot, A.R. Jacques	1727-1781				French economist, PU
Venizelos, Eleutherios	1864-1936	65	140		Greek prime minister
Victor Emanuel II (Italy)	1820-1878	100	225	420	King of Sardinia
Victor Emanuel III	1869-1947	50	110	200	King of Italy
Victoria (England)	1819-1901	200	635	900	DS-$750, $1500, SDS-2X
Vishinsky, Andrei	1883-1954	75	140		Soviet foreign minister
Waldegrave, James	1715-1763				English statesman, PU
Walpole, Robert	1676-1745	80	150	300	First prime minister England
Weizmann, Chaim	1874-1952	500	1225	2500	President of Israel

Name	db/dd	Sig.	LS/DS	ALS	Comments
William III (England)	1650-1702	700	1500	2650	
William IV (England)	1765-1837	100	285	400	SDS-2X, s. of George III
William (Wilhelm) I	1797-1888	100	250	375	King of Prussia
William II	1859-1941	200	400	500	Emperor of Germany
Wilson, Sir Harold	1916-	30	60	125	British Labour statesman
Zaimis, Alexander	1855-1936	50	100	200	Greek prime minister

Science & Technology

WHAT YOU NEED TO KNOW

* An area of the hobby that generally attracts collectors with similar backgrounds, some of the signatures of noble participants in medicine, science and technology are not only extremely valuable, but also difficult to find.

* Ironically, collecting in this area of the hobby may require some research. While many scientists such as Niels Bohr, Humphry Davy , and Elihu Thomson, are unfamiliar to most, the names of Thomas Edison, Isaac Newton, and Alexander Graham Bell are common to our vernacular.

* The signatures of those individuals who have contributed significantly in the field of medicine, science and technology is a fascinating area to collect. With discoveries and innovations, in numerous areas, almost on a daily basis this area is not only dynamic but exciting for collectors.

* Like so many areas of the hobby, form plays a significant factor in determining value. An original mathematical manuscript from French physicist Andre Marie Ampere or a document concerning the dosages of Mesothorium by PSI radiation signed by Marie Curie are always going to have a far greater value than a simple signature

MARKET FACTS

* Many of the innovators of key products and processes have been overlooked in the autograph market.

 * Autographed material from individuals such as the Swiss psychiatrist Carl Jung have shown significant price appreciation in all forms. While Jung and Freud autographed material are probably no surprise in their appreciation other notables such as B.F. Skinner - an outstanding signer through the mail during his lifetime, have also shown increased interest from collectors.

TRENDS

* This area, while showing strong broad-based increases, is prone to having certain individuals, such as Albert Einstein exhibit dramatic price increases in certain forms. The simple signature of Einstein appreciated nearly three fold to that of Louis Pasteur in the last twenty-five years.

* Outstanding manuscripts, documents and letters have been consistently available in the market over the past few decades.

* There is an inconsistency in the pricing of items in the ALS form - primarily for

key figures.

* There has been a tendency by some dealers to over exaggerate the importance of some material found in this area.

* A benefit of collecting in this area is that pricing - minus the ALS form, is relatively consistent, as is the appreciation.

* This market continues to lack a significant international presence necessary to stabilize certain values.

Note: The values listed below reflect material of average content. Key documents relating to a major theory or discovery often command a greater value (market dependent) that can only be gleaned through market research.

Abbreviations: AF - all forms, ESPV = exhibits significant pricing variations, NP = Nobel Prize, PU = pricing undetermined, RS = responsive signer

Name	db/dd	Sig.	DS	ALS	SP	Comments
Abel, John Jacob	1857-1938					U.S. biochemist, PU
Adams, John Couch	1819-1892	45	90	150		English astronomer
Adler, Alfred	1870-1937	125	550	1250	200	Austrian psychologist
Agassiz, Jean Louis R.	1807-1873	100	125	300	650	Swiss-born US paleontologist
Aiken, Howard	1900-1973	30	50	145	75	U.S. mathematician
Alexanderson, Ernst	1878-1975	50	125	225	175	High frequency alternator inven.
Alford, Andrew	1904-	20	35	70	40	Localizer antenna system inov.
Alvarez, Luis Walter	1911-1988	20	40	100	35	Radio distance & direction
Ampere, Andre-Marie	1775-1836	185	450	1500		Electrodynamics scientist
Anderson, Carl D.	1905-1991	25	60		60	U.S. physicist, NP
Angstrom, Anders J.	1814-1874	155	325	700		Swedish astrophysicist
Arkwright, Richard	1732-1792					English inventor
Armstrong, Edwin H.	1890-1954	80	225	450	275	Dev. method high freq. oscil.
Arrhenius, Svante A.	1859-1927	150	300	500		Swedish scientist
Aston, Francis W.	1877-1945	35	75	150	70	English physicist
Atanasoff, John V.	1903-1995	20	40	80	50	U.S. (ABC) computer pioneer
Attenborough, David	1926-	25	65	150	50	English traveler, zoologist
Axelrod, Julius	1912-	20	40	100	30	U.S. neuropharmacologist, NP
Avogardo, Amedeo	1776-1856	110	300	1100		Chemist, physicist
Babbage, Charles	1792-1871	200	400	600		English mathematician
Baekeland, Leo Hendrik	1863-1944	40	60	150	75	Synthetic resins dev., "Bakelite"
Baird, John L.	1888-1946	150	300		365	Scottish electrical eng.
Banting, Fredrick Grant	1891-1941	600	900	1500	1000	Canadian physician, insulin dev.
Bardeen, John	1908-1991	35	60	120	45	Transistor developer, NP
Barnard, Christian	1922-	30	65	125	50	S.African surg., first heart trans.
Basov, Nikolai G.	1912-	25	60		50	Soviet physicist
Beckman, Arnold O.	1900-	30	45	85	50	Developed acidity testing equip.
Becquerel, A.C.	1788-1878	375	800	1000		Electrochemical pioneer, phys.
Becquerel, A.H.	1852-1908	200	500	600		Physicist, uranium radioactivity

Name	db/dd	Sig.	DS	ALS	SP	Comments
Bell, Alexander Graham	1847-1922	400	1200	3000	3000	U.S. telephone pioneer, inven.
Bennett, Willard H.	1903-1987	20	40	110	50	Dev. radio frequency mass spe.
Benz, Karl F.	1844-1929					Ger. automobile eng., PU
Berdeen, John	1908-1991	30	50	150	45	Co-inventor of transistor
Berg, Paul	1926-	20	50		35	U.S. molecular biologist
Berliner, Emile	1851-1929	60	100	235	100	Dev. microphone & gramo.
Bernard, Claude	1813-1878	150	400	675		French physiologist
Bernoulli, Daniel	1700-1782	800	2200	2750		Swiss mathematician, gases
Berry, Clifford	1918-1963	40	75	180	60	Co-inventor first digital compute
Berzellus, Jons Jakob	1779-1848	100	175	525		Chemist, dev. chem. symbols
Bessel, Fredrich	1784-1846	135	250			German astronomer
Bessemer, Henry	1813-1898	40	65	225	100	U.S. Inventor, Bessemer steel
Best, Charles	1899-1978	55	150		125	Canadian physiologist
Bichat, Marie F.	1771-1802					French physician, PU
Bieriot, Louis	1872-1936	70	115	275	145	French engineer, aviator, inven.
Binet, Alfred	1857-1911	175	350			French psychologist
Binning, Gerd Karl	1947-	20	50	100	50	Dev,. scanning tun. microscope
Bird, Forrest	1921-	15	40	85	40	Dev. medical respirators
Black, Harold Stephen	1898-	30	40	85	40	Negative feedback amplifier
Black, Joseph	1728-1799					Scottish physicist, scarce, PU
Blumberg, Baruch S.	1925-	25	40	65	40	Dev. hepatitis B vaccine
Bohr, Aage	1922-	25	75		50	Danish physicist
Bohr, Niels	1885-1962	375				ESPV - all forms, quan. theorist
Borelli, Giovanni	1608-1679					Italian scientist, PU
Born, Max	1882-1970	200	350	600	300	German physicist
Bosch, Carl	1874-1940	65	150			German chemist
Bose, Satyendranath	1894-1974	30	100	225	100	Physicist, chemist
Bowditch, Nathaniel	1773-1838	100	265	475		U.S. astronomer
Brattain, Walter H.	1902-1987	35	55	165	50	Transistor innovator
Brenner, Sidney	1927-	25	45		30	South African scientist
Breuer, Josef	1842-1925					Viennese physician, PU
Broglie, Louis de	1893-1987	30	60	120	300	French physicist, wave theorist
Broglie, Maurice de	1875-1960	40	85		70	French physicist
Brown, Rachel Fuller	1898-1980	25	50	135	50	Mystatin developer
Buchner, Eduard	1860-1917					German chemist, PU
Bunsen, Robert	1811-1899	200	450	1000	1325	Ger. chemist, Bunsen burner
Burbank, Luther	1849-1926	125	300	325	200	Plant patent program contributor
Burckhalter, Joseph H.	1912-	20	40	65	35	FITC developer
Burroughs, William S.	1857-1898	150	400	825		Calculating machine dev.
Burton, William Meriam	1865-1954	45	90	200	100	Developed gasoline manufac.
Bush, Vannevar	1890-1974	50	200	300	150	U.S. elec.engin., anal. compute
Byron, Augusta Ada	1815-1851					English mathematician, PU
Calmette, Albert	1863-1933	55	125			French bacteriologist
Calvin, Melvin	1911-	20	40		25	U.S. chemist, NP
Camras, Marvin	1916-1995	25	45	120	50	U.S. inventor, magnetic tape
Cannizzaro, Stanislao	1826-1910	125	250	400		Italian chemist, atomic weights
Cannon, Annie	1863-1941	50	100		170	U.S. astronomer, stars spectra
Carlson, Chester F.	1906-1968	30	75	150	75	Electrophotography pioneer
Carnot, Sadi	1796-1832					French scientist, PU
Carothers, Wallace H.	1896-1937	65	110	250	125	Synthetic fiber innovator
Carrel, Alexis	1873-1944	80	200	325	100	French surgeon, biologist

Name	db/dd	Sig.	DS	ALS	SP	Comments
Carrier, Willis Haviland	1876-1950	50	125	200	130	Air-conditioning systems
Carson, Rachel	1907-1964	75	225	300	250	U.S. marine biologist
Cartwright, Edmund	1743-1823					British inventor, PU
Carver, George Wash.	1864-1943	225	800	1000		U.S. botanist, chemist, educator
Cavendish, Henry	1731-1810	275	570	1625		British chemist, disc. hydrogen
Chadwick, James	1891-1974	100	200	500	250	British physicist, disco. neutron
Chain, Ernst	1906-1979	30	55		45	Ger.-born British biochemist
Chapin, Darly	1906-1995	25	50	150	45	U.S. physicist, solar energy cell
Charcot, Jean M.	1825-1893	100	200	600		French neurologist
Charles, Jacques	1746-1823					French physicist, PU
Cherenkov, Pavel	1904-					Soviet physicist, PU
Claude, Albert	1899-1983	35	80	170	60	Founder of modern cell biology
Clausius, Rudolf	1822-1888	45	100	200		German physicist
Cockcroft, John D.	1897-1967	75	100	275	100	British nuclear physicist
Colton, George B.	1923-	15	40	65	25	Oral contracept. pioneer, "pill"
Compton, Arthur	1892-1962	100	200	300	100	U.S. physicist
Conover, Lloyd H.	1923-	10	35	60	30	Tetracycline creator
Coolidge, William D.	1873-1974	50	90	175	125	Vacuum tube developer
Cooper, Leon	1930-	20	45		30	U.S. physicist, NP
Cornforth, John	1917-	25	50		35	Australian chemist, NP
Cottrell, Frederick G.	1877-1948	50	100	225	70	Electrostatic precipitator
Cousteau, Jacques Y.	1910-1997	65	175	250	175	Marine explorer, Aqualung
Cray, Seymour	1925-1996	25	80	125	70	Supercomputer pioneer
Crick, Francis	1916-	50	125		70	Brit. molecular biologist, NP, $
Crookes, William	1832-1919	120	155	200		British physicist, chemist, inven.
Cugnot, Nicolas-J.	1728-1804					French engineer. PU
Curie, Marie	1867-1934	1200	2650	5565		Polish/Fr.chemist, SDS-3X
Curie, Pierre	1859-1906	1500	3475			Fr. phys., w. Marie, ESPV
Curtiss, Glenn	1878-1930	260	450			U.S. aeronautical inven., ESPV
Cushing, Harvey	1869-1939	170	450	700		U.S. neurologist
Cuvier, Georges	1769-1832	75	300			French anatomist
Daimler, Gottlieb	1834-1900	450	1270	2225		Ger.engineer, inven., auto.
Dalton, John	1766-1844	150	470	1000		Brit. physicist, chemist, at. table
Damadian, Raymond V.	1936-	20	40	70	30	Cancer detection apparatus
Daniell, John	1790-1845	100	200	275		British chemist, elec. cell
Dart, Raymond	1893-1988	30	75		50	Paleontologist
Darwin, Charles	1809-1882	675	2400	2750		Brit. natural., evolutionist, ESPV
Davy, Humphry	1778-1829	125	350	675		Brit. chemist, SALS - 5 - 10X
De Forest, Lee	1873-1961	300	1350	1650	1200	Audion amplifier,SALS- 5 - 10X
Deere, John	1804-1886					(see Business)
De Havilland, Geoffrey	1882-1965					British aircraft designer, PU
Deipoci, Enrico	1710-1770	40	800	1000		Italian physicist
Delbruck, Max	1907-1981	30	50	125	50	U.S. pioneer molecular genetics
De Vries, Hugo	1848-1935	40	75		60	Dutch botanist, osmosis
Dewar, James	1842-1923	50	100		70	Scottish chemist, thermos
Diesel, Rudolf	1858-1913	1000	2675	3000		German mechanical engineer
Djerassi, Carl	1923-	10	25	55	25	Oral contraceptives
Dobzhansky, Theo.	1900-1975	40	125		70	U.S. geneticist
Domagk, Gerhard	1895-1964	45	150		75	German pathologist, NP
Doppler, Christian	1803-1853	160	350	800		Austrian physicist, Doppler
Dow, Herbert Henry	1866-1930	75	125	275	100	Bromine developer

Name	db/dd	Sig.	DS	ALS	SP	Comments
Draper, Charles Stark	1901-1987	25	40	115	60	Gyroscopic equipment innov.
Durant, Graham J.	1934-	10	25	40	20	Cimetidine (Tagamet) developer
Eastman, George	1854-1932					(see Business)
Eckert, Jr., J. Presper	1919-1995	20	45	100	50	Co-inventor Eniac computer
Edgerton, Harold E.	1903-	20	35	70	30	Stroboscope pioneer
Edison, Thomas	1847-1931	500	1350		2250	U.S. inventor, ESPV
Ehrlich, Paul	1854-1915	400	1300	2000	1500	Ger. bacteriologist, immun. pio.
Einstein, Albert	1879-1955	1200	3250	3500		Ger./U.S. physicist, SALS-3X

Albert Einstein

* Einstein, a German-born US physicist formulated the theories of relativity, along with working on radiation physics and thermodynamics.

* In 1905 he published a special theory of relativity, and in 1915 issued his general theory of relativity.

* Einstein won the Nobel Prize for Physics in 1921.

* Einstein's conception of the basic laws governing the universe was outlined in his unified field theory made public in 1953.

* Einstein's autographed material is by far the most popularly collected of his field.

* Letters of interesting content do often enter the market, however their prices reflect the great interest and demand for his material.

* Typewritten letters in German are the most common form encountered. Handwritten letters are rare especially those containing significant content - science or Jewish causes.

* Einstein did use form letters, most surrounding atomic issues, that bear printed signatures. These are relatively easy to detect as such.

* While Einstein was a popular subject of photographs, finding an autographed quality piece can be harder to find than letters. Some signed sketches do occasionally enter the market but they are not as popular as a signed photograph.

* Common letterhead: "THE INSTITUTE FOR ADVANCED STUDY, PRINCETON, NEW JERSEY", also his personal blind embossed four-line letterhead, "A. EINSTEIN, 112 MERCER STREET, PRINCETON, NEW JERSEY, U.S.A."

* Common form: "A. Einstein"

Recent Offerings: TLS, 1950, science content - $3, 995; ALS, 1945, good content - $9,900; SP, 8" x 10", B&W - $6,995; SP, 5" x 7", inscribed, B&W - $7,500

Name	db/dd	Sig.	DS	ALS	SP	Comments
Elion, Gertrude B.	1918-	25	70	150	40	DNA blocking drugs innovator
Elton, Charles	1900-1991	25	60		40	British ecologist
Emmet, John C.	1938-	10	25	40	20	Cimetidine (Tagamet) developer
Enders, John F.	1897-1985	35	75	125	50	U.S. virologist, vaccine pioneer
Ericsson, John	1803-1889	100	200	500		Propeller innovator
Esaki, Leo	1925-	20	50		30	Japanese physicist, NP

Name	db/dd	Sig.	DS	ALS	SP	Comments
Euler, Leonhard	1707-1783	1050				Swiss math., cal. , ESPV, scarce
Fahrenheit, Gabriel	1686-1736	3200	8000	15000		Ger. physicist, Fahrenheit scale
Faraday, Michael	1791-1867	175	375	725		British physicist, chemist
Farnsworth, Philo Taylor	1906-1971					TV sys. pioneer, ESPV, PU
Fermat, Pierre de	1601-1665					Fr. mathematician, PU, scarce
Fermi, Enrico	1901-1954	500	1750	3100		Italian/U.S. physicist, ESPV
Ferraris, Gallileo	1847-1897					Ital. physicist, electrical eng., PU
Feynman, Richard	1918-1988	30	40	100	35	U.S. physicist, writer
Fischer, Emil	1852-1919	200				German chemist, NP
Fischer, Hans	1881-1945	75	175			German chemist, NP
Flammarion, Camille	1842-1925	50	75	175	200	French astronomer
Fleming, Alexander	1881-1955	225	500	1650	1000	British bacteriologist, penicillin
Florey, Howard	1898-1968	25	50		40	Australian pathologist, NP
Ford, Henry	1863-1947					(see Business)
Forrester, Jay W.	1918-	15	30	55	25	Magnetic storage pioneer
Foucault, Jean B.L.	1819-1868					French physicist, PU
Fourier, Jean B.J.	1768-1830	350	700	1500		Fr. mathematician, SALS-5-10X
Franck, James	1882-1964	45	110	275	140	Ger. physicist, quantum theorist
Frege, Friedrich	1848-1925	75	150			German philosopher
Fresnel, Augustin	1788-1827					French physicist, PU
Freud, Anna	1895-1982	225	450			Aust. psychoanalysis
Freud, Sigmund	1856-1939	1725	4750	5150	10000	Aust. psychiatrist, SALS-2-2.5X
Frisch, Karl	1886-1982	20	30		25	Austrian zoologist, NP
Fulton, Robert	1745-1815	400	1200	2500		U.S. gunsmith, inventor
Galileo, Galilei	1564-1642					Ita. astronomer, PU, rare
Gallo, Robert	1937-	20	45		59	U.S. scientist, AIDS
Galton, Francis	1822-1911					English scientist, eugenics, PU
Galvani, Luigi	1737-1798	2500	3625			Italian physicist, fdr. galvanism
Ganellin, C. Robin	1934-	10	25	40	20	Cimetidine (Tagamet) developer
Gauss, Carl Friedrich	1777-1855	125	300	1150		German physicist, mathematics
Gay-Lussac, Joseph	1778-1850	100	300	1000		French chemist, physicist
Geiger, Hans	1882-1945	150	350	700		German physicist, G. counter
Gell-Mann, Murray	1929-	20	50		35	U.S. physicist, NP
Gesell, Arnold	1880-1961	25	50		40	U.S. psychologist
Gibbs, Josiah W.	1839-1903	150	450			U.S. theoretical physicist, chem.
Giffard,, Henri	1825-1882					French inventor, dirigible, PU
Gilbert, Walter	1932-	20	45		30	U.S. molecular biologist, NP
Ginsburg, Charles P.	1920-	10	30	50	25	Videotape recorder pioneer
Glaser, Donald	1926-	25	50		40	U.S. physicist, NP
Goddard, Robert H.	1882-1945	400	1600	1750		U.S. physicist, father rocketry
Goethals, George W.	1858-1928	200	650	1200		U.S. army eng., built Pan. Canal
Gogli, Camillo	1843-1926	100				Italian cell biologist
Goodyear, Charles	1800-1860	325	1600	4500		Vulcanization developer
Gorgas, William C.	1854-1920	140	200	350	225	U.S. sanitarian, U.S. army surg.
Gould, Gordon	1920-	20	45	80	50	Optically pumped laser ampli.
Gould, Stephen J.	1941-	20	50		30	U.S. paleontologist
Greatbatch, Wilson	1919-	25	40	75	40	Medical cardiac pacemaker dev.
Greene, Leonard M.	1918-	20	35	65	35	Airplane stall warning device in.
Guerin, Camille	1872-1961					French bacteriologist

Name	db/dd	Sig.	DS	ALS	SP	Comments
Haber, Fritz	1868-1934	40	75			German chemist
Haeckel, Ernest	1834-1919	65	150	300		German zoologist, evolutionist
Hahn, Otto	1879-1968	150	500	2250	400	German chemist, atomic fission
Hailey, Edmund	1656-1742	4000				British astronomer, ESPV
Haldane, J.B.S.	1892-1964	60	150	225	125	British scientist, geneticist
Hale, George	1868-1938	35	100	200		U.S. astronomer
Hall, Charles Martin	1863-1914	75	150	300		Aluminum manufacturing pio.
Hall, James	1761-1832	200	400	750		British geologist, chemist
Hall, Robert N.	1919-	15	45	100	40	High voltage/power semicon.
Haller, Albrecht	1708-1777					Swiss physician, neurology, PU
Halley, Edmond	1656-1742					English scientist, PU
Hanford, W.E. "Butch"	1908-	25	40	75	30	Polyurethane pioneer
Harvey, William	1578-1657	1125	4000	13500		English physician, anatomist
Hawking, Stephen	1942-					English physicist, ESPV, PU
Hazen, Elizabeth Lee	1885-1975	35	50	145	45	Nystatin pioneer
Heisenberg, Werner	1901-1976	50	250	800	150	German physicist, matrix mech.
Helmholtz, Hermann v.	1821-1894	175	500	650		German physicist, anatomist
Hench, Phillip	1896-1965	25	50	100	35	U.S. physician, NP
Henry, Joseph	1797-1878	75	150	250		U.S. physicist
Henry, William	1774-1836	100	200	300		British chemist
Herschel, John F.	1792-1871	150	225			English scientist
Herschel, William	1738-1822	165	450	725		British astronomer, dis. Uranus
Hertz, Heinrich	1857-1894	125	260	600		German physicist
Hess, Victor	1883-1964	20	40	100	30	Austrian physicist, NP
Hewish, Antony	1924-	20	35		25	Brit. radio astronomer, NP
Hewlett, William R.	1913-	30	75	150	40	Var. frequency oscillation gen.
Higonnet, Rene Alph.	1902-1983	30	60	125	50	Photo composing machine
Hilbert, David	1862-1943	150	300	550	200	German mathematician
Hillier, James	1915-	25	45	125	30	Electron lens correction device
Hofstadter, Robert	1915-1990	20	40	50	30	U.S. high-energy physicist
Holland, John P.	1840-1914	75	150	275		Irish engineer, submarines
Hollerith, Herman	1869-1929	65	110	265	125	Modern data processing pio.
Holmes, Donald Fletch.	1910-1980	30	60	125	45	Polyurethane pioneer
Hoover, William	1849-1932	50	110	250	70	U.S. manufacturer, vacuum
Houdry, Eugene J.	1892-1962	50	125	200	60	Catalytic cracking of petroleum
Hoyle. Frederick	1915-	25	50		30	English astronomer
Hubble, Edwin P.	1889-1953	25	125	250	100	U.S. astronomer
Humboldt, Alexander v.	1769-1859	100	200	350		German explorer, naturalist
Hutton, James	1726-1797					Scottish geologist, PU
Huxley, Julian	1887-1975	50	150	250	75	British biologist
Huxley, Thomas Henry	1825-1895	50	150	225		English scientist, humanist
ves, Frederic	1856-1937	50	130			U.S. inventor, halftone process
Jacob, Francois	1920-	20	45		30	French biochemist, NP
Jacuzzi, Candido	1903-1986	25	50		35	U.S. engineer
Jeans, James	1877-1946	20	50	140	35	Brit. mathematician
Jeffreys, Alec	1950-	20	40		25	British geneticist
Jenner, Edward	1749-1823	500	1000	2000		Brit. physician, dis. vaccination
Jessop, William	1745-1814	150	275			British canal engineer
Jenner, William	1815-1898	40	100	275		Brit. physician, pathol. anatomist
Joliot-Curie, Frederic	1900-1958	100	400	500	275	Fr. physicist, radioactivity theor.

Name	db/dd	Sig.	DS	ALS	SP	Comments
Joliot-Curie, Irene	1897-1956	50	200	250		French physicist, w. Frederic
Josephson, Brian	1940-	15	30		20	British physicist, NP
Joule, James P.	1818-1889	65	170	250		British physicist
Julian, Percy F.	1899-1975	50	130	225	75	Synthesis of cortisone
Jung, Carl	1875-1961	600	2200	4250	2500	Swiss psychiatrist, analytical
Junkers, Hugo	1859-1935	75	200	300		German airplane designer
Kay, John	1704-1764					British inventor, PU
Keck, Donald B.	1941-	20	40	75	25	Fused silica optical waveguide
Kekule v. Stradonitz, F	1829-1896	100	200	300		German chemist
Kenny, Sister Elizabeth	1886-1952	200	400	500	300	Australian nurse, polio treatment
Kepler, Johannes	1571-1630					German astronomer, PU
Kettering, Charles Fran.	1875-1958	125	200	300	150	Engine starting/ignition devices
Kilby, Jack S.	1923-	25	40	75	50	Miniaturized electronic circuits
Kitasato, Shibasaburo	1852-1931					Japanese bacteriologist, PU
Klaproth, Martin	1743-1817					German chemist, PU
Klein, Melanie	1882-1960	30	65		45	Austrian child psychologist
Koch, Robert	1843-1910	375	775	1325		German bacteriologist, NP
Kohler, Georges	1946-1995	50	150	275	100	German immunologist
Kolff, Willem J.	1911-	25	50	75	45	Artificial-kidney dialysis machine
Korolev, Sergei	1906-1966					Soviet designer, PU, ESPV
Krebs, Hans	1900-1981	20	45		30	Brit. biochemist, NP
Kroeber, Alfred	1876-1960	40	100		60	U.S. anthropologist
Kwolek, Stephanie	1923-	15	30	50	25	Kevlar (5X stronger than steel)
Lagrange, Joseph	1736-1813	215	435			French geometer, astronomer
Laing, R. D.	1927-1989	20	45		30	Scottish psychoanalyst
Lamarck, Jean B.	1744-1829	500	1000	1250		French naturalist, evol. theorist
Lamb, Willis	1913-	20	40		25	U.S. physicist, NP
Land, Edwin Herbert	1909-1991	100	250	375	200	Polaroid camera developer, ES
Landsteiner, Karl	1868-1943	50	100	200		Austrian immunologist
Langmuir, Irving	1881-1957	50	100	200	100	Incandescent electric lamp
Laplace, Pierre S.	1749-1827	500	1000			French astronomer, physicist
Lavoisier, Antoine	1743-1794	650				Fr. chemist, DS - rare, AF scarce
Lawrence, Ernest O.	1901-1958	100	250	400	200	Method/apparatus for ions
Leakey, Louis	1903-1972	50	150	250	100	British paleoanthropologist
Leakey, Mary	1913-1996	60	135		70	British paleoanthropologist
Leakey, Richard	1944-	100	200		155	British archeologist
Lear, William P.	1902-1978	50	125	200	100	Automobile radio dev., Learjet
Leclanche, Georges	1839-1882					French engineer, PU
Ledley, Robert S.	1926-	15	35	70	25	Entire body CAT scanner
Leeuwenhoek, Anton.	1632-1723					Dutch microscopist, PU
Leibniz, Gottfried	1646-1716					German mathematician, PU
Lejeune, Jerome	1927-1994	40	100	200	50	Fr. geneticist, Down's syndrom.
Lemaitre, Georges	1894-1966	60	150			Belgian cosmologist, Big Bang
Levi-Montalcini, Rita	1909-	25	75		45	Italian neurologist
Levi-Strauss, Claude	1908-1990					French anthropologist
Liebig, Justus von	1803-1873	275	700	1350		German chemist,quan. organic
Lilienthal, Otto	1848-1896	650	1575	2500		German aviation pioneer
Lippershey, Hans	1570-1619					Dutch lens maker, PU
Lippmann, Gabriel	1845-1921					French doctor, NP, PU
Lister, Joseph	1827-1912	250	500	800		Brit. pio. of antiseptic surgery

Name	db/dd	Sig.	DS	ALS	SP	Comments
Lorenz, Konrad	1903-1989	25	75		40	Austrian ethologist, NP
Lorenz,Ludwig	1829-1891					Danish mathematician, PU
Lowell, Percival	1855-1916	25	50	100	60	U.S. astronomer, Pluto theorist
Lumiere, Louis	1864-1984	200	350		350	French cinematographer
Lumiere, Auguste	1862-1954	500	1200		700	French cinematograph inventor
Lyell, Charles	1797-1875	125	250	450		Scottish geologist
Lysenko, Trofim	1898-1976					Soviet biologist, PU
Macintosh, Charles	1766-1843					Scottish chemist
Maiman, Theodore H.	1927-	20	40	65	30	Ruby Laser Systems
Malinowski, Bronslaw	1884-1942					Anthropologist
Mannheim, Karl	1893-1947					Hungarian sociologist
Marconi, Guglielmo	1874-1937	250	1000	2000	1000	Italian physicist, wireless tele.
Marsh, Othniel	1831-1899					U.S. paleontologist
Marx, Karl	1818-1883					German philosopher, PU
Maskelyne, Nevil	1732-1811	100	200	400		English astronomer
Mauchly, John W.	1908-1980	30	100	150	50	U.S. co-inventor of Eniac
Maurer, Robert D.	1924-	20	40	55	25	Fused silica optical waveguide
Maxim, Hiram	1840-1916	100	200	300		US inventor, machine gun
Maxwell, James Clark	1831-1879	100	200	325		British physicist, electricity theo.
Mayer, Julius	1814-1878	75	175	300		German physicist
Mayer, Maria Goeppert	1906-1972	40	100	175	50	U.S. geneticist, mob. genetic
McAdam, John	1756-1836	100	200	275		Scottish engineer, road sur.
McClintock, Barbara	1902-1992	40	100		60	U.S. geneticist
McCormick, Cyrus	1809-1884	320	1000	1200		Reaper, grain not grim
Mechnikov, Ilya	1845-1916					Russian scientist, NP, PU
Medawar, Peter	1915-1987	30	50		35	Immunologist, NP
Meitner, Lise	1878-1968	125	300	500		Austrian physicist, atomic theo.
Mendel, Gregor J.	1822-1884	500	1000	2000		Austrian botanist, genetics pio.
Mendeleyev, Dmitri	1834-1907	500	1200	2000		Russian chemist, dev. PTE
Menninger, Karl	1893-1990	30	75	150	40	U.S. psychiatrist
Mergenthaler, Ottmar	1854-1899	125	250	425		Linotype, printing bar machine
Mesmer, Franz	1734-1815	175	350	600		German physician, theorist
Messerschmitt, Willy	1898-1978					German airplane designer, PU
Messier, Charles	1730-1817					French astronomer, PU
Michelson, Albert A.	1852-1931	125	250	500	150	U.S. physicist
Millikan, Robert A.	1868-1953	100	200	400	250	U.S. physicist
Millman, Irving	1923-	25	60	125	40	Hepatitis B vaccine
Mitchell, R.J.	1895-1937	125	250		200	British aircraft designer
Morgan, Thomas Hunt	1866-1945	125	250	500	160	U.S. geneticist, embryologist
Morley, Edward	1838-1923	65	150	300		U.S. physicist
Morse, Samuel F. B.	1791-1872	500	1500	2650	5000	Telegraph signals
Moseley, Henry	1887-1915					English physicist, scarce, PU
Mossbauer, Rudolf	1929-	25	50		35	German physicist, NP
Mott, Nevill	1905-	25	50		35	English physicist
Moyer, Andrew J.	1899-1959	40	75	100	50	Penicillin production innovator
Moyroud, Louis Marius	1914-	15	35	45	25	Photo composing machine
Mulliken, Robert	1896-1986	45	140		50	U.S. chemist, NP
Nansen, Fridtjof	1861-1930	150	300	400		Norwegian explorer & sci., NP
Newton, Issac	1642-1727	2000	4000	8000		English nat. philo., SLS-2-3X
Noyce, Robert N.	1927-1990	30	75	125	50	Semiconductor device-and-lead

Name	db/dd	Sig.	DS	ALS	SP	Comments

The Alfred B. Nobel Prize

* Alfred B. Nobel (1833-1896), inventor of dynamite, bequeathed $9 million, the interest of which was to be distributed yearly to those judged to have benefited humankind in chemistry, literature, physics, medicine-physiology and the promotion of peace.

* Prizes were first awarded in 1901.

* The first Nobel Memorial Prize in Economic Science was awarded in 1969. It was funded by the central bank of Sweden.

* Each prize is now worth about $1 million.

* Awards were not given every year.

* Collecting autographed material from recipients of the Nobel Prize is not only popular but has proven a valuable endeavor over the past few decades.

Name	db/dd	Sig.	DS	ALS	SP	Comments
Olsen, Kenneth H.						(see Business Leaders)
Oppenheimer, J. Robert	1904-1967	750	1750	4000	1500	U.S. phys., scarce in most forms
Ostwald, Wilhelm	1853-1932	70	140	275	150	German physical chemist
Otis, Elisha Graves	1811-1861	150	400	750		Elevator pioneer
Otto, Nikolaus August	1832-1891	250	600	1200		Gas Motor Engine
Page, Robert Morris	1903-1992	25	75	150	60	U.S. physicist, radar developer
Parker, Louis W.	1906-	25	60	125	30	Television receiver
Parsons, John T.	1913-	15	25	40	25	Numerical control of machine
Pasteur, Louis	1822-1895	600	1000	2000	3000	French chemist, pasteurization
Patterson, Clair C.	1922-1995	30	60	150	50	U.S. geochemist
Paul, Les	1915-	25	50		75	U.S. inventor, electric guitar
Pauli, Wolfgang	1900-1958	45	100		70	Austrian physicist, NP
Pauling, Linus	1901-1994	50	300	500	100	U.S. chemist, political activist
Pavlov, Ivan	1849-1936	800	2000			Russian physiologist
Perrin, Jean	1870-1942	75	175	325		French physicist, NP
Petrie, Flinders	1853-1942	125	250			English archeologist
Piccard, Auguste	1884-1962					Swiss scientist, PU
Pitman, Issac	1813-1897					English teacher, inventor, PU
Planck, Max	1858-1947	150	350	1000	350	German physicist, quan. theorist
Plank, Charles J.	1915-	20	40	75	40	Gasoline and petroleum prod.
Plunkett, Roy J.	1910-1994	30	60	150	60	U.S. chemist, created "Teflon"
Poincare, Henri	1854-1912	75	150	275	150	French mathematician, physicist
Popper, Karl	1902-	40	100		65	Austrian philosopher
Powell, Cecil	1903-1969	100	200		125	English physicist, NP
Priestley, Joseph	1733-1804	450	1250	2500		British chemist, disc. oxygen
Prokhorov, Aleksandr	1916-					Russian physicist, PU
Rabi, Isidor Isaac	1899-1986	50	100	150	75	U.S. physicist, pio. atomic exp.
Ramsay, William	1852-1916	50	125			Scottish chemist
Reed, Walter S.	1851-1902	500	1200	4250		U.S. army pathologist, bacter.
Reich, Wilhelm	1897-1957	125	300	500	200	Austrian doctor
Remington, Eliphalet	1793-1861	250	500	875		U.S. inventor

Name	db/dd	Sig.	DS	ALS	SP	Comments
Remington, Philo	1816-1889	175	400	700		U.S. inventor and businessman
Richter, Burton	1931-	25	50		35	U.S. physicist, NP
Richter, Charles F.	1900-1985	35	75		50	U.S. seismologist
Riemann, Bernhard	1826-1866	125	325	1000		German mathematician, calculus
Rines, Robert H.	1922-	20	50	75	30	High-definition radar pioneer
Roentgen, Wilhelm	1845-1923	600	1500	3000		German physicist, disc. the X ray
Rogers, Carl	1902-1987	35	80		45	U.S. psychologist
Roget, Peter	1779-1869					English physician, PU
Rohrer, Heinrich	1933-	15	30	50	20	Scanning tunneling microscope
Rosinski, Edward J.	1921-	10	25	40	20	Gasoline and petroleum pioneer
Rubin, Benjamin A.	1917-	15	30	55	25	Bifurcated vaccination needle
Rush, Benjamin	1745-1813	175	250			U.S. physician
Russell, Bertrand	1872-1970	100	250	450	210	English phil. and mathematician
Rutherford, Ernest	1871-1937	200	500	1000	250	British physicist, atomic nucleus
Ryle, Martin	1918-1984	35	100		50	English radioastronomer, NP
Sakharov, Andrei	1921-1989	300	650			Soviet physicist
Sabin, Albert B.	1906-1993	35	125	150	125	Russian/U.S. oral polio vaccine
Sagan, Carl	1934-1996	25	60	125	50	U.S. astronomer, writer
Salk, Jonas	1914-1995	50	200	350	200	U.S. developer polio vaccine
Sanger, Frederick	1918-	25	50		40	English biochemist
Sarett, Lewis Hastings	1917-	20	40	65	35	Proc. of treating pregene com.
Sarnoff, David	1891-1971	100	350	700	150	Broadcast pioneer
Schiaparelli, Giovanni	1835-1910	150	400	1200		Italian astronomer
Schliemann, Heinrich	1822-1890	250	625			German archeologist
Schrodinger, Erwin	1887-1961	55	135		75	Austrian physicist, NP
Schultz, Peter C.	1942-	15	30	50	25	Fused silica optical waveguide
Schweitzer, Albert	1875-1965	175	600	1125	800	French theologian, philosopher
Schwinger, Julian	1918-	20	40		30	U.S. quantum physicist, NP
Secchi, Angelo	1818-1878	150	375	800		Italian astronomer
Seiwald, Robert J.	1925-	15	30	50	25	FITC
Semon, Waldo	1898-	20	50	75	40	PVC plastisols
Shapley, Harlow	1885-1972	50	100	200	75	U.S. astronomer, SDS-2-3X
Sheehan, John C.	1915-1992	30	65	100	50	Semisynthetic penicillin
Shockley, William Brad.	1910-1989	50	125	150	100	Transistor
Shoemaker, Eugen	1928-1997	50			100	U.S. planetary geo., comet fndr.
Sikorsky, Igor I.	1889-1972					(see Aviation)
Simon, Herbert	1916-	20	40		35	U.S. social scientist, NP
Singer, Isaac	1811-1875	750	1850			U.S. inventor, sewing machine
Skinner, B.F.	1903-1990	30	75		75	U.S. psychologist
Smith, Adam	1723-1790					Scottish economist, PU
Smith, John Maynard	1920-					British biologist, ESS, PU
Smith, William	1769-1839					British geologist,PU
Snow, C.P.	1905-1980	30	75		60	English physicist
Sommeller, Germain	1815-1871					French engineer. PU
Sopwith, Thomas	1888-1989	100	200		150	Biplane designer
Sorensen, Soren	1868-1939	50	100	215		Danish chemist
Sperry, Elmer A.	1860-1930	200	400	600	200	Ship's Gyroscopic compass
Sperry, Roger	1913-1994	25	50	75	45	U.S. brain expert, mind theorist
Spock, Benjamin	1903-1998	30	100	175	60	U.S. pediatrician
Stanley, William	1858-1916	85	175	250		Electric transformer
Stark, Johannes	1874-1957	45	100	200	100	German physicist

Name	db/dd	Sig.	DS	ALS	SP	Comments
Steinmetz, Charles P.	1865-1923	75	150	400	125	German/U.S. elect. eng., GE
Stephenson, George	1781-1848	200	375	750		English engineer
Steptoe, Patrick	1913-1988	35	80		45	English obstetrician
Stewart, Frederick	1904-1993	35	100	200	100	British botanist, cell biologist
Stibitz, George R.	1904-1995	40	125	250	75	U.S., inv. first digital computer
Stokes, George	1819-1903	60	120	250		Irish physicist
Svedberg, Theodor	1884-1971	45	100		60	Swedish chemist
Synge, Richard	1914-	25	60		40	British biochemist
Szent-Gyorgyl, Albert	1893-1986	40	100		60	U.S. biochemist, NP
Szilard, Leo	1898-1964	45	150	300		Hungarian/U.S. physicist
Tabern, Donalee L.	1900-1974	20	50	75	30	Thiobarbituric acid derivatives
Talbot, William	1800-1877	300	600	900		English photography pioneer
Taylor, Frederick	1856-1915					U.S. engineer, PU
Teller, Edward	1908-	40	100	250	100	U.S. physicist
Tesla, Nikola	1856-1943	500	1000	1200	1000	Serb./U.S. electrical engineer
Thompson, John	1860-1940	125	300	650		U.S. inventor, machine gun
Thomson, Elihu	1853-1937	500	1000	1650		U.S. inventor
Thomson, George	1892-1975	50	125			English physicist, NP
Thomson, J.J.	1856-1940					English physicist, electron, PU
Thomson, William	1824-1907	125	250	400	225	Br. mathematician, (Lord Kelvin)
Tinbergen, Niko	1907-	25	55		35	Dutch zoologist. NP
Tishler, Max	1906-	15	30	40	20	Riboflavin and sulfaquinoxaline
Tobin, James	1918-	20	40		30	U.S. economist, NP
Townes, Charles Hard	1915-	25	45	75	40	Masers
Trevithick, Richard	1771-1833	60	120			British engineer
Turing, Alan	1912-1954					English mathematician, PU
Tyndall, John	1820-1893	60	120	175		Irish physicist
Urey, Harold	1893-1981	100	200	300		U.S. chemist
Vail, Alfred	1807-1859					U.S. communications pio., PU
van de Graaff, Robert	1901-1967	75	150	300	125	U.S. physicist
Vane, John	1927-	20	40		30	British pharmacologist, NP, RS
Virchow, Rudolf	1821-1902	225	500	1000		Ger. pathologist, fdr. cell. path.
Volta, Alessandro	1745-1827	500	2500	3000		Italian physicist, electricity pio.
Volwiler, Ernest H.	1893-1992	25	45	125	40	Thiobarbituric acid derivatives
Von Braun, Werner	1912-1977	200	500	725	400	German/U.S., rockets developer
Von Neumann, John	1903-1957	125	250	475	175	U.S. scientist
Waksman, Selman	1888-1973	50	100	150	65	U.S. biochemist
Wallace, Alfred Russell	1823-1913	100	200	450	225	British naturalist, evolutionist
Wang, An	1920-1990	25	50	80	50	Magnetic pulse controlling dev.
Warburg, Otto	1878-1976	130	250			German biochemist, NP
Wasserman, August von	1866-1925	75	150	300	135	German bacteriologist
Watt, James E.	1736-1819	450	900	2000		British mechanical engineer
Weber, Max	1864-1920	125	240			German sociologist
Weber, Wilhelm	1804-1891	100	200	370		German physicist
Wegener, Alfred L.	1880-1930	65	130	220	80	German meteorologist
Weismann, August	1834-1914	120	225	375		German biologist
Westinghouse, George	1846-1914					Steam-powered brake dev., PU
Whipple, George	1878-1976	50	100		65	U.S. physiologist

Name	db/dd	Sig.	DS	ALS	SP	Comments
Whitney, Eli	1765-1825	700	2250	4000		Cotton gin
Wiener, Norbert	1894-1964	35	90	185	75	U.S. mathematician, cybernetics
Wigner, Eugene	1902-1995	25	50	150	50	U.S. quantum theorist, NP
Wilkins, Maurice	1916-	25	45		30	British scientist, NP
Williams, Robert R.	1886-1965	35	70	125	50	Isolation of Vitamin B1
Wilson, Edward	1929-	20	40		30	U.S. zoologist
Wohler, Friedrich	1800-1882	145	275	465		German chemist
Wollaston, William	1766-1828					British chemist, PU
Woodward, Robert	1917-1979	30	75		50	U.S. chemist, NP
Wright, Orville & Wilbur						(see Aviation)
Wright, Sewall	1889-1988	30	60	100	50	U.S. evolutionary theorist
Wundt, Wilhelm	1832-1920	100	200	300		German physiologist
Yersin, Alexandre	1863-1943	60	145			Swiss bacteriologist
Zeiss, Carl	1816-1888					German optician, PU
Zeppelin, Ferdinand von	1838-1917	300	1100	2000	1000	German soldier, aeronaut
Zernike, Frits	1888-1966	55	125		75	Dutch physicist, NP
Zsigmondy, Richard	1865-1929	145	265	400		Austrian chemist, NP
Zworykin, Vladimir Kos.	1889-1982	50	150	250	100	Cathode ray tube

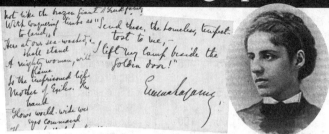

JUSTICES OF THE SUPREME COURT OF THE UNITED STATES

WHAT YOU NEED TO KNOW

* In some instance an individual's entire reputation as a Supreme Court justice can be associated with a single controversial ruling. For example Roger B. Taney, Dred Scott v. Sanford decision of 1857.

* The courts are associated with the name of the chief justice. For example, the Warren Court.

* Justices have very diverse backgrounds.

* Some collectors prefer photographs signed by the entire court, most of which can be found dating back to the Chase Court. In some instances no official group photo was taken.

* It was customary to destroy the judicial papers of a justice upon death. In later years however most were donated to a university or institution.

MARKET FACTS

* The autographs of Supreme Court justices have exhibited consistent increases in value over the past twenty five years.

* The market has shown significant price variations in form - a sign of unfamiliarity by both dealers and collectors.

* Handwritten letters are the form in greatest demand.

* The market is driven by the signatures of the greatest justices, such as Oliver Wendell Holmes, Jr. and John Marshall.

* Forgeries are scarce.

* Obtaining a full set of signatures from every member of the court is extremely difficult.

TRENDS

* Justices often respond to autograph requests with chamber cards. These read "Supreme Court of the United States, Washington, D, C. 20543," include an

embossed eagle (left corner) and a notation "Chambers of Justice... or Chambers of the Chief justice". These cards can vary in size and are popular with collectors.

JUSTICES OF THE SUPREME COURT OF
THE UNITED STATES REFERENCE CHART

* Key:
* = Scarce, ** - Rare, *** = Available, **** = Common
Abbreviations: f. = father of; LD = limited demand, CC = Continental Congress, USHR = United States House of Representatives, AG = attorney general, AOPYS = average opinions per years of service, RU = relatively unknown, CJ = Chief Justice, GW = George Washington

Justices	Tenure	Appt. by.	Comments
Baldwin, Henry	1830 - 44	A. Jackson	** Plagued by problems
Barbour, Philip	1836 - 41	A. Jackson	** Limited legacy
Black, Hugo	1937 - 71	F. Roosevelt	**** Prolific writer
Blackmun, Harry	1970-94	R. Nixon	**** Speaker & writer
Blair, John	1789-96	G. Washington	** Limited participation
Blatchford, Samuel	1882-93	C. Arthur	*** Diligent & productive
Bradley, Joseph	1870-92	U. Grant	*** Intellectual, prolific
Brandeis, Louis	1916-39	W. Wilson	* Significant demand
Brennan, William	1956-90	D. Eisenhower	**** Controversial
Brewer, David	1889-1910	B. Harrison	*** Prolific, died suddenly
Breyer, Stephen	1994 -	W. Clinton	**** Unpredictable
Brown, Henry	1890-1906	B. Harrison	* Scarce in later material
Burger, Warren E. *	1969-87	R. Nixon	** Balanced, art enthusiast
Burton, Harold H.	1945-58	H. Truman	**** Court historian
Butler, Pierce	1923-39	W. Harding	*** Stubborn, religious
Byrnes, James F.	1941-42	F. Roosevelt	**** Gov. SC; Sec./state
Campbell, John A.	1853-61	F. Pierce	* CSA officer, very wise
Cardozo, Benjamin N.	1932-38	H. Hoover	* Prolific, strong demand
Catron, John	1837-65	M. Van Buren	* LD
Chase, Salmon P. *	1864-73	A. Lincoln	*** Gov. OH; Sec./treasury
Chase, Samuel	1796-1811	G. Washington	*** Controversial
Clark, Tom C.	1949-67	H. Truman	**** Historian/.f. R. Clark
Clarke, John H.	1916-22	W. Wilson	** Advocate world peace
Clifford, Nathan	1858-81	J. Buchanan	*** Prolific, LD
Curtis, Benjamin	1851-57	M. Fillmore	*** Resigned from court
Cushing, William	1790-1810	G. Washington	** Last Pres. appointee
Daniel, Peter V.	1842-60	M. Van Buren	* LD, slavery advocate
Davis, David	1862-77	A. Lincoln	*** USS/IL, independent
Day, William R.	1903-22	T. Roosevelt	*** Active, baseball fan
Douglas, William O.	1939-75	F. Roosevelt	**** Controversial
Duval, Gabriel	1811-36	J. Madison	*** LD, spelling variations
Ellsworth, Oliver*	1796-1800	G. Washington	*** CC, USS, hated writing
Field, Stephen J.	1863-97	A. Lincoln	*** LD
Fortas, Abe	1965-69	L. Johnson	**** LD, Violinist
Frankfurter, Felix	1939-62	F. Roosevelt	** Illegible writing - 1960s

Justices	Tenure	Appt. by.	Comments
Fuller, Melville W. *	1888-1910	G. Cleveland	*** Reclusive
Ginsburg, Ruth Bader	1993-	B. Clinton	**** Detailed, opera lover
Goldberg, Arthur J.	1962-65	J. Kennedy	****Sec./labor, UN ambas.
Gray, Horace	1881-1902	C. Arthur	*** Scholar, historian
Grier, Robert C.	1846-70	J. Polk	* LD
Harlan, John Marshall	1877-1911	R. Hayes	*** Judicial activist
Harlan, John Marshall	1955-71	D. Eisenhower	*** Prolific, federalist
Harrison, Robert H.	1789-90	G. Washington	* Declined to serve
Holmes, Oliver W.	1902-32	T. Roosevelt	*** Strong demand
Hughes, Charles E. *	1910-16	W. Taft	*** Gov. NY, Sec./state
	1930-41	H. Hoover	
Hunt, Ward	1872-82	U. Grant	** LD
Iredell, James	1790-99	G. Washington	* Very prolific
Jackson, Howell E.	1893-95	B. Harrison	* USS, served 15 months
Jackson, Robert H.	1941-54	F. Roosevelt	****Negotiator, AG
Jay, John *	1789-95	G. Washington	* Prolific, statesman
Johnson, Thomas	1792-93	G. Washington	* CC, served 14 months
Johnson, William	1804-34	T. Jefferson	* Disenter
Kennedy, Anthony M.	1987 -	R. Reagan	****Accessible
Lamar, Joseph R.	1911-16	W. Taft	* Prolific, yet short term
Lamar, Lucius Q.C.	1888-93	G. Cleveland	*** Sec./interior, LD
Livingston, Brockholst	1807-23	T. Jefferson	* Prolific & brilliant writer
Lurton, Horace	1910-14	W. Taft	* Oldest jurist,prolific, LD
Marshall, John *	1801-35	J. Adams	* USHR, Sec./state
Marshall, Thurgood	1967-92	L. Johnson	**** First African-American
Matthews, Stanley	1881-89	J. Garfield	*** USS, LD
McKenna, Joseph	1898-1925	W. McKinley	*** USHR, reclusive
McKinley, John	1838-52	M. Van Buren	* USS, prolific
McLean, John	1830-61	A. Jackson	*** Postmaster General
McReynolds, James	1914-41	W. Wilson	***AG , controversial
Miller, Samuel	1862-90	A. Lincoln	*** Prolific
Minton, Sherman	1949-56	H. Truman	*** USS, popular
Moody, William H.	1906-10	T. Roosevelt	** USHR,Sec./navy, AG
Moore, Alfred	1800-04	J. Adams	* LD, delivered 1 opinion
Murphy, Frank	1940-49	F. Roosevelt	**** AG, mayor of Detroit
Nelson, Samuel	1845-72	J. Tyler	* LD
O'Connor, Sandra Day	1981-	R. Reagan	**** First woman justice
Paterson, William	1793-1806	G. Washington	* USS, Gov. NJ, statesman
Peckham, Rufus	1896-1909	G. Cleveland	* Private outside of court
Pitney, Mahlon	1912-22	W. Taft	* USHR, controversial
Powell, Lewis F. , Jr.	1972-87	R. Nixon	**** Popular, educator
Reed, Stanley F.	1938-57	F. Roosevelt	**** Solicitor general
Rehnquist, William H. *	1972-	R. Nixon	**** Author
Roberts, Owen J.	1930-45	H. Hoover	**** Special counsel
Rutledge, John *	1790-91,95	G. Washington	* Twice appointed, recluse
Rutledge, Wiley B.	1943-49	F. Roosevelt	* Educator, died at age 55
Sanford, Edward T.	1923-30	W. Harding	* Gifted speaker
Scalia, Anton	1986-	R. Reagan	**Elusive signer, educator
Shiras, George	1892-1903	B. Harrison	** LD, reclusive
Souter, David H.	1990-	G. Bush	**** Served NH Sup. Court
Stevens, John P.	1975-	G. Ford	**** Educator
Stewart, Potter	1959-81	D. Eisenhower	****Prolific

Justices	Tenure	Appt. by.	Comments
Stone, Harlan F. *	1925-46	C. Coolidge	**** Educator, AG
Story, Joseph	1812-45	J. Madison	* Sig. demand, author
Strong, William	1870-80	U. Grant	* Skilled & articulate
Sutherland, George	1922-38	W. Harding	**** USHR, USS, articulate
Swayne, Noah H.	1862-81	A. Lincoln	*** Active in Ohio politics
Taft, William H. *	1921-30	W. Harding	*** See U.S. Presidents
Taney, Roger B. *	1836-64	A. Jackson	*** AG. Sec./War, ill health
Thomas, Clarence	1991-	G. Bush	**** Dir. EEOC
Thompson, Smith	1823-43	J. Monroe	*** Rare from court years
Todd, Thomas	1807-26	T. Jefferson	* LD, wrote very little
Trimble, Robert	1826-28	J.Q. Adams	* Most papers destroyed
Van Devanter, Willis	1910-37	W. Taft	*** AOPYS - 13, farmer
Vinson, Fred M. *	1946-53	H. Truman	* USHR, Sec./treasury
Waite, Morrison R. *	1874-88	U. Grant	*** RU before court years
Warren, Earl *	1953-69	D. Eisenhower	*** Gov. CA, effective CJ
Washington, Bushrod	1799-1829	J. Adams	* Meticulous, nephew GW
Wayne, James M.	1835-67	A. Jackson	* USHR, mayor Savannah
White, Byron R.	1962-93	J. Kennedy	**** Pro football player
White, Edward D. *	1894-1921	G. Cleveland	* USS, strong demand
Whittaker, Charles E.	1957-62	D. Eisenhower	*** Ill health in later years
Wilson, James	1789-98	G. Washington	* Signer DOI
Woodbury, Levi	1845-51	J. Polk	*** USS, Sec./navy, LD
Woods, William B.	1881-87	R. Hayes	*Brig. Gen., papers lost

Name	db/dd	Sig	DS	ALS	SP	Comments
Baldwin, Henry	1780-1844	45	100	240		SALS-2X
Barbour, Phillip P.	1783-1841	75	150	265		
Black, Hugo L.	1886-1971	45	110	255	100	TLS - $150
Blackmun, Harry A.	1908-	40	260	275	75	
Blair, John	1732-1800	250	800	1500		Signer of Constitution
Blatchford, Samuel	1820-1893	45	135	210		
Bradley, Joseph P.	1813-1892	60	125	225	160	
Brandeis, Louis D.	1856-1941	200	650	800	1300	SP - $800
Brennan, William J., Jr.	1906-1997	80	125	160	85	
Brewer, David J .	1837-1910	50	100	200	75	
Breyer, Stephen	1938-	20	35	125	40	
Brown, Henry B.	1836-1913	75	150	250	175	
Burger, Warren E.	1907-1995	50	220	250	80	
Burton, Harold H.	1888-1964	50	175	335	100	USS
Butler, Pierce	1866-1939	50	100	250	75	ANS - $300
Byrnes, James F.	1879-1972	35	105	240	60	
Campbell, John A.	1811-1889	120	225	350		
Cardozo, Benjamin N.	1870-1938	150	325	715	850	Distinct handwriting
Catron, John	1786-1865	75	150	250		
Chase, Salmon P.	1808-1873	100	200	350	650	
Chase, Samuel	1741-1811	300	500	1000		Signer DOI, SALS-2-X
Clark, Tom C.	1899-1977	35	110	125	100	
Clarke, John H.	1857-1945	100	200	350	175	
Clifford, Nathan	1803-1881	80	185	250	150	AG (Polk)
Curtis, Benjamin R.	1809-1874	50	165	265		
Cushing, William	1732-1810					Pricing undetermined
Daniel, Peter V.	1784-1860	45	140	250		

Name	db/dd	Sig	DS	ALS	SP	Comments
Davis, David	1815-1886	75	300	350		Lincoln confidant
Day, William R.	1849-1923	45	90	135	65	Often at the ballpark!
Devanter, Willis Van	1859-1941	100	200	300	250	NOT prolific
Douglas, William O.	1898-1980	75	150	310	200	
Duvall, Gabriel	1752-1844	50	150	300		
Ellsworth, Oliver	1745-1807	120	315	500		
Field, Stephen J.	1816-1899	100	150	300	250	
Fortas, Abe	1910-1982	25	125	180	100	Responsive signer!
Frankfurter, Felix	1882-1965	150	700	1200	800	
Fuller, Melville W.	1833-1910	100	200	300	200	
Ginsburg, Ruth Bader	1933-	30	40	140	40	
Goldberg, Arthur J.	1908-1990	50	150	200	115	
Gray, Horace	1828-1902	30	75	170	40	
Grier, Robert C.	1794-1870	100	250	450		
Harlan, John M.	1833-1911	55	100	175	100	
Harlan, John Marshall	1899-1971	60	100	150	125	TLS-$350, AQS - $425
Holmes, Oliver W.	1841-1935	235	450	1500	650	A master of his craft!
Hughes, Charles E.	1862-1948	50	200	400	250	
Hughes, Charles E.	1862-1948	45	145	250	175	
Hunt, Ward	1810-1886	70	125	200		
Iredell, James	1751-1799					Pricing undetermined
Jackson, Howell E.	1832-1895	60	125	250	125	
Jackson, Robert H.	1892-1954	55	200	375	125	Nuremberg participant
Jay, John	1745-1829	385	1325	2650		ALS - 2.5X
Johnson, Thomas	1732-1819					Pricing undetermined
Johnson, William	1771-1834	100	300	815		
Kennedy, Anthony M.	1936-	30	60	150	50	
Lamar, Joseph R.	1857-1916	50	100	200	100	
Lamar, Lucius Q.C.	1825-1893	60	125	250		USS
Livingston, Henry B.	1757-1823	150	325	500		
Lurton, Horace H.	1844-1914	55	180	250		
Marshall, John	1755-1835	450	1850	5250		ADS (10 sigs)$11K
Marshall, Thurgood	1908-1993	125	300	300	200	
Matthews, Stanley	1824-1889	45	150	275		
McKenna, Joseph	1843-1926	35	50	80	40	
McKinley, John	1780-1852	100	200	300		Health problems
McLean, John	1785-1861	75	225	300		
McReynolds, James C.	1862-1946	50	100	150	75	
Miller, Samuel F.	1816-1890	100	200	300		
Minton, Sherman	1890-1965	45	145	200	90	
Moody, William H.	1853-1917	50	125	175	65	
Moore, Alfred	1755-1810	3750				
Murphy, Frank	1890-1949	60	180	300	125	
Nelson, Samuel	1792-1873	60	165	250		
O'Connor, Sandra Day	1930-	35	175	250	50	
Paterson, William	1745-1806					Signer of Constitution
Peckham, Rufus W.	1838-1909	55	125	200	125	
Pitney, Mahlon	1858-1924	50	75	150	40	
Powell, Lewis F., Jr.	1907-1998	40	125	175	75	
Reed, Stanley F.	1884-1980	45	100	175	80	
Rehnquist, William H.	1924-	45	130	250	100	
Roberts, Owen J.	1875-1955	50	175	225	100	

Name	db/dd	Sig	DS	ALS	SP	Comments
Rutledge, John	1739-1800	195	600	1775		SOC, refused apt.1795
Rutledge, Wiley B.	1894-1949	40	135	275	85	
Sanford, Edward T.	1865-1930	100	200	300	175	
Scalia, Antonin	1936-		45	100	200	60
Shiras, George, Jr.	1832-1924	100	250	400	200	
Souter, David H.	1939-	35	75	175	50	
Stevens, John Paul	1920-	30	100	160	70	
Stewart, Potter	1915-1985	45	105	175	100	
Stone, Harlan F.	1872-1946	75	250	325	225	
Story, Joseph	1779-1845	100	200	350		
Strong, William	1808-1895	85	175	300		
Sutherland, George	1862-1942	75	150	300	200	
Swayne, Noah H.	1804-1884	50	125	200		
Taft, William H.	1857-1930					(See U.S. Presidents)
Taney, Roger B.	1777-1864	75	275	595		
Thomas, Clarence	1948-	25	40	115	40	
Thompson, Smith	1768-1843	100	200	385		
Todd, Thomas	1765-1826					Prices undetermined
Trimble, Robert	1777-1828					Prices undetermined
Vinson, Fred M.	1890-1953	100	200	440	225	
Waite, Morrison R.	1816-1888	100	200	250	125	SALS-2X
Warren, Earl	1891-1974	65	250	225	250	
Washington, Bushrod	1762-1829	125	350	775		
Wayne, James M.	1790-1867	100	225	475		SP scarce
White, Byron R.	1917-	45	120	175	60	
White, Edward D.	1845-1921	50	190	225	135	
White, Edward D.	1845-1921	75	200	250	150	
Whittaker, Charles E.	1901-1973	50	75	170	85	
Wilson, James *	1742-1798	725	1062	1600		DS - $800
Woodbury, Levi	1789-1851	60	150	265		
Woods, William B.	1824-1887	100	200	400	150	Scarce in all forms

* (See DOI & Constitution)

UNITED STATES MILITARY

WHAT YOU NEED TO KNOW

* As defined the military; of or relating to soldiers, arms or war, has existed for centuries.

* Each country has their own unique military structured to meet their particular needs.

* The Department of Defense (DOD) was previously the War Department, established by Congress in 1789.

* In 1798 a separate Navy Department was created. Under the National Security Act of 1947 they merged.

* The Secretary of Defense - a cabinet-level position, was established as the principal assistant to the President and in charge of the DOD.

* As one might anticipate, many military documents are "classified," with content only being available through copies upon declassification.

* The chain of command runs from the President to the Secretary of Defense, through the Joint Chiefs of Staff to the commanders-in-chief of the unified and specified commands.

* If you are going to participate in this sector, one is advised to research an individual's background, participation-engagements, commands, and post-military career activities.

MARKET FACTS

* The autographed material of military figures is popular and similar to coinage, commonly traded in a related market.

* The market form of choice, when available, is the signed photograph of a military leader in uniform.

* There has been little modern-day forgeries encountered in this niche of the market, however machine-signed items are common particularly with active officers.

* Since this niche of the hobby is funded by taxpayers, the response rate to

autograph requests is often higher than that of other areas.

* An individual's promotions, decorations, and assignments - regardless of legitimacy or justification, can impact value.

TRENDS

* Similar to other countries, military leaders of the United States are primarily encountered in our own market. The exception being that of a popular niche, such as Napoleon's Generals, or prominent military leaders, such as Bernard Montgomery.

* Collectors also continue to select key niches in this market to build collections around such as "Aces" and "Medal of Honor Winners."

* Material entering the market, especially from obscure participants, has shown increasing inconsistency in value.

UNITED STATES MILITARY, (See also Revolutionary War and Civil War)

Notes:
> * Assorted selected entries appear - not intended to be comprehensive.
> * Some inconsistent abbreviations exist also due to space restrictions
> *The pricing for many entries is undetermined due to the lack of material entering the market. Collectors have expressed the desire for the entry to appear here, regardless of a formal value, for reference use.

NAME	Dates	Sig.	DS	ALS	SP	Principal Wars
Abrams, Creighton	1914-1974	30		150	75	WWII, Korea, Vietnam
Almond, Edward	1892-1979	20		75	40	WWI, WWII, Korean
Arnold, Henry "Hap"	1886-1950	60	200		175	WWI, WWII
Atkinson, Henry	1782-1842					1812, Black Hawk, PU
Bainbridge, William	1774-1833	150	300	575		Quasi War, 1812
Blandy, William H. G.	1890-1954	40	110		55	WWI, WWII
Bliss, Tasker	1853-1930					Span.-Amer., WWI, PU
Boatner, Haydon L.	1900-	15	30		25	WWII, Korea
Boyd, John P.	1764-1830					India, 1812, PU
Bradley, Omar	1893-1981	110	250		175	WWI, WWII
Brereton, Lewis H.	1890-1967	45	150		65	WWI, WWII
Brown, George S.	1918-1978	20	50		35	WWII, Korea
Brown, Jacob J.	1775-1828					1812, PU
Brown, Wilson	1882-1957	40	100		60	WWI, WWII
Bullard, Robert L.	1861-1947	35	70		65	Spanish-American
Burke, Arleigh A.	1901-?	20	50	70	40	WWII, Korean
Butler, Smedley D.	1881-1940	60	125		100	Spanish-American, WWI
Butler, William O.	1791-1880	60	200			1812, Mexican-Amer.

NAME	Dates	Sig.	DS	ALS	SP	Principal Wars
Callaghan, Daniel J.	1890-1942	50			100	WWI, WWII
Carlson, Evans F.	1896-1947	40	80		50	WWI, WWII
Carpender, Arthur S.	1884-1960	30	70		40	WWI, WWII
Cates, Clifton B.	1893-1970	15	30	55	25	WWI, WWII
Chaffee, Adna R.	1884-1941	70	180	225		Cuban, WWI
Chauncey, Issac	1772-1840	25	85	100		France, 1812
Chennault, Claire L.	1890-1958	400		600	500	WWI, WWII
Childs, Thomas	1796-1853	20	50	75		1812, Seminole
Chynoweth, Bradford G.	1890-1986	15	65	50	40	WWII
Clark, Mark	1896-1985	40	165	300	85	WWI, WWII, Korea
Clark, William	1770-1838	25	80	100		Indian, 1812
Clay, Lucius	1897-1978	30	100		100	WWII
Coffee, John	Unknown					1812, Creek, PU
Collins, Joseph L.	1896-?					WWI, WWII, PU
Coulter, John B.	1891-?	15	30		20	WWI, WWII
Cushman, Robert	1914-1985	20	40		25	WWII, Vietnam
Dade, Francis L.	c.1793-1835					Florida, PU
Davis, Jefferson	1808-1889	535	1375	1650	2500	CSA President
Decatur, Stephen	1779-1820	950	2350	4000		Quasi, 1812, ESPV
Del Valle, Pedro A.	1893-1978	15	25		25	WWII
Denfeld, Louis E.	1891-1972	10	25		25	WWI, WWII
Devereux, James P.	b.1903	20	55	100		WWII
Devers, Jacob L.	1887-1979	30	50		40	WWII, RS
Dickman, Joseph T.	1857-1928	225	450	740		Apache, WWI
Dodd, Francis T.	1899-1973	10	25		20	WWII, Korean
Doniphan, Alexander W.	1808-1887	100	200	360		Mexican War
Doolittle, James H.	1896-	50	160		85	WWI, WWII
Eaker, Ira C.	1896-1987	40	50	125	125	WWI, WWII
Eichelberger, Robert L.	1886-1961	25	60		50	WWI, WWII
Fletcher, Frank J.	1885-1973	25	60	125	55	WWI, WWII
Flipper, Henry O.	1856-1940	25	50	100		Controversial
Foss, Joseph J.	1915-	25	75	100	60	WWII
Foulois, Benjamin D.	1879-1967	30	60	100	50	Spanish-American
Funston, Frederick	1865-1917	100	200	300		Cuban Insurrection
Gaines, Edmund P.	1777-1849	75	165	215		1812, Seminole
Geiger, Roy S.	1885-1947	50	100	200		WWI, WWII
Gerow, Leonard T.	1888-1972	25	65	130	50	WWI, WWII
Ghormley, Robert L.	1883-1958	25	55		40	WWI, WWII
Giffen, Robert C.	1886-1962	20	50	65	30	WWI, WWII
Goethals, George W.	1858-1928	200	460			Spanish, WWI
Grattan, John L.	1830-1854					Sioux, PU, scarce
Graves, William S.	1865-1940	45	100		75	WWI
Griner, George W.	1895-	15	40			WWI, WWII
Griswold, Oscar W.	1886-1959	15	30			WWI, WWII
Gruenther, Alfred M.	1899-1983	20	40		40	WWI, WWII
Haig, Alexander M.	1924-	15	30		40	Vietnam
Hale, Willis	1893-1961	30	75		50	WWII

NAME	Dates	Sig.	DS	ALS	SP	Principal Wars
Hall, Charles P.	1886-1953	35	70	150		WWI, WWII
Halsey, William F.	1882-1959	75	200	250	200	WWI, WWII
Hansell, Haywood	1909-					WWII, PU
Harbord, James G.	1866-1947	75	150	200	125	WWI, COB, RCA
Harmon, Ernest N.	1894-1979	25	60	120	30	WWI, WWII
Hart, Thomas C.	1877-1971	20	55	125	35	WWI, WWII
Hasbrouck, Robert W.	1896-1985	30	115		60	WWI, WWII
Hester, John H.	1886-1976	30	60		40	WWII
Hewitt, Henry K.	1887-1972	25	50	100		WWI, WWII
Hines, John L.	1868-1968	40	115			Spanish, WWI
Hodge, John R.	1893-1963	30	65		50	WWI, WWII
Hodges, Courtney H.	1887-1966	65	120		75	WWI, WWII
Holcomb, Thomas	1879-1965	35	75		75	WWI, WWII
Hull, Isaac	1773-1843	200	500	600		Quasi, 1812
Hunter, Charles	1906-1978	30	75	100	50	WWII
Johnson, Richard M.	1780-1850					1812, PU
Johnson, Sir William	1715-1774					French & Indian, PU
Jones, David C.	1921-	15	40		25	WWII, Korean
Jones, Thomas	1790-1858	30	75			1812, Mexican

Chairman of the Joint Chiefs of Staff, 1949-2001

Omar N. Bradley, USA	1949-53
Arthur W. Radford, USN	1953-57
Nathan F. Twining, USAF	1957-60
Lyman L. Lemnitzer, USA	1960-62
Maxwell D. Taylor, USA	1962-64
Earle G. Wheeler, USA	1964-70
Thomas H. Moorer, USN	1970-74
George S. Brown, USAF	1974-78
David C. Jones, USAF	1978-82
John W. Vessey, Jr., USA	1982-85
William J. Crowe, USN	1985-89
Colin L. Powell, USA	1989-93
John Shalikashvili, USA	1993-97
H. Hugh Shelton, USA	1997-2001
Richard B. Myers, USAF	2001- present

NAME	Dates	Sig.	DS	ALS	SP	Principal Wars
Kearny, Stephen	1794-1848	100	225	300		1812, Mexican
Kenney, George C.	1889-1977	25	60		50	WWI, WWII
Keyes, Geoffrey	1886-1967	60	120		75	WWII
Kimmel, Husband E.	1882-1968	325			600	WWI, WWII, P. Harbor
King, Edward P.	1884-1958	50	120	240		WWI, WWII, POW
King, Ernest	1878-1956	35	100	225	100	WWI, WWII
Kinkaid, Thomas C.	1888-1972	25	70	140	35	WWI, WWII
Krueger, Walter	1881-1967	50	100	200	70	WWI, WWII
Lawrence, James	1781-1813					Tripolitan, scarce, PU
Lee, Willis A.	1888-1945	55	120	200		WWI, WWII
LeMay, Curtis	1906-	25	55		60	WWII
Lemnitzer, Lyman L.	1899-1988	30	50	100	40	WWII, Korean

NAME	Dates	Sig.	DS	ALS	SP	Principal Wars
Liggett, Hunter	1857-1935	35	70	120		WWI
Lucas, John P.	1890-1949	65	130	215		WWI, WWII
McCain, John S.	1884-1945	50	100		85	WWI, WWII
McConnell, John P.	1908-1986					WWII, PU
MacArthur, Douglas	1880-1964	240	550	700	500	WWI, WWII
MacDonough, Thomas	1783-1825	100	250			Quasi, 1812
McGiffen, Philo	1860-1897					Sino-French, scarce
McMorris, Charles H.	1890-1954	60	130	200	75	WWI, WWII
McNair, Lesley J.	1883-1944	70	150	225		WWI, WWII
Macomb, Alexander	1782-1841					1812, Seminole, PU
Mahan, Dennis	1802-1871	75	150	250		Theorist
March, Peyton C.	1864-1955	45	100	200	75	WWI
Merrill, Aaron	1890-1961	35	70	150	60	WWI, WWII
Merrill, Frank D.	1903-1955	40	100	165		WWII
Middleton, Troy H.	1889-1976	50	130		100	WWI, WWII
Mitchell, William "Billy"	1879-1936	250	1000	1150		WWI
Mitscher, Marc A.	1887-1947	300	650		600	WWI, WWII
Montgomery, Alfred E.	1891-1961	30	65		45	WWII
Mueller, Paul J.	1892-1964	25	60		40	WWII
Nimitz, Chester W.	1885-1966	150	300		400	WWI, WWII
Norstad, Lauris	1907-1988	25	50		45	WWII
Oldendorf, Jesse B.	1887-1974	40	100		65	WWI, WWII
Palmer, John M.	1870-1955	60	150	260		WWI, WWII
Parker, George	1889-1968	30	65		40	WWI, WWII
Patch, Alexander	1889-1945	75	150	300	180	WWI, WWII
Pate, Randolph M.	1898-1961	40	100	200	70	WWII, Korean
Patrick, Mason M.	1863-1942	50	110	200	75	WWI
Patton, George S.	1885-1945	1000	2000	3250		WWI, WWII
Pepperell, William	1696-1759	100	200	300		French & Indian
Perry, Matthew C.	1794-1858	425	800	1500		1812, Algerian
Perry, Oliver H.	1785-1819					1812, rare, PU
Pershing, John J.	1860-1948	125		350	375	Mexican, WWI
Pick, Lewis A.	1890-1956	30	90		50	WWI, WWII
Pike, Zebulon	1779-1813	250	565	1000		1812
Porter, David	1780-1843	50	150	275		Quasi, 1812
Powell, Colin L.	1937-	25	100		100	Vietnam, Kuwait
Quitman, John A.	1798-1858	30	55			Mexican
Radford, Arthur W.	1896-1973	50	100	200	65	WWI, WWII
Reed, Walter	1851-1902	375	700		650	Physician
Reid, Samuel C.	1783-1861	40	85			Quasi, 1812
Richardson, Robert C.	1882-1954	100	225		200	WWI, WWII
Rickenbacker, Edward	1890-1973	125	250	450	275	WWI, WWII
Ridgway, Matthew	1895-	75	150	220	130	WWI, WWII
Rockwell, Francis	1886-1979	25	60	100	30	WWI, WWII
Rodgers, John	1772-1838	100	225	300		Quasi, 1812
Rodman, Thomas	1815-1871					Ordanance special., PU

NAME	Dates	Sig.	DS	ALS	SP	Principal Wars
Ryan, John D.	1915-1983	20	40		25	WWII
Schwarzkopf, H. Norman	1934-		30	100		75	Vietnam, Kuwait
Scott, Hugh L.	1853-1934	35	70	125		Indian, WWI
Sheperd, Lemuel C.	1896-1990	25	50	100	35	WWI, WWII
Sherman, Forrest P.	1896-1951	35	75	125	50	WWI, WWII
Sherman, Frederick C.	1888-1957	20	40	100	35	WWI, WWII
Short, Walter	1880-1949	20	40	55	30	WWI, WWII
Shoup, David	1904-1983	25	40	75	40	WWII
Sibert, Franklin C.	1891-					WWII, PU
Simpson, William H.	1888-1980	25	75	200	50	WWI, WWII
Sims, William S.	1858-1936	40	100	150	60	WWI
Smith, Charles B.	1916-	20	40		30	WWII, Korean
Smith, Holland M.	1882-1967	50	100	175	70	WWI, WWII
Smith, Julian C.	1885-?	20	40			WWII
Smith, Oliver P.	1893-?	40	75	125	50	WWI, WWII
Smith, Persifor F.	1798-1858	40	80	150		Seminole, Mexican
Smith, Ralph C.	1893-?	25	50	100		WWI, WWII
Smith, Walter B.	1895-1961	40	75	130	55	WWI, WWII
Smyth, Alexander	1765-1830	25	40			1812
Somervell, Brehon B.	1892-1955	25	50	75	30	WWI, WWII
Sprague, Clifton A.	1896-1955	50	80			WWI, WWII
Sprague, Thomas L.	1894-1972	25	60	100	40	WWI, WWII
Spruance, Raymond A.	1886-1969	50	100	150	70	WWII, ambassador
Standley, William H.	1872-1963	40	75	125	50	WWII, ambassador
Stewart, Charles	1778-1869	100	200	300		Quasi, 1812
Stilwell, Joseph	1883-1946	150	300	500	300	WWI, WWII
Stockton, Robert F.	1795-1866	100	200	300		1812, Mexican
Stratemeyer, George E.	1890-1969	25	40	75	40	WWII, Korean
Sultan, Daniel I.	1885-1947	40	75	125		WWI, WWII
Summerall, Charles	1867-1955	50	100	200	75	Spanish, WWI
Swift, Innis	1882-1953	30	50	75	40	WWI, WWII
Swing, Joseph	1894-1984	25	45		35	WWI, WWII
Taylor, Maxwell	1901-1987	30	75	125	65	WWII, Korean, ambass.
Theobald, Robert A.	1884-1957					WWI, WWII, PU
Travis, William B.	1809-1836	2500				Texas, ESPV
Truscott, Lucian K.	1895-1965	50	100	150	75	WWI, WWII
Tunner, William H.	1906-1983	20	40	75	30	WWII, Korean
Turner, Richmond	1885-1961	40	80	150	60	WWI, WWII
Twining, Nathan F.	1897-1982	45	125	175	75	WWI, WWII
Vandegrift, Alexander A.	1887-1973	50	100	150	75	WWII
Vandenburg, Hoyt S.	1899-1954	50	125	200	100	WWII, Korean
Van Fleet, James A.	1892-	25	50	115	50	WWI, WWII, Korean
Van Rensselaer, Steph.	1764-1839	50	125	200	80	1812, RPI, USHR
Wagner, Arthur L.	1853-1905	35	70	100	50	Indian, Spanish-Amer.
Wainwright, Jonathan	1883-1953	125	250		250	WWI, WWII. MOH
Walker, Frank R.	1899-1976	25	45	70	35	WWII
Walker, Walton H.	1889-1950	35	70	125	70	WWI, WWII
Wedemeyer, Albert C.	1896-1990	30	125		115	WWII

NAME	Dates	Sig.	DS	ALS	SP	Principal Wars
Westmoreland, William	1914-	20	50	100	50	WWII, Korean
White, Thomas D.	1901-1965	35	75	125	50	WWII
Wilkinson, Theodore S.	1888-1946	70	150			WWI, WWII, MOH
Winder, William H.	1775-1824	25	60	100		1812
Wood, Leonard	1860-1927	50	100	150	150	WWI, PC
Worth, William J.	1794-1849	30	75	125		1812, Mexican

WORLD MILITARY - TEST CHAPTER

WHAT YOU NEED TO KNOW

* As defined the military; of or relating to soldiers, arms or war, has existed for centuries.

* Each country has their own unique military structured to meet their particular needs.

MARKET FACTS

* The autographed material of military figures is popular and similar to coinage, commonly traded in a related market.

TRENDS

* Similar to other countries, military leaders of the United States are primarily encountered in our own market. The exception being that of a popular niche, such as Napoleon's Generals, or prominent military leaders, such as Bernard Montgomery.

WORLD MILITARY - 1700 - Present

Notes:
* Due to space restrictions not all formal titles are included with each entry.
* Some inconsistent abbreviations exist also due to space restrictions
*The pricing for many entries is undetermined due to the lack of material entering the market. Collectors have expressed the desire for the entry to appear here, regardless of a formal value, for reference use.
* The hobby of autograph collecting is popular around the world and price guides
such as this should begin to reflect this aspect. As part of an attempt to enhance future editions, we are interested in compiling data reagrding the following entries.

Name	db/dd	Sig.	DS	ALS	SP	Comments
Abbas Mirza	1783-1833					Persian general, PU
Abd-el-Kader	1808-1883					Algerian ruler, PU
Abd-el-Krim	1881-1963					Moroccan Berber leader, PU
Abd-er-Rahman Khan	1844-1901					Emir of Afghanistan, PU
Abdullah et Taaisha	1846-1899					"The Khalifa", Sudanese gen.
Abe, Hiroaki	1889-1949					Japanese admiral, PU
Abe, Noruyuki	1875-1953					Japanese general, PU
Abrial, Jean-Marie Chas.	1879-1962					French admiral, PU
Adachi, Hatazo	1884-1947					Japanese general, PU
Adan, Avraham "Bren"	1926-					Israeli general, PU
Adenauer, Konrad	1876-1967	50	175	250	150	W. German chancellor
Agha Mohammed Khan	1720-1797					Persian general , ruler, KIA . PU
Aguinaldo, Emilio	1869-1964	125	150	200	150	Philip. revolutionary
Ahmad Shah Durani	1722-1772					Afghan general, chieftain, PU
Akbar Khan	?-1849					Afghan general, PU
Akiyama, Saneyuki	1868-1918					Japanese admiral, PU
Akiyama, Yoshifuru	1859-1930					Japanese general,PU
Alanbrooke, Sir Alan F.	1883-1963					British field marshal, PU
Albert, Archduke of Aus.	1817-1895					Austrian field marshal, PU
Alekseev, Mikhail V.	1857-1918					Russian general, PU
Alexander I (Pavlovich)	1777-1825		1300	1000		Russian czar
Alexander of Battenberg	1857-1893					Prince of Bulgaria, PU
Alexander of Tunis	1891-1969	75	125	175	120	British field marshal
Allenby, Edmund H. H.	1861-1936	75	160		200	British field marshall, ESPV
Allende Gossens, S.	1908-1973	50	140	275	100	Chilean Marxist pres., ousted
Alompra	1714-1760					Burmese monarch, PU
Alvinczy, Josef	1735-1810					Austrian field marshall, PU
Ambrosio, Vittorio	1879-1958					Italian general, PU
Anami, Korechika	1887-1945					Japanese general, PU
Anderson, Kenneth A.	1891-1959					British general, PU
Annunzio, Gabriele d'	1863-1938					Italian adventurer, PU
Anson, George Lord	1697-1762					"Father of the British Navy", PU
Aosta, Amedeo U.	1898-1942					Italian general, PU
Aosta, Emanuele F.	1869-1931					Italian field marshal, PU
Arabi Pasha	1839-1911					Egyptian army officer, PU
Araki, Sadao	1877-1966					Japanese general, PU
Ardant Du Picq, Charles	1831-1870					French army officer, PU
Arentschildt, Alexander	1806-1881					Hannoverian general, PU
Ariga, Kosaku	1897-1945					Japanese naval officer, PU
Arima, Masafumi	1895-1944					Legendary Japanese Adm., PU
Arnim, Jurgen von	1889-1971					German panzer general, PU
Artigas, Jose Gervasio	1764-1850					Uruguayan gen., PU
Asaka, Yasuhiko	1887 - ?					Japanese general, PU
Asquith, Herbert H.	1852-1928	40	75	125	150	British liberal prime minister
Ataturk, Kemal	1881-1938					Founder of modern Turkey, PU
Attlee, Clement	1883-1967	50	150	225	100	British leader, prime minister
Auchinleck, Claude J.	1884-1981	50	100		1000	British field marshal, "The Auk"
Augereau, Pierre Fran.	1757-1816					Fr. Marshal of the Empire, PU
Aung San	1916-1947					Burmese political leader, PU
Bach-Zelewski, Erich v.	1898-1972					German general, PU
Baden-Powell, Robert	1857-1941	175	350	400		British general, "B-P",

Name	db/dd	Sig.	DS	ALS	SP	Comments
Bader, Douglas Robert	1910-1982					British air force officer, PU
Badoglio, Pietro	1871-1956					Italian field marshal, PU
Bagration, Peter I.	1765-1812					Russian general, PU
Baird, Sir David	1757-1829					British general, PU
Baker, Valentine	1827-1887					British/Turkish general, PU
Bakunin, Mikhail	1814-1876					Russian revolutionary, PU
Balbo, Italo	1896-1940					Italian air marshall, PU
Balfour, Arthur J.	1848-1930	60	125	125	100	British foreign secretary Ballivian,
Jose	1804-1852					Bolivian general, statesman, PU
Baraguay D'Hilliers, Ach.	1795-1878					Marshal of France, PU
Baratieri, Oreste	1841-1901					Italian general, PU
Barclay de Tolly, Mikhail	1761-1818					Russian field marshal, PU
Barclay, Robert H.	1785-1837					British naval officer, PU
Barnard, Sir Henry W.	1799-1857					British general, PU
Barre, Georges	1886-1970					French general, PU
Barreiro, Jose Maria	1793-1819					Spanish general, PU
Barrios, Justo Rufino	1835-1885	65	150			Guatemalan dictator
Barth, Jean	1650-1702					French admiral,PU
Bastico, Ettore	1876-1972					Italian marshal, PU
Batista y Zaldivar, Fulge	1901-1973	175			200	Cuban president, dictator
Battenberg, Prince Lou.	1854-1921					British admiral, PU
Bayerlein, Fritz	1899-1970					German general, PU
Bazaine, Achille Fran.	1811-1888					Marshal of France, PU
Beatty, David, 1st Earl	1871-1936					British admiral, PU
Beaufre, Andre	1902-1973					French general, PU
Beauharnais, Eugene d.	1781-1824					French general, PU
Beaulieu, Jean Pierre d.	1725-1819					Austrian general, PU
Beaverbrook, Lord	1879-1964	40	100		50	British financier, statesman
Beck, Ludwig	1880-1944					Ger. gen., plotted Hitler's a., PU
Begin, Menachem	1913-1992	100	200		200	Israeli prime minister,RS
Bellegarde, Count Hein.	1756-1845					Austrian field marshal, PU
Below, Fritz von	1853-1918					German general, PU
Below, Otto von	1857-1944					German general, PU
Ben-Gurion, David	1886-1973	225	500		500	First PM of Israel, SDS-2X
Benedek, Ludwig Aug.	1804-1881					Austrian field marshal, PU
Benes, Eduard	1884-1948					Czech. president, PU
Bennigsen, Count Lev.	1745-1826					Russian general, PU
Berenguer, Damaso	1873-1953					Spanish general, statesman, PU
Beresford, Charles W. d.	1846-1919					British admiral, PU
Beresford, William Carr,	1768-1854					British general, PU
Beresford-Peirse, Noel	1888-1953					British general, PU
Bevan, Aneurin	1897-1960					British labor party leader, PU
Bevin, Ernest	1881-1951	30	50	100	50	British labor party leader
Bismarck, Otto von	1815-1898	300	600			Ger. states., "Iron Chancellor"
Blum, Leon	1872-1950	30	60	125	50	French socialist leader, writer
Bolivar, Simon	1783-1830	500				South American revolutionary
Brandt, Willy	1913-1992	30	100	200	100	Ger., chancellor of W.Germany
Brezhnev, Leonid	1906-1982	500			600	Soviet leader, 1964-1982
Briand, Aristide	1862-1932					French foreign minister, PU
Cabrera, Ramon	1806-1877					Spanish Carlist general, PU
Cadorna, Luigi	1850-1928					Italian general, PU

Name	db/dd	Sig.	DS	ALS	SP	Comments
Cadorna, Raffaele	1815-1897					Italian general,PU
Calder, Sir Robert	1745-1818					British admiral, PU
Calleja Del Rey, Felix M.	1759-1828					Spanish Colonial governor, PU
Cambridge, George W.	1819-1904					British field marshal, PU
Campbell, Sir Archibald	1769-1843					British general, PU
Campbell, Sir Colin,	1792-1863					British field marshal, PU
Campero, Narisco	1815-1896					Bolivian general, PU
Campioni, Inigo	1878-1944					Italian admiral, PU
Canaris, Wilhelm	1887-1945					German admiral, PU
Caneva, Carlo	1845-1922					Italian general,PU
Canterac, Jose	1785-1835					Spanish general, PU
Capelle, Edouard von	1855-1931					German admiral, PU
Capello, Lugi Attilio	1859-1941					Italian general, PU
Carden, Sir Sackville H.	1857-1930					British admiral, PU
Cardigan, James Tho.	1797-1868					British general, politician,PU
Carnot, Lazare Nicolas	1753-1823					French general, PU
Carpenter, Alfred Nich.	1881-1955					British admiral, PU
Carranza, Venustiano	1859-1920					Mexican statesman, PU
Carrera, Jose Miguel de	1785-1821					Chilean general, PU
Carton De Wiart, Adrian	1880-1963					British general, PU
Castelnau, N. M. J. E. C.	1851-1944					French general, PU
Castlereagh, Robert	1769-1822	35				British foreign secretary
Caulaincourt, Arm. A. .	1773-1827					French general, PU
Cavagnari, Domenico	1876-1966					Italian admiral, PU
Cavallero, Ugo	1880-1943					Italian field marshal,PU
Cavan, Frederick R. .	1865-1946					British field marshal, PU
Caviglia, Enrico	1862-1945					Italian field marshal, PU
Caviur, Camillo Benso	1810-1861					Italian statesman, PU
Ceausescu, Nicolae	1918-1989	75			150	Communist leader
Cervera y Topete, P.	1839-1909					Spanish admiral, PU
Cetshwayo	1827-1884					Zulu monarch,PU
Ch'en, Ch'eng	1898-?					Nationalist Chinese gen., PU
Ch'en, Chiung-ming	1878-1933					Chinese warlord, PU
Ch'en, Yu-ch-eng	1836-1862					Chinese Taiping general, PU
Chakkour, Youssef	1928-					Syrian general, PU
Chamberlain, Austen	1863-1937	50			125	British statesman
Chamberlain, Neville	1869-1940	75	200		200	British Con. , PM,SDS-2X
Championnet, Jean A.E	.1762-1800					French general, PU
Chang, Fa-k'uei	1896-?					Nationalist Chinese general, PU
Chang, Hsueh-liang	1898-?					Chinese warlord, PU
Chang, Hsun	1854-1923					Chinese warlord, PU
Chang, Lo-hsing	?-1863					Chinese rebel leader, PU
Chang, Tso-lin	1873-1928					Chinese warlord, PU
Chang, Tsung-ch'ang	1881-1933					Chinese warlord, PU
Chard, John Rouse Mer.	1847-1897					British army officer, PU
Charles, Louis John	1771-1847					Austrian field marshall, PU
Chasse, David Hendryk	1765-1849					Dutch general, PU
Chauvel, Henry George	1865-1945					Australian general, PU
Chelmsford, Fred. A. T.	1827-1905					British general, PU
Chen, Yi	1901-1972					Communist Chinese mar., PU
Chetwode, Sir Phillip W.	1869-1950					British field marshal, PU
Chiang Kai-shek	1887-1975	200				Nationalist Chinese president

Name	db/dd	Sig.	DS	ALS	SP	Comments
Cho, Isamu	1895-1945					Japanese general, PU
Chu, Teh	1886-1976					Communist Chinese mar., PU
Church, Sir Richard	1784-1873					British army officer in Greek, PU
Churchill, Winston	1874-1965	850	1750	4000	3500	SDS-5X,SALS-2-3X, SB-$2300
Cialdini, Enrico	1813-1892					Italian general, PU
Ciano, Galeazzo	1903-1944	75				Italian fascist foreign minister
Clam-Gallas, Eduard von	1805-1891					Austrian general, PU
Clausewitz, Karl Maria	1780-1831					Prussian general, theorist, PU
Clemenceau, Georges	1841-1929	100			200	French statesman
Clerfayt, Charles Jos.	1733-1798					Austrian field marshal, PU
Climo, Skipton Hill	1868-1937					British general, PU
Clinton, William Henry	1769-1846					British general, PU
Clive, Robert	1725-1774	300				First adm. of Bengal
Cobbe, Sir Alexander S.	1870-1931					British general, PU
Cochise c.	1812-1974					American Apache Indian , PU
Cochrane, Thomas	1775-1860					British admiral, PU
Cockburn, Sir George	1772-1853					British admiral,PU
Codrington, Sir Edward	1770-1851					British admiral, PU
Colbert, Jean Baptiste	1619-1683					French statesman, PU
Colborne, Sir John	1778-1863					British field marshal, PU
Colley, Sir George P.	1835-1881					British general, PU
Collins, Michael	1890-1922					Irish revolutionary, PU
Collishaw, Raymond	1893-1976					Canadian air vm British ser., PU
Congreve, Sir William	1772-1828					British artillery officer, PU
Coningham, Sir Arthur	1895-1948					British air marshal, PU
Conrad Von Hotzen., F.	1852-1925					Austro-Hung. field marshal, PU
Coote, E. (Brave Heart)	1728-1783					British general, PU
Cotton, Sir Stapleton	1773-1865					British field marshal,PU
Crace, Sir John C.	1887-1968					British admiral, PU
Cradock, Sir C. G. F. M.	1862-1914					British admiral, PU
Craufurd, Robert	1764-1812					English gen., "Black Bob", PU
Crazy Horse	c.1849-1877					Oglala Sioux war chief, PU
Cromwell, Oliver	1599-1658		6000			Lord Protector of England
Cronje, Pieter A.c	.1835-1911					Boer general, PU
Crutchley, Victor A.C.	1893-1986					British admiral, PU
Cumberland, William A.	1721-1765					British prince and general, PU
Cunningham, Sir Alan G.	1887-1983					British general, PU
Cunningham, Sir And.	1883-1963					British admiral, PU
Cunningham, Sir John	1885-1962					British admiral, PU
Curzon of Kedleston	1859-1925					Viceroy of India, PU
Daigo, Tadashige	1891-1947					Japanese admiral, PU
Daladier, Edouard	1884-1970	35	75	150	75	French radical socialist politician
Danton, Georges	1759-1794					French Revolutionist, PU
Davout, Louis Nicolas	1770-1823					Fr. Marshal of the Empire, PU
Dayan, Moshe	1815-1981	125	250		200	Israeli general, politician
De Gasperi, Alcide	1881-1954					Italian prime minister, PU
De Gaulle, Charles	1890-1970		1275	2500		French general, ESPV
De Robeck, Sir John M.	1862-1928					British admiral, PU
De Valera, Eamon	1882-1975					Irish/U.S. statesman, PU
De Wet, Christiaan R.	1854-1922					Boer general, PU
Deng Xiaoping	1904-1997	975				Paramount leader of China

Name	db/dd	Sig.	DS	ALS	SP	Comments
Desaix de Veygoux, C.	1768-1800					"The Just Sultan", PU
Dessalines, Jean Jacq.	c.1746-1806					Haitian general and ruler, PU
Dewa, Shigeto	1856-1930					Japanese admiral, PU
Diaz, Armando	1861-1928					Italian marshal, PU
Dietl. Eduard	1890-1944					German general, PU
Dietrich, Josef	1892-1966					German general, PU
Dingiswayo	c.1770-1818					Mtetwa chieftain, PU
Dinh Diem, Ngo	1901-1963					US. Vietnamese president, PU
Dinuzulu	1868-1913					Zulku chieftain, PU
Disraeli, Benjamin	1804-1881	175	300	500		British prime minister, SALS-2X
Dobell, Sir Charles Mac.	1869-1954					British general, PU
Dohihara, Kenji	1883-1948					Japanese general, PU
Dollfuss, Engelbert	1892-1934					Austrian chancellor, PU
Dollman, Friedrich	1876-1944					German general, PU
Donitz, Karl	1891-1980	100	225		200	German admiral, TSS-$350
Douhet, Giulio	1869-1930					Italian army officer, PU
Dowding, Hugh C. T.	1882-1970					British air marshal,PU
Dreyfus, Alfred	1859-1935	160	350	900		French army officer, SALS-2X
Drouet d'Erlon, Jean B.	1765-1844					Marshal of France, PU
Dubcek, Alexander	1921-1992	75	150	225	100	Czech. statesman
Dumouriez, Charles F.	1739-1823					French general, PU
Dunmore, John Murray	1732-1809					British colonial governor, PU
Ebert, Friedrich	1871-1925					Social Democrat, PU
Eden, Sir Anthony	1897-1977	50	125		75	British foreign secretary, PM
Ehrensvard, Earl August	1745-1800					Swedish admiral, PU
Eichorn, Hermann von	1848-1918					German field marshal,PU
Einem, Karl von	1853-1934					German general, PU
Emmich, Otto von	1848-1915					German general,PU
Enomoto, Takeaki	1836-1908					Japanese admiral, PU
Enver, Pasha	1881-1922					Turkish general, PU
Erhard, Ludwig	1897-1977	50	100	200	75	W. German chancellor
Estaing, Count C.H.T.	1729-1794					French admiral
Falkenhausen, Ludwig	1840-1936					German general, PU
Falkenhayn, Erich von	1861-1922					German general, PU
Falkenhorst, Nikolaus	1885-1968					German general, PU
Fayolle, Marie Emile	1852-1928					Marshall of France, PU
Feng Tzu-ts'ai	1818-1903					Chinese general, PU
Feng, Kuo-chang	1859-1919					Chinese warlord, PU
Feng, Yu-hsiang	1882-1948					Chinese warlord, PU
Fink, Friedrich August	1718-1766					Prussian general,PU
Fisher, John Arbuthnot	1841-1920					British admiral, PU
Foch, Ferdinand	1851-1929					French field marshal, PU
Fonck, Paul Rene	1894-1953					French officer, PU
Franchet D'Esperey,.F	1856-1942					Marshal of France,PU
Franco, Francisco	1892-1975	250				Spanish leader, dictator
Franco-Bahamonde, F.	1892-1975					Spanish general, dictator, PU
Frederick Charles, Prin.	1828-1885					Prussian prince, field mars., PU
Frederick William, Prince	1882-1951					German general, PU
Fredrick II, the Great	1712-1786	500	1000	2000		Prussian monarch
French, John Denton P.	1852-1925					British general, PU

Name	db/dd	Sig.	DS	ALS	SP	Comments
Freyberg, Bernard Cyril	1889-1963					New Zealand general, PU
Friedeburg, Hans Georg von						German general, PU
Friessner, Johannes	1892-1971					German general, PU
Fritsch, Baron Werner	1880-1939					German military officer, PU
Fromm, Friedrich	1888-1945					German general, PU
Frontenac, Louis de	1620-1698					French gov. New France, PU
Frunze, Mikhail Vasily.	1885-1925					Russian revolutionary gen., PU
Fujii, Koichi	1858-1926					Japanese admiral, PU
Fujiwara, Iwaichi	1908-					Japanese general, PU
Fukuda, Hikosuke	1875-1959					Japanese general, PU
Fukuda, Masataro	1866-1932					Japanese general, PU
Fukudome, Shigeru	1891-1971					Japanese admiral, PU
Fuller, John F. Charles	1878-1964					British general, theorist, PU
Gaitskell, Hugh	1906-1963					Brit. labor party leader, PU
Gall	c.1840-1894					American Sioux war chief, PU
Galland, Adolf	1912-					German air force general, PU
Gallieni, Joseph Simon	1849-1916					Mar.France (posthumous), PU
Gallwitz, Max Von	1852-1932					German general, PU
Gambetta, Leon	1838-1882					French statesman, politician, PU
Gamelin, Maurice Gust.	1872-1958					French general, PU
Gandhi, Indira	1917-1984	175	300	350	250	P.M. of India, SALS-2X, RS
Gandhi, Mohandas K.	1869-1948	600	1150	1825	2750	Indian political leader
Garibaldi, Giuseppe	1807-1882	150	350	375	800	Italian patriot, soldier
Gatacre, Sir William F.	1843-1905					British general, PU
Genda, Minoru	1904-1989					Japanese naval air officer, PU
Geronimo	1829-1909	5000			5000	American/Chiricahua Apache
Giap, Vo Nguyen	1912-					Vietnamese gen., PU
Gladstone, William E.	1809-1898	60	125	300	125	British prime minister, SALS-2X
Glubb, Sir John Bagot	1897-1986					British army officer, PU
Goebbels, Paul Joseph	1897-1945	400	1100	1500	1200	Nazi propagandist, SALS-2-3X
Goltz, Count Kolmar	1843-1916					German field marshal, PU
Gordon, Charles Geo.	1833-1885					British general, PU
Goring, Hermann W.	1893-1946		1200	2150	1200	German Reichsmarschall
Gottwald, Klement	1896-1953					Czech. Communist leader, PU
Gough, Hubert de la P.	1870-1963					British general, PU
Gough, Hugh	1779-1869					British field marshal, PU
Gribeauval, Jean Bapt.	1715-1789					French artillery officer, PU
Groener, Wilhelm	1867-1939					German general, statesman, PU
Grouchy, Emmanuel M.	1766-1847					Fr. Marshal of the Empire, PU
Guderian, Heinz	1888-1953					German general, PU
Guevara, Che (Ernesto)	1928-1967	500	1000			Guerilla leader, Cuban rev.
Guibert, Jacques Ant.	1743-1790					Fr. army officer, theorist, PU
Haig, Douglas, 1st Earl	1861-1926					British field marshal, PU
Haldane, Richard Burd.	1856-1928					British statesman, military, PU
Halder, Franz	1884-1972					German general, PU
Hamilton, Sir Ian Stand.	1853-1947					British general, PU
Hammarskjold, Dag	1905-1961	150	300	700		Swedish, UN Sec. gen. SDS-2X
Han, Fu-ch u	1890-1938					Chinese warlord, PU
Hanaya, Tadashi	1894-1957					Japanese general, PU
Hara, Chuichi	1889-1964					Japanese admiral, PU

Name	db/dd	Sig.	DS	ALS	SP	Comments
Hara, Tameichi	1900-					Japanese naval officer, PU
Harris, Sir Arthur Travers	1892-1984					British air marshal, PU
Hasegawa, Kiyoshi	1883-1970					Japanese admiral, PU
Hasegawa, Yoshimichi	1850-1924					Japanese field marshal, PU
Hashimoto, Gun	1886-1963					Japanese general, PU
Hashimoto, Kingoro	1890-1957					Japanese army officer, PU
Hashimoto, Mochitsura	1909-					Japanese naval officer, PU
Hata, Shunroku	1879-1962					Japanese field marshal, PU
Hattori, Takushiro	1901-1960					Japanese army officer, PU
Hausen, Max Klemens	1846-1922					German general, PU
Hausser, Paul	1880-1972					German general, PU
Havelock, Sir Henry	1795-1857					British general, PU
Haviland, William	1718-1784					British general, PU
Hawke, Edward, Baron	1705-1781					British admiral, PU
Hayashi, Senjuro	1876-1942					Japanese general, PU
Herriot, Edouard	1872-1957					Fr. radical socialist leader, PU
Herzi, Theodor	1860-1904					Founder modern Zionism, PU
Hidaka, Sonojo	1848-1932					Japanese admiral, PU
Higashikuni, Naruhiko	1887-?					Japanese general, PU
Higuchi, Kichiro	1888-1970					Japanese general, PU
Hill, Sir Rowland	1772-1842					British general, PU
Himmler, Heinrich	1900-1945	450	1100	2000	800	Head of Nazi SS and Gestapo
Hindenburg, Paul von	1847-1934	175	400	500	500	German field marshall WWI
Hipper, Franz von	1863-1932					German admiral, PU
Hirose, Takeo	1868-1904					Japanese naval officer, PU
Hitler, Adolph	1889-1945	1500	2500		2500	LS-$3750, APPT.-$2500
Ho Chi Minh	1890-1969	700	1500		2000	N. Vietnamese pres.
Ho Long	1896-1967					Com. Chinese marshal, PU
Ho Ying-ch'in	1890-?					Nationalist Chinese general, PU
Hoche, Louis Lazare	1768-1797					French general, PU
Hoepner, Erich	1886-1944					Ger. gen., inv. assasin. plot,PU
Hoffman, Max	1869-1927					German general, PU
Homma, Masaharu	1887-1946					Japanese general, PU
Honda, Masaki	1889-1964					Japanese general, PU
Honjo, Shigeru	1876-1945					Japanese general, PU
Horii, Tomitaro	1890-1942					Japanese general, PU
Hosogaya, Boshiro	1888-1964					Japanese admiral, PU
Hu Lin-i	1812-1861					Chinese general, PU
Hu Tsung-nan	1895-1962					Chinese Nationalist general, PU
Huang, Hsing	1874-1916					Chinese rebel, PU
Hung Hsiu-ch uan	1814-1864					Chinese rebel leader, PU
Hung Ta-ch uan	1823-1852					Chinese rebel leader, PU
Hutier, Oskar von	1857-1934					German general, PU
Hyakutake, Haruyoshi	1888-1947					Japanese general, PU
Ichido, Hyoe	1855-1931					Japanese general, PU
Ichiki, Kiyono	1892-1942					Japanese army officer, PU
Iida, Shojiro	1888-?					Japanese general, PU
Ijichi, Hikojiro	1859-1912					Japanese admiral, PU
Ijichi, Kosuke	1855-1917					Japanese general, PU
Ijuin, Goro	1852-1921					Japanese admiral, PU
Ijuin, Matsuji	1893-1944					Japanese admiral, PU

Name	db/dd	Sig.	DS	ALS	SP	Comments
Imai, Takeo	1898-?					Japanese army officer, PU
Imamura, Hitoshi	1886-1968					Japanese general, PU
Immelmann, Max	1890-1916					Ger. lit., "The Eagle of Lille", PU
Imoto, Kumao	1903-?					Japanese army officer, PU
Inada, Masazumi	1896-?					Japanese general, PU
Inoguchi, Toshihira	1896-1944					Japanese admiral, PU
Inonu, Rashid Ismet	1884-1973					Turkish general, statesman, PU
Inoue, Hikaru	1851-1908					Japanese general, PU
Inoue, Ikutaro	1872-1965					Japanese general, PU
Inoue, Shigeyoshi	1889-?					Japanese admiral, PU
Ishihara, Kanji	1886-1949					Japanese general, PU
Ishimaru, Tota	1881-1942					Japanese naval officer, PU
Isogai, Rensuke	1886-1967					Japanese general, PU
Itagaki, Seishiro	1885-1946					Japanese general, PU
Ito, Seiichi	1890-1945					Japanese admiral, PU
Ito, Sukemaro	1834-1906					Japanese admiral, PU
Ito, Yuko	1843-1914					Japanese admiral, PU
Ivanov, Nicholas Yudo.	1851-1919					Russian general, PU
Iwakuro, Hideo	1897-1970					Japanese general, PU
Jameson, Sir Leander S.	1852-1917					British colonial adventurer, PU
Jellicoe, John Rush.l	1859-1935					British admiral, PU
Jinnah, Muhammad Ali	1876-1948					First gov.-gen.of Pakistan, PU
Jodl, Alfred	1890-1946					German general, PU
Jofre, Joseph Jacques	1852-1931					Marshal of France, PU
John, Archduke of Aus.	1782-1859					Austrain army leader, PU
Jomini, Antoine Henri	1779-1869					Swiss-French gen.,, PU
Joseph, Chief	c.1840-1904					American Nez Perce chief, PU
Joubert, Petrus Jacobus	1831-1900					Boer general, politician, PU
Jourdan, Jean-Baptiste	1762-1833					Fr. Marshal of the Empire, PU
Juarez, Benito	1806-1872	500	1250			Mexican ldr., DS-$750, $1400
Junot, Jean Andoche	1771-1813					French general, PU
Kabayama, Sukenori	1837-1922					Japanese general, PU
Kagesa, Sadaaki	1893-1948					Japanese general, PU
Kakuta, Kakuji	1890-1944					Japanese admiral, PU
Kamimura, Hikonojo	1849-1916					Japanese admiral, PU
Kanaris, Konstantinos	1790-1877					Greek admiral, statesman, PU
Kanin, Kotoshito	1865-1945					Japanese field marshal, PU
Karageorge	1762-1817					Serbian general, ruler, PU
Katakura, Tadashi	1898-?					Japanese general, PU
Kataoka, Shichiro	1854-1920					Japanese admiral, PU
Kato, Kanji	1870-1939					Japanese admiral, PU
Kato, Tomosaburo	1861-1923					Japanese admiral, PU
Katsu, Awa	1823-1899					Japanese naval officer, PU
Katsura, Taro	1847-1913					Japanese gen., statesman, PU
Kawabe, Masakazu	1886-1965					Japanese general, PU
Kawabe, Torahiro	1890-1960					Japanese general, PU
Kawaguchi, Kiyotake	1892-1961					Japanese general, PU
Kawakami, Soroku	1848-1899					Japanese general, PU
Kawamura, Kageaki	1850-1926					Japanese field marshal, PU
Kawamura, Sumiyoshi	1836-1904					Japanese admiral, PU

Name	db/dd	Sig.	DS	ALS	SP	Comments
Keitel, Wilhelm	1882-1946	325	700	1400	700	German general
Kellermann, Francois E.	1735-1820					Fr. Marshal of the Empire, PU
Kerensky, Aleksandr	1881-1970	250	750	1500		Russ. hd. of prov. gov. (1917).
Kesselring, Albert von	1885-1960	125	475		200	German field mnarshal
Keyes, Roger John B.	1872-1945					British admiral, PU
Khomeini, Ruhollah	1900-1989	475				Iranian ldr., "ayatollah"
Khrushchev, Nikita	1894-1971	300	500			Sec. Communist party, USSR
Kigoshi, Yasutsama	1854-1932					Japanese general, PU
Kim Il Sung	1910-					North Korean ruler, PU
Kim Il Sung	1912-1994					N. Korean dictator, PU
Kim Kwang Hyop	c.1910-					North Korean general, PU
Kim Ung	c.1910-?					North Korean general, PU
Kimura, Heitaro	1888-1948					Japanese general, PU
Kimura, Masatomi	1891-1960					Japanese admiral, PU
Kinashi, Takakzu	1902-1944					Japanese naval officer, PU
Kitchener, Horatio H.	1850-1916					British field marshal, PU
Kleber, Jean-Baptiste	1753-1800					French general, PU
Kluck, Alexander von	1846-1934					German general, PU
Kluge, Gunther von	1882-1944					German field marshal, PU
Kodama, Gentaro	1852-1906					Japanese general, PU
Koga, Mineichi	1885-1944					Japanese admiral, PU
Koiso, Kuniaki	1880-1950					Japanese general, PU
Kolchak, Aleksandr V.	1874-1920					Russian admiral, PU
Komatsubara, Michitaro	1886-1940					Japanese general, PU
Kondo, Nobutake	1886-1953					Japanese admiral, PU
Kosciusko, Tadeusz A.	1746-1817					Polish general, PU
Kossuth, Lajos	1802-1894		825			Key figure Hungarian revolution
Kropotkin, Pyotr	1842-1921		400	775		Russian anarchist
Kun, Bela	1886-c.1939					Hungarian member, PU
Kuribayashi, Tadamichi	1891-1945					Japanese general, PU
Kurita, Takeo	1889-1977					Japanese admiral, PU
Kuroki, Takemoti	1844-1923					Japanese general, PU
Kuropatkin, Aleksei N.	1848-1925					Russian general, PU
Kuroshima, Kameto	1893-1965					Japanese admiral, PU
Kusaka, Jin'ichi	1889-1972					Japanese admiral, PU
Kusaka, Ryunosuke	1892-1971					Japanese admiral, PU
Kutuzov, Mikhail I. G.	1745-1813					Russian field marshal, PU
La Marmora, Alfonso F.	1804-1878					Italian general, PU
Lally, Thomas Arthur	1702-1766					French general, PU
Lannes, Jean	1769-1809					Marshal of the Empire, PU
Lanrezac, Charles Louis	1852-1925					French general, PU
Lasalle, Count Antoine	1775-1809					French general, PU
Lattre de Tassigny, Jean	1889-1952					Marshal of France, PU
Laval, Pierre	1883-1945					French politician, PU
Law, Andrew Bonar	1858-1923	30	75	150		Britishpolitician
Lawrence, Thomas E.	1888-1935	600	1100	3500	2650	"Lawrence of Arabia", SALS-2X
Leeb, Wilhelm Ritter v.	1876-1956					German field marshal, PU
Lefebvre, Francis Jos.	1755-1820					Fr. marshal of the Empire, PU
Leman, Gerard Mathieu	1851-1920					Belgian general, PU
Lenin, Vladimir Ilyich	1870-1924			30000		Rus. rev.,Ldr. SALS-$30000
Lesseps, Ferdinand de	1805-1894	150	250	500		Fr., Suez Canal, AQS-$385

Name	db/dd	Sig.	DS	ALS	SP	Comments
Lettow-Vorbeck, Paul E.	1870-1964					German general, PU
Levesque, Rene	1922-1987					Canadian premier, PU
LI Hsiu-ch'eng	1824-1864					Chinese rebel general, PU
LI Hsu-pin	1817-1858					Chinese general, PU
LI Tsung-jen	1891-1969					Nat. Chinese general, PU
LI Yuan-hung	1864-1928					Chinese warlord, PU
Liddell Hart, Sir Basil H.	1895-1970					British army officer, PU
Liman von Sanders, O.	1855-1929					German general, PU
Lin Piao	1907-1971					Chinese communist marshal, PU
Litvinov, Maxim	1876-1951					Polish/Russian rev., PU
Liu Chih	1892-?					Chinese Nationalist general, PU
Liu Chih-tan	1902-1936					Communist Chinese, PU
LIU K'un-yi	1830-1902					Hunan army general, PU
Liu Po-ch'eng	1892-?					Chinese Com. marshal, PU
Lloyd George, David	1863-1945	75	200	400	250	British Liberal party PM
Lu Cheng-ts'ao	1904-					Communist Chin. general, PU
Ludendorff, Erich	1865-1937					German general, PU
Luxemburg, Rosa	1871-1919					German revolutionary, PU
Lyautey, Louis Hubert	1854-1934					French marshal, PU
Ma Chan-shan	1885-1950					Nationalist Chinese general, PU
Ma Pu-fang	1903-					Nationalist Chinese general, PU
Maarios III	1913-1977					Greek , Pres. Cyprus, PU
MacDonald, J. Ramsay	1866-1937	75	150	225	200	Brit., First Labor party PM
Macdonald, Jacques E.	1765-1840					Fr. marshal of the Empire, PU
Mack Von Leiberich, K.	1752-1828					Austrian general, PU
Mackensen, August von	1849-1945					German field marshal, PU
Macmahon, Marie Edme	1808-1893					Marshal of France, PU
MacMillan, Harold	1895-1986	30	75	150	50	British prime minister
Magsaysay, Ramon	1907-1957					Filipino soldier, statesman, PU
Maistre, Paul Andre M.	1858-1922					French general, PU
Makino, Shiro	1893-1945					Japanese general, PU
Mangin, Charles Marie	1866-1925					French general, PU
Mannerheim, Carl Gus.	1867-1951					Russian and Finnish soldier, PU
Manstein, Erich von	1887-1973					German field marshal, PU
Manteuffel, Baron Ed.	1809-1885					Prussian field marshal, PU
Manteuffel, Baron H.	1897-1978					German general, PU
Mao Tse-tung	1893-1976					Chinese statesman, PU
Marat, Jean Paul	1743-1793					French revolutionary, PU
Marlborough, John C.	1650-1722					British captain general, PU
Marmount, Auguste F.	1774-1852					French marshal, PU
Marti, Jose	1853-1895					Cuban patriot, poet, PU
Maruyama, Masao	1889-1957					Japanese general, PU
Masaryk, Jan	1886-1948	100	200	300		Czech. foreign minister
Masaryk, Thomas G.	1850-1937	150	300	600		Czech. statesman
Massena, Andre	1758-1817					French marshal, PU
Matsui, Iwane	1878-1948					Japanese general, PU
Matsumoto, Yawara	1860-c.1925					Japanese admiral, PU
Matsumura, Tatsuo	1868-1932					Japanese admiral, PU
Matsutani, Makoto	1903-					Japanese army officer, PU
Maude, Sir Frederick S.	1864-1917					British general, PU
Maunoury, Michael J.	1847-1923					French general, PU

Name	db/dd	Sig.	DS	ALS	SP	Comments
Mazaki, Jinsaburo	1876-1956					Japanese general, PU
Mazarin, Jules	1602-1661					French cardinal, prime min., PU
Mazzini, Giusseppe	1805-1872			1100		Italian reformer, SALS-2X
Mboya, Tom	1930-1969					Kenyan political leader, PU
Medici III, Cosimo I de	1642-1723		1500			Grand Duke of Italy
Medici, Cosimo I de	1519-1574					Duke of Florence, PU
Medicis, Catherine de	1519-1589					French, PU
Meir, Golda	1898-1978	125	300	600		FDC-$95, SALS-3-4X
Mello, Custodoio Jose	1840-1902					Brazilian admiral, PU
Mengele, Josef	1911-1994	3695				Nazi,"The Angel of Death"
Methuen, Paul Sanford	1845-1932					British general, PU
Metternich, Klemens W.	1773-1859	100	275	450		Austrian statesman
Mikawa, Gun'ichi	1890-					Japanese admiral, PU
Minami, Jiro	1874-1957					Japanese general, PU
Minie, Claude E	1804-1879					French officer, inventor, PU
Misu, Sotaro	1855-1921					Japanese admiral, PU
Mitterrand, Francois	1916-1996	25	50	75	40	French president
Miura, Goro	1846-1926					Japanese general, PU
Mobutu Sese Seko	1930-1997					Zaire (Congo) president, PU
Model, Walther	1891-1945					German field marshal, PU
Mollet, Guy	1905-1975	25	50	100	60	French, social politician
Moltke, Count Helmuth	1848-1916					German general, PU
Moltke, Count Helmuth	1800-1891					German field marshal, PU
Monash, Sir John	1865-1931					Australian general, PU
Moncey, Bon Adrien	1754-1842					French revolutionary, PU
Monro, Sir Charles C.	1860-1929					British general, PU
Montcalm, Louis-Jos.	1712-1759					French general, PU
Montgomery, Bernard L.	1887-1976	125	350		375	SDS-7X, ESPV
Moreau, Jean Victor M.	1763-1813					French general, PU
Mori, Takashi	1894-1945					Japanese general, PU
Mortier, Edouard Adol.	1768-1835					French marshal, PU
Mountbatten, Louis Fr.	1900-1976	125	250	335	225	Brit. admiral, SDS-3-4X
Murakami, Kakuichi	1862-1927					Japanese admiral, PU
Murat, Joachim, King	1767-1815					French marshal, PU
Murray, Sir Archibald J.	1860-1945					British general, PU
Mussolini, Benito	1883-1945	375	600	3000	1200	Italian facist dictator
Mutaguchi, Ren'ya	1888-1966					Japanese general, PU
Muto, Akiro	1892-1948					Japanese general, PU
Muto, Nobuyoshi	1866-1933					Japanese field marshal, PU
Nagano, Osami	1880-1947					Japanese admiral, PU
Nagata, Tetsuzan	1884-1935					Japanese general, PU
Nagy, Imre	c.1896-1958	75	200		150	Communist premier
Nakamuta, Kuranosuke	1837-1916					Japanese admiral, PU
Nana Sahib (Dandu P.)	c.1821-1860					Indian ruler, PU
Napier, Charles James	1782-1853					British general, PU
Napier, Robert Cornelis	1810-1890					British field marshal, PU
Napoleon I (Bonaparte)	1769-1821	700	1856	16500		Emperor of the French, SDS-4X
Narvaez, Ramon Maria	1800-1868					Spanish general and statesman
Nashiha, Tokicki	1850-1923					Japanese admiral, PU
Nasser, Gamal Abdel	1918-1970	100	200	350	250	Egyptian pres., SDS-2X
Naumo, Chuichi	1886-1944					Japanese admiral, PU

Name	db/dd	Sig.	DS	ALS	SP	Comments
Ne Win	1911-					Burmese general, PU
Nehru, Jawaharial	1889-1964	150	400	700	400	Indian prime minister
Ney, Michel, Prince	1769-1815					"Le Rougeaud, ... Brave", PU
Nicholas (Romanov),	1856-1929					Russian general, PU
Nieh Jung-chen	1899-?					Com. Chinese marshal, PU
Nieh Shih-ch'eng	?-1900					Chinese general, PU
Nishi, Kanjiro	1846-1912					Japanese general, PU
Nishimura, Shoji	1889-1944					Japanese admiral, PU
Nivelle, Robert Georges	1856-1924					French general, PU
Nkrumah, Kwame	1909-1972					First prime minister of Ghana, PU
Nogi, Maresuke	1843-1912					Japanese general, PU
North, Frederick	1732-1792	125	400	600		British prime minister
Nozu, Michitsura	1841-1907					Japanese field marshal, PU
Nuri as-said	1888-1958					Arab general, Iraqi states., PU
O'Connell, Daniel	1775-1847	150	300	700		Irish ldr., "The Liberator"
O'Higgins, Bernardo	1776-1842					Chilean patriot, PU
Obata, Hideyoshi	1880-1944					Japanese general, PU
Ogawa, Mataji	1848-1909					Japanese general, PU
Oguri, Kozaburo	1868-1944					Japanese admiral, PU
Oi, Shigemoto	1863-1951					Japanese general, PU
Okada, Keisuke	1868-1952					Japanese admiral, PU
Okamura, Yasuji	1884-1966					Japanese general, PU
Oku, Yasukata	1846-1930					Japanese field marshal, PU
Okubo, Haruno	1846-1915					Japanese general, PU
Omori, Sentaro	1894-?					Japanese admiral, PU
Omura, Masujiro	1824-1869					Japanese statesman, PU
Onishi, Takijiro	1891-1945					Japanese admiral, PU
Osako, Naotoshi	1844-1927					Japanese general, PU
Oshima, Hiroshi	1885-?					Japanese general, diplomat, PU
Oshima, Hisanao	1848-1928					Japanese general, PU
Oshima, Yoshimasa	1850-1926					Japanese general, PU
Osman Nuri Pasha	1832-1900					Turkish general, PU
Otani, Kikuro	1855-1923					Japanese general, PU
Oudinot, Nicolas Cha.	1767-1847					French marshal, PU
Outram, Sir James	1803-1863					British general, PU
Oyama, Iwao	1842-1916					Japanese field marshal, PU
Ozawa, Jisaburo	1886-1966					Japanese admiral, PU
P'eng Teh-huai	1898-1974					Com. Chinese marshal, PU
Paderewski, Ignance	1860-1941	150	400	500	400	Polish, Sig. - $95, ESPV
Paget, Sir Henry William	1768-1854					English field marshal, PU
Pai Ch'ung-hsi	1893-1966					Nationalist Chinese general, PU
Pakenham, Sir Edward	1778-1815					British general, PU
Palikao, Charles Guill.	1796-1878					French general, PU
Palmerston, Viscount	1784-1865	50	100	150		British Whig-liberal PM
Paoli, Pasquale	1725-1807					Corsican general, PU
Papagos, Alexandros	1883-1955					Greek field marshal, PU
Papandreou, Andreas	1919-1996					Greek leftist politician, PU
Papandreou, Georgios	1888-1968					Greek politician,PM, PU
Papen, Franz von	1879-1969	75	200	275	150	German politician
Papoulas, Anastasios	1859-1935					Greek general, PU

Name	db/dd	Sig.	DS	ALS	SP	Comments
Parnell, Charles Stewart	1846-1891					Irish nationalist leader, PU
Paulus, Friedrich von	1890-1957					German field marshal, PU
Pearson, Lester	1897-1972	50	100	200	100	Canadian diplomat, Liberal
Peel, Robert	1788-1850	75	150	200		British prime minister
Perignon, Dominique C.	1754-1818					French marshal, PU
Peron, Juan	1895-1974	150	450	500	500	President of Argentina
Petain, Henri Philippe	1856-1951					Marshal of France, PU
Peter I the Great	1672-1725					Russian ruler, PU
Petlyura, Simon	1879-1926					Ukrainian general , PU
Pichegru, Charles	1761-1804					French general, PU
Picot, Auguste Henri	1756-1793					French general, PU
Picton, Sir Thomas	1758-1815					English general, PU
Piekhanov, Georgi	1857-1918					Russian revolutionary, PU
Pilsudski, Joseph	1867-1935	125	300	500	275	Polish statesman
Pineau, Christian	1905-1995					French Resistance leader, PU
Pitt, William the Elder	1708-1778					British statesman, PU
Pitt, William the Younger	1759-1806	150	300	500		British prime minister
Plumer, herbert Charles	1857-1932					British field marshal, PU
Poincare, Raymond	1860-1934	50	100	130	100	French statesman
Pompidou, Georges	1911-1974	25	50		40	French Gaulist political leader
Poniatowski, Prince J.	1762-1813					Polish-French marshal, PU
Potemkin, Grigori	1739-1791					Russian field marshall, PU
Pretorius, Andries Wil.	1798-1853					Boer general, statesman, PU
Pretorius, Marthinus W.	1819-1901					Boer general, statesman, PU
Prittwitz und Graffron, M.	1848-1917					German general, PU
Putnik, Radomir	1847-1917					Serbian general, PU
Rabin, Yitzhak	1922-1995	150	300	700	275	Israel P.M., ESPV, SDS-2X
Radetzky, Josef W.	1766-1858					Austrian field marshal, PU
Radzievskiy, Aleksei I.	1911-1978					Russian general, PU
Raeder, Erich	1876-1960					German admiral, PU
Raglan, Fitzroy James	1788-1855					British field marshal, PU
Rami I	?-1809					Siamese monarch, PU
Rathenau, Walter	1867-1922					German industrialist, PU
Rennenkampf, Pavel K.	1854-1918					Russian general, PU
Reynaud, Paul	1878-1966					French statesman, PU
Rhee, Syngman	1875-1965	200	450	900	300	First pres. of S. Korea
Rhodes, Cecil	1853-1902	150	275	400		British imperialist
Riall, Phineas	1775-1850					British general, PU
Richelieu, Cradinal de	1585-1642		1000	2250		French states., SDS-$3500
Richthofen, Baron M.	1892-1918					German, "The Red Baron", PU
Richtofen, Baron Wolf.	1895-1945					German air force general, PU
Roberts, Sir Frederick	1832-1914					British field marshal, PU
Robertson, Sir William	1860-1933					British field marshal, PU
Robespierre, Maximillan	1758-1794	1250	4000			French Revolution leader
Rokossovski, Konstan.	1896-1968					Marshal of the Soviet Union, PU
Rommel, Erwin	1891-1944	800	1600	3000	2500	"The Desert Fox", ESPV
Roon, Albrecht Theo.	1803-1879					Prussian field marshal, PU
Ross, Robert	1766-1814					British general, PU
Rundstedt, Karl Rudolf	1875-1953					German field marshal, PU
Rupprecht, Crown	1869-1955					German general, PU
Russell, John	1792-1878					British prime minister, PU

Name	db/dd	Sig.	DS	ALS	SP	Comments
Sa'ud, abd al-'Aziz ibn	c.1880-1953					Saudi Arabian ruler, PU
Sadat, Anwar al-	1918-1981	100	200		300	Egyptian president, ESPV
Saigo, Takamori	1827-1877					Japanese field marshal, PU
Saigo, Tsugumichi	1843-1902					Japanese general, PU
Saint-Cyr, Laurent G.	1764-1830					French marshal, PU
Saito, Yoshitsugu	1890-1944					Japanese general, PU
Sakai, Takashi	1887-1946					Japanese general, PU
Sakamoto, Toshiatsu	1858-1941					Japanese admiral, PU
Sakuma, Tsutomi	1879-1910					Japanese naval officer, PU
Sakurai, Seizo	1889-?					Japanese general, PU
Salazar, Antonio de	1889-1970					Dictator of Portugal, PU
Samejima, Shigeo	1849-1928					Japanese general, PU
Samejima, Tomoshige	1889-1966					Japanese admiral, PU
Samori, Toure	c.1835-1900					Dioula war chief, ruler, PU
Samsonov, Aleksandr	1859-1914					Russian general, PU
San Martin, Jose de	1778-1850					Latin American general, PU
Sandwich, Edward M.	1625-1672					English admiral, PU
Sano, Tadayoshi	1889-1945					Japanese general, PU
Santa Anna, Antonio L.	1794-1876			1600		Mexican general, ANS-$800
Sato Kenryo	1895-1975					Japanese general, PU
Sato, Eisaku	1901-1975	30	75	150	50	Japanese prime minister
Sato, Kojiro	1862-1927					Japanese general, PU
Sato, Kotoku	1893-1959					Japanese general, PU
Sato, Tetsutaro	1866-1942					Japanese admiral, theorist, PU
Saud, Abdul Aziz Ibn	c.1880-1953					King of Saudi Arabi, PU
Saxe, Hermann Maurice	1696-1750					Marshal of France, PU
Scharnhorst, Gerhard	1755-1813					Prussian general, PU
Scheer, Reinhard	1863-1928					German admiral, PU
Scheidemann, Philipp	1865-1939					German Social leader, PU
Schlieffen, Count Alfred	1833-1913					Prussian-German general, PU
Schuman, Robert	1886-1963					French statesman, PU
Schuschnigg, Kurt	1897-1977	50	100	200	75	Austrian chancellor
Schwarzenberg, Karl P.	1771-1820					Austrian field marshal, PU
Seeckt, Hans von	1866-1936					German general, PU
Seng-Kuo-Lin-Ch'in	?-1865					Mongol/Chinese general, PU
Senger und Etterlin, Fri.	1891-1963					German general, PU
Serurier, Count Jean	1741-1819					French Marshal, PU
Seymour, Edward H.	1840-1929					British naval officer, PU
Sforza, Carlo	1872-1952					Italian foreign minister, PU
Shaka	c.1787-1828					Zulu monarch, PU
Shaoqi, Liu	c.1898-1974					Chinese Communist leader, PU
Sher Ali Khan	1825-1879					Afghan ruler, PU
Shibayama, Yahachi	1850-1924					Japanese admiral, PU
Shih Ta-k'ai	1821-1863					Chinese rebel general, PU
Shimada, Shigetaro	1883-?					Japanese admiral, PU
Shimanura, Hayao	1858-1923					Japanese admiral, PU
Shiozawa, Koichi	1881-1943					Japanese admiral, PU
Shirakawa, Yoshinori	1868-1932					Japanese general, PU
Shrapnel, Henry	1761-1842					British general, PU
Sitting Bull	c.1831-1890				15000	Sioux leader
Skorzeny, Otto	1908-1975					German SS officer, PU
Slessor, Sir John C.	1897-1979					British air marshal, PU

Name	db/dd	Sig.	DS	ALS	SP	Comments
Slim, Sir William Joseph	1891-1970					British field marshal, PU
Smith, Sir Henry George	1787-1860					British general, PU
Smith-Dorrien, Sir Hor.	1858-1930					British general, PU
Smuts, Jan C.	1870-1950					S. African statesman, PM, PU
Somerville, Sir James	1882-1949					British admiral, PU
Soubise, Charles de R.	1715-1787					Marshal of France, PU
Soult, Nicolas Jean	1769-1851					Marshal General of France, PU
Spaak, Paul Henri	1899-1972	25	50	75	35	Belgian, socialist leader
Spee, Count Maximilian	1861-1914					German admiral, PU
Speidel, Hans	1897-1987					German general, PU
Stalin, Joseph	1879-1953	1750	5000			Soviet, Sig/ w Pushkin-$5000
Stauffenberg, Count K.	1907-1944					German soldier, PU
Stresemann, Gustav	1878-1929					German chancellor, PU
Student, Kurt	1890-1978					German general, PU
Suchet, Louis Gabriel	1770-1826					French Marshal, PU
Suetaka, Kamezo	1884-1955					Japanese general, PU
Sugiyama, Hajime	1880-1945					Japanese field marshal,PU
Sukamo	1901-1970	100				First president of Indonesian
Sun Ch'uan-feng	1884-1935					Chinese general, warlord,PU
Sun Yat-sen	1866-1925	750	1100	1750		Chinese revolutionary
Sung Che-yuen	1885-1940					Nationalist Chinese general,PU
Suvorov, Alexander V.	1729-1800					Russian field marshal,PU
Suzuki, Kantaro	1868-1948					Japanese admiral,PU
Suzuki, Keiji	1897-1967					Japanese general,PU
Suzuki, Soroku	1865-1940					Japanese general, PU
Suzuki, Sosaku	1891-1945					Japanese general, PU
Tachibana, Koichiro	1861-1929					Japanese general, PU
Tai Li	1895-1946					Nationalist Chinese general, PU
Takagi, Sokichi	1893-?					Japanese admiral, PU
Takagi, Takeo	1892-1944					Japanese admiral, PU
Takahashi, Ibo	1888-1947					Japanese admiral,PU
Takarabe, Takeshi	1867-1949					Japanese admiral,PU
Tal, Israel	1924-					Israeli general,PU
Talleyrand, Charles de	1754-1838	200	500			French statesman, diplomat
Tamon, Jiro	1878-1934					Japanese general, PU
Tamura, Iyozo	1854-1903					Japanese general,PU
Tanaka, Giichi	1863-1929					Japanese general,PU
Tanaka, Raizo	1892-1969					Japanese admiral,PU
Tanaka, Ryukichi	1893-?					Japanese general,PU
Tanaka, Shin'ichi	1893-?					Japanese general,PU
Tanaka, Shizuichi	1887-1945					Japanese general,PU
Tani, Tateki	1837-1911					Japanese general,PU
Tantia Topi	c.1810-1859					Indian rebel leader, PU
Tatekawa, Yoshitsugu	1880-1945					Japanese general, PU
Tatsumi, Naobumi	1845-1907					Japanese general, PU
Tedder, Sir Arthur W.	1890-1967					British air marshal, PU
Tegetthoff, Count W.	1827-1871					Austrian admiral, PU
Terauchi, Hisaichi	1879-1946					Japanese general, PU
Terauchi, Makakata	1852-1919					Japanese field marshal, PU
Thant, U	1909-1974	50	150	300		UN secretary-general
Thielmann, Baron J.	1765-1824					Saxon general,PU

Name	db/dd	Sig.	DS	ALS	SP	Comments
Timoshenko, Semen K.	1895-1970					Marshal of the Soviet Union,PU
Tirpitz, Alfred von	1849-1930					German admiral,PU
Tito, Josip Broz	1892-1980	100	200	300	250	President of Yugoslavia
Todleben, Count Franz	1818-1884					Russian general, PU
Togliatti, Imiro	1893-1964					Italian Communist party ldr., PU
Togo, Heihachiro	1848-1934					Japanese admiral, PU
Tojo, Hideki	1885-1948					Japanese statesman, PU
Tojo, Hideki	1884-1948					Japanese general, PM,PU
Tomioka, Sadatoshi	1897-1970					Japanese admiral, PU
Topete Y Carballo, Juan	1821-1885					Spanish admiral, statesman,PU
Townshend, Sir Charles	1861-1924					British general, PU
Toyoda, Soemu	1885-1957					Japanese admiral, PU
Trenchard, Hugh Mont.	1873-1956					British air marshal, PU
Trotsky, Leon	1879-1940		4500			Russian revolutionary
Troubridge, Sir Ernest	1862-1926					British admiral, PU
Trujilio Molina, Rafael .	1891-1961	75	150		300	Dom. Rep. dictator, ESPV
Ts'ai O	1882-1916					Chinese warlord, PU
Ts'ao K'un	1862-1928					Chinese general, politician, PU
Tseng Kuo-feng	1811-1872					Chinese statesman, general, PU
Tshombe, Moise K.	1919-1969	50	100		100	Congo premier (Zaire)
Tso Tsung-t'ang	1812-1885					Chinese statesman, general, PU
Tsuboi, Kozo	1843-1898					Japanese admiral, PU
Tsuchihashi, Yuitsu	1891-?					Japanese general, PU
Tsuchiya, Mitsuharu	1848-1920					Japanese general, PU
Tu Wen-hsiu	?-1873					Chinese rebel leader, PU
Tuan Ch'i-jui	1865-1936					Chinese warlord , PU
Tukhachevsky, Mikhail	1893-1937					Russian general, military, PU
Ueda, Kenkichi	1875-1962					Japanese general, PU
Uehara, Yusaku	1856-1933					Japanese field marshal, PU
Ugaki, Matome	1890-1945					Japanese admiral, PU
Ulbricht, Walter	1893-1973					German Dem. Republic, PU
Umezu, Yoshijiro	1882-1949					Japanese general, PU
Uriu, Sotokichi	1857-1937					Japanese admiral, PU
Ushijima, Mitsuru	1887-1945					Japanese general, PU
Ushiroku, Jun	1884-?					Japanese general, PU
Vandamme, Dominique	1770-1830					French general, PU
Vasilevskii, Aleksander	1895-1977					Marshal of the Soviet Union, PU
Venizelos, Eleutherios	1864-1936					Greek statesman, PU
Verwoerd, Hendrik F.	1901-1966	100	200			S. African prime minister
Victor-Perrin, Claude	1764-1841					Fr. marshal of the Empire, PU
Villeneuve, Pierre Chas.	1763-1806					French admiral, PU
Wachi, Takaji	1891-?					Japanese general, PU
Waldersee, Alfred von	1832-1904					German field marshal, PU
Wavell, Archibald P.	1883-1950					British field marshal, PU
Wei Ch'ang-hui	?-1856					Chinese rebel general, PU
Wei Li-haung	1897-?					Nationalist Chinese general, PU
Weizmann, Chaim	1874-1952		1500	2475		Zionist leader, first Israeli pres.
Wellington, Arthur W.	1769-1852					British field marshal, PU
Wemanekaf, Ford W.	1760-1856					Bavarian general, PU

Name	db/dd	Sig.	DS	ALS	SP	Comments
Weygand, Maxime	1867-1965					French general, PU
Weyler Y Nicolau, Val.	1838-1930					Spanish general, PU
White, Sir George Stuart	1835-1912					British field marshal, PU
Wilhelm, Crown Prince	1882-1951					German general, PU
Wilson, Harold	1916-1995	50	125	150	75	British Labor party leader
Wilson, Henry Maitland	1881-1964					British field marshal, PU
Wilson, Sir Henry H.	1864-1922					British field marshal, PU
Wingate, Orde Charles	1903-1944					British general, PU
Wittgenstein, Ludwig A.	1769-1843					Russian field marshal, PU
Witzleben, Erwin von	1881-1944					German field marshal, PU
Wolfe, James	1727-1759					British general, PU
Wolseley, Sir Garnet J.	1833-1913					British field marshal, PU
Wood, Sir Henry Evelyn	1838-1919					British field marshal, PU
Wrangel, Pyotr Niko.	1878-1928					Russian general, PU
Wrede, Prince Karl Phil.	1767-1838					Bavarian field marshall, PU
Wu P'ei-fu	1873-1939					Chinese warlord, PU
Wurmser, Count Dag.	1724-1797					Austrian general, PU
Wurttemberg, Albrecht	1865-1939					German field marshal, PU
Yamada, Otozo	1881-1965					Japanese general, PU
Yamagata, Aritomo	1838-1922					Japanese field marshal, PU
Yamaguchi, Tamon	1892-1942					Japanese admiral, PU
Yamaji, Motoharu	1841-1897					Japanese general, PU
Yamamoto, Gonnohyoe	1852-1933					Japanese admiral, PU
Yamamoto, Isoroku	1884-1943					Japanese admiral, PU
Yamanshi, Hanzo	1864-1944					Japanese general, PU
Yamashita, Gentaro	1863-1931					Japanese admiral, PU
Yamashita, Tomoyuki	1888-1946					Japanese admiral, PU
Yamaya, Tanin	1866-1940					Japanese admiral, PU
Yanagawa, Heisuke	1879-1945					Japanese general, PU
Yang Hu-ch'eng	?-1949					Chinese warlord, PU
Yang, Hsiu-ch'ing	c.1817-1856					Chinese rebel general, PU
Yanushkevich, Nikolai	1868-1918					Russian general, PU
Yashiro, Rokuro	1860-1930					Japanese admiral, PU
Ye Jianying	1899-					Com. Chinese marshal, PU
Yeh T'ing	?-1946					Com. Chinese general, PU
Yen Hsi-shan	1883-1960					Chinese warlord, PU
Yokoyama, Shizuo	1890-1961					Japanese general, PU
Yonai, Mitsumasa	1880-1948					Japanese admiral, PU
Yorck von Wartenburg,J.	1759-1830					Pru. general field marshal, PU
York and Albany, Fr.	1763-1827					British field marshal, PU
Yuan Shih-k'ai	c.1859-1916					Chinese general, statesman, PU
Yudenich, Nikolai N.	1862-1933					Russian general, PU
Yuhi, Mitsue	1860-1940					Japanese general, PU
Zapata, Emilianoc.	1879-1919		1600	1750		Mexican revolutionary
Zhilinsky, Yakov Greg.	1853-c.1920					Russian general, PU
Zhou Enial	1898-1976					Chinese diplomat, PM., PU
Zhukov, Georgi Konst.	1896-1974					Marshal of the Soviet Union, PU
Zieten, Count Hans E.	1770-1848					Prussian field marshal, PU

Section Three

ACADEMY AWARDS -
ALPHABETICAL REFERENCE GUIDE

While there are many references for Academy Award winners available to collectors, most are often done chronologically. As one collector told me, "It's nice to have a chronological list of award winners, but since I collect in this area , I often don't have the time to review such a list before making a purchase." "An alphabetical list is far more useful for my needs," he continued. So here it is, in checklist form, for your use!

Abbreviations: BA = Best Actor, BD = Best Director, BP = Best Picture, BSA = Best Supporting Actor, BSAS = Best Supporting Actress

Name	Category/Subject	Year
☐ A Beautiful Mind	BP	2001
☐ A Man for All Seasons	BP	1966
☐ Abraham, F, Murray	BA - Amadeus	1984
☐ Albertson, Jack	BSA - The Subject Was Roses	1968
☐ All About Eve	BP	1950
☐ All Quiet on the Western Front	BP	1930
☐ All The King's Men	BP	1949
☐ Allen, Woody	BD - Annie Hall	1977
☐ Amadeus	BP	1984
☐ Ameche, Don	BSA - Cocoon	1985
☐ American Beauty	BP	1999
☐ An American in Paris	BP	1951
☐ Andrews, Julie	BAS - Mary Poppins	1964
☐ Annie Hall	BP	1977
☐ Arliss, George	BA - Disraeli	1930
☐ Around the World in 80 days	BP	1956
☐ Ashcroft, Peggy	BSAS - A Passage to India	1984
☐ Astor, Mary	BSAS - The Great Lie	1941
☐ Attenborough, Richard	BD - Ghandi	1982
☐ Avildsen, John G.	BD - Rocky	1976
☐ Bainter, Fay	BSAS - Jezebel	1938
☐ Balsam, Martin	BSA - A Thousand Clowns	1965
☐ Bancroft, Anne	BAS - The Miracle Worker	1962
☐ Barrymore, Ethel	BSAS - None But the Lonely Heart	1944
☐ Barrymore, Lionel	BA - A Free Soul	1931
☐ Basinger, Kim	BSAS - L.A. Confidential	1997
☐ Bates, Kathy	BAS - Misery	1990
☐ Baxter, Anne	BSAS - The Razor's Edge	1946
☐ Baxter, Warner	BA- In Old Arizona	1929

Name	Category/Subject	Year
☐ Beatty, Warren	BD - Reds	1981
☐ Beery, Wallace	BA - The Champ	1932
☐ Begley, Ed	BSA - Sweet Bird of Youth	1962
☐ Ben - Hur	BP	1959
☐ Benigni, Roberto	BA - Life is Beautiful	1998
☐ Benton, Robert	BD - Kramer vs. Kramer	1979
☐ Bergman, Ingrid	BSAS - Murder on the Orient Express	1974
☐ Bergman, Ingrid	BAS - Gaslight	1944
☐ Bergman, Ingrid	BAS - Anastasia	1956
☐ Berry, Halle	BAS - Monster's Ball	2001
☐ Bertolucci, Bernardo	BD - The Last Emperor	1987
☐ Binoche, Juliette	BSAS - The English Patient	1996
☐ Bogart, Humphrey	BA - The African *ueen	1951
☐ Booth, Shirley	BAS - Come Back Little Sheba	1952
☐ Borgnine, Ernest	BA - Marty	1955
☐ Borzage, Frank	BD - Bad Girl	1932
☐ Borzage, Frank	BD - Seventh Heaven	1928
☐ Brady, Alice	BSAS - In Old Chicago	1937
☐ Brando, Marlon	BA - The Godfather	1972
☐ Brando, Marlon	BA - On the Waterfront	1954
☐ Braveheart	BP	1995
☐ Brennan, Walter	BSA - The Westerner	1940
☐ Brennan, Walter	BSA - Kentucky	1938
☐ Brennan, Walter	BSA - Come and Get It	1936
☐ Broadbent, Jim	BSA - Iris	2001
☐ Broadway Melody	BP	1929
☐ Brody, Adrien	BA - The Pianist	2002
☐ Brooks, James L.	BD - Terms of Endearment	1983
☐ Brynner, Yul	BA - The King and I	1956
☐ Burns, George	BSA - The Sunshine Boys	1975
☐ Burstyn, Ellen	BSAS - Alice Doesn't Live Here Any...	1974
☐ Buttons, Red	BSA - Sayonara	1957
☐ Cage, Nicholas	BA - Leaving Las Vegas	1995
☐ Cagney, James	BA - Yankee Doodle Dandy	1942
☐ Caine, Michael	BSA - The Cider House Rules	1999
☐ Caine, Michael	BSA - Hannah and Her Sisters	1986
☐ Cameron, James	BD - Titanic	1997
☐ Capra, Frank	BD - Mr. Deeds Goes to Town	1936
☐ Capra, Frank	BD - You Can't Take It With You	1938
☐ Carney, Art	BA - Harry and Tonto	1974
☐ Casablanca	BP	1943
☐ Cavalcade	BP	1933
☐ Chakiris, George	BSA - West Side Story	1961
☐ Chariots of Fire	BP	1981
☐ Cher	BAS - Moonstruck	1987
☐ Chicago	BP	2002

Name	Category/Subject	Year
☐ Christie, Julie	BAS - Darling	1965
☐ Cimarron	BP	1931
☐ Cimino, Michael	BD - The Deer Hunter	1978
☐ Coburn, Charles	BSA - The More the Merrier	1943
☐ Coburn, James	BSA - Affliction	1998
☐ Colbert, Claudette	BAS - It Happened One Night	1934
☐ Colman, Ronald	BA - A Double Life	1947
☐ Connelly, Jennifer	BSAS - A Beautiful Mind	2001
☐ Connery, Sean	BSA - The Untouchables	1987
☐ Cooper, Chris	BSA - Adaption	2002
☐ Cooper, Gary	BA - Sergeant York	1941
☐ Cooper, Gary	BA - High Noon	1952
☐ Coppola, Francis Ford	BD - The Godfather Part II	1974
☐ Costner, Kevin	BD - Dances with Wolves	1990
☐ Crawford, Broderick	BA - All The King's Men	1949
☐ Crawford, Joan	BAS - Mildred Pierce	1945
☐ Crisp, Donald	BSA - How Green Was My Valley	1941
☐ Crosby, Bing	BA - Going My Way	1944
☐ Crowe, Russell	BA - Gladiator	2000
☐ Cukor, George	BD - My Fair Lady	1964
☐ Curtiz, Michael	BD - Casablanca	1943
☐ Dances with Wolves	BP	1990
☐ Darwell, Jane	BSAS - The Grapes of Wrath	1940
☐ Davis, Bette	BAS - Dangerous	1935
☐ Davis, Bette	BAS - Jezebel	1938
☐ Davis, Geena	BSAS - The Accidental Tourist	1988
☐ Day-Lewis, Daniel	BA - My Left Foot	1989
☐ DeHavilland, Olivia	BAS - The Heiress	1949
☐ DeHavilland, Olivia	BAS - The Best Years of Our Lives	1946
☐ DelTorio, Benicio	BSA - Traffic	2000
☐ Demme, Jonathan	BD - The Silence of the Lambs	1991
☐ Dench, Judi	BSAS - Shakespeare in Love	1998
☐ DeNiro, Robert	BSA - The Godfather Part II	1974
☐ DeNiro, Robert	BA - Raging Bull	1980
☐ Dennis, Sandy	BSAS - Who's Afraid of Virginia Woolf?	1966
☐ Donat, Robert	BA - Goodbye, Mr. Chips	1939
☐ Douglas, Melvyn	BSA - Being There	1979
☐ Douglas, Melvyn	BSA - Hud	1963
☐ Douglas, Michael	BA - Wall Street	1987
☐ Dressler, Marie	BAS - Min and Bill	1931
☐ Dreyfuss, Richard	BA - The Goodbye Girl	1977
☐ Driving Miss Daisy	BP	1989
☐ Dukakis, Olympia	BSAS - Moonstruck	1987
☐ Duke, Patty	BSAS - The Miracle Worker	1962
☐ Dunaway, Faye	BAS - Network	1976
☐ Dunn, James	BSA - A Tree Grows in Brooklyn	1945

Name	Category/Subject	Year
☐ Duvall, Robert	BA - Tender Mercies	1983
☐ Eastwood, Clint	BD - Unforgiven	1992
☐ Ferrer, Jose	BA - Cyrano de Bergerac	1950
☐ Field, Sally	BAS - Norma Rae	1979
☐ Field, Sally	BAS - Places in the Heart	1984
☐ Finch, Peter	BA - Network	1976
☐ Fitzgerald, Barry	BSA - Going My Way	1944
☐ Fleming, Victor	BD - Gone With The Wind	1939
☐ Fletcher, Louise	BAS - One Flew Over the Cuckoo's Nest	1975
☐ Fonda, Henry	BA - On Golden Pond	1981
☐ Fonda, Jane	BAS - Klute	1971
☐ Fonda, Jane	BAS - Coming Home	1978
☐ Fontaine, Joan	BAS - Suspicion	1941
☐ Ford, John	BD - The Informer	1935
☐ Ford, John	BD - The Quiet Man	1952
☐ Ford, John	BD - How Green Was My Valley	1941
☐ Ford, John	BD - The Grapes of Wrath	1940
☐ Forman, Milos	BD - One Flew Over the Cuckoo's Nest	1975
☐ Forman, Milos	BD - Amadeus	1984
☐ Forrest Gump	BP	1994
☐ Fosse, Bob	BD - Cabaret	1972
☐ Foster, Jodie	BAS - The Accused	1988
☐ Foster, Jodie	BAS - The Silence of the Lambs	1991
☐ Fricker, Brenda	BSAS - My Left Foot	1989
☐ Friedkin, William	BD - The French Connection	1971
☐ From Here to Eternity	BP	1953
☐ Gable, Clark	BA - It Happened One Night	1934
☐ Garson, Greer	BAS - Mrs. Miniver	1942
☐ Gaynor, Janet	BAS-Seventh Heaven, Sunrise, St...	1928
☐ Gentleman's Agreement	BP	1947
☐ Ghandi	BP	1982
☐ Gibson, Mel	BD - Braveheart	1995
☐ Gielgud, John	BSA - Arthur	1981
☐ Gigi	BP	1958
☐ Gladiator	BP	2000
☐ Going My Way	BP	1944
☐ Goldberg, Whoopi	BSAS - Ghost	1990
☐ Gone With The Wind	BP	1939
☐ Gooding, Jr., Cuba	BSA - Jerry Maguire	1996
☐ Gordon, Ruth	BSAS - Rosemary's Baby	1968
☐ Gossett, Jr., Louis	BSA - An Officer and a Gentleman	1982
☐ Grahame, Gloria	BSAS - The Bad and the Beautiful	1952
☐ Grand Hotel	BP	1932
☐ Grant, Lee	BSAS - Shampoo	1975

Name	Category/Subject	Year
☐ Grey, Joel	BSA - Cabaret	1972
☐ Griffith, Hugh	BSA - Ben - Hur	1959
☐ Guinness, Alec	BA - The Bridge on the River Kwai	1957
☐ Gwenn, Edmund	BSA - Miracle on 34th Street	1947
☐ Hackman, Gene	BSA - Unforgiven	1992
☐ Hackman, Gene	BA - The French Connection	1971
☐ Hamlet	BP	1948
☐ Hanks, Tom	BA - Forrest Gump	1994
☐ Hanks, Tom	BA - Philadelphia	1993
☐ Harden, Marcia Gay	BSAS - Pollock	2000
☐ Harrison, Rex	BA - My Fair Lady	1964
☐ Hawn, Goldie	BSAS - Cactus Flower	1969
☐ Hayes, Helen	BAS - The Sin of Madelon Claudet	1932
☐ Hayward, Susan	BAS - I Want to Live!	1958
☐ Heckart, Eileen	BSAS - Butterflies Are Free	1972
☐ Heflin, Van	BSA - Johnny Eager	1942
☐ Hepburn, Audrey	BAS - Roman Holiday	1953
☐ Hepburn, Katharine	BAS - The Lion in Winter	1968
☐ Hepburn, Katharine	BAS - Guess Who's Coming to Dinner	1967
☐ Hepburn, Katherine	BAS - On Golden Pond	1981
☐ Hepburn, Katherine	BAS - Morning Glory	1933
☐ Heston, Charlton	BA - Ben - Hur	1959
☐ Heyes, Helen	BSAS - Airport	1970
☐ Hill, George Roy	BD - The Sting	1973
☐ Hiller, Wendy	BSAS - Separate Tables	1958
☐ Hoffman, Dustin	BD - Rain Man	1988
☐ Hoffman, Dustin	BA - Kramer vs. Kramer	1979
☐ Holden, William	BA - Stalag 17	1953
☐ Holliday, Judy	BAS - Born Yesterday	1950
☐ Holm, Celeste	BSAS - Gentleman's Agreement	1947
☐ Hopkins, Anthony	BA - The Silence of the Lambs	1991
☐ Houseman, John	BSA - The Paper Chase	1973
☐ How Green Was My Valley	BP	1941
☐ Howard, Ron	BD - A Beautiful Mind	2001
☐ Hull, Josephine	BSAS - Harvey	1950
☐ Hunt, Helen	BAS - As Good as it Gets	1997
☐ Hunt, Linda	BSAS - The Year of Living Dangerously	1983
☐ Hunt, William	BA - Kiss of the Spider Woman	1985
☐ Hunter, Holly	BAS - The Piano	1993
☐ Hunter, Kim	BSAS - A Streetcar Named Desire	1951
☐ Huston, Anjelica	BSAS - Prizzi's Honor	1985
☐ Huston, John	BD - The Treasure of the Sierra Madre	1948
☐ Huston, Walter	BSA - The Treasure of the Sierra Madre	1948
☐ Hutton, Timothy	BSA - Ordinary Poeple	1980
☐ In the Heat of the Night	BP	1967

Name	Category/Subject	Year
Irons, Jeremy	BA - Reversal of Fortune	1990
It Happened One Night	BP	1934
Ives, Burl	BSA - The Big Country	1958
Jackson, Glenda	BAS - A Touch of Class	1973
Jackson, Glenda	BAS - Women in Love	1970
Jagger, Dean	BSA - Twelve O'Clock High	1949
Jannings, Emil	BA - The Way of All Flesh, The Last ...	1928
Johnson, Ben	BSA - The Last Picture Show	1971
Jolie, Angelina	BSAS - Girl, Interrupted	1999
Jones, Jennifer	BAS - The Song of Bernadette	1943
Jones, Shirley	BSAS - Elmer Gantry	1960
Jones, Tommy Lee	BSA - The Fugitive	1993
Kazan, Elia	BD - On the Waterfront	1954
Kazan, Elia	BD - Gentleman's Agreement	1947
Keaton, Diane	BAS - Annie Hall	1977
Kedrova, Lila	BSAS - Zorba the Greek	1964
Kelly, Grace	BAS - The Country Girl	1954
Kennedy, George	BSA - Cool Hand Luke	1967
Kidman, Nicole	BAS - The Hours	2002
Kingsley, Ben	BA - Ghandi	1982
Kline, Kevin	BSA - A Fish Called Wanda	1988
Kramer vs. Kramer	BP	1979
Lancaster, Burt	BA - Elmer Gantry	1960
Landau, Martin	BSA - Ed Wood	1994
Lange, Jessica	BAS - Blue Sky	1994
Lange, Jessica	BSAS - Tootsie	1982
Laughton, Charles	BA - The Private Life of Henry VIII	1933
Lawrence of Arabia	BP	1962
Leachman, Cloris	BSA S- The Last Picture Show	1971
Lean, David	BD - Lawrence of Arabia	1962
Lean, David	BD - The Bridge on the River Kwai	1957
Leigh, Vivien	BAS - A Streetcar Named Desire	1951
Leigh, Vivien	BAS - Gone With The Wind	1939
Lemmon, Jack	BA - Save the Tiger	1973
Lemmon, Jack	BSA - Mister Roberts	1955
Levinson, Barry	BD - Rain Man	1988
Lloyd, Frank	BD - Cavalcade	1933
Lloyd, Frank	BD - The Devine Lady	1929
Loren, Sophia	BAS - Two Women	1961
Lukas, Paul	BA - Watch On The Rhine	1943
MacLaine, Shirley	BAS - Terms of Endearment	1983
Magnani, Anna	BAS - The Rose Tattoo	1955
Malden, Karl	BSA - A Streetcar Named Desire	1951

Name	Category/Subject	Year
☐ Malone, Dorothy	BSAS - Written on the Wind	1956
☐ Mankiewicz, Joseph	BD - A Letter to Three Wives	1949
☐ Mankiewicz, Joseph	BD - All About Eve	1950
☐ Mann, Delbert	BD - Marty	1955
☐ March, Frederic	BA - Dr. Jekyll and Mr. Hyde	1932
☐ March, Frederic	BA - The Best Years of Our Lives	1946
☐ Marty	BP	1955
☐ Marvin, Lee	BA - Cat Ballou	1965
☐ Mathau, Walter	BSA - The Fortune Cookie	1966
☐ Matlin, Marlee	BAS - Children of a Lesser God	1986
☐ McCambridge, Mercedes	BSAS - All The King's Men	1949
☐ McCarey, Leo	BD - The Awful Truth	1937
☐ McCarey, Leo	BD - Going My Way	1944
☐ McDaniel, Hattie	BSAS - Gone With The Wind	1939
☐ McDormand, Frances	BAS - Fargo	1996
☐ McLaglen, Victor	BA - The Informer	1935
☐ Mendes, Sam	BD - American Beauty	1999
☐ Midnight Cowboy	BP	1969
☐ Milestone, Lewis	BD - All Quiet on the Western Front	1930
☐ Milestone, Lewis	BD - Two Arabian Knights	1928
☐ Milland, Ray	BA - The Lost Weekend	1945
☐ Mills, John	BSA - Ryan's Daughter	1970
☐ Minghella, Anthony	BD - The English Patient	1996
☐ Minnelli, Liza	BAS - Cabaret	1972
☐ Minnelli, Vincente	BD - Gigi	1958
☐ Mitchell, Thomas	BSA - Stagecoach	1939
☐ Miyoshi Umeki	BSAS - Sayonara	1957
☐ Moreno, Rita	BSAS - West Side Story	1961
☐ Mrs. Miniver	BP	1942
☐ Muni, Paul	BA - The Story of Louis Pasteur	1936
☐ Mutiny on the Bounty	BP	1935
☐ My Fair Lady	BP	1964
☐ Neal, Patricia	BAS - Hud	1963
☐ Newman, Paul	BA - The Color of Money	1986
☐ Ngor, Haing S.	BSA - The Killing Fields	1984
☐ Nichols, Mike	BD - The Graduate	1967
☐ Nicholson, Jack	BA - One Flew Over the Cuckoo's Nest	1975
☐ Nicholson, Jack	BA - As Good as it Gets	1997
☐ Nicholson, Jack	BSA - Terms of Endearment	1983
☐ Niven, David	BA - Separate Tables	1958
☐ O'Brien, Edmond	BSA - The Barefoot Contessa	1954
☐ O'Neal, Tatum	BSAS - Paper Moon	1973
☐ Oliver!	BP	1968
☐ Olivier, Laurence	BA - Hamlet	1948
☐ On the Waterfront	BP	1954

Name	Category/Subject	Year
☐ One Flew Over the Cuckoo's Nest BP		1975
☐ Ordinary People	BP	1980
☐ Out of Africa	BP	1985
☐ Pacino, Al	BA - Scent of a Woman	1992
☐ Page, Geraldine	BAS - The Trip to Bountiful	1985
☐ Palance, Jack	BSA - City Slickers	1991
☐ Paltrow, Gwyneth	BAS - Shakespeare in Love	1998
☐ Pa☐uin, Anna	BSAS - The Piano	1993
☐ Parsons, Estelle	BSAS - Bonnie and Clyde	1967
☐ Patton	BP	1970
☐ Paxinou, Katina	BSAS - For Whom the Bell Tolls	1943
☐ Peck, Gregory	BA - To Kill a Mockingbird	1962
☐ Pesci, Joe	BSA - Goodfellas	1990
☐ Pickford, Mary	BAS - Coquette	1929
☐ Platoon	BP	1986
☐ Poitier, Sidney	BA - Lilies of the Field	1963
☐ Polanski, Roman	BD - The Pianist	2002
☐ Pollack, Sydney	BD - Out of Africa	1985
☐ Quinn, Anthony	BSA - Viva Zapata!	1952
☐ Quinn, Anthony	BSA - Lust for Life	1956
☐ Rain Man	BP	1988
☐ Ranier, Luise	BAS - The Great Ziegfeld	1936
☐ Ranier, Luise	BAS - The Good Earth	1937
☐ Rebecca	BP	1940
☐ Redford, Robert	BD - Ordinary Poeple	1980
☐ Redgrave, Vanessa	BSAS - Julia	1977
☐ Reed, Carol	BD - Oliver!	1968
☐ Reed, Donna	BSAS - From Here to Eternity	1953
☐ Revere, Anne	BSAS - National Velvet	1945
☐ Richardson, Tony	BD - Tom Jones	1963
☐ Robards, Jason	BSA - Julia	1977
☐ Robards, Jason	BSA - All the President's Men	1976
☐ Robbins, Jerome	BD - West Side Story	1961
☐ Roberts, Julia	BAS - Erin Brockovich	2000
☐ Robertson, Cliff	BA - Charly	1968
☐ Rocky	BP	1976
☐ Rogers, Ginger	BAS - Kitty Foyle	1940
☐ Ruehl, Mercedes	BSAS - The Fisher King	1991
☐ Rush, Geoffrey	BA - Shine	1996
☐ Russell, Harold	BSA - The Best Years of Our Lives	1946
☐ Rutherford, Margaret	BSAS - The V.I.P.s	1963
☐ Saint, Eva Marie	BSAS - On the Waterfront	1954
☐ Sanders, George	BSA - All About Eve	1950

Name	Category/Subject	Year
☐ Sarandon, Susan	BAS - Dead Man Walking	1995
☐ Schaffner, Franklin J.	BD - Patton	1970
☐ Schell, Maximilian	BA - Judgment at Nuremberg	1961
☐ Schildkraut, Joseph	BSA - The Life of Emile Zola	1937
☐ Schindler's List	BP	1993
☐ Schlesinger, John	BD - Midnight Cowboy	1969
☐ Scofield, Paul	BA - A Man for All Seasons	1966
☐ Scott, George C.	BA - Patton	1970
☐ Shakespeare in Love	BP	1998
☐ Shearer, Norma	BAS- The Divorcee	1930
☐ Signoret, Simone	BAS - Room at the Top	1959
☐ Sinatra, Frank	BSA - From Here to Eternity	1953
☐ Smith, Maggie	BSAS - California Suite	1978
☐ Smith, Maggie	BAS - The Prime of Miss Jean Brodie	1969
☐ Soderbergh, Steven	BD - Traffic	2000
☐ Sondergaard, Gale	BSAS - Anthony Adverse	1936
☐ Sorvino, Mira	BSAS - Mighty Aphrodite	1995
☐ Spacek, Sissy	BAS - Coal Miner's Daughter	1980
☐ Spacey, Kevin	BSA - The Usual Suspects	1995
☐ Spacey, Kevin	BA - American Beauty	1999
☐ Spielberg, Steven	BD - Schindler's List	1993
☐ Spielberg, Steven	BD - Saving Private Ryan	1998
☐ Stapleton, Maureen	BSAS - Reds	1981
☐ Steenburgen, Mary	BSAS - Melvin and Howard	1980
☐ Steiger, Rod	BA - In the Heat of the Night	1967
☐ Stevens, George	BD - Giant	1956
☐ Stevens, George	BD - A Place in the Sun	1951
☐ Stewart, James	BA - The Philadelphia Story	1940
☐ Stone, Oliver	BD - Platoon	1986
☐ Stone, Oliver	BD - Born on the Fourth of July	1989
☐ Straight, Beatrice	BSAS - Network	1976
☐ Streep, Meryl	BSAS - Kramer vs. Kramer	1979
☐ Streep, Meryl	BAS - Sophie's Choice	1982
☐ Streisand, Barbra	BAS - Funny Girl	1968
☐ Swank, Hilary	BAS - Boys Don't Cry	1999
☐ Tandy, Jessica	BAS - Driving Miss Daisy	1989
☐ Taurog, Norman	BD- Skippy	1931
☐ Taylor, Elizabeth	BAS - Butterfield 8	1960
☐ Taylor, Elizabeth	BAS - Who's Afraid of Virginia Woolf?	1966
☐ Terms of Endearment	BP	1983
☐ The Apartment	BP	1960
☐ The Best Years of Our Lives	BP	1946
☐ The Bridge on the River Kwai	BP	1957
☐ The Deer Hunter	BP	1978
☐ The English Patient	BP	1996
☐ The French Connection	BP	1971

Name	Category/Subject	Year
☐ The Godfather	BP	1972
☐ The Godfather Part II	BP	1974
☐ The Great Ziegfeld	BP	1936
☐ The Greatest Show on Earth	BP	1952
☐ The Last Emperor	BP	1987
☐ The Life of Emile Zola	BP	1937
☐ The Lost Weekend	BP	1945
☐ The Silence of the Lambs	BP	1991
☐ The Sound of Music	BP	1965
☐ The Sting	BP	1973
☐ Thompson, Emma	BAS - Howard's End	1992
☐ Titanic	BP	1997
☐ Tom Jones	BP	1963
☐ Tomei, Marisa	BSAS - My Cousin Vinny	1992
☐ Tracy, Spencer	BA - Boys Town	1938
☐ Tracy, Spencer	BA - Captains Courageous	1937
☐ Trevor, Claire	BSAS - Key Largo	1948
☐ Unforgiven	BP	1992
☐ Ustinov, Peter	BSA - Spartacus	1960
☐ Ustinov, Peter	BSA - Topkapi	1964
☐ Van Fleet, Jo	BSAS - East of Eden	1955
☐ Voight, Jon	BA - Coming Home	1978
☐ Walken, Christopher	BSA - The Deer Hunter	1978
☐ Washington, Denzel	BSA - Glory	1989
☐ Washington, Denzel	BA - Training Day	2001
☐ Wayne, John	BA - True Grit	1969
☐ West Side Story	BP	1961
☐ Wiest, Dianne	BSAS - Hannah and Her Sisters	1986
☐ Wiest, Dianne	BSAS - Bullets Over Broadway	1994
☐ Wilder, Billy	BD - The Lost Weekend	1945
☐ Wilder, Billy	BD - The Apartment	1960
☐ Williams, Robin	BSA - Good Will Hunting	1997
☐ Wings	BP	1928
☐ Winters, Shelley	BSAS - The Diary of Anne Frank	1959
☐ Winters, Shelley	BSAS - A Patch of Blue	1965
☐ Wise, Robert	BD - The Sound of Music	1965
☐ Wise, Robert	BD - West Side Story	1961
☐ Woodward, Joanne	BAS - The Three Faces of Eve	1957
☐ Wright, Teresa	BSAS - Mrs. Miniver	1942
☐ Wyler, William	BD - The Best Years of Our Lives	1946
☐ Wyler, William	BD - Mrs. Miniver	1942
☐ Wyler, William	BD - Ben - Hur	1959
☐ Wyman, Jane	BAS - Johnny Belinda	1948
☐ You Can't Take It With You	BP	1938

Name	Category/Subject	Year
☐ Young, Gig	BSA - They Shoot Horses, Don't They?	1969
☐ Young, Loretta	BAS - The Farmer's Daughter	1947
☐ Zemeckis, Robert	BD - Forrest Gump	1994
☐ Zeta-Jones, Catherine	BSAS - Chicago	2002
☐ Zinnemann, Fred	BD - A Man for All Seasons	1966
☐ Zinnemann, Fred	BD - From Here to Eternity	1953

The Manuscript Society

PROFESSIONAL

AUTOGRAPH

ORGANIZATIONS

THE MANUSCRIPT SOCIETY

THE MANUSCRIPT SOCIETY was founded in 1948 as the *National Society of Autograph Collectors*, and has grown to an international membership of more than 1,800 including dealers, private collectors, scholars, authors, and caretakers of public collections such as librarians, archivists, and curators. There are also many historical societies, museums, special libraries and academic libraries that are institutional members.

The Society publishes two quarterly publications, *MANUSCRIPTS* and *THE MANUSCRIPT SOCIETY NEWS*, which are sent to each member without charge. *MANUSCRIPTS* is a journal with an established reputation for excellent scholarly and collector articles reflecting the diverse interests in the field of autographs and manuscripts. Issues offer views on the principal areas of historical and literary collecting, present auction results, list new members and publicize sources of autographs through dealer and auctioneer advertisements. The *NEWS* features information on the whole contemporary world of autographs, including important discoveries, acquisitions, trends, disasters, preservation, upcoming sales, legal questions, thefts, forgeries, replevin actions and exhibits, as well as news about the Society and its members. Collectors and scholars seeking or offering manuscript material are permitted to place their notices in a special section.

The Society's chief activity is a five-day annual meeting, held in a community offering good manuscript resources for viewing. The programs feature exhibitions, panel discussions, speakers of note, tours and social occasions for fellowship and interchange of ideas. Major cities have alternated with smaller communities as the locales for these meetings so as to provide a varied view of the manuscript resources available. Five annual meetings have been held abroad: London in 1970 and 1986, Ottawa in 1978, Dublin in 1991 and Edinburgh in 1996.

Local chapters in the Twin Cities, Washington and Southern California offer members a chance to meet with others in their area. All members in good standing may belong to a chapter.

A comprehensive monograph titled *AUTOGRAPHS AND MANUSCRIPTS: A COLLECTOR'S MANUAL*, was published under the auspices of The Manuscript Society by Charles Scribner's Sons in 1978. Its long definitive articles on many aspects of collecting, arranging and preserving manuscript material – all of them written by experts in their fields – have caused the book to be hailed as a classic treatment of the subject. In 1984 Greenwood Press published *MANU-SCRIPTS: THE FIRST TWENTY YEARS*, an anthology of 50 memorable articles from the Society's journal. THE *AUTOGRAPH COLLECTOR'S CHECKLIST* was published by the Society in 1990, providing lists to aid collectors in a number of popular collecting fields. HISTORY IN YOUR HANDS, a 50-year history of the Society and autograph collecting in general, was published in 1997.

To celebrate the bicentennial of the United States, in 1975 and 1976 a traveling exhibit was sponsored by the Society in cooperation with the Smithsonian Institution. It consisted of documents written during the early months of the Revolution, which were loaned to the exhibit by members of the Society from their own collections. The Society also has aided members involved in litigation over contested ownership of manuscript material where the rights of individuals to own historic documents have been questioned.

The Manuscript Society welcomes new members. The annual individual or institutional membership fee is $45. Contributing memberships at $100, sustaining memberships at $250, benefactor memberships at $500, and life memberships at $2,000 help to further Society interests. Memberships are on a calendar year basis; new members joining after July 1 may pay half the annual rate. All monies go to support the publication program, to aid in the defense of individuals against government agencies in replevin suits, and to maintain the expenses of managing Society affairs.

The Manuscript Society
Edward C. Oetting
Executive Director
1960 E. Fairmont Drive
Tempe, AZ 85282-2844
Visit our Web site at: http://www.manuscript.org

PADA

The Professional Autograph Dealers Association, Inc. (PADA) is an organization of knowledgeable, experienced, and ethical dealers in historic autograph material. Established in 1995 by many of the nation's leading dealers, PADA is dedicated to maintaining the highest standards of business ethics, professionalism and service in the autograph industry. Its members seek to establish a marketplace for autographs, in which collectors can buy and sell with confidence and receive informed, accurate advice.

PADA has a stringent code of ethics to which its members must adhere. PADA dealers are required to provide a money-back guarantee of authenticity on all the autographs they sell. In addition, they must conscientiously authenticate and accurately describe all autographs; they must conduct their businesses honestly, fairly, and with integrity; and they must make every effort to promote customer satisfaction.

Membership in PADA is limited to dealers who abide by its code of ethics and who have demonstrated expertise and integrity in buying and selling autographs. All applicants for membership are carefully screened. Applicants must have been in the autograph business for at least three years; most PADA members have far more experience than this.

PADA also seeks to encourage interest in, and appreciation of, autographs. It maintains an informational Web site (www.padaweb.org) where its complete code of ethics can be found. The site also presents the Monthly Catalog, a new list every month of autographs offered by PADA members. The Monthly Catalog provides an excellent sampling of the fine and varied autograph material handled by PADA dealers. The Web site also lists all PADA members, along with their areas of special expertise, and contains links to their individual e-mail addresses and Web sites. Further expansion of PADA's Web site is planned, including the addition of a library of information that will be helpful to autograph collectors.

Every April PADA holds an autograph show in New York City that is considered by many the nation's premier autograph show. The organization is planning other shows across the country, and details about all PADA shows can be found on its Web site. PADA also plans to issue publications on autographs that will be useful to collectors.

PADA dealers are an unrivaled source for autographs. Collectively, they offer a large and diverse assortment of material in all price ranges. Among the specialties of PADA members are U.S. history, including presidents and military leaders; world history; music; literature; the fine and performing arts; science and medicine; exploration; aviation; business and finance; and vintage theater and entertainment.

PADA members can provide collectors with other valuable services. With their many years of experience, they can answer questions about autograph collecting and offer advice on all aspects of the field. They can discuss proper methods for storing and displaying autographs and can help locate an expert conservator, when one is needed. Individual members of PADA offer authentication services and appraisals of autographs. They can act as agents for collectors and libraries at auctions.

PADA dealers also represent a significant market for purchasing autographs, whether single items or entire collections. They buy autographs outright, offering a fair price and immediate payment. PADA dealers also take autographs on consignment, acting as agents for their sale. PADA's code of ethics requires members to adhere to the highest professional standards when they are buying autographs, assuring the seller of courteous and honest treatment.

Whether you are buying or selling autographs, if you do business with a PADA member, you can be sure that you are dealing with a reliable individual who has a commitment to quality, service and integrity. PADA dealers look forward to sharing with you the excitement and rewards of autograph collecting and helping you find the autographs that you will treasure for years to come.

For a free brochure and membership directory, write to:
The Professional Autograph Dealers Association, Inc.
P.O. Box 1729, Murray Hill Station
New York, NY 10016
Visit our Web site at: www.padaweb.org

UACC

The Universal Autograph Collectors Club, Inc. (UACC) is the world's largest organization for autograph collectors with over 2,000 members in more than 27 countries. Founded in 1965, the UACC is a federally approved nonprofit organization whose purpose is to educate members and the public about all aspects of autograph collecting through its publications, shows, conventions and seminars. Unlike other organizations, the UACC Executive Board is not made up of dealers but, rather, of collectors. They are elected by the membership.

By joining the UACC, you will receive our renowned 64-page bimonthly journal, *The Pen and Quill,* which features articles and news on autographs in all areas. These include our famous signature studies (articles on authentic, secretarial, autopen, rubber-stamped, facsimile and forged signatures), as well as interesting historical footnotes using collectors' documents and stories of in-person encounters with the celebrities of the time. This information gives the collector better information in order to make decisions in purchasing good quality material.

To this end, the UACC also boasts the largest Autograph Dealer's registry, known as UACC Registered Dealers. These 200+ individuals or companies have provided information regarding their business for publication, including how long they have been involved in the field and if they have any ethics violations. This information is posted on the UACC Web site at www.uacc.org along with other important information you should know about each dealer. These dealers are the leaders in the field of autographs and, as such, they fully support the UACC and its goals. Each year we give a Distinguished Dealer Award to one of our dealers that excels in service to the industry.

Speaking of the Internet, the UACC was the first organization to establish a fully interactive Web site, which includes autograph news, membership information, Registered Dealer information, the Hall of Shame, Constitution and Code of Ethics, show schedules and more.

The UACC was also the first organization to institute a Code of Ethics by which each member agrees to abide as a condition of membership. Our code is the toughest in the industry and has resolved over 95% of the complaints filed by the membership. Our extensive ethics files have been used and applauded by numerous law enforcement agencies. Our active Ethics Board works for the protection of the membership.

Each year the UACC presents a number of awards to individuals that have given of themselves each year for the betterment of the hobby. These include literary awards, collector of the year awards, the president's quality award and the coveted UACC Distinguished Service Award.

Our members are also given FREE classified ads in our journal as well as opportunities to purchase uncommon autographic material and reference works at affordable prices. There is also our annual auction that benefits the membership.

We sponsor shows around the United States and in England, as well as a yearly convention, and are the only organization that accepts Visa and Mastercard for membership or anything else for that matter.

Our best resource is our membership. When shared, the combined knowledge and experience of our members makes the UACC the best organization for the informed collector.

To learn more about the UACC, write for a brochure and membership information to:
UACC
P.O. Box 6181
Washington, DC 20044-6181
or visit our Web site at: www.uacc.org
We hope you will join our universe of fellow collectors soon.

Key Civil War Battles and Campaigns

* Understanding the key battles and campaigns of the Civil War is a necessity for autograph and document collectors, for without this information, no accurate value/significance could ever be placed on a particular item.

* Another point to remember is that Northerners named battles after nearby bodies of water, while Southerners after nearby places. Therefore the Union fought at Bull Run Creek, while the Confederacy battled at Manassas.

Military Operations - A Brief Non-comprehensive Overview

First Bull Run

On July 21, 1861 forces met near Manassas, VA to wage the first major land battle.

Other Activities of 1861/Early 1862

Wilson's Creek (August 10, 1861), Pea Ridge, Ark. (March, 1862)

Grant in the West, Spring 1862

Fort Henry and Fort Donelson, on the Tennessee and Cumberland rivers (February, 1862), Island No. 10 in the Mississippi (March 16-April 7, 1862), Shiloh Church (April 6, 7, 1862), Corinth (May, 1862), and New Orleans (April 26, 1862).

Peninsular (March, 1862)

Monitor and Merrimack (March 9, 1862), Shenandoah Valley (March to June 1862), Yorktown (May 4, 1862), Williamsburg (May 5, 1862), Seven Pines (May 31 - June 1, 1862) and Seven Days (June 26 - July 1, 1862)

Second Bull Run

Cedar Mountain (August 9, 1862) and Manassas Junction (August 29, 30, 1862)

Perryville and Antietam

Perryville, KY (October 8, 1862) and Sharpsburg, MD, along Antietam Creek (September 17-19, 1862)

Vicksburg

Grant failed (December 1862, January-March 1863), but was successful May - July 4, 1863.

Chancellorsville

Chancellorsville (May 1-4, 1863) - Jackson mortally wounded.

Gettysburg

Gettysburg, PA (July 1-July 3, 1863)

Chickamauga and Chattanooga

Chattanooga (September, 1863), Chickamauga Creek (September 19-20, 1863), Lookout Mountain and Missionary Ridge (November 24-25, 1863)

Virginia Campaigns of 1864-65

Wilderness (May-June, 1864), Cold Harbor (June 3, 1864), Petersburg (June 15-18, 1864), Cedar Creek (October 19, 1864), Petersburg (March, 1865)

Georgia and Carolina

Kennesaw Mountain (June 27, 1864), Atlanta (September, 1864), Savannah (December 21, 1864), Franklin, TN (November 30, 1864), Nashville, TN (December 15-16, 1864), Bentonville, NC (March 19-21, 1865), Raleigh, NC (April 13, 1865).

Surrender at Appomattox Court House (April 9, 1865)

A Selected Cast Summary of Popular Vintage Prime Time Television

A popular area of collecting is television cast photos. Driven in recent years by syndication and nostalgic cable channels, a new generation of fans has emerged. Children are now tuning in to shows their parents and even grandparents grew up watching. This increased interest in vintage television has even carried over into the autograph market.

Let's face it: Television – when compared to radio and movies – is a relatively new form. Although many of the early pioneers of this art form are now deceased, others are still with us. Signatures of deceased stars like Lucille Ball, Milton Berle and George Burns remain affordable and plentiful. Collectors who grew up on this art form can easily assemble an impressive autograph collection.

While autographed cast photographs are the most desirable, assemblages of signatures in a variety of forms can be equally as impressive and cost effective. Due to association, the prime cast members of a show are of greatest interest to television aficionados, but a comprehensive grouping of key characters can make for a grand display. Whatever direction you may choose, this area of collecting is simply a lot of fun!

Notes:

* This list is not intended to be comprehensive or all-inclusive. "Vintage," as described in these listings, is considered prior to 1980. In most cases, primary characters are listed first. Key character actors are also included, with many in multiple listings due to studio contractual agreements. Actors who have won Academy Awards, such as George Burns, Art Carney, Sally Field, Michael Douglas, Ernest Borgnine, etc. are always in demand.

❑ Abbott and Costello Show, The
Cast: Bud Abbott, Lou Costello, Hillary Brooke, Sid Fields, Gordon Jones, Joe Kirk, Joe Besser. Hints: Abbott and Costello are both highly sought; all others signatures easy, with the exception of Besser, who was a member of The Three Stooges; Costello died in 1959 and Abbott passed away in 1974.

❑ Adam 12
Cast: Martin Milner, Kent McCord, William Boyett, Gary Crosby, William Stevens, Jack Hogan, Mikki Jamison, Claude Johnson. Hints: Milner is sought more for previous roles; during the show's run both Milner and McCord answered mail requests with facsimile signatures.

❑ Addams Family, The
Cast: Carolyn Jones, John Astin, Jackie Coogan, Ted Cassidy, Blossom Rock, Ken Weatherwax, Lisa Loring, Felix Silla. Hints: All are fairly easy, with Coogan being the most sought after.

❑ Adventures in Paradise
Cast: Gardner McKay, Weaver Levy, Linda Lawson, Henry Slate, James Holden, George Tobias, Sondi Sodsai, Lani Kai, Guy Stockwell, Marcel Hillaire.

❑ Adventures of Ellery Queen, The
Cast: Richard Hart, Lee Bowman, Florenz Ames, George Nader, Les Tremayne, Lee Phillips, Jim Hutton, David Wayne, Tom Reese, John Hillerman, Ken Swofford, Ike Glee. Hints: Hart died suddenly in 1951 – a tough signature!

❑ Adventures of Ozzie & Harriet, The
Cast: Ozzie Nelson, Harriet Nelson, David Nelson, Eric "Ricky" Nelson, Don DeFore, Parley Baer, Lyle Talbot, Mary Jane Croft, Frank Cady, Skip Young, Gordon Jones, June Blair, Kristin Harmon, James Stacy, Joe Flynn, Constance Harper, Jack Wagner, Charlene Salerno, Ivan Bonar, Greg Dawson, Sean Morgan. Hints: All the Nelsons are sought after, with Ricky being the key; Ricky was a prolific signer before his tragic death.

❑ Adventures of Rin Tin Tin, The
Cast: Lee Aaker, James Brown, Joe Sawyer, Rand Brooks.

❑ Adventures of Superman, The
Cast: George Reeves, Phyllis Coates, Noel Neill, Jack Larson, John Hamilton, Robert Shayne. Hints: Reeves is the key – a tough signature to acquire over the years, not only due to his Superman participation, but also because of his appearance in "Gone with the Wind." Reeves died in 1959.

❑ Adventures of Wild Bill Hickok, The
Cast: Guy Madison, Andy Devine.

❑ Aldrich Family, The
Cast: Robert Casey, Richard Tyler, Henry Girard, Ken Nelson, Bobby Ellis, House Jameson, Lois Wilson, Nancy Carroll, Barbara Robbins, Charita Bauer, Mary Malone, June Dayton and others.

❑ Alice
Cast: Linda Lavin, Philip McKeon, Vic Tayback, Polly Holliday, Beth Howland, Diane Ladd, Celia Weston and others. Hint: all signatures easy to acquire.

❑ All in the Family
Cast: Carroll O'Connor, Jean Stapleton, Sally Struthers, Rob Reiner, Isabel Sanford, Mel Stewart and others. Hints: One of the best television shows ever, with a cast to match; all signatures are plentiful; O'Connor sent out facsimile signed photographs during periods of increased fan mail.

❑ Amos 'n' Andy
Cast: Alvin Childress, Spencer Williams, Tim Moore, Johnny Lee, Ernestine Wade, Horace Stewart, Amanda Randolph, Lillian Randolph.

❑ Andy Griffith Show, The

Cast: Andy Griffith, Ronny Howard, Don Knotts, Frances Bavier, Elinor Donahue, Jim Nabors, Anita Corsaut, George Lindsey, Howard McNear, Hal Smith, Jack Dodson, Paul Hartman, Betty Lynn, Jack Burns, Hope Summers. Hints: Extremely popular with collectors; Griffith has varied responses over the years; Howard signs in-person; Knotts also has varied responses; Bavier is the least plentiful and most expensive; don't overlook some great character actors.

❑ Batman

Cast: Adam West, Burt Ward, Alan Napier, Madge Blake, Neil Hamilton, Stafford Repp, Yvonne Craig and others. Hints: Both West and Ward have attended autograph shows.

❑ Beverly Hillbillies, The

Cast: Buddy Ebsen, Irene Ryan, Donna Douglas, Max Baer Jr., Raymond Bailey, Nancy Kulp, Bea Benaderet, Harriet MacGibbon and others. Hints: Ryan is the key signature; Ebsen signed for years and is plentiful, as is Douglas; Baer is a very reluctant signer.

❑ Bewitched

Cast: Elizabeth Montgomery, Dick York, Dick Sargent, Agnes Moorehead, David White, Irene Vernon, Kasey Rogers and others. Hints: Montgomery is the key. Her signature is plentiful in the market and can easily be found on signed checks.

❑ Big Valley, The

Cast: Barbara Stanwyck, Richard Long, Peter Breck, Lee Majors, Linda Evans, Napoleon Whiting. Hints: The entire cast often complied with autograph requests; it was Majors' first acting role.

❑ Bob Newhart Show, The

Cast: Bob Newhart, Suzanne Pleshette, Bill Daily, Peter Bonerz, Marcia Wallace and others. Hints: All cast members are good signers.

❑ Bonanza

Cast: Lorne Greene, Michael Landon, Dan Blocker, Pernell Roberts, Victor Sen Yung, Ray Teal, David Canary, Lou Frizzell, Mitch Vogel, Tim Matheson. Hints: Blocker is the key signature – he died prior to the 1972-73 season; during the years of the show, they answered requests with facsimile signed cast photos; Greene and Landon were never easy through the mail.

❑ Brady Bunch, The

Cast: Robert Reed, Florence Henderson, Ann B. Davis, Maureen McCormick, Eve Plumb, Susan Olsen, Barry Williams, Christopher Knight, Mike Lookinland. Hints: Reed is the key signature; all other members are good signers.

❑ Carol Burnett Show, The

Cast: Carol Burnett, Harvey Korman, Lyle Waggoner, Vicki Lawrence, Tim

Conway and others. Hints: A great cast, all of whom willingly comply with autograph requests; Burnett can be tough through the mail.

❑ Charlie's Angels
Cast: Kate Jackson, Farrah Fawcett-Majors, Jaclyn Smith, Cheryl Ladd, Shelly Hack, Tanya Roberts, David Doyle and John Forsythe. Hints: All cast members are good signers with the exception of Fawcett-Majors, who left the show in 1977.

❑ Chico and the Man
Cast: Jack Albertson, Freddie Prinze, Scatman Crothers, Bonnie Boland, Issac Ruiz, Ronny Graham, Della Reese, Gabriel Melgar, Charo. Hints: Prinze, who died in 1977, is the key signature here; his signed material can be tough to find.

❑ CHiPs
Cast: Larry Wilcox, Erik Estrada, Robert Pine, Lew Saunders, Brodie Greer and others. Hints: Autographs of the entire cast are easy to acquire.

❑ Combat
Cast: Rick Jason, Vic Morrow, Pierre Jalbert, Jack Hogan, Dick Peabody, Steven Rigers, Conlon Carter, Shecky Greene, Tom Lowell. Hints: Morrow is the key signature – he died tragically during a movie shoot.

❑ Dallas
Cast: Larry Hagman, Barbara Bel Geddes, Jim Davis, Patrick Duffy, Victoria Principal, Charlene Tilton, Lind Gray, Steve Kanaly, Ken Kercheval, Tina Louise, David Wayne, Keenan Wynn, David Ackroyd, Ted Schackelford, Joan Van Ark, Barbara Babcock and many others. Hints: Hagman is the key signature and can be elusive at times; all others are plentiful.

❑ Daniel Boone
Cast: Fess Parker, Albert Salmi, Ed Ames, Patricia Blair, Veronica Cartwright, Darby Hinton, Dal McKennon, Robert Logan, Don Pedro Colley, Roosevelt Grier, Jimmy Dean. Hints: Parker is the key signature – he has always been accommodating to collectors.

❑ Danny Thomas Show, The (a.k.a. Make Room for Daddy)
Cast: Danny Thomas, Jean Hagen, Marjorie Lord, Rusty Hamer, Sherry Jackson, Penny Parker, Angela Cartwright, Amanda Randolph, and many others. Hints: Thomas, a television legend, is the key signature.

❑ Death Valley Days
Host: Stanley Andrews, Ronald Reagan, Robert Taylor, Dale Robertson, Merle Haggard. Hints: A good following exists for all these cast members; Reagan was only on the show for one season (1965-66).

❑ Dennis the Menace
Cast: Jay North, Herbert Anderson, Gloria Henry, Joseph Kearns, Sylvia Field, Gil

Smith, Irene Tedrow, Billy Booth, Gale Gordon, Sara Seeger. Hints: North is the most popular; Kearns died before completing the 1961-1962 season; all other signatures are plentiful.

❑ Dick Van Dyke Show, The

Cast: Dick Van Dyke, Mary Tyler Moore, Rose Marie, Morey Amsterdam, Larry Mathews, Richard Deacon, Jerry Paris, Ann Morgan Guilbert, Carl Reiner. Hints: An extremely popular show; Van Dyke and Moore are the key signatures – of the two, Moore is the tougher; all other signatures can be found.

❑ Dr. Kildare

Cast: Richard Chamberlain, Raymond Massey, Eddie Ryder, Jud Taylor, John Patrick, Lee Kurty. Hints: Key signatures are Chamberlain and Massey – both could be elusive.

❑ Donna Reed Show, The

Cast: Donna Reed, Carl Betz, Shelley Fabares, Paul Petersen, Patty Petersen, Bob Crane, Ann McCrea, Janet Langard, Darryl Richard. Hints: All signatures generally available; Fabares of "Johnny Angel" fame pursued a recording contract – as did other cast members.

❑ Doris Day Show, The

Cast: Doris Day, Denver Pyle, Fran Ryan, James Hampton, Philip Brown, Todd Starke, Naomi Stevens, Rose Marie, McLean Stevenson, Paul Smith, Kaye Ballard, Bernie Kopell. Hints: Day has always been a great signer; a nice group of character actors here – many went on to greater fame.

❑ Dragnet

Cast: Jack Webb, Barton Yarborough, Barney Phillips, Herb Ellis, Ben Alexander, Harry Morgan. Hints: Webb is the key signature; during the show's run both Webb and Morgan answered requests with facsimile signed photos.

❑ Dukes of Hazzard, The

Cast: Tom Wopat, John Schneider, Catherine Bach, Denver Pyle, James Best, Sorrell Booke, Sonny Schroyer, Ben Jones, Rick Hurst and Waylon Jennings (voice only). Hints: A good mix of actors, all of whom are easy to acquire.

❑ Dynasty

Cast: John Forsythe, Linda Evans, Pamela Sue Martin, Al Corley, Bo Hopkins, Pamela Bellwood, Kathy Krutzman, John James, Lloyd Bochner, Dale Robertson, Wayne Northrop, Lee Bergere. Hints: All cast signatures generally available in the market.

❑ Eight is Enough

Cast: Dick Van Patten, Diana Hyland, Betty Buckley, Adam Rich, Willie Aames, Connie Needham, Dianne Kay, Susan Richardson, Laurie Walters, Lani O'Grady, Grant Goodeve, Michael Thoma, Virginia Vincent, Jennifer Darling, Brian Patrick

Clarke, John Prather, Michael Goodrow, Ralph Macchio. Hints: The signatures of all cast members are generally available.

❏ Emergency!
Cast: Robert Fuller, Julie London, Bobby Troup, Kevin Tighe, Randolph Mantooth, Ron Pinkard, Michael Norell, Tim Donnelly, Marco Lopez, Mike Stoker. Hints: The signatures of all cast members are generally available; Troup was a former bandleader.

❏ Family Affair
Cast: Brian Keith, Sebastian Cabot, Anissa Jones, Johnnie Whitaker, Kathy Garver, Nancy Walker. Hints: Following the tragic deaths of some cast members, completing an assemblage of signatures will be a challenge. During the show's run, Keith answered requests with a facsimile signed photograph.

❏ Father Knows Best
Cast: Robert Young, Jane Wyatt, Elinor Donahue, Billy Gray, Lauren Chapin, Sarah Selby, Robert Foulk, Vivi Jannis, Yvonne Lime, Paul Wallace, Jimmy Bates, Roger Smith, Robert Chapman, Sue George, Roberta (Jymme) Shore. Hints: Young is the key signature.

❏ Flipper
Cast: Brian Kelly, Luke Halpin, Tommy Norden, Andy Devine, Ulla Stromstedt. Hints: The signatures of all cast members are generally available.

❏ Fugitive, The
Cast: David Janssen, Barry Morse, Jacqueline Scott, Bill Raisch. Hints: Janssen is the key signature – he was generally an elusive signer; all other signatures are generally available.

❏ George Burns and Gracie Allen Show, The
Cast: George Burns, Gracie Allen, Bea Benaderet, Hal March, John Brown, Fred Clark, Larry Keating, Bill Goodwin, Harry Von Zell, Ralph Seadon, Ronnie Burns, Judi Meredith. Hints: Vintage signed photos of Burns and Allen are highly sought by collectors – facsimiles do exist.

❏ Get Smart
Cast: Don Adams, Barbara Feldon, Edward Platt, Dave Ketchum, Stacy Keach, Bernie Kopell, King Moody, Dick Gautier, Robert Karvelas, Jane Dulo. Hint: "Would you believe?" Adams answered most signature requests with facsimile signed photos; all other cast members were good signers.

❏ Gilligan's Island
Cast: Bob Denver, Alan Hale Jr., Jim Backus, Natalie Schafer, Tina Louise, Russell Johnson, Dawn Wells. Hints: One of the most popular syndicated programs of all time; Hale is the key signature, followed by Schafer and Backus; all other cast members have attended autograph shows; Louise is a reluctant signer.

❏ Gomer Pyle, U.S.M.C.

Cast: Jim Nabors, Frank Sutton, Ronnie Schell, Roy Stuart, Ted Bessell, Barbara Stuart, William Christopher, Forrest Compton, Allan Melvin, Tommy Leonetti, Larry Hovis. Hints: Sutton is the key signature; Nabors has always been a great signer; the show used a stable of studio actors, many of whom went on to gain fame in other roles.

❏ Good Times

Cast: Esther Rolle, John Amos, Jimmie Walker, Ja'net DuBois, Ralph Carter, BernNadette Stanis, Moses Gunn, Johnny Brown, Janet Jackson, Ben Powers, Theodore Wilson. Hints: The signatures of all cast members are generally available.

❏ Green Acres

Cast: Eddie Albert, Eva Gabor, Pat Buttram, Tom Lester, Alvy Moore, Hank Patterson, Barbara Pepper, Fran Ryan, Frank Cady, Kay E. Kuter, Sid Melton, Mary Grace Canfield, Judy McConnell. Hints: Albert and Gabor are the key signatures – both can be a challenge; the show included a great stable of CBS character actors.

❏ Gunsmoke

Cast: James Arness, Milburn Stone, Amanda Blake, Dennis Weaver, Ken Curtis, Burt Reynolds, Glenn Strange, Roger Ewing, Buck Taylor, Dabbs Greer, James Nusser, Charles Seel, Howard Culver, Tom Brown, John Harper, Hank Patterson, Sarah Selby, Ted Jordan, Roy Roberts, Woody Chambliss, Charles Wagenheim, Frank Ryan. Hints: A television classic, Gunsmoke ran for 20 years; Arness is both the key signature and easiest to acquire; Weaver left in 1964; original autographed cast photos (Arness, Stone, Blake and Weaver) are scarce and highly sought after.

❏ Happy Days

Cast: Ronny Howard, Henry Winkler, Tom Bosley, Marion Ross, Anson Williams, Donny Most, Erin Moran, Gavan O'Herlihy, Randolph Roberts, Neil J. Schwartz, Beatrice Colen, Linda Purl, Misty Rowe, Tita Bell, Pat Morita, Al Molinaro, Scott Baio, Lynda Goodfriend, Cathy Silvers, Ted McGinley. Hints: The signatures of all cast members are generally available; Howard can be elusive; Winkler has answered requests with facsimile signed photographs.

❏ Have Gun – Will Travel

Cast: Richard Boone, Kam Tong, Lisa Lu. Hints: Boone was never an easy signature to acquire.

❏ Hawaii Five-O

Cast: Jack Lord, James MacArthur, Kam Fong, Zulu, Richard Denning, Al Harrington, Harry Endo, Al Eban, Maggi Parker, Peggy Ryan, Herman Wedemeyer, Morgan White, Glenn Cannon, Khigh Dhiegh, William Smith, Moe Keale, Sharon Farrell, Jim Bird. Hints: Lord is the key – he often answered requests with facsimile signed photographs; MacArthur also is sought for his role in Tarzan; the signatures of all other cast members are generally available.

❏ Hawaiian Eye
Cast: Bob Conrad, Anthony Eisley, Connie Stevens, Poncie Ponce, Grant Williams, Mel Prestidge, Doug Mossman, Troy Donahue. Hints: Conrad is the key signature; the show had a good stable of Warner Brothers actors – Stevens, Donahue, etc.

❏ Hawk
Cast: Burt Reynolds, Wayne Grice, Bruce Glover, Leon Janney. Hints: Reynolds is the key signature.

❏ Hazel
Cast: Shirley Booth, Don DeFore, Whitney Blake, Maudine Prickett, Howard Smith, Bobby Buntrock and many others. Hints: Booth is the key signature – she was never much for answering fan mail; all others signatures of cast members are generally available.

❏ Hill Street Blues
Cast: Daniel J. Travanti, Michael Conrad, Michael Warren, Charles Haid, Veronica Hamel, Bruce Weitz, Rene Enriguez, Kiel Martin, Taurean Blacque, James Sikking, Joe Spano, Betty Thomas, Barbara Babcock, Barbara Bosson and others. Hints: The signatures of all cast members are generally available.

❏ Hogan's Heroes
Cast: Bob Crane, Werner Klemperer, John Banner, Robert Clary, Richard Dawson, Ivan Dixon, Kenneth Washington, Larry Hovis, Cynthia Lynn, Sigrid Valdis. Hints: Crane is the key, and is a tough signature to find – however, he did answer his fan mail; Banner is also a difficult signature; all other cast members should prove easy to acquire.

❏ Honeymooners, The
Cast: Jackie Gleason, Art Carney, Audrey Meadows, Joyce Randolph, Sheila MacRae, Jane Kean. Hints: A television classic – Gleason is the key signature; all cast members are generally available; original cast autographed photos are always in demand.

❏ I Dream of Jeannie
Cast: Barbara Eden, Larry Hagman, Bill Daily, Hayden Rorke, Philip Ober, Karen Sharpe, Barton MacLane, Emmaline Henry, Vinton Hayworth. Hints: Hagman is the key signature; all cast members are generally available, including Eden – she has answered requests with facsimile signed photographs.

❏ I Love Lucy
Cast: Lucille Ball, Desi Arnaz, Vivian Vance, William Frawley, Richard Keith, Mary Jane Croft, Frank Nelson. Hints: Unparalleled in the history of television – a CBS

classic; the entire cast is key – Frawley is the toughest to find; any autographed cast photo – scarce or assemblage – is in demand.

☐ Ironside
Cast: Raymond Burr, Don Galloway, Barbara Anderson, Don Mitchell, Elizabeth Baur, Gene Lyons, Johnny Seven, Joan Pringle. Hints: Burr is the key signature – he was always elusive when it came to autograph requests; original cast photos with Anderson, who left in 1971, are not easy to find.

☐ Jeffersons, The
Cast: Sherman Hemsley, Isabel Sanford, Roxie Roker, Franklin Cover, Berlinda Tolbert, Paul Benedict and others. Hints: The signatures of all cast members are generally available.

☐ Knots Landing
Cast: Ted Shackelford, Joan Van Ark, James Houghton, Kim Lankford, Don Murray, Michele Lee, John Pleshette, Constance McCashin, Keith Talbert, Pat Peterson, Steve Shaw and many others. Hints: The signatures of all cast members are generally available.

☐ Kojak
Cast: Telly Savalas, Dan Frazer, Kevin Dobson, George Savalas, Vince Conti, Mark Russell. Hints: Savalas is the key signature – he was never great at answering fan mail.

☐ Lassie
Cast: Tommy Rettig, Jan Clayton, George Cleveland, Donald Keeler, Paul Maxey, Jon Provost, Arthur Space, Cloris Leachman, June Lockhart, Hugh Reilly, Todd Ferrell, Andy Clyde, Robert Bray, Jed Allen, Jack De Mave. Hints: The signatures of all cast members are generally available.

☐ Laverne & Shirley
Cast: Penny Marshall, Cindy Williams, Eddie Mekka, Phil Foster, David L. Lander, Michael McKean, Betty Garrett and others. Hints: The signatures of all cast members are generally available.

☐ Leave It to Beaver
Cast: Barbara Billingsley, Hugh Beaumont, Jerry Mathers, Tony Dow, Ken Osmond, Stanley Fatara, Richard Deacon and others. Hints: The signatures of all cast members are generally available.

☐ Little House on the Prairie
Cast: Michael Landon, Karen Grassle, Melissa Gilbert, Melissa Sue Anderson, Lindsay Greenbush, Sidney Greenbush, Karl Swenson, Richard Bull, Katherine MacGregor, Alison Arngrim, Jonathan Gilbert, Kevin Hagen, Dabbs Greer, Charlotte Stewart, Victor French, Ted Gehring, Bonnie Bartlett, Merlin Olsen and many others. Hints: Landon is the key signature – he was always an elusive signer;

Olsen is a member of the NFL Football Hall of Fame; the signatures of all other cast members are generally available.

Lone Ranger, The
Cast: Clayton Moore, John Hart and Jay Silverheels. Hints: Moore was always a great signer.

Lost in Space
Cast: Guy Williams, June Lockhart, Mark Goddard, Marta Kristen, Billy Mumy, Angela Cartwright, Jonathan Harris, Bob May. Hints: Williams is the key signature.

Love Boat, The
Cast: Gavin MacLeod, Bernie Kopell, Fred Grandy, Ted Lange, Lauren Tewes, Jill Whelan. Hints: The signatures of all cast members are generally available; Grandy served in the U.S. House of Representatives.

Lucy-Desi Comedy Hour, The
Cast: Lucille Ball, Desi Arnaz, Vivian Vance, William Frawley and Richard Keith. Hints: See "I Love Lucy."

Lucy Show, The
Cast: Lucille Ball, Vivian Vance, Charles Lane, Gale Gordon, Dick Martin, Candy Moore, Jimmy Garrett, Ralph Hart, Roy Roberts, Mary Jane Croft, Lucie Arnaz, Desi Arnaz Jr. Hints: See "I Love Lucy."

M*A*S*H
Cast: Alan Alda, Wayne Rogers, Loretta Swit, Larry Linville, Gary Burghoff, McLean Stevenson, William Christopher, Jamie Farr, Harry Morgan, Mike Farrell, David Ogden Stiers; also Karen Philipp, Tim Brown, Patrick Adriarte, John Orchard, Linda Meiklejohn, Herb Voland, Odessa Cleveland, Marcia Strassman, Kelly Jean Peters, Kellye Nakahara and many others. Hints: Despite the fact that some of the cast is deceased, Stiers is still the toughest signature to acquire.

Magnum, P.I.
Cast: Tom Selleck, John Hillerman, Roger Mosley, Larry Manetti and Orson Welles (voice). Hints: The signatures of all cast members are generally available; the voice is not.

Man From U.N.C. L. E., The
Cast: Robert Vaughn, David McCallum, Leo Carroll and Barbara Moore. Hints: The signatures of all cast members are generally available.

Mannix
Cast: Mike Connors, Joseph Campanella, Gail Fisher, Robert Reed. Hints: The signatures of all cast members are generally available.

Many Loves of Dobie Gillis, The
Cast: Dwayne Hickman, Bob Demver, Frank Faylen, Florida Friebus, Sheila James and many others. Hints: The signatures of all cast members are generally available; Denver now charges for his signature.

Marcus Welby, M.D.
Cast: Robert Young, James Brolin, Elena Verdugo and others. Hints: Young is the key signature – he came out of retirement to play the role; Brolin is a temperamental signer.

Mary Tyler Moore Show, The
Cast: Mary Tyler Moore, Ed Asner, Ted Knight, Gavin MacLeod, Valerie Harper, Cloris Leachman, Lisa Gerritsen, John Amos, Georgia Engel, Betty White, Joyce Bulifant, Priscilla Morrill, Robbie Rist. Hints: Moore and Knight are the key signatures; all other cast members are generally available.

Maude
Cast: Beatrice Arthur, Bill Macy, Adrienne Barbeau, Brian Morrison, Kraig Metzinger, Conrad Bain, Rue McClanahan, Esther Rolle, John Amos, Fred Grandy, Chris Liccardello and others. Hints: The signatures of all cast members are generally available.

Maverick
Cast: James Garner, Jack Kelly, Diane Brewster, Roger Moore, Robert Colbert. Hints: Garner is the key signature; the signatures of all cast members are generally available.

McCloud
Cast: Dennis Weaver, J.D. Cannon, Terry Carter, Diane Muldaur, Ken Lynch. Hints: Weaver is the key signature; the signatures of all cast members are generally available.

McHale's Navy
Cast: Ernest Borgnine, Joe Flynn, Tim Conway, Carl Ballantine, Gary Vinson, Billy Sands, Edson Stroll and many others. Hints: Borgnine is the key signature – he often answers requests with facsimile signed photographs; the signatures of all cast members are generally available.

Mission: Impossible
Cast: Steven Hill, Barbara Bain, Martin Landau, Greg Morris, Peter Lupus, Peter Graves, Leonard Nimoy, Sam Elliott, Lesley Ann Warren, Lynda Day George, Barbara Anderson. Hints: The signatures of all cast members are generally available.

Mod Squad, The
Cast: Michael Cole, Clarence Williams III, Peggy Lipton, Tige Andrews. Hints: The signatures of all cast members are generally available.

❏ Monkees, The
Cast: David Jones, Peter Tork, Mickey Dolenz and Mike Nesmith. Hints: The signatures of all cast members are generally available; Nesmith is the toughest signature.

❏ Munsters, The
Cast: Fred Gwynne, Yvonne DeCarlo, Al Lewis, Butch Patrick, Beverly Owen, Pat Priest. Hints: Gwynne is the key signature; all others are generally available.

❏ My Three Sons
Cast: Fred MacMurray, Tim Considine, Don Grady, Stanley Livingstone, William Frawley, William Demarest, Meredith MacRae, Barry Livingston, Tina Cole and others. Hints: MacMurray, Frawley (see I Love Lucy) and Demarest are key signatures, all others are generally available.

❏ Saturday Night Live
Cast: Chevy Chase, John Belushi, Dan Aykroyd, Gilda Radner, Garrett Morris, Jane Curtin, Laraine Newman, Bill Murray, Albert Brooks, Gary Weis and many, many others. Hints: The original cast is most sought after – key signatures Belushi and Radner; many talented cast members followed, including Joe Piscopo, Eddie Murphy, Billy Crystal, Martin Short, Dennis Miller, Phil Hartman (deceased), Dana Carvey, Mike Myers, Chris Farley (deceased), Chris Rock, Adam Sandler, just to name a few.

❏ Odd Couple, The
Cast: Tony Randall, Jack Klugman, Al Molinaro, Gary Walberg, Larry Gelman, Archie Hahn and others. Hints: The signatures of all cast members are generally available.

❏ Partridge Family, The
Cast: Shirley Jones, David Cassidy, Susan Dey, Danny Bonaduce, Jeremy Gelbwaks, Brain Foster, Suzanne Crough, David Madden, Ricky Segall, Alan Bursky. Hints: Cassidy is the key signature; the signatures of all other cast members are generally available.

❏ Perry Mason
Cast: (1957-66) Raymond Burr, Barbara Hale, William Hopper, Ray Collins, Wesley Lau, Richard Anderson and William Talman. Hints: Raymond Burr is the key signature; Tallman can be tough to find; the signatures of all other cast members are generally available.

❏ Petticoat Junction
Cast: Bea Benaderet, Edgar Buchanan, Jeannine Riley, Gunilla Hutton, Meredith MacRae, Pat Woodell, Lori Saunders, Linda Kaye, Smiley Burnette, Rufe Davis, Charles Lane, Frank Cady and many others. Hints: Benaderet passed away during the 1968-69 season; many talented CBS character actors found their way to the Junction.

Rawhide
Cast: Clint Eastwood, Eric Fleming, Sheb Wooley, Paul Brinegar, Steve Raines, Rocky Shahan, James Murdock and others. Hints: Eastwood is the key signature – watch for "ghost" signatures.

Real McCoys, The
Cast: Walter Brennan, Richard Crenna, Kathy Nolan, Lydia Reed, Mike Winkleman, Tony Martinez, Andy Clyde, Madge Blake, and others. Hints: Brennan, a multiple Oscar winner, is the key signature; the signatures of all other cast members are generally available.

Rockford Files, The
Cast: James Garner, Noah Beery Jr., Joe Santos, Gretchen Corbett, Stuart Margolin, Bo Hopkins, Tom Atkins, James Luisi, Tom Selleck. Hints: Garner is the key signature.

Route 66
Cast: Martin Milner, George Maharis, Glenn Corbett. Hints: The signatures of all cast members are generally available.

Rowan & Martin's Laugh-In
Cast: Dan Rowan, Dick Martin, Gary Owens, Ruth Buzzi, Judy Carne, Eileen Brennan, Goldie Hawn, Arte Johnson, Henry Gibson, Roddy-Maude Roxby, Jo Anne Worley and many, many others. Hints: Rowan is the key signature; the signatures of all other cast members are generally available.

Sanford and Son
Cast: Redd Foxx, Desmond Wilson, Slappy White, Don Bexley, Hal Williams, Gregory Sierra, Nathaniel Taylor, LaWanda Page and others. Hints: Foxx is the key signature and can be difficult to find.

77 Sunset Strip
Cast: Efrem Zimbalist Jr., Roger Smith, Edd Byrnes, Louis Quinn, Jacqueline Beer, Byron Keith, Richard Long, Alison Long, Robert Logan, Joan Staley. Hints: The signatures of all cast members are generally available; Zimbalist is a temperamental signer; Byrnes charges for his signature.

Six Million Dollar Man, The
Cast: Lee Majors, Richard Anderson, Alan Oppenheimer, Martin Brooks. Hints: The signatures of all cast members are generally available.

60 Minutes
Cast: Mike Wallace, Harry Reasoner, Morley Safer, Dan Rather, Andy Rooney, Ed Bradley and others. Hints: Original cast members can be difficult to acquire; Wallace is elusive, Reasoner sent out facsimile signed photographs, Safer doesn't answer his mail, Rather has always been difficult by mail, Rooney is just plain difficult to deal with, and Bradley ignores requests. Fortunately for collec-

tors, replacement members have been responsive to collectors.

❑ Star Trek
Cast: William Shatner, Leonard Nimoy, DeForest Kelley, Grace Lee Whitney, George Takei, Nichelle Nichols, James Doohan, Majel Barrett, Walter Koenig and others. Hints: Pick up a copy of the UACC publication *The Study of Star Trek Autographs* by Al Wittnebert; forgeries and facsimiles are common.

❑ Starsky and Hutch
Cast: Paul Michael Glaser, David Soul, Bernie Hamilton, Antonio Fargas. Hints: The signatures of all cast members are generally available.

❑ Streets of San Francisco, The
Cast: Karl Malden, Michael Douglas, Richard Hatch, Lee Harris. Hints: Malden is the key signature and Douglas is a difficult signature to acquire.

❑ Taxi
Cast: Judd Hirsch, Jeff Conaway, Danny DeVito, Marilu Henner, Tony Danza, Randall Carver, Andy Kaufman, Christopher Lloyd. Hints: Kaufman is the key signature; Hirsch and DeVito are reluctant signers; Lloyd answers requests with a facsimile signed photograph.

❑ That Girl
Cast: Marlo Thomas, Ted Bessell, Lew Parker, Rosemary DeCamp, Bonnie Scott, Dabney Coleman, Bernie Kopell, Carolyn Daniels, Alice Borden, Ronnie Schell, George Carlin, Don Penny, Ruth Buzzi. Hints: The signatures of all cast members are generally available.

❑ Three's Company
Cast: John Ritter, Joyce DeWitt, Suzanne Somers, Audra Lindley, Norman Fell, Richard Kline, Don Knotts, Anne Wedgeworth, Jenilee Harrison and others. Hints: The signatures of all cast members are generally available.

❑ Tonight Show Starring Johnny Carson, The
Cast: Johnny Carson, Ed McMahon, Skitch Henderson, Milton DeLugg, Doc Severinsen, Tommy Newsome and others. Hints: Carson is the key signature and can be a challenging acquisition – for years he answered requests with a facsimile signed photograph.

❑ Untouchables, The
Cast: Robert Stack, Jerry Paris, Abel Fernandez, Nick Georgiade, Anthony George, Paul Picerni, Steve London, Bruce Gordon. Hints: The signatures of all cast members are generally available.

❑ Virginian, The
Cast: Lee J. Cobb, James Drury, Doug McClure, Gary Clarke, Pippa Scott, Roberta Shore, Randy Boone, Clu Gulager and many others. Hints: Cobb is the

key signature; the signatures of all other cast members are generally available.

❏ Voyage to the Bottom of the Sea
Cast: Richard Basehart, David Hedison, Robert Dowdell, Henry Kulky, Terry Becker, Allan Hunt, Del Monroe, Paul Trinka, Richard Bull. Hints: Basehart is the key signature; the signatures of all other cast members are generally available.

❏ WKRP in Cincinnati
Cast: Gary Sandy, Gordon Jump, Howard Hesseman, Loni Anderson, Richard Sanders, Jan Smithers, Tim Reid, Frank Bonner. Hints: The signatures of all cast members are generally available; Anderson often answers mail requests with a facsimile signed photograph.

❏ Wagon Train
Cast: Ward Bond, Robert Horton, Terry Wilson, Frank McGrath, Scott Miller, John McIntire, Michael Burns, Robert Fuller. Hints: Autographed original cast photographs are scarce; Bond died in 1961 and can be a difficult signature to acquire; Horton stayed until 1962.

❏ Waltons, The
Cast: Ralph Waite, Michael Learned, Will Geer, Ellen Corby, Richard Thomas, Robert Wightman, Judy Norton-Taylor, David Harper, Kami Cotler, Jon Walmsley, Mary Elizabeth McDonough, Eric Scott, Joe Conley, Ronnie Edwards, John Crawford, Helen Kleeb, Mary Jackson, Lynn Hamilton and others. Hints: Autographed original cast photographs are difficult to find; key signatures are Corby and Geer (both deceased); Thomas often answered requests with facsimile signed photographs.

❏ Welcome Back, Kotter
Cast: Gabe Kaplan, John Travolta, Marcia Strassman, Robert Hegyes, Lawrence Hilton-Jacobs, Ron Palillo, John White and others. Hints: The signatures of all cast members are generally available; Travolta is the key signature.

❏ Wild Wild West, The
Cast: Robert Conrad, Ross Martin, Michael Dunn. Hints: Autographed original cast photographs of Conrad and Martin are difficult to find; Conrad often answered mail requests with facsimile signed photographs; Martin was an elusive signer.

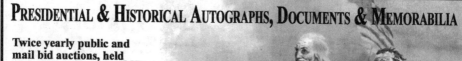

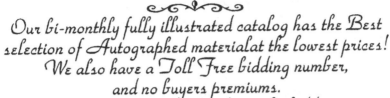

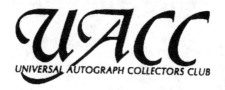

THESE MEN LIVED BY THEIR REPUTATION

SO DO WE

Signature House
SINCE 1994

In ten years we have grown in quality, integrity and our willingness to please our customers.

We have built our name on reliability. Our bidders receive a lifetime guarantee of authenticity plus our exclusive Golden Guarantee. Consignors receive current market information and free appraisals plus the most competitive rates available.

Would you rather sell your collectibles now? Whether you have one autograph or a collection, you can have your check tomorrow.

Contact us for a catalog.

Gil & Karen Griggs
407 Liberty Avenue
Bridgeport, WV 26330
Phone: (304) 842-3386   Fax: (304) 842-3001
email: editor@signaturehouse.net
website: www.signaturehouse.net

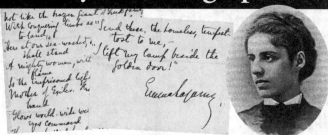

ABOUT THE AUTHOR

Mark Allen Baker is a respected author and historian whose work has appeared in more than one hundred periodicals. He is the author of twelve books, including the *Baseball Autograph Handbook, Auto Racing, Collector's Guide to Celebrity Autographs* and *Goldmine Price Guide to Rock 'n' Roll Memorabilia.* His work has been referenced and featured in numerous major publications including *Sports Illustrated* and *USA TODAY.* Baker also has been a featured guest on many radio and television shows including Metro TV (NY) and VH-1.

A graduate of the State University of New York, Baker also has worked in a variety of finance, marketing, sales and executive management positions for the General Electric Corporation, Genigraphics Corporation and Pansophic Systems Incorporated. Additionally, Baker has done postgraduate work at George Washington University and taught seminars at both R.I.T. and M.I.T. He has been a featured speaker at various engagements including the Hemingway Days Writers Conference.

Additional biographical data can be found in numerous professional directories including *Who's Who in the East, Who's Who in Entertainment* and *Who's Who in America.*